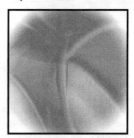

Business Rules Applied

Business Better Systems Using the Business Rules Approach

Barbara von Halle

WILEY COMPUTER PUBLISHING

John Wiley & Sons, Inc.

New York • Chichester • Weinheim • Brisbane • Singapore • Toronto

Publisher: Robert Ipsen
Editor: Robert Elliot
Developmental Editor: Emilie Herman
Managing Editor: John Atkins
Associate New Media Editor: Brian Snapp
Text Design & Composition: Publishers' Design and Production Services, Inc.

Designations used by companies to distinguish their products are often claimed as trademarks. In all instances where John Wiley & Sons, Inc., is aware of a claim, the product names appear in initial capital or ALL CAPITAL LETTERS. Readers, however, should contact the appropriate companies for more complete information regarding trademarks and registration.

This book is printed on acid-free paper. ∞

Published by John Wiley & Sons, Inc., New York

Published simultaneously in Canada.

Chapter 13 and 14 includes text and screen shots copyrighted by the following vendors: HNC Software (p. 476–489). ©2001 Brokat Technologies; ILOG, Inc. (489–491). ©2001 ILOG Inc.; Usoft, Inc. (433–450). ©2001 Ness Usoft Group; Versata, Inc. (p. 450–471) ©2001 Versata, Inc.

This publication is designed to provide accurate and authoritative information in regard to the subject matter covered. It is sold with the understanding that the publisher is not engaged in professional services. If professional advice or other expert assistance is required, the services of a competent professional person should be sought.

Library of Congress Cataloging-in-Publication Data:

Von Halle, Barbara.
    Business rules applied : building better systems using the business rules approach /
Barbara von Halle.
        p. cm.
    Includes index.
    ISBN 0-471-41293-7 (pbk. : alk. paper)
    1. Business.   2. Industrial management.   3. Business—Data processing.   4. Industrial
management—Data processing.   I. Title.

HD31 .V594   2001
658—dc21

2001046536

Printed in the United States of America.

10 9 8 7 6 5 4 3 2 1

Advance Praise for
Business Rules Applied

"Today's fast-paced, competitive business environment demands flexible applications that can be adapted to meet changing business requirements. Insurance companies, financial institutions and other policy intensive organizations must develop applications that allow the easy modification and implementation of business and regulatory policy. Telecommunications companies must design their customer relationship management and billing systems to support frequent new product and service offerings. Application service providers must be able to rapidly customize their software to meet the unique business requirements of each individual customer. More and more companies are looking to business rules for the answer.

Business rule technology delivers a key technical capability. However, like other technologies that promise to simplify and speed application development—object-oriented languages like Java and C#, platforms like J2EE and .NET, and data representations like XML—business rule technology alone cannot ensure a successful application. The promise of more flexible, adaptable applications, where business rules are managed separate from the application, can only be realized by good application design. Business rule technology vendors provide powerful enabling tools—but the success of the application depends on a thorough understanding of business requirements and an application design that implements those requirements.

Little information is available today addressing the design and development of business rule applications. How should business rules be identified? How should they be represented? At what phase should they be integrated into the system development life cycle? How do business rules work with object-oriented applications and relational databases? How are business rules implemented in applications? These are among the issues addressed by *Business Rules Applied*. As Barbara von Halle's bestselling *Handbook of Relational Database Design* guided data analysts and data base administrators, this book will help business analysts and developers build applications using business rules. This is an important book for those looking to implement business rule technology."

Colleen McClintock
JRules Product Manager, ILOG, Inc.

"With her book *Business Rules Applied*, Barbara von Halle puts the information systems design discipline at a higher level. Placing rules as a third design principle between data modeling and workflow concepts, she bridges a gap that until now has only been bridged by the object-oriented modeling techniques like UML. The book takes the reader all the way from early business level requirements analysis to the precise actual realization of the system. The author takes a step-by-step approach, describing the rules analysis and design process in regular terms of the IT professional. This book opens up a new world to anybody interested in capturing business logic in a structured way and from a business perspective.

For every phase of development the book explains how to position the rules perspective in relation to the 'normal' way of working when modeling data and process only. Through crisp and clear guidelines and working from a detailed real-world case, the methodology described is truly effectuated for the reader. With this book von Halle opens up the business rules way of thinking to a wider audience. It offers a new and practical perspective on information systems development, that every software engineer and business systems analyst should add to his toolkit."

Paul Mallens
Author of the *USoft Approach to Business Rules Automation*
Delft University of Technology, the Netherlands

To kindergarten tee-ball players everywhere.

Contents

Foreword

Business rule systems—*evolutionary* or *revolutionary*? The best answer is "yes." I say that without tongue in cheek.

The really big changes are always based on a matter of degrees. Small quantitative differences can become large qualitative ones. A football game, as they say, can be won by inches. Heat water to 99 degrees Centigrade, and you still have a liquid. Heat it a bit more, though, and you get something quite different.

The Business Rule Approach has been in a long period of incubation, gradually heating up degree-by-degree all through the 1990s. Refinements in the approach have come in many small increments by dedicated pioneers in out-of-the-spotlight corners of the IT world. But for those of us fortunate enough to have participated in this process, we have always known the approach would eventually come into its own in a big way. As I've said many times in my lectures and seminars, *business rules are inevitable!*

Why? Well, Barbara is about to tell you why. Just plunge into Part 1 and you'll quickly get the picture. No need for me to repeat that here.

Here's where I want to focus: small quantitative differences producing big qualitative ones. Heat the water just a bit more, and you get steam. Harness that steam on an industrial scale, and you get a source of new power far beyond anything before. The trick from a business point of view, of course, is all in the timing. The winners usually wait until the approach is proven, but jump in before competitors.

As I write this today, that's exactly where we are in the Business Rule Approach. As Barbara's book demonstrates, there is a whole new source of power to meet IT needs in the 21st century—business rule *methodology*. Barbara lays this out in wholesome detail in Parts 2 through 5 of her book.

I also agree with her when she points out that you don't necessarily need a new engine to benefit from that. But let me be straight about this. I believe there *is* a rule engine in your future—and probably sooner than you think.

"If things would only slow down some," you might say, "coding rules in procedural languages would work just fine." But therein lies the flaw. With each passing year, doing business is inexorably moving *faster*, not slower. And there's no sign of that letting up. I believe your business will inevitably move toward knowledge automation—*rule engines*—simply because it is already feeling so much heat. Quantitative differences produce qualitative ones.

Back now to the original question: Business rule systems—*evolutionary* or *revolutionary*? Like I said, the answer is yes. Let me quote Barbara on this. In the Summary of Chapter 3 she writes, "At first glance, you may believe that this book does not contain any new ideas. This is a natural first impression because you have always dealt with all aspects of a system, regardless of what you called those aspects or which is your favorite system development paradigm. However, this book proposes that the Rule Track . . . makes all the difference in the world in the world to the *business* itself" [emphasis mine]. There you have it—evolutionary yet revolutionary.

Just one more thing before I close. On a personal note, let me thank *you*, Barbara, for all those regular Friday afternoon phone discussions on business rules back in the early- and mid-1990s when I was writing (incubating, really) *The Business Rule Book*. On a cabinet in my office I have a note from that period predicting that you would write a book about business rule methodology for IT professionals by the year 2000. (Really true—the ink is even faded.) Just one question: *Why were you a year or two late?* No matter, it was worth waiting for!

Ronald G. Ross
Principal, Business Rule Solutions, LLC
Executive Editor, www.BRCommunity.com

Preface

A business rules approach to systems development promises to be the most practical and desirable way to build systems. It can help you build better, easily changeable systems faster than any previous approach. This book provides a step-by-step practical approach for building systems using a business rules approach.

The timing of the emergence of a business rules approach is compelling. Adaptability is a subtle but powerful change in the way we build systems. As a parallel, let's look at how the emergence of relational concepts and corresponding technology took place. Ted Codd documented his relational model in a landmark paper in 1970. Subsequently, small software vendors created database management systems based on a subset of the concepts of the relational model. Shortly after that, major software vendors did the same. Around that time, authors like C.J. Date published books and gave presentations that explained the concepts of the new software to the IT industry. Eventually, people such as Candy Fleming and I published books and gave courses in how a practitioner can proceed from gathering requirements to using the new software for creating relational databases.

Relational technology flourished for many reasons:

- It was theoretically sound.

- Software vendors understood the theory, to some extent, and delivered commercial products.

- IT notables, such as C.J. Date, eloquently explained the theory, benefits, and practicality of relational products to the IT industry.

- Other practitioners gained early experience and developed step-by-step approaches for using the new software.

Let's now evaluate the evolution of the business rules approach. Ted Codd laid the groundwork for the integrity aspect of the relational model back in 1970. While this aspect has not been fully deployed by relational DBMS vendors, it had made strides through triggers and stored procedures and in research under the auspices of active database systems.

Innovative software vendors (such as Versata Inc, Brokat Technologies, USoft Inc., ILOG Inc., The Haley Enterprise, and Rule Machines Inc.) incorporated those concepts into a type of software product called commercial rules technology. These products are used mostly by application developers, less so by database professionals, because the product environments promote the idea that those integrity constraints, the business rules, are part of the application development world.

In addition, Ronald G. Ross has published further theory on the classification and grammar of the various types of integrity constraints, or business rules. C.J. Date published a book for IT practitioners that explains the history of the business rule phenomenon as it relates to the relational model, as well as the adoption process for software vendors. He further acknowledges that, while specification of constraints (business rules) can be part of a fully matured relational database management system, there are benefits to doing so in a middle tier that manages the rules independently of the DBMS.

So, as for the business rules approach:

- It is theoretically sound.
- Vendors understand the theory, to some extent, and are delivering commercial products.
- C.J. Date and Ronald G. Ross have explained the theory and product capabilities to the IT Industry.

It is now time for a step-by-step approach for applying the theory to technology in the world of e-business, Web-based, object-oriented, and relational database systems development. This book combines best practice systems design principles plus adherence to the principles of a business rules approach, thereby enriching what you already know how to do.

A system built according to the business rules approach has many advantages over other systems. However, given the pressures of e-commerce, the most important advantage is that a business rules system is designed to easily accommodate changes in the business with minimal disruption. Therefore, this book introduces a new emphasis and formalism around capturing, validating, and automating the rules of the business so that the business can easily change those rules as it sees fit.

The methodology in this book builds on familiar methodologies such as structured systems analysis, information engineering, and object-orientation so that readers can easily add a business rules approach to existing practices. The most significant aspect of this book is the introduction of a rule track into a systems development methodology. The steps, guidelines, techniques, and examples of activities in this track guide the reader in understanding what business rules are, why they are important to the business, why it is important not to bury the business rules in code again, and how to analyze and deliver the rules as a valuable, changeable aspect of the resulting system.

Defining the Business Rules Approach

A business rules approach is merely a formal way of managing and automating an organization's business rules so that the business behaves and evolves as its leaders intend. Essentially, a business rules system is an automated system in which you separate the rules, logically, perhaps physically, and share them across data stores, user interfaces, and applications.

You can apply most of the concepts in this book regardless of whether you utilize special rules technology, although use of such technology will deliver the most immediate and long-lasting benefits. As a starting point, during scoping for example, you will pay special attention to the business motivation for your project. Aspects of this motivation may include objectives, goals, strategies, tactics, and policies. These are the fundamental justification for the rules you uncover, deliver, and change during the systems development effort.

During the discovery of requirements, you will seek important decisions behind the target system and dissect these into atomic rules, capturing them in a rules repository. You can extend an existing repository, utilize an existing CASE tool, or build a simple rules database.

Moving into analysis, you become involved in steps and techniques specifically aimed at verifying the quality of rules, connecting rules to information and knowledge, and understanding dependencies among rules.

Finally, in the design phase, you consider implementation options, paying close attention to those that allow you to deliver the rules in a way that accomplishes four significant objectives:

- *Separate* rules from the rest of the system so you can reuse them
- *Trace* rules to the reasons they exist as well as to where they are implemented
- *Externalize* rules so everyone can know what they are
- *Position* rules for change at any time

Why We Wrote This Book

Some of you may be veteran software and database engineers. You may suspect that you are now poised at the brink of a monumental moment in software engineering history. This moment represents a natural next step, compelled by business momentum. Consider the impact of the relational model, in its theoretical elegance and corresponding technology, on the ability to deliver more flexible database and applications more quickly. Then, consider the following.

In 1988, Candace Fleming and I completed a book, *Handbook of Relational Database Design* (1989), that contains a step-by-step approach for building logical data models and transforming them into stable relational databases. The approach focuses on understanding the business rules surrounding those database designs. In 1989, the phrase "business rules" was not an upcoming buzzword. Even so, we strongly urged readers to take a methodological approach to capturing, documenting, and implementing those business rules.

The good news is that readers successfully followed that step-by-step database design approach, and created stable relational databases. The bad news is that those practitioners also ended up with an intriguing collection of leftover business rules. What to do with them? Specifically, who is responsible for implementing and evolving them and in what manner?

It comes as no surprise that these leftover business rules emerged as a fertile battleground over which database designers and application developers have waged territorial wars. These wars still go on today. So, the step-by-step approach in that book, while it focused on business rules, remained unfinished and unresolved, because it did not make a very formal separation between modeling the data and gathering business rules. This book, however, introduces a very clear separation by adding enough discipline to the rule aspect that it becomes a rule track.

The rule track leads you to fascinating new possibilities, precisely because the methodology delivers, for analysis and management, a business rules asset. You will learn that the business rules asset may turn out to be the most important deliverable that information technology professionals can deliver back to the business.

This book is the result of intense collaboration among a team of people who have practiced various aspects of a business rules approach.

Over the past eight to ten years, each of us developed various techniques, deliverables, and arguments for developing systems using a business rules approach. In addition to our own experience, we spoke to rules technology vendors and their customers. We also spoke to people who have built their own rules software or incorporated a business rules approach into traditional systems development.

In this way, the methodology in this book has been tested in various forms at various places. The intent in pulling it all together is to introduce a practical, step-by-step approach by which other people can also be successful with a business rules approach. Another justification for the book was to publicize the advances made by commercial rules technology vendors and products. Our hope is that readers will adopt the business rules approach and will be able to utilize rules technology in a practical manner.

How This Book Is Organized

The structure of this book is straightforward. Part 1, "Business Rule Basics," contains ruidmentary material for understanding and justifying a business rules approach for developing systems. Part 2, "Getting Started on a Business Rules Project," assists in scoping and planning your business rules project. Part 3, "Discovery," contains details for discovering system requirements. Part 4, "Analysis," presents details for analyzing the three parts of a business rules system: rules, data, and process. Finally, Part 5 discusses design alternatives, first for the general case and also for specific rule product environments.

The book is organized into these five parts because it is meant to be read and used by practitioners who may have little or no knowledge of how to build a system following a business rules approach. With this in mind, Part 1 is appropriate for all readers because it provides the foundation for reading all other parts of the book. Specifically, Chapter 1, "The Need for a Business Rules Approach," begins by presenting compelling benefits for considering a business rules approach to systems development. If the benefits seem worth pursuing, Chapter 2, "Business Rule Concepts," explains the terms and concepts, for the non-technical reader, behind a business rules approach. Once the reader understands the terms and concepts, Chapter 3, "Introduction to Business Rule Methodology," provides a manager's view of a system development methodology enhanced with considerations for leveraging a business rules approach.

The remainder of the book, Parts 2 through 5 are similar to each other in that each contains a step-by-step methodological approach for one phase in the development of a system using a business rules approach. Each part covers one phase of this approach. Part 2 addresses the Scoping and Planning effort for a system to be developed using a business rules approach, or even parts of a business rules approach. Part 3 presents steps by which a practitioner can discover requirements for a system scoped in Part 2. Part 4 takes the practitioner into the analysis of those requirements, paying special attention to the emergence of rules as an important and visible aspect of the system. Part 5 completes the approach by leading the practitioner through steps, techniques, and examples for designing and implementing the business rules system.

As you can see, these parts are in the sequence in which a practitioner would carry out a systems development project using a business rules approach if the development process were to occur one phase at a time. In reality, due to the popularity of iterative and incremental systems development, the project team may be carrying out several phases in parallel and iteratively. Nevertheless, for instructional purposes, these parts represent one phase distinct from the one before and after it. In this way, the practitioner gains an understanding of how the deliverables from each phase lead to the subsequent phase in an orderly, intelligent manner.

Because Parts 2 through 5 represent a sequential, step-by-step methodology, the chapters within each part are related to each other and presented in a deliberate sequence. For example, the two chapters in Part 2, (Chapter 4, "Scoping for Success," and Chapter 5, "Project Planning with Business Rules,") represent the first activities in starting a business rules systems development project. These activities include first those needed to scope the project and second, those for developing a plan by which to accomplish the scoped project.

Likewise, the chapters in Part 3 all deal with the discovery of initial requirements for the project. Specifically, the Chapter 6, "Discovering Initial Requirements," describes a way of discovering general requirements by adding a step for uncovering the decisions made within the execution of a business event. Chapter 7, "Discovering Rules and Data," focuses more specifically on the discovery of detailed rules behind those decisions and the data needed to execute those rules. Because the formalism of rule discovery is new with a business rules approach, Chapter 8 provides the reader with a way of doing so using facilitated sessions with business experts.

Part 4 takes the reader beyond the initial discovery of requirements into the analysis of those requirements. Each chapter in this Part analyzes a different aspect of the system: its data, its rules, and its surrounding process. The sequence of these chapters is significant. Chapter 9, "Analyzing Data," begins by analyzing data because the data foundation is very cruical to the delivery of a stable system capable of handling changeable rules. Chapter 10, "Analyzing Rules," analyzes rules because rule analysis may influence the analysis of the system process. Chapter 11, "Analyzing Process," concludes Part 4 by explaining the process component of the system and how it may be different had you not first analyzed the decisions, rules, and data.

Finally, Part 5 represents the real-world tangible deliverable of a system based on a business rules approach. The chapters, again, are in a deliberate sequence. Chapter 12, "Designing for a Business Rules Approach," discusses the overall system design considerations, with emphasis on how to design the new rule aspect. Chapter 13, "Implementing Business Rule Systems Using Data-Change-Oriented Rules Products," repeats the generic design steps from Chapter 12, but this time illustrates how each step occurs using selected commercial data-change-oriented rules products. Chapter 14, "Implementing Business Rule Systems Using Service-Oriented Products," does likewise, this time using selected commercial service-oriented rules products.

There is no doubt that the most important chapter in the book is Chapter 15, "Rule Management." This chapter comes last only for two reasons. The first is that you may not fully appreciate the value of rule management unless you first understand rules and how to leverage them in systems designed for business change. The second reason is that, while you may build a business rules system without formal rule management by following Chapters 4 through 14, you are likely to want to leverage the benefits of rule management for the next business rules system. Specifically, when your first business rules system is successful, you will want to use its rules and approach as a foundation for building more business rules systems and also incrementally building a business rules asset.

Most of you will not read this book from start to finish. Rather, you will use it as a reference for topics most relevant to your interest in a business rules approach and your responsibilities on a business rules system development project. Following are some suggestions for approaching the book:

- Project managers should read Chapters 1 through 3 to appreciate why a business rules approach is superior to approaches without a rules emphasis, to understand the concepts behind business rules, and to gain a management-level perspective of a full life cycle development approach. Project managers should also read Chapters 4 and 5 if you have decided (or been appointed) to oversee the development, using a business rules approach, of a specific system. A project manager can skip Chapters 6 through 14, unless you will be performing or critiquing the rule-oriented deliverables. However, Chapter 15 is crucial reading for the project manager so that project team documents and leverages the rule-related deliverables, standards, and the rules themselves.

- Analysts should also read Chapters 1 through 5 to understand the justification for a business rules approach, how systems development is different in a business rules approach, and how the target project was scoped and planned. Chapters 6 and 7 are the instructions for the analyst who will be gathering requirements for the target system and provide an understanding of how to add a focus on rules.

    While an analyst can gather rules from knowledgeable people with one-one-one interviews, formal facilitated rule sessions are often the most productive means for doing so, where the rules are to be based on business consensus. With this in mind, Chapter 8 leads the analyst through the important differences between a traditional requirements-gathering meeting or set of requirements interviews and a facilitated session. From here, the chapter contains specific steps and techniques for conducting a rule-facilitated session as a quick and reliable means for uncovering initial rule sets within a business context.

For the analyst who is responsible for delivering high-quality data requirements and new rule requirements, Chapters 9 and 10 are crucial reading. An analyst responsible for process analysis should read Chapters 10 and 11 to understand how the process may change based on the influence of rules analysis.

No doubt a common challenge within most organizations is that people don't know the rules. The rules are buried in executing code. When this is the case, an analyst may be charged with excavating these rules from system source code. A white paper on the companion Web site called "Discovering Rules through Business Rule Mining" is for these analysts and provides an overview for how to accomplish this, sample deliverables using one commercial product, and useful techniques.

- Naturally, an analyst will want to document the analytical results and relate these to rules. Therefore, Chapter 15 is required reading for all analysts so that analysis deliverables can be captured properly and used by designers and business people.

- Designers and implementers again should review Chapters 1 through 3 for the justification, concepts, and methodology overview. Perhaps the designers have the most challenging responsibility in a business rules approach because the new goal is to better coordinate the implementation of rules so as to enable change on demand. Therefore, a designer can skip the detailed chapters on discovery and analysis and proceed to the design approach covered in Part 5. The designer should carefully read Chapter 12 and apply the recommendations in this chapter to the organization's target technology choices. A designer with a vision for the future will appreciate the advantages of commercial rules technology presented in Chapter 12 and may influence the organization to consider conducting a pilot using one or more of these products. A database designer should read the white paper on the companion Web site called "Designing Relational Databases" to review important database design principles in the context of a business rules system. The designer should also read Chapter 15 to document the design deliverables so as to enable impact analysis when rule changes occur.

- The technologist and methodologist will find this book a useful primer for understanding today's commercial rules technology and where it is headed in the future. The technologist and methodologist should read Chapters 1 through 3 for foundational understanding of a business rules approach, its benefits, as well as for insights into commercial rules products that leverage the approach. Of most importance to the technologist and methodologist is Chapter 12, to better understand generic rule design, and Chapters 13 and 14 for a practical perspective on exactly how to deploy commercial rules products within the framework of a business rules methodology. As is true for all audiences, the technologist and methodologist should read Chapter 15 on managing rules to understand how commercial rules technology enables rule changes, especially when supported with proper rule management practices.

Products Featured in This Book

Technology is rarely a silver bullet. But a great idea today may have limited value without supporting technology to escalate its availability and adaptability. So, too, with a business rules approach. It is best leveraged and sometimes most justified when supporting technology drives its principles.

For this reason, we include representative product examples in the book. These include USoft Inc. and Versata Inc. products as examples of data-change-oriented rules technology and Ilog Inc. and HNC Software products as examples of service-oriented rules technology. In some cases, vendors provided solutions to our Case Study within our publication timeframe. In other cases, vendors were not able to do so. Our apologies to vendors we did not yet know about, but you are invited to publish their solutions to our case study on the companion Web site.

This book is not meant to serve as an endorsement of one product over another. The participating vendors and products are representative of the business rules technology space at this time. We are grateful to their ideas and willingness to contribute to the book so that readers can better understand technology alternatives.

We included products with the following characteristics:

- Embrace the understanding of a business rules approach to systems development (not merely an e-business focus)
- Provide some aspects of rule management
- Operate within standard software and hardware environments
- Have excited and positive customer testimonials
- Enable changeable rules within systems
- Are model-driven, be these data models or object models or both
- Can interface with various Web browsers and data storage mechanisms, such as files and relational databases
- Either provide a complimentary rule service to an application or full rule-oriented application development.

How to Use This Book as Rules Technology Matures

The emergence of commercial rules products, while gaining in popularity, has only just begun. Yet, these span a range of business requirements, from supporting distributed objects to centralizing sophisticated rule bases. These products, and the theoretical philosophy behind them, offer very desirable alternatives for delivering application systems.

Some commercial rules products are still in their infancy. No doubt, they will mature and new products will emerge. The authors expect major software vendors to enter the market and new niche vendors to shine. In particular, in the next few years, expect new developments and enhancements to include broader rule types and better, more useable rule management facilities.

Wherever possible, the methodology in this book specifically separates technology-independent from technology-oriented tasks. Moreover, even within the technology-oriented tasks, the book presents technology-neutral tasks and decisions, unbiased (in intent) from existing products. The design steps take into consideration the facilities of ideal business rules products, facilities common among today's business rules products, and the advances expected over time. Equally important, the book includes insights for how to implement a business rules system without business rules products. This allows you to select implementation options that best fit current needs with a vision toward the future. In this way, you can leverage the philosophy and advantages of a business rules approach in the absence of proper technology, and progress more easily into newer emerging products.

What's on the Web Site

This book is a glimpse into a better way to build systems, especially when developing e-focused, adaptable systems. As such, the book is a starting point for entering in the world of changeable systems and a foundation upon which to build business rule successes.

Because a business rules approach as a philosophy, set of methods, and tools is evolving quickly, a companion Web site at www.wiley.com/compbooks/vonhalle will keep readers abreast of products, techniques, and experiences.

In particular, the Web site is a door to a full business rules library and services, consisting of:

- Full description of the VCI Case Study referenced throughout the book
- Implementations of the VCI Case Study, using products featured in the book as well as products not featured in the book
- White papers with more detail on selected techniques presented in the book
- Real-world experiences and lessons learned when using the approach in this book
- Predictions and trends in commercial rules technology, as they arise
- Links to related Web sites

From Here

There is no doubt that this book will cause excitement and appreciation for a business rules approach as the best way to deliver changeable systems for business growth. Changeable systems, built from a foundation of rules, put the business back in control of itself so it can guide its way through changing times.

We hope that this book instills continuing technological advances in existing rule-related products and in the introduction of robust meta data management and repository products for managing rules. We also hope that rule software companies embrace the important aspects in this book behind a business rules approach, and teach them to their clients. It will be most useful if many of the concepts and techniques within these pages become a yardstick by which to measure rules products, software development approaches, and the quality of new systems themselves.

Very importantly, we want this book to initiate meaningful discussions and debates over the role of object orientation, data orientation, and rules orientation, so as to appreciate the benefits of each and so that the ideal compromise for the business becomes reality and business-as-usual.

Of most importance is that this book enables readers to proceed with confidence through the business rules systems development process by adapting the steps, guidelines, and techniques in this book to fit your organizational culture and business needs.

This is not merely a book to explain business rule concepts or even to justify a business rules approach. Rather, it is a book for the day-to-day practitioner by which you can utilize rules for the benefit of the business. It is our hope that this book, by leading to business rule success stories, will be a constant reference for those readers who use it to make a difference to the business community. In this way, everyone should win (business people and IT people) and everyone keeps on winning because the rules can and should easily keep on changing.

Acknowledgments

Without a doubt, this book would not be possible were it not for the efforts and moral support of many special people. For starters, I would like to express my gratitude to early reviewers, Neela Waghmare, Nancy Shipley, and Chip Didden, who pored over initial manuscripts, submitted questions, and worked on solutions to the case study. I am indebted to Grace Van Etten who also reviewed chapters, especially regarding technical points. A very special thank you goes to Janet Wall and Linda Nieporent who devised the detailed case study and its solution, giving the book a fun but realistic target business rules system. There is a special thank you to Linda Nieporent who devised useful rule techniques and created various case study solution documentation. Additional gratitude goes to Art Moore and Janet Wall for assisting in the coordination of contributors and to Janet Wall for coordinating vendor correspondence.

I also want to offer a sincere expression of gratitude to Janet Wall, Art Moore, and Neville Haggerty, all of whom wrote many versions of various chapters, mostly during nonworking hours. They never seemed to get tired of working on this book.

All of us who worked on the book are grateful for the contributions and dedication of business rules vendors in exploring and implementing our case study. Without their contributions, the book would be deficient in alternatives in a full business rules solution. We are especially grateful for their patience with our questions through email and conference calls. From ILOG Inc., we want to thank Colleen McClintock and Steven Paulin. From USoft Inc., we appreciate the incredibly quick and thorough response from Sjors Niesten and Rob Haarst. From HNC Software, we owe our thanks to Ken Mollay, Vince Emery, Eric Odell, and Tom Goering. From Versata Inc., we are indebted to Steven Sweeting for working on the case study against difficult deadlines as well as his support and encouragement throughout the book project. We would also like to thank Tony Phillips, formerly of Versata Inc., who wrote a valuable Versata methodology document.

The truth is that this book would never have been possible without the encouragement and support of every employee of Knowledge Partners Inc. (KPI). Only because KPI employees were willing to take on some of my regular job responsibilities was I able to dedicate significant time to the book. Other employees graciously accepted that the book writing would impact my ability to participate in all company activities. Therefore, in one way or another, all KPI employees made a sacrifice for this book. I am, as always, amazed at and humbled by their unending and sincere support.

I would like to extend a very special thank you to Bob Elliott of Wiley and Sons who encouraged me throughout the years to eventually write a business rules book. Also deserving recognition is Emilie Herman of Wiley and Sons, whose regular encouragement, support, and advice assisted every step of the way.

No one can write a business rule book without giving tremendous credit to Ronald G. Ross. His intellectual depth, publications, teaching, consulting, and persistence in the field of business rules have created tremendous opportunity for business rule practitioners and vendors.

Every book project has its unplanned challenges. Sadly, as this book neared its completion, I was diagnosed unexpectedly with breast cancer. I am forever grateful to Dr. Vivien Chou whose diligence and intuition would not let go of a cancer that seemed to defy detection. As a result of the diagnosis, my life was changed forever and it was sometimes difficult to keep up with book deadlines amid medical appointments. I am therefore grateful to medical doctors, Dr. Robert Goodman, Dr. Jan Huston, and Dr. Richard Michaelson, who were flexible with my schedule. In particular, the caring and cheerful attitudes of John Tirado and Lauralee Curcione in the radiation department kept my spirits in the right place, day after day after day. I am also grateful to everyone within KPI, my family, and Wiley (especially Emilie Herman), whose support and caring during this time allowed me to complete the project as originally scheduled.

As always, I am personally indebted to my husband of 24 years, Mike von Halle, for his never-ending belief in and support for me. Without his dedication and assistance in both our personal and business lives, this book would never have been possible.

About the Authors

Barbara von Halle is the founder of Knowledge Partners, Inc. (KPI). She plays many roles in the company, from strategic planning to career development of employees. She is best known for pioneering in the world of Data Architecture and Business Rules through writings and consulting work. In 1996, she received the honored Outstanding Individual Achievement Award from the International Data Management Association. She was a leading contributing editor for Database Programming and Design magazine, co-authored *The Handbook of Relational Database Design,* and co-edited *The Handbook of Data Management.*

About the Contributors

Neville Haggerty is a Principal Consultant with Knowledge Partners, Inc. He has 34 years of experience in information management. For the past 17 years, he has held information technology management consultant positions specializing in facilitating communications between business and information technology people. Most recently, Neville introduced clients to templates for capturing business requirements, extended System Architect to include the capture of business rules, and facilitated rule scoping sessions. Neville has been utilizing these skills and techniques in soliciting and storing business rules for various business rule projects.

    Art Moore is a Principal with Knowledge Partners, Inc. He has experience in consulting practice management, methodology development, project management, and delivery oversight in information architecture, data warehousing, and a business rules approach to systems specification. He played a key role in developing and testing a business rule mining methodology. Most recently, he has been applying formal facilitation skills to the soliciting of business rules.

Linda (Jeney) Nieporent is a Principal Consultant with Knowledge Partners, Inc. She has seven years of experience as a consultant, instructor, and speaker in data architecture and business rules, including working for a CASE tool vendor. Assisting clients in soliciting data requirements and business rules, she creates corresponding data models and correlates them to rules. Most recently, she has been integrating business rules analysis into data modeling activities and exploring how rules technology vendors support the implementation of rule-oriented systems.

Janet Wall is a Principal with Knowledge Partners, Inc., and provides leadership in business development, employee mentoring, and development of Intellectual Property. Previously, Janet was Director of IRM and of Applications Development for a pharmaceutical research institute. Janet has been a key member of member of a business rule methodology team. She coordinates business rule experiences and deliverables and assists in future methodology development.

Business Rule Basics

The Need for a Business Rules Approach

What differentiates human behavior from that of other known life forms? One answer is our freedom to make choices (Peck 1993). While we apply rules to facts and utilize knowledge to make sensible choices, we also rely on emotions and logic. Because everyone has a different guidance system, we each react differently when faced with identical circumstances.

Businesses also make decisions based on facts, and for those decisions to be of high quality, the logical rules must also be of high quality. For a business to make consistent decisions, it relies on consistent, high-quality rules and facts that are available to decision makers and systems. These rules and facts are known as *business rules*. When business people and information systems have access to appropriate business rules at the opportune moment, they can make informed choices in a timely manner. Business rules, then, serve as the guidance system that influences the collective behavior of an organization's people and information systems.

A *business rules approach* is a formal way of managing and automating an organization's business rules so that the business behaves and evolves as its leaders intend. This book will help you build systems based on a business rules approach. When you do this, not only can the business make consistent, smart choices, it can also respond more quickly to change by instigating changes in those rules as it sees fit. A business rules approach to systems development allows the business to automate its own intelligent logic better, as well as to introduce change from within itself and learn better and faster how to reach its goals.

This chapter will illustrate the importance of incorporating business rules into your everyday practices, define what the business rules approach includes and how it can benefit your organization, explain the role of rules technology in this framework, and get you started on the path to implementing a business rules approach in your company.

The Importance of Business Rules

An enterprise operates according to many different kinds of rules, such as legal mandates and rules it constructs for itself. Naturally, business rules are of most value when they represent the best thoughts of the enterprise's best thinkers. Most enterprises craft a unique set of business rules for guiding its areas of core competence to differentiate itself from its competition. These areas often include customer relationship management or product marketing.

Unfortunately, too often business rules are inaccessible or, worse, unknown. This is the case when business rules are buried in legacy code, for which there is little or no documentation. It is scary to think of the rules executing on behalf of a business that remain hidden from those who use those systems and from those who want to make changes in that logic. When such rules are inaccessible or unknown, people (including systems developers) make assumptions about them that may be incorrect or inconsistent. Such assumptions lead to behavior (human or electronic) that is not well orchestrated, not effectively focused on common objectives, and certainly not capable of easy changes and adaptability.

It is also important for the business to be able to change. After all, humans are very capable of assimilating new knowledge, correcting old knowledge, applying it to behavior, and evaluating the results. This is called learning. Humans have a great affinity for learning and businesses today need to capitalize on that ability to remain healthy and competitive.

Needless to say, the pace of change today, largely due to technology breakthroughs, has reached unprecedented heights. Now, more than ever, the business and its people need to learn more, learn it quickly, and redefine relationships and automated procedures.

What this means is that you need to build systems differently in one respect. The business needs systems in which the rules are: separated from other components so everyone knows *that* they exist; externalized so everyone knows *what* the rules are; traceable to their origins and their implementations so everyone knows *where* the rules come from; and deliberately positioned for change so everyone knows *how to improve* them.

These are the four principles of the business rules approach:

- *Separate rules
- *Trace rules
- *Externalize rules
- *Position rules for change

We will go into greater depth on each principle later in this chapter.

If you deliver systems that do not support these principles, the business itself is no longer in the driver's seat in effecting business change! That's because you will continue to separate the business from its ability to reason, the underlying guidance system by which it carries out and justifies its activities. When the business loses memory of its business rules, it has difficulty experimenting with change, learning, growing smarter, and exhibiting more consistent insightful behavior. This is a dangerous position for today's businesses.

A Moment in Time

In 1988, there were many unknowns relating to relational technology futures. Which relational products would survive? Which would evolve fastest to provide originally missing functionality? Which products would emerge to support large data and transaction volumes, distributed systems?

We stand at the same frontier today with respect to business rules technology futures. Those of us who grew up in the relational paradigm shift can only be excited about what is about to occur.

Without a doubt, commercial rules technology, like relational technology, will serve as a monumental step forward in the evolution of systems design and implementation. Not only does commercial rules technology promise to deliver better changeable systems faster, it has the promise of putting the business back in touch with itself, by unearthing and externalizing its own rules, which are the foundation of its own decision-making capacity.

You now take one more giant step beyond the legacy that resulted from the introduction of relational technology. Specifically, you gather those leftover business rules that created a battleground over which database designers and application developers have waged war and over which software vendors have agonized. You acknowledge that the solution to this war did not lie within information engineering or within object-orientation, nor is it adequately addressed by UML (Unified Modeling Language) or (eXtensible Modeling Language) XML. Yet the war will be waged in greater magnitude in front of the world over the Internet.

The solution lies in a change in philosophy, in a business rules approach to methodology, management, and technology. A business rules approach may deliver to the business the most important business advantage: its own logic in changeable technology.

Regardless of how far and how fast commercial rules technology advances, a crucial aspect of delivering higher quality application systems (especially ones that will become visible to customers and partners via the Internet) is to start collecting and managing the rules of the business. It is no longer desirable to bury rules in specifications and program code where they are locked away, requiring costly intervention and overhead to effect change. You can no longer deliver the rules in a format that is inaccessible and not understood by a business audience. You can no longer leave the business rules in bondage where they become lost.

The collection of rules across an enterprise encompasses its collective intelligence. An organization's business rules, captured and analyzed and challenged and automated in a business-oriented way, not only determine who an organization is . . . but what it can become. Behind the business rules approach lurks the opportunity to capture the business rules and challenge them. The business rules collection becomes a magnet for serious analysis. A business rules approach becomes focused mental activity aimed at achieving important business objectives. Eventually, the best thought patterns of the enterprise could become business rules, the inspiration and primary guidance system for collective behavior. And the business rule itself becomes the instrument of change. The authors predict that a business rules approach to systems development will turn out to be a competitive advantage for any business enterprise that undertakes it.

Applying Lessons Learned about Business Rules

Witnessing a kindergarten T-ball game as a first-time spectator, you learn quickly that if you do not know the rules of the game, you will not be able to interpret the behavior of the players. This is also true of business organizations. For starters, in kindergarten T-ball, a batter continues to bat even after incurring three strikes. You learn quickly that there is a rule that every batter *will* remain at bat until the batter hits a fair ball. Second, a batter will get to first base even if someone tags the batter out or if the ball reaches the person at first base before the runner does. That's because another rule mandates that every batter *will get to first base*, at least, no matter what.

An interesting consequence of these rules is that the half-inning is not over after three outs, because there is no concept of an out, hence no rules about outs. Again, you need to learn that the half-inning ends, according to another rule, when every team member has had an opportunity at bat. Of course, applying the previous rules, this implies that every member will eventually hit the ball and every member will eventually run at least to first base. This, of course, could take forever, which would definitely be stressful to a spectator who has other activities to do on that day. So, it is useful for you to know the rule that declares the end of the game to be one and a half hours after it starts, no matter what. And as for declaring a winner, another rule mandates that every game be automatically declared a tie. There are no winners or losers.

If you did not know these rules, you would certainly be confused because you might presume that kindergarten T-ball follows the rules of other forms of baseball. Therefore, you may mistakenly feel sadness at a third strike, if you were rooting for that team. Or you may unknowingly encourage a runner to run fast enough to beat the ball to first base because you believe the runner needs to do so to get to first base. The truth is that, according to the rules, it makes no difference whether the runner beats the ball to first base. Even worse, you might even try to count the runs in an effort to keep a meaningless score.

Why these rules? The rules of kindergarten T-ball are crafted to meet the common objectives of the sport. These are for players to learn what it means to be part of a team, for players to learn how to hit the ball and in which direction to run, and for players to learn how to catch and throw the ball. There are no objectives for winning a game or for computing batting averages. In fact, to introduce rules for doing either of these could even be harmful to the objectives.

Viewing a kindergarten T-ball game as an enterprise or culture, complete with events (someone hits a ball, someone actually catches a ball), rules, and players, you can apply the following ten lessons learned from the rules of kindergarten T-ball to your own organization:

1. Business rules are the basis for orderly behavior among all players.

2. Business rules influence not only the behavior of players but of onlookers.

3. Business rules teach and instill confidence; they lead to greater productivity in decision-making.

4. Business rules can relieve stress because they explain results.

5. Business rules guide the players' freedom of choice.

6. Business rules guide behavior so common objectives are more likely to be met.

7. Business rules are best leveraged when shared in a consistent manner among all relevant players.

8. Business rules can motivate players or demotivate them.

9. Business rules determine the likelihood of achieving common goals.

10. Business rules are mechanisms by which an organization changes itself.

What Is a Business Rules Approach?

A *business rules approach* is a methodology—and possibly special technology—by which you capture, challenge, publish, automate, and change rules from a strategic business perspective. The result is a *business rules system*, an automated system in which the rules are separated, logically and perhaps physically, from other aspects of the system and shared across data stores, user interfaces, and perhaps applications.

As you can see, at the heart of a business rules approach is an appreciation for rules as a valuable asset for a business organization. In fact, a business rules approach to systems development elevates the importance of business rules to the business and carries that importance into the organization's systems development function and approach.

In some cases, organizations are truly leveraging the business rules approach by incorporating it into business process engineering or reengineering initiatives. To these organizations, a business rules approach is an avenue through which to drive change across large business scopes.

Business rules are a formal expression of knowledge or preference, a guidance system for steering behavior (a transaction) in a desired direction. On the grand scale, business rules, then, are the guidance system that influences the collective behavior of an organization's people and information systems.

A business rules approach aims to deliver that guidance system as externalized rules, automated as an integral and active component in systems architecture. Therein lies the new emphasis: a knowledge-focused way of designing new systems. It is no longer acceptable to bury that knowledge deep in code where no one knows what it is. It is equally no longer acceptable to have that knowledge locked in bondage where it cannot change on demand.

A business rules approach, by deploying technology so that it externalizes and manages the thinking or decision-making capacity of an organization, empowers the business to use that technology as an extension of intellectual power.

Where the Business Rules Approach Is Effective

The pressures facing many businesses today can seem insurmountable. Most of these pressures require changes in the way the business operates through its underlying automated systems. Even more challenging is the realization that customers, competitors, or legislative requirements impose many of these pressures. The following nine common scenarios in today's business world can be improved by applying a business rules approach:

1. **The business needs to change, but its systems are barriers to change**. Most of today's operating systems are similar to black boxes because there is a lack of documentation and knowledge about them. Without proper documentation and knowledge, the task of upgrading the systems is time-consuming and costly at best, and impossible at worst. The lack of knowledge of internal and buried system logic became apparent in the costs of the Y2K projects. Also, the average shelf life of a software release is measured in months and customer expectations have accelerated. The need to deliver upgrades to software is greater than ever before.

2. **New legislative mandates and directions are underway that not only require adherence, but also open the doors to new business opportunities.** Adherence to new legislative mandates usually requires changes to existing systems. New business opportunities may require changes to existing systems or the building of new systems. For example, the healthcare industry is an example of changing rules and emerging opportunities. In the area of healthcare providers, new types of medical benefits and rules for payment and pricing have emerged. Also, in pharmaceutical research, for example, some changes involve reducing clinical trial times for treatment possibilities for life-threatening diseases.

3. **Emerging products, services, and partnerships are arising out of the Internet marketplace.** For example, BtoB (business to business) relationships are emerging through the Web where the rules of these relationships need defining and will evolve over time.

4. **Virtual competition looms.** Virtual competition can appear if similar products and services are available through a competitor who has only a Web presence, not a walk-in presence.

5. **Mergers and acquisitions are prominent**. When this occurs, there is a need to consolidate information, customer bases, and purchases, all requiring evaluation of existing policies, practices, and rules.

6. **Business process reengineering continues**. Some of these efforts sometimes aim to create a consistent global perspective for a given process. Or a BPR effort can aim for a customer-centric process. Regardless, these efforts take a top-down view to streamline a business, make it more effective and smarter. BPR initiatives often change culture and strive for consistent or at least visible policies and rules across organizational barriers.

7. **The application backlog is unending**. There is an increasing desire for e-business applications. IT functions need to develop new systems and change existing ones faster than ever before.

8. **There continues to be a never-ending shortage of application system developers.** This is especially true for the Web development world. Resources become more expensive.

9. **There are shortcomings of other approaches and technologies.** These include information engineering and object-orientation.

Implementing the Business Rules Approach Now

There are many motivating factors in today's fast-paced, e-oriented business world to take an evolutionary step forward in systems development. Merely consider the far-reaching influence, promise, and pace of the Internet, in business and personal life. It's enough to make your head spin.

New dot-com companies have but a short time to prove their worthiness. Traditional (non-dot-com) companies strive to conquer the Web, to be among the first to provide customer service, entice new customers and partners, and introduce new or enhanced services. The Web page is the new calling card. Competition is a mouse click away from your customer. The Internet is leveling some marketplaces and confusing others.

Regardless, the software behind the Web page is the new business image and often the first touch with the customer. The world of e-transactions is moving faster than ever and changing as it moves. How can you keep up with the business? Is there a simple but elegant alternative to how you historically have built systems?

A business rules approach to systems development promises to be the most practical and desirable way to build systems from now on. A business rules approach builds better, changeable systems faster than any previous approach. The time has come to capitalize on the promises of building systems using a business rules approach.

This seems also to be the opinion of C. J. Date, who states as the first sentence in his recent book, "An exciting new technology called business rules is beginning to have a major impact on the I/T industry—more precisely, on the way we develop and maintain computer applications" (Date 2000). He further suggests the eventual impact of a business rules approach when he states later, "business rules can be seen in some respects as the next (and giant) evolutionary step in implementing the [original relational vision]."

John E. Mann expresses a similar opinion (Mann 2000). "The Internet is apparently creating many cases in which the rules-based approach is the only one that makes sense."

Unique Aspects of Business Rules Approach

Taking the business rules approach offers three unique benefits:

- The rule track
- Integration of object-orientation, information engineering, and rule formalism
- Correlation of rules to business motivation (strategy, objectives, goals, tactics)

The most unique aspect of a business rules approach is the introduction of a rule track. It represents the set of rules behind the interactions and over the data, where the rules are managed as a separate, externalized, logical component.

You can choose business rules technology that is designed specifically to manage the execution of a rule collection. Alternately, you can utilize nonbusiness rules technology, even homegrown Java, but in a way that leverages the concepts and advantages of a business rules system.

The second unique characteristic of a business rules approach is that it represents the integration of object-orientation, information engineering, and rule formalisms.

The third unique characteristic of a business rules approach is that it correlates the underlying rules to many aspects of business motivation. These include goals, objectives, strategy, and tactics. In this way, the business can evaluate the effectiveness of the rules in guiding the business toward its desired ends.

Advantages of Building Systems Using a Business Rules Approach

At a glance, ten advantages of building systems using a business rules approach include:

Simplicity. A business rules approach is simple to understand both for business and technical people. Specifically, the concept of a rule, even different classifications of rules, is fairly intuitive. Business people may not be overly interested in data models, process models, or object models. But they are definitely quite interested in business policies and rules. Indeed, it is through policies and rules that business leaders steer the business.

Theoretical base. The concept of rules as protecting data integrity has its origins in the relational model. Additional research has been conducted into active database systems. There is certainly much theory and practical experience with rules from the field of knowledge engineering.

Small number of necessary, nontechnical concepts. At the core of a business rules approach is the rule itself. There are a few concepts around a rule, such as decisions, rule patterns, rule families, and rule clauses. A decision is simply a logical grouping of rules. Rules can be grouped together into rule patterns for analysis purposes based on similar clauses in the rules. Rule patterns can be grouped together into rule families based on similar output from the rule. And, of course, rules are comprised of one or more rule clauses.

Rule independence. A business rules approach aims to express rules in a syntax that is independent of technology and applications. While there is no industry standard for expressing rules, this book provides sample templates.

Ease of application development. With the emergence of commercial rules technology, various kinds of rule processing are made easier. With some products, the application calls the rule product when the application needs a decision to be made based on the execution of underlying rules. With other products, the rule product supports the execution of rules as a result of data changes. In either case, a rule professional defines the rules once and these are executed on behalf of an application as needed.

Rule reuse. If you choose to use commercial rules products, rules managed within them can be reused by various transactions and can interface with a variety of browsers, database management system (DBMS) products, and other kinds of software. Therefore, you can define and implement a rule, or set of rules, only once, but have those rules active for various purposes. You can even test the rules before you develop the rest of the application. Even if you do not use a commercial rules product, you can design your system so that rules are grouped in logical ways and can be reused and shared.

Simplified systems design. A business rules approach aims to separate core process flow from rule execution. This creates two separate flows: one for rules and one for system execution sequence. You design a business rules system around essential intellectual process flow. That is, by focusing on rules, an analyst can distinguish the absolute dependencies among rules from those that are interesting from a performance or user-preference perspective. In this way, rule execution can be delegated to special rules technology (or homegrown rules capability) while the core system flow (without the rules) is designed by a system designer. In this way, there may be fewer necessary deliverables and possibly less need for coding, depending on target technology. That is, with some commercial rules products, analysts capture the integrity and computational rules of the system and developers express them as declarative rules rather than procedural program code. Some commercial rules products manage these rules, compile them, and determine the point of execution, in much the same way that relational products manage data, select among appropriate access paths, compile access paths, and execute those paths. It may take weeks or months to discover what the rules ought to be, depending on the availability of business expertise. However, once you capture and document a rule, you can implement it in rules technology within a matter of hours. Those hours are spent determining where and how to implement a rule. If you were doing this with previous procedural approaches, you would likely implement the rule, not only using procedural code, but often in various programs or methods. Commercial rules products allow you to implement common rules in one place or even to share common clauses among rules.

Dynamic rules. While rule changes may not be instantaneously possible, you can change a business rules system easily. A rule developer can change one rule at a time, or many rules at a time, and have that change available to all relevant business transactions, again depending on target technology. In this way, a business rules system becomes a platform for business change. The rules themselves become the instruments of business adaptability.

Performance. Commercial rules products are designed specifically to manage and execute rules. Thus, they contain internal logic for how best to do so and for delivering optimum performance.

Incremental systems delivery. A business rules system can be delivered quite easily in incremental pieces. If the first increment includes a solid data foundation, cast with the future in mind, incremental system releases become the delivery of upgraded or additional rule sets to an existing infrastructure.

Benefits to the Business

Most of you realize that technology alone is rarely, if ever, a silver bullet. Yet technology deployed with intelligence becomes interesting and powerful. When you deploy technology so that it externalizes and manages the decision-making capacity or the rules of an organization, imagine the possibilities. You empower the business to use that technology as an extension of intellectual power.

In particular, there are six benefits to the business audience of a business rules approach:

- Change is no longer unnecessarily disruptive and costly.

- Business people are closer to the system specifications.

- Business rules are documented and accessible through a repository, no longer hidden in code. When business rules are in an accessible repository, they serve as a mentor to people operating in a collaborative work environment. Business people know where to find the rules.

- When error messages match to the business rules themselves, business people are able to act with complete knowledge, explanations, and business justifications behind a transaction.

- Systems are delivered faster and for less cost.

- Conclusions reached from data warehousing or data mining are more meaningful when you can associate them with active business rules. The correlation of trends or results to the underlying business rules provides a mechanism by which the business can experiment with changed rules so as to change results.

Benefits to Software Engineers

Software engineers also realize at least eleven benefits in applying a business rules approach. These include:

- A business rules approach can shorten development time because there may be less to do, commercial rules products are often easy to use, and you can reuse rule code.

- A business rules approach delivers systems that are designed to accommodate change.

- Developers can enter business rules into rules technology without needing to understand the full span of the processes using the rules.

- A business rules approach narrows the communication gap between requirements, analysis, and design.

- If application code is generated from rules there is less coding by humans, and consequently less opportunity for error. With less need to code, developers are free to focus more on business requirements.

- Because you can change rules easily, there is little need to freeze requirements. Instead, you can focus efforts on determining the priority of the rule change and proper authorization for doing so.

- A rules layer is a natural layer between the user interface and the database layers. It allows for the opportunity to experiment with rules technology.

- A business rules approach adds to existing methodologies the one link that has always been missing and that, it turns out, may be the most important of all.

- Developing a business rules system can be more cost effective than customizing packages.

- A business rules approach enables rule enforcement across technology environments allowing for migrations from one technology to another and interfaces to multiple technologies.

- A business rules approach positions you for technology evolution.

How Can a Business Rules Approach Deliver These Benefits?

The business rules approach in this book is based on the four very simple principles mentioned earlier, which together deliver the benefits above. This book refers to these principles as the STEP principles. They are:

(S) Separate. This means that you separate the rules from all other aspects of the requirements and in the system itself. You do this primarily so you can reuse rules. That is, if you manage them as an individual asset, you can apply techniques specific for optimizing them and you can change rules independently of other aspects of the system. This includes, optionally, separating rules into rules technology so rule processing is efficient.

(T) Trace. This means that you maintain a connection from each rule in two directions. The first direction is toward its origins. A rule has origins in aspects of the business's motivation, such as business missions, goals, objectives, strategies, tactics, and policies. You will also keep track of specific metrics, which will be the yardstick by which the business wants to measure the effectiveness of a rule in guiding the organization. Therefore, you will trace a rule to its origins so you can determine, over time, whether the rule remains a correct rule by which the organization wishes to steer its course. The second direction to trace is the rule's implementation. You do this so that you can assess the impact of rule changes. That is, you record all of the places where the rule is executed. For systems, this may include cross-references from the rule to object methods, to DBMS triggers, and various other implementation options. For human execution of a rule, this may include cross-references to policy and procedures manuals.

(E) Externalize. This means that you express a rule in a format understandable to nontechnical, business audiences and that you make the rule available to these audiences. You do this so that everyone knows what the rules are, where to find out what they are, and is able to optimize them. Doing this allows business leaders to inspect rules and consider challenging them or measuring their effectiveness from time to time.

(P) Position. This means that you always position a rule for change precisely because you expect rules to change as a regular course of doing business. You do this so that rule changes happen easily and quickly. Positioning a rule for change can mean implementing it in a technology that allows for easy change, such as a commercial rules product. Even without using a commercial rules product, positioning a rule for change means being able to conduct impact analysis when a rule needs to change, such that you know which business events, decisions, and organizations are impacted by the change. It also means that the data foundation supporting the rule is built in a flexible manner such that rule changes should not require expensive and time-consuming database changes.

Table 1.1   STEP Principles and Their Purposes

STEP PRINCIPLE	PURPOSE OF THE PRINCIPLE
Separate rules	• To reuse rules • To apply special techniques to optimize rule quality • To change rules independently of other system aspects
Trace rules	• To determine, over time, if the rule remains a correct rule for guiding the business • To assess the impact of rule changes
Externalize rules	• To allow everyone to know where rules can be known • To allow everyone to know what the rules are • To allow everyone to challenge the rules
Position rules for change	• To enable easy rule changes • To enable quick rule changes

Keep these STEP principles in mind because they will keep you honest in your own business rules approach. You can compromise any one of them at any time and for valid reasons. But should you do so, do it in an informed manner. That is, make sure you can justify the price paid and the benefits lost.

Table 1.1 contains the benefits of each STEP principle. Using it can help you determine what aspects of this methodology you can leave out, what sacrifices need to be made, and what benefits can be missed.

When an organization coordinates the management and automation of its business rules in a rigorous way, the rules become an organizational intellectual asset. When the organization automates those rules across platforms, the business rule becomes an instantaneous and consistent guidance system, the electronic nervous system of the learning organization. If the organization can change those rules at will, the rules become a strategic tool for charting the future.

Before proceeding with this book, ask yourself the following questions:

- Does your organization change itself, from time to time? Might such a change be as small as a change in one rule at a time?

- When the organization wants to change a rule, how does the IT function respond? Does the IT function know where the rule is enforced? If so, is it enforced in a variety of technologies, thereby requiring several sets of skills and testing?

- How long does it take to make such a change? How much does it cost?

- Are there rules that cannot realistically be traced to all of their automated components or that are too expensive to change?

- Are these answers reasonable in today's business environment?

A business rules approach is part of the solution for changing these answers.

Barriers to a Business Rules Approach

Many simple and valuable ideas are met with resistance. While there are many reasons for resistance even to good ideas, the two major barriers are cultural discomfort and profit motive, that is, cultural discomfort and price-driven resistance.

Cultural discomfort arises because an organization is accustomed to developing systems according to in-house traditions (or lack thereof) and the pride that accompanies current practices. The idea of changing those traditions, even for a better way, may seem, at first, like an admission of failure. It is sometimes difficult to perceive the fine-tuning of an already successful approach as a sign of leadership.

As a comparison, it may be interesting to contemplate the original resistance to relational technology. When relational products emerged on the marketplace, some visible industry commentators proclaimed that the relational model could not work at all, or could not work well. As a small admission, some resistors hesitantly accepted that perhaps relational technology was appropriate for query systems, but that it certainly was inappropriate for transactional systems. Many people found it difficult to accept the fact that a DBMS optimizer could select a valid access path and perhaps do so better than an experienced programmer. Other people could not imagine a DBMS that did not rely on visible intrarecord pointers because these people could not conceive that a DBMS without such visible pointers could ever perform acceptably. Most of these resistances were either untrue or have been overcome.

Profit-driven resistance is interesting because today's business world is accustomed to reducing all ideas to profit potential. Without very short-term profit realization, good ideas and approaches are slow to gain acceptance. The fast-paced world wants to see profit benefits well predicted and immediate, if possible.

The good news about a business rules approach is that it overcomes both kinds of resistances. From a cultural perspective, there is no doubt that most current systems development practices are seriously lacking in effective management and automation of business rules. Therefore, regardless of an organization's favorite systems development approach, it is lacking in this regard, but so is everyone else. There need not be a sense of personal or organizational failure. It is simply a maturation process.

Not only that, but the impetus for cultural change usually requires the pain of changing to be less than the pain of not changing. Because the business world now needs new systems that can change on demand, the pain of not adopting a business rules approach may quickly become worse than the cultural implications of endorsing the business rules approach. Further, John E. Mann of Patricia Seybold Group (Mann 2000) states that evolution to a new approach becomes attractive when there are pressures of change and uncertainty, products deliver on a promise, and customer experiences with the approach and products are positive. No doubt today businesses face change and uncertainty. There are rules-technology products delivering on the promises of the business rules approach. There are a growing number of positive and successful customer experiences.

There is another cultural consideration. It is highly likely that your competitors are already investigating a business rules approach and corresponding technology. If these organizations benefit from the advantages in this chapter, other organizations who do not do so will be at a disadvantage and may need to catch up to remain competitive.

The profit motive is also present. As indicated throughout this book, a business rules approach (depending on target technology) can deliver systems faster. More importantly, it can deliver systems designed for change.

There is one more consideration to ponder. Relational technology made its initial successful entrance into the general IT community when it proved to satisfy a need not satisfied well enough by other approaches. In this case, relational first emerged as a technology for supporting decision-support, query-oriented systems. Structured DBMS products, such as hierarchical or network DBMS products, did not do this well at all and other approaches, such as inverted file technology, did not do this well enough. So, there was an immediate market need that was satisfied by relational technology. From here, the relational approach and corresponding products found their way into transactional systems and now into data warehousing capabilities.

As a corollary, the business rules approach makes its initial successful entrance because it satisfies the business's need to work with systems that can change easily, especially where the business leaders themselves more directly guide those changes. A business rules approach begins with the language of the business people and traces those requirements to an implementation that allows for easy changes. This is a niche that is badly needed now. Over time, a business rules approach will become the standard way of developing almost all systems.

The Role of Rules Technology

The term *commercial rules technology* means specialized software for managing and executing rules. A business rules approach leads to dynamically changeable systems primarily because commercial rules technology today enables us to do so. The advantages of commercial rules technology include:

- Reducing the need to write code
- Reducing development time
- Reducing bugs
- Enabling quick rule enhancements
- Delivering rules independent of databases, middleware, and presentation layer
- Delivering visible rules (no longer hidden)
- Enabling rule reuse
- Enabling single point rule specification
- Automating rule execution.

When you first introduced a relational database management system into your organization, you deployed technology that externalized and managed the informational asset of the organization. With a business rules approach, you deploy technology so that it externalizes and manages the thinking or decision-making capacity.

Like relational DBMS products in the past, commercial rules technology should only get better with time, as vendors understand more about the idiosyncrasies of effective rule management and execution. After all, application programmers cannot do global optimization of a rule within a rule set with each program fix in the same way that rule-specific software can.

A major advantage to using commercial rules technology is that it requires you to write less code. Writing code is time-consuming, error prone, and costly. For these reasons, changes are also time-consuming, and expensive.

This book is not meant to be a thorough reference on current and emerging commercial rules technology. However, for the purpose of the methodology, the book divides the world of such products into two broad categories, which are quite different from each other: data-change-oriented and service-oriented.

A *data-change-oriented rules product* executes rules when a running application touches data for which rules have been declared. With this approach, as an application attempts to update data, the rules capability watches for conditions that must be true about the data as well as conditions that should cause a reaction, such as the creation of new data. Vendors in this category of rules products include Versata Inc. and USoft Inc.

The Versata Logic Server (VLS) supports declarative rules that are bound to the data or object model and that become part of Java objects. The rules are not implemented as triggers or stored procedures in the DBMS! The rules execute automatically when an application wants to create, update, and delete data. The VLS is able to refer to the current and prior data values in the midst of a transaction.

In a USoft environment, you capture rules in USoft's repository. From here, the rules are translated into executable code that will execute automatically for any situation to which the rule applies. Again, this is because the rules are bound to the underlying data such that any application that attempts to update, delete, or create that data will invoke all appropriate rule execution.

A *service-oriented rules product* executes rules upon request by a running application, not because the application directly attempted to touch data. In this case, the rules service waits until an application calls on it to apply rules to data. The rules are not bound to a data or object structure. Usually, the application passes the data to the rules service, the rules service may also retrieve and update data from a database or objects, the rules service executes the rules, and the rules service sends the results of the rule execution back to the calling application. The application can then decide to abort the transaction, update the database, or carry out other actions. You can see that these rules are not bound to data structures. They are free-floating. The actions prescribed in such rules apply to in-memory data values. The rule designer assigns the rules to rule sets. The data objects are loaded into memory and bound to the working storage of the rules products prior to invocation of the rules services. Products in the service-oriented category include HNC Software's Blaze Advisor and ILOG Inc.'s Jrules.

You will need to decide whether to use a commercial rules product or not, and if so which one. You should consider that it is most advantageous to use a commercial rules product in any of six circumstances, as when:

- The rules change frequently.
- The rules need to change quickly.
- The rules are complex and better supported by such a product.
- The rules are to be shared and consistently applied across transactions.
- Other system software, such as operating systems, browsers, and DBMS products, will deliver new releases and your system must continue to function with new releases without unnecessary interruptions.
- The performance of rule execution is acceptable, perhaps superior, in a rules product.

TESTIMONIALS FOR THE BUSINESS RULES APPROACH

The most useful testimonials on the success of the business rules approach are from customers of commercial rules technology products.

Versata
John Mann reported benefits touted by Versata customers such as:

> Applications created with Versata were much easier to change than those created by ordinary programs . . . the only task is to add or change business rules.
> Applications developed with Versata were free of random bugs that plague programs written by hand.
> Versata defines an overall plan and structure for an application.

A major hotel chain, in an effort to develop a major Java application, obtained development efforts ranging from six to eight months and costing $250–400k. Instead, the chain developed the application using Versata as a means to deliver an enterprise class Java application without requiring sophisticated Java expertise. Not only was the project successful, but it led the way to more development using a business rules approach and the Versata product.

USoft
Likewise, USoft customers report benefits such as:

> Rules are expressed only once and managed explicitly.
> Rules are automatically combined at execution time into a full process.
> Rules execute automatically as determined by the rules software, not by programmers.
> Rules are independent of database, middleware, and Graphical User Interfaces (GUIs).
> Rules are no longer hidden, but well documented and understood.
> Lines of code are drastically reduced.
> Automatic reuse of rules by other applications and components is a great advantage.

For example, Carolyn Jackson, a USoft client, says, "We have found the business rules approach makes it easy to make changes. Adjustments can be made quickly without disrupting or delaying the overall development schedule." As she points out, "Probably for the first time ever we are anticipating a finished development which comes in on time, is completed for the agreed price and will actually do more than we originally requested."

As David Kail says "Using USoft Developer has allowed us to successfully replace the previous legacy systems and provides us with a system which we can keep up to date with the ever-changing business requirements."

ILOG

Inovant, the IT and processing services subsidiary of Visa International, incorporated ILOG JRules business rule software into portions of Inovant's new Web-based profile management system. ILOG JRules will allow Inovant to better manage and maintain the business policies that support Visa's electronic interaction with its 21,000 member banks. The new profile management system is part of Inovant's overall reengineering of VisaNet, the world's largest and most sophisticated consumer financial transaction processing system. Inovant operates the global transaction-processing network supporting Visa branded products. ILOG JRules will be used to automate complex validation tasks associated with Visa's 21,000 member profiles.

"We manage a tremendously complex global transaction processing system, and as we reengineer that system to meet the rapidly growing payment volume generated by Visa, we need tools like ILOG JRules that can bring greater efficiencies to the system," said Dimitri Karavias, senior vice president of VisaNet Management Systems at Inovant. "We selected ILOG JRules because it is flexible and easy to embed, allows us to dynamically change our member profile management application, has the performance to support our highly demanding transaction volume, and reduces the development cost of making changes to the profile management system." The customizable rule language support in the product will allow nontechnical personnel at Inovant to quickly update business rules that correlate to bank-specific programs in response to changing market and customer needs. Both ILOG rule engines (for C++ and Java) are becoming widely used throughout the telecommunications industry for alarm filtering and correlation, customer billing and billing mediation, and customer relationship management.

Chordiant Software will use ILOG JRules business rule engine software to implement consistent business policies across CRM applications and customer touchpoints—a feature that will help Chordiant customers build closer customer relationships by targeting their service and product offerings. "We selected ILOG JRules because its flexibility allowed us to integrate the technology in record time—crucial for fast deployment—and the customizable business rule language support will allow us to offer a solution that business people can use," said Sam Spadafora, CEO for Chordiant Software. "Customers are demanding more personalized Web experiences and the ability to receive the right offer at the right time based on their need. ILOG's JRules will help us to deliver that one-to-one marketing."

Annuncio Software Inc. selected ILOG JRules business rule engine to enhance Annuncio Bright's ability to tailor marketing promotions and campaigns. Annuncio Bright makes it easy for e-marketers to target marketing offers and merchandising messages without requiring help from IT staff. ILOG

JRules provides the flexibility that marketers need to create rule-based promotions, including cross-sell and up-sell campaigns, content specific to a company's merchandising and promotions. "Rule-based merchandising and web personalization are important core technologies of our Annuncio Bright product," said Didier Moretti, chief executive officer and founder, Annuncio Software Inc. "We initially selected ILOG JRules because it was flexible and easy to embed, speeding our time to market. The customizable business rule language feature in ILOG JRules should enhance our ability to create an e-merchandising campaign-specific business rule language that our customers will easily understand."

Vodafone TeleCommerce (NYSE: VOD) is using the ILOG JRules business rule engine to manage billing rules in Billit, the new Vodafone billing solution. Billit enables real-time customer billing for the use of communications services, including content commerce and mobile IP (Internet Protocol). Initially, Billit will be deployed inside the Vodafone group.

Formerly known as Mannesmann TeleCommerce, Vodafone TeleCommerce developed Billit in just eight months, and plans to replace existing billing systems with the new solution. "We were extremely impressed by the flexibility offered by ILOG Rules for managing the billing logic in our product," said Dr. Jürgen Lemke, the Billit project manager at Vodafone. "We could tell ILOG JRules was written specifically for this sort of deployment because its highly intuitive development environment let us quickly do exactly what we wanted to do. Moreover, its openness will enable our customers to easily adapt the product to their needs for many years to come."

Applying the Business Rules Approach

Essentially, there are three ways to apply the business rules approach:

Discovery and analysis. Follow a business rules approach for discovering requirements and analyzing them. Then, deliver a traditional process or object model, data model, and rules correlated to those models for your designers.

Discovery, analysis, and design. Follow a business rules approach for discovering requirements, analyzing them, and designing the system such that you deliver a design that specifically separates rule-execution components from the rest of your system.

Discovery, analysis, design, and implementation in a commercial rules product. Follow a business rules approach for discovering requirements, analyzing them, designing and implementing the rules in commercial rules technology.

Table 1.2 summarizes the benefits of each application.

Table 1.2   Benefits of Applying the Business Rules Approach

APPLICATION	BENEFIT	HOW BENEFITS CAN BE ACHIEVED
Using the business rules approach only for discovery and analysis (not design and implementation)	Delivers crisper business the business requirements and brings the business audience closer to the requirements process Externalizes organizational knowledge which can be expressed as rules Provides an avenue for improved decision-making because rules are known Positions the organization for rules technology	Capture data, process, and rules as separate kinds of requirements Extract rules from legacy code, where applicable Analyze data, process, and rules according to specific techniques to improve their quality Tie rules to business motivation (goals, objectives, strategy) and to mechanisms for measuring related business progress Capture, publish, and manage rules through a repository Establish a rule stewardship program in line with business process reengineering initiatives Drive data from rules Wrap process around rules Conduct rule analysis Ensure traceability of business requirement to rule to its implementation
Using the business rules approach for discovery, analysis, and design (but not using commercial rules technology)	All of the above plus: Enables easier rule changes	All of the above plus: Separate rule execution code from core process code Deliver flexible data structures, capable of accommodating new data requirements for new or changed rules
Using the business rules approach for discovery, analysis, design, and implementation with commercial rules technology	All of the above plus: Substantially increases initial development productivity Enables easy incremental systems delivery Delivers a system that is designed to be a significant instrument of change, not a hindrance to it	All of the above plus: Reduce lines of code (by not writing detailed code for managing rule execution) Test rules or rule sets before full data is available and before full application is available Execute rules automatically through rules technology

(continues)

Table 1.2   *(continued)*

APPLICATION	BENEFIT	HOW BENEFITS CAN BE ACHIEVED
	Significantly reduces cost and time for system maintenance	Force a single point of rule specification
	Enables consistent rules enforcement across technology environments	
	Positions the organization for technology evolution (as database, application, and middleware technology mature, they are expected to include business rule enforcement, rule-related functionalitys, and rule-related performance enhancements).	

The first option implies that you believe the business rules approach provides a missing link in your requirements and analysis process. In this case, you follow the methodology so that your deliverables include the new considerations for rules and integrate rules with process or objects and data. You pass these analysis deliverables to designers who then design systems in their usual way, but integrate the rule specifications into the design deliverables, perhaps by including rules as part of the specifications for object methods, for example. If this is the case, follow the methodology in this book through to Chapter 11. This option allows you to separate rules from data and process from an analytical perspective leading to higher quality requirements and bringing the business audience closer to the requirements process. Regardless of what your designers do with the rules, you should aim to trace them to business objectives and their implementations, make them accessible to business people, and hope that developers position them for easy change.

The second option takes this idea one step further. If you select this option, you believe that the business rules approach not only adds value to your requirements and analysis process, but you also want to design your system so that you separate the rule component from the core process flow. If this is the case, follow the methodology in this book through to Chapter 12. Request that developers create software components that execute rules and that can be shared by other application components. This option allows you to separate rules from data and process through to the design aspect so that the executable version of rules is reusable. Be sure, again, to trace the rules to business objectives and their implementations, make them easily accessible to the business community, and encourage developers to position them for change.

The third option is the most ideal because it takes full advantage of the business rules approach all the way through to implementation. This is similar to the way that relational DBMS products take full advantage of databases designed following relational principles. The third option, by using technology specifically aimed at managing and executing rules, can significantly shorten development time and reduce the time it takes to make changes later. This option allows you to separate rules from data and process all the way through to implementation in a rather effortless manner. In this case, follow the methodology in this book through Chapter 14. Commercial rules products automatically trace rules to their implementation and you may also be able to record the rules' connections to business objectives. You will still need to take extra steps to make rules available to business people. The rules product will render the rules easy to change and will likely deliver efficient rule-processing.

Regardless of the option you choose, following is a summary of the kinds of rule-related techniques introduced in this book to guide you in delivering high-quality rules in your system:

1. Identify decisions behind business events.

2. Decompose decisions into atomic rules.

3. Classify, name rules and write them according to templates.

4. Improve the quality of rules through determination of inconsistencies and overlaps and redundancies.

5. Classify rules into rule patterns.

6. Determine dependencies among rule executions.

7. Position rules always for change.

Alternately, you may evolve similar techniques that work best for you.

Where to Go from Here

So far we have made certain assumptions:

- You want to build better systems faster.

- You want to build systems capable of easily accommodating change.

- You have a fixed amount of time and money.

- You probably practice iterative development and parallel execution.

- Many of you follow an object-oriented approach to systems development.

The purpose of this book is to define a practical path by which you can be successful in developing business rules systems within your constraints and culture. You have already started your journey into the world of business rules by buying this book. Now, follow these six simple steps:

Step 1: Select a target system or small part of a system for which to experiment with a business rules approach. Choose one for which a simple data or object class model will do and whose rules are simple, known, or accessible. Margaret Thorpe of ILOG Inc. at the Business Rules Forum Conference in November 1997 provided an insight. "The most important rules are likely to be in marketing, selling, production and delivery, invoicing, customer service, customer relationship management, and regulatory compliance because these tend to be high volume and heavy in customer interface." Today, add to that list business-to-business partnering on the Web. Surely, you can find a subset of a system and begin to search for rules.

Step 2: Select a commercial rules product to use in a prototype. To quickly select a product, review Chapter 12 to gain an understanding of the differences among products. Contact a vendor mentioned in this book and discuss their product's capabilities.

Step 3: Follow the methodology in this book and build a prototype. How you follow the methodology in this book depends upon which application of a business rules approach in Table 1.2 you choose. Option 1 implies following the steps in Chapters 4, 5, 6, 7, 9, 10, and 11. Option 2 adds to these the steps in Chapter 12. Option 3 adds yet to these the steps in Chapter 13 or 14 along with product-specific considerations.

Step 4: Experiment with rules. Allow the business people to see a system tightly controlled with rules versus a version, which allows more freedom of choice.

Step 5: Change rules. Learn how the business reacts to change when it can quickly change a rule.

Step 6: Evaluate the experience for others. Capture development metrics and also change management metrics. Document the skills gained and the lessons learned.

As you can see, the book presents chapters for following a business rules approach from scoping (Chapter 4), planning (Chapter 5), discovering requirements (Chapters 6, 7, and 8), analyzing requirements (Chapters 9, 10, and 11), designing for rules (Chapters 12, 13, and 14), and managing rules (Chapter 15). Chapter 3 summarizes these steps so you can see the difference in emphasis in a business rules approach.

Most importantly, the methodology in this book provides the missing ingredient from other methodologies, which is the collection of steps, techniques, and guidelines for capturing and automating business rules in a strategic way.

Summary

The IT industry has lacked a formal approach to managing, analyzing, and automating all of those business rules. A Business Rules Approach to Systems Development may prove to be the most practical and desirable way to build systems from now on, as it promises to deliver better changeable systems faster. At the heart of a business rules approach to systems development is an appreciation for rules as a valuable resource for a business organization. Commercial rules technology has the promise of putting the business back in touch with itself, by unearthing and externalizing its own rules, which are the foundation of its own decision-making capacity. A business rules approach to systems development elevates the importance of business rules to the business and carries that importance into the organization's systems development function and approach.

A business rules approach leads to a system equipped to change rules, add new rules, and retire old rules. A business rules approach manages and delivers with new rigor the tangible rules of the business, positioned for change. A business rules approach puts the business back in charge of its destiny. So, rule discovery and rule change become a continuous dialog with the business community, a normal way of doing business, a normal way of building systems, and that's where most businesses need to go now. A business rules approach to systems development will turn out to be a competitive advantage for a business enterprise. Your competitors are probably already investigating the advantages of a business rules approach.

As you read this book, keep in mind that shared rules and shared data result in shared knowledge. Shared knowledge makes for a smarter learning enterprise. A smarter learning enterprise is not only empowered to change, but is intellectually positioned to become whatever it envisions for itself.

Through a business rules approach, humans and systems in an enterprise inherit a guidance system that originates from the experience and thinking of its leaders. Each actor in the enterprise becomes a possessor of such knowledge. An enterprise with an automated business rules asset becomes master of its fate because it controls its intelligence and stewards change through information technology.

Business Rule Concepts

Once upon a time, people lived in a world without business rules.

Probably not true. Probably not even desirable.

Of course, people lived in a world without computers (as impossible as that may seem to some), but never without business rules. The term *business rules* loosely means the rules or policies of the business; they guide the business in its activities. In the everyday business world, the following statements are business rules or business policies:

- An employee with five years with the company is entitled to four weeks of paid vacation.

- An employee with fewer than four years with the company is entitled to three weeks of paid vacation.

- An employee with fewer than six months with the company is not entitled to paid vacation without special permission.

- Stock options vest one-third each year over three years.

- A visit to a medical professional within the healthcare plan network costs $10.

- A visit to a medical professional not within the healthcare plan network will cost the employee a deductible of $500 and 20 percent of all expenses after that up to a maximum of $5,000 after which the employee will incur 100 percent of the costs.

- A customer with outstanding payment due must pay in full prior to a new order being shipped.

- A preferred customer automatically receives express shipping on all orders.

So, informally speaking, business rules are the guidelines and mandatory policies that govern interactions among employees, customers, suppliers, and automated systems. But, what is a business rule, *formally* speaking?

This chapter introduces the definition and classifications of business rules that will be used throughout the book. This chapter also includes a first look at the case study, which will give you a brief overview of how to implement rules.

Formally Defining Business Rules

There is no industry standard definition for the term *business rule*, or even for *rule*. This book adopts the definition put forth by the Business Rules Group (2000): "A *business rule* is a statement that defines or constrains some aspect of the business. It is intended to assert business structure or to control or influence the behavior of the business." The Guide Business Rule Project Team is a group of individuals dedicated to standardizing the terms surrounding the concept of business rules (www.businessrulesgroup .org).

For now, then, think of business rules as the set of conditions that govern a business event so that it occurs in a way that is acceptable to the business. That is, a business event is unsuccessful when it fails to meet the business's rules for a successful business event. The business leaders determine the difference between a successful and unsuccessful business event. They do this by stating rules that define all possible and permissible conditions for a successful business event along with those that are not permissible.

If it helps, consider the business event from a database perspective. That is, database updates represent the finalization of a business event in that the database holds the evidence, such as an order scheduled for shipment, that the business event has occurred to successful completion. The business event should not go to successful completion if the conditions surrounding it do not measure up to the business's rules or requirements. For example, if the target business event is the placing of an order, the order should not be entered into the database (that is, accepted as an approved order) unless the items ordered are valid, the items ordered are available for shipment in the desired timeframe, and the financial agreement between the customer and the business is acceptable.

Whether you consider a business rules approach to be a methodology for the business people or for systems development people, the business rules perspective focuses on the "thinking" or "decision-making capacity" of the organization. The business organization sets the rules by which relevant parties, such as customers, suppliers, employees, and corresponding systems, are to behave. The rules (or absence of rules) represent the degrees of freedom that an organization allows for its customers, employees, and partners. In the latter case, the business organization may allow the supplier or customer to establish (and change) his or her own rules of interaction. Doing so allows for customized interfaces to Web-based applications, for example.

Classifying Business Rules

There are different types of statements that qualify as business rules according to the definition above. Unfortunately, there is no universal business rule classification scheme. Table 2.1 documents business rule classification schemes proposed by various individuals and organizations. It is not important for you to know these classification schemes, only to understand that there are many of them and perhaps more to come. However, if you read Chapters 13 and 14—which contains implementations of this book's case study in commercial rules products—you may want to refer to Table 2.1 to better understand a particular product's solution.

The usefulness of a business rule classification scheme depends on the purposes served by it for the intended audience. A business rule classification scheme is helpful in discovering rules, analyzing them, and even designing for them.

Some rule classification schemes are intended for application developer audiences. These may contain classifications that differentiate validation rules from referential integrity rules, for example, because there is usually a difference between these two types from a programming perspective. A programmer may code for validation rules, but referential integrity rules may be enforced in the DBMS. Look at the Versata rule classifications in Table 2.1 as an example of classifications that may be more meaningful to application developers.

Table 2.1   Classifications of Business Rules

SOURCE	BUSINESS RULE CLASSIFICATION SCHEME
Business Rules Group (2000)	Derivation: a statement of knowledge that is derived from other knowledge in the business • Mathematical calculation • Inference Structural assertion: a defined concept or a statement of a fact that expresses some aspect of the structure of the enterprise. This encompasses both terms and the facts assembled from these terms. • Terms • Facts Action assertion: a statement of a constraint or condition that limits or controls the actions of the enterprise • Authorization • Condition • Integrity constraint
Ross (2001)	• Facts • Terms • Rules • Constraints • Derivations • Inferences • Timing • Sequence • Heuristics

(continues)

Table 2.1   Classifications of Business Rules

SOURCE	BUSINESS RULE CLASSIFICATION SCHEME
General Data Analysis Rule Types	Attribute rules • Uniqueness • Optionality (null) • Value check Computations Inferences Multi-entity-attribute constraints Relationship rules • Cardinality • Optionality • Referential integrity • Counts of cardinality
C. J. Date (2000)	• Constraint • State constraint • Transition constraint • Stimulus/response • Derivation • Computation • Inference
C. J. Date (2000)	Chris Date further proposes another scheme for constraints that is based on the structure of the data itself • Domain constraints • Column constraints • Table constraints (constraints within one table) • Database constraints (constraints among two or more tables)
Versata Inc.	• Referential integrity rules • Derivations (attribute computations) • Validation (attribute mandatory/optional values, min, max) • Constraint (attribute-to-attribute constraints within one entity?) • Action/event • Presentation rules
USoft Inc. (Mallens [1997])	• Restriction rules: business constraints on the information to be stored, what is not allowed • Behavior rules: how the system is to behave in given situations, what the system should do automatically • Deductive rules: how information should be derived or calculated • Presentation rules: how the system presents itself to the user, how work and tasks are to be organized • Instruction rules: how the user is to operate the system in certain situations

Other rule classification schemes are intended for database audiences. These may contain classifications that differential rules for tables versus rules for columns because these may have different performance implications, for starters. Look at C. J. Date's (2000) more formal rule classifications in Table 2.1 for examples of these.

Still another way to classify rules is to divide rules into entity rules, attribute rules, and relationship rules. Such a classification scheme is most intuitive to data analysts and data modelers because these people would prefer to document relationship rules with the relationship and attribute rules with the attribute, for example. Note that Table 2.1 makes reference to the most familiar types of attribute and relationship rules (attribute uniqueness, attribute optionality, attribute value checks, relationship cardinality, relationship optionality, and relationship referential integrity). Table 2.1 also includes reference to more complex rules (attribute computations, attribute inferences, relationship counts, and multi-entity-attribute constraints) which are sometimes captured by data modelers and sometimes not a variation of this kind of rule classification scheme can be found in Moriarty (1998).

A pure business rules approach does not distinguish among rules based on who captures them or whether the rules are simple or complex. This leads to other rule classifications more closely aligned with a rule audience such that these classification schemes are based on the intent and intellectual properties of the rule itself. These classification schemes ignore distinctions based on who captures them, where they are programmed, and which data model or database constructs they most relate to. Examples of these, in Table 2.1, are in Ross (1997) and in the Business Rules Group (2000).

It certainly is not the intent of this book to suggest unnecessarily another business rule classification scheme. However, this book uses one intended for the business audience (not technical professionals) and specifically for use during the discovery of rules and their validation. With this in mind, the business rule classification scheme serves the following purposes:

- Explains the full range of business rules that you are looking to capture.

- Simplifies and guides the business audience efficiently through a useful sequence for discovering rules.

- Enables business people to express each kind of business rule in its own kind of sentence template for better clarity.

Figure 2.1 depicts a high-level business rule classification scheme used in the remainder of this book. You do not need to use this scheme. Feel free to adopt a scheme

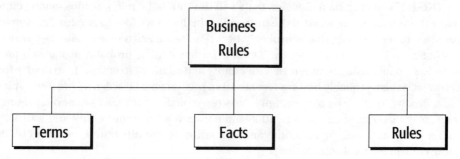

Figure 2.1   A high-level business rule classification scheme.

that best suits your most important audience and serves your most important purposes. Notice that Figure 2.1 divides the world of business rules into only three major categories: terms, facts, and rules.

Terms

A *term* is a noun or noun phrase with an agreed upon definition. You will later see that terms are referenced in other types of business rules. A term can define any one of the following:

- A concept, such as *customer*
- A property of a concept, such as *customer-credit-rating-code*
- A value, such as *female*
- A value set, such as *Days-of-the-American-Workweek (Mon, Tues, Wed, Thurs, Fri)*

(Note: If you are a data modeler, terms will turn out to be entities, attributes, domains, or constants. In the examples above, Customer will probably become an entity. Customer-credit-rating-code will probably become an attribute of a Customer entity. The third example, "female" is probably a constant used in a rule expression. The fourth example is a set of values that may become a domain.)

Facts

A *fact* is a statement that connects terms, through prepositions and verb phrases, into sensible, business-relevant observations. You will later see that facts are also referenced in other types of business rules. Examples of facts are:

- Customer can place order.
- Order is for line item.
- Line item is for a product.
- Customer qualifies for customer-credit-rating-code.

The terms and facts are the semantics behind the rules. They will also become the foundation for a logical data model and physical database and perhaps a business object model.

(Note: If you are a data modeler, facts will turn out to be relationships among entities or the association of an attribute to an entity. In the above four examples, "customer can place order" is a fact that is probably best represented as a relationship between a Customer entity and an Order entity. "Order is for line item" is probably also best represented as a relationship between an Order entity and a Line Item entity. "Line item is for a product" is also probably best represented as a relationship between a Line Item entity and a Product entity. The last example, "customer qualifies for customer-credit-rating-code" may materialize as a m:n relationship between a Customer entity and a Credit-Rating entity and will then become an association of the attribute Customer-credit-rating-code in the Customer entity.)

Rules

The third classification, rules, is where the excitement lies in a business rules approach. A *rule* is a declarative statement that applies logic or computation to information values. A rule results either in the discovery of new information or a decision about taking action. Examples of rules are:

- The order-total-dollar-amount is the sum of the line item dollar amounts.

- A new customer must not place an order whose order-total-dollar-amount exceeds $1000.

- Shipment of an order for an existing customer who has not paid their last invoice, will be delayed until that payment is received.

So, a rule will turn out to be executable logic that uses information as input and creates, as output, either information or action. Figure 2.2 deconstructs the three classifications further. Table 2.2 summarizes these classifications and offers examples of each. It also includes additional classifications that will be covered in the next section of this chapter.

Classifications of Rules

As a business event or use case takes place, a business person may inject rules to control its execution and that there are, at least, four possible ways that a rule can guide a business event. Specifically, a rule can do one of the following within the context of the business event:

- Present information about the business event.
- Constrain information created by the business event.
- Initiate an action outside the boundary of the target system or business event.
- Create new information from existing information.

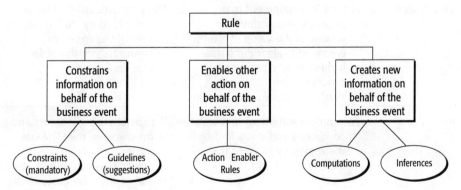

Figure 2.2 Rule classification scheme.

Table 2.2   Business Rule Classifications Used

BUSINESS RULE CLASSIFICATION	SIMPLE DEFINITION OF BUSINESS RULE CLASSIFICATION	EXAMPLES
Term	A noun or noun phrase with an agreed upon definition.	Customer Customer credit rating code "female" Days of the American Work Week (Mon, Tues, Wed, Thurs, Fri)
Fact	A statement that connects terms, through prepositions and verbs, into sensible business-relevant observations.	Customer can place order. Order is for line item. Line item is for a product. Customer qualifies for customer-credit-rating-code.
Mandatory constraint	A complete statement that expresses an unconditional circumstance that must be true or not true for the business event to complete with integrity.	A customer *must* not have more than 10 open orders at one time. The total dollar amount of a customer order *must* not be greater than the customer's single order credit limit amount.
Guideline	A complete statement that expresses a warning about a circumstance that should be true or not true.	A customer *should* not have more than 10 open orders at one time.
Action enabler	A complete statement that tests conditions and upon finding them true, initiates another business event, message, or other activity.	If a customer order is valid, then initiate the Place Order business event. If a customer is high risk, then notify the customer services manager.
Computation	A complete statement that provides an algorithm for arriving at the value of a term where such algorithms may include sum, difference, product, quotient, count, maximum, minimum, average.	The total-amount-due for an order is computed as the sum of the line-item amount(s) for the order plus tax
Inference	A complete statement that tests conditions and upon finding them true, establishes the truth of a new fact.	If a customer has no outstanding invoices, then the customer is of preferred status. If a customer is of preferred status, then the customer's order qualifies for a 20 percent discount.

These classifications indicate what the rule intends to do from a business person's point of view.

One category of rules not included in Figure 2.2 is the presentation rule. A *presentation rule* simply describes how a piece of information is to be displayed to a human. In his book, C. J. Date (2000) further refines these into field labels, field alignment, background and foreground colors, fonts, heights and widths, captions, edit masks, field defaults, and table fields. While these kinds of rules are certainly important, they are the least important to this book. They are included because they appear as a classification of rules within some commercial business rules products.

The rule classifications you are likely to spend the most time on as you follow this book are computations, constraints, and inferences. There are three reasons why these tend to require most of your attention. The first reason is that computations and inferences create knowledge while constraints restrict or guide behavior. These tend to be of greater business significance than the presenting of information. The second reason is that these three classifications of rules are also the ones for which responsibility for capture and implementation has been split or under debate between database and application professionals. The third reason is that computations, inferences, and mandatory constraints are the kinds of rules most frequently supported in commercial rules products.

Constraints

A constraint can be a mandatory restriction or suggested restriction on the behavior of the business event. A *mandatory constraint* is a complete statement that expresses an unconditional circumstance that must be true or not true for the business event to complete with integrity. Examples of mandatory constraints are:

- A customer *must* not have more than 10 open orders at one time.

- The total dollar amount of a customer order *must* not be greater than the customer's single order credit limit amount.

Throughout the methodology chapters, you will work with a case study representing an Internet-based theme park service for after school children. In anticipation of that, this chapter also includes example rules from that case study since you may want to refer back to this chapter as you progress through the case study.

Examples of mandatory constraints for the case study include:

- Member login ID must be in the set of required Member IDs for a member to enter the park.

- Member password must be the correct password for that member for the member to enter the park.

- The member must have theme park allowed time remaining for the member to enter the park.

- The guardian billing status must be acceptable for the member to enter the park.

Guidelines

A *guideline* is a complete statement that expresses a warning about a circumstance that should be true or not true. A guideline does not force the circumstance to be true or not true, but merely warns about it, allowing the human to make the decision. Because a guideline only warns and does not reject, it provides a freedom of choice.

An example of a guideline is:

A customer should not have more than 10 open orders at one time.

This book includes guidelines as a classification of rules because they are often very important to the business community. Some commercial rules products do not support the management and specification of guideline rules, which means the developer usually translates them into warning messages.

Action Enablers

The third category is action enablers. An *action enabler* is a complete statement that tests conditions and upon finding them true, initiates another business event, message, or other activity. That is, an action enabler initiates a new action external to the scope of the system or increment under study.

Examples of action enablers are:

- If a customer order is valid, then initiate the Place Order process.
- If a customer is high risk, then notify the customer services manager.

Examples of an action enabler from the case study is:

- If a member is too old for this theme park, initiate the action of recommending other suitable theme parks.

Action-enabler rules can be used in some commercial rules products to create an event-oriented sequence of workflow steps. It may be helpful to think of mandatory constraints and action enablers as opposites. Mandatory constraints stop an event from completing. Action enablers start an event.

The fourth category includes those rules that create new information from existing information. There are two types under this category, computations and inferences.

Computations

A *computation* is a complete statement that provides an algorithm for arriving at the value of a term where such algorithms may include sum, difference, product, quotient, count, maximum, minimum, average.

An example of a computation rule is:

- The total-amount-due for an order is computed as the sum of the line-item amount(s) for the order plus tax.

An example of a computation rule from the case study is:

- The guardian prepaid hours is computed as the total money paid divided by the theme park hourly rate.

The result of executing a computation rule is to create a new piece of information. This book uses the term *knowledge* to mean a piece of information created by a rule. That is, the information is not simply known by looking at it or reading it, it needs to be created according to a rule of some sort. In this case, the new piece of information is a new value for an attribute, such as total-customer-order-dollar-amount. Later, the logical data model, perhaps the database design and the object model, may reflect these new information pieces.

Inferences

An *inference* is a complete statement that tests conditions and upon finding them true, establishes the truth of a new fact.

Examples of inferences are:

- If a customer has no outstanding invoices, then the customer is of preferred status.
- If a customer is of preferred status, then the customer's order qualifies for a 20 percent discount.

Examples of inferences from the case study are:

- If the member has completed their homework, time is added to their theme park allowed time.
- If the guardian has a poor credit rating, guardian billing method is set to prepay.

The result of executing an inference rule is to create a new piece of information, therefore knowledge. This new piece of information, in database terms, can either be a new instance of an entity (for example, a new instance of the preferred customer entity) or a new instance of an attribute (for example, a new value for customer-order-discount-amount). Therefore, as you collect and analyze rules, keep in mind that when you discover database action within the scope of the system or target increment, classify the corresponding rule as an inference. In this book, an inference rule results in the setting of the value of something based on conditions, even if the value is set as a result of a computation. Therefore, a rule such as the first one above from the case study is classified as a inference rule even though the value of theme park allowed time may be the result of computing the sum of a previous theme park allowed time and additional bonus time due to completing homework.

Again, the logical data model and, perhaps, the database and object model, may contain these new pieces of information.

Using the definition of business rules in this chapter, all business rules are about data. That is, terms define data concepts and details, facts define associations among data, constraints and guidelines test data values, computations arrive at a data value, inferences arrive at a data conclusion, and action enablers evaluate data values prior to initiating action.

Expressing Business Rules

Figure 2.3 illustrates that a business rule can actually be expressed in four different forms, each for a different audience. A rule starts its life usually as a piece of business conversation, which is the case if the rule comes from people. In this form, the rule is simply someone's expression of a concept perceived as policy or a rule. In this form, the policy statement is informal, without discipline. It is simply a first attempt at communicating that there may be a policy or rule to discuss.

The second form is a natural language form whose audience is the business community, but for which you attempt to add some discipline. It is important to keep in mind that business rules have a business flavor, regardless of how you choose to implement them. You can see by the figure that you want to capture a natural language form of a rule only if the rule is relevant to your scope. You also want to express the rule as an atomic thought, discussed in Chapter 10 on analyzing rules, and in declarative form (stating what is to be done, not how).

The third form is a rule specification language whose audience is business and technical people. This form is a declarative disciplined way of expressing what the rule is to accomplish, but not how to accomplish it. By the time you translate a rule into this form, it has all of the properties of a good quality rule, which are also discussed in Chapter 10. Ideally, this form is the basis from which to generate executable rule code. Unfortunately, there is no standard rule specification language. There are various rule languages proposed as part of other modeling approaches.

This brings us to the fourth form, a rule implementation language that is the machine-executable version of the rule whose audience is the target technology. The rule implementation language may actually be a procedural language. It is most useful when the natural language form and the specification language are declarative, nonprocedural.

Figure 2.3   Types of rule expressions.

Using Rule Templates

Rule templates are disciplined patterns by which a business rule is expressed as a combination of rule clauses. A simple *rule clause* is of the form:

<term1> <operator> <term2>.

As a review, a term is a noun or noun phrase with an agreed-upon definition. These include concepts (customer), property of a concept (customer-credit-rating-code), value (female), and value set (Mon, Tues, Wed, Thurs, Fri).

An *operator* is any operator that makes sense for the particular term type. The subsequent terms and operators will exist only if they make business sense. An outstanding text on a classification scheme of rule clauses is Ross (1997).

An example of a rule clause is Customer-credit-rating-code = "A", where there are two terms (customer-credit-rating-code and "A") and one operator (=).

Another example is Sum (line items for an order) where there is one term (line items for an order), which represents a fact between two terms (order and line item) and one operator (sum).

Obviously, you can paste together rule clauses to create all kinds of complicated rules. Dependencies surface among rules when the result of one rule is a rule clause that is tested in another rule. You will discover the importance of rule dependencies during rule analysis.

In this book, the structured rule language templates link together rule clauses for expressing rules when it is useful to do so. If a rule is too complex to express in that manner, feel free to resort to natural language, scientific notation, or whatever format makes the most sense.

If you wanted to be sophisticated in your rule classification scheme, you could classify each rule clause according to what it does. For example, some rule clauses simply compare one value to another. Another rule clause represents a particular type of computation, such as a sum or difference. Ross (1997) is an excellent source for reference here.

To keep it simple, if you use the business rule classification scheme in this chapter, there are seven different kinds of business rule classifications needing templates: terms, facts, mandatory constraints, guidelines, inferences, action enablers, and computations. First, we present them at a macro level, in terms of rule clauses. Then, Table 2.3 provides details into the kinds of rule clauses that might appear in each business rule template.

Using Rule Clauses

Rule clauses connect you to the data foundation, one way or another. That is because an automated rule references various pieces of information in a database or file (tables, columns, relationships, and so on). A designer needs to understand those references. Specifically, should any piece of information referenced in a rule clause change in value, it is possible that the rule should fire and verify that the database still remains in compliance with business rules or policy. This is fundamentally a new concept in system design and a value brought forth by commercial data–oriented rules products. (The

Table 2.3 Business Rule Templates

BUSINESS RULE CLASSIFICATION	DETAILED DEFINITION OF BUSINESS RULE CLASSIFICATION	RULE TEMPLATE
Term	Noun or noun phrase with an agreed-upon definition, can be divided into: • Concept, object class, entity • Property, detail, attribute • Value • Value set	\<term\> IS DEFINED AS \<text\>
Fact	Statement connecting terms into sensible, business-relevant observations: • Entity-to-entity relationship • Entity-to-attribute assignment • Supertype-to-subtype connection	\<term1\> IS A \<term2\> \<term1\> \<verb\> \<term2\> \<term1\> IS COMPOSED OF \<term2\> \<term1\> IS A ROLE PLAYED BY \<term2\> \<term1\> HAS A PROPERTY OF \<term2\>
Computation	Statement providing algorithm on numeric data for arriving at the value of a term. Computes the value of one term. May reference many terms in formula.	\<term1\> IS COMPUTED AS \<formula\>
Mandatory constraint	Statement expressing circumstances that must be true of input information.	\<term1\> MUST HAVE \<at least, at most, exactly *n* of\> \<term2\> \<term1\> MUST BE \<comparison\> \<term2\>, \<value\>, \<value list\> \<term1\> MUST BE IN LIST \<a,b,c\> \<term1\> MUST NOT BE IN LIST \<a,b,c\> IF \<rule phrase(s)\> THEN \<constraint of any of the above types\>
Guideline	Statement expressing circum-stances that must be true of input information	\<term1\> SHOULD HAVE \<at least, at most, exactly *n* of\> \<term2\> \<term1\> SHOULD BE \<comparison\> \<term2\>, \<value\>, \<value list\> \<term1\> SHOULD BE IN LIST \<a,b,c\> \<term1\> SHOULD NOT BE IN LIST \<a,b,c\>

Table 2.3 (*continued*)

BUSINESS RULE CLASSIFICATION	DETAILED DEFINITION OF BUSINESS RULE CLASSIFICATION	RULE TEMPLATE
Guideline (*cont.*)		IF <rule phrase(s)> THEN <any of the above guideline types>
Inferred knowledge	Statement expressing circumstances that lead to a new piece of information	IF <term1> <operator> <term2, value, value list> AND <again> THEN <term3> <operator> <term4> Where operator can be: Comparison (=, not =, =<, >=, <>) In, not in Has quantity <at least *n*, at most *n*, exactly *n* > of
Action enabler	Statement expressing circumstances that lead to external event.	IF <term1> <operator> <term2> THEN <action>

difference between data-oriented and service-oriented rules products was covered in Chapter 1.)

Ronald G. Ross came to the realization that an individual rule actually governs multiple database activities. That is, if any clause in a rule changes its truth value (e.g., a data element changes its value), the rules should fire. This may mean that the rule fires as a result of a column update, a row insert, or a row delete.

A business rules system, if it is to have a data-oriented perspective, needs to know all such database activities such that, should any business event initiate any of those data changes, the corresponding (and hence, shared) rule will fire automatically.

With commercial data-oriented rules products today, this can be automatic. With other kinds of development products, it is not. If you are designing your application without such a product, you may consider designing your objects and methods around that concept.

If you do not design your object/methods around the attachment of rules to database events, you need to be sure you are not disintegrating the data integrity. You may choose not to attach rules to database events if rules serve as guidance or advisors rather than as constraints over the execution of the business event.

The methodology in this book provides guidelines for preserving the connection from rules to database activities, if this is useful to your system.

Using Rule Names for Identification

Because rules are worth capturing, managing, and changing, it is helpful not only to give them an identifier such as a Rule ID, which is an arbitrary number that stays with the rule forever, but also a meaningful name.

A simple rule-naming convention is to include in the rule name the classification for a rule (e.g., constraint, guideline, computation, inference, or action enabler) and also the name of the information it most closely governs. You can put the information name first and the rule classification at the end of the rule name. If that combination is not unique, you may need descriptor words in between.

For example, a rule name of "Guardian Credit Rating Inferred Knowledge" indicates that the rule governs the setting of the value for Guardian Credit Rating and that this rule is an inferred knowledge rule.

Likewise, a rule name of "Guardian Billing Status Constraint" indicates a rule that constrains a business event based on the value of the Guardian Billing Status.

Consider the following three rule names:

- Theme park allowed time constraint
- Theme park allowed time for homework inferred knowledge
- Theme park allowed time for chores inferred knowledge.

You can immediately deduce that each rule is most closely related to the theme park allowed time (which you will see is the amount of time a member can spend in the theme park). The first one is a constraint, so it rejects a business event based on its conditions. The second two are inferred knowledge rules. These rule names contain descriptor words (specifically "for homework" and "for chores") so you can tell them apart (they are two different rules). You also may deduce that one of them infers a value for theme park allowed time based on whether the member has completed homework while the other does so based on whether the member has completed pre-assigned chores.

Using Workflow Rules

There is another classification of rules, known as *workflow rules*, sometimes called *process automation rules*. Workflow rules are statements that measure conditions and determine appropriate action. In that way, they are similar to action-enabler rules. Workflow rules is a term usually used to represent the rules governing the transition of work responsibility among long-running business events to manage multiple transactions over time. The business rules mentioned in the rest of this chapter and the remainder of this book are the rules within an individual transaction.

For example, the entire order processing business event may move from confirmed order (confirmed by the customer) to approved order (approved by an internal manager), fulfilled order (items packed from inventory), shipped order (items sent to customer), invoiced order (bill sent to customer), and paid order (order paid for by customer). Workflow rules monitor the progress of the order processing business event and schedule the next set of processing to the appropriate person or automated system.

The term *business rules*, as used in this book, refers to the rules that execute within each of those sets of processing, the rules within an individual transaction.

The distinction is not always obvious, hence there is overlap sometimes between the functionality of a commercial rules product and a commercial workflow product.

For the purposes of this book, think of workflow rules as those that sit above the entire long business event and direct the processes to responsible parties (such as a person or automated system). The business rules act within the processes to complete it and report the results to the workflow environment, which then schedules the next process.

An Alternate View of Business Rules

If you prefer, you can view business rules as the integrity rules surrounding the creation of data on behalf of business events. As such, the idea of business rules has a theoretical foundation in the *relational model*. The relational model was introduced by Dr. Codd in a landmark paper in 1970. Although many people think of the relational model as a technological breakthrough, the model itself is an intellectual concept, independent of technology. It consists of three components, one of which addresses the concept of business rules under a different name. It is important to understand these components so as to better understand the role of business rules in systems development today.

One component of the relational model is the *data structure*. The data structure is the organizational nature of the data as perceived by users. A second component of the relational model is the *data manipulation.* The data manipulation represents the types of operations users can request of the data in the data structure. A third component is the *data integrity* component. (Pay attention to this one!) The data integrity is the set of rules that govern how the data in the data structure behave when it is manipulated. All three components are important.

Sadly, the relational integrity component of the relational model may be the least known and least understood. And yet, without adequate data integrity support, the data can lose meaning and value, possibly becoming incorrect, incomplete, or misleading. Many readers have experienced such deterioration in data quality.

If anyone doubts the implications of careless attention to data integrity, simply count the millions of dollars spent today and for the foreseeable future in cleaning existing data en route to exposing it in data warehouse environments. The cost of poor data quality is astronomical to businesses today. The truth is that data integrity is a very simple concept to acknowledge and endorse. But it can be complicated in its full implications.

Today, database professionals, using mostly DDL (Data Definition Language), create the data structure along with a subset of the data integrity. Most commonly, database professionals usually create data integrity enforcement for aspects of data integrity support that are available in the target relational DBMS product.

On the other hand, application professionals code the statements within applications that perform operations on the data. The application professionals also enforce aspects of the data integrity within the application, especially those not supported in the DDL for the target database.

In this way, the data structure has become the responsibility of the database professional. The data manipulation has become the responsibility of the application development professional. However, responsibility for the data integrity component usually remains unclear, debatable, and often split between the two groups of professionals. Traditionally, there has been a lack of standard discipline for capturing and enforcing all rules behind data integrity.

This lack of standard discipline should be most alarming. After all, the data integrity component may, in fact, be the most important component of a system.

At the very least, a business rules approach to systems development integrates the capture and documentation of data integrity (rules) such that you can apply better discipline to their enforcement.

Business rule concepts, then, are details behind the data integrity component of the relational model. As such, business rule concepts do not imply specific technical approaches for rule storage or rule execution strategies. But there are interesting disciplined properties about rules.

First, rules are organized into predicates in much the same way that data is organized into relations. Second, consider that relational tables have six special characteristics, as follows:

- Columns are single-valued
- Entries in columns are of the same kind
- Each row is unique
- Sequence of columns left to right is insignificant
- Sequence of rows top to bottom is insignificant
- Each column has a unique name.

Rules can be perceived as also having special properties, as follows:

- A rule results in only one conclusion. That conclusion for a mandatory constraint is a yes or no answer as to whether the conditions of the constraint are met. The conclusion for an inference is a new piece of information. The conclusion for a computation is a computed value.
- Entries in rule clauses are terms and operators.
- Each rule is unique.
- Sequence of clauses in a rule is insignificant.
- Sequence of rules is insignificant, unless otherwise stated.

These properties contribute to rules being intuitive, easy to validate, and flexible with respect to execution strategies.

The rules and predicates define permissible states. They are not a specification for a rule language any more than the relational manipulation component is a specification for a data access language. Most commercial rules products require support in the rule language for all relational operators to be able to enforce a complete set of possible rules.

Business rule concepts do not dictate how rules are to be implemented by a given product. Business rule concepts do mean, however, that there is great benefit if rules are enforced without the developer needing to be aware of rule implementation details. The methodology in this book helps you preserve the principles of a business rules approach even when implementing with immature commercial rules products or none at all.

How Does a Business Rules System Differ from an Expert System?

Simply put, a *business rules system* is a computerized system that assists in the management and execution of the business rules (computational and integrity validation) logic in running the business.

A *knowledge-based system* or *expert system* is a special classification of information system with certain characteristics. These systems tend to have five characteristics that distinguish them from other kinds of systems.

First, they address very complex decision-making activities, where the goal is to make a determination or judgment about a situation with complex logic behind it. Second, these systems can deal with uncertainty of knowledge, including the probability of decisions or confidence levels of conclusions. Third, the rules in these systems are usually inference rules, where one decision may require the execution of hundreds or thousands of inference rules. Fourth, the corresponding rule software usually includes an inference engine that determines the sequence of rule execution based on forward- or backward-chaining algorithms for arriving at a goal. Fifth, rule execution is usually not tied to database activities. That is, the rules reference the data in making inferences, but do not govern database updates per se.

Sample applications within this classification of information systems include: diagnosis, assessment, advising, classification, control, and design.

A business rules system is emerging as a classification of information system with very different characteristics. First, a business rules system addresses simple decision-making activities, typical of those found in day-to-day operational business events of a business. For business rules systems, the goal is simply to make a determination or judgment as to whether a business event should be accepted or not. Second, a business rules system deals only with certain knowledge. That is, either a rule results in a definite new value or a definite true or false answer. There are no guesses, no maybes, or confidence factors. Third, rules in business rules systems can be of many classifications, including guidelines, computations, constraints, inferences, and action enablers. They ultimately aim to protect the integrity of database changes during the course of a business event. Fourth, rule software for a business rules system usually ties rules to the execution of data updates, often without an inference engine.

Sample applications for a business rules system include most of the e-business applications, such as order entry, order tracking, and claims processing.

There is a gray line emerging between the two. Some assessment problems, such as processing a loan application, can be supported with either an expert system or a business rules system. The number and complexity of rules, performance implications, and other requirements would determine which way such applications ought to be developed.

How Do You Best Implement Rules?

At a very simple glance, there are three different ways to implement rules: commercial rules product, application code, and the DBMS.

The first and most exciting is in a commercial rules product. This is the most exciting opportunity for many reasons. First, as a separate piece of software, the product can manage the rules as artifacts with an existence independent of process flow and data considerations. Second, this means that there may be an opportunity to share these rules across application systems in much the same way that database management systems allow databases to be shared across application systems. Keep in mind, however, that databases cannot be shared unless they are designed to be shared. The same is true of rules.

Third, rule-specific software is designed deliberately to manage and execute rules properly and efficiently. While each commercial product may vary significantly from others, they also have very strong desirable characteristics with respect to executing rules, more so than homegrown application code can likely provide. This idea is similar to the concept that optimizers in relational database management systems are more intelligent about data access than a homegrown program can be because the optimizer has more information available to it than the programmer had at program-writing time. Also, as the nature of specific databases changes (volume changes, for example), the optimizer can update its knowledge and change its access strategy accordingly.

Likewise, rule-specific software is more intelligent about rule execution than a homegrown program is likely to be because it, too, has more information available to it than the programmer had at program-writing time. Also, like relational database optimizers, rule-specific software may be capable of looking at the whole picture for a rule (when it should execute, where it should execute, what else is impacted). In addition, in a rule-specific software environment, rules are always perceived by programs or by people as rules and nothing else, usually in declarative or simple form.

The second option for implementing rules is to include them in the application-specific logic. Usually, this means incorporating them as parts of methods within application object classes. This implementation does not have the advantage of utilizing rule statistics for intelligent processing and also buries the rules deep within application code. To gain some benefits to a business rules approach, at the very least, you would maintain a cross-reference from each rule to the object class or method in which it is implemented. If you desired that the rules should execute for all transactions touching rule-related data, this functionality would require sophisticated design on your part.

The third option is to implement rules in the DBMS, either as triggers or stored procedures or other product-specific options. This solution covers the firing of rules for all transactions touching rule-related data in that database (if this is desirable), but it does not provide the opportunity for optimizing overall rule execution based on rule statistics and it does not allow for easy sharing of rules across DBMS products.

Enforcement of rules becomes complicated when you mix the options. If you have some rules in rule-specific software, some in application procedural code, and some in DBMS code, each one has a different implementation language. Therefore, making rule changes to a system will require several different kinds of technical professionals, a great deal of coordination, and more involved testing.

Your goal is to use this book to find a better way. More details on these considerations are found in Chapter 12.

Sample Business Rules from the Case Study

Although you have not yet reviewed the case study, we would like to give you a glimpse of what is to come in the remaining chapters. Read the following as if you are analyzing documentation from interviews and you are looking for business rules, classifying them, and researching them to the best of your ability.

Terms

From the case study, let's consider seven terms:

- Invoice late fee amount:
  - Computed term
  - Definition: an amount of money applied to an invoice when payment of previous invoice(s) is late
  - Computation rule for the computed term: is computed as 10 percent of an invoice amount with a minimum amount of $5
- Invoice volume discount amount:
  - Base or computed term, may not know at first
  - Definition: amount of money subtracted from total invoice due amount based on selected discount criteria applied to an invoice prior to other discounts
- Bounced check fee amount:
  - Base term if it is a fixed amount without a computation
  - Definition: a fixed amount of money applied to all members when a check is returned
- Invoice member total park time amount:
  - Computed term
  - Definition: billable amount of time spent in the park for each member
  - Computation rule for the computed term: is computed as the sum of member time used in park rounded up to the nearest 15 minutes
- Usage:
  - Base term
  - Definition: amount of time a member spends in the park for an invoice period
  - Domain: minutes
- Additional member discount amount:
  - Base term
  - Definition: amount of discount applied if a guardian has more than one member, set to 15 percent, applied to the member(s) with the lowest balance applied after volume discounts
- Invoice payment amount:
  - Base term
  - Definition: amount of money a guardian submits for an invoice and it is applied to the oldest invoice first

Facts

Facts that may arise from studying a detailed description of the case study might be:

- An invoice contains the amount of billable time spent in each park

- An invoice contains fees and deducted time for that month
- An invoice contains discount information (multiple children, volume, employee discount)
- An invoice contains the total in each park for each member

Rules

The case study is rich in rules. Consider each classification.

- Mandatory constraint rules:
  - An employee discount is only available to children of an employee.
  - There is only one invoice per guardian per month.
  - Invoices are due on the 25th of the month.
- Action-enabler rules:
  - Invoices are generated on the first business day of the month.
  - Account status is checked on a daily basis.
  - If guardian payment method is automatic method then authorize payment for the invoice amount.
- Computation rules:
  - The member's base fee for a park is computed as the hourly fee times the number of hours the member spent in the park.
  - The member's volume discount amount is computed as the product of standard volume discount rate times the number of hours the member spent in a park over the volume discount threshold for that park.
  - A guardian's monthly invoice total is computed as the sum of all their member monthly invoice totals.
- Inference rules:
  - If an invoice is more than 65 days overdue then the account is not in good standing.
  - If a new rate for a guardian is proposed and an announcement has been made to the guardian one month prior to invoice date, then new rate is in effect.

You may be uncertain as to whether a statement represents a rule or not. Consider the following from the case study.

- Nonrules:
  - A guardian receives only one invoice for all their members: This is simply how many to produce/print/send, not a rule, as defined in this chapter.
  - The invoice has four sections: general information, member detail, outstanding invoices, and payments. This is simply how to organize output, not a rule.
  - Late fees are applied at the end of the invoice: This is simply where to print them.

Summary

This chapter introduced the basic concepts about business rules, such as what are they, what classifications exist, how to express them, and theoretical foundations. Business rules are the set of conditions that govern a business event so that it occurs in a way that is acceptable to the business. We recommend that you establish a business rule classification scheme for the business audience specifically for use during rule discovery and rule validation. A business rule classification scheme that works for a business audience includes terms, facts, mandatory constraints, guidelines, computations, inferences, and action enablers. The system may need to know all database activities such that, should any business event initiate any of those data changes, the corresponding (and hence, shared) rule will fire automatically.

You now understand what business rules are and how they govern business events. The next chapter, therefore, provides an overview for how to incorporate business rule concepts and automation techniques into your current systems development approach.

Introduction to Business Rule Methodology

This chapter provides an understanding of the complete business rule methodology detailed in the remainder of the book. If you are a project manager or methodologist, you will find this chapter useful in understanding the differences behind a business rules approach compared to other common approaches. If you are a practitioner, such as an analyst or designer or programmer, this chapter serves as an introduction to the practices that are covered in the remainder of the book.

What Is a Business Rule Methodology?

A *business rule methodology* is a set of phases, steps, techniques, and guidelines for delivering a business rules systems. As Chapter 1 stated, a business rules system is an automated system that separates the rules of the business logically, perhaps physically, from other aspects of the system and shares them across data stores, user interfaces, and applications.

While there are many reasons to build a business rules system, the two primary reasons are to significantly shorten development time and to deliver a system that is designed for change. To achieve these differences, you need a systems development methodology that divides the problem domain into at least three separate but integrally related aspects: data, process, and rules. Essentially, this book leads you through the tasks of separating these aspects from each other, optimizing each in its own right, integrating them back together for a holistic solution, and supporting the solution with enabling technology.

Building a business rules system requires a business rule methodology because rules don't surface on their own, don't disconnect themselves from other system artifacts, don't optimize themselves, and don't maintain themselves over time. Therefore, a business rules approach, when compared to other systems development approaches, places more emphasis and importance and discipline on the formalizing of the rules of the business and, hence, the delivery of those rules within corresponding changeable system logic.

It turns out that rules, more than objects and even data, are where the new excitement is. That's because rules represent the underpinnings of the organization's culture and decision-making power. Rules utilize information so as to make decisions, create new knowledge, and take intelligent action. What can be more important and exciting than that?

In fact, you will discover that the rules emerge as the most important system aspect from a business person's perspective. That's because businesses today want and need to change and rules are an important way through which the business changes. You, as an IT professional, either enable the business to change or stifle it by the way you deliver rules within your systems. You either bury the rules hopelessly in program code where they remain resistant to change. Or you deliberately liberate them for scrutiny and easy change.

The goal of a business rule methodology, then, is to start by separating these three aspects of a system: rules, data, and process considerations. Obviously, most of this book is dedicated to the steps and techniques for separating and managing rules. That's because, as important as rules are to the business, they represent the aspect most often neglected or without formalism in other methodologies. A unique benefit to a business rules approach is that it has tentacles in both business and systems development communities. For the business community, a business rules approach is a methodology by which business leaders utilize rules as instruments of proactive and creative organizational change. You will see glimpses of this in Chapter 4, "Scoping for Success." In Chapter 4, when you scope a proposed business rules system, you give careful attention, not only to the business motivation for the system, but to the important role played by the rules in guiding the business toward its objectives. It is beyond the scope of this book to provide a methodology for incorporating a business rules approach into a business process reengineering (BPR) methodology. However, Chapter 4 provides the starting point by which you can introduce business rules into your existing BPR approach.

The remainder of this chapter presents an overview of the tracks and phases in building a business rules system. A quick overview of the tracks first provides a basis for understanding the discussions about the phases. Note that each phase consists of steps, guidelines, and deliverables for each track.

If you are a seasoned systems developer, you may conclude that your systems development approach already addresses all of the items discussed in this chapter. The difference is that a business rules approach recognizes all five types of rules from Chapter 2 in four important ways. The first recognition that is part of the entire methodology is that rules are an asset, worthy of being captured formally. The second realization is that rules are to be managed with care throughout their lifetime. The third, and perhaps most important, recognition is that rules are meant to change on a regular basis so as to hit business objectives more effectively or aim for new ones. The fourth realization is that rules must be readily accessible to everyone who needs to know them, behave by them, and change with them.

Benefits of Using a Business Rule Methodology

Ideally, a system built according to a business rule methodology should, by design, exhibit the following desirable characteristics:

- Is developed faster than nonbusiness rules systems

- Is based on a very stable data model where the data is shared across application and organizational boundaries

- Is based on rules that are shared across application and organizational boundaries (no more unnecessary "application" silos)

- Is developed around the essential core process flow (based on rule dependencies), allowing for freedom of choice in other types of process flow

- Allows for various technology architectures and designs for rule automation (that may change over time, even if the rules themselves don't change)

- Includes traceability from business objectives to requirements to automated rules

- Minimizes the inclusion of rules as part of nonrule deliverables

- Exhibits the new economy of system changes, such that changes in rules are easy to make.

In case you missed the last and most important point, rule changes are easy.

How a Business Rule Methodology Differs from Other Methodologies

The most significant differences in a business rule methodology were summarized in Chapter 1 as the four STEP principles. As a reminder, the differences are that a business rule methodology simply aims to separate, trace, externalize, and position rules for change in every phase, track, and step of the methodology. Each of the methodology chapters in this book (Chapters 4 through 12) contains a figure depicting how the phase and track within the chapter addresses the four STEP principles of the business rules approach.

At a casual glance, the most obvious difference in a business rule methodology is the very existence of a rule track. The rule track focuses only on rules and how those rules relate to other aspects of the system.

Naturally, you can choose to omit or modify the steps in the rule track, as perhaps you have been doing until now. However, when you do so, you need also to recognize that you will be sacrificing some of the benefits of a business rules approach. The sacrifice may sometimes be worth it because business life is not perfect. There are limitations to time, technology, money, knowledge, and skill sets that may render such sacrifices necessary. Nevertheless, as a knowledgeable business rule practitioner, you can make such sacrifices with a complete understanding of their implications. You will be in a good position to know when those sacrifices are necessary for other business reasons.

For easy reference, Table 3.1 summarizes the major differences in a business rule methodology by phase. Not all of these differences occur in the rule track. Some may occur in the process or data track, but each track has tentacles into the rule track. These

Table 3.1 Differences in a Business Rule Methodology by Phase

DIFFERENCE IN METHODOLOGY	SCOPING PHASE	PLANNING PHASE	DISCOVERY PHASE	ANALYSIS PHASE	DESIGN PHASE
Separate rules	Plan for rule management	Include tasks for discovering, analyzing, designing, and delivering rules	Decompose business events into decision	Recognize rules as separate from but related to data, object, and process models Decompose rules into atomic rules Understand required rule flow before the rest of the system flow Produce a workflow of the core process that invokes shared decisions and rules	Implement rules separate from core process flow Generate executable rules from a commercial rules product
Trace rules	Emphasize and formalize business context behind rules	Include four new rule roles (rule analyst, rule designer, rule implementor, and rule integrator)	Correlate decisions and rules to business context Associate decisions and rules with use cases	Create rule-enriched logical data model Reference rules in the rule-enriched logical data model Uncover rule dependencies Reconnect rules to business motivation and optimize them Make sure the process, decision, and rules remain faithful to business objectives	Correlate rule specifications to implementations

Externalize rules	Establish business purposes for managing rules	Establish rule standards Establish rules repository	Identify concrete scenarios requiring rules Express rules in natural language Name rules Classify rules	Create state transition diagrams and enhanced workflow diagrams to show decisions and rules, objects and data Resolve rule inconsistencies, overlaps, and redundancies	Include natural language rules as error messages
Position rules for change	Begin a solid information architecture	Test and deploy commercial rules products	Correlate rules to information referenced and created Give rules well-defined jurisdictions and consensus Avoid premature commitment to execution sequence	Establish well-defined rule jurisdictions and consensus Represent rule-materialized knowledge in the rule-enriched logical data model Discover alternate workflows Uncover business preferences in workflow Explore detailed rule flow, as necessary	Favor changeable rule implementation over rigid ones Deliver databases capable of change

differences will become more understandable and important as you read the remainder of the book.

Even though systems development approaches have evolved over time, there are three major evolutionary steps that stand out:

- Structured systems analysis (with a process perspective)

- Information engineering (with a data perspective)

- Object orientation (with a combination of data and process perspective)

Let's review these quickly so you can better understand, not only the value of a business rules approach, but how it represents the next logical step forward.

Structured systems analysis provided discipline to the algorithmic or functional aspect of the system, but it did not elevate the importance of the information or data aspect. As a result, systems built following structured systems analysis were likely to deliver application-specific, narrow-focused databases that proliferated over the years into expensive information chaos.

Therefore, *information engineering* emerged to add to the functional aspect, a strong and strategic data-orientation. Following an information engineering approach, organizations were more likely to deliver databases designed to accommodate the needs of multiple applications and business groups. Doing so reduced the proliferation of duplicate and inconsistent databases, when done properly. Of course, delivering such high quality databases takes time and skill. Not only that, a shortcoming of the functional aspect of information engineering is that it does not take advantage of distributed processing opportunities and current development technology.

Also, often, in practice, information engineering resulted in high quality databases, but the reintegration of data and process was not always smooth. Therefore, recently, an *object-orientated approach* became popular that combines the functional and data aspects into one abstraction. Object orientation allows a developer to focus on one abstraction (the object or object class) that combines the data and functional aspects. A shortcoming of object orientation is that, without retaining a strong data perspective in practice, it can result in databases that do not reflect good database design principles. These principles are important if you want to deliver high quality databases, especially those capable of supporting business change.

Emergence of Rules

There continue to be emotional debates over the advantages and disadvantages of information engineering versus object-orientation techniques. Suffice it to say, however, that a recognized shortcoming is that neither separates, externalizes, traces, and positions the underlying rules for change.

So, while information engineering may produce more stable databases and object orientation may lend itself to iterative development of distributed systems and a combination of both addresses both aspects, neither approach delivers very changeable systems. That's because both miss the formalized capture of business decisions, guiding policies, and externalized rules, not to mention dependencies among rules and from rules to business direction. Even data-oriented approaches tend not to capture or manage computed data values, complex data constraints spanning data entities or objects, and data materialized through inference rules.

Therefore, adding to either approach, a business rules approach to either information engineering or object-orientation or a combination is an improvement, addressing an obvious missing link.

Does a Business Rules Approach Necessitate Yet a New Systems Development Methodology?

It is worth noting that the time is right for considering a business rule methodology as the natural next step in the path from structured systems analysis, information engineering, object orientation, and finally to a business rules approach.

Not only that, but the business rules approach in this book deliberately combines the benefits of all three philosophies (object-oriented, data-oriented, and rule-oriented). The only new piece (or new emphasis) is the rule orientation. The good news is that a business rule methodology does not represent a major change, but merely a change in emphasis, an enhancement to proven principles. In this way, business rules become the integrating factor that can tie everything (and every technology professional) together nicely, not to mention the business itself.

Some readers will groan at the thought of analyzing and designing three areas: data, process or objects, and rules. Could this result in analysis paralysis and unending arguments among three possible teams? The truth is that to ignore one at the expense of another simply compromises quality. More than that, the pace of business today compels you to pay greater homage to the intelligence behind the enterprise, to bring that out in a forward-thinking way, and not to lose sight of techniques from the past that remain valuable.

Separating rules and data and process allows three different sets of techniques to fine-tune and optimize each piece. To ignore one set of techniques delivers only a partially leveraged system. Integrating all three aspects together comes later in the methodology process, as it should.

In a world where time to delivery is measured in months and where the business needs to change itself or its underlying technology in a heartbeat, there can be no other way. The rules must emerge in importance or the business itself will suffer. The information used and knowledge created by the rules must also emerge as important or the business will operate in a chaotic state. The process or objects that tie it all together must remain important or delivery becomes questionable.

Naturally, the payback to a business rule methodology has three perspectives to it, one for each core aspect. These paybacks are the ability to reuse (copying and customizing) business classes and components, reuse (sharing) of rules, and reuse (sharing) of databases. But these three things are not the same things. Each looks different. Each serves different purposes. And, perhaps each should be implemented in technology specifically aimed at optimizing it. So, a business rules approach positions your organization for a more intelligent technological future.

Relationship between Business Rules Approach and Object-Orientation

Because object-orientation is popular today and will be for the foreseeable future, let's now consider how it relates to a business rules approach. Simply stated, an *object-oriented approach to software development* represents a way of thinking about a problem domain by expressing it in abstractions (objects or object classes) in the vocabulary of the problem space. This is in contrast to former structured systems analysis, which approached a problem domain through abstractions depicting its functional decomposition. It is partly in contrast to an information engineering approach that dealt with part of the problem domain by representing part of it through functional abstractions.

However, information engineering also approached a problem by understanding its data requirements that represent the problem domain in its vocabulary. So, in that respect, object-orientation and the data portion of information engineering have similarities. They both attempt to describe the problem space in business vocabulary, using familiar concepts such as customer, product, service, order, and so on.

A difference emerges because of the difference in purpose. The object or class model *combines* the data and process requirements into one abstraction for the purpose of eventually designing executable program code for an application software environment. The data model *separates* data from process for the purpose of eventually designing databases for a database management software environment. Subsequently, a data professional develops a data model based on strict semantic and integrity principles, some of which aim to better understand the data and some of which aim to represent that data in a form easily adaptable to database technology. So, concepts such as primary and foreign keys, referential integrity, and normalization, while they aid in gaining a full understanding of the data, are often criticized as being too relational technology–centric for many people.

A business object model, on the other hand, represents much of the same business concepts as a logical data model without necessarily imparting to them the concepts of primary and foreign keys, referential integrity rules, and normalization. So, a preliminary business object model and a logical data model may look similar at some point. But, the logical data model, if the analyst follows good data modeling principles, evolves into a deliverable that best represents data for database implementation. The business object model, when an analyst and designer follows object-oriented principles, evolves into a deliverable that best represents the organization of logic for application software implementation. The important point is that these are fundamentally different models.

There is much debate as to whether a systems development project requires both a data model and an object model and how such models should relate to each other, let alone how the team manages that relationship. It is certainly not the intention of this book to settle this debate. However, it is important to re-emphasize that each of these models serves different and valid purposes. Object models are excellent from which to design system logic. If you want to leverage data, you need to separate it from process so as to analyze it and improve it and optimize it beyond the boundaries of that process.

There are many benefits to an object-oriented approach to systems development: It decomposes the problem in abstractions representing the vocabulary of the business, it is often applied for iterative development, it is often applied for incremental development, it leads to design of distributed collaborative units, which is appropriate for today's technology environments and for the future.

So, think of *object-oriented analysis* as defining the problem domain using abstractions representing business vocabulary, called business objects. Looked at simply, object-oriented design is usually the process of inventing additional abstractions, called infrastructure objects, to solve the problem so that software works. Rules, then, are intellectual specifications about the business objects. Therefore, you can create a business object model, use its terms to express rules, but the business object model is not a replacement for a logical data model that assists in designing databases.

Where Is the Object Track?

As indicated earlier in this chapter, the business rule methodology in this book is comprised of four tracks: data, process, rules, and technology. With the popularity and benefits of object-orientation, the question arises: Where is the object track?

Essentially, the object track is absorbed in the process track. That's because most of the object-oriented models and techniques aim to analyze, design, and deliver the dynamic aspects of a system: its execution sequence and how responsibilities are assigned to participating software object classes.

The process track is not called the object track because there are other ways to analyze and design process (such as structured systems analysis), which may, at times, be equally or more appropriate within the process track.

In particular, you will find references in this book to process decomposition diagrams as a useful technique in scoping a project. That's because a process decomposition diagram may provide a very useful top-down view of the scope of the system.

So suffice it to say that the business rule methodology in this book takes the liberty of borrowing from techniques that work. It favors object-oriented techniques often since these are most popular and very beneficial. It also includes other techniques because these, too, are useful.

Role of Objects in a Rule-Empowered Enterprise

When you embark on a business rule methodology, you begin to unleash the power of rules in guiding the business. But beyond that the role and purpose of objects becomes magnified. Objects become the mechanism for what they were meant to be, not stretched to represent data or to encapsulate rules. In fact, the harmony between objects and rules plus the harmony between rules and data means that objects bring about the overall process that ties it all together. You will hear this many times throughout this book, but consider that a process is guided by policies, policies are implemented through rules, rules refer to information or knowledge, and rules create knowledge or initiate action. Objects are the glue that holds the whole process together.

Adding Rules to an Object-Oriented Approach

Can you simply add rules to an object-oriented approach? The answer is yes and no. Of course, you can always add rules to an approach that does not contain sufficient formalism and emphasis on them. The important principles of a business rules approach are to separate the rules, trace them to business motivation and implementation, externalize them for all audiences, and position them for change. If you want to add a rule focus to your object-oriented approach, keep these four principles in mind and consider the following three aspects of most object-oriented projects.

The first is that object-orientation aims to encapsulate the internals of an object from its interface. On the other hand, a business rules approach advocates that rules not be encapsulated or hidden, but be broadcast or externalized for all to know. So, you need to find a way to do this.

The second is that object-orientation contains methods within objects for carrying out functionality, which is a natural place to implement rules. However, most object-oriented development environments require procedural coding, which does not lend itself most easily to the changing of rules. So, you need to find a way to minimize the need for procedural coding.

The third is the decision as to how to assign rules to objects. You can create an object for each rule that would soon become a management nightmare. Or, you can group rules together and assign them to an object, such as all rules for a decision belong to one object. Alternately, you can group rules into entity-based objects. There are endless possibilities. You need to decide on an organizational standard approach.

However, to most easily benefit from all four principles, special software aimed specifically at managing and executing rules may seem more desirable, either for your first business rules system or a subsequent one.

In the absence of using such software, you can craft an object-oriented approach toward rules as long as you take extra steps in separating rules from core process flow, tracing rules to business reasons and implementations, externalizing rules for the business audience, and positioning rules for change by knowing how to conduct impact analysis.

This book contains insights for these in appropriate chapters.

Relationship between a Business Rules Approach and Iterative Systems Development

Iterative systems development is a term that means repetition of a whole series of systems development phases. For example, you may carry out discovery, analysis, design, and implementation, and then deliberately start over again in discovery. You start over to incrementally add realizations that surfaced and to carry those realizations through to implementation.

Iterative development for the processing carried out by objects may not only makes sense, but it may be the only way that makes sense. The whole dynamic nature of Web development may best be served by iterative development because such dynamics cannot always be predicted.

E-business systems, especially, *BtoB (business to business)* systems are often developed in iterative fashion. This is because such systems are either very complex in nature or not well defined because they represent new business territory. For example, if the rules are undefined as to how a customer and supplier are to partner on the Web, iterative development allows for prototyping and managing incremental learning and delivery of the relationship. Object-oriented approaches often incorporate an iterative flavor to the development life cycle.

The first iteration of development is usually not intended to be complete. In fact, many people say that an object model is rarely correct after only a single attempt. The iterative software development process is one of continual iteration. This means that different parts of an object model can be at different stages of completion at a point in time.

When someone uncovers a deficiency, the analyst, designer, or developer returns to an earlier stage to make adjustments.

A business rules approach, by recognizing a delivery increment as a set of business events and underlying rules, allows you to limit the aspect of the system for which you need to do this. If you deliver those rules in a changeable manner, you can add to them and change them as the relationship with the business customers and partners matures.

Iterative development makes sense for the dynamic aspects because these cannot always be well known ahead of time, and they will also change over time. Dynamic aspects of a system also vary from organization to organization in terms of desired sequence, transaction volumes, and data volumes, not to mention technology and hours of operation. So iterative development makes sense to test variations until one emerges as the optimum.

On the other hand, iterative development is not a good approach for delivering a stable data architecture. Consider that the data model is more like a static aspect and is also difficult to change. Therefore, because it is static, it can be known ahead of time, although knowing it requires time and effort. For this reason, this book cautions that it may not be in your best interests to approach data architecture in an iterative fashion. Therefore, this book includes steps for developing a data architecture whereby you aim to understand the full data scope as early and as much as possible.

The use of prototyping and iteration is most useful for suggesting different designs. In particular, for those pieces you are designing procedurally, you may want to prototype first, including screens and screen flow and procedural object interaction. Note that you can test rules separately. In fact, if you are using a commercial rules product, you can test rules for correctness and completeness first and for performance second. You can try various prototypes for a database design when seeking best performance, but good analysis is needed to get a starting point that will be stable over time.

Therefore, to prototype and iterate for a business rules system, consider even using existing flat files (while the data professionals are busy analyzing and designing the eventual database) and consider a commercial rules product, even if you will code the rules into procedural object code for your production system.

It seems reasonable that successful iterative systems development, to be effective and efficient, requires a solid data architecture, a strategy for delivering that data architecture incrementally to support delivery increments, and reusable changeable decisions and rules.

Overview of Business Rules Methodology

We will now summarize the steps in the full methodology of this book. Pay special attention to the steps in the rule track, but also see how the other tracks change in subtle ways to allow for rules. Asterisks (*) indicate those steps that are new for rules or are revised to accommodate rules.

Scoping Steps

Following is one set of steps for scoping, rather than separate steps per track. This indicates that there is not a significant difference in scoping for a business rules approach.

However, step 3 in scoping is influenced by a business rules approach because step 3 is where you uncover the full business context against which you will uncover and measure the value of rules:

1. Do initial research
2. Develop initial scope statement
3. Investigate full business context (*)
4. Identify business events
5. Identify stakeholders
6. Identify locations
7. Identify event response processes
8. Identify business performance metrics
9. Identify data subjects
10. Identify additional requirements
11. Identify business constraints
12. Identify technical constraints
13. Identify business and technical risks
14. Prioritize business requirements
15. Determine architectural alternatives
16. Select architectural solution
17. Create scope diagram
18. Estimate organizational infrastructure and required resources
19. Create project charter document
20. Gain commitment.

Scoping is followed by two sets of steps for discovering requirements. One set is for discovering initial requirements and one set is for discovering rules and data together. Steps for discovering initial requirements include:

1. Create use-case descriptions
2. Add concrete scenarios
3. Identify decisions (*)
4. Complete the Conceptual Model

The steps for discovering rules and data include:

1. Identify rule sources (*)
2. Select a rule discovery roadmap (*)
3. Select or confirm rule standards (*)
4. Plan rule discovery time and commitment (*)

5. Discover rules through the roadmap (*)

6. Authenticate the rules (*)

7. Give rules business value (*)

8. Define terms (*)

9. Define facts (*)

10. Begin a term/fact model

11. Add concrete scenarios (*)

Note that the steps for discovering initial requirements contain only one new step to accommodate rules and that is a step for uncovering decisions behind business events. Decisions are a framework for organizing detailed rules. Also note that most of the steps for discovering rules and data together are new or revised to accommodate a business rules approach.

Analysis Steps

There are three separate sets of steps for analyzing rules, data, and process. The fact that there are three sets of steps highlights the fact that there are different analysis techniques for each track and different, but related deliverables. Note that all of the steps for analyzing rules are new. Some of the steps for analyzing data are new or revised because there is overlap between understanding data integrity constraints and uncovering more complicated constraints. Therefore, you need to coordinate well the gathering of traditional business rules about the data with the gathering of more complex rules about the business processes using the data. Many of the steps for analyzing process are revised by taking a business rules approach. That's because you want to separate the details of rule execution from the core process flow. The rule execution flow may also influence the overall process flow.

Steps for analyzing rules:

1. Make each rule atomic (*)

2. Understand the underlying rule patterns (*)

3. Remove redundant rules (*)

4. Resolve overlaps among rules (*)

5. Resolve inconsistencies among rules (*)

6. Ensure completeness among rules (*)

7. Identify dependencies among rules (*)

8. Refine the process based on rule family dependencies or data activities (*)

9. Optimize the rules for the business (*)

Steps for analyzing data:

1. Identify candidate entities

2. Determine relationships among entities

3. Identify primary and alternate keys

4. Propagate foreign keys

5. Determine key business rules (*)

6. Add attributes

7. Normalize attributes

8. Analyze relationships

9. Determine detailed rules (*)

10. Combine with related logical models

11. Integrate data models with broader business perspectives

12. Anticipate the future in the model

13. Identify rule-created entities (*)

14. Identify rule-created relationships (*)

15. Identify rule-created attributes (*)

16. Correlate rules with the rule-enriched logical data model (*)

Steps for analyzing process:

1. Uncover and expand a preliminary core process flow

2. Assign decisions and rules to the rules capability (*)

3. Confirm the essential core process flow (*)

4. Consider alternative core process flows

5. Create a simple workflow diagram to show maximum concurrency for the core process flow

6. Finalize the preferred core process flow

7. Create a simple workflow diagram for the core process flow (*)

8. Revise core workflow diagram using concrete scenarios

9. Reference business context (again!) (*)

10. Confirm the core workflow diagrams

11. Study important state transitions

12. Round out all tracks (*)

13. Create other process analysis deliverables for the core process flow

14. Create a workflow diagram for the rule flow, if necessary (*)

Design Steps

Following is a set of steps for designing the system. Admittedly, it does not contain details for designing screens and core process flow because these are the same as for a nonbusiness rules system. Instead, it contains a set of steps for designing rule automation and all of these steps are new. It also contains steps for designing high-quality relational databases since this is important in delivering changeable systems. The asterisk in step 4 for relational database design is a reminder to coordinate rule enforcement in the database tier with the rule designer.

The steps for designing for rules include:

1. Confirm your architecture, but sharpen it with a rules capability (*).
2. Determine the basic requirements for your rules capability (*).
3. Determine if you will acquire a commercial rules product (*).
4. If not, determine if you will develop your own rules capability (*).
5. Determine in which tier to enforce rules (*).
6. Design for rules in a commercial data-oriented rules product (*).
7. Design for rules in a homegrown data-oriented rules capability (*).
8. Design for rules in a commercial service-oriented rules product (*).
9. Design for rules in a homegrown service-oriented rules capability (*).
10. Tune the database.
11. Tune the rules (*).
12. Tune the rules by moving rule enforcement to another tier (*).
13. Tune the rules by duplicating rule enforcement (*).
14. Tune the rules by changing rule templates (*).
15. Design the rest of the system.

Steps for designing the relational database:

1. Determine tables.
2. Determine columns.
3. Adapt storage structure to product environment.
4. Design for rules (*).
5. Analyze business events served by the database.
6. Consider access paths for the business events.
7. Tune the invisible options.
8. Tune the visible storage structures.

Business Rule Methodology Tracks

The overall goal of this book is to provide the project manager and technical professionals with the steps needed to deliver a business rules system with confidence. Therefore, the remainder of this book (Parts 2 to 5) are dedicated to doing just that. Each methodology chapter addresses a specific phase or track with steps, guidelines, and examples by which a reader can learn and gain confidence. Each methodology step also contains a solution for a case study that continues throughout the book to a final implementation by participating vendors.

Project Managers will find Parts 2 and 3 most interesting. Business analysts, data analysts, rule analysis, and object analysts should read Parts 3 and 4. Designers and architects should read Parts 4 and 5.

With this in mind, let's review the four tracks.

Figure 3.1 highlights the four tracks in a business rules approach. The technology track focuses on the logical and physical separation of the target system into technology tiers, even if the environment does not include rule-specific technology products. You can choose commercial rules technology that specifically manages the execution of the rule collection. Alternately, you can utilize nonrule technology, but in a way that leverages the concepts and advantages of a business rule system.

The focus of the process track is the dynamic characteristics of the system, which include the sequencing of the system logic, but devoid of the rules guiding those interactions. The focus of the data track is the vocabulary and grammar that business events and transactions are about. A business rule methodology specifically removes rule considerations from the data and process tracks. It introduces a third track, the rule track, that stands on its own to a large extent.

What this means is that the steps you normally follow when designing databases, designing for process flow, and delivering user interfaces will change when you do it according to a business rules approach. Specifically, the data and process tracks are reduced in content because they are devoid of rule details. However, the data and process tracks integrate with the rule track in important ways. Therefore, the focus of the new rule track is to separate out the set of computations, constraints, inferences, guidelines, and action-enabling rules that utilize the information to guide actions.

Technology Track

The technology track includes steps for the selection, customization, and support of technology so as to leverage the business rules approach. While you can utilize any technologies to implement business rules (including COBOL against flat files), this book introduces the reader to rule-centric technologies that enable quicker delivery of and easier changes to business rules systems.

For the most part, this book presumes you will be using an Internet or Web front end, a relational DBMS, commercial rule-oriented technology perhaps, and Case or repository technology.

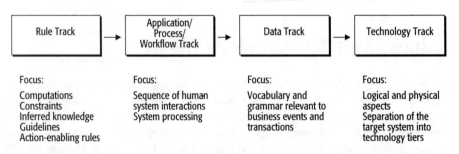

Figure 3.1   Business rules methodology tracks.

Process Track

The process track focuses on understanding actor interactions, the sequence of interactions between humans and the system, as well as interactions between the system and other automated pieces, such as databases or other systems. Therefore, as you follow the steps within the process track, you will deliver a list of all business events served by the target system, the business event's associated business process, and finally to the decisions that are made on behalf of the process in servicing the business event. As soon as you transition from understanding the event's process to uncovering the decisions behind the event, you transition from the process track into the rule track. Hopefully, you can imagine that the transition from business events to processes to decisions to rules is a natural one.

Data Track

The data track produces the data models and eventual database. When you follow the steps in the data track, you uncover the vocabulary and grammar with which the rules are expressed and you create a stable data structure to represent that vocabulary. Specifically, as you uncover rules, you make sure each word or phrase is represented in the data model and database. Hopefully, you can understand that the transition from rule collection to data constructs is likewise also a very natural one.

For now, keep in mind that a data model and eventual database for a business rule system may have important differences from those for nonbusiness rule systems. Parts 4 and 5 of this book, Analysis and Design, highlight these crucial distinctions.

Following the steps in the data track, you organize the terms and facts into a stable data structure, using architectural data analysis and design principles. But you deliver a data structure with minimal rules in it. From here, the steps lead you to analyze the data structure for long-term stability in the face of business change. Because of the importance of the data foundation, the data track in this book contains steps for developing as stable a database as possible, as early as possible. The goal is to identify implementable data increments that enable structural database growth over time with minimal interruption to the business. The ability for the data structure to support business change and future directions is important enough to discuss further.

Businesses today need to change quickly, either reactively or proactively. To accommodate such changes in existing systems is usually very time-consuming and expensive. Historically, the most expensive systems changes have been those that require a change in the system's logic (such as, in a computation rule, inference rule, or constraint rule, for example) or require a change in data structure (such as, move attributes around, add attributes, change keys, add tables).

Let's look first at changes in the system's logic. In the past, making changes to a system's logic was a time-consuming task because a programmer had to find all relevant procedural code (could be in many places), change it, and test it. However, rules positioned for change through rule technology enable dynamic changes to logic centrally managed as declarative rules. Therefore, when you express much of the system logic as declarative rules, changes to those rules require significantly less time, therefore cost less money, and have a quicker positive impact on the business itself.

Let's now look at changes in data structure. These can remain very time-consuming and expensive, even when using commercial rules technology. First, the data change has to be analyzed and designed. Major data structural changes may require data unloads and reloads. In addition, corresponding system logic may also need changing. If you express much of the system logic as declarative rules, these changes may require less time than otherwise. However, the structural data changes are still as time-consuming and expensive as ever. Therefore, structural data changes become the most significant changes, causing the most disruption.

Suffice it to say that, with business rule systems development, the economics change. If rule changes become easy, data changes can emerge as the most significant barrier, by far, to business change, if database design does not occur properly.

The data track in this book not only highlights the importance of the underlying data model, but provides techniques for ensuring that the initial data model remains stable over time. The data track addresses this by understanding the entire data scope from the beginning and by identifying those aspects of its data structure that you need to design with the future in mind. It makes little sense to position the rules for change and then allow tomorrow's data foundation to remain a significant barrier to that change!

Consider that it is a very serious mistake to simply reverse-engineer existing data structures into a model from which to move forward. That's because such a model reflects current data requirements possibly in a very narrow, application-biased perspective. With such databases as a foundation, the business's demand for adding or modifying rules will require serious database changes. This defeats the whole purpose, and undermines a major advantage of building a business rules system in the first place.

A business rules system should be one that accommodates change on purpose. A data structure that does not include future vision will stifle change.

Rule Track

A fourth track, then, represents the set of rules behind the interactions and over the data, where the rules are managed as a logical component, separate from the core process flow and separate from the data. The rule track focuses on the capture, analysis, automation, and change of the business's rules. These rules are the foundational logic that guides decisions and actions within the business organization and now within a business rules system. By crafting the rules of the business as a deliverable, the business people are at the helm of systems development, governing the behavior of its humans and its systems. Through specification of these rules, the business experts preordain the answers to standard or anticipated business situations that may arise within a business event. At the same time, the business experts can selectively omit rules for those decisions that are better left to the creativity of human choice, rather than to predefined rules. The rule track aims to externalize the business's rules of operation so that the entire business community and its automated systems can think and act spontaneously and more intelligently.

By separating the rules from the data and process, you move the learning curve for the business people closer to the people. The documented rules serve as error messages when they are violated. The rules serve as a basis for future analysis because it is through experimenting with rules that the business leaders challenge and change business behavior.

The rule track starts with steps for discovering rules behind a business event or behind the decisions for that event. It includes steps for reducing those rules to a minimal but complete set. It leads you to analyze dependencies among rules as well as correlations from rules to data items and database operations. As you can see, the business rules approach delivers a very integrated solution to systems development, by definition. That's because the methodology requires that expression of a rule always relates to items in the data or business object model. This fosters an unbreakable connection between the two. There is literally no way to disintegrate the logic of the target system (its rules) from the underlying data foundation.

The rule track, like all tracks, is prevalent in all phases of the methodology. Starting with the scoping phase, for example, the rule track is evident as you seek the business context for rules, such as objectives and policies. In the discovery phase, the rule track includes steps for capturing decisions that may represent logical groups of rules. In the analysis phase, the methodology includes steps for reducing those rules to a minimal but complete set. During analysis, you analyze dependencies among rules as well as correlations from rules to data items and database operations.

With an understanding of the four tracks, let's now look at how the tracks fit within the methodology phases.

Business Rule Methodology Phases

A business rules approach to systems development, like most systems development methodologies, has six conceptually different phases (even if done incrementally). These are shown in Figure 3.2 as scope, plan, discover, analyze, design, and deliver. The figure shows that each phase has steps and deliverables for each of the four tracks.

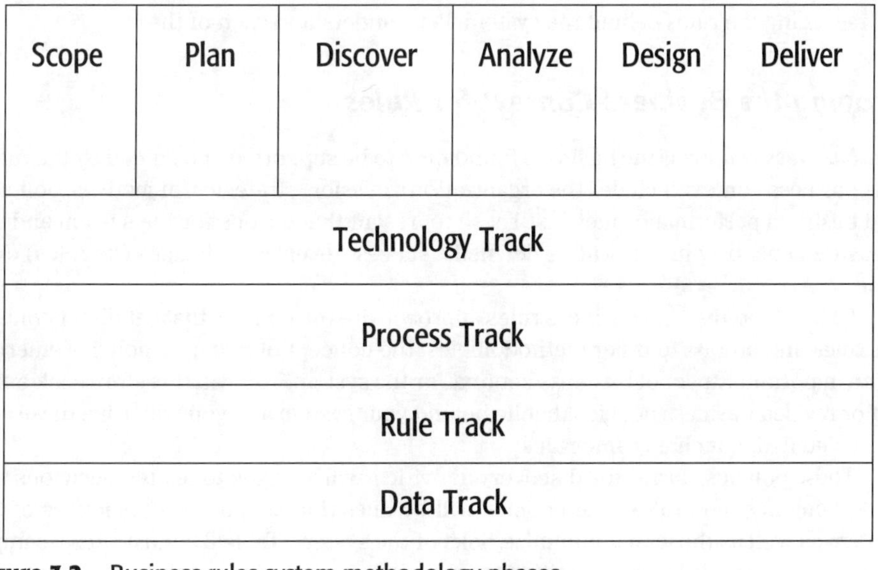

Scope	Plan	Discover	Analyze	Design	Deliver

Technology Track

Process Track

Rule Track

Data Track

Figure 3.2   Business rules system methodology phases.

Figure 3.2 does not intend to suggest an old-fashioned waterfall approach to systems development. However, for tutorial purposes, it is important that you understand the conceptual differences among the phases. For example, it is very important to do a thorough job with scoping and planning. Keep in mind that a business rules approach aims to deliver up front a strong architectural foundation (to accommodate future business changes). This means that incremental systems delivery may become the adding, changing, and retiring of rules or rule sets within that foundation. This requires that the first increment include the stabilizing aspects of the information architecture, rule jurisdictions, and rule stewardship. When this is so, the discovery phase can occur in incremental pieces, followed by analysis, design, and delivery, while more discovery occurs in parallel.

Scoping Phase

Scoping is the process of capturing high-level business requirements and boundaries for a new or enhanced information system. In this respect, the scoping phase for a business rule system is not unlike that of other kinds of systems. During scoping, this book leads you in solidifying two important aspects of scope. The first is the identification of business events, correlated to target system releases. Incremental delivery units defined along the boundaries of business events results in incremental deliveries that are of business value.

The second scope is that of the data scope, with an understanding of the extent of data-sharing across the organization. Understanding the data scope allows you to plan the data analysis, design, and implementation such that it will accommodate current and future business needs and user communities.

From a business rules perspective, there are three business rule–oriented considerations during scoping. The first is the business context for the eventual business rules. The second consideration is the set of scoping deliverables in preparation for rules, specifically the identification of policies as precursors to rules. The third is the purpose for managing the rules behind the system. Let's understand each of these.

Scoping the Business Context for Rules

The *business context* is the business foundation to be supported and guided by the rules. The business context includes the organization's mission, strategies, objectives, policies, and business performance metrics. These represent the reasons for the system and the measurements by which it will be deemed a success, even as it changes (its rules) over time.

Of most interest to a business rules approach are the policies that set direct context for rules. In contrast to other methodologies, the concept of business policies emerges as an important aspect of business context for the system. You will therefore seek existing or revised business policies that lie behind your system and you will drive these into more detailed, but changeable rules.

These policies, during the discovery activities, will lead you to related decisions and underlying business rules. The policies will be ones that support the objectives of the system as well as those that minimize risks of the system. Table 3.2 illustrates a sample risk mitigation table, with risk mitigation policies.

Table 3.2   Sample Risk Mitigation Table with Policies

ID	RISK	MITIGATING POLICIES
R1	The unintended release of the identities of member children.	The identities of member children will not be released to any external person or organization. Every industry-standard precaution must be taken to safeguard sensitive customer information. We must conform to all country and state regulations.
R2	Members will not continue to use the park's services if they perceive that entrance times are excessive or that the pace of game-playing is too slow.	Actual versus planned enrollments must be measured daily. System response times must be monitored for comparison to VCI service-level standards. The technical architecture must be scalable and quickly upgradable.
R3	Members will not continue to use the park's services if they don't find the games and other services enjoyable.	Retain the services of a child-learning consultancy to help select games and other services. Develop policies and procedures for measuring member satisfaction.
R4	Late or nonpayment of bills by customers.	Credit-checking policies, procedures, and rules must be developed to identify guardians who represent a credit risk.
R5	Children attempt to enroll friends.	Develop policies and procedures for validating the identities of external parties during the enrollment process.

Purpose for Managing Rules behind the System

For a business rules system, it is important to determine, with the sponsor and stakeholders, why there is a desire to manage the rules. For example, do the stakeholders want to employ rule management to achieve one or more of the following:

- Deliver shared rules across organizational boundaries of the stakeholders
- Resolve undesirable inconsistencies among discovered rules
- Identify where it is appropriate for rules to be inconsistent
- Resolve inconsistencies in business objectives
- Create rules for new processes.

Another important difference during the scoping phase is the planning for rule management, including methodology, repository, and organizational infrastructure. This brings you to the planning phase.

Planning Phase

Often the planning phase is simply the last part of the scoping phase. During planning, you create a project plan for building the business rules system. Naturally, a project plan for a business rules system includes an emphasis on the following:

- Separating rules throughout discovery, analysis, design, and delivery
- Tracing rules from business origin to system implementation
- Externalizing rules for all audiences through a rules repository
- Positioning rules for change by utilizing or simulating rule-related technology.

To achieve an emphasis on the above items, there are at least five aspects of your project plan that are needed to accommodate a business rules approach.

The first aspect to consider is the set of tasks for establishing rule standards. The second is the set of tasks and guidelines specifically for discovering, analyzing, designing, and delivering automated rules as a separately managed asset. The third incorporates the opportunity to test and deploy commercial rules technology.

The fourth new aspect to your project plan addresses at least four new roles for dealing with rules. A *rule analyst* is responsible for capturing rules from business conversations, documents, or program code. A *rule designer* is responsible for determining where rules are to be enforced within application architecture. A *rule implementer* is accountable for coding the executable rules, although application developers or database administrators, depending on where the rules are implemented, may play this role. A *rule integrator* or manager analyzes rules across business events and across applications to ensure high-quality rules for the organization. This role probably also selects and manages the repository into which rules are entered and from which rules are managed.

The fifth new aspect is the set of tasks for your rule repository. These include documentation of meta data and rule repository requirements, a rule metamodel, and the decision on a rule-storage mechanism. You will need a rules repository user guide, and perhaps training materials. If your project involves excavating rules from existing systems, you will need procedures on how to do this, and perhaps training materials here also. You may need to know the priority sequence in which to seek rules from people or from program code. If you are fortunate, you will include tasks for establishing a rule stewardship program that identifies formally those roles in the organization that accept responsibility for policy, which leads to responsibility for rules.

Discovery Phase

The discovery phase uncovers detailed system requirements, but remains technology neutral. For ease of understanding, this book divides the discovery phase into two pieces. The first is the discovery of initial requirements. The second is the discovery of rules and data.

This book specifically separates the discovery phase from the analysis phase for one simple reason: Discovery refers to the uncovering of those requirements, not the analyzing of them.

The purpose of discovering initial requirements is to document only the essential aspects of the system behavior because these lead you to the discovery of the underlying data and rules. For our purposes, essential aspects of system behavior include five items: the tasks or activities behind each business event, the decisions made on behalf of those tasks or activities, the information referenced in making those decisions, the knowledge created or judgments made by those decisions, and finally, real or imaginary event scenarios for testing completeness of the system behavior.

A significant difference in a business rules approach emerges when, during the discovery phase, you shift from discovering system behavior to unearthing decisions and rules behind business events. That is, you quickly shift your focus from events and processes (the doing aspect) to the discovery and formal analysis of the decision-making (the intellectual aspect) behind a business event.

Therefore, the purpose of discovering rules and data is to begin (and never stop!) capturing rules, and also to solidify the information and knowledge behind them. Keep in mind, then, that rule discovery will and should be an iterative process. In a business rule world, rule discovery, essentially, never ends. After all, it is not really just a phase. You intend to build an information system designed to change its rules, add new ones, and retire old ones. So, rule discovery is a continuous dialog with the business community and that's good.

Many previous systems development approaches start with understanding the sequence of user interactions, sequence of processes behind those interactions, and perhaps which object classes accept accountability for certain functionality. In a business rules approach, however, much of this is temporarily put on hold while you move quickly to discovering the organizational intelligence behind the event. The reason is that no one can truly understand the "essential or mandatory sequence of user interaction" until you have uncovered the underlying essential rule set and corresponding stable data model. More than that, if using commercial rules products, you may not need to design for objects or classes to execute rules. Rule execution may be handled by a rule service or rule development environment. There is no sense in designing for things you need not implement yourself!

The discovery phase has a heavy business community focus. You can discover rules either from business people or from legacy code. The goal of rule discovery is simply to find out what the rules are or what someone thinks they are or ought to be. You aim to express the rules in the business community's language so the business audience understands them. You manage and report on the rules in much the same way data analysts manage and report on existing data elements in systems or on screens and reports.

Analysis Phase

The analysis phase applies discipline to artifacts collected in each track. Specifically, the steps in the rule track apply familiar and new discipline to the rule collection, in much the same way that data analysis adds discipline to a collection of data elements. The methodology steps of rule analysis lead you to find rule inconsistencies and redundancies. It includes steps for producing rule dependency chains, which unearth the essential "thinking flow" that emerges from knowing the rules.

During the analysis phase, you determine which decisions and underlying rules are to be shared across organizational and application boundaries. The important concept to realize during discovery is that business events follow policies and require decisions to be made. When rules execute, they reference pieces of information and may create new pieces of information, called knowledge, in order to carry out decisions. All of these intellectual assets (decisions, rules, base information, and rule-created knowledge) can be shared across organizational boundaries, with proper analysis, when appropriate for the business.

The analysis phase includes tasks for analyzing rules into high quality rule sets, creating a rule-enriched logical data model, assessing the quality of source data, and mining rules from source systems, if appropriate. You may validate rules through rule validation workshops.

Rule analysis also has a business-orientation in the final step. Here, you bring rule problems back to the business audience, refine the rules, and optimize them for the business. Remember that, in a business rules system, you can change the rules later. You do, however, want to be sure that the rules within each new system increment are free of inconsistencies and do not contain rules that seem to serve no business purpose or detract from hitting business objectives.

The rule analysis steps lead you from the rule dependency chains back to the workflow interaction and sequence. Specifically, the rule dependency chains may refine the initial sequence of user interaction (the preliminary workflow) to preserve the essential sequence of rule dependencies. From here, the steps lead you to introduce to that underlying essential sequence, alternative sequences for other reasons, such as performance or increased customer satisfaction. Once again, the transition from rule analysis back to process analysis is quite natural.

Finally, in the analysis phase, there are steps for building the data model from the terms and facts behind the rules. Again, the transition from rules to data is very natural. However, most importantly, the Data Analysis steps lead to analyzing the model with the future in mind where that future may hold changes in policies and rules. There are steps for evolving the system's data model into one that can serve a cross-organizational business perspective.

The balance between analysis and design is as controversial as always, even in a business rules approach. This book proposes that thorough analysis is desirable for high-quality database designs. Process design and rule design can happen iteratively, sometimes with little formal analysis.

Design Phase

Within the rule track, the design phase includes steps for classifying rules into types where those types can be assigned to implementation options. A rule may be implemented in the presentation layer, middle layer, database layer, or a combination. The rule design steps lead the rule designer in determining how to implement those rules in those layers. Options include commercial rules technology, homegrown code, DBMS stored procedures and triggers, and so on. For rules that will not be enforced using business rules technology, there are steps by which the designer will correlate them to corresponding data operations (insert, update, delete) to ensure that each rule fires in every instance. In this way (unlike previous systems development approaches) the execution of rules transcends transactional and application boundaries. Also, correlating rules to data operations enables future impact analysis when a rule changes.

THE ZACHMAN FRAMEWORK AND A BUSINESS RULE METHODOLOGY

For readers who are proponents of the Zachman Framework for Information Architecture, it is beyond the scope of this book to discuss an in-depth analysis of where business rules fit within the Framework. An excellent source for opinions on this matter is www.zifa.com and www.businessrulesgroup.org.

This book simply presumes that scoping and discovery deliverables belong in Zachman rows 1 and 2. Analysis deliverables belong in Zachman row 3. Design deliverables are from Zachman row 4. Business rules themselves are somewhere in column 6, the motivation column. There are different opinions as to which row business rules live. If determining which row business rules belong is important to your organization or project, we recommend you refer to the two Web sites above.

Therefore, during the design phase, you assign rules to the target technology, design the database for its target technology perhaps, design rule support within the DBMS, and design core system flow around rule dependency chains. Someone designs utilities while others translate conversion specifications to physical descriptions. You install, customize, and test target technology and you are ready to go.

This book recognizes that your target technology may be not rule-oriented technology at all. If this is the case, the design phase may include the design of shared program code to enforce rules (outside or within the DBMS) and that, the database design team may be a key player here. You are aiming for well-managed rule automation. This ensures that rules are no longer redundantly (and possibly inconsistently) implemented many times over in application code.

It is impossible for one book to cover implementation details for all possible development environments. Therefore, Chapter 12 presents a generic business rules design methodology that can be tailored to product-specific environments. This book, then, serves as a starting point for building business rules systems.

Delivery Phase

During the delivery phase, you enter data definitions into database technology and perhaps also into rules technology. Someone loads the databases, codes objects, creates screens and Web pages, and defines and redefines rules. Users are trained and begin testing. You add and modify rules, as needed. The next delivery increment can then begin. While it is beyond the scope of this book to provide details on various implementations, Chapters 13 and 14 contain examples using representative commercial rule products.

Summary

At first glance, you may believe that this book does not contain any new ideas. This is a natural first impression because you have always dealt with all aspects of a system, regardless of what you called those aspects or which is your favorite systems development paradigm. However, this book proposes that the rule track—including rule discovery, analysis, design, and delivery—makes all the difference in the world to the business itself. That's because the rule track makes the business rules tangible to the business, hence they become instruments of change. The resulting system is able to grow with the business rather than become a legacy hindrance to business advancement.

Unlike previous systems development approaches, a business rule methodology recognizes that no one can truly understand the "essential or mandatory" sequence of user interaction until you have uncovered the underlying essential rule set and corresponding stable data model. Therefore, a project plan for a business rules system includes the rule-oriented emphasis and roles specified in this chapter. Pay special attention to these, because within them small changes in philosophy, focus, techniques, and even products come into play. It is within these that very small changes take place. But these are the small changes that bring about the big differences in the business itself. These are the changes that externalize and manage the policies and rules of the business, so that the business can become what it wants to become, so that information technology becomes the weapon of change and not a barrier to future possibilities.

The business rule differences in this chapter are:

- You remove rule considerations from the data and application tracks and introduce a rule track that stands on its own to a large extent.
- The process track, wraps core process flow around rule dependencies.
- The data track supports the rule track.
- The technology track leverages the separation of rule execution from core process flow.
- Rule changes become easier.
- Once you uncover the essential rule dependencies, you can refine the sequence of user interaction to preserve that sequence and introduce to it alternative sequences for other reasons.

A business rules approach puts the business people at the helm of the business and also at the helm of systems development. The business people steer the behavior of resulting systems by supplying, adding, changing, or archiving rule requests so as to effect business change. Business change, then, ceases to be disruptive to systems delivery and to the business itself. Instead, business change becomes a proactive, strategic, business weapon. The business rule becomes the fuel to energize the business change.

The methodology chapters contain techniques aimed at separating, tracing, externalizing, and positioning rules for change. Some of these may be familiar. Some will seem more formal than you have experienced. Some may be new to you. Some may seem excessive, but remember that the goal is to leverage the rules of the business as instruments of business change. Of most importance is the overall management of rules, covered in Chapter 15.

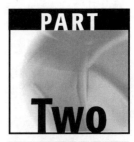
Getting Started on a
Business Rules Project

Scoping for Success

You now stand at the beginning of an exciting new information systems development project. You are at this point because someone in the business community, with funding (a sponsor), has a business need that may be addressed by building (or altering an existing) automated information system. Your first responsibility is to solicit and document a common understanding of the new information system's business requirements. These are what the information system is all about, what it is not about, and the cost and benefits of building and supporting it.

It is very important to do a thorough job with scoping and planning. Keep in mind that a business rules approach aims to deliver up front a strong architectural foundation expressly to accommodate future business changes. This means that incremental systems delivery often becomes the adding, changing, and retiring of rules or rule sets within that foundation. This requires that the first increment include the stabilizing aspects of the information architecture, rule jurisdictions, and rule stewardship. When this is so, the discovery phase can occur in incremental pieces, followed by analysis, design, and delivery, while more discovery occurs in parallel. In fact, you can iterate from discovery to analysis to design and delivery and back to rediscovery of rules. You can, in your iterations, add rules and change rules. But to do so nimbly requires a solid information architecture. So, scoping takes an early look into the informational scope of the project.

Scoping is the first phase of your project, as shown in Figure 4.1.

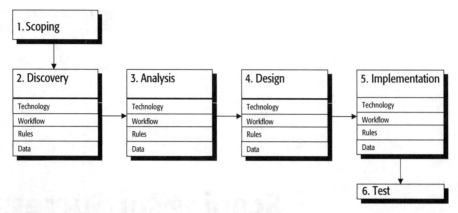

Figure 4.1   Business rule systems methodology phases.

What Is Scoping?

Scoping is the process of capturing high-level *business requirements* and boundaries for a new or enhanced information system. If you do not establish a common understanding of the information system's objectives among stakeholders at the outset, the chances for completing a successful information system development effort are at great risk.

The business requirements documented during the scoping phase represent the high-level objectives of the project's executive sponsor and other project stakeholders (Wiegers 1999). The high-level business requirements define the vision and objectives of the new information system and constitute the business case for the commitment of money and people to build it. The business requirements from the scoping phase establish the priorities of the next phase, the discovery phase.

How Is Scoping Different in a Business Rules Approach?

The scoping process in a business rules project is much the same as in other successful information systems development methods. There are, however, four important differences, which appeared in Table 3.1:

1. Separating rules by planning for rule management.
2. Tracing rules by emphasizing and formalizing business context.
3. Externalizing rules by establishing business purposes for managing rules.
4. Positioning rules for change by beginning to build a solid information architecture.

Naturally, these relate to the fact that you focus on rules as separate artifacts just as some of you have, for a long time now, focused on data and its structure as a separate asset. The differences support the four principles of the business rules approach: separate, trace, externalize, and position rules for change. Let's look at each of these differences.

Separating Rules by Planning for Rule Management

The first difference supports the separation of rules from other considerations by including the planning for formal or informal rule management. Will you manage rules within this project only or across projects? Regardless, you need to scope your rule management requirements and include tasks in your project plan for providing the right level of rule management support. These tasks may include evaluation of rule meta data, development of a rule metamodel, a decision on where to store rules, a rule repository user guide and training, rule mining procedures and training for excavating rules from program code, and procedures for rule stewardship.

Tracing Rules by Emphasizing and Formalizing Business Context

The second difference supports the tracing of rules to their origins, the business context. The scoping phase supports this difference by placing an emphasis and formalism on the business context for the eventual rules. The business context explains why the business is sponsoring this project, in the first place. More than that, the *business context* is the business foundation to be supported and guided by the rules. But, business context plays a much more prevalent role throughout the development of a business rules system. That's because, business rules are, in fact, an ongoing deliverable of the business context itself.

The business context includes the organization's mission, strategies, objectives, policies, and business performance metrics. These represent the reasons for the system and the measurements by which it will be deemed a success, even as it changes (its rules) over time. As you proceed through this book, you will learn that policies lead to decisions and decisions are comprised of rules. Thus, there is a very definite path from business context (project justification) eventually to rules. A business rules approach, from the very beginning, starts to weave this path. The business rule objectives should be in support of the organization's strategic objectives as spelled out in the current year's business plan.

Therefore, business context is of special importance if the business community is to leverage the business rules approach. Recall that, while systems developers view a business rules approach as a shift in emphasis for developing faster, more changeable systems, the business community sees it as a mechanism by which to utilize instruments of proactive and creative organizational change. Therefore, the potential impact on the business of the business rules approach starts in the scoping phase with the uncovering of business context. Specifically, the steps in the scoping phase lead you in recognizing (hence capturing) policies and tactics as precursors to the rules. In general, your goal is to capture policies or tactics during the scoping phase and their underlying rules during the discovery phase. In practice, you may be capturing both during both phases. This leads to the identification of policies as precursors to rules. Most systems development methodologies include common deliverables in a scoping phase. It is most useful to create, as the major deliverable from scoping, a project charter. Typically, a project charter includes reasons (benefits) for the system, business events to be handled by the system, high-level data subjects behind the business events, and risks.

Something that is important to a business rules system, and beginning in scoping, is that you begin to identify policies. These policies, during the discovery activities, will lead you to related decisions and underlying business rules. The policies will be ones that support the objectives of the system as well as those that minimize risks of the system.

Externalizing Rules by Establishing a Business Purpose for Managing Rules

The third difference supports the externalization of rules for all audiences and is represented by the identification of the purpose for managing the rules behind the system. Why is the organization taking a step toward rule management? What is the organization's purpose in wanting to manage its rules better, even if this is the only or first project for doing so? When you know the answer to this question, you can plan, in the next chapter, the infrastructure you need for appropriate rule management. Reasons for managing rules better might be to:

- Deliver shared rules across organizational boundaries of the stakeholders
- Resolve undesirable inconsistencies among discovered rules
- Identify where it is appropriate for rules to be inconsistent from one organization to another
- Resolve inconsistencies in business objectives
- Create rules to support new business processes.

Positioning Rules for Change by Beginning to Build a Solid Information Architecture

A fourth difference supports the principle of positioning rules for change by focusing on a solid architectural foundation, particularly for the data track. Accordingly, you will notice that the scoping phase contains steps for understanding the data scope early. You can do this by taking an object perspective, identifying important high-level business objects that are of interest to the target project. You can also do this by taking a data perspective, identifying data subjects, conceptual data entities, and a preliminary depiction of a conceptual data model. This book advocates that a solid information architecture is an important deliverable in your first system increment. If you deliver such a foundation early, incremental system deliveries can mostly be new or changed rule sets, without serious architectural interruptions. If you embark on iterative, incremental development (as is recommended by most experts), you will want a solid information architecture beneath your system. Your increments and iterations may evolve variations in process flow, screen design, and certainly now in rule executions, but it is very difficult to make changes (even in prototyping) to a database design.

The total difference is the faithfulness to the four principles of the business rules approach (separate, trace, externalize, and position rules for change). Scoping begins to separate rules from other aspects of the system by starting with business context. Scoping traces rules by tying them to strategies, objectives, goals, risks, and other factors they aim to support. Scoping externalizes aspects of rules by gaining commitment on the related elements of business context. Scoping positions rules for change by planning for rule management.

Scoping is the very first step in the methodology and sets the stage for the subsequent phases. As such, the rule track becomes evident as a new emphasis with new formalism, and distinguishes business rules systems development from other approaches.

What Is the Purpose of Scoping?

The purpose of scoping is to capture high-level business requirements and establish project boundaries at the beginning. First, good estimates of project schedule and cost require a solid understanding of the business requirements. Second, prioritizing business requirements solidifies the implementation plan. This plan defines the business functions addressed in each release of the information system. Third, in the absence of a well-executed scoping phase, the project is highly susceptible to drift in priority and scope, with subsequent liabilities and risks. Fourth, business requirements are the essential inputs to the design and coding tasks later in the development process. For example, business requirements are the basis for creating test cases.

In this book, for ease of discussion, we make a differentiation between scoping and planning, although you may, in practice, consider planning to be part of the scoping phase. For our purposes, we consider scoping to include only the essential deliverables needed to put boundaries around the target information systems project. We consider the planning activities to be the details for how the project will be carried out, once the scope of essential deliverables has been decided.

What Are the Deliverables of Scoping?

The primary deliverable in this book from the scoping phase is a project charter. The project charter answers, at the very beginning of the project, the most fundamental questions about the target information system and its associated development project. These include:

- Who will use the system and what business benefits will they realize?
- How will the success of the system be measured?
- What are the business and technical risks and constraints associated with development of the system and how will you deal with them?
- How long will it take and how much will it cost?

Please note that, although the project manager is responsible for the tasks that lead to the creation of the project charter, its content is the responsibility of the executive sponsor and of the business and technical partners.

Project Charter Content

The *project charter* is a specification of your executive sponsor and partners' business requirements for the new or enhanced information system. The project charter makes the business case for the project. Figure 4.2 is a sample table of contents for a project charter.

I. Purpose of the Project

II. Business Context
   A. Organizational Mission
   B. Strategies
   C. Objectives
   D. Policies Supporting Objectives
   E. Business Performance Metrics
   F. External Factors

III. Scope
   A. Stakeholders (people and organizations)
   B. Locations
   C. Interfacing Information Systems and Databases
   D. Business Events
   E. Event Response Processes
   F. Data Subjects
      1. Conceptual Data Entities
      2. Conceptual Model
   G. Additional Requirements
   H. Architectural Solution
      1. Alternative Technical Solutions
      2. Preferred Technical Solution
   I. Scope Diagram

IV. Constraints
   A. Business Constraints
   B. Technical Constraints

V. Risks and Mitigations

VI. Project Plan
   A. Organizational Infrastructure (roles and responsibilities, authorities)
   B. Organizational Resources (involvement and expectations)
   C. Detailed Project Plan
   D. Estimated Costs

Figure 4.2   Sample table of contents for a project charter.

What Are the Steps in Scoping?

The intent of this chapter is to present one specific set of scoping steps that has proven successful. These scoping steps flow naturally into the next phase, the discovery phase. This chapter presents only an overview of the scoping phase and is not meant to be a comprehensive reference for scoping an information systems development project. Rather, this chapter emphasizes those steps and deliverables specifically pertinent to subsequent discovery of business rules. Figure 4.3 summarizes the scoping steps in this chapter.

Note that you may be more comfortable using a scoping approach that you have already used successfully. If so, please be sure you understand the concepts outlined previously in this chapter. How is Project Scoping Different Using a Business Rules Approach? Also, read the Summary: The Business Rule Difference in Scoping. These two sections highlight ideas and deliverables that are specific to a business rules approach that may be missing or under-emphasized in other approaches. You will want to consider adopting these rule-enhanced tasks and techniques into your development process.

Please note that even though the scoping process is presented here as a series of sequential steps, you are likely to do many of them in parallel.

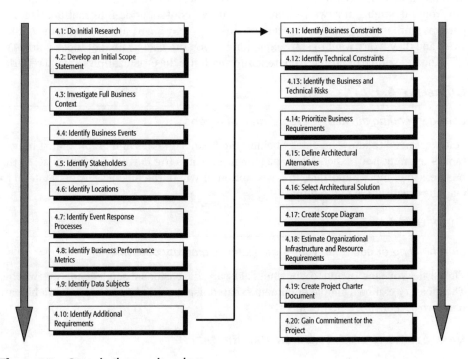

Figure 4.3 Steps in the scoping phase.

STEP 4.1: DO INITIAL RESEARCH

The purpose of doing research at the outset of a project is to ground business analysts and other team members in the business and technical environments of the target information system.

GUIDELINE 4.1.1

Gather and study existing documentation on the business and technical environment.

Some of the sources to explore include:

- The current year's strategic business plan
- Policy and procedure manuals
- Existing process models, data models and data dictionaries
- Existing system documentation
- Industry-specific magazines and periodicals
- Internal newsletters and intranet Web pages
- Industry- or organization-specific glossaries of terms
- Current and planned IT technology.

In some cases, the organization may have commissioned studies of the target business function in the past by the IT organization or a consulting firm. If so, read the output from the studies for two reasons. First, it can contain good information. Second, perhaps more important, the subject matter experts may have participated in the earlier work and they won't want to start explaining to you the background of those studies.

Another source of business context information is the organization's annual reports.

GUIDELINE 4.1.2

Consider reading the last two years' annual reports.

You don't need to know all details behind the financial tables and graphs. Most important is learning how executive management explains the current performance of the business and, more important, the description of where the business leaders intend to lead the organization in the future.

GUIDELINE 4.1.3

Start building or adding to your organization's glossary of terms.

The earlier you start or add to a business glossary, the easier subsequent analysis will be. The glossary can be a simple document created using a word processor or can be part of a formal repository environment.

CASE STUDY: STEP 4.1—DO INITIAL RESEARCH

You are commissioned to build a business rules system for a new enterprise called Virtual Children Incorporated, or VCI.

Case Study Instructions:

- Gather business documentation and summarize it.
- Document mission, objectives, strategies, policies if possible.

Case Study Solution:

You uncover several documents explaining the organization for which you are building a business rules system. These include the founders' video, initial business plan, and minutes from organizational meetings. You summarize the following:

Essentially, VCI is a virtual world for children at home after school. VCI is an Internet-based park for such children. It is referred to as VCI Park. The VCI employees who support the park behind the scenes and provide guidance to the members are called park rangers. Guardians are the customers who enroll their children. If a guardian does not have access to the Internet, an admittance park ranger can enroll a child on behalf of the guardian.

Guardians can control the children's entrance into VCI on a daily basis, if desired. Again, admittance park rangers can do so, if needed. Children have to be between 6 and 15 years old. Guardians pay a monthly fee for VCI service per child, depending on which park services the guardian wishes their child to access.

A child whose guardian enrolls them in VCI is called a member and has an entrance pass. The entrance pass is validated every day when the member enters the VCI premises through VCI's Web page. Once inside the premises, the member can visit any or all of the following services within the park:

- Theme park, which has games in it
- Librarian function, which assists the member in searching the Internet for school research
- Tutorial function, which provides the member with homework assistance
- University function, through which the member can attend distance learning classes and receive certificates or credit

The first service VCI will offer is the theme park service.

The theme park contains strategy games (chess, checkers, other), intellectual games (memory challengers, math problems), and entertainment videos, which are age-appropriate. The park does not have any games or videos of a violent or sexual nature. An active security force for inappropriate language or messages monitors all conversations between a member and park rangers.

When a member arrives at the park gate, the member presents an entrance pass (that is, identification) and is acknowledged. The entrance ranger asks the member pertinent questions for the day, selected by the guardian. These can be the same questions every day or the guardian can change them. Questions are selected by the guardian from a menu. For the sake of simplicity, the first release of the VCI system will allow guardians to choose from four questions. (The advanced reader can design the system to allow for an unlimited number of questions of unlimited content.) The four questions are:

- Did you finish your written homework (in one subject or all subjects) for today? (yes or no)

- Did you complete your (specific or all) chores for today? (yes or no)

- Did you complete (a specific or all) activities for today (yes or no)

- What grade (A, B, C, D, F) did you receive on a test (in subject of choice) today?

Depending on the answer to each question, the member will receive a time allotment for visiting the theme park, as set up by the guardian. The questions and their answers are emailed to the guardian. Should the guardian discover that the member was not truthful in the answers (for example, the member did not really finish homework), the guardian can disable or reduce the hours allowed in the theme park for future days.

You are designing the VCI passage system that is responsible for:

- Member enrollment into the park system

- Member entrance into the park

- Member exit from the park

- Guardian communications about usage of the park

- Invoicing customers for services used by members.

STEP 4.2: DEVELOP AN INITIAL SCOPE STATEMENT

The scope of the target information system is a statement, from the executive sponsor's perspective, of what is included in the information system and what is not. A *scope statement* includes definition of stakeholders (persons, organizational functions), business processes, locations, systems, and data that are within the target system's boundaries and those that are not. Therefore, this chapter leads you to define for the scope the business events, event response processes, data subjects, and additional requirements. It includes steps for determining alternative technical solutions and a preferred solution as part of the final agreement of scope. The chapter suggests you augment the scope statement with a scope diagram, often called a *context diagram.*

The purpose of an initial scope statement is to jumpstart the project. It is a tangible early deliverable that involves the key participants and solidifies the thinking behind the project's business requirements. Think of the initial scope statement as an early checkpoint for making sure that you understand the information system needs of your sponsor and business partners and what their expectations are for the project.

GUIDELINE 4.2.1

Keep the initial scope statement short.

Limit the initial scope statement to a short narrative document, usually no more than a few pages in length. The initial scope statement actually represents the seed and starting point of the project charter document that you produce as a final deliverable of the scoping phase. The content of the initial scope statement is the responsibility of the executive sponsor. That said, it is important to gather, as well, the ideas and opinions of the other project participants. You need to understand persons and organizational functions of interest to the project, with emphasis on how organizational knowledge relates to your ability to discover, analyze, design, and leverage the organization's rules that will ultimately guide the system's behavior.

You will later engage these people in developing a more complete definition of project scope, as described in steps 4.3 to 4.20. Specifically, over the course of this chapter, you will expand and refine the scope until the project charter ultimately supercedes everything in the initial scope statement.

GUIDELINE 4.2.2

Be specific in content for the scope statement.

Include a short description of the general purpose for target information system, organizational mission, high-level business objectives for the target system, tactics or policies for achieving the objectives, suggested scope of a first release of the system, the stakeholders, constraints, and known risks with mitigation strategies (tactics and policies for minimizing risks).

The case study includes an example of an initial scope statement. The explanation of each section in it appears in subsequent steps in this chapter.

There are several ways to solicit input from your executive sponsor, champion, business, and technical partners. One way is to interview the executive sponsor with the champion, business, and technical partners also present. Another is to meet first with the business and technical partners, develop a draft initial scope statement, and then submit it to the executive sponsor for approval. A third is to conduct a facilitated initial scope session.

GUIDELINE 4.2.3

Consider utilizing a facilitated session.

Consider utilizing a facilitated session as a mechanism for composing the initial scope statement under the following circumstances: the project is extremely large, the project is broad in impact across the organization, or political issues need to be resolved right away.

Include the sponsor, champion, and partners in the facilitated session, and aim at gaining consensus on key issues right at the outset.

Distribute the initial scope statement document to the executive sponsor, business champion, and business and technical partners for review and comment. Schedule follow-up calls or meetings to gain everyone's comments and approval.

CASE STUDY: STEP 4.2—DEVELOP INITIAL SCOPE STATEMENT

Case Study Instructions:

- Create an initial scope statement for the VCI passage system

Case Study Solution:
Initial Scope Statement VCI Passage System

> **Purpose:** Founded in 2001, Virtual Child International (VCI) provides services to guardians of school-age children. VCI's service, VCI Park, is unique. There are no other organizations offering competitive services at this time. VCI's mission is to keep after-school children safe, connected, and productive via the Internet.

Guardians can enroll children as members of VCI Park. Members can access the park's games and other offerings via the Internet.

The initial release of the VCI passage system will be designed to offer guardians an easy way to enroll school children as members of the VCI theme park. Once enrolled, the system will provide access for each member child to a virtual world of games, tutoring, and other services. The system will allow guardians to communicate with VCI about services and will bill them monthly for the services and time their members have used.

Organizational Mission: Keep after-school children safe, connected, and productive through an Internet connection while VCI makes a profit.

High-level Business Goals: Note that objectives, as defined later, should be measurable, and so on. So maybe *goal* is a better term here.

- VCI will be the first to offer Web-based after-school services for children.
- VCI services will be safe for children.
- Guardian satisfaction is a high priority.

More Specific Goals: More specific objectives with supporting policies of the first release of the VSI system are documented in Table 4.1.

Scope of First Release of System: The first release of the VCI passage system will support enrolling new members, controlling member entrance to the theme park, and invoicing guardians for park services.

Stakeholders: Table 4.2 depicts the stakeholders of the VCI passage system.

Constraints: There is limited venture capital available for developing the first release of the system.

Table 4.1   Goal-Policy Table

GOALS	TACTIC OR POLICY FOR ACHIEVING GOALS
Provide easy-to-use enrollment process for guardians located anywhere in the world	All known information about an existing guardian (such as credit rating) will be accessible to the enrollment process. All location information about a guardian will include international address fields.
Monitor member entrance to and exit from the park.	All communications between a member and park rangers will be recorded for quality assurance and reference. Time used by members in the park will be recorded.
Create accurate bills for the time a member has used in the park.	Billing calculations will be published and applied to all invoices. Billing accuracy is of the highest importance.
Insure all communications with guardians are friendly and timely.	All communications with a guardian and park rangers will be recorded for quality assurance and reference.

Table 4.2 Stakeholder Table

STAKEHOLDER TYPE	STAKEHOLDERS
Actors	Guardians Park rangers (admittance and entrance rangers) Member children
Business champion	VCI's enrollment director
Business partners	VCI personnel director VCI park activities director A representative of the venture capital group
Technical partners	Information resource management manager Rule manager IT application development manager IT technical support manager
Other	Government regulatory agencies

- The Internet will be used for the enrollment and billing processes and for all communications with customers and members.

Risks and mitigating policies: Refer to Table 4.3 for descriptions of the dangers that the VCI passage system might encounter and the policies that should be proposed for avoiding each risk or mitigating its effects should the problem occur.

Table 4.3 VCI Risks and Mitigating Policies

RISK	RISK DESCRIPTION	TACTIC OR POLICY FOR MITIGATING RISKS
Risk 1	The unintended release of the identities of member children.	The identities of member children must not be released to any external person or organization. Every industry-standard precaution must be taken to safeguard sensitive member information. VCI must conform to all international, national, and local security regulations.
Risk 2	Members will not continue to use the park's services if they perceive that entrance times are excessive or that the pace of game-playing is too slow.	Actual versus planned enrollments must be measured daily. System response times must be monitored for comparison to VCI service-level standards. The technical architecture must be scalable and quickly upgradable.

(continues)

Table 4.3   VCI Risks and Mitigating Policies (*Continued*)

RISK	RISK DESCRIPTION	TACTIC OR POLICY FOR MITIGATING RISKS
Risk 3	Members will not continue to use the park's services if they don't find the games and other services enjoyable.	VCI will retain the services of a child-learning consultancy to help select games and other services. VCI will develop policies and procedures for measuring member satisfaction.
Risk 4	Late or nonpayment of bills by customers.	Credit-checking policies, procedures, and rules must be developed to identify guardians who represent a credit risk.
Risk 5	Children attempt to enroll friends.	VCI must develop policies and procedures for validating the identities of external parties during the enrollment process.

STEP 4.3: INVESTIGATE FULL BUSINESS CONTEXT

Business context defines the external and internal environments within which you will be building the target information system and within which it will be used. From a business rules perspective, one important goal of the scoping phase is to understand and document the business context for the rules you will discover, analyze, and implement in later phases. The business context behind business rules is the business foundation to be supported and guided by the rules. The business context is the backdrop against which all rules should be cast, changed, and justified. Without understanding business context, full justification for the project (and for each rule behind it) is in question.

The Business Rules Group offers excellent advice in "Organizing Business Plans: The Standard Model for Business Rule Motivation" (www.businessrulesgroup.org). They state, "the basic idea is to develop a business model for the elements of the business plan before system design or technological development is begun." They further state that there are no standard elements for business plans and no inclusion of business rules in common business planning approaches. To address this void, they produced the business rule motivation model, which is an excellent reference for step 4.3 where you investigate the full business context for the target project and its rules.

The business context, then, includes organization's mission, vision, strategies, goals, tactics, objectives, and policies. The Business Rules Group eloquently organizes these elements into means and ends. *Ends* comprise the organizational wish list, what an organization wants to achieve. *Means* are mechanisms for achieving the ends. In this regard, ends include vision, goals, and objectives, whereas means include mission, strategy, tactics, business policies, and business rules. They take this one step further and associate mission (means) with vision (end), strategy (means) with goal (end), tactic (means) with objective (end), and ultimately tie business policies and rules to both means and ends.

It is beyond the purpose of this book to devise a business plan. Therefore, we will not explore all of the above elements in detail. It is also likely that, as a member of a targeted systems development project, you may not have the authority to develop or improve current business plans. Most likely, you will need to make do or improvise with a subset of business plan elements.

With this in mind, let's take a look at a likely subset of these and how you can use them to define a business context behind your target system and its rules.

GUIDELINE 4.3.1

Document specific aspects of business motivation.

Document aspects of business context, such as mission, objectives, tactics, strategies, and policies, if known. The quotes in this section are from "Organizing Business Plans: The Standard Model for Business Rule Motivation."

Using the Business Rules Group's definitions, a *vision* is "a statement about the future state of the enterprise, without regard to how it is to be achieved." Often, vision statements seem too fuzzy to be overly useful for our purposes here.

A *goal*, according to the Business Rules Group, is "a statement or condition of the enterprise to be brought about or sustained through appropriate means." An example they provide is "To deliver pizzas in an expedient amount of time." While useful for business planning, this may be too vague for our purposes.

An *objective* is "a statement of attainable, time-targeted, and measurable target that the enterprise seeks to meet in order to achieve its Goals." Therefore, the following is an objective: Increase repeat customer business by 15 percent by the end of the year. To be measurable, there must be a definition of "repeat customer business" and the units for measuring it. Objectives are very useful to a business rules approach because they provide a mechanism for measuring the effectiveness of rules aimed at achieving them.

Therefore, consider a mission, which "indicates the ongoing operational activity of the enterprise." It should contain action, product or service, and customer, hence is more specific. The following represents a mission statement: To provide customers worldwide with the best service on the highest quality consumer electronics products at competitive prices. Here the action is "to provide," the product or service is "the best service on the highest quality consumer electronics products at competitive prices," and the customer is "customers worldwide."

A *strategy* "represents the essential Course of Action to achieve Ends—Goals in particular . . . represents the right approach to achieve its Goals, given the environmental constraints and risks the enterprise faces." A sample strategy may be: Ship orders as quickly as possible.

A *tactic* is a course of action that represents part of the detailing of strategies. An example is: Form a partnership with a shipping company that can deliver our orders overnight to any location.

Finally, a *policy* aims to guide the enterprise and is less specific than its underlying rules. Think of a policy as a high-level prescription for a desired result, usually one that the organization knows it can achieve or wishes to achieve. As an example of a policy: Ship for next day arrival at the customer's location all orders received before 4 P.M.

Therefore policies are actually precursors to rules. Note that a policy does not inform you of how exactly to behave according to it. In order to know how to behave in accordance with a policy, you need to know the rules behind it since the rules are very explicit in prescribing terms and conditions for the desired behavior. In this example, a rule that supports the policy is: If an order is entered by 4 P.M. on a business day, and if stock is available, and if customer credit is okay, then the order must be shipped for arrival at the customer location by noon on the next business day. Note that this rule gives precise conditions to check (Is it prior to 4 P.M. on a business day? Is stock available? Is customer credit okay?) as well as precise action (ship order for arrival at the customer location by noon on the next business day).

During the discovery phase, you will need to solidify the precise meaning of every term in those conditions and actions so as to deliver a rule without ambiguity. For starters, you will agonize over the meanings of order, 4 P.M., business day, stock, available, customer credit, OK, shipped, shipped for arrival, customer, customer location, noon, and next business day.

Table 4.4 pulls together a partial business context from the examples above. It is a partial business context because not all elements are present. Therefore, there may be gaps in business justification or assumptions. However, it represents elements that you are likely to uncover, leaving out those that are often elusive. Pay special attention to the fact that the policy does indeed set the stage for rules. In the above example, the policy guides the behavior of shipping orders such that orders received before 4 P.M. must be shipped for next day arrival at the customer's location. To be most specific, try to write a policy statement to include at least five intellectual pieces. They include the following:

- The desired guided behavior
- The enforcement level of the policy
- The party most closely responsible for adhering to the policy
- The jurisdiction over which the policy is valid
- The policy's rationale.

The first is the desired guided behavior. For example, the desired behavior encouraged by the policy in Table 4.4 is that orders received before 4 P.M. must be shipped for next day arrival at the customer's location.

The second intellectual piece is the enforcement level of the policy. Is the policy merely a guideline or is it mandatory? In the example, the question is, Must such orders

Table 4.4   Rule within a Partial Business Context

Mission	To provide customers worldwide with the best service on the highest quality consumer electronics products at competitive prices.
Objective	To increase repeat customer business by 15% by the end of the year.
Strategy	Ship customer orders as quickly as possible.
Tactic	Employ a shipping service to deliver 95% of customer orders by the next day after receipt of order.
Policy	We will ship all orders entered before 4 P.M. for next day arrival at customer locations.
Rule	If a customer order is entered by 4 P.M. on a business day, and if stock is available, and if customer credit is OK, then the order must be shipped for arrival at the customer's location by noon of the next business day.

be shipped for next day arrival or is it merely a recommendation? The wording of the policy should indicate Must versus Should.

The third intellectual piece of a policy is the party most closely responsible for adhering to the policy. The responsible party can be named in the policy or can be connected to it as a valid piece of meta data.

The fourth intellectual piece is the jurisdiction over which the policy is valid. The jurisdiction can be geographical boundary or organizational boundary. In our example, does this policy apply to all orders received at any location? Like the responsible party, the jurisdiction of a policy can be included in its wording or as meta data associated with it.

A fifth intellectual piece is the policy's rationale, which is usually to achieve a desired result (goal or objective) or to minimize a risk. The policy in Table 4.4 would be more specific (that is, explicitly contains all five properties) if written as:

The Shipping department must fulfill and ship all orders from any customer located anywhere received before 4 P.M. for next day arrival at the customer's location in order to maintain customer satisfaction.

You will be reminded again during the discovery phase that a policy usually has closely associated decisions that clarify the policy. In this example, a related decision is: Is a customer order received before 4 P.M.?

Business context also includes external and internal factors. *External factors* include the extraprise (suppliers, customers, partners), regulatory authorities, or situations, such as current and predicted market share, that impact the organization and how it conducts its business. Internal factors include the intraprise, which is made up of formal and informal, permanent and temporary organizational structures or traditions. These impact the organization's conduct.

Business context is very important to understand because business context starts from the top of the business's motivation (that is, its reason for existence) down to the justification for the business's every rule. In reality, eventually you should ask: Why is each rule needed? The answer must be that the rule is congruent with its business environment. That is, the rule in some way, eventually, supports a business objective, minimizes a risk, and does this in congruence with organizational policy.

Your organization's strategic business plan is the best place to look for mission, objectives, and strategies. Tactics may be found in organization-specific documents. Policies may be found elsewhere, in policy manuals, or may be unwritten. Rules are usually hidden in various documents, program code, or in peoples' heads, but you will now be responsible for finding and managing them better. This is why rules are often elusive. You will need to be diligent in your subsequent search for and analysis of rules. Otherwise the corresponding strategies, objectives, and policies are in jeopardy. And without the strategies, objectives, and policies, the rules are in jeopardy. Worst case, the organization is disintegrated in its plans, its motivations, and therefore in its very intelligence.

An organization can introduce change by changing who or how tasks are done to achieve difference in speed and interfaces, but the most important changes are changes in policies or rules.

For more insights into the full business context behind business rules, refer to work published by Ronald G. Ross (1997) and visit www.businessrulesgroup.org.

Other items to investigate in order to understand the business context around your business rules system are:

Communities of practice. Persons with an interest in the outcome of the system development effort are called *stakeholders*. It is important to understand your system's stakeholders. Some stakeholders represent separate communities of practice. A *community of practice* is an informal group of people bound together by shared job experience and expertise. A large organization will contain many such groups. Two examples include sales representatives and disability insurance claim representatives. Your approach to gathering requirements will differ if your project focuses on a single community of practice versus involving the cooperation of more than one group. For more information on communities of practice, see Brown and Duguid (2000).

Political boundaries of rules. When determining the political boundaries for an information system, consider the political boundaries for the rules within that system. During the discovery phase you will begin to capture rules from the stakeholders of your target information system. Yet the organizations or people who set those rules may not be these same stakeholders. That is, the rules for your information system may actually originate externally to those who will use the information system. When this is the case, you may need to deal with political issues in determining which rules are the right ones and who is authorized to say so.

Proprietary nature of the rules. Some rules may be dictated by a regulatory agency. Others may represent industry-wide best practices. However, the majority of the rules, and the most important ones, are likely to be proprietary to your organization. They represent how management differentiates your business from that of competitors. For example, your product return policies may be more liberal than those of your competition with an objective of attracting new customers. Be aware that there may be resistance to documenting and acknowledging proprietary rules. You may need political assistance in soliciting and validating rules that are unique to the business. This is where you may need the political clout of your sponsor.

Locations. The stakeholders of your target system may be physically located in a number of places. Your Web customers can be anywhere in the world. The applicability of a rule may depend on a customer's location or the state in which a branch office is doing business. For example, the enforcement of sales tax rules may depend on regulations in your customer's state.

Sources of rules. You will be capturing rules from a number of sources. You can gather rules from conversations, interviews, or facilitated sessions. Or you may capture them from relevant documents, such as policy and procedure manuals. Business rules buried in legacy systems code and files present a special challenge. You may need to excavate those rules from poorly designed, nondocumented code. Chapter 10 provides a step-by-step process for doing this. You should document the source of each business rule as a part of its definition.

Rule classification. You will need a method of classifying rules. This book offers a rule classification scheme in Chapter 2 that has been useful. Your success with a rules approach is not based on which rule classification scheme you choose, but rather on the fact that you use one and use it consistently.

What rules to capture. Chapter 2 introduced you to the various classifications of rules. You may want to capture and manage all rules relevant to the target information system. Or you can limit yourself to computation rules and constraint rules, leaving inference rules and action-enabling rules as part of process and program specifications.

Rule complexity. If the decisions and rules are extremely complex and are designed to solve complicated intellectual problems, a more sophisticated approach to rule capture, analysis, and design (such as, knowledge engineering or expert systems development) may be appropriate.

Tacit knowledge. Tacit knowledge is the decision-making capacity buried within the minds of people or within existing systems but needs to be made accessible. To transition tacit knowledge into implicit knowledge, you will need a means of publishing rules and making them easily accessible.

Rule consistency. If there is a desire to achieve consistency in how decisions are made, then capturing the rules and gaining consensus becomes important.

Power to the people. Are people empowered and knowledgeable in how business decisions ought to be made? You need to be sure you have the right people approving the rule sets.

Decision scope. If there is a desire to leverage organizational decision-making capacity across boundaries (organizational, application, and geographical), you may need a rule management board to enforce consistent rules with technology to enable automation of rules across applications.

Improving decisions. If there is a desire to analyze, over time, organizational decision-making capability in order to learn and improve, then you will want to implement rules in a technology that enables easy rule changes.

Speed of change. If there is a need for faster deployment of changes in the way the business makes those decisions, rule engine technology may be a good choice.

CASE STUDY: STEP 4.3—INVESTIGATE FULL BUSINESS CONTEXT

Case Study Instructions:

- Document mission, strategies, objectives, and policies as they relate to the target VCI system.

Case Study Solution:
In order to build a successful business the founders of VCI have defined business strategies and tactics/policies in their business plan. They have not made a clear distinction between a policy and a tactic, so we simply document them as they are. The following is a partial list.

- **Mission:** Keep after-school children safe, connected, and productive through an Internet connection while VCI makes a profit.
  - Objective 1: VCI will service 1,000 guardians by year-end.

    Strategy 1.1: VCI should be the first to offer Web-based after-school services for children.

Strategy 1.2: Guardian satisfaction must be given high priority.

Policy 1.2.1: It should be easy for guardians to communicate with VCI via the Web or phone.

Policy 1.2.2: Guardians should receive an immediate response to all inquiries.

Policy 1.2.3: VCI must solicit feedback about guardian satisfaction on a regular basis.

■ Objective #2: VCI will service 2,000 members within 6 months.

Strategy 2.1: The safety of children will be assured.

Policy 2.1.1: The identities of the children using VCI services must be protected.

Strategy 2.2: The VCI system will be easy for children to use.

Policy 2.2.1: Members must receive immediate on-screen assistance.

STEP 4.4 IDENTIFY BUSINESS EVENTS

Starting the definition of a system by identifying business events is a technique recommended in many methodologies. According to McMenamin and Palmer (1984), a *business event* is an activity in the business environment, external to the proposed system that requires a response from the proposed system. There are also temporal events. A *temporal event* is an event that is initiated by the passing of time such as a monthly pay cycle.

An initial focus on business events offers several advantages. Business people are familiar with their organization's business events and are comfortable talking in terms of those events. The list of events to which a system must respond helps define the system's scope. If you are familiar with documenting use cases in gathering requirements, a business event is the starting point for finding use cases.

Identifying business events leads to confirming the stakeholders in the external world who initiate each event. We use the term *actor* to mean a stakeholder who sets business activities in motion by initiating a business event. An actor is someone or something that interacts with the target information system and receives benefits from it. Note that an automated information system itself can also be an actor. For example, a system that at the end of the business day informs its parent financial institution about the risk position of that system's owning organization is an actor.

You can use business events as one means of partitioning system implementation into useful staged releases. In this way, each release represents a set of complete system interactions on behalf of one kind of actor, for example, customers or vendors.

Business events can be categorized as either external or temporal. External events are those that arrive from the world outside the system. Examples of external events include hits on the organization's Web site and customer orders. Temporal events are those that are driven by the arrival of a predetermined date or time. For example, the creation of customer invoices might be initiated at the end of each business day.

GUIDELINE 4.4.1

Name each business event.

Name each business event using the naming convention actor/verb/noun or noun phrase. For instance, "Customer Places New Order" and "Prospect Requests Information". Name each temporal business event as "Time to verb/noun or noun phrase" for instance, "Time to Bill Customers".

Create a brief description for each event and make an estimate of how many occurrences of the event can be expected.

CASE STUDY: STEP 4.4—IDENTIFY BUSINESS EVENTS

Case Study Instructions:

- Identify business events for the VCI passage system.

Case Study Solution:

The first release of the VCI passage system will automate the following business events:

- Guardian enrolls member
- Member requests entrance into the park
- Member exits from the park
- Guardian requests park usage information

Table 4.5 is an event description table for the first business event.

STEP 4.5: IDENTIFY STAKEHOLDERS

As stated earlier, a stakeholder is a person (a role) with an interest in the outcome of an information system development effort.

GUIDELINE 4.5.1

Name each stakeholder.

Give each stakeholder a name that is meaningful to the business.

Table 4.5 VCI Business Event Table

BUSINESS EVENT	DESCRIPTION
Guardian enrolls member	Potential customers (guardians) contact VCI with the intention of requesting information about the services that VCI can provide for children in their care. To take advantage of a VCI service, a guardian must enroll each child as a member. Guardians can enroll a new member child using the VCI Web site, via email, or by phone.
Event type	External
Initiating actors	Guardians Admission park rangers (acting for a guardian)
Frequency	100/day growing at 10% per quarter

GUIDELINE 4.5.2

Define each stakeholder.

There are several categories of stakeholder. You should identify each category, and include examples in your definitions.

An *actor* is a person who interacts with the target system and benefits from the functions it performs. For instance, a sales representative requesting and receiving order status information on his/her customers is an actor.

A *direct consumer* is a kind of actor. A direct consumer is a person who uses the system's functions or outputs as part of their job responsibilities. For example, the sales specialist who receives a sales representative's request and sends the information back to the representative's PDA is a direct consumer. In the past, direct consumers were usually employees of the organization, but with Web-based systems, direct consumers can be anyone authorized to access the target system's functions. For example, if you use your bank's Web site to manage your checking account, then you are a direct consumer of the bank's online system.

A *participant* is a person whose input and support are needed throughout the project. For example, your participants will include subject matter experts who will assist in defining your project's scope.

An *external stakeholder* is a person or organization who has an interest in the target system or in some way influences its design and operation. For example, regulatory authorities and government agencies who specify rules that must be accommodated in a system's functions are external stakeholders.

In some cases, one person may fulfill more than one of these roles. For instance, a business partner (someone who is requesting the system) may need the new system's functionality so badly that he/she may be your project's acting champion (someone who fights political and economic battles to see that the system can be built).

CASE STUDY: STEP 4.5—IDENTIFY STAKEHOLDERS

Case Study Instructions:

- Identify stakeholder definitions for the VCI passage system.

Case Study Solution:
Table 4.6 defines the VCI stakeholder, guardian.

Table 4.6 VCI Stakeholder Table

STAKEHOLDER	DEFINITION	TYPE	ALIASES	EXAMPLES
Guardian	A guardian is defined as the person who, or organization that, has legal responsibility for a child. A guardian becomes a customer of VCI when he/she enrolls a child as a member.	Actor	Customer	Birth parent Foster parent Grandparent Court-appointed guardian

STEP 4.6: IDENTIFY LOCATIONS

The stakeholders of the target system may be physically located in a number of places.

GUIDELINE 4.6.1

Identify relevant locations.

You should include locations that are geographical places, virtual or electronic addresses, or addresses where voice communications occur. Maps or other graphics can be helpful.

By identifying locations, you can begin to scope the size and distribution of the system's community as well as the roles of these people and their skill sets. Also, the applicability of a business rule may depend on the location of a business unit.

CASE STUDY: STEP 4.6—IDENTIFY LOCATIONS

Case Study Instructions:

- Identify locations for VCI.

Case Study Solution:
Table 4.7 is an example of a location definition

STEP 4.7: IDENTIFY EVENT RESPONSE PROCESSES

According to McMenamin and Palmer, a business process encompasses all of the detailed processing needed to service one business event. A business event is represented by a set of data elements. It is the arrival and recognition of this data by the system that triggers a business process. A business process triggered by a business event is called an *event response process*. Note that if you find yourself identifying more than one set of event-related information, you are probably dealing with more than one business event (Essential Requirements).

At this point you are not interested in all of the detailed steps involved with handling a business event. The reason you identify event-response processes is to understand, early in the project, the nature of data usage within the target system and at its interfaces. Document the information created by the system, who uses that information, and to where (another point of automation) the information is sent by the system.

Table 4.7 VCI Location Table

LOCATION	DESCRIPTION	TYPE	ALIAS	EXAMPLES
VCI corporate headquarters	The VCI corporate headquarters is defined as the physical location of VCI senior management and where corporate administrative services are carried out.	Internal	Home office	Fresno, CA

GUIDELINE 4.7.1

Identify and name the event-response process for each event.

This is a straightforward task. For each event, consider the response the information system must provide. For example, if the event is "Sales Representative Requests Order Status", then the event-response process might be "Respond to Order Status Information Request". Make your names as specific as possible. Avoid names like "Process Requests." This name doesn't convey solid information about the nature of the response processing.

Name the event response processes using a verb/noun or noun phrase. For example, the process triggered by the event "Client Makes Trade" should be "Execute Client Trade."

GUIDELINE 4.7.2

Define each event response process.

In this step, focus on the information that each event-response process receives, the event itself, and its information outputs.

Name an event's data content using a noun or noun phrase, such as "Customer Discount Information" or "Item Availability Request."

Name event-response process outputs using a high-level *data subject* or *conceptual entity* or business object name, such as "Invoice" or "New Customer."

A useful way to document business events and response processes is to create a business event/event-response process table used in the case study.

CASE STUDY: STEP 4.7–IDENTIFY BUSINESS EVENT RESPONSE PROCESSES

Case Study Instructions:

■ Create a business event/event-response process table for the VCI passage system.

Case Study Solution:
Table 4.8 illustrates the VCI passage system: business event/event-response process table.

Table 4.8   VCI Event-Response Process Table

BUSINESS EVENT	INFORMATION INPUT	EVENT RESPONSE PROCESS	INFORMATION OUTPUT	OUTPUT DESTINATION
Guardian enrolls member	Guardian: guardian information	Enroll member	Guardian credit confirmation Request for new information, if needed	Guardian
	Guardian: member information			Database

Table 4.8   *(Continued)*

BUSINESS EVENT	INFORMATION INPUT	EVENT RESPONSE PROCESS	INFORMATION OUTPUT	OUTPUT DESTINATION
		Membership	Guardian qualification confirmation Recommendations if member not qualified	
	System: service information		Estimated charges information	Guardian
	System: confirmation information		Scheduled entrance date	Guardian Entrance system Billing system
			Membership information	Entrance system Billing system Customer database

STEP 4.8: IDENTIFY BUSINESS PERFORMANCE METRICS

A *business performance metric* is a piece of information useful in measuring how well an organization is doing in meeting its business objectives. Performance metrics should be easy to define if your system's objectives are linked to your organization's business objectives as spelled out in the strategic business plan. For example, if a business objective states that the number of new customers should be increased by 10 percent over the previous year, then your system will need a way to flag new customers and to calculate the percentage of new to repeat customers versus numbers for last year's results. Business performance metrics are often called key performance indicators or KPIs.

GUIDELINE 4.8.1

Document important information about each event response process.

For each event response process, identify and document business performance metrics.

Identify possible pieces of information that are useful in determining the effectiveness of the event, the response process, or policies behind them.

CASE STUDY: STEP 4.8—IDENTIFY BUSINESS PERFORMANCE METRICS

Case Study Instructions:

- Create a table of business metrics for the VCI passage system.

Case Study Solution:

You may decide to capture the number of times a parent begins to sign up a member to the program but doesn't complete it. You may decide to capture the number of questions asked by members during invocation of a particular game or the number of compliments or complaints about a game. These metrics result in additional information requirements and are documented in Table 4.9. They provide the basis for ongoing improvement of the event and process, and possibly the establishment of new business rules.

STEP 4.9: IDENTIFY DATA SUBJECTS OR HIGH-LEVEL BUSINESS OBJECTS

For the purposes of scoping, a *business object* is a business term that is important or at the heart of the target system. You can start a list with definitions of business objects about which the system is to be built, such as Guardian, Member, Park Services, and so on.

If you prefer to take a more data-oriented approach, rather than high-level business objects, identify the data subjects (or high-level data entities) that relate to your target system. There is not much difference between a high-level business object and a data entity, at this point. That's because business objects represent an abstraction of the problem domain in terms of the things in that domain. (As object-oriented development progresses, however, the meaning of object and of class changes as they evolve into elements of system design.)

Also, there is a long-practiced disciplined way of using data subjects as a practical means of dividing up a large data scope into deliverable pieces. For this reason, this chapter goes into detail about how to start with data subjects and drive them into detailed data constructs.

A *data subject* is a high-level categorization and grouping of business information where the categorization is based on data-oriented, not function- or process-oriented,

Table 4.9 VCI Business Performance Metrics

BUSINESS PERFORMANCE METRIC	DESCRIPTION
Name of Metric	Total enrolled members
Business performance objective	Enroll 2,000 members within 6 months of opening the park.
Computation rule	Total enrolled members is computed as the numeric total of all active members whose guardian has a good account standing.
Frequency	Once per week.

boundaries. Data-oriented boundaries illustrate how best to carve up an organization's data asset.

The division of the data into subjects is useful because doing so enables you to:

- Start communications with business people about data without regard to function, program, or organization.

- Minimize overlap of data analysis efforts that will be started later.

- Prioritize the delivery of subject area databases. In this way, it helps to identify logical groupings of event response processes (those focused on the same subject areas) that can form the basis for cleanly partitioned, incremental releases of system functionality.

The criteria for high-quality data subject definitions are:

- The set of data subjects covers the entire scope of the enterprise. All the organization's information is included.

- Each data subject is mutually exclusive of every other subject area in scope and content.

- The data in each data subject spans all business processes, functions, and systems.

- Each data subject represents a resource significant to the business. It is encompassing in scope, substantial in complexity, and of enduring value (from Ross 1997).

- There is a higher degree of affinity, cohesiveness, and density of relationships within a data subject than among data subjects.

- The number of relationships between the data subject and other data subjects is minimal. These relationships are mostly optional versus mandatory and/or access is low across those relationships.

- Each data subject represents a very high level supertype (right below the seven highest levels of supertypes: Who, What, Where, How, When, Why).

GUIDELINE 4.9.1

Define each data subject.

Using the data subject definition criteria above, identify and document the data subjects within the project scope.

If you will be using a data modeling tool, you should understand constraints the tool places on data within a data subject. For example, in one tool a data subject is one model/diagram. In another it is a view in a portion of a model/diagram. Sometimes an entity may or may not be allowed to be part of more than one subject area, even as a visiting entity.

GUIDELINE 4.9.2

Start a list of conceptual entities.

Start a list of conceptual entities (based on business processes) within each data subject. It is never too early to start to understand the data environment. In Step 4.7 you defined the information inputs to each event response process and its outputs. Use your process input and output definitions to help you start a list of conceptual entities.

GUIDELINE 4.9.3

Create a preliminary conceptual data model.

You should consider creating an initial data model from the system-related information your team has documented so far. If the target business area has been studied and modeled before, you should evaluate this work and reuse as much as possible. Refer to Chapter 9 for a definition of conceptual data model.

Even if your system will be accessing existing databases (hence, you will not be responsible for designing them), it is useful to create a preliminary conceptual data model. That's because a comparison of your conceptual data model to the existing database design may highlight constraints or restrictions with the database that your project may need to consider.

CASE STUDY: STEP 4.9—IDENTIFY DATA SUBJECTS

Case Study Instructions:

- Identify the major data subjects in the VCI passage system.
- Begin defining conceptual data entities.
- Begin to create a conceptual data model for the VCI passage system.

Case Study Solution:

From your initial understanding of the business events, it seems that your system will touch on at least four data subjects: Person, Account, Service, and Location. Table 4.10 defines one of these.

As for the data subjects, the Person data subject seems to have conceptual data entities for Member, Guardian, and Park Ranger. The Account data subject will probably contain billing-related data entities. The Service data subject would contain entities for the various areas in the park into which a guardian can enroll a child. Based on your past experience in building information architecture based on data subjects, you suspect that

Table 4.10 VCI Preliminary Data Subject Definitions

DATA SUBJECT	DESCRIPTION
Name	Account
Description	An account is defined as a legally binding agreement between VCI and a customer.
Examples	Memberships
Candidate conceptual data entities	Membership
Conceptual entity examples	Membership for Susan Schneider, logon Id 2113

Table 4.11 VCI Candidate Conceptual Entities

CONCEPTUAL ENTITY	
Name	Membership
Description	A membership is a type of account. A membership account is defined as an agreement between VCI and a customer (guardian) for services provided to an after-school member child. A membership identifies the customer, the member child, and the services to which the member child has access. A membership is for a single child.
Examples	Membership # 213 for Susan Schneider, logon ID 2113
Known data quality problems	None

your system will probably contain data belonging to a Location data subject. This data subject will include information about mailing addresses, fax phone numbers, email addresses, voice phone numbers, and so on. Table 4.11 illustrates a sample table for documenting candidate conceptual entities. Figure 4.4 depicts an early conceptual data model for VCI.

STEP 4.10: IDENTIFY ADDITIONAL REQUIREMENTS

By additional requirements, we mean desires about the system not directly related to what it is to do. For example, additional requirements can include a specific presentation look and feel based on the need for ease of training because of high employee turnover.

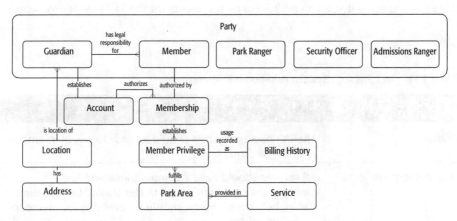

Figure 4.4 VCI early conceptual data model.

Guideline 4.10.1

Include additional requirements.

Additional requirements include:

- Usability (how easy must the information system's features be to use and user support like Help facilities, user documentation)

- Performance (how quickly the information system needs to respond)

- Availability (how many hours per day, days per week, weeks per month, the information system needs to be available for the users to use)

- Capacity (how much data the information system needs to handle, how many users the system needs to service, locations of users to service, how many transactions the system needs to process in a specific amount of time)

- Security (what functions protect the information system and its data from unauthorized access).

You need to understand stakeholder thinking about the system's additional requirements. For example, because the VCI system will be used by children and their guardians who may not be accustomed to using a computer, the information system's design must emphasize ease of use.

These requirements are the basis for a service level agreement (SLA) document. The purpose of an SLA is to establish a level-of-service agreement between users of the system and the IT support organization. This agreement includes definitions of actor and VCI responsibilities and for each VCI service component, its measurement criteria, and the levels of performance that can be expected.

Case Study: Step 4.10–Identify Additional Requirements

Case Study Instructions:

- Identify additional requirements for the VCI passage system.

Case Study Solution:
Table 4.12 begins to document additional requirements for the VCI passage system.

Table 4.12   VCI Passage System Additional Requirements

ADDITIONAL REQUIREMENTS	
Name	The VCI passage system should be easy to use by members and guardians.
Related requirements	All screens should have a common look and feel. Online assistance from a park ranger should be available. Call-in help desk support should be available for members and guardians.

STEP 4.11: IDENTIFY BUSINESS CONSTRAINTS

Constraints are restrictions placed on the project and can be of a business nature or technical nature. For instance, on the technical side, an Internet-based solution may be a constraint because of the adoption of the Internet by competitors. Examples of business constraints may be limitations imposed by budget limitations or by business culture. This step leads you in uncovering business and technical constraints.

Review the list of constraints identified by the executive sponsor, champion, and business and technical partners and documented in the initial scope statement. Based on a better understanding of the business context, consider expanding that list of business constraints that could impact your project.

GUIDELINE 4.11.1

Be specific in defining business constraints.

Include as business constraints those related to projects this one is dependent on, time constraints, competition, and projects depending on this one.

Additional business-related constraints may include:

- In-progress initiatives upon which this project may be dependent
- A time constraint based on external factors, such as a business competitor's offering
- Dependence of another project on the results of this one.

CASE STUDY: STEP 4.11—IDENTIFY BUSINESS CONSTRAINTS

Case Study Instructions:

- Create a table of business constraints for the VCI passage system.

Case Study Solution:

It is understood that a potential competitor is looking for venture capital. This startup company has hired developers and has retained a well-known educational consulting firm. It is very important that VCI be the first to offer after-school services for children. It is critical to build a substantial customer base quickly. A sample business constraint table is documented in Table 4.13.

STEP 4.12: IDENTIFY TECHNICAL CONSTRAINTS

In this step, aim to understand the current and proposed technical environment. With the business and technical partners, identify technology-related constraints that did not

Table 4.13   VCI Passage System Business Constraints

BUSINESS CONSTRAINTS	
Name	The VCI passage system must be operational 6 months from the project start date.
Rationale	Potential competitors are seeking venture capital for a similar Web-based service.

surface earlier. You can conduct an investigation into the current technical environment in parallel with your investigation into business constraints. As you uncover the kind of data and processes within scope, you can begin assessing the current technical situation. From here you can identify and interview the appropriate technical experts, either individually or in groups.

GUIDELINE 4.12.1

Be specific in defining technical constraints.

Consider existing systems, migration issues, interfacing systems and technology, standards, skills, information availability, information quality, information integration, distribution of processes.

Therefore, questions you can ask are:

- What systems, if any, currently support identified business events and processes?
- Are portions of processes partially implemented in several systems, and are there significant system migration issues to consider?
- What systems would need to be interfaced with, and what technology are they implemented in?
- Are there existing technology strategies and standards to consider?
- What technical skills will be required and are they available?
- What is the availability of information that has been identified as required to support the event response processes? Is some of the data not currently available, or very difficult to get, or of known bad quality?
- Will data have to be integrated from multiple sources?
- Which processes require support for many distributed users? Is a new technical infrastructure needed for them?

When soliciting technical constraints, be aware that business partners may be very well aware, from a consumer or "system client" perspective, of current technical barriers, although sometimes these barriers can be overcome. These people are not, however, likely to have complete knowledge of the underlying technical issues, or barriers to their resolution. Therefore, be sure to include technical partners in these discussions.

Pay attention to the availability and accessibility of data sources, if known. Pay attention to the quality of data sources, if known. Consider early investigation of data quality by formation of a data quality function that is one step ahead of the development team.

CASE STUDY: STEP 4.12—IDENTIFY TECHNICAL CONSTRAINTS

Case Study Instructions:

- Create a table of technical constraints for the VCI passage system.

Case Study Solution:

The director of enrollment has done marketing research aimed at estimating the numbers of children who would be prospects for the services VCI plans to offer. One important factor is whether a child has access to a computer and if the computer is capable of reaching the Internet. In your discussions with the director of enrollment, she confirms

Table 4.14   VCI Technical Constraint Definition

TECHNICAL CONSTRAINTS	
Name	The VCI passage system must be accessible using all Web browsers.
Rationale	Because VCI does not control the software that customers and members will use to access our system (and because we do not want to download software to customer computers), the system's functions must be compatible with Microsoft, Netscape, and Mac browsers (including the current software releases and two previous releases). Features specific to one browser product cannot be used in the design.

your suspicion that many children, although they have Internet access, are not using powerful computers or the latest versions of their browser software.

As a result, you specify that your system must support multiple browser products including back releases of each and that features proprietary to one browser product should not be used in the design. See Table 4.14.

As a result of this important constraint, VCI has written a policy that states that all user accessible systems must be designed so that no software needs be loaded into a customer's or member's computer in order to access and use the system.

STEP 4.13: IDENTIFY THE BUSINESS AND TECHNICAL RISKS

New and enhanced information systems bring business benefits, the benefits that provide the business motivation for the system investment. However, as with any course of action, there can also be undesirable outcomes. As much as possible you should anticipate risks and have plans in place for how to mitigate their effects should the need arise.

GUIDELINE 4.13.1

Be specific in defining risks.

For each business event, describe the risks that could threaten the project's success. Risks are the dangers that can have a negative impact on the successful development of an information system, its implementation, or its operation. That is, a *risk* is an exposure to the chance of injury or loss, to put oneself in danger. Thus, risks are opportunities for failure. This step leads you in documenting each risk along with suggestions for how each risk can be avoided or how its effects can be mitigated.

GUIDELINE 4.13.2

Be specific in defining mitigating policies.

For each risk, identify policies intended to mitigate its effects. As you will see, you can mitigate risks by introducing new policies. Policies for addressing risk may be the precursor to underlying business rules.

The idea that business policy statements exist to address risk is from the work of Ross (1997). Another important step, also from Ross, is mapping each policy statement back to the business objectives, defined earlier, that it supports. This gives the reason and basis for a particular policy in response to a particular risk. The identified policies should, in turn, support the objectives established for the system.

CASE STUDY: STEP 4.13–IDENTIFY BUSINESS AND TECHNICAL RISKS

Case Study Instructions:

- Identify risks for the VCI passage system along with mitigation policies for each risk.

Case Study Solution:

Suppose, in the case study, the participants identify the risk that a customer may decide that some of the VCI Park games are too violent. To minimize the impact of this risk, we need to propose risk mitigation strategies and policies shown in Table 4.15.

STEP 4.14: PRIORITIZE BUSINESS REQUIREMENTS

In most cases it will not be possible or desirable to implement all the functionality of a new information system at one time. So you will need a way to partition the system's functions into a set of releases that will deliver new system capabilities incrementally over a period of time. There are a number of techniques you can use to help you create a schedule of system releases.

Table 4.15 VCI Passage System Business Risk Definitions

ID	BUSINESS RISK	TACTIC OR POLICY FOR MITIGATING RISKS
Risk 6	A guardian may find some of the games inappropriate for their children.	Guardian service must be given the highest priority.
		The system should display for the guardian a thorough explanation of each game before the guardian is asked to select the games for the child.
		VCI should create and support an independent body of parents to evaluate games, assign a rating to them and provide descriptions.
		The system must provide a mechanism by which guardians share comments on the games with each other.
		There must be standard procedures for handling customer complaints.

The first criterion you must consider will be the business needs of the organization. At this point in the scoping process you have documented the system's business requirements. One set of requirements specifies the business events that the system must handle. With the executive sponsor, champion, business and technical partners, prioritize the business events based on business needs.

GUIDELINE 4.14.1

Be sure to understand business priorities.

If the business requirements priorities are obvious, you may need only a formal discussion. If priorities are not clear, consider conducting a facilitated session.

Where priorities are not clear or there are differing opinions, consider asking stakeholders to place each event into a simple matrix. The two placement criteria are:

- Must Have, the system cannot function without this event, versus Nice-to-Have, desirable but not a major factor for system success
- Now, this event must be in the first release, versus Later, can be delivered in a later release.

CASE STUDY: STEP 4.14–PRIORITIZE BUSINESS REQUIREMENTS

Case Study Instructions:

- Create a matrix of prioritized business requirements for the VCI passage system.

Case Study Solution:

The matrix in Table 4.16 shows the outcome of a facilitated session in which the executive sponsor and business partners have come to agreement on their priorities for the sequence in which the system should process business events. Table 4.17 illustrates a complete business event table for VCI with business events assigned to system releases.

STEP 4.15: DEFINE ARCHITECTURAL ALTERNATIVES

In the best of all worlds, you would deliver everything that is important or desirable to all stakeholders. Most likely, though, you will not be able to deliver all functionality

Table 4.16   VCI Prioritized Business Requirements

	NOW	LATER
Must Have	Guardian enrolls child Guardian changes member services Member requests entrance to park Member exits from park Bill for services	Measure customer satisfaction
Nice to Have	Measure system performance	Evaluate services offered by competitors

Table 4.17 Business Events to System Releases

BUSINESS EVENT IDENTIFIER	BUSINESS EVENT NAME	BUSINESS PROCESS NAME	ACTOR(S) WHO CAN INITIATE	SYSTEM RELEASE IDENTIFIER
1	Request to enroll member	Enroll member	Guardian	Release 1
			Park ranger	Release 2
			Park ranger	Release 2
2	Request to unenroll member	Unenroll member	Guardian	Release 2
			Park ranger	Release 1
3	Request to view current charges	Publish charges	Guardian	Release 1
			Park ranger	Release 1
4	Maintain member privileges	Add/update member questions for park entrance	Guardian	Release 1
			Park ranger	Release 1
5	Request to view member activities	Publish member activities	Guardian	Release 1
6	Request to enter VCI Park	Admit member to VCI Park	Member	Release 1
		Answer entrance questions	Member	Release 1
7	Request to enter theme park	Admit member to theme park	Member	Release 1
8	Request to begin tutoring session	Conduct tutoring session	Member	Release 2
9	Request librarian service	Librarian service	Member	Release 2
10	Request to attend university class	University class admittance	Member	Release 3

No.	Service	Detail	Actor	Release
11	Market special deals for park services	Special deals for new parks	Park ranger	Release 3
		Special deals for existing guardians	Park ranger	Release 3
12	Issue invoices	Calculate fees for all members for each guardian	Park ranger	Release 1
13	Receive payments	Log check payments received by guardians	Park ranger	Release 1
		Log credit card payments and check automatic withdrawals for each guardian		Release 1
		Partial payment	Park ranger	Release 1
		Bounced check	Park ranger	Release 1
14	Add new park services	Provide new marketing information and sample entrance questions for new park service		Release 3
15	Change existing park service rates		Park ranger	Release 2

immediately. Some requirements will be scheduled for later releases, and maybe some "nice to have" functionality will not be feasible within the foreseeable future.

Defining the preferred technical approach and release strategy is a matter of balancing business needs and priorities against technical feasibility, cost, time, organizational and perhaps even legal constraints.

You may want to decide early on the characteristics of the overall technical approach to the solution. For example, do you use commercial rules technology at all? Do you centralize all the data and application processing in one place, or distribute these? Are there system migration issues to be considered? Does an existing legacy system represent a total constraint on some requirements, and will you have to interface or collaborate with that system to accomplish some or all of the required functions? What is the impact of all this?

GUIDELINE 4.15.1

Prepare a business process to business information matrix.

From the previous scoping steps, you have gathered the documentation you need to establish solution alternatives. You know which processes share the same information, and the business priority of supporting each with the new system. You can group these together, in terms of which processes use the same information in the same way (create, read, update, and delete). This matrix is called a CRUD matrix.

A CRUD matrix can help you come to two conclusions. The first is the set of processes that represent natural groups, from both a logical *and* technical perspective, and so might be implemented together incrementally if it turns out not to be feasible to implement all processes immediately. The second is the set of processes affected by the same technical issues and risks, especially in terms of data availability and quality, which translate into feasibility and cost to implement.

GUIDELINE 4.15.2

Prepare additional matrices.

Additional matrices can assist stakeholders in making system release partitioning decisions. One matrix may group event response processes by the constraints and risks associated with them, with an estimate of what will be required to address the constraints and risks. An estimate of costs and time is helpful. You may want to establish estimated time ranges of, for example, a few months, 6 months to a year, over a year, and also ranges of cost.

Compare the results of this analysis with the business-assigned priorities for implementing these processes. You are likely to see a very limited set of feasible alternatives emerge (and for purely practical purposes you'll want to limit the number you analyze), that fall in one of the four typical quadrants that are sometimes useful to plot and categorize by:

- Quick and easy to implement but little business impact/value
- Difficult and costly to implement but high business impact/value
- High time and cost, and low impact/value
- Low time and cost, and high impact/value

CASE STUDY: STEP 4.15—DEFINE ARCHITECTURAL ALTERNATIVES

Case Study Instructions:

- Create a CRUD matrix of event-response to conceptual data entity for the VCI passage system.
- Create a table of technical constraints.

Case Study Solution:

Table 4.18 is a CRUD matrix of event-response process to conceptual data entity.

Table 4.18   VCI CRUD Matrix of Event-Response Process to Conceptual Entity

EVENT RESPONSE PROCESS	CUSTOMER INFORMATION	MEMBERSHIP INFORMATION	SERVICE INFORMATION	BILLING INFORMATION
Enroll member	Create	Create	Read	Create
Admit member to the park	Read	Read	Read	Update
Allow member exit		Read	Read	Update
Bill customer	Read	Read	Read	Update

In one way, as a new initiative, VCI is fortunate in not having legacy systems constraints to consider. VCI business people have, however, identified technical constraints in setting up the VCI University processes. These include the identification of educational Web sites and establishing linkages with specific portions of these sites. Obviously, a business constraint is the successful negotiation of contracts with the owners of the selected sites. Resolution of these constraints is estimated to occur within acceptable timeframes, available resources and current technical capabilities. See Table 4.19.

Table 4.19   VCI Technical Constraints

PROCESSES	CONSTRAINTS	RISKS	TIME ESTIMATE	COST ESTIMATE
Identify sites	Minimum time of qualified people	Poor selections leading to low University Services usage	3 months	$50,000
Negotiate contracts	Minimum time of qualified people	Undesirable contract terms leading to low profitability	6 months	$70,000
Establish links to selected sites	Limited Web developer staff—no budget for contractors	Basic park services will be delayed	3 months	$150,000

This book's purpose and scope is to focus on a business rules approach to system definition and development, and to keep the case study reasonably manageable. With this in mind, VCI, in addition to using a business rules driven requirements-gathering approach, has settled on a Web-based, centrally managed system, implemented with commercial rules technology. VCI recognizes that accessing the park in particular, but in fact the whole system, is rich in rules. To provide flexibility of services and the ability to rapidly enhance the system's functionality in the future, a business rules approach is a must. VCI will choose a rules engine or engines as part of its technical solution.

STEP 4.16: SELECT ARCHITECTURAL SOLUTION

In this step, present your analysis of solution alternatives to the group of stakeholders. Guide them in selecting the one that represents the best balance of business value, cost, time, and risk.

GUIDELINE 4.16.1

Consider a facilitated session.

Finally, document the decision on which alternative, or variation of one, has been selected. Include a description of the selected alternative and a brief mention of the alternatives not chosen.

CASE STUDY: STEP 4.16—SELECT ARCHITECTURAL SOLUTION

Case Study Instructions:

■ Write a summary of the preferred approach to the VCI passage system.

Case Study Solution:
VCI will be offering Web-based services and they will use the Web for communications with customers and members as much as possible. They have chosen to build and maintain their systems using a commercial rules product. Their technical architecture will be designed for scalability based on estimates of customer and services growth. Based on their perceived window of opportunity in the market place, available resources and issues of technical feasibility, VCI management has decided on providing basic park services along with the necessary enrollment and billing functions in the initial system release. Two more releases will follow over the next year.

STEP 4.17: CREATE SCOPE DIAGRAM

A *scope diagram* is your first visual representation of the information system. Its purpose is to depict the target system from the actors' points of view. It depicts the system's boundaries and its business environment.

GUIDELINE 4.17.1

Include human actors.

It is most useful to show human actors on the left side of the diagram. Additional actors, which include other information systems and databases, are placed on the right side of the diagram. A large rectangular symbol in the center represents the boundary of the information system under consideration. The lines connecting actors to the system are the business events initiated by an actor or are events initiated within the system communicating something of value to an actor.

Notice that scope diagrams do not try to show how processing is done. That comes later using other diagrams and text description.

CASE STUDY: STEP 4.17—CREATE SCOPE DIAGRAM

Case Study Instructions:

- Create a scope diagram for the VCI passage system.

Case Study Solution:
Figure 4.5 illustrates a scope diagram using a use-case diagram.

STEP 4.18: ESTIMATE ORGANIZATIONAL INFRASTRUCTURE AND RESOURCE REQUIREMENTS

You will need a preliminary analysis of resources, costs, and timeframes. At this point, that analysis is a first cut, high-level project plan/schedule for the discovery phase along with estimates for the succeeding phases. Once final commitment is gained in step 4.20, you will add more detail to the project plan either as the last step in scoping (the first

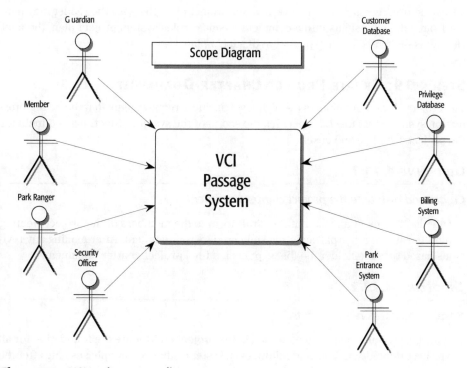

Figure 4.5 VCI project scope diagram.

step in planning) or as the first step in discovery. For now, you need to consider at a high level the following.

Establish the organizational and process infrastructure necessary to execute the project successfully. This includes the issue resolution process. The issue resolution process is the approach to identifying, ranking, escalating and resolving questions related to system cost and time frames, as well as organizational, technical or other unforeseen barriers or issues that may arise.

Define a project organization chart.

Document a change management process for controlling the cycle of requesting, investigating, estimating, authorizing, and implementing changes in business requirements, resources, and schedules through the course of the project.

Establish a communications plan for normal reporting of project status for reviewing project risks and their mitigation.

For most information systems projects, you establish processes for managing information about your data and process requirements and models. For a business rules system, you need to do the same for business rules. You will begin to plan the business rules management processes. Because business rules management is a new focus, it is the subject of Chapter 15, Rule Management.

Establish a steering committee of stakeholders to whom you can target important scope issues, questions, priorities, and changes. Use this steering committee to resolve issues and keep the project on target. On a regular basis, weekly or monthly, give them a formal presentation of project status, successes, and issues.

A project plan explains the project organization, schedule and estimates of the required resources. Therefore, there are scoping steps for determining organizational infrastructure, resources, and an associated project plan. Because the reader may benefit from detailed insights into a complete business rules system project plan, the next chapter is dedicated to an explanation of such a plan.

STEP 4.19: CREATE PROJECT CHARTER DOCUMENT

The project charter documents the high-level business requirements that the target information system must meet. It specifies the scope of the system's functions and includes the project schedule and costs.

GUIDELINE 4.19.1

Create and distribute the project charter document.

Create the document and submit it in draft form to the members of the project steering committee and to other participating stakeholders for comment. After making any revisions based on stakeholder feedback, publish a final project charter document.

GUIDELINE 4.19.2

Baseline business requirements.

The business requirements documented in the project charter are the foundation for all the project-related activities that follow, even system enhancement phases long after the initial system has been delivered. As the project progresses and the business environment evolves, it is inevitable that changes to the original requirements will be needed. Establish the business requirements as stated in the project charter as the baseline against which all requests for change are judged.

CASE STUDY: STEP 4.19—CREATE A PROJECT CHARTER DOCUMENT

The project charter is, essentially, the compilation of all the preceding deliverables, so it is not repeated here in the case study.

STEP 4.20: GAIN COMMITMENT FOR THE PROJECT

During the scoping phase you have been working closely with your project's sponsor and its other stakeholders. Since the project charter focuses on the business needs of the organization, the sponsor and business partners have been the source of most of the document's content. The members of the project steering committee have participated in decisions about scope, priorities, and resources. When stakeholders read your completed project charter, there should be no surprises in it for them. Once they review the document, you should have formal commitment to proceed.

Summary

Meeting the objectives of a scoping phase is essential to the success of any information system development effort, whether you are using a business rules approach or not. The information gathered and the decisions made become the foundation for all project activities that follow.

In the scoping phase you work very closely with your executive sponsor, business champion, and with your business and technical partners. The purpose is to elicit specific answers to specific questions. Those questions include: who (sponsors, partners, stakeholders, experts, actors), what (information), when (business events), where (locations), how (event-response processes), and why (mission, strategy, objectives, policies).

The most important difference in a business rules driven approach is a heavy and formal emphasis on Why. As with other development approaches, the *whys* establish the ultimate justification and basis for the project, but for a business rules approach, the whys do even more. The whys are the business context leading to the business rules you will gather and analyze in the discovery and analysis phases. The business context defines the desired outcomes (business success), how to measure those outcomes (business performance metrics), and, most importantly, how to guide the business (and its information systems) toward achieving those objectives (the role of the business rules). A complete business context includes ends (vision, goal, objective) and means (mission, strategy, tactic), guidance (policies, rules), influences (external, internal), rule classifications, rule complexity, rule consistency needs, tacit knowledge reserves, people power, decision scope, decision improvement needs, and need for speed of change.

Some other specific considerations that are unique to a business rules project and that you may need to address in scoping:

- You may need to educate the sponsor on the benefits of a business rules approach.

- You may need to identify business objectives met by taking a business rules approach.

- You will need to identify the source for the rules of the system: people, documents, or systems.

- You may need to deal with the political complexity that the system will use rules that are set by people outside the system's political scope.

- You may need to take special precautions of rules that are of a very proprietary nature.

- You may need to limit the classifications of rules you capture and manage based on the business's desire and ability to invest in rule management.

The other important difference in a business rules approach is in the planning for rules management as an important part of the organizational and infrastructure planning that takes place at the end of the scoping phase. It is this emphasis and this groundwork in the scoping phase that lays the foundation for rule discovery, and for successful business control and management of the deployed rules over time, which is the final and biggest payoff of a business rules approach.

The next chapter guides you in building the project plan for the scoped system.

Project Planning with Business Rules

You arrived at this point because you (or someone else) have developed a project charter that outlines the purpose, business context, scope, constraints, risks, and success criteria for delivering your target business rules system. You need now to be very specific about deliverables, timeframes, and resources needed to deliver that system as expected.

What Is Project Planning?

Recall from Chapter 4 that this book separates scoping from planning simply because it may be easier to explain. It may also prove useful to determine the scope first and then to plan the details on delivering the target system for that scope.

Effective project planning and project management usually makes the difference between a successful and an unsuccessful project. A project plan outlines the deliverables, the tasks required to achieve those deliverables, the timeframes in which those deliverables are expected to be accomplished, and the resources required to accomplish those tasks (people and financial). The *project plan* is a living set of methods, tools, and documents that allow the project manager to effectively execute and control the various aspects of the project.

A project plan is the most important tool with which a project manager leads the entire project team and sets expectations within and outside the team regarding delivery of the business rules system. Except in rare cases, it is usually acceptable for deviations in the plan to occur due to unforeseen circumstances. Even so, the project plan is the mechanism for measuring the impact of those deviations and for devising corrective or alternative plans for achieving the final goal. Since change is inevitable, a change management process is needed to track and control the changes and record the impact. Therefore, the initial project plan is an estimate based on known factors as to how the entire project will occur. The formal incorporation of a business rules aspect to the project may present new tasks and skills that may also result in deviations from the first plan. Therefore, at the completion of a phase of the project, revisit and refine the existing estimates for the next phase.

The project manager should keep metrics on the productivity of the business rule aspects of the project. These metrics provide realistic input into project plans for future business rules projects. For example, consider keeping track of how many rules you discover per facilitated session or per average size legacy program, how long it takes to verify a rule with a business audience, and, eventually, how long it takes to implement a rule in different enforcement options.

How Is Project Planning Different for a Business Rules Approach?

You can see from the task lists in this chapter that a business rules system development project is, in many ways, much like any other full life cycle development project. However, there are at least five aspects of your project plan depicted in Table 3.1 that are needed to accommodate a business rules approach:

- Separating rules by including tasks for discovering, analyzing, designing, and delivering automated rules as a separately managed asset.

- Tracing rules by including four new roles for dealing with rules (rule analyst, rule designer, rule implementer, rule integrator).

- Externalizing rules by establishing rule standards, expressing rules in natural language, naming and classifying rules.

- Externalizing rules by establishing a rules repository.

- Positioning rules for change by incorporating the opportunity to test and deploy commercial rules technology.

Let's look at each of these differences.

The first difference supports the idea of separating rules from other aspects of the system, at least conceptually and perhaps physically. In this regard, a difference is the set of tasks specifically for discovering, analyzing, designing, and delivering automated rules as a separately managed asset. Details on these are found in the methodology chapters which are Chapters 4 through 14.

The second difference aims to support the principle of tracing rules from origins to implementations. The third difference supports the idea of externalizing rules for all audiences and is supported in the project plan by the set of tasks for establishing rule standards. These are covered in detail in Chapter 15. The fourth difference also supports externalization of rules and is the set of tasks for your rules repository, covered in Chapter 15. These include documentation of meta data and rule repository requirements, a rule metamodel, and the decision on a rule storage mechanism. You will need a rule repository user guide, and perhaps training materials. If your project involves excavating rules from existing systems, you will need procedures on how to do this, and perhaps training materials here also. You may need to know the priority sequence in which to seek rules (from people or from program code). If you are fortunate, you will include tasks for establishing a rule stewardship program that identifies formally those roles in the organization that accept responsibility for policy, which leads to responsibility for rules.

The fifth difference enables the positioning of rules for change. This is supported by a project plan that incorporates the opportunity to test and deploy commercial rules technology.

When you have completed these tasks, you are ready for the discovery phase.

For tutorial purposes, this chapter presents the project plan in a rigid waterfall approach, where each phase appears quite separate from the other in the plan. In truth, especially if following object-oriented, iterative, incremental development, your project may not happen this way at all. You may naturally iterate among design alternatives for process flow and, definitely, for rule evolution and correction. So, as indicated in Chapter 4, you may have concurrent discovery tracks, analysis tracks, and so on. You may take one increment through iterative development and back to discovery and analysis again in which you refine and correct rules. Each methodology chapter contains a section on how to incorporate its concepts into an iterative development approach.

However, the purpose of this book is to present the different tasks, guidelines, and deliverables for a business rules approach. The simplest way to do this is to assume, for now, that phases are separate, deliverables are separate, so that we can explain them better.

What Are the Purposes of Project Planning?

The overall purposes for a project plan, then, are to:

- Formalize the scope and definition of the final deliverable(s), so you have a basis for issue management, change control, risk management.
- Highlight important interim deliverables and timeframes (schedule), so you can set tangible expectations to project sponsors and stakeholders.
- Establish critical checkpoints (milestones) against which to monitor progress or adjust the plan over time, as needed.
- Gain an understanding of knowledge and skills needed and of time commitments required.
- Depict task dependencies, so you can be proactive in accommodating deviations in schedule.

What Are the Deliverables from Project Planning?

While the primary deliverable is the project plan, there are other deliverables that may be useful to the business rule project manager. These include:

- Team policy document
- Team organization chart
- Team communication procedures document
- Team knowledge sharing procedures document
- Change management procedures document
- Issue log procedures
- Steering committee procedures
- High-level architecture solution paper or diagram
- Meta data and rule repository requirements
- Detailed project schedule

We will now examine each of these in greater detail.

Team Policy Document

This document outlines guidelines and rules for the project team members. For example, it includes policies and procedures regarding vacation time, holidays, working from home, personal time, flex time, and training time.

Team Organization Chart

This chart establishes the roles and responsibilities, with reporting accountability, for the various functions needed to deliver a business rules system. Let's look more closely at the roles and responsibilities of the project team members. At the very least, consider four new roles because of your emphasis on business rules. A *rule analyst* is responsible for capturing rules from business conversations, documents, or program code. A *rule designer* is responsible for determining where rules are to be enforced within an application architecture. A *rule implementer* is accountable for coding the executable rules, although this role will likely be played by application developers or database administrators, depending on where the rules are implemented. A *rule integrator* or manager is the role for analyzing rules across business events and across applications to ensure high quality rules for the organization. This role probably also selects and manages the repository into which rules are entered and from which rules are managed.

Team Communication Procedures Document

These include the frequency and format of status reports and status meetings. It also may include procedures for submitting changes to the project plan.

For large projects, the project manager may want to conduct formal weekly meetings with the leaders of each team within the team organization. Each team leader may want to conduct a weekly formal meeting with team members. On a monthly basis, the project manager may wish to hold a full team meeting. The purpose of full team meetings is to review project status and share accomplishments among the teams to foster a strong sense of teamwork, respect, and support.

Team Knowledge Sharing Procedures Document

These are procedures by which the project team shares knowledge gained about the business area under study and about the business rules approach itself. You can accomplish the sharing of team knowledge through informal procedures or through formal procedures regarding a regularly scheduled series of knowledge sharing meetings. You may also want to introduce formal procedures for posting final deliverables.

Consider creating a knowledge center about the business rules project. A *knowledge center* is a single point of communication whereby a person can discover intellectual capital pertaining to the project or aspects of the project. Your knowledge center can be an internal Web page from which interested parties can gain access to interesting project collateral, such as the latest project plan, the current status of project deliverables, completed project deliverables, project methodologies, and project personnel. The knowledge center can serve as a training mechanism in that people can use it to learn about the benefits and progress of a business rule methodology.

Change Management Procedures Document

These include mechanisms whereby the project sponsor or project members register formal requests for changes in scope. People can log requested scope changes into a change management system or database from which the project manager can negotiate changes in project plan for accommodating acceptable requests for change management.

Consider creating your own change management system. You can do so using standard desktop software and provide access to the system via Web browsers. The project manager or change manager reviews the change requests on a regular basis and brings them to the attention of people empowered to approve the request, delay it, or not approve it.

Issue Log Procedures

These include mechanisms whereby project members can record issues needing resolution prior to proceeding with the project plan. An *issue* is a situation that may cause a change in the team's ability to meet deadlines for and quality of deliverables. When issues require collaboration among team members or with outside members, the project manager can call a meeting and come to resolution, hopefully before deadlines are missed. The project manager should prioritize changes and issues, make sure they are well documented, and review them on a regular basis. The project manager should also devise an escalation plan and an issue resolution plan.

Again, consider creating your own issue logging system using standard desktop software. Provide access to the system to project team members and, perhaps, the public at large. As the project or change manager, review the issues on a regular basis and prioritize them. Then bring the issues to the attention of people empowered to resolve them and those whose collaboration is needed for resolution.

A useful way to prioritize issues is into the following categories:

High priority. If unresolved, the issue will delay a dependent deliverable.

Medium priority. The issue needs resolving, but will not delay a deliverable.

Low priority. The issue needs resolving, but resolution can wait indefinitely.

Steering Committee Procedures

This document includes procedures to be followed by the project steering committee. It may include meeting frequencies and durations, locations, mission of the steering committee, membership on the committee, responsibilities of members, voting procedures on scope changes, issues, and rule-related resolutions. The purpose of the steering committee is to be sure the project remains focused on its plan and, if the plan changes, it remains faithful to the business priorities.

High-Level Architecture Solution Paper or Diagram

This document can be produced during scoping or during planning. Regardless, it represents more details and explanation about the preferred solution outlined in the project charter. For a business rules project, it should include the technology tiers, meta data technology, rule storage technology, existing systems and databases, and interfaces among all relevant aspects. The architecture solution paper or diagram need not, at this time, specify particular products, unless they are already known. Products can be evaluated and selected later in the project.

Meta Data and Rule Repository Requirements

A special rule-related deliverable that may be most useful if delivered during planning is the set of meta data and rule repository requirements. During planning, you may decide to develop a rule metamodel and make a decision regarding a rule storage mechanism.

Detailed Project Schedule

This contains the tasks, timeframes, and resources needed for the project. The characteristics of a high-quality project plan are:

- Tasks are at a high enough level to tie to deliverables but not low enough to specify the "how-to." Also, tasks are granular enough to be achievable within a general time constraint. For example, many project managers advocate that each task be achievable within a duration of 40–80 hours.

- Estimates are created by the teams responsible for the deliverable and take into account vacation schedules and other commitments by team members.

- Dependencies are easily determined and are feasible.

- There is a contingency factor built into each high-level deliverable for unforeseen circumstances.

- There are checkpoints for intrateam and interteam deliverables.

- Resources are leveled (not overallocated).

Important Objectives in Business Rules Project Planning

Your goal is to deliver a business rules system that adheres to good software engineering principles. Good software engineering principles include database, rule, and (most likely) object design principles. However, you also want to leverage the benefits of the business rules approach by enabling *rapid* and *iterative* application development without compromising quality and the ability of the business to introduce change in a minimally disruptive manner.

Your project plan, then, should include tasks and deliverables for the following:

- A system release strategy that allows for clean system partitions so as to deliver reasonably sized, but complete, increments of business value.

- A system design that accommodates reasonable and continuous business change by separating, externalizing, tracing, and positioning rules for change.

- A solid data foundation from start to finish.

In this chapter, we look more closely, through the eyes of the project manager, at the anticipated deliverables for each phase of the business rule methodology.

We proposed in Chapter 4 that the deliverable for the scoping phase be a project charter. The deliverables for the project planning portion of the project charter are the ten items we've just discussed.

In the sample project plans below, the tasks with asterisks are those tailored to a business rules development project. These tasks are either new tasks or are familiar tasks modified to accommodate the new rule perspective. While these may seem like a lot of new items to consider, they are relatively simple and result in faster, changeable systems.

Sample Project Plan for the Scoping and Planning Phase

Table 5.1 depicts a sample project plan for the scoping and planning aspects.

Table 5.1   Sample Project Plan for Scoping Phase

1 SCOPING	MORE DETAILS
1.1 Verify existing sponsor	
1.2(*) Establish project team organizational structure	Project manager
	Data quality team (archeologists, data inspectors)

(continues)

Table 5.1   Sample Project Plan for Scoping Phase (*Continued*)

1	SCOPING	MORE DETAILS
		Data team (DAs, DBAs, conversion programmers, testers) Application process team (modelers, graphics designers, Web developers, testers) Rule team (rule analysts, rule designers, rule developers, rule integrator, rule testers) Technology team (architects, programmers) User support team
1.3	Establish team policies	
1.4	Establish team communications procedures	
1.5	Establish preliminary scope statement with sponsor	
1.6	Conduct workshop to create project charter	
1.7	Formalize steering committee procedures	
1.8	Create system context diagram	
1.9	Develop or validate high level technology solution (including rule technology)	
1.10	Establish issue management procedures	
1.11	Establish change management procedures	
1.12	Finalize project charter	Refer to Chapter 4
1.13	Develop detailed project schedule	Use this one for starting point

Deliverables for the Discovery Phase

For the discovery phase, this chapter divides the deliverables along the four tracks as follows:

- Discovery process track
  - Event response description for each business event (such as use cases, process decomposition, state transition diagrams)
  - Decisions behind each business event
  - Concrete scenarios for each business event
  - Refined conceptual model for the system
  - CRUD of conceptual data entities to business event
- Discovery rule track
  - Rules in business language categorized by conceptual data model entity or business object
  - Rule repository and user guide
  - Rule mining procedures and user guide (if applicable) to execavate rules from program code
  - Prioritized rule sources (people and code)
  - Rule stewardship program
- Discovery data track
  - File/table inventory reports of existing files and tables
  - Data subject description document
  - Conceptual model (data and process) and CRUD
  - Prioritized data sources (existing files and tables)
  - Information stewardship program
- Discovery technology track
  - Technology architecture diagram including data pipelines and possibly rule technology
  - Technology selection for business rule mining, business rule repository, and model management
  - Technology requirements document
  - Validated and refined technical solution

Most of the deliverables specific to a business rules project lie within the rule track. If you choose to store rules in a rules repository, you will need a rule repository user guide, and perhaps training materials. If your project involves excavating rules from existing systems, you will need procedures on how to do this, and perhaps training materials. You may need to know the priority sequence in which to seek rules (from people or from program code). If you are fortunate, you will establish a rule stewardship program, which identifies formally those roles in the organization that accept responsibility for policy, which leads to responsibility for rules.

Sample Project Plan for the Discovery Phase

Table 5.2 provides a sample project plan for the discovery phase.

Table 5.2   Sample Project Plan for the Discovery Phase

2	DISCOVERY	MORE DETAILS
2.1	Process track	
2.1.1(*)	Conduct archeology (existing system and data)	
		Collect artifacts for each system
		Register artifacts into archeology tool
		Create system flows of existing system
		Create system CRUDs of existing system
		Analyze system statistics of existing system
2.1.2(*)	Prioritize target programs for rule mining	
		Document file/table inventory of existing system
2.1.3	Prioritize target files/tables for data source quality assessment	
2.2	Rule Track	
2.2.1(*)	Establish rule standards	Identify reasons and audiences for business rule classification
		Determine a business rule classification scheme(s) for rule discovery, rule analysis, rule design, and rule implementation
		Establish rule templates for expressing rules
		Decide on meta data for rule discovery, rule analysis, rule design, rule implementation, business access
		Design a business rule metamodel
		Establish rule naming conventions
		Build/buy/extend decision on a business rule repository
2.2.2	Determine where to capture terms and definitions	Data dictionary Case tool Repository
2.2.3	Determine tools for creating application models, data models, other models, matrices	Case tools

Table 5.2 (*Continued*)

2	DISCOVERY	MORE DETAILS
2.2.4(*)	Create, install, or extend business rule repository	
		Document rule repository requirements
		Review rule metamodel
		Create rule repository database
		Create rule repository functionality and screens
		Create rule repository user guide
		Create rule repository training
		Offer rule repository training
2.2.5	Create interfaces among meta data management products, if appropriate	
2.2.6(*)	Solidify a rule mining methodology	
		Create rule mining user guide (optional)
		Create rule mining training
		Offer rule mining training
2.2.7(*)	Begin rule mining	
2.2.8(*)	Solidify a discovery Methodology	
		Create rule discovery user guide (optional)
		Create rule discovery training
		Offer rule discovery training
2.2.9(*)	Conduct rule discovery workshops	
		Prework
		Execute workshops
		Postwork
2.2.10(*)	Publish final rule discovery deliverables	Business events/use-case matrix Business process matrix Use-case diagram

(continues)

Table 5.2   Sample Project Plan for the Discovery Phase (*Continued*)

2	DISCOVERY	MORE DETAILS
		Interaction description or process decomposition diagram Concrete use cases Business event to entity CRUD Rules in repository
2.2.11	Create requirements traceability document	
2.3	Data track	
2.3.1	Solidify a conceptual modeling methodology	
		Create a conceptual modeling user guide (optional)
		Create conceptual modeling training
		Offer conceptual modeling training
2.3.2	Define or refine data subjects	
2.3.3	Create conceptual data and process model or business object model	
2.3.4	Begin data source quality assessment	
2.4	Technology track	
2.4.1	Confirm requirements for performance, capacity, availability, testing	
2.4.2	Create technology diagram of tiers	
2.4.3	Select tools for rule mining, rule repository, model management	

Deliverables for the Analysis Phase

Moving onto the analysis phase, this chapter again divides deliverables into four tracks.

- Analysis process track
  - Simple workflow diagram devoid of detailed rule processing
  - State transition diagram for entities or business objects of importance
  - Final set of concrete scenarios
  - A class model for the core process of each business event, so you can proceed with object-oriented design for them
  - A sequence diagram for classes involved in the core process of each business event, so you can proceed with object-oriented design for them
  - A class model for the rule flow, if you are building your own rules capability
  - A sequence diagram for classes involved in rule flow, if you are building your own rules capability
  - Workflow diagram (for each actor a workflow, window flow)
- Analysis rule track
  - Rule management procedures
  - Validated rules analyzed for semantic quality and expressed in template format stored in the rule repository (from workshop and mining)
  - Rule dependency chains
  - Rule/data activity correlations
- Analysis data track
  - Data source quality reports
  - Logical entity relationship data model, business object model, or rule-enriched logical data model
  - Synonym list
  - Logical data conversion specifications
  - Data integration and standardization issues
  - Documentation and recommendations on options in multitiered data architecture
  - Data distribution requirements
  - Requirements for storing historic data
  - Requirements to meet auditing requirements
  - Estimated data volumes
  - Data backup and recovery requirements
  - Data security requirements
- Analysis technology track
  - Results for technology proofs-of-concepts

- Validated and refined technical solutions and selections
- Beginning of technology architecture implementation

Again, most of the rule-related deliverables appear in the rule track. During analysis, you will want rule management procedures by which rule analysts can add, suggest changes to, and delete or archive rules. Perhaps these procedures should extend to allowing business experts to do the same, or at least, to suggest rule changes. A rule management function would evaluate those suggestions and verify with appropriate business experts (rule stewards) that such changes are good for the business. From there, the rule manager would assemble the design teams to discuss how and where rule changes occur.

Also in the rule track, during analysis, you study discovered rules for poor-quality rules and poor quality rule sets (inconsistencies, incompleteness). You are likely to express the rules in a format more disciplined than the natural language format used during discovery with business people.

Rule (family) dependency chains represent the inherent relationships among rules, specifically when the output of one rule is the input to another rule. These dependency chains represent "knowledge dependencies" (hence represent mandatory sequence of execution). Rule dependency chains are valuable to database and rule designers. The database designers will use these to study data access paths. Rule designers will use these to study rule implementation alternatives. Process and object analysts will study them in search of core process flow.

Within the technology track, the plan includes opportunities to conduct proofs of concept. If you are embarking on excavating rules from legacy code, select an automation tool and test it out, gathering metrics by which to refine your project plan. Likewise, if you will be employing rule technology, bring in the target product and conduct a 4–6 week pilot to validate feasibility and establish development metrics by which to adjust your project estimates.

Sample Project Plan for the Analysis Phase

Table 5.3 suggests a sample project plan for the analysis phase.

Table 5.3   Sample Project Plan for the Analysis Phase

3	ANALYSIS	MORE DETAIL
3.1	Process track	
3.1.1(*)	Solidify application process methodology (altered with a rules approach)	
		Create an analysis user guide (optional)
		Create training program
		Offer application process flow training

Table 5.3   (*Continued*)

3	ANALYSIS	MORE DETAIL
3.1.2	Create process flow deliverables	Actor process flow, showing parallel and serial processes Actor window flow Actor pages and navigation specs
3.2	Rule track	
3.2.1(*)	Determine rule procedures	
3.2.2(*)	Solidify rule analysis methodology	
		Create rule analysis user guide (optional)
		Create rule analysis training
		Offer rule analysis training
3.2.3(*)	Solidify rule optimization methodology	
		Create rule optimization user guide (optional)
		Create Rule optimization training
		Offer rule optimization training
3.2.4(*)	Complete rule mining	
3.2.5(*)	Complete rule analysis	Confirm essential rule set Create a rule-enriched logical data model Establish a CRUD from rule to entities, attributes, relationships Depict the rule (family) dependency chains (Modify actor process flows based on the rule chains)
3.2.6(*)	Complete rule optimization deliverables	Tie rules to business objectives Identify metrics for measuring usefulness of rules Tie metrics to data warehouse requirements Optimize rules to meet business objectives
3.2.7(*)	Conduct rule validation workshops	
		Prework
		Execute workshops
		Postwork

(*continues*)

Table 5.3   Sample Project Plan for the Analysis Phase (*Continued*)

3	ANALYSIS	MORE DETAIL
3.2.8(*)	Finalize rules in repository	
3.3	Data track	
3.3.1	Complete data source quality assessment	
3.3.2	Determine history and archive requirements for data	
3.3.3(*)	Solidify data analysis methodology (logical data modeling) altered with a rules approach	
		Create data analysis user guide (optional)
		Create data analysis training
		Offer data analysis training
3.3.4	Create logical data model	
3.3.5	Integrate logical data model with enterprise data model	
3.3.5	Create entity life cycle diagrams, as needed (for rule completeness)	
3.3.6	Estimate data volumes	
3.3.7	Begin data conversion specifications	
3.4	Technology track	
3.4.1(*)	Select preferred technology choices (including rule technology)	
3.4.2	Conduct proofs of concepts with technology choices	
3.4.3	Refine technology diagram with product specifics	
3.4.4	Identify needed interfaces among technology platforms	

Deliverables for the Design Phase

As for design, this chapter recommends the following deliverables:

- Design process track
  - Workflow: for each actor's windowflow, Web pages, and navigation
  - Detailed screen design revised due to rule dependency chains
  - User views designed
  - User transactions, reports, and queries designed
  - User guides
  - System release strategy
- Design rule track
  - A rule technology diagram, showing the various layers (highlighting those in which rules execute)
  - Physical rule design, consisting of
    - Assignment of rules to layers
    - Specifications for how the rules layer works
    - Implementation specifications for rules in the rules layer
    - Implementation specifications for rules in the database layer (triggers, etc.)
    - Insights into how the rules layer communicates with other layers.
- Design data track
  - Access path diagrams for important events
  - Database structural design
  - Database technical designs (indexing, clustering, partitioning)
  - Database space calculations
  - Database backup, recovery, load utility designs
  - Database disaster recovery design
  - Physical conversion/transformation specifications
  - Database and client security design
  - Standardized allowed value implementation
  - Ongoing data quality assessments and reports
  - Database and transaction volumes
  - Storage estimates
  - Database rule design, where rules are implemented in the database or centralized
- Design technology track
  - Technology installed and customized to client needs
  - Technology practice guides for technical support
  - Production deployment document
  - Production support document

You will notice rule-related deliverables in the process track. Specifically, screen flow design is tailored around rule dependency chains. Within the data track, there is a deliverable for mapping rules to technology and for providing database support for rule design where rules are to be enforced through the DBMS. Keep in mind that this may also mean the creation of shared program code to enforce rules (outside the DBMS) and that, if so, the database design team may be a key player here. That is, you are aiming for centralized rule management. Centralized rule management ensures that rules are no longer redundantly (and possibly inconsistently) implemented many times over in application code.

Sample Project Plan for Design

Table 5.4 is a sample project plan for the design phase.

Table 5.4   Sample Project Plan for the Design Phase

4	DESIGN	MORE DETAIL
4.1	Process track	
4.1.1	Confirm division of business events into system releases	
4.1.2(*)	Solidify application design methodology (altered with a rules approach)	
		Create application process flow design user guide (optional)
		Create application process flow training
		Offer application process flow design training
4.1.3	Create application design deliverables	Actor screen/page designs Actor page navigation/action designs Nonrule functions design deliverables Interaction descriptions between use-case and database or external system
4.1.4	Create user guides for actors	
4.1.5	Create use-case descriptions for interactions among automated components (ones not automatically handled by the commercial rules technology)	

Table 5.4 *(Continued)*

4	DESIGN	MORE DETAIL
4.1.6	Design object models as needed to support procedural execution and interfaces not handled by the business rule technology	
4.2	Rule track	
4.2.1(*)	Solidify rule design methodology	
		Create rule design user guide (optional)
		Create rule design training
		Offer rule design training
4.2.2	Walk through the mapping of rule classifications to target technology options	Workstation rule enforcement Rule technology rule enforcement (rule middle layer) enforcement DBMS rule enforcement (triggers, stored procedures) Shared object enforcement Application-object enforcement No enforcement (manual)
4.2.3(*)	Create rule design deliverables	Matrix of rule to enforcement mechanism Multi-entity rule design CRUD rules for database insert/update/delete
4.2.3	Design for nondeclarative rule support	
4.3	Data track	
4.3.1(*)	Solidify database design methodology (altered with a rules approach)	
		Create database design user guide (optional)
		Create database design training
		Conduct database design training

(continues)

Table 5.4   Sample Project Plan for the Design Phase (*Continued*)

4	DESIGN	MORE DETAIL
4.3.2	Design database(s)	Databases Tables Storage structures (space, partitions, indexes, locking, etc.) Views Rule technology query objects
4.3.3	Design database utilities	
4.3.4	Create physical data conversion specifications	
4.3.5	Create data conversion programs	
4.4	Technology track	
4.4.1(*)	Install and customize all technology	
4.4.2	Create technology practice guides for technical support personnel	
4.4.3	Create user support model	
4.4.4	Train technical support personnel	
5	Implementation	Product-specific tasks here

A Project Plan for a Comprehensive Business Rule Project

If you combine the above project plans, you have a sample task list that can be used as a starting point for a comprehensive business rules project. You can then decide which aspects of your project should occur in iterative fashion.

The tasks take into consideration that you want strong data resource management, you are migrating data from an existing source to the new system source, you want to ensure that the quality of the source and target data is excellent, and that you will utilize facilitated sessions to add speed and quality to consensus deliverables.

During the analysis phase, the project plan shows tasks for analyzing rules into high-quality rule sets, creating the logical data model, assessing the quality of source data, and mining rules from source systems, if appropriate. Rules are validated through rule validation workshops. You make the decision whether to optimize the rule set for the business prior to initial rule implementation or to do so later. Data conversion specifications are written during this phase also.

During the design phase, rules are assigned to the target technology, the database is designed for its target technology, and process flow is designed. Utilities are designed and conversion specifications become physically oriented. Target technology is installed, customized, tested, and ready to go.

During implementation, data definitions are entered into rule technology, databases are loaded, screens are created, core process flow is coded, and rules are defined and redefined. Users are trained and begin testing.

New and modified rules can be added as needed.

The next delivery increment can then begin.

Characteristics of a Good Project Manager

The project manager for a business rules project must have all the qualities of a good project manager plus an appreciation and knowledge of the business rules life cycle. Specifically, such a person should have the following professional traits:

- Excellent planner and team facilitator
- Excellent communication skills within and outside the project team
- Excellent leadership skills
- Ability to influence, collaborate, negotiate, compromise, and enforce difficult decisions
- Ability to resourcefully, effectively, and efficiently deal with problems
- Appreciation for data as an organizational asset
- Appreciation for rules as an organizational asset

Considerations for Iterative and Parallel Systems Development

Iterative development is the process whereby you conduct discovery, analysis, design, and implementation for an increment and then revisit discovery, analysis, design, and implementation for that increment based on what you learned the first (or second or third, etc.) time around. This book uses the term *parallel development* to mean the process of carrying out the phases for multiple increments at one time or even carrying out the steps in each phase at the same time, rather than sequentially.

A business rules approach lends itself very well to iterative development, more than most other approaches. This is because the business rules approach is based on the concept that discovery of rules never ends because the business itself is always changing and getting smarter, hopefully. So, if you discover rules, group them into decisions, and share those decisions among relevant processes or use cases, you should be able to add or change a rule and have that change apply to all appropriate processes or use cases.

Therefore, you can deploy iterative development to experiment with variations in screen flow, business rule logic flow, and actual rule content until the business people are happy.

However, it is very difficult to develop a solid data architecture iteratively. That's because changes to physical databases can be time-consuming and costly, maybe prohibitively so. For example, if you have very large databases and you want to change a column, you may need to drop the table, which drops all related views. You will then need to reload the table, recreate indices, and recreate views and other dependent items. So whereas changes to rules are usually very fast (the updating of simple declarative code in some cases) and changes in system code are less fast, changes in database designs become the most time-consuming.

Therefore, if you want to capitalize on iterative development, this book recommends that you first gain a solid understanding of your scope. Second, while you iterate through the first increment in detail (its screen flow, business rule logic flow, and so on), you develop a broad perspective of the final data architecture. Doing so will allow you to outline the foundational points of the data architecture so that you can implement them in a way that allows you to add to it for other increments, but without major data structure changes and corresponding disruptions.

This is very important. It means that the data analysts and data architects will be understanding a larger picture of the target system than the scope of the first increment. While this may slow down the delivery of the first increment, you should make up that time later because subsequent increments should be easier to accommodate. This means that you must not constrain data analysts and data architects to one increment at a time. They need to consider the data requirements for all of them as much as possible, as early as possible.

As a testimonial, consider: "It took Yet2.Com several weeks to understand and build its internal processes and data model correctly, but that time was compensated for by decidedly reduced testing and ability to handle change. . . . There are two parts to speed-to-market: How fast you can get the first release online and how fast you can roll out changes in the future. . . . Yet2.Com at first saw a 25–30 percent improvement in productivity, but now, while making changes, the doubled or tripled speed the company is now experiencing is truly paying off" (Mann 2000).

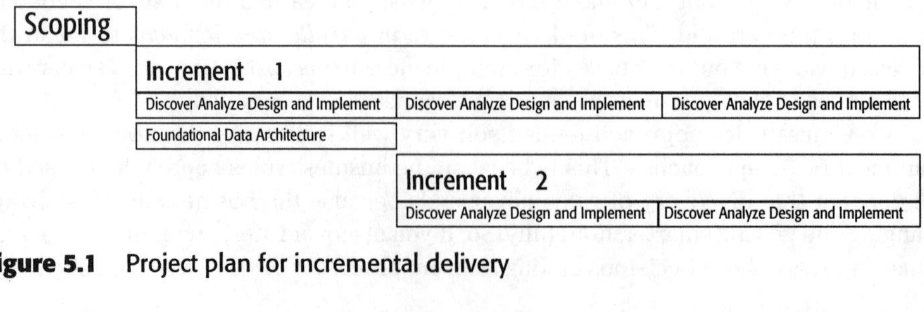

Figure 5.1 Project plan for incremental delivery

Keeping this in mind, Figure 5.1 suggests an increment approach to delivery following a business rules approach. It shows that scoping should be mostly defined before starting an increment. It shows increment one having three iterations through discovery, analysis, design, and implementation. However, it indicates that the foundational data architecture should be begun and completed before you start another increment. Many more increments can happen in parallel and each can have many more interactions.

Summary

By now you may be aware of the subtle but important benefits that are achievable when you manage business rules as a separate component. For example:

- A business user should be able to query a rule repository in many ways. The repository can produce a history of the rule, an explanation of the business objectives it aims to serve.

- A business rules approach puts the business people at the helm of the business and also at the helm of systems development. The business people steer the behavior of resulting systems by supplying, adding, changing, or archiving rules so as to effect business change.

- Business change, then, ceases to be disruptive to systems delivery and to the business itself. Instead, business change becomes a proactive, strategic, business weapon. The business rule becomes the fuel to energize the business change.

Pay special attention to the tasks in the plans above marked with asterisks because it is within these tasks that change in philosophy, focus, techniques, and even products come into play. It is within these tasks that very small changes take place. These are the changes that will make all the difference in the world to your business organization. These are the changes that separate, trace, externalize, and position for change the policies and rules of the business . . . so that the business can become what it wants to become . . . so that information technology becomes a strategic enabler the weapon of change and no longer a barrier to future possibilities.

Discovery

Discovering Initial Requirements

You may have arrived at the discovery phase from various previous points. There may have been a prior business process engineering or reengineering effort. Or you may have completed the scoping steps outlined in Chapter 4. Regardless, the discovery phase begins when there is a defined project scope to develop a target information system, a business commitment to build the information system, a detailed plan for how to proceed, and a desire to develop the information system with a business rules approach.

Figure 6.1 reminds you of where the discovery phase fits with respect to the other phases in the methodology. Note that the discovery phase addresses the discovery of requirements in four tracks: process, data, technology, and rules. This chapter focuses

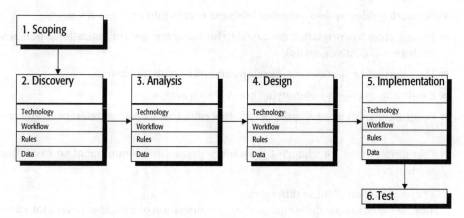

Figure 6.1 Business rule systems methodology phases.

mostly on the discovery of requirements in the process track as a starting point. Because the discovery process in this book places new emphasis on the rules track, you will want to address the concepts in Chapter 15 for managing rules.

What Is the Discovery of Initial Requirements?

In this book, the discovery of initial requirements means gaining a preliminary understanding of four aspects: potential process flow (most likely through documenting use-case descriptions), instances for testing purposes (through collecting concrete scenarios), intellectual decision-making behind the process (through capture of decisions), and the potential for sharing information (through developing a conceptual model).

For tutorial purposes, and to provide a new emphasis on rules, this book separates the discovery of process-oriented (who, when, where, and how) requirements from data (what) and rules (why). In reality, you may discover them all at once, most likely over several iterations.

How Is Discovery of Initial Requirements Different for a Business Rules Approach?

Most of you will notice that the first two steps in this chapter (create use-case descriptions and identify concrete scenarios) are similar to how you would begin discovering requirements for most object-oriented and even non-object-oriented development efforts. The third step, perhaps may seem new to you. It represents the discovery of decisions, rather than moving directly to an initial discovery of objects or of sequences of responsibilities among objects. This shift in emphasis occurs because of six subtle differences in discovering initial requirements for a business rules approach outlined in Table 3.1:

- Separating rules by decomposing business events into business decisions.
- Tracing rules by correlating decisions to business context (organizational policies, strategies, objectives, goals).
- Tracing rules by associating decisions and rules with use cases.
- Externalizing rules by identifying concrete scenarios.
- Positioning rules for change by correlating rules to information referenced and created.
- Positioning rules for change by avoiding premature commitment to execution sequence.

Let's look at each of these differences.

The first, most unique difference is the decomposition of a business event into a set of activities, but focusing first on those activities that are decision-rich. The second difference is that you make sure the decisions occur in concert with business context, such as organizational policies, strategies, and objectives. Because you perceive a process primarily as a series of decisions, you focus early on policies (if any and if known) for each decision. After all, if there is a decision to be made about something, there probably is a policy to guide the decision (somewhere). Otherwise, why would the organization bother making the decision? Further, if you have done your scoping and discovery activities with diligence, the policy should provide a lot of useful information such as: What does it intend for the result to be? Is it a mandatory policy or a guideline only? Who is most responsible for the policy? Over what jurisdiction does it apply? And, most important of all, what is its rationale? In other words, you are rounding out the motivation and intelligence behind the decision to make sure it has maximum business value.

The third difference is that you will associate rules or decisions to those use cases that rely on them. You will learn that decisions and rules may be shared across use cases, much like information may be shared.

Next is the fourth difference which is the identification of a more complete set of concrete use cases to be sure that every rule can be tested.

This brings you to the fifth difference, which is avoidance of premature commitment to execution sequence. That is, you do not obsess over sequence of activities or tasks at this time. You want to understand the decisions (intelligence) behind the event first, and only later on work out how communications happen among objects to carry out that intelligence.

The sixth difference is a focus on the information referenced and knowledge created by the business event, or actually on the decisions employed by a business event.

Later, during the analysis phase, you will determine which of those decisions (and underlying rules) are to be shared across organizational and application boundaries. That's because the rules are the thinking behind the business event. When a rule executes, it references pieces of information. It may create a new piece of information called knowledge. Decisions, rules, information, and rule-created knowledge are intellectual assets. All can be shared across organizational boundaries, with proper analysis, when appropriate for the business. All of these intellectual assets are important focal points in a business rules approach.

What Is the Purpose of Discovering Initial Requirements?

The purpose of discovering initial requirements is twofold. The first point is to gain an initial understanding for how the business community would like the system's process to flow. The second is to get started early in understanding the decisions, policies, and rules behind the process. The goal is to do so without considering target technology, although you will soon see that commercial rules technology can shorten this discovery time. The second goal is to develop as few deliverables as possible without sacrificing your understanding of the target system.

It is usually natural to begin by understanding in more detail how the business community perceives the system's process flow. An investigation into a preliminary system process flow leads you to the rules. The question now is, How much investigation and discovery about the process flow is needed in a business rules approach? The answer is probably less than is needed for traditional systems development, depending on target technology.

This chapter proposes that you uncover three essential aspects related to the process behind the business event: the tasks or activities behind each business event if doing so is helpful; a sample of the real or imaginary event scenarios for unraveling and testing completeness of the process; and the decisions made on behalf of those tasks or activities to lead you to rules. The premise is that you need to understand the decisions and rules before you determine whether they will execute through object-oriented code or through other rule-oriented approaches.

This chapter does, however, encourage you to begin or refine a term-fact model in the discovery process so that you have a semantic foundation for the decisions and rules. This can be a business object model or a conceptual data model. *Business objects,* according to Paul Harmon and Mark Watson (1997), are "the kinds of things that end users talk about.... Business objects include things like employees, sales orders, accounts, machines, rejection slips, and company sites." They are distinguished from *infrastructure objects,* which they define as "classes that the developer creates to assure that the software works. Therefore, a business object model contains terms and facts familiar to the business person and about which decisions are made and rules are executed. You will develop class models (and other object-oriented deliverables) during process analysis in Chapter 11.

Even if you develop a business object model, this chapter also encourages you to develop a conceptual data model because a stable information architecture is critical to future business rule changes. The earlier you begin understanding it, the better. Figure 6.2

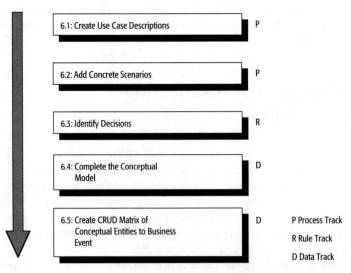

Figure 6.2   The steps of the discovering initial requirements phase.

provides the details behind the discovery of initial requirements. Note that steps 6.1 and 6.2 address deliverables in the process track because these steps deal with event-response process details and corresponding scenarios. Step 6.3, because it involves identifying decisions, takes you into the rule track. Step 6.4, because it starts or evolves a conceptual data model, takes you into the data track. Step 6.5, by creating or evolving a CRUD matrix between conceptual entities and business events, ties together the data track and the process track. Because you will use this CRUD matrix as input to designing stable, shared databases, Figure 6.2 denotes step 6.5 as a deliverable that belongs more in the data track rather than in the process track.

What Are the Deliverables of Discovering Initial Requirements?

In this book, we separate the discovery of process (this chapter) from that of rules and data (Chapter 7). You can, of course, combine the steps in these two chapters into one discovery effort. This chapter divides them here merely for ease of explanation. Should you decide not to follow the steps in this chapter, but to follow your own approach for discovering initial requirements, the separation of rule discovery into its own chapter provides an easy reference by which you can incorporate Chapter 7's concepts into your own requirements-gathering approach.

Below are the possible deliverables for the discovery of process in the process track.

- Use-case descriptions for the human interactions with each business event
- Concrete scenarios for each business event
- Decisions behind each business event
- Terms and facts
  - Business object model
  - Refined conceptual model
- CRUD matrix of conceptual data entities or business objects to business events.

At this time, you may also want to consider that a deliverable from the technology track is a technology architecture vision paper or diagram.

What Are the Steps in Discovering Initial Requirements?

The intent of this chapter is to present one set of steps and deliverables that should suffice in discovering initial requirements so that you can move quickly into rules. This chapter contains requirements techniques that are common and span systems development paradigms, such as use cases and scenarios. You should add steps and deliverables that are familiar to and successful within your organization for gathering requirements.

STEP 6.1: DESCRIBE THE EVENT RESPONSE PROCESS DETAILS BY CREATING USE-CASE DESCRIPTIONS

As part of the scoping phase, you created an event-response process table. You begin the discovery phase by reviewing this table for each business event within the initial scope so that you can proceed to understand it in more detail.

Specifically, in step 6.1 you aim to understand the details behind the event-response process sufficiently enough to get started uncovering rules. There are many ways of doing this, although the most popular way today is the creation of use-case descriptions. Some people argue that older techniques, such as functional decomposition diagrams, are desirable because they depict the system functionality from a top-down perspective, allowing you to see the whole picture of functionality. Other people argue that such techniques do not lend themselves well to the eventual creation of distributed component-based systems. The truth is that there are many approaches for understanding the event-response process and all have merits. It is not the purpose of this book to contribute to the debates as to whether one is preferable over another or whether, in fact, you should use more than one technique. Instead, this chapter focuses mostly on use-case descriptions because they are common and gaining in popularity. However, the chapter also illustrates possible solutions using other alternatives.

A use-case description represents a typical sequence of interactions that may carry out a business event. According to Paul Harmon and Mike Watson (1997), a *use-case description* provides a generic, step-by-step description of the interaction between an actor and a use case. If you review Figure 4.5, it actually depicts eight use cases, one for each interaction between the VCI system and human or electronic actors.

A use-case description is generic in that it does not name a specific person but an actor or role. A use-case description usually contains a normal sequence of interactions and alternate sequences to handle error conditions, for example.

Table 6.1 illustrates a sample use-case template (Phillips 2000). Note that it contains a place for adding business rules to the use case. Because a rule may be relevant to more than one use case, it would be ideal if you can connect a use-case description to each relevant rule and have the rule repository print out the rules onto the use-case description.

Table 6.1 Sample Use-Case Template from Versata

USE CASE NAME:
Version: 0.1
Status: Draft
Project/Problem Domain: Agency Administration System
Author: Jacobson
Owner: Ms. Noma

Table 6.1 *(Continued)*

USE CASE DETAILS:

Purpose
To create a new Agency and associate an Administrator

Actors

Agency Administrator

Agency Administration Supervisor

Credit Check Bureau

Trigger Events & Message Contents

A "New Agency" request form is received by the Agency Administrator (via fax or email) from one of the Branch Offices

(average 5 per week, 1 hour per request)

Use Case Description

Preconditions:

Agency must not already exist

Administrator must be Active

Post conditions:

Agency Active

Intermediate States:

Awaiting credit check

Process Steps and Flow (Scenarios):

Actor Actions (external events)	System Response
Select "Agency Request" input	Display "Agency Request" form
Input Agency Details	Validate Agency Details
	Generate Agency ID
	Request Agency Credit Check from credit bureau
	Set Status to "Pending Credit Check"
	Save details and notify Actor
Receive credit details	Set Agency Status to "Pending Authorization" or "Failed Credit Check"

(continues)

Table 6.1   Sample Use-Case Template from Versata (*Continued*)

Input Administrator ID	Validate Administrator exists and is "Active"
	Associate Administrator with Agency
	Set Agency Status to "Pending Authorization"

Business Rules (for each process and data object)

(see data objects for attribute data types)

If Agency must have a Credit Score over 6.9 to be approved

If the Agency Rating is Gold, the Administrator must be a Grade 5 or above

Exceptions or Special Conditions (maybe more business rules)

If the selected Administrator is not active or qualified, an alternative Administrator is selected by head office.

Data (data objects, attributes, message flows)

Agency

Administrator

Credit Bureau List

Associated Reference Materials

Administrator's Handbook

Acceptance Criteria for Use Case (for testing)

Each Agency may have 3 contact addresses but only 1 current billing address

Part entries of Agency details should be retrievable for later completion

Example

Implementation Issues

Remarks

Open Items & Risks

Keep in mind as you write use-case descriptions that you are not overly concerned with absolute sequence at this point. You are simply gaining an understanding of a typical sequence as suggested by members of the business community. You will use your use-case descriptions first as a fast path to discovering the decisions and rules behind the event. When you later analyze rules (Chapter 10), you will methodologically uncover the essential sequence in which the system must uncover related knowledge when servicing an event. The essential sequence becomes the sequence in which decisions and rules need to execute. You will, then, combine the essential rule sequence with overall core process flow in Chapter 11.

GUIDELINE 6.1.1

Simply use whatever technique assists you in soliciting from a business person a reasonable sequence in which the business event may be serviced.

Although this chapter favors use-case descriptions, use whatever approach works best for your organization. It is not the purpose of this book to critique the various approaches and their merits and shortcomings. Some organizations may prefer process decomposition diagrams. Still others may prefer system response tables. For complex, multiorganization and multisystem processes, a swim lane diagram may be helpful. However, use-case descriptions and analysis are the most popular and usually the most useful for today's component-based, distributed computing environments.

CASE STUDY: STEP 6.1—DESCRIBE THE EVENT-RESPONSE PROCESS DETAILS BY CREATING USE-CASE DESCRIPTIONS

Case Study Instructions:

- Write a use-case description for the interaction between guardian and the system for the business event Guardian Enrolls Member.

Case Study Solution:
If you refer back to the case study description in Step 4.1, most of the documentation describes concepts behind the business event Member Requests Entrance to the Park. So, you need to find additional documentation and talk to business experts about how a guardian enrolls a member. This can be done in a facilitated session or through one-on-one interviews.

Based on what you learn, you create a preliminary use-case description shown in Figure 6.3.

STEP 6.2: ADD CONCRETE SCENARIOS

The term *concrete scenario* means an imaginary or actual instance of a business event or use case. Collecting scenarios is an effective and fun way of starting or solidifying a conversation about the business event. Later, concrete scenarios prove useful for validating that you have described all of the required processing of the system and eventually all of its rules.

Solicit scenarios from business people. Business people can have fun coming up with creative scenarios. These can be used later as test cases for a system prototype. For example, suggest that the business person bring the last 50 transactions that would have been processed by the system. Be sure to include successful and unsuccessful transactions.

Suppose your business audience for the Internet Park may propose the following scenarios for the business event Guardian Enrolls Member:

Scenario 1: Mary is a single parent with a 14-year-old daughter. She wants to enroll her daughter in all theme park functions. Her daughter always does her homework and

Normal Sequence:

1. Guardian accesses the VCI Web page.

2. Guardian accesses the enrollment Web page.

3. Guardian enters guardian information.

4. System qualifies guardian (decisions and rules!).

5. Guardian enters member information.

6. System qualifies member for enrollment in the park (decision and rules!).

7. System displays the complete enrollment screen.

8. Guardian approves the enrollment.

Alternate Sequences:

(a) Guardian is not known. The system initiates a use case for "Enter new guardian."

(b) Guardian has bad credit. The system sets the guardian's payment method to prepay status and sends a message to the guardian indicating that a payment for a prespecified amount is needed before the member will be able to enter VCI Park.

(c) Member is too young. The system sends a message that the member is not age-appropriate for this park.

(d) Member is too old. The system initiates a use case for "Recommend other parks."

(e) Guardian does not have access to the Internet.

Figure 6.3   Preliminary guardian enrolls member use-case description.

her chores, so Mary merely wants to ask the daughter, prior to park admission, if her daughter received any good grades that day. Her daughter can have 1 hour in the game park every day but gets an extra 30 minutes for every good grade. Mary is a new customer. We don't know if she is a good credit risk or not.

Scenario 2: John and Barb want to enroll a 10-year-old boy. He is to be tutored in reading for 30 minutes a day using the tutoring function of the park before he can enter the game park. His reading skill level is age 8. He can have 1 hour of access to the game park per day. John and Barb are existing customers with another child enrolled. Past history indicates that they do not have good credit.

CASE STUDY: STEP 6.2—ADD CONCRETE SCENARIOS

Case Study Instructions:

- Create simple concrete scenarios for the event Member Requests Entrance into the Park. Be creative so as to include all different possibilities.

Case Study Solution:

Below are very simple concrete scenarios for the business event, Member Requests Entrance into the Park. Later, in the next chapter, when you uncover rules, you will proceed with more complicated concrete scenarios.

1. Bob G. has enrolled his daughter Kylie, who is 10 years old and is a VCI member. Bob has signed up his daughter for the theme park and the Spanish tutorial. Bob has entered the following questions to be answered by Kylie when she logs in to VCI Park:

    - Have you completed your homework?

    - Have you helped your mother with your chores?

2. Ted H. has signed up his two children as members. It seems that he is quite concerned that his children complete all their homework and all their chores before entering the VCI park system. Some of the questions that he has asked them to answer are:

    Questions to Peter:

    - Have you completed your homework today?

    - Have you cleaned up your room today?

    - Have you done two of your assigned chores (identified on the refrigerator) today?

    - You had a Math Test yesterday. If you received your test results today, what grade did you receive?

    Questions to Tricia:

    - Have you completed your homework today?

    - Have you cleaned up your room today?

    - Have you done two of your assigned chores (identified on the refrigerator) today?

    - You had a spelling test two days ago. If you received your test results today, what grade did you receive?

3. George S. has two nephews, Brian and Al, who he has signed up as members. George has entered questions to ensure that his nephews complete their homework and do well in school. The questions he has entered for his nephews are: (Note: they are the same for both of his members.)

    - Have you completed your homework?

    - What grade did you get on your Geography test today?

4. Janet W is a guardian with VCI. She has enrolled her grandchild, Nancy (age 8) as a member to VCI. Janet has prepaid for 8 hours (480 minutes) for her granddaughter's time in the VCI park system. Janet has asked her granddaughter the following questions:

- Have you read a book today for 15 minutes?

- Have you completed your homework for today?

STEP 6.3: IDENTIFY DECISIONS

In this book, a *decision* is a judgment to be made. For example, one decision may be determining whether a customer is of preferred status. This decision relates to customer. Think of other decisions, such as, is a product in stock? Can an order be shipped to a desired location within the requested timeframe? These are all decisions that a system (or human) may need to make when servicing a customer request for an order (a business event).

Sometimes a decision is simply the execution of one rule. For example, if the decision is that a product is always in stock simply if there is one or more of the product on the shelf, the decision is made by executing one rule. That rule is: If the quantity on the shelf of a product is greater than 0, then the product is in stock.

Often, however, a decision results from the execution of many rules. As an example, suppose the business adopts a policy that the last 10 products on the shelf are to be sent to preferred customers only. The policy can be enforced by two different rules, each compliant with the policy. One rule states that if you are a preferred customer, the product is in stock if there is one or more on the shelf. The other rule states that if you are not a preferred customer, the product is considered in stock only if there are eleven or more on the shelf, because the business needs to reserve ten for the preferred customers.

Now, you search for evidence of decisions or rules. You can do this in at least two ways: studying policies or studying event details, or both.

GUIDELINE 6.3.1

Review policies from scoping in search of decisions. Remember to review policies related to objectives as well as those meant to mitigate risks.

You can begin by reviewing the policies uncovered as part of the scoping phase. Start with the policies behind the business event that aim for the objectives. Do any of those policies apply to the business event? If so, do those policies imply that a decision needs to be made so as to be compliant with the policy?

As an example, Chapter 4 introduced the following possible policy: Orders received before 4 P.M. must be shipped for next day arrival at the customer's location. Recall that, in this example, related considerations are: What constitutes an order? What does it mean for an order to be received? What does it mean for an order to be received before 4 P.M.? And what does it mean to ship an order for next day arrival at a customer location? Therefore, if you were performing step 6.3, Identify Decisions, for the business event Order Is Received and the event-response process Fulfill Order, you could start by discussing the following considerations that arise from studying policies.

- What constitutes an order?
  - This will lead to the rules verifying that mandatory information for order processing is present.
- What does it mean for an order to be received?
  - This may lead to rules that determine that the source of the order is valid for meeting this next day shipment policy: fax? phone? email? Web?
- What does it mean for an order to be received before 4 P.M.?
  - This will lead to rules that test the order's timestamp.
  - This will lead to rules that test the receive time against the time in a standard time zone.
- What does it mean to ship an order for next day arrival at a customer location?
  - You can also proceed to reviewing the policies whose aim is to mitigate risks. In Chapter 4, you uncovered the following risk: the unintended release of the identity of member children. An associated policy is: The identity of member children must not be released to any external person or organization. Therefore, if you were performing step 6.3, Identify Decisions, for a business event involving the request of the identity a member, you could investigate the following:
- What information constitutes the identity of a member?
  - This will lead to rules that validate the unique identity of a member.
- What is an external person?
  - This will lead to rules that determine whether an actor is an external versus internal person.
- What constitutes an external organization?
  - This will lead to rules that determine whether an actor represents an organization that is external versus internal.

GUIDELINE 6.3.2

Study event details in search of decisions.

The second way to search for decisions is to look more closely at event details, such as response interactions, a use-case description, low-level processes in a process decomposition diagram, or even concrete scenarios in search of processes driven by decision-making activity.

GUIDELINE 6.3.3

Start with discovering decisions rather than proceeding directly to discovering rules under certain circumstances.

If the business event or a use case seems riddled with decision-making activity (that is, decisions are made about many business nouns) or if the business event or use case happens over a long timeframe, you may want to start by first understanding the kinds of decisions made rather than jumping right into the discovery of detailed rules. Also, sometimes the initial business audience is aware of high-level decisions (for example, about customer or customer credit checking), but does not know the specific details as to how such decisions are made. In these cases, it is useful to identify decisions first and rules later.

GUIDELINE 6.3.4

For each step in the use-case description, determine if there is any mental processing or "thinking" involved.

Look for the following thinking-oriented words, such as:

> Check
>
> Qualify
>
> Compute
>
> Calculate
>
> Estimate
>
> Evaluate
>
> Determine
>
> Assess
>
> Compare
>
> Verify
>
> Validate
>
> Confirm
>
> Decide
>
> Diagnose
>
> Process.

These words suggest that there are rules or decisions behind them. If, however, the step is one of "provide information" or "carry out action," there may be no rules behind it. Look back to Figure 6.3. Notice that steps 4 and 6 contain the word "qualifies." Therefore, these are marked as representing steps in which the system makes decisions (see the parentheses). There may also be hints at hidden decisions in the alternate sequences.

GUIDELINE 6.3.5

Identify the primary business noun (term) about which each decision is made.

As examples, review the decisions listed below:

- Is *customer* <u>known?</u>
- Does *customer* <u>have a good credit rating?</u>

- Is *product* <u>known?</u>
- Is *product* <u>available for an order?</u>
- Is *product* <u>shippable as requested for an order?</u>

Notice that each decision is about a business noun (such as customer or product). These are shown above in italics. Also note that the decision itself is about a state that the noun may or may not be in (such as *known, have good credit rating*). These are shown above with an underscore.

GUIDELINE 6.3.6

Be sure that each primary business noun (term) has a place in the conceptual data model or business object model.

Most of the time, you will want to make sure there is an entity in the conceptual data model or an object in the business object model for each primary business noun. In some cases, the primary business noun may best be a role played by an entity in the conceptual data model or a subclass in a business object model. This might be the case for a primary business noun of Customer, which is represented as a role of a Business Party entity in the conceptual data model.

From a list of decisions, you can proceed to the next chapter where you will uncover the rules behind each decision.

GUIDELINE 6.3.7

Collect the following meta data for each decision or computation: Decision made; information referenced for decision; knowledge created by the decision; action taken, if any.

You will discover later that most decisions (and rules) do not belong only to one business event or activity, but actually execute over and over again throughout many processes, events, and use cases. A value of the business rules approach is to identify and manage this reuse of decisions and rules to minimize coding, aim for consistency, and facilitate business changes in decisions or rules.

Specifically, decisions and rules have an existence independent of business event, use case, process, transaction, and so on, in much the same way that data have an existence that transcends these considerations.

A useful way to record decisions is with a *decision matrix*, which records each decision, information needed, knowledge created, and whether the materialization of that decision is within the target scope of the current release.

GUIDELINE 6.3.8

Document decisions that occur outside the boundaries of the target system.

Many times there will be decisions that are made by other systems or by humans.

GUIDELINE 6.3.9

Start a list of issues surrounding each decision.

Hopefully, you will address these issues when you gather rules behind the decisions, discussed in the next chapter.

CASE STUDY: STEP 6.3–IDENTIFY DECISIONS

Case Study Instructions:

- Identify the decisions made for each step in a use-case description for Member Requests Entrance into the Park.

- Identify primary business nouns.

- Walk through scenarios with a business person to learn more details about those decisions.

- Fill out a decision matrix.

Case Study Solution:

Figure 6.4 shows a simple, preliminary use-case description for Member Requests Entrance to Park.

You identify a preliminary set of decisions for each step of the use case, as shown in Table 6.2.

To identify primary business nouns, in studying these decisions, two primary business nouns emerge: Guardian and Member.

Let's now walk through the scenarios with a business person. What kinds of decisions are made; which decisions admit the member; which deny access to member?

1. Bob—Kylie

    A. Is login accepted (yes or no)—Yes

    B. Is billing status Credit or Prepay—Credit

    C. What is default time allowed—20 minutes in theme park; 20 minutes in tutorial

---

Normal Sequence:

1. Member accesses the VCI Web page.
2. Member presents entrance pass (identification).
3. System qualifies member.
4. System presents member-specific questions to member.
5. Member answers questions.
6. System qualifies member answers to questions.
7. System qualifies guardian billing.
8. System enables member to enter park.

Figure 6.4   Preliminary member requests entrance to park use-case description.

Table 6.2 Task Decision Table

USE CASE STEP	DECISION	RULE
1. Member accesses the VCI Web page.	None	
2 Member presents entrance pass (identification)	None	
3. System qualifies member	Is member login *accepted*?	
4. System presents member-specific questions to member	None	
5. Member answers questions	None	
6. System qualifies member answers to questions	Is homework *done*? Is chore *done*? Is activity *done*? Is subject grade *acceptable*?	
7. System sends member answers to guardian	None	
8. System qualifies guardian billing	Does guardian have money *sufficient to pay for member entrance*?	
9. System enables entrance to park	None	

    D. What are the member responses to questions

Homework—Yes → Add 10 minutes to default time in theme park

Chores—No → Deduct 5 minutes from theme park allowance

  2. Ted—Peter

    A. Login accepted—Yes

    B. Credit/Prepay—Credit

    C. Default time allowed—0 minutes

    D. Responses

      ■ Homework—Yes → 30 minutes in theme park

      ■ Cleaned Room—Yes → 15 minutes in theme park

      ■ Chores—Yes → 15 minutes in theme park

      ■ Math Test—C → 15 minutes in math tutorial before entering theme park

  3. Ted—Tricia

    A. Login accepted—Yes

    B. Credit/Prepay—Credit

    C. Default time allowed—0 minutes

    D. Responses

- Homework—Yes → 30 minutes in theme park

- Cleaned room—Yes → 15 minutes in theme park

- Chores—No → Deduct 15 minutes from theme park allowance

- Spelling Test—B → 5 minutes in theme park

4. George—Brian

    A. Login accepted—Yes

    B. Credit/Prepay—Credit

    C. Default time allowed—30 minutes in theme park; 20 minutes in library park

    D. Responses

- Homework—Yes → allow default time in park

- Geography Test—B → allow default time in park

5. George—Al

    A. Login accepted—Yes

    B. Credit/Prepay—Credit

    C. Default time allowed—30 minutes in theme park; 20 minutes in library park

    D. Responses

- Homework—No → No time in theme park; allow default time in library park

- Geography Test—C → No theme park allowance all week

6. Janet—Nancy

    A. Login accepted—Yes

    B. Credit/Prepay—Prepay

    C. Default time allowed—20 minutes in theme park, 30 minutes in math tutorial

    D. Prepaid time remaining—110 minutes

    E. Responses

- Read Book—Yes → allow default time in both parks

- Homework—Yes → allow default time in both parks

- Practiced piano—No → must spend 15 minutes in tutorial before entering theme park

    Note: Nancy is well within her prepaid allotment. At most she will use 50 minutes and will have at least 60 minutes remaining in the prepaid account.

STEP 6.4: COMPLETE THE CONCEPTUAL MODEL

In step 6.4, you carry out discovery activities appropriate for the data track by refining the conceptual model you started during the scoping phase or starting one if you did not already do so. In this book, a *conceptual data model* is a high-level view of information requirements.

The conceptual model described in this book borrows from former ideas of information engineering. Some practitioners may not be in favor of creating a conceptual model because many systems are developed today, following an object-oriented approach that gives low or no priority to information engineering concepts. We include a conceptual model in our deliverables because, without careful attention to the underlying information architecture, you are likely to proliferate poor quality databases. In a world where business rules can change easily, poor quality databases become serious barriers to business growth. To minimize the risk that the database will inhibit rule changes, the conceptual model represents the scope information requirements extended beyond the target information system scope wherever possible. Doing so positions you to deliver databases that can be shared across organizational and application boundaries with minimal disruption to the business. Doing so also positions you to develop data structures that will support a wide variety of new rules. By creating a conceptual data model, you are able to divide the information requirements into segments that can be planned, scoped, analyzed, designed, and implemented in increments over time.

Note that you can also enhance your business object model at this point to extend beyond the scope of your target system. However, your business object model, if you create one, will likely serve as a foundation for adding infrastructure objects, and iteratively refining so that it serves the processing needs of the system well. The processing needs and the data needs are not the same. You will apply different criteria to the analysis and design of objects to leverage them than you will to the analysis and design of databases to leverage them. Object models, in one way or another, aim to serve the dynamic aspect of the system and ought to be developed iteratively with the dynamic nature in mind. Attention is given to object models in Analyzing Process, Chapter 11. Data models, on the other hand, aim to serve the static informational structure of the system and are difficult to develop iteratively, as changes to data structures are expensive and time-consuming.

GUIDELINE 6.4.1

At a minimum, the conceptual model should consist of three deliverables: a conceptual data model, a conceptual process model, and a CRUD matrix showing information (entity), usage (create, update, delete, read, or usage) of the lowest levels in the conceptual process model.

The benefits of creating a conceptual model for a broad scope include:

- Enabling the integration of eventual databases (with few surprises)

- Serving as the focal point for all data requirements for all projects eventually

- Serving as insight into business-knowledgeable sources to be included in data analysis activities (that is, to scope the specific data analysis project)

- Communicating the breadth of business data to business people and to IT professionals

- Solidifying proposed data subject boundaries

- Establishing early stewardship boundaries over information.

GUIDELINE 6.4.2

For a business rules system, the conceptual data model should include major entities that are of interest to the scope under consideration.

The focus in creating a conceptual data model is on common business semantics, that is, data names, data meanings, and data relationships. It can show abstract supertypes (such as business party) with business-specific subtypes. It need include only the most prominent subtypes. Many-to-many relationships need not be resolved in a conceptual data model, unless doing so adds to business understanding. It shows cardinality of relationships but not optionality. Except for abstract supertypes, all entity and attribute names reflect business terms. Where interesting, obvious attributes are shown within entities, if known. Codes or flags are not shown as entities or attributes. The model should be complete enough to influence design but not enough to serve as a final design specification. (For more details on the items mentioned in this paragraph, refer to Chapter 9.)

If you do not create a conceptual data model during the discovery phase, you are likely to spend more time getting started in building your detailed logical data model. Moreover, the absence of a conceptual data model means that the seams among subjects are unclear, thus possibly resulting in duplicate and inconsistent analysis efforts.

GUIDELINE 6.4.3

Typically, a conceptual process model is a functional decomposition diagram with supporting text.

The functional decomposition diagram is usually decomposed down to the level necessary to indicate creation of an entity. Keep in mind that these functions are not system functions, but business functions. The reason you want a conceptual process (business function) model is because you want to understand the possibility of sharing data across business functions. This book does not favor one process or functional modeling approach over another.

GUIDELINE 6.4.4

The CRUD matrix should depict business event to conceptual entities.

A *CRUD matrix of conceptual entities to business events* is a correlation of each business event to the conceptual entities it creates, updates, reads, or deletes. This provides an early idea of the scope of the data foundation that is needed for each incremental delivery. You do not need to deliver the entire data foundation with the first release. However, you need to deliver foundational data structures against which future data pieces can be added with little negative impact on the system.

If you do not create a conceptual process model and the CRUD matrix between processes and entities, your detailed logical data model created during the analysis phase may not reflect a broad enough scope to be stable.

CASE STUDY: STEP 6.4—BEGIN TO CREATE OR REFINE THE CONCEPTUAL MODEL

Case Study Instructions:

- Update the conceptual data model with new information gained.

Case Study Solution:

Figure 6.5 depicts a possible preliminary conceptual data model based on what you have uncovered so far. Table 6.3 proposes a partial CRUD, showing the business event, Member Requests Entrance to Park, and its usage of conceptual data entities.

Considerations for Iterative and Parallel Systems Development

Some of the concepts addressed in this chapter (use cases, concrete scenarios, decisions, and the terms and facts referenced in decisions) will evolve throughout all phases of development. Specifically, you will correct and add details to use cases. You may add

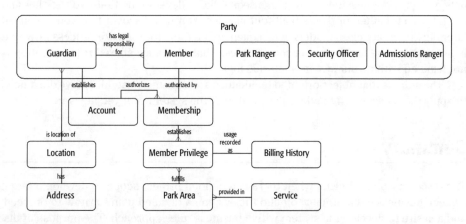

Figure 6.5 Preliminary conceptual data model.

Table 6.3 CRUD Matrix, Business Event to Business Entity

BUSINESS EVENT	BUSINESS PARTY ENTITY	GUARDIAN ENTITY	MEMBER ENTITY	MEMBERSHIP ENTITY	MEMBER PRIVILEGE ENTITY
Guardian Enrolls Member	C, R	C, R, U	C	C	C

more use cases. You will revisit concrete scenarios, adding more to ensure completeness. Decisions (and rules) will be added and changed. Especially if using commercial rules products (or building your own rules component), you will be able to change and add rules quickly for prototyping. Data can be added or changed in each phase, although not all data changes are easy to accommodate. This is why a solid information architecture assists in enabling a smooth iterative development experience, because it minimizes the costly and negative impact of data changes.

Within this part of discovery, you can carry out the steps in this chapter in parallel, if useful. For example, if you will be developing all of your own object-oriented code, you may want to develop use cases and concrete scenarios in parallel. Subsequently, you may want to work on decisions and the terms and facts within them in parallel. You might even focus on all four items in parallel:

- Use-case descriptions to use as a basis in analysis for sequence diagrams and class diagrams.

- Concrete scenarios to check for completeness.

- Decisions employed by the use case to create a starting point for rule discovery.

- Terms and facts referenced in decisions to use as a basis in analysis to refine the class and sequence diagrams and begin a logical data model.

If, instead, you will be deploying your system using certain commercial rules products, you may address these four items sequentially, develop the first two together and the last two together, or develop all four at once. You will discover that you may need later only to create class models and sequence diagrams for the core process flow that is not responsible for executing shared rules. That's because shared rule execution is not handled within your system's internal logic.

The point is that object-oriented techniques are extremely useful, but we don't need to apply them necessarily to the rules portion of the system. Not yet, anyway.

Summary

The discovery phase begins when there is a defined project scope to develop a target system, business commitment to build the system, a detailed plan for how to proceed, and a desire to develop the system with a business rules approach. The purpose of discovering initial requirements is to document aspects of the system's process that includes five items: typical details behind each business event; decisions made behind those interactions; information referenced in making those decisions; the knowledge created by those decisions; and sample real or imaginary event scenarios for testing completeness of the process.

The significant difference in a business rules approach lies in the unearthing of decisions behind business events. That is, you begin, even during the discovery phase, to focus on the decision-making (intellectual processing) behind a business event as the starting point for uncovering detailed rules (and thought processes) behind each decision. What this means is that a business rules approach places emphasis on the intelligence (computations, constraints, inferences) required to handle a business event. Later, you will want to determine the process by which those decisions and rules are executed and which ones are to be shared across organizational and application boundaries.

While you begin by studying the sequence of interactions, you are truly not concerned with actual sequence at this point in time. You are only looking for a way that will lead you to the rules behind the event. When you later analyze the rules (Chapter 10), you will methodically uncover the essential sequence of processing behind the event. The *essential processing sequence* represents the sequence in which the system must uncover related knowledge (or decisions) when servicing an event.

Traditional systems development methodologies usually do not include a formal capturing or analysis of decisions and relating them to business context, such as goals, objectives, strategies, and policies.

During the discovery phase, you should create a conceptual model. This provides an early idea of the scope of the data foundation that is needed for each incremental delivery. You do not need to deliver the entire data foundation with the first release. However, you need to deliver foundational data structures against which future data pieces can be added with little negative impact on the system.

At this point, you have an understanding of your use cases, the decisions behind them, sample concrete scenarios, a semblance of semantics through the identification of terms. You are now ready for the next chapter. In Chapter 7, you seek the detailed rules and information pieces behind each use-case and possibly shared across them.

Discovering Rules and Data

You arrived at the discovery of rules and data because you have already completed the other aspects of the discovery phase. That is, from the scoping phase, you know the delivery increments of the target system through identification of business context, business events, event-response processes, stakeholders, data subjects, constraints, and other requirements. You have also gained an understanding of the expected behavior of each increment through the understanding of the details behind each event-response process, decisions behind the tasks, and documentation of concrete scenarios. Most likely, you began documenting use-case descriptions, although, if useful, you created process decomposition diagrams, system response tables, or other means. The most interesting activity so far may be the discovery of the decisions behind each business event. Decisions represent executable thinking, which eventually decomposes into a set of rules.

What Is the Discovery of Rules and Data?

Simply stated, the discovery of rules and data is the process of capturing the detailed intellectual decision-making capacity behind the way the business wants to handle business events. The rules are the decisions (which result in knowledge or action) and the data is the information needed to make those decisions.

You are now positioned to search for those rules and the information behind the decisions. Figure 7.1 is repeated so you remain aware of where the discovery phase fits into the whole business rule systems development methodology. In theory, the discovery phase follows the scoping phase and is completed before you start the analysis

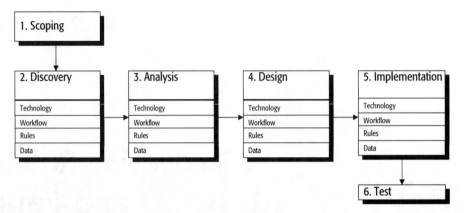

Figure 7.1   Business rule systems methodology phases.

phase. The analysis phase, then, addresses the output of the discovery phase, with new emphasis and discipline on rules.

During rule discovery, you must determine the kinds of rules you want to discover and manage formally. You will need rule-naming conventions. You will also need to decide how to express rules.

For the Internet Theme Park, you want to manage, as stand-alone rules, complex constraints, guidelines, computations, inferences, and action-enabler rules. You will store them in a homegrown rules repository. Rule names will indicate the classification for a rule (constraint, guideline, computation, inference, or action enabler) and the information it most closely governs.

Just as you can do top-down and bottom-up process discovery as well as top-down and bottom-up data discovery, you can also do top-down and bottom-up rule discovery. Top-down rule discovery would begin with business context, perhaps from mission, and drive down toward policies and to rules. Bottom-up rule discovery would begin with system interactions or use cases and search for decisions and rules. For most readers, the bottom-up rule discovery path will be most useful because you are focusing on system requirements and human interactions with the system. However, while this chapter starts with the bottom-up approach, it ends with top-down considerations.

How Is Rule and Data Discovery Different for a Business Rules Approach?

It is probably valid to say that rule discovery makes all the difference in the world between a business rules system and a nonbusiness rules system. The five characteristics of rule discovery that sets a business rules approach apart from all others and depicted in Table 3.1, are:

- Separating rules by discovering them as distinct from other system artifacts.

- Tracing rules by relating them to business context (organizational policies, strategies, tactics, goals, objectives).

- Externalizing rules by expressing them in natural language and in templates, naming them and classifying them.

- Positioning rules for change by giving them well-defined jurisdictions and establishing business consensus.

- Positioning rules for change by associating them with the knowledge they reference and the knowledge they create.

These five differences support the four principles of the business rules approach: separate rules, trace rules, externalize rules, and position rules for change. Let's look at each difference and how it relates to the discovery of rules and data.

The first difference is that rule discovery is true to the principle of separating rules from other artifacts simply because rule discovery discovers rules, making them tangible from the start. The second difference may be the most important because it traces rules to their origins and justifications. That is, rule discovery relates rules to the business context they support. This means making sure each rule relates appropriately to policies, strategies, tactics, risk, or objectives.

The third difference is in support of externalizing rules for all audiences. Thus, rule discovery expresses rules in natural language, translates them to templates for clarity if useful, gives them meaningful names, and classifies them based on what each intends to do.

The fourth difference is that rule discovery is faithful to the principle of positioning rules for change because it authenticates rules by making sure each rule has a well-defined jurisdiction and that business leaders are in consensus about the rule.

The fifth difference also positions rules for change by associating rules with the knowledge referenced and created.

For reference, Figure 7.2 shows the details of rule and data discovery. Note that steps 7.1 through 7.7 focus almost entirely on various aspects of discovering rules. These steps include tasks, guidelines, and techniques specifically aimed at uncovering rules, documenting them, and ensuring that they bring value to the business. These steps are

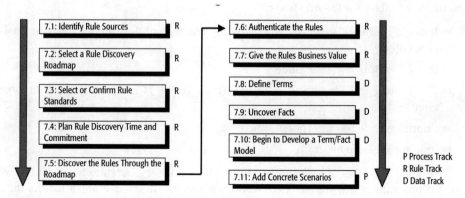

Figure 7.2   Steps for discovering rules and data.

the starting point through which rules become a business asset, an organizational instrument of change.

Steps 7.8 and 7.10 use the rules to validate and enhance the data model and data semantics. Step 7.11 continues to add to concrete scenarios as you get deeper into rules because you want to be sure you have mechanisms for testing them. Figure 7.2 depicts step 7.11 as part of the process track. This chapter looks at each step in detail.

What Is the Purpose of Discovering Rules and Data?

The purpose of discovering rules and data is to begin (and never stop!) capturing rules, and also to solidify the data behind the rules. Keep in mind, then, that rule discovery will and should be an iterative process. In a business rule world, rule discovery, essentially, never ends (it is not really just a phase). You intend to build an information system designed to change its rules, add new ones, and retire old ones. So, rule discovery is a continuous dialog with the business community and that's good.

If you are like most of us, you are likely to find that you begin to discover both rules and data together at first. Don't be confused. Data and rules, while they can be analyzed separately, are intimately related. In 1989, Fleming and von Halle prescribed an approach to logical data modeling that purposely collected and proposed related business rules along the way. The approach did not make a very formal separation between modeling the data and gathering business rules.

This chapter, however, makes more of a separation, by adding enough discipline to the rule aspect that it becomes a rule track.

What Are the Deliverables from Rule and Data Discovery?

The steps, guidelines, and techniques in this chapter focus mainly on the discovery of rules and data, hence the rule track and the data track. Repeated for your convenience are the deliverables for the rule track:

- Rules in business language categorized by conceptual data model entity or business object
- Rule repository and user guide
- Rule mining procedures and user guide (if applicable) to excavate rules from program code
- Prioritized rule sources (people and code)
- Rule stewardship program.

We present insights into alternatives for a rules repository and rule change and stewardship program in Chapter 15. Repeated here also are the deliverables for the data track.

- File/table inventory reports of existing files and tables also if migrating from existing systems

- Data subject description document

- Conceptual model (data and process and CRUD)

- Prioritized data sources (existing files and tables) if migrating from existing systems

- Information stewardship program

This chapter continues the development of a conceptual model and begins a detailed logical data model. You will need file/table inventory reports if you will be migrating or referencing data from existing automated sources. You will also, then, need a list of prioritized data sources should there be more than one source for specific data. While the information stewardship program is a deliverable out of discovery, this book focuses mainly on the rule track. For the reader interested in information stewardship approaches, we recommend Larry English's book and Web site.

What Are the Steps in Rule and Data Discovery?

This chapter contains steps, deliverables, and techniques for discovering the rule and data requirements so you can add them to other requirements to gain a full understanding of the target system.

Most of this chapter is dedicated to ways of discovering rules and rule-related information because these are the ingredients missing in other systems development approaches.

STEP 7.1: IDENTIFY RULE SOURCES

A *rule source* is a place to go to begin to find rules.

GUIDELINE 7.1.1

Classify rule sources into three basic types: person, document, code.

A person who serves as a rule source may be a business knowledge worker or business decision-maker. When you select a person to be a source for rules, be sure it is someone who knows the rules, knows how to research the rules, or is empowered to create rules for the target business event.

A *document that serves as a rule source* may be a procedure manual, legal contract, legal mandate publication, systems documentation, or business and system documentation.

We use the term *code as a possible rule source* to mean application source code, database code (such as triggers and stored procedures), data definition language, data manipulation language, and any source code that contains guidelines, computations, inferences, or constraints.

GUIDELINE 7.1.2

Identify the optimum mechanisms for interfacing with the different types of rule sources.

If your rule sources are people, you can interface with people in many ways, including electronic communications, video communications, voice communications, face-to-face interviews, and facilitated sessions. You will need to select the optimum choice.

If your rule sources are program code, you can inspect the code manually or you can use automated tools to assist. (Refer to the companion Web page for a white paper called "Discovering Rules through Business Rule Mining" for more specifics on how to excavate rules from code using a tool-assisted approach.)

CASE STUDY: STEP 7.1—IDENTIFY RULE SOURCES

Case Study Instructions:

- Identify appropriate rule sources for the business event Member Requests Entrance to the Park, specifically the use case between the member and the VCI passage system.
- Classify them into persons, documents, and code.
- Identify the appropriate mechanism for interfacing with the rule sources.

Case Study Solution:
For rule sources, you evaluate whether you need to involve representatives from the following VCI functions:

- Guardian Services (assists guardians in enrollments, provides communications to guardians, answers guardians' concern)—yes
- Member Services (assists members in entering the park and using all facilities)—yes
- Marketing (establishes pricing schemes and special deals, determines target guardians and members, monitors growth in guardianship and membership)—no
- Finance (invoices guardians, manages accounts/payable and accounts/receivable, payroll, and so on)—yes
- Credit department (coordinates outside credit checks, maintains internal credit issues and credit-rating schemes)—no
- Theme park department (manages the theme park activity)—yes
- Library department (manages the library activity)—no
- Tutorial department (manages the tutorial activity)—no
- University department (manages the university activity)—no.

To categorize rules sources, the above sources are people. Further, you are fortunate that VCI does not have legacy systems from which you need to discover or mine rules so there are no rule sources that are code. As for documents that can serve as rule sources, Guardian Services has produced a preliminary Member Enrollment Guide, but has not yet created a Member Entrance to the Park Guide. The credit department has many memos for you to read pertaining to guardian credit checking, should that play a role in entrance to the park. The finance department also has designed reports for guardian account analysis that you can look at.

As for how you will interface with the above people, you decide to have a facilitated rule and data discovery session with the above participants. So, you will study Chapter 8 very carefully for insights into how to plan, conduct, and conclude those sessions.

STEP 7.2: SELECT A RULE DISCOVERY ROADMAP

A *rule discovery roadmap* is a description of the journey you will take with the rule sources in search of rules. A rule discovery roadmap consists of the rule-related deliverables you will produce, a prescription for and samples of those deliverables, and steps for how you will lead from the starting point to interim deliverables to a set of rules.

Simply put, the reason you create a rule discovery roadmap is that rules do not come to the surface by themselves. They are usually hidden, not clearly understood, and sometimes, merely alluded to. You must lead business experts (or program and data inspectors) in articulating the rules or in finding them within documents or code.

The reason to craft carefully a roadmap by which to discover rules is to determine exactly what you will do as you interface with the sources for rules be those sources people, documents, or code. Therefore, you need to establish the rule discovery roadmap so you know how you are to work with the rules sources in discovering what the relevant rules are.

If your rule sources are people, the rule discovery roadmap assists you in leading business experts, in an efficient manner, from their current understanding of the business to a collection of relevant rules. You also want to do so in a way that can easily be learned and transferred to others so that the rule discovery process is repeatable and predictable. That's because rule discovery never ends. The business will want to retire rules, change them, and add to them over time. A rule discovery roadmap provides the foundation for doing so.

GUIDELINE 7.2.1

Select the appropriate approach rule discovery roadmap based on the types of rule sources for the project's scope; the organization's culture, including current requirements and analysis techniques that the organization is comfortable developing; and deliverables the organization is comfortable reviewing or can reuse.

Seek the answers to the following questions to better understand your organization's culture and familiarity with information systems development deliverables. What, if any, business process engineering or software engineering methodologies have been successful in your organization? Consider integrating the deliverables from these into the rule discovery roadmap. Because many of you follow object-oriented approaches, this chapter highlights how to proceed from use-case descriptions to rules. Even if you do not follow an object-oriented approach, you can still employ use-case descriptions and use them as a starting point for discovering rules.

What types of process-model deliverables have you created during scoping or in the discovery of system behavior? It is best to use process modeling approaches and deliverables that are familiar to your participants, although a roadmap from use-case descriptions to rules is a common one.

How does your organization prefer to gather requirements? Is there a preference for rapid application development, traditional waterfall development, or other? For rapid application development, you may want to incorporate the simulation of rules using rules technology during rule discovery activities. For traditional requirements gathering, you may also choose to simulate rules quickly, although documentation of rules into the rules repository may suffice.

Is rules technology to be part of the production environment? If so, you may want to learn more about the target product and the vendor's recommended approach to rule discovery. Then you can tailor your rule discovery roadmap and deliverables to those that lend themselves very naturally to a specific automated environment.

Does your organization endorse an enterprise (or large-scoped) information architecture? If so, be sure to include the deliverables from that architecture as a foundation for your conceptual model and detailed logical data model to leverage rule-sharing across organizational boundaries.

In this book, we name rule discovery roadmaps according to their starting points. You can deploy a mission-policy roadmap, which starts with business mission and moves to policies, then to rules. You can devise an event-decision roadmap, which starts with business event and proceeds to decisions, then to rules. Figure 7.3 illustrates an approach for this roadmap. You can craft a use-case-decision roadmap, which starts with a use case and proceeds to decisions, then to rules. See Figure 7.4 for an idea on how to do that. Or you can choose a process-decomposition-decision roadmap, which begins with a traditional process decomposition diagram and proceeds to decisions, then to rules. You can also create a workflow-decision roadmap, which begins with a workflow deliverable and seeks rules at various points. A data-analysis-rule roadmap starts with the data model and uses it to search for rules.

Table 7.1 depicts various kinds of rule discovery roadmaps and when each may be most appropriate.

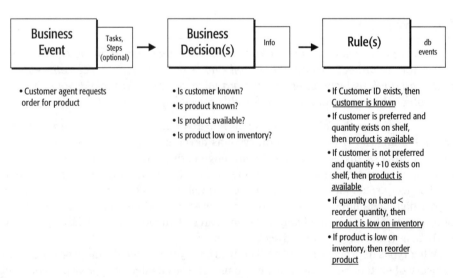

Figure 7.3 Event-decision roadmap.

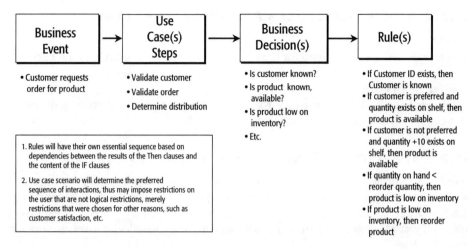

Figure 7.4   Use-case decision roadmap.

Table 7.1   Rule Discovery Roadmap Recommendations

RULE DISCOVERY ROADMAP	RECOMMENDED WHEN
Event-decision roadmap	The organization does not utilize use cases as a technique, perhaps uses structured requirements and analysis approaches or no formal approaches.
Use-case-decision roadmap	The organization already utilizes use cases as a requirements-gathering and analysis technique.
Process-decomposition-decision roadmap	The organization already utilizes process decomposition as a requirements-gathering and analysis technique.
Workflow-decision roadmap	The organization creates a workflow deliverables (such as swim lane model) or the target business area is a workflow intensive process.
Data-analysis-decision roadmap	The organization has an existing logical data model for the target system or the target production environment is to include a data-change-oriented rules product.
Mission-policy	Rule sources are high-level decision-makers and the project is part of a business-processing reengineering effort.

CASE STUDY: STEP 7.2—SELECT A RULE DISCOVERY ROADMAP

Case Study Instructions:
Select a rule discovery roadmap for the facilitated session on Entrance to the Park.

Case Study Solution:
You decide to embark on the use-case roadmap, but you will do so by isolating decisions because decisions can transcend a use case.

STEP 7.3: SELECT OR CONFIRM RULE STANDARDS

Before discovering rules, you need to have rule standards in place. In particular, you need to determine the classification of the rules you are looking to discover and manage. Specifically, you need to determine whether you will collect all classifications of rules or if you will collect only those rules that are implemented declaratively in your target technology.

GUIDELINE 7.3.1

Consider collecting all classifications of rules presented in Chapter 2, regardless of whether you can support them declaratively in your target environment.

Capturing all rules as declarative rules allows you to analyze and optimize them, regardless of how you implement them. Doing so is also likely to provide better insights into how you can best implement them.

GUIDELINE 7.3.2

Establish or confirm a rule classification scheme.

At the very minimum, you will need a rule classification scheme to help business people understand and express rules. Throughout this book, we use the classification scheme from Chapter 2 for this purpose:

- Constraints
- Guidelines
- Inferred knowledge rules
- Computations
- Action enablers.

GUIDELINE 7.3.3

Decide or confirm where to store rules during the discovery process.

Use your rules repository for the discovery process (see Chapter 15). An exception may be if you are conducting facilitated rule discovery sessions (Chapter 8) in which case you may want an interim storage mechanism for the session participants prior to entering the rules into the repository.

GUIDELINE 7.3.4

Agree on a rule-naming convention for the discovery phase that will be used also in the analysis phase.

It is much easier, with rules as with data, to adopt a naming convention early and stick to it. Review the naming conventions in Chapter 2.

GUIDELINE 7.3.5

Determine which rules to express in the data model, which to express as rules, and which to express in both.

The reason you want to determine this is so you can assign responsibilities properly. The data analyst will capture those rules that you decide to store in the data model or its meta data. The rule analyst will capture those rules that you decide to store as rules and not in the data model or its meta data.

We recommend that you capture as rules, separate from the data model, all rules that do not change the data structure. Likewise, we recommend that you capture in the data model or its meta data, those rules that change the way you would structure the data or those rules that have a standard representation within your data modeling tool.

With this in mind, it is most natural to include as data model constructs or data model meta data, relationship cardinality, optionality, and referential integrity rules and attribute uniqueness and optionality.

Likewise, it is most natural to include as rules (not as part of the data model), multiattribute or multientity constraints, attribute computation rules, inference rules, and attribute domain validation rules (sometimes known as domain definitions) and value sets. However, if your data-modeling tool has a natural place to store domain value sets, you may choose to store them with the data model.

GUIDELINE 7.3.6

Confirm that, for those rules you will express as rules rather than as data model constructs, you will first do so in free form natural language.

Regardless of the ambiguity of natural language, experience shows that it is always useful to express rules in the most natural free form manner for the business audience.

GUIDELINE 7.3.7

Determine rule templates for those rules you will express as rules in language.

Let's use the templates presented in Chapter 2.

GUIDELINE 7.3.8

When expressing rules in template form, be sure the terms are logical terms, not programming or database terms.

The terms in templated rules should match constructs in the logical data model because these rules serve as logical specifications to rule or application implementers.

GUIDELINE 7.3.9

Confirm or establish rule-stewardship procedures.

The concept of rule stewardship is discussed in detail in Chapter 15, Rule Management. For the purpose of this chapter, you need to determine who to hold accountable for validating discovered rules and how you will resolve conflicts. A formal rule stewardship program establishes permanent business people whose jobs include, within their area of responsibility, evaluating rule changes, validating new rules, and negotiating rule conflicts. If you do not have a formal rule stewardship program, you may want to establish an informal one among the project stakeholders for the purpose of rule discovery and later rule analysis.

GUIDELINE 7.3.10

Be prepared to capture meta data about rules.

Each organization will determine the kinds of meta data to capture about rules, depending on how the organization positions those rules. That is, are the rules for documentation purposes, for change management, or for initiating change? Refer to Chapter 15 for an overview of rule meta data that has proven to be useful.

CASE STUDY: STEP 7.3—SELECT OR CONFIRM RULE STANDARDS

Case Study Instructions:

- Determine which classifications of rules to capture.
- Confirm where you will store the rules during discovery and then during analysis.
- Decide on a rule-naming convention.
- Determine which rules will be documented in the data model meta data and which will be documented as stand-alone rules.
- Confirm rule templates for expressing those rules you will document as stand-alone rules when you will document both a natural language version and a templated version.

Case Study Solution:
As for rule classifications, you decide to capture all classifications: constraints, guidelines, inferences, computations, and action enablers.

You will capture them in a word processor during the rule discovery workshop and transfer them to a homegrown rules repository for the analysis phase.

You will follow the rule-naming convention presented in Chapter 2.

The logical data model meta data will house relationship cardinality, optionality, and referential integrity rules, as well as attribute null and uniqueness rules. The rules repository will house relationship optionality rules, attribute domain value rules, and all other rules.

You will use the templates mentioned in Chapter 2.

STEP 7.4: PLAN RULE DISCOVERY TIME AND COMMITMENT

You are now ready to plan your rule sessions, be they sessions with business people, with policy documents, or with computer code.

GUIDELINE 7.4.1

Craft an efficient schedule by which to carry out the interfaces with the rule sources.

When rule sources are people, you need to schedule access to them. Hopefully, these are important and busy people so you need to plan your time with them early and you need to have your rule discovery roadmap well defined so as not to waste their time.

GUIDELINE 7.4.2

Insure that the plan is optimal for the organization's culture, especially for those parts where business experts are to provide insight into and confirm resulting rules.

A suggestion here is to conduct facilitated sessions for rule discovery and subsequent rule confirmation. Another suggestion is to establish a rule stewardship program through which there is a natural hierarchy of rule issue resolution. This allows you to escalate disagreements on rules and resolve them quickly and appropriately.

CASE STUDY: STEP 7.4—PLAN RULE DISCOVERY TIME AND COMMITMENT

Refer to Chapter 8 for planning the workshop.

STEP 7.5: DISCOVER THE RULES THROUGH THE ROADMAP

This is simply the step by which you step through the discovery process, using the rule sources for finding rules. Let's walk through sample steps in the use-case roadmap:

1. Review with a business person the target use-case description.

2. For each step, determine if the system makes decisions to carry out the step. You may also decide whether, if the human makes decisions to carry out the step, you want to record decisions that are not automated. Sometimes, these decisions are out of scope, as you will see in the case study below.

3. For each step in which the system makes a decision, ask the business person to identify those circumstances for the business event, activity, or system response that are not acceptable. These will be constraints, those rules that prevent the business event from completing successfully. For example, perhaps the order-total dollar amount cannot exceed the customer's credit limit amount. Perhaps the customer must have a certain credit rating to pay by credit. Capture these as decisions, which means express them, as "Is *primary business noun* in *state x*?" Refer to Chapter 6 for more details.

4. For each step in which the system makes a decision, ask the business person about the kinds of warnings the system should give, even if it does not reject the

business event. Perhaps the order-total dollar amount is permitted to exceed the customer's credit limit for a preferred customer, although it should not be permitted without human input to that decision (human override to the warning). These are guideline rules. Capture these also as decisions, if useful.

5. For each step in which the system makes a decision, ask the business person to identify those circumstances that might occur and which do not reject the business event (constraints) or give warning (guidelines), but which alter the way the business event occurs. These questions lead to inferred knowledge rules. For example, if the customer pays for the order before shipment, does the order qualify for a 20 percent discount? You may want to abstract these up to decisions also, identifying a primary business noun and a corresponding state for it.

6. Ask the business person to identify those terms in the above rules that are calculated values. This leads you to computation rules.

7. Finally, ask the business person for those circumstances within a business event that should initiate another business event (hence, business process). You may need to ask the business person for these by asking for other circumstances that might occur that don't alter the original business event, but which require action by another. For example, if a product inventory amount dips below a reorder target, the inventory reorder process should order more inventory.

8. Start a list of issues, as they arise.

GUIDELINE 7.5.1

Don't be concerned about not catching all of the rules.

Remember that rule discovery never ends. Moreover, in rule analysis, you will check completeness of rules through the use of rule patterns and through data model inspection.

GUIDELINE 7.5.2

Don't be concerned if you find policies rather than rules.

Up to this point, the chapter assumes that you can capture rules from your audience. However, if your audience is comprised of high-level managers, you may not be able to capture rules at all, but may find policies instead. This is common and nothing to worry about. After all, discovery really aims to find knowledge and knowledge is not always clear, succinct, and detailed at the start. You may, in fact, discover a combination of policies and rules from your audience.

Your goal is to capture intellectual decision-making or computing capability in a manner that is as unambiguous as possible. If you capture only a policy, because the audience does not know the detailed rules, document the policy and seek corresponding rules from other people later. If you capture rules that are not atomic (they can be broken into smaller rules), don't worry about that now. It is more important to capture them in a form that the audience is comfortable with. You can always translate them into another form later.

An example is that a business person, for the case study, may state that the employee discount must be applied after volume discount and after additional member discount. This will resolve itself into several rules, but you don't need to do this resolution during discovery.

You can apply most of the guidelines in this chapter to policies as well as rules.

GUIDELINE 7.5.3

Establish a business-grouping scheme for rules.

A *business-grouping* scheme for rules is simply a way to list rules together that have a business connection in common. Recall that business rules are first and foremost for business people. It is important not to forget to provide a mechanism by which business people can group and analyze rules in useful collections. You may find it valuable to determine, with the business audience, the kinds of business categorization and grouping they would like to use in generating reports on the rules.

Consider connecting each rule to each of the following:

- Business events that are guided by it

- Business organizational areas that rely on it

- Information systems that relies on it

- Business value (see below)

When you discover and document rules, the rules may not be the best rules for the business event or for the business objectives. You need to decide whether the business people will rethink the rules during the rule discovery phase or whether they will do so later. Regardless, at some point you will lead the business in rethinking the rules. Hopefully this will become a normal part of improving the business. However, we discuss the optimization of rules in Chapter 10.

CASE STUDY: STEP 7.5–DISCOVER THE RULES

Case Study Instructions:

- Document or review the decisions behind the use case between member and the VCI passage system in the business event, Member Requests Entrance to the Park.

- For each decision, identify constraints. Do so by looking at each decision and investigating circumstances within the event that are not acceptable. Write the constraint rule in natural language.

- For each decision, identify guideline rules. These are warnings, which may arise during the event. Again, do so by looking at each decision. Identify circumstances for that decision that should lead to warnings, but which will not stop the event from proceeding. Write the guideline rule in natural language.

- Identify inferred knowledge rules. Start by going through each decision in search of circumstances, which may arise, leading to inferred knowledge. Also identify the conclusion of those circumstances. Write the inferred knowledge rule in natural language.

- Identify computation rules. Start by identifying data values that are computed for each decision. Make sure you either document computation rules for these or inferred knowledge rules that compute them.

- Identify action-enabler rules that initiate action external to the business event. Do this by noting conditions within the business event that may initiate external actions. Write the action enabler in natural language.

- Identify issues, if any.

- Name each rule.

- Write rules in template form.

Case Study Solution:
Fortunately, in Step 6.3, you already studied the use-case description and uncovered decisions behind it. Revisit Table 6.2. Keep in mind that this table is a working tool only. In your rules repository, decisions may be associated with (shared across) many activities. There appear to be six decisions that require supporting rules.

Search for constraint rules. Starting with the first decision (Is Member Login Accepted?), you ask the participants if there are constraints by which this decision would prevent the member from entering the park. That is, are there circumstances that must be true (or must not be true) about the member login for the member to enter the park.

Your participants indicate that, indeed, two constraints come to mind. First, the member login ID must be in the set of registered member IDs. Second, the member's password must be the correct password for that member. Refer to Table 7.2 to see these two constraints added to the Decision and Rules Table.

Table 7.2 Decisions and Rules for Business Event Member Requests Entrance to Park

DECISION	RULE	RULE CLASSIFICATION
Is member login *accepted*?	Input Member Login ID must be in the set of Member Login IDs	Constraint
	Input Member Password must match the Member Login Password	Constraint
Is theme park time *remaining*?	Theme park allowed time must be > 0	Constraint
Is homework *done*?	If answer to homework question = yes then add member homework bonus time to theme park allowed time	Inferred knowledge
	If answer to homework question = no then subtract member homework deduct time from theme park allowed time	Inferred knowledge
Is chore *done*?	If answer to chore question = yes then add member chore bonus time to theme park allowed time.	Inferred knowledge

Table 7.2 (*Continued*)

DECISION	RULE	RULE CLASSIFICATION
	If answer to chore question = no then subtract member chore deduct time from theme park allowed time.	Inferred knowledge
Is activity *done*?	If answer to activity question = yes then add member activity bonus time to theme park allowed time	Inferred knowledge
	If answer to activity question = no then subtract member activity bonus time from theme park allowed time	Inferred knowledge
Is subject grade *acceptable*?	If answer to subject grade question >= guardian grade threshold then add grade bonus time to theme park allowed time	Inferred knowledge
	If answer to subject grade question < guardian grade threshold then subtract grade deduct time from theme park allowed time	Inferred knowledge
	If answer to subject grade question < guardian grade threshold then add tutor bonus time to tutorial park allowed time	Inferred knowledge (Not first release)
Is guardian-billing status *sufficient to pay for member entrance*?	Guardian billing status must be sufficient for member entrance	Constraint
Is guardian-billing status *sufficient to pay for member entrance*?	If guardian payment method is credit and guardian credit rating is good, then guardian-billing status is sufficient for park entrance	Inferred knowledge
	If guardian credit rating code is "A" then guardian credit rating is good	Inferred knowledge
	If guardian is VCI employee then guardian credit rating is good	Inferred knowledge
	If guardian payment method is prepay and guardian prepaid hours >= member theme park allowed time then guardian billing status is sufficient	Inferred knowledge
	Guardian prepaid hours is computed as (to be determined)	Computation

It turns out that the member ID and member password are established during a different event, Guardian Enrolls Member. Notice that we made these two constraints rather than combining them into one (where member ID must match and the member password must match) because we want atomic rules. It is possible that, in the future, the rule for validating member ID may change independently of the rule for validating member password.

You move onto the next set of decisions, those about homework, chores, activities, and subject grades. Again, you ask the participants if there are any constraints relating to these decisions that would prevent a member from entering the park. The participants begin discussing that these decisions may impact the amount of time a member is allowed to spend in the park. In fact, inference rules begin to surface that either add or detract time from the theme park time remaining for the member. (You can choose to pursue these inference rules at this point or postpone them.) You decide to postpone discussions about inference rules but this discussion leads you to conclude that there is at least one constraint related to these decisions. That constraint is that, after these decisions are known, there must be theme park time remaining for the member to be allowed to enter the park. That is, if these decisions result in zero time allowed in the theme park, the member must be prevented from entering the theme park. Again, Table 7.2 contains this constraint.

Finally, you move to the last decision. Does the guardian have money *sufficient to pay for member entrance*? There is much discussion here, perhaps disagreement. Participants discuss various ways to determine whether the billing status of the guardian is acceptable for the member to enter the park. So, you conclude that there is at least one overriding constraint that comes to mind. Specifically, the guardian billing status must be acceptable (for member entrance). How it becomes acceptable seems to be determined by a series of inference rules. Table 7.2 shows this constraint.

You now search for guideline rules. Yet, your participants find no circumstances that give rise to warnings. Therefore, as yet, there are no guideline rules.

You begin seeking inference rules. Again, you start with one decision at a time and ask if there are circumstances that may occur that would lead to other circumstances.

Beginning with the first decision (Is member login accepted?), participants cannot think of related inference rules. What this means is that this decision is determined by two constraints and no other rules.

Moving on to the decisions about homework, chores, activities, and grades, again many inference rules resurface. For starters, participants indicate that if the guardian wants to reward a child for doing their homework, the guardian can specify that the child gets more time in the theme park. Alternately, the guardian can restrict a child who did not do their homework by subtracting time in the theme park. The same is true for members who do their chores or complete activities. You add these six inference rules to the Decisions and Rules Table in Table 7.2.

As for the school grades, the participants decide not only to allow the guardian to reward good grades with extra time in the theme park and deduct time for poor grades, but also to require tutorial time for poor grades. You point out that the tutorial feature is not available in the first release of the system, but you add the three inference rules to Table 7.2.

Moving on to the final decision for this business event (Does guardian have money sufficient to pay for member entrance?), more inference rules surface. You learn that, if a guardian is authorized to pay by credit and they have a good credit rating with VCI, the entrance is allowed because there is a strong likelihood the guardian will pay. On the other hand, if the guardian is not allowed to pay by credit and must prepay, the system needs to determine if the guardian has paid enough money to cover the time allowed to the member requesting park entrance. Finally, participants decide that guardians who are employees always have sufficient billing status for their members to enter the park. Thus, you now have three more inference rules in Table 7.2. (Hopefully, you are beginning to see how the rules guide the organization's behavior and that a change in rules can change financial and other results.)

Further discussion concludes that the decision (and corresponding rules) for determining if a guardian is authorized for payment by credit occurs outside the scope of this business event, in another business event.

You now seek computation rules. The following terms are computed: Member Theme Park Time Allowed and Member Tutorial Park Time Allowed. You have already identified the inferred knowledge rule that computes each of these. You also point out that Guardian Prepaid Hours is probably a computed value where the Guardian Prepaid Amount is divided by the hourly rate. Since participants are unsure of how exactly to compute this amount, you leave the computation rule undefined in Table 7.2.

You move on to action enablers that initiate external events. Your participants look for external events that might be initiated by this business event. There are none.

As for issues, your participants identify the following:

- Issue 1: How many characters should a member password be?
- Issue 2: Should members be required to change their password? If so, at what frequency?
- Issue 3: Should anyone at VCI know a member's password?
- Issue 4: Computation rule for Guardian Prepaid Hours is missing.

Table 7.3 contains the names of each rule.

Let's examine rule templates for rules 1 and 14.

Rule 1 is a constraint rule that states that "Input Member Login ID must be in the set of Member Login IDs." Referring to Chapter 2, you have five templates to choose from to express the constraint more formally. These templates are as follows:

- <term1> MUST HAVE <at least, at most, exactly n of> <term2>
- <term1> MUST BE <comparison> <term2>, <value>, <value list>
- <term1> MUST BE IN LIST <a,b,c>
- <term1> MUST NOT BE IN LIST <a,b,c>
- IF <rule phrase(s)> THEN <constraint of any of the above types>

The term that Rule 1 constrains is the Actor's Member Login ID, which is what the actor enters on the screen. So you would substitute "Actor's Member Login ID" for <term 1> in your selected template. Rule 1 states that Member Login ID must be in the set of Login IDs. Therefore, you must substitute for this phrase the name of an Entity.attribute set in your logical data model. Assume your logical data model has an entity called Member and that entity has an attribute called Member-Login-ID. The login ID entered by the actor must match one of the login IDs in this set of attributes. Rule 1 best fits template 3.

Table 7.3 Decision-Rule Table with Rule Names

RULE NAME	RULE CLASSIFICATION	RULE IN NATURAL LANGUAGE	RULE NUMBER
Member login ID park entrance constraint	Constraint	Input Member Login ID must be in the set of Member Login IDs	Rule 1
Member password park entrance constraint	Constraint	Input Member Password must match the Member Login Password	Rule 2
Theme park time remaining constraint	Constraint	Theme park allowed must be > 0	Rule 3
Theme park allowed time for home-work inferred knowledge	Inferred knowledge	If answer to homework question = yes then add member homework bonus time to theme park allowed time	Rule 4
Theme park disallowed time for homework inferred knowledge	Inferred knowledge	If answer to homework question = no then subtract member homework deduct time from theme park allowed time	Rule 5
Theme park allowed time for chores inferred knowledge	Inferred knowledge	If answer to chore question = yes then add member chore bonus time to theme park allowed time	Rule 6
Theme park disallowed time for chores inferred knowledge	Inferred knowledge	If answer to chore question = no then subtract member chore deduct time from theme park allowed time	Rule 7
Theme park allowed time for activity inferred knowledge	Inferred knowledge	If answer to activity question = yes then add member activity bonus time to theme park allowed time	Rule 8
Theme park disallowed time for activity inferred knowledge	Inferred knowledge	If answer to activity question = no then subtract member activity bonus time from theme park allowed time	Rule 9

Name	Type	Rule	Rule #
Theme park allowed time for grade inferred knowledge	Inferred knowledge	If answer to subject grade question >= guardian grade threshold then add grade bonus time to theme park allowed time	Rule 10
Theme park disallowed time for grade inferred knowledge	Inferred knowledge	If answer to subject grade question < guardian grade threshold then subtract grade deduct time from theme park allowed time	Rule 11
Tutorial park allowed time for grade inferred knowledge	Inferred knowledge	If answer to subject grade question < guardian grade threshold then add tutor bonus time to tutorial park allowed time	Rule 12
Guardian billing status constraint	Constraint	Guardian billing status must be sufficient for member entrance	Rule 13
Guardian billing status for park entrance inferred knowledge	Inferred knowledge	If guardian payment method is credit and guardian credit rating is good, then guardian-billing status is sufficient for park entrance	Rule 14
Guardian credit rating inferred knowledge	Inferred knowledge	If guardian credit rating code is "A" then guardian credit rating is good	Rule 15
Employee guardian credit rating inferred knowledge	Inferred knowledge	If guardian is VCI employee then guardian credit rating is good	Rule 16
Prepay guardian billing status for park entrance inferred knowledge	Inferred knowledge	If guardian payment method is prepay and guardian prepaid hours >= member theme park allowed time then guardian billing status is sufficient for park entrance	Rule 17
Guardian prepaid hours computation	Computation	Guardian prepaid hours is computed as (to be determined)	Rule 18

You use the template and substitute for <a,b,c> the name of the set of attributes to search:

```
Actor's Member Login ID MUST BE IN LIST <Member.Member-Login-ID>.
```

Rule 14 is an Inferred Knowledge Rule and states "If guardian payment method is credit and guardian credit rating is good, then guardian-billing status is sufficient for park entrance." There is one template in Chapter 3 for Inferred Knowledge Rules as follows:

```
IF <term1> <operator> <term2, value, value list> AND <again> THEN
   <term3> <operator> <term4>
```

Where operator can be:

■ Comparison (=, not =, =<, >=, <,>)

■ In, not in

■ Has quantity <at least n, at most n, exactly n> of

In this case, <term 1> is guardian payment method. Assume you have represented this in your logical data model as an attribute within the Guardian entity called Guardian.payment-method-type-name. The natural language rule has an operator of "is", which you substitute with "=". The <term 2> is the value credit so you substitute the value "credit" in your rule template, provided that this is how you will store that value in the database. (For example, if you stored only Guardian.payment-method-type-code, you would need to compare to a code value, such as "CR" for credit.)

Moving onto <again>, you see that another term is guardian credit rating. This, in your data model, is Guardian.credit-rating-measurement-code as an attribute in a Guardian entity. The operator again is "is", which you replace with "=". Then, the other term refers to the value "good" so if you are storing it that way in your database, you simply substitute "good" for "good." (Note that Rule 15 sets the value of Guardian.credit-rating-measurement-code based on a value of another attribute, Guardian.credit-rating-code. Here, you assume that there may be many other rules by which the inferred attribute of Guardian.credit-rating-measurement-code is set.)

Finally, <term 5> is "guardian billing status", which translates in your data model to an inferred attribute called Guardian.billing-status-name. And <term 6> translates into a literal of "sufficient". Your templated rule is:

If Guardian.payment-method-type-name = "credit" and Guardian.credit-rating-measurement-code = "good" then Guardian.billing-status-name = "sufficient"

STEP 7.6: AUTHENTICATE THE RULES

The phrase *authenticate the rules* means to make sure the rule is positioned to guide all relevant business behavior. Specifically, it means making the rule active where the business leaders want it to be and congruent with the business context discussed in Chapter 4. Essentially, there are two important aspects in authenticating rules: jurisdiction and consensus. Both should be part of a rule stewardship program. The first is full rule jurisdiction.

GUIDELINE 7.6.1

Verify full jurisdiction of each rule.

A rule's *jurisdiction* refers to the territory over which the rule guides behavior so that common business objectives are more likely to be achieved. The jurisdiction can be expressed as:

- Geographical locations where the rule is relevant (such as by state, country, continent, planet)
- Political boundaries over which the rule is relevant (such as corporate, division, department)
- Types of actors for which the rule is relevant (such as preferred customers, undesirable customers).

The second aspect of authenticating rules is identifying its governing parties. *Governing parties* are those people and organizations who can change the rule or whose consensus is needed prior to changing a rule. A governing party can be:

- Regulatory agency
- Overall enterprise
- Division
- Organizational representative
- End customer.

GUIDELINE 7.6.2

Gain consensus from stakeholders or approval from the steward for each rule.

This is part of a rule stewardship program also. Once the rule seems appropriate for guiding business behavior, once its full jurisdiction is determined, all stakeholders (those who are impacted by it) or a representative board of stakeholders should provide consensus if the rule is to represent consensus opinion.

In some cases, consensus is not appropriate, for example where a rule is mandated. This happens for regulatory rules and for rules that aim for consistency and change from higher political bodies.

CASE STUDY: STEP 7.6—AUTHENTICATE THE RULES

Case Study Instructions:

- Verify the jurisdiction for each rule.
- Identify the participants who need to approve each rule.

Case Study Solution:
Upon inspection, all participants agree that all of the rules should be enforced for all guardians and all members in all locations. Discussion ensued as to how guardian credit is established, since this may vary among countries. However, the establishment of

guardian credit is not within the scope of Member Requests Entrance to the Park, but merely the checking of guardian credit.

Member Services should approve the following rules: Rules 1, 2, and 3, since these relate to the login procedures. Member Services should also approve Rules 4, 5, 6, 7, 8, 9, 10, 11, 12, and 13, since these relate to how members answer their guardian's questions.

Member Services and Finance should approve the rules about determining billing status of guardians, which are Rules 14, 15, 16, 17, and 18.

STEP 7.7: GIVE THE RULES BUSINESS VALUE

You now drive the business context of the rules to completion. That is, you complete the business circle so that the rules have value. If possible, tie each rule to the policies it implements. Doing so allows future analysis of policies (do they continue to support changing objectives, for example) as well as analysis of rules (do they, in fact, support those policies).

GUIDELINE 7.7.1

Connect each rule to policies implemented by the rule, if known.

Provide a mechanism in the rules repository for connecting rules to policies. Policies don't often change (although they may change), but rules behind them may change more often to better implement the results desired from policy.

GUIDELINE 7.7.2

Determine the business value for each rule.

In the absence of formal policies, at least consider connecting rules to common business motivations:

- Be compliant with regulatory mandates
- Value (delight) to the customer
- Increase revenue
- Increase profit
- Minimize risk
- Open new opportunities.

While doing this is not as precise as tying rules to policies, it is a first step toward documenting why the organization is enforcing or suggesting a specific rule.

For example, suppose you have a rule that allows a preferred customer to take the last item on a shelf. This rule exists not for compliance to regulatory requirements, but to delight the customer. If someone requests a change to that rule, the rule steward should evaluate the change as to whether it has a positive or negative impact on delighting the customer or whether the idea of delighting the customer is no longer a priority.

Connecting rules by these kinds of business value is also useful for analyzing effectiveness of the rules. In one case, there was a rule aimed to delight a customer by making every conversation pleasant and complete. However, there was another rule aimed at increasing profit, which constrained the amount of time a customer service representative could spend in conversation with a customer. These rules were in conflict in that, depending on which one the customer service representative followed, one of the business values was possibly jeopardized.

Case Study: Step 7.7—Give Rules Business Value

Case Study Instructions:

- Connect each rule to relevant policies, if known.
- Connect each rule to other business motivations, if possible.

Case Study Solution:
The solution is shown in Table 7.4.

Step 7.8: Define Terms

Recall from Chapter 2 that a term is a noun or noun phrase with an agreed-upon definition. Terms represent concepts that the business can know about. A term can be a common term, industry-specific term, or organization-specific term. Examples of terms are: customer, customer credit code, and customer total dollar amount.

Guideline 7.8.1

Make sure there is a business definition for each term.

Avoid writing rules or policies for which terms are not well defined. If terms are not defined, the policy or rule will be ambiguous. When this cannot be avoided, keep a list of undefined terms. Do not consider a rule or policy complete until all of the terms are defined and the definitions are documented in an accessible manner. Make a note of the source of the term's definition, should you need more clarification.

In the past, definitions of terms were captured in a data dictionary. Today, analysts capture term definitions in data modeling tools, object modeling tools, and repository products. You will need to determine where term definitions are first defined, especially if you are creating many kinds of models.

Guideline 7.8.2

Create a synonym list for terms.

Often different participants in an organization will use different names for the same term. Start a synonym list, but have a standard term that you will use in all rule expressions.

Guideline 7.8.3

If you are creating a business object model, make sure each term has a home in it.

It may not be necessary from a rule perspective to create a business object model. However, many readers will feel comfortable with doing so during discovery. If so, make sure you have a class for each term or a class in which an attribute for each term will belong.

Table 7.4 Rules Tied to Policy and Other Motivations

RULE NAME	RULE CLASSIFICATION	RULE IN NATURAL LANGUAGE	POLICY IMPLEMENTED BY THE RULE	HIGH-LEVEL BUSINESS MOTIVATION AIMED FOR BY THE RULE
Member login ID park entrance constraint	Constraint	Input Member Login ID must be in the set of Member Login IDs	VCI must conform to all international, national, and local security regulations	Minimize security risk
Member password park entrance constraint	Constraint	Input Member Password must match the Member Login Password	VCI must conform to all international, national, and local security regulations	Minimize security risk
Theme park allowed time constraint	Constraint	Theme park allowed time must be > 0		Provide customer (guardian) value
Theme park allowed time for homework inferred knowledge	Inferred knowledge	If answer to homework question = yes then add member homework bonus time to theme park allowed time	Time usage in the park will be recorded	Provide customer (guardian) value
Theme park disallowed time for homework inferred knowledge	Inferred knowledge	If answer to homework question = no then subtract member homework deduct time from theme park allowed time	Time usage in the park will be recorded	Provide customer (guardian) value
Theme park allowed time for chores inferred knowledge	Inferred knowledge	If answer to chore question = yes then add member chore bonus time to theme park allowed time	Time usage in the park will be recorded	Provide customer (guardian) value

Theme park disallowed time for chores inferred knowledge	Inferred knowledge	If answer to chore question = no then subtract member chore deduct time from theme park allowed time	Time usage in the park will be recorded	Provide customer (guardian) value
Theme park allowed time for activity inferred knowledge	Inferred knowledge	If answer to activity question = yes then add member activity bonus time to theme park allowed time	Time usage in the park will be recorded	Provide customer (guardian) value
Theme park disallowed time for activity inferred knowledge	Inferred knowledge	If answer to activity question = no then subtract member activity bonus time from theme park allowed time	Time usage in the park will be recorded	Provide customer (guardian) value
Theme park allowed time for grade inferred knowledge	Inferred knowledge	If answer to subject grade question >= guardian grade threshold then add grade bonus time to theme park allowed time	Time usage in the park will be recorded	Provide customer (guardian) value
Theme park disallowed time for grade inferred knowledge	Inferred knowledge	If answer to subject grade question < guardian grade threshold then subtract grade deduct time from theme park allowed time	Time usage in the park will be recorded	Provide customer (guardian) value
Tutorial park allowed time for grade inferred knowledge	Inferred knowledge	If answer to subject grade question < guardian grade threshold then add tutor bonus time to tutorial park allowed time	Time usage in the park will be recorded	Provide value to Customer Open new opportunities (use of remedial services)
Guardian billing status constraint	Constraint	Guardian billing status must be sufficient for member entrance		Minimize financial risk

continues

Table 7.4 Rules Tied to Policy and Other Motivations (*Continued*)

RULE NAME	RULE CLASSIFICATION	RULE IN NATURAL LANGUAGE	POLICY IMPLEMENTED BY THE RULE	HIGH-LEVEL BUSINESS MOTIVATION AIMED FOR BY THE RULE
Credit guardian billing status for park entrance inferred knowledge	Inferred knowledge	If guardian payment method is credit and guardian credit rating is good, then guardian-billing status is sufficient for park entrance		Minimize financial risk
Credit guardian credit rating inferred knowledge	Inferred knowledge	If guardian credit rating code is "A" then guardian credit rating is good		Minimize financial risk
Employee guardian credit rating inferred knowledge	Inferred knowledge	If guardian is VCI employee then guardian credit rating is good		Provide employee satisfaction
Prepay guardian billing status for park entrance inferred knowledge	Inferred knowledge	If guardian payment method is prepay and guardian prepaid hours >= member theme park allowed time then guardian billing status is sufficient for park entrance		Minimize financial risk
Guardian prepaid hours	Computation	Guardian prepaid hours are computed as (to be determined)		Minimize financial risk

GUIDELINE 7.8.4

If and when someone is creating a rule-enriched logical data model (Chapter 9), make sure each term in each rule is an entity or attribute in it.

You do not need to create a rule-enriched logical data model during discovery, although this book advocates that you create one during analysis. However, as you capture rules, if analysts are evolving a rule-enriched logical data model, be sure the noun is a business entity or attribute that has already been defined and understood. If you have an information stewardship program, make a note of its steward.

CASE STUDY: STEP 7.8—DEFINE TERMS

Case Study Instructions:

- Identify terms in rules 1 and 14 that you will need to define.
- Provide reasonable definitions for those terms.

Case Study Solution:

Rule 1: Input member login ID must be in the set of Member Login IDs.
Terms:

- Member: a person between the ages of 6 and 15 who is enrolled in VCI park services (probably an entity in the data model)
- Member login ID: a preassigned character string that uniquely identifies a member to the VCI park system (probably an attribute of member).

Rule 14: If guardian payment method is credit and guardian credit rating is good, then guardian-billing status is sufficient for park entrance.
Terms:

- Guardian: a person over 18 who enrolls a member in VCI park services (probably an entity in the data model)
- Guardian payment method: method by which a guardian has been approved to pay for VCI services, most likely to include prepay and credit (probably an attribute of Guardian).
- "Credit": a value allowed for guardian payment method when VCI has obtained credit method, such as a charge card number (probably a constraint on the values allowed by guardian payment method, an element of a domain set)
- Guardian credit rating: represents a value assigned to a guardian after VCI does credit checks or as a result of good or bad guardian payment history with VCI (probably an attribute of Guardian)
- "Good": a value allowed for a guardian credit rating after credit evaluation, but you don't see any formalized rules for setting its value yet (probably a constraint on the values allowed by guardian credit rating and inferred by inference rules)
- Guardian billing status: represents a value assigned to a guardian so as to determine eligibility of building up additional charges, in this case it seems like part of a conclusion reached by formal rules (probably an inferred attribute of Guardian)

■ "Sufficient for park entrance": a value assigned to guardian billing status as a result of executing formal rules (probably a constraint on the values allowed by guardian billing status and inferred by inference rules)

STEP 7.9: UNCOVER FACTS

Recall that a *fact* is a complete statement connecting terms (via verbs or prepositions) into sensible, business-relevant observations. Facts represent all that the business can know about terms. Examples of facts are: a customer places order, a customer qualifies for a credit-code, and a customer is worth a customer total dollar amount.

GUIDELINE 7.9.1

Search for facts that give each rule the proper context.

Facts are difficult to find. You may not find them until a data analyst builds the detailed data model. But, for example, consider the following computation rule:

A customer order total dollar amount is computed as the sum of all line item total amounts plus shipping and handling costs plus tax.

The facts that lay hidden, that provide full context are:

■ Customer places order

■ Customer order is worth a total dollar amount

■ Customer order has line item

■ Line item has a total amount

■ Customer order has shipping costs

■ Customer order has handling costs (might be different from shipping costs)

■ Customer order has tax amount

GUIDELINE 7.9.2

If and when someone creates the rule-enriched logical data model, make sure all base facts needed for the rule are in it.

The above facts will become apparent when a data analyst organizes them as entities and attributes in a detailed data model. The connection of terms, facts, and rules becomes clear when you create a rule-enriched data model, depicting all information attributes, all knowledge (rule-created) attributes, and all rules.

This leads us to the next step, where we gather terms and facts into a structural model.

CASE STUDY: 7.9—UNCOVER FACTS

Case Study Instructions:

■ Identify facts behind rules 1 and 14.

■ Identify whether those facts are computed (by computation rules) or inferred (by inferred knowledge rules).

- Identify constraints on those facts.
- Begin identifying possible facts underlying the rules.

Case Study Solution:
You uncover the following facts:

- Member "is identified" by Member ID.
- Member "passes security check" with Member Password.
- Guardian "is assigned" Guardian Payment Method.
- Guardian payment method "can be" "credit". (Can it be anything else?)
- Guardian "qualifies for" Guardian Credit Rating.
- Guardian "earns" Guardian Billing Status.
- Guardian Billing Status "can be" "sufficient for park entrance". (Can it be anything else?)

You take a preliminary guess at the nature of those facts. Base facts are facts whose values are not computed or inferred by a rule.

- Member "is identified" by Member ID (probably a base fact).
- Member "passes security check" with Member Password (probably a base fact).
- Guardian "is assigned" Guardian Payment Method (probably a base fact).
- Guardian payment method "can be" "credit". (Can it be anything else?) (May be a domain constraint.)
- Guardian "qualifies for" Guardian Credit Rating (probably a base fact).
- Guardian "earns" Guardian Billing Status (inferred fact).
- Guardian Billing Status "can be" "sufficient for park entrance". (Can it be anything else?) (May be a domain constraint.)

Constraints on fact values that you uncovered so far include:

- Guardian Payment Method must be one of (credit, prepay, or what else?)
- Guardian Credit Rating must be one of (good, or what else?)
- Guardian Billing Status must be one of (sufficient for park entrance, or what else?)

A preliminary list of facts (connections among the terms above) for all discovered rules is:

- Member is identified by login.
- Member confirms identity through member password.
- Member qualifies for theme park allowed time.
- Member entrance session has answer to homework question.
- Member has specified by guardian homework bonus time.
- Member has specified by guardian homework deduct time.
- Member entrance session has answer to chore question.

- Member has specified by guardian chore bonus time.
- Member has specified by guardian chore deduct time.
- Member entrance session has answer to activity question.
- Member has specified by guardian activity bonus time.
- Member has specified by guardian activity deduct time.
- Member entrance session has answer to subject grade question.
- Member has specified by guardian grade threshold.
- Member has specified by guardian grade bonus time.
- Member has specified by guardian grade deduct time.
- Member has specified by guardian grade tutor bonus time.
- Member has tutorial park time allowed.
- Guardian qualifies for guardian payment method.
- Guardian has credit rating code.
- Guardian qualifies for guardian billing status.
- Guardian can be VCI employee.
- Guardian who is prepay has prepaid hours.

The next step here is to convert the above business-oriented terms into logical terms and create a corresponding term/fact model.

STEP 7.10: BEGIN TO DEVELOP A TERM/FACT MODEL

A *term/fact model* is a representation of the terms and facts comprising the vocabulary of the business. In the absence of creating a term/fact model, you can simply capture term and fact definitions in a word-processing document or repository. However, this book encourages you to create a model of the terms and facts, not just their definitions, because a model depicts more clearly how they are all related semantically.

In particular, in this chapter, you are interested in the vocabulary used to express rules. There are at least three different ways to express a term/fact model:

- Using a fact-oriented approach (such as object-role modeling)
- Using a business object model devoid of methods
- Using a logical data model (usually an entity-relationship model).

In truth, a fact-oriented approach that aims to create a model from disciplined elementary facts is often more intuitive to a business audience than an object (class) model or a logical data model. That's because a fact-oriented model is much like a diagramming of sentences.

The definition of a fact, in the context of a fact-oriented approach, is the same as the definition in our book. Therefore, sample fact types from the case study are: Guardian enrolls Member, Member requests entrance to Park, and Member is known by First Name. Figure 7.5 shows what a fact model might look like for these three facts. In this diagram, the ovals represent terms and the boxes represent predicates that connect

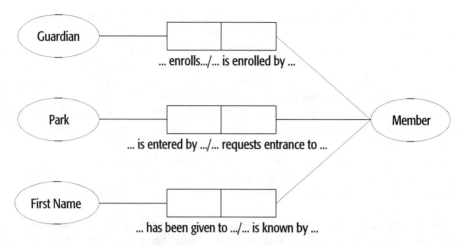

Figure 7.5   Sample term/fact model.

terms together into meaningful sentences. Notice that there are three facts and four terms. Notice also that Member is a term involved in three facts. Most important, notice that a term/fact model like this one does not differentiate between a term that is probably an entity (such as Guardian, Member, and Park) and a term that is probably an attribute (such as First Name). The distinction between an entity and an attribute is not important. What is important is that terms are named and defined and connected through facts. The business audience does not need to care about whether a term is to be an entity or an attribute.

In a similar vein, notice that the terms are not organized within object classes again because the business audience does not really need to care about object classes. The business audience simply needs to identify terms and facts referenced in rules and their definitions. The rest (organizing them into entities and attributes or object classes) is the responsibility of analysts or designers, not business people.

As you can see, a term/fact model can be a model that diagrams atomic sentence structures so that business people understand the terms and facts and their relationships to each other. This may be ideal for business audiences, although often the diagrams become quite busy.

If you are most comfortable with object-oriented techniques, you can create a business object model as your initial term/fact model, in which case your business object model depicts the terms and facts only, organized into object classes. However there is no need at this time to depict operations or methods for those classes. You are only concerned about terms and facts. A business object model as a tool for representing terms and facts is only a temporary solution. The reason is that you are not likely to maintain the business object model over time, because you are more likely to use it as a starting point for design. This means you may add to it infrastructure object classes (such as interface classes and control classes) where infrastructure objects are those needed to make software work. Thus, you are likely to evolve an initial business object model into a model more appropriate from which to develop software and less appropriate as one to represent the pure semantics of the terms and facts referenced in rules.

This book, therefore, strongly suggests that you develop a detailed logical data model (an entity-relationship model) as a foundation for your information architecture and that this model serve as your permanent, living model of terms and facts behind your rules. There are three reasons for this recommendation. First, a term/fact model may become too complicated very quickly for depicting terms and facts, although some tools can produce summary models. Second, the business object model is not usually a permanent, living deliverable. Third, the logical data model is usually a permanent, living deliverable and also lends itself nicely to the database design process, which is very important in this book for building changeable systems. Therefore, you can start developing this model at this point, representing terms and facts as entities, attributes, and relationships.

At the risk of being repetitive, it is important to emphasize that the purpose of an object (class) model and that of a logical data model are significantly different. The object class model is a blueprint around which to design and create executable system code, whereas the logical data model is a blueprint around which to design databases. These two different purposes are equally important, but each addresses a different challenge with different techniques. The confusion arises because both models need to represent the terms and facts of the problem or solution domain, but for different purposes. Because the semantic purity of the terms and facts is crucial to the integrity of rules, this book recommends that the logical data model be the source for term and fact definitions.

As introduced in Chapter 9, a logical data model is a philosophy and set of techniques for representing information requirements independent of how they are accessed, who accesses them, and whether or not such access is computerized. If you will not be designing a database for your target system, you should still develop a logical data model (as discussed in Chapter 9), but you need not include all relational considerations in it. You can keep it in a less technical and disciplined manner.

GUIDELINE 7.10.1

Tie each rule to the information it references.

During the discovery of initial system requirements, in Step 6.6, you may have created a CRUD matrix, which indicated information referenced by the system in servicing a business event. Now, in the discovery of rules and data, you take that idea one step further. You study each rule to better understand the information it references so as to perform its role in the decision-making behind the business event.

Remember that rules reference pieces of information to determine compliance to a constraint or a guideline, compute a formula, or qualification for an inferred knowledge rule or action-enabler rule. In your rules repository, associate each rule to those pieces of information (or knowledge, created by another rule) that the rule references in order to execute its logic. Doing so allows you to perform impact analysis should any of those pieces of information change in any way (data type, length, meaning, computation, and so on).

GUIDELINE 7.10.2

Tie each rule to the information it materializes.

A subtle, but most valuable (sometimes hidden) aspect of rules is that they can create information, called knowledge. Now you associate each rule with the knowledge it creates, if any. A computation rule creates a value for the computed attribute. An inferred knowledge rule creates an existence of an entity, sets a flag, or sets another attribute value. A guideline and a constraint and action enabler create a truth value. A *truth value* is a yes or no indicator denoting whether the constraint or guideline is violated or whether the conditions for action are met. Each atomic rule, then, creates only one piece of new information or knowledge. Tie each rule to this knowledge it creates so you can perform impact analysis. This will prove useful also as you move into rule analysis.

In summary, then, for computations, connect the rule to the attribute whose value it computes. For inferences, connect the rule to the attribute whose value it infers or to the entity whose existence it infers. For constraints, connect the rule to the entity or attribute that may violate it. For guidelines, connect the rule to the entity or attribute that may violate it. For action enablers, connect the rule to the action it enables. Consider creating a decision-rule-information matrix.

GUIDELINE 7.10.3

An alternative to tying each rule to the specific information it references or knowledge it creates is to group rules according to the data entity they are most closely associated with.

You can be very precise and devise a mechanism for normalizing the truth value of a rule to a data entity. Or you can simply group rules by the data entity that seems most intuitive.

Table 7.5 is a sample rule report from USoft based on the case study. In this report, business object is synonymous with data entity. The rule ID appears to have a numerical sequence within another grouping. The rule type is the USoft rule classification scheme. Note that they have assigned a useful description, priority, and a natural language definition of each rule. They have nicely associated each rule to the business motivation that justifies it.

CASE STUDY: STEP 7.10—BEGIN TO DEVELOP DETAILED LOGICAL DATA MODEL OR TERM/FACT MODEL

Case Study Instructions:

- Create a table that correlates each rule to knowledge it creates, if any.
- Create a table that correlates each rule to information or knowledge it refers to.
- Create the full detailed logical data model during analysis.

Case Study Solution:
Table 7.6 shows a table of rules to information and knowledge referenced as well as knowledge created.

Table 7.5 Rules per Table or Object in USoft's Teamwork

BUSINESS OBJECT	RULE ID	TYPE	SHORT DESCRIPTION	PRIORITY	MOTIVATION	DEFINITION
General	PRK013	Other Type	member communication	Should Have	BAN INAPPROPRIATE LANGUAGE	Communication can only be between a park ranger and a member. VCI monitors this communication for language content.
Invoice	INV001	Behavior	invoice date	Would Have	INVOICING POLICY	Invoice date is the first business day of the month.
Invoice	INV002	Restriction	one invoice a month	Would Have	INVOICING POLICY	One invoice is created per month per guardian, not per member.
Invoice	INV003	Restriction	account not in good standing	Would Have	INVOICING POLICY	An account is not in good standing if an invoice is more than 65 days overdue.
Invoice	INV004	Deduction	volume discounts	Would Have	DISCOUNT POLICY	Volume discounts are applied to current fees on a daily basis.
Invoice	INV005	Deduction	total charge for guardian	Must Have	INVOICING POLICY	The total charges for the month for a guardian are the sum of the charges for each member.
Invoice	INV006	Deduction	base fee	Must Have	FEE POLICY	The base fee for a park is the hourly fee times the number of hours spent in the park (rounded up to the nearest quarter hour).
Invoice	INV007	Deduction	base = final	Must Have	DISCOUNT POLICY	Without discounts base fee equals final fee.
Invoice	INV008	Deduction	total charge per member	Must Have	INVOICING POLICY	The total charges for the month per member are the sum of the final fees for each invoice item in a member section.

Park usage	PRK005	Combination	entrance park questions	Must Have	WEB REQUIREMENT	A guardian must enter "Entrance to Park Questions". More specific: <Document: Entrance to Park Scenarios.doc> A member cannot enter a park unless the enrollment process is completed including the credit check and the guardian has entered their desired "Entrance to Park Questions." Many mentioned that VCI does provide some examples or templates of questions to assist the guardian. </Document: Entrance to Park Scenarios.doc>
Park usage	PRK006	Combination	enrollment	Must Have	WEB REQUIREMENT	Guardian sets default time per park.
Park usage	PRK007	Combination	enrollment	Must Have	WEB REQUIREMENT	Default time can be changed any time.
Park usage	PRK008	Behavior	enrollment	Must Have	WEB REQUIREMENT	When a prepaid guardian attempts to allocate more time in the theme park than allocated in the bank, display a warning message.
Park usage	PRK101	Restriction	possible responses	Must Have	REQUIREMENT VERSION 1	Currently, possible responses on entrance questions can be: (Y)es and (N)o.
Party	PRK001	Presentation	enrollment	Must Have	WEB REQUIREMENT	Enrollment information may be entered by the guardian or by a park ranger on behalf of a guardian.
Party	PRK002	Restriction	guardian is a relative	Must Have	REQUIREMENT VERSION 1	A guardian may be a parent, grandparent, or other relative.

continues

Table 7.5 Rules per Table or Object in USoft's Teamwork (*Continued*)

BUSINESS OBJECT	RULE ID	TYPE	SHORT DESCRIPTION	PRIORITY	MOTIVATION	DEFINITION
Party	PRK003.1	Behavior	default application status	Must Have	CREDIT RATING POLICY	When guardian enrollment data is entered, online or by a park ranger, the default value of the guardians application status is (P)ending.
Party	PRK003.10	Behavior	mail entrance pass	Should Have	PROJECT REQUIREMENT	Once the application status of a prospective guardian is "Accepted", send a mail with the entrance pass (user/password) to a new VCI member.
Party	PRK003.2	Behavior	employee accepted	Must Have	CREDIT RATING POLICY	VCI employees signing up as guardians automatically get the (A)ccepted application status.
Party	PRK003.3	Behavior	prepayment accepted	Must Have	CREDIT RATING POLICY	Guardians with prepayment billing method get the "Accepted" application status.
Party	PRK003.4	Other Type	mail credit service	Must Have	CREDIT RATING POLICY	At the end of each working day, all data of guardians with the "Pending" application status are mailed to our credit service bureau, for the external credit check. This includes corresponding account data.
Party	PRK003.5	Instruction	credit service ratings	Must Have	PROJECT REQUIREMENT	When credit ratings are received (via email or snail mail) from our credit service bureau, these ratings will be entered in the system by our park rangers.
Party	PRK003.6	Restriction	credit ratings	Must Have	CREDIT RATING POLICY	Credit ratings can be: (E)xcellent, (F)air, and (P)oor. These values are to be selected from a dropdown list box.

	ID	Type	Name	Priority	Policy	Description
Party	PRK003.7	Behavior	poor credit rating rejected	Must Have	CREDIT RATING POLICY	Guardians with (P)oor credit rating get the (R)ejected application status.
Party	PRK003.8	Behavior	fair credit rating accepted	Must Have	CREDIT RATING POLICY	Guardians with (F)air or (E)xcellent credit rating, get the (A)ccepted application status.
Party	PRK003.9	Behavior	fair credit rating prepay	Should Have	CREDIT RATING POLICY	Accounts of guardians with (F)air credit rating get the (P)repay billing method code
Party	PRK004	Presentation	member enrollment	Must Have	WEB REQUIREMENT	A guardian must supply the following information to enroll the member: guardian name, address, social security number, billing method, payment information, method of communication, member name, member SSN, member DOB, relationship of guardian to member. Guardian info is shown on the Enroll as a Guardian task. The billing method and payment information are shown on the Account Info info task.
Party	PTY001	Restriction	birth is in the past	Must Have	CONSISTENCY	A date of birth is be in the past.
Party	PTY002	Restriction	member between 6 and 15 years old	Must Have	CUSTOMER POLICY	A member must be between 6 and 15 years old. A member is allowed to use the VCI Park from the day of his or her 6th birthday, until the end of the month of his or her 16th birthday.
Party	PTY003	Restriction	subtyping	Must Have	CUSTOMER POLICY	A Party is either a Member or an Adult.
Party	PTY004	Restriction	subtyping	Must Have	CUSTOMER POLICY	An Adult is a Guardian or a Park Ranger or both.

Table 7.6 Rules and Information Reference, Knowledge Created

RULE NAME	RULE CLASSIFICATION	RULE IN NATURAL LANGUAGE	KNOWLEDGE CREATED	KNOWLEDGE/INFORMATION REFERENCED
Member login ID park entrance constraint	Constraint	Input Member Login ID must be in the set of Member Login IDs		Member login ID
Member password park entrance constraint	Constraint	Input Member Password must match the Member Login Password		Member password
Theme park allowed time constraint	Constraint	Theme park allowed time must be > 0		Theme park allowed time
Theme park allowed time for homework inferred knowledge		If answer to homework question = yes then add member homework bonus time to theme park allowed time	Theme park allowed time	Answer to homework question Member homework bonus time
Theme park disallowed time for homework inferred knowledge		If answer to homework question = no then subtract member homework deduct time from theme park allowed time	Theme park allowed time	Answer to homework question Member homework deduct time
Theme park allowed time for chores inferred knowledge		If answer to chore question = yes then add member chore bonus time to theme park allowed time	Theme park allowed time	Answer to chore question Member chore bonus time
Theme park disallowed time for chores inferred knowledge		If answer to chore question = no then subtract member chore deduct time from theme park allowed time	Theme park allowed time	Answer to chore question Member chore deduct time
Theme park allowed time for activity inferred knowledge		If answer to activity question = yes then add member activity bonus time to theme park allowed time	Theme park allowed time	Answer to activity question Member activity bonus time

Theme park disallowed time for activity inferred knowledge	If answer to activity question = no then subtract member activity deduct time from theme park allowed time	Theme park allowed time	Answer to activity question Member activity deduct time
Theme park allowed time for grade inferred knowledge	If answer to subject grade question >= guardian grade threshold then add member grade bonus time to theme park allowed time	Theme park allowed time	Answer to subject grade question Guardian grade threshold Member grade bonus time
Theme park disallowed time for grade inferred knowledge	If answer to subject grade question < guardian grade threshold then subtract member grade deduct time from theme park allowed time	Theme park allowed time	Answer to subject grade question Guardian grade threshold Member grade deduct time
Tutorial park allowed time for grade inferred knowledge	If answer to subject grade question < guardian grade threshold then add tutor bonus time to tutorial park allowed time	Tutorial park allowed time	Answer to subject grade question Guardian grade threshold Tutor bonus time
Guardian billing status constraint	Guardian billing status must be sufficient for member entrance		Guardian billing status
Credit guardian billing status for park entrance inferred knowledge	If guardian payment method is credit and guardian credit rating is good, then guardian-billing status is sufficient for park entrance	Guardian billing status	Guardian billing status Guardian credit rating
Credit guardian credit rating inferred knowledge	If guardian credit rating code is "A" then guardian credit rating is good	Guardian credit rating	Guardian credit rating
Employee guardian credit rating inferred knowledge	If guardian is VCI employee then guardian credit rating is good	Guardian credit rating	Guardian

continues

Table 7.6 Rules and Information Reference, Knowledge Created (*Continued*)

RULE NAME	RULE CLASSIFICATION	RULE IN NATURAL LANGUAGE	KNOWLEDGE CREATED	KNOWLEDGE/INFORMATION REFERENCED
Prepay guardian billing status for park entrance inferred knowledge		If guardian payment method is prepay and guardian prepaid hours >= member theme park allowed time then guardian billing status is sufficient for park entrance	Guardian billing status	Guardian payment method Guardian prepaid hours Member theme park allowed time
Guardian prepaid hours	Computation	Guardian prepaid hours are computed as (to be determined)	Guardian prepaid hours	To be determined

Take a moment to appreciate the value of Table 7.6. Suppose the business decided to change the valid values for "answer to chore question" from "yes/no" to a list of chores the member has completed. The business would want to know which rules rely on the answer to that question and would those rules need to be reworded. You could select all of the rules that reference the "answer to chore question" to identify relevant rules for change.

Likewise, suppose VCI decided to offer free time to the park for certain situations. It may be useful to produce a list of rules that set a value to "theme park allowed time" to see which of those rules should change so as to add more time to the allowed park time.

If you do not capture this correlation in discovery, you may do so in analysis.

STEP 7.11: ADD CONCRETE SCENARIOS

You have been adding concrete scenarios throughout the discovery phase. As you uncover rules, it is important to be sure you can test that they are the correct rules for business results and, later, that the system has implemented them properly.

GUIDELINE 7.11.1

Verify that you have a scenario that will test each rule.

As you add rules, review and update scenarios to be sure each rule is tested. It is probably useful to keep track of which scenarios test which rules. This may actually decrease the cost and time during system testing since you will not need to test for full transaction loads, but only a full set of scenarios that will test each rule.

CASE STUDY: STEP 7.11—ADD CONCRETE SCENARIOS

Case Study Instructions:

- Review the concrete scenarios you have collected so far and associate each one with rules they test.

- Identify those rules for which you don't yet have scenarios to test.

Case Study Solution:
Consider Table 7.7, which correlates the scenarios with the rules.

Table 7.7   Correlating Scenarios with Rules

RULE	WHAT RULE IS ABOUT	BOB-KYLE	TED-PETER	TED-TRICIA	GEORGE-BRIAN	GEORGE-AL	JANET-NANCY
R1	Login ID	X	X	X	X	X	X
R2	Password	X	X	X	X	X	X

continues

Table 7.7 Correlating Scenarios with Rules (*Continued*)

RULE	WHAT RULE IS ABOUT	BOB-KYLE	TED-PETER	TED-TRICIA	GEORGE-BRIAN	GEORGE-AL	JANET-NANCY
R3	Password	X	X	X	X	X	X
R4	Time in park > 0	X	X	X	X	X	X
R5	Homework, yes	X	X	X	X		X
R6	Homework, no					X	
R7	Chores, yes		X				
R8	Chores, no	X		X			X
R9	Activity, yes		X	X			X
R10	Activity, no						
R11	Grade okay			X	X		
R12	Grade not okay, hurts theme park						
R13	Grade not okay, needs tutorial park		X			X	
R14	Credit guardian	X	X	X	X	X	
R15	Credit guardian	X	X	X	X	X	
R16	Employee guardian						
R17	Prepay guardian						X
R18	Guardian prepaid hours						X

This is an interesting exercise. Some rules are tested by every scenario, usually the basic rules that apply to every instance (such as login procedures). There are three rules for which you have no scenarios. Rule 10 deducts theme park time for a member who does not do an activity. Rule 12 deducts theme park time for a member who does not receive an acceptable grade. You do have scenarios for rule 13, which requires such a member to go to the tutorial park. You should ask whether rules 10 and 12 are relevant still. If so, create scenarios to test them. Finally, you are also missing a scenario to test rule 16, which deals with a guardian who is a VCI employee.

If you are missing scenarios to test rules, you will not be sure that the rules are implemented properly in the system. Also, you will not have a sure way of testing changes to those rules over time.

Scenarios are cost-effective because a set of scenarios that covers all rules allows you to test system enhancements without creating huge volumes of test data.

Considerations for Iterative and Parallel Systems Development

There is very little that is rigid in rule discovery. Expect almost all of the concepts addressed in this chapter to change over time, whether this occurs during the life of a system increment, your first release of the project, or afterwards. Concepts that may change are rule sources (new people, old systems, more rules mined from systems), rule roadmaps (no need to stick to just one), concrete scenarios (add to them, change them), rule jurisdictions (challenge them), and even rule consensus (encourage disagreements to test rules against business objectives). Therefore, formal or informal rule discovery is, by definition, ongoing, and hence a fundamental impetus for iterative systems development.

You should be able to add, change, and delete rules from the decisions that group them, test out your new set of rules, and continue to refine them. This is especially possible when using commercial rules technology. In fact, often you can test the rules without testing the rest of the application.

The most rigid concepts, by definition, are the terms and facts behind the rules. You cannot change the meaning of a term without wreaking havoc upon all of the rules that reference it or create it. Therefore, while iterative development can discover new rule sources and new rules, analyze them, design them, deploy them, and start all over again, the whole foundation falls apart when the underlying data semantics and semantically stable structure changes. This is why, again, a stable information architecture is required not only for iterative development, but also for eventual changeable production systems.

But the rules must be free to change at any time. And iterative development is a way to test that freedom. How long does it take you to challenge a rule, assess the impact of changing it, change it, and test that change?

Summary

During rule discovery, you dig deeper into tasks, looking for knowledge-intensive activities where decisions are made or computations executed. The activities themselves and their sequence are not yet important. Decisions and rules take priority as they represent executable thinking. Activities and execution sequence will wrap around the rules later.

Discovery ends where it begins, with business context. In this way, you solidify the reason for a rule's existence, the motivation behind instituting it, and the value it is expected to deliver to the business. After all, every rule costs money. Every rule should earn its keep. Every rule is an instrument of business change and an element of organizational intelligence.

Without a business rules approach, we have always addressed these requirements, but not as artifacts separate from data and process. As we separate the rules from other artifacts, we will be able to perform more advanced analysis of them and leverage new rule-oriented technology. Perhaps you can envision that a formal approach to fully understanding and managing business rules is very important to the intelligent enterprise.

Key concepts from this chapter are:

- Before getting started in discovering rules, you need to have business rule standards in place.

- You need to decide whether you will rethink the rules during rule discovery or whether you will rethink them later. Regardless, at some point you will lead the business in rethinking the rules.

- Hopefully, you will be changing rules often, be it adding, retiring, or updating rules. This is where your business-grouping scheme for rules pays off.

- Every rule should earn its keep by guiding behavior in predictable ways towards meeting business objectives.

The next chapter provides details on how to conduct rule discovery through facilitated sessions.

Discovering Rules through Facilitated Sessions

When you reach this point, you are ready to discover rules for your target business rules systems development project. Moreover, you are fortunate enough to be able to do so through face-to-face communications with business experts who have made a commitment to provide input.

This chapter provides steps and guidelines for gathering rules through a technique called *facilitated sessions*. Facilitated sessions are most useful and effective for situations where there is business value not only in discovering rules, but in gaining consensus that the discovered rules are the preferred rules. Therefore, facilitated sessions for rule discovery are recommended for processes and responsibilities that are split across multiple functions or individuals. Facilitated rule discovery sessions are also recommended even if you do not expect to discover different perspectives on the decisions and rules behind a business event. Because the facilitated rule discovery session uncovers how the participants envision the decision-making behind the business event, you are likely to find surprises and disconnects in the way people assume "things work." Therefore, the fastest way to surface and resolve these differences is to work through them with the relevant business experts together at one time.

Therefore, there are two sets of circumstances that should lead you to discovering rules through facilitated sessions. The first is when the business wants to operate with rules that have been approved via a consensus of a group of people. For rules that should not be consensus-driven, you will need to identify the organizational role or function that should have the ultimate accountability or expertise for those rules. The second set of circumstances that benefit from facilitated rule discovery sessions is when responsibilities for carrying out a business event are shared or split organizationally.

This chapter introduces the basics of conducting a facilitated session aimed at discovering rules. While you may apply facilitated session for the purpose of discovering project scope and nonrule requirements, this chapter discusses facilitation sessions focused only on the rules (with strong relationship to data requirements). This is not to say that you cannot, through facilitated sessions, gather requirements in multiple tracks, such as process, data, rule, and other requirements. However, for large projects, we have found that you will typically host many facilitated sessions aimed specifically at rule gathering and fewer sessions on the other requirements. In fact, rule discovery sessions should become part of the business culture as the rules are expected always to be changing. Therefore, this chapter focuses mostly on using facilitated sessions as a means to discover the rules.

The facilitation approach in this chapter is derived from the FAST facilitation methodology developed and taught by MG Rush Systems, Inc. You can find information about the FAST methodology at www.mgrush.com. Specifically, we use Gary Rush's ideas about session preparation, session parts, and roles, for example. We extend his methodology to focus more specifically on rule discovery. Even if you already have experience conducting facilitated sessions for other purposes, please read this chapter because the concept of rule discovery influences every step.

What Is a Facilitated Rule Discovery Session?

A *facilitated session* is a formal approach for hastening the process of collecting and gaining concurrence on topics under discussion. It aims to consolidate and confirm information, turn opinion into agreement, and evolve agreement into consensus for action. A facilitated session among empowered business experts exploits group intelligence and can arrive at very effective results. Therefore, a *facilitated rule discovery session* is a facilitated session that embodies the *process* for soliciting and documenting business input from session participants into a collection of commonly understood policies or rules.

A facilitated session is different from most meetings in three important ways. First, it is structured in a manner proven to achieve preplanned results. Second, its structure can be customized to meet the needs of rule discovery. Third, a facilitated session has very defined roles. The most obvious role is the facilitator who is responsible for the process of the session. A *facilitator* is someone who is trained to structure and plan the session(s), guiding it toward that objective. The facilitator, however, is neutral with respect to the output of the session.

The *scribe* (sometimes called a documenter) records work products created and decisions made during the session, without bias or additional annotations. The *session participants* are people who have business knowledge (which, in this chapter, means knowledge of the business event, its decisions, and underlying rules). The session participants are empowered to make decisions about conflicting or new rules. The participants come together trusting the facilitator to steer them professionally toward the goal of capturing agreed-upon rules. The session may include session *observers* who merely listen, learn about the facilitation process, or evaluate the facilitator and the process.

Roles in a Facilitated Rule Discovery Session

As you have seen, there are a number of roles involved in the successful execution of a facilitated rule discovery session. Those are summarized below:

Facilitator. Neutral person responsible for overall planning of the session(s), establishing the agenda, and guiding the actual session(s) toward production of the deliverables. The facilitator leads the session so that participants produce the basic content of raw rules. Final packaging of these results and distribution is beyond the scope of the facilitated session and not the responsibility of the facilitator.

Executive Sponsor. Leadership and financial sponsor of the business rules systems development initiative to which facilitated rule discovery is being applied. This person is responsible for overall scope and purpose, communicating support and ensuring expectations are properly communicated to participants. The executive sponsor may kick off the initial session, but does not normally participate, unless the sessions deal with policy issues for which the sponsor is directly responsible.

Methodologist. Person responsible for defining the rule discovery roadmap. This role does not participate in the rule discovery sessions regarding content, but does resolve questions about rule discovery, and rules in general. The facilitator may also be the methodologist, but may not be any other role.

Scribe. Neutral role responsible for recording the results of the sessions, and final packaging of deliverables. The methodologist in this role may assist the scribe. Participants review the session notes for accuracy only. The scribe must be familiar and competent with automated facilitation tools, and responsible for their effective use in the session.

Business Partner. The business manager who has been tasked by the sponsor and given responsibility for successful execution of the business aspects of the project to which the rule discovery facilitation is applied. Along with the technical partner, this person is responsible for facilities and scheduling, ensuring the availability of the executive sponsor and participants for presession, session activities, and final review of deliverables. This role may or may not also be a subject matter expert or stakeholder participant.

Technical Partner. The technical manager who has been given responsibility for successful execution of the technical aspects of the project to which the facilitated rule discovery is applied. This person shares responsibilities with the business partner regarding scheduling and availability of people. This role does not normally require a subject matter expert or stakeholder participant.

Participant. The subject matter expert and/or stakeholder assigned to participate actively in the session(s). This person possesses the knowledge and authority to define or refine business events, decisions, and rules under discussion in collaboration with the other participants. This person is responsible, with the other participants, for creation of the session deliverables.

Observer. A neutral party who may observe the session for the purpose of being informed, learning the process, or critiquing the process. This person is not allowed to participate.

How Is a Facilitated Session Different for Rule Discovery?

Facilitated sessions can be used for many purposes. All facilitated sessions have similar structure, roles, and ground rules. The differences in applying facilitated sessions for rule discovery are twofold. First, the methodology followed during the session is a roadmap specifically aimed at gathering rules in a group setting. Second, the ultimate deliverable is a set of rules to support the target business events.

A facilitated session for rule discovery differs from other facilitated sessions in four ways, in compliance with the four principles of the business rules approach:

- Separating rules by aiming to discover consensus-driven business rules and policies
- Tracing rules by requiring a rule analyst to focus on the life cycle of a rule and serve as methodologist
- Externalizing rules by expressing them in business language
- Positioning rules for change by including a data analyst to listen for terms and possibly uncover hidden facts.

Let's look at each of these differences.

The first difference supports the separating of rules by seeking to discover consensus-driven policies and rules. The second difference supports the tracing of rules by requiring a *rule analyst* to focus on the life cycle of a rule as it progresses in the session, from its birth in unstructured business conversation to formalized policies or rules. In rule discovery sessions, the rule analyst serves as the methodologist for the sessions.

The third difference supports the externalizing of rules by expressing rules in business language for a business audience. And the fourth difference supports the positioning of rules for change by adding a *data analyst* who listens for terms (possibly uncovers hidden facts) and prepares for the creation of a logical data model.

What Is the Purpose of a Facilitated Rule Discovery Session?

The purpose of a facilitated rule discovery session is to gather, evaluate, and gain consensus on an initial set of rules that should govern the business events to be handled by the target system. Facilitated sessions, because they are a disciplined group working session, are useful because they limit the possibility of gathering conflicting rules among the participants. In addition, facilitated rule discovery sessions accelerate rule capture and save time in reviewing and evaluating rules. In summary, the disciplined group discussions tend to yield better quality rules.

What Are the Deliverables from a Facilitated Rule Discovery Session?

Think of a rule discovery session as having three phases, the planning phase, the conducting phase, and the follow-up phase.

The deliverables of the planning phase of a facilitated rule discovery session are:

- Selected and documented rule discovery roadmap
- Session agenda
- Annotated session agenda for the facilitator
- Risks of the session and corresponding mitigation strategies
- Invitation letter to participants
- Completed checklist of logistics.

The deliverables of the conducting phase of a facilitated rule discovery session are dependent on the rule discovery roadmap. Using the event-decision roadmap (see Chapter 7), the deliverables are:

- Refined list of events
- Refined list of decisions
- List of rules (possibly stored in a rule repository)
- List of defined terms
- List of action items, assigned to a participant if appropriate
- List of outstanding issues, each one assigned to a participant with a date for resolution
- Other deliverables needed to arrive at rules, as needed
- Simulated rules, if possible.

The deliverables of the follow-up phase to an interactive business session are:

- Resolutions to open items
- Finalized formatted session results.

What Are the Steps In Planning and Conducting a Facilitated Rule Discovery Session?

This chapter presents an introduction to the steps in all phases of facilitated rule discovery sessions. Please keep in mind that this chapter is not meant to be a comprehensive reference by which to become a trained rule discovery facilitator. For an excellent and thorough grounding in facilitation, we recommend the FAST facilitation-training program. You can find more information on that at www.mgrush.com.

That said, simply stated, a facilitated rule discovery session involves three phases. The first phase, planning the rule discovery session, addresses the justification and process for the session, focusing on its desired deliverables. During this phase, the facilitator confirms the purpose and scope of the session, identifies participants, devises the roadmap that will lead participants to rules, creates an agenda for the session, anticipates risks about the session, establishes logistics for the session, invites participants, interviews them, and finally, briefs them prior to the session, if needed. The roadmap is the session agenda, without the introduction and wrap-up sections.

The second phase, conducting the rule discovery session, is the actual execution of the rule discovery roadmap that results in the initial set of rules. Conducting the rule discovery session includes delivering an introduction to the session, executing the rule discovery roadmap, and a formal review of the session itself.

The third phase, completing follow-up activities, is extremely important as it involves documenting the group's decisions and resolving open issues.

Figure 8.1 illustrates the details of discovering rules through facilitated rule discovery sessions.

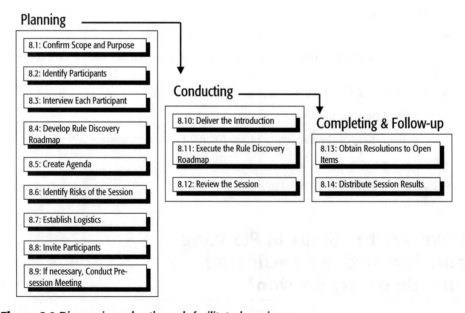

Figure 8.1 Discovering rules through facilitated sessions.

Phase 1: Planning the Facilitated Rule Discovery Session

Thorough planning and preparation are key to the success of any facilitated session. The purpose of this planning and preparation is to:

- Confirm management commitment
- Define purpose, scope, and objectives
- Develop preliminary estimates and schedule—maybe you'll need more than one session, for example
- Become familiar with the target business area
- Prepare participants
- Build agendas
- Determine deliverables for each workshop/session
- Determine approach
- Develop session estimates and schedule.

STEP 8.1: CONFIRM PURPOSE AND SCOPE OF THE SESSION

As a first step, you, the facilitator, should meet with the business and technical partners. If the project is purely a business initiative without a definite systems development effort, there may be no technical partner. However, the steps that follow address a systems development project, using a business rules approach.

While you can utilize facilitated sessions to establish scope for your project, we are primarily outlining the approach to deploying facilitated sessions for rule discovery. Therefore, the first step in planning for this session is to obtain or confirm, from the executive sponsor, a preliminary, high-level statement of the overall scope and purpose of the project and of the facilitated session itself.

GUIDELINE 8.1.1

The purpose and scope of the facilitated session should include the target business events and an appropriate subset of the business event that will fit comfortably into the session timeframe.

The purpose and scope of the facilitated session should be to capture rules for a subset of the target business rules system. Consider focusing on one business event or use case. As indicated in Chapter 7, identify the use cases for a business event. Develop a use-case description for each which describes the typical sequence as well as alternate sequences. Aim to uncover the decisions and rules behind each step in a use-case description.

Alternately, consider dividing the business event into an appropriate set of decisions. You can aim to discover rules for one decision at a time. In some cases, a business event may involve one major decision. This might be the case if a business event is very simple. For example, consider this business event: a request by a customer to see if a product is in stock. In this case, there is one decision: Is the product in stock? One way to slice this business event and decision into smaller pieces is to consider the conditions that are needed (on the If side of an inference rule) to arrive at the results (on the Then side of an inference rule) where the result is either "in stock" or "out of stock." The facilitated session could start by identifying the conditions to be evaluated and then move to consider all possible tests on those conditions. In this case, conditions may be:

- Is customer of preferred status?
- Is customer an employee?
- Is customer a shareholder?
- Is quantity-on-hand above special-customer-limit?
- Is quantity-on-hand above normal-customer-limit?

You can also decide to focus on certain conditions that may occur during the course of the business event.

CASE STUDY: STEP 8.1—CONFIRM PURPOSE AND SCOPE OF SESSION

Case Study Instructions:

- Assume you are planning your first facilitated rule discovery session for the VCI case study. The sponsor is the CEO. Together, you decide to limit the focus of the first rule discovery session to one business event and one of its subtasks.

Case Study Solution:
Scope of first facilitated rule discovery session:

- Business event: Enroll Member
- Subtask: Check Guardian Credit

Purpose of first facilitated rule discovery session:

- Capture all decisions and rules for checking guardian credit.

STEP 8.2: IDENTIFY PARTICIPANTS

The project will require a business partner and technical partner, although selection of partners may not, in fact, be final until planning is complete. The business and technical partners may then recommend participants whom the executive sponsor approves. The participants, in interviews, may make suggestions for yet additional useful participants. Depending on the organization, the partners will accept or adjust the modified list of possible participants and obtain final approval from the executive sponsor.

GUIDELINE 8.2.1

Be sure the participants represent the full business breadth behind the rules.

If multiple departments or business units may be involved in setting or following the underlying rules, be sure each is represented.

GUIDELINE 8.2.2

Be sure that participants are familiar with their business area, have access to the rules required to execute target business events, and are empowered to discuss and resolve rule inconsistencies or issues.

Participants must be able to participate actively in the session for the session to be productive.

CASE STUDY: STEP 8.2—IDENTIFY PARTICIPANTS

Case Study Instructions:

- For the initial rule discovery session, you evaluate the organization chart for VCI. While VCI is a virtual company, it has the following organizational functions, determine who should be represented at the rule discovery session:

Guardian Services. Assists guardians in enrollments, provides communications to guardians, answers guardians' concern.

Member Services. Assists members in entering the park and using all facilities.

Marketing. Establishes pricing schemes and special deals, determines target guardians and members, monitors growth in guardianship and membership.

Finance. Invoices guardians, manages accounts payable and accounts receivable, payroll, and so on.

Credit department. Coordinates outside credit checks, maintains internal credit issues and credit-rating schemes.

Theme Park department. Manages the theme park activity.

Library department. Manages the library activity.

Tutorial department. Manages the tutorial activity.

University department. Manages the university activity.

- Determine the title of each attendee who should attend from each organizational function.

Case Study Solution:
The latter three functions do not exist yet as these are future offerings. The Member Services function may not have much involvement in guardian credit checking. Therefore, the functions that should attend are: Guardian Services, Finance, Marketing, and Credit department.

  Because VCI is a new business, many of the decisions and rules have not yet been determined, although some policies have been set. To be sure that participants are empowered to set initial rules, the participants should be the lead manager of each of the three participating functions or should be a designee that the lead manager has empowered with decision-making authority.

STEP 8.3: INTERVIEW EACH PARTICIPANT

There are two purposes for interviews with participants. The first is to establish your understanding of the target scope and of the participants. The second is to validate that you have the right participants.

GUIDELINE 8.3.1

Brief each participant on the purpose and scope of the facilitated session, with emphasis on the rule discovery methodology and their role in that process.

In particular, ask each participant about:

- Their role in the target business scope
- Their concerns about the session, or issues/obstacles they think may impact it or its results
- Their expectations for the session
- Their opinion on who should and shouldn't attend, and why
- Any schedule conflicts. Even though the time and final agenda for the session may not be cast in stone at this point, you should have a general sense of it and know approximately when it will be final.

Provide each participant with a summary of the facilitated session approach and roles involved should also be provided. In addition, ask each participant to bring to the session relevant materials, such as report samples, etc.

If there is also a project team who is responsible for requirements, analysis and design of the system, separate from the participants, interview the requirements team, too. You may be able to interview the lead players on the requirements team as a group.

CASE STUDY: STEP 8.3–INTERVIEW EACH PARTICIPANT

Case Study Instructions:

- Document the interview with the head of the Credit department, Greg.

Case Study Solution:

- Name: Greg
- Date of interview: September 1, 2001
- Title: Vice President, Credit Department
- Role: Set credit limits, set credit ratings, coordinate outside credit searches, publish current list of bad credit guardians
- Concerns: Guardian Services is likely to want to be more lenient with guardian credit. Finance will be less lenient. Marketing will also want very lenient credit rules so as to expand the market.
- Expectations: The decisions behind checking the guardian credit are likely to be straightforward, but the rules may become controversial. Greg hopes that his opinion on rules is the one that the group approves.

- Who should and should not attend: Greg wishes that Mike, of the Finance department, were attending the session for support. Greg is not sure that Art, of the Marketing department should be attending.

- Schedule conflicts: not available for 5 days after payments due since he is very busy then updating the poor credit guardian list with those who are late with payments.

STEP 8.4: DEVELOP RULE DISCOVERY ROADMAP

In this step, you select the rule discovery roadmap that you believe suits the target audience. Chapter 7 presented various rule discovery roadmaps, which are simply the steps, deliverables, and techniques by which you proceed from a business starting point to a set of rules. The business starting point can be a business event, a business process, a use case, or another business concept familiar to your audience.

GUIDELINE 8.4.1

Confirm the purpose to be served by the rules to be discovered.

With the sponsor and partners, discuss whether the session aims to:

- Share rules among participants
- Find or resolve consistency in rules among participants
- Identify areas where there should be inconsistency in rules
- Find or resolve consistency in business objectives
- Create rules for new processes where there currently are none.

GUIDELINE 8.4.2

Confirm the classifications of rules you are to discover in the facilitated rule discovery session.

Revisit the rule classification scheme in Chapter 2. Confirm those classifications to be discussed in the session.

GUIDELINE 8.4.3

For those classifications, be prepared with rule templates.

The rule templates (with guidelines for how to use them) will educate the participants in how to express rules in a consistent manner. Revisit the rule templates in Chapter 2.

GUIDELINE 8.4.4

Select a rule discovery roadmap that will work best with your participants.

For a facilitated rule discovery session it is even more important to carefully define your rule discovery roadmap. You have limited time to spend with all the right participants, so you want to be extremely efficient. To be efficient, you need a rule discovery roadmap that you can walk through with participants comfortably and to which they can easily relate. It must be compatible with the organization's culture. Most importantly, you want to capture the rules, evaluate them for quality as a group, and tie them to business context and metrics. After all, herein lies the true business value in a business rules approach.

GUIDELINE 8.4.5

Draw a flowchart diagram depicting the rule discovery process for the session. Use this throughout the session.

This is extremely useful to reorient intense rule discovery conversations and get the participants back on track.

GUIDELINE 8.4.6

Decide on a rules repository for use during the rule discovery session.

If you will be using a formal rules repository for rule management, you can enter discovered rules directly into it and display rule entry screens on the wall. Then, at the convenient times, you can generate rule reports for review by participants.

Another alternative is simply to write rules on large sheets of paper hung up on walls around the room. During the process, the scribe or a rule analyst can enter the rules into a formal rules repository or rule database or rule document.

GUIDELINE 8.4.7

Investigate usefulness and availability of commercial rules technology for simulating rule sets.

A very successful approach is to have a database designer and rule implementer attend the facilitated session. Afterwards, these two people can create a prototype application in which the discovered rules execute against test data. A demonstration of the prototype can be considered a session deliverable.

CASE STUDY: STEP 8.4—DEVISE RULE DISCOVERY ROADMAP

Case Study Instructions:

- Determine, with the sponsor and partners, whether the goal is to collect rules that are to be shared among participating groups, consistent among the groups, allowed to be inconsistent, to support consistent business objectives, and whether you are to craft rules for new processes.
- Determine the classifications of rules to capture.
- Create appropriate rule templates.
- Select a rule discovery roadmap.
- Decide on a rules repository for the sessions.

Case Study Solution:
The CEO ordains that you are to aim for consistency among participants wherever consistency makes business sense. Where it does not make business sense, you are to document that.

After discussions with the CEO and the participants, you decide to capture:

- Computations
- Inferences
- Constraints
- Action enablers
- Guidelines (lower priority)

You will use the rule templates in Chapter 2.

You select the event-decision roadmap and customize it for this session. This means, your rule discovery roadmap will lead your participants as follows:

- Review the target business event and its subtask under discussion.
- Review and refine a list of business metrics for measuring the effectiveness of the target business event or its underlying process.
- Walk through the business event, its tasks and steps.
- Identify the decisions made on behalf of each task or step.
- Uncover rules behind those decisions as constraints, guidelines, inferred knowledge, computations, and action enablers.
- Define terms in the rules. (You may want to have a logical data model available, if there is one.)
- Identify concrete scenarios if some come to mind.
- Tie each rule to a business policy, if possible.

You decide simply to write the rules on flip charts positioned throughout the room. The scribe will capture these in an electronic document for distribution. For the second session, you decide to investigate use of rules technology to simulate the rules. At that session, you will give a demonstration of how the first set of captured rules behaves in a rule product. For the second session, then, you will capture rules on the flip charts and also in the rules technology for immediate viewing of a resulting system.

STEP 8.5: CREATE THE AGENDA

As you develop more information about the participants, the overall background of the project, and the expectations for the deliverables, shape a specific agenda for the session or series of sessions, based on the rule discovery roadmap.

GUIDELINE 8.5.1

Create a separate copy of the session agenda for your own contingency notes and details on how you will approach and conduct each step.

Once you finalize the agenda, create an annotated version with special instructions to yourself. Specifically, include full details on how you will conduct each agenda step, including a breakdown of the substeps you will take, if any, and expected time for each. Include ideas on issues or situations that may arise and how you plan to handle them.

Be sure it includes estimated timeframes for each part of the agenda and descriptions for all deliverables.

The agenda is truly the responsibility of the facilitator. You may wish to review the agenda with the business and technical partners, but you, as the facilitator, must be comfortable with the agenda.

CASE STUDY: STEP 8.5—CREATE THE AGENDA

Case Study Instructions:

Create an agenda for the first rule discovery session.

Case Study Solution:
You craft the following agenda:

9:00–9:30	Introduction
9:30–10:00	CEO welcome
10:00–10:15	Review agenda and ground rules
10:15–10:30	Break
10:30–11:00	Business event, metrics
11:00–12:00	Decisions
12:00–1:00	Lunch
1:00–5:00	Rules

STEP 8.6: IDENTIFY RISKS OF THE SESSION

The facilitator and partners must also identify possible risks associated with the session(s). These include risks associated with cultural issues, such as organizational size and complexity. Risks include logistical issues, political issues, and those associated with the newness and complexity of project. Risks also include issues associated with the newness and complexity of the rule discovery roadmap and concerns about the skill and agendas of the participants.

GUIDELINE 8.6.1

For each issue identified, a risk mitigation strategy needs to be identified, and referenced in the annotated agenda as needed.

CASE STUDY: STEP 8.6—IDENTIFY RISKS OF THE SESSION

Case Study Instructions:

- Identify risks for the first session.
- Identify a risk mitigation strategy for each risk.

Case Study Solution:
After the interviews, you document the following likely risks:

- Different functions may have different and conflicting rules.
- Some rules may not be under the jurisdiction of the participants.

- A participant may not be able or willing to attend the full session.
- A participant may not be qualified to address the decisions and rules.
- Some rules may be guidelines only and not enforced.
- Business terminology may be different among participants, making rule expression difficult.
- New rules may require organizational change.
- New rules may require commitment of partnerships with the outside world.
- Data behind a rule may not be available or dependable.
- The conflicting objectives of some participants may generate the need for special management and resolution approaches.
- In rare cases, it may be determined that someone identified as a participant may, based on initial fact-finding, be expected to be more disruptive than helpful to the process and should not attend.

You document the risk mitigation strategies in Table 8.1.

Table 8.1 Risk Mitigation Strategies

RISK ID	RISK	MITIGATION
Risk 1	Different participating functions may have different and conflicting rules.	Rules are tied eventually to objectives. Determination is made as to whether the functions have different objectives and, if so, whether those objectives are conflicting.
Risk 2	Some rules may not be under the jurisdiction of the participants.	Rules outside the participant jurisdiction are taken to the executive steering committee.
Risk 3	A participant may not be able or willing to attend the entire session.	The facilitator requests a replacement participant.
Risk 4	A participant may not be qualified to address the decisions and rules.	The facilitator requests a replacement participant.
Risk 5	Some rules may be guidelines and not enforced.	Discussions determine whether the rule should enable human decision or whether consistent enforcement is needed.
Risk 6	Business terminology may be different among participants, making rule expression difficult.	Standardized terms must be used in rules.

continues

Table 8.1 Risk Mitigation Strategies (*Continued*)

RISK ID	RISK	MITIGATION
Risk 7	New rules may require organizational change.	Rules requiring organizational change are submitted to the executive steering committee.
Risk 8	There may be disagreement among participants on rules.	Plan specific conflict resolutions techniques (such as methods of voting and of counting votes) in advance, and a clear idea as to what types of conflicts are to be resolved in the session, which are to become action items for escalation to the steering committee, and which are to be the subject of action items for further research by one or more of the participants.
Risk 9	New rules may require commitment of partnerships with the outside world.	Rules requiring external change are submitted to the executive steering committee for approval.
Risk 10	Data behind a rule may not be available or dependable.	Data issues are documented and brought to the executive steering committee.
Risk 11	A participant is disruptive.	The facilitator requests a replacement.

STEP 8.7: ESTABLISH LOGISTICS

As the agenda and participants are finalized, so too must logistics for the session(s) be decided. This includes ensuring that proper facilities and material are available, and that all participants are scheduled and prepared with the appropriate materials.

GUIDELINE 8.7.1

If possible, arrange to hold the session offsite.

Offsite rule discovery sessions are the most productive because participants are not easily distracted by other work duties. If need be, others can reach them in emergency situations via beepers or cell phones (but not *during* the session). Be sure to publish a phone number where participants can receive messages and to arrange for Internet or email connections during breaks.

GUIDELINE 8.7.2

Choose a room layout most conducive to rule discovery sessions.

The room can be set up to encourage different communication styles. For example, a room set up as a classroom encourages instructor-student discussions, but mostly instructor presentation. This is least optimal for facilitated sessions. The best arrangement is likely to be a room arranged with tables in a horseshoe formation, which encourages equal participation. The facilitator can stand at the center of the horseshoe. This option may prove most valuable if there will be various flip charts and wall hangings for participants to be viewing during the session.

GUIDELINE 8.7.3

Create a checklist of room preparation and scheduling actions necessary so the meeting runs smoothly in terms of logistics and facilities.

Use the following list as a starting point:

- Address, building, room, sign-in requirements; also notify security desk for visitor passes, if needed
- Room size, ventilation, lighting, furniture, and layout appropriate (u-shaped layout of tables around center area for facilitation visuals)
- Schedule for meals, refreshments, including adequate coffee and water (don't give cookies and sweets in the afternoon; give fruit, cheese, nuts, etc.)
- Material sent in advance, handouts, schedule
- Directions to the location
- Accommodations, transportation
- Materials
- White board(s)
- Flip chart(s) and easels
- Numerous colored markers appropriate to the surface(s)
- Marker clean-up supplies (erasers, fluids, paper towels)
- Visual display equipment
- Handouts for the participants
- Paper and pens for the participants
- Name tents
- Facilitation hardware and software availability and setup as appropriate; also ensure it is functioning
- Adhesive tape for taping up flip-chart pages
- Sufficient wall space for these (and check that it can be used for this purpose)
- Magnetic or self-adhering paper, or plastic notes or erasable surface objects for modeling data, workflow, etc.

GUIDELINE 8.7.4

Inspect, approve, and become familiar with the room prior to the session.

This guideline may sound trivial, but there should be no logistical surprises for the facilitator. The facilitator, during the session, will be most effective spending all energy on the process of the session.

GUIDELINE 8.7.5

Meet with the scribe and other people to discuss their participation during the session.

The facilitator should meet with the scribe(s), as well as attending business analysts and data analysts who may be acting as methodologists or observers, to ensure they understand their roles in the session. The scribes record, during the session, only what is covered and agreed upon by the group. The facilitator also ensures that any special facilitation tools, such as facilitation software, is well understood and will be effectively utilized. The rule analyst captures, by writing down on large sheets for all to see and posting these about, raw candidate rule statements or facts that surface. The rule analyst or data analyst jots down nouns (candidate terms) as they are mentioned.

STEP 8.8: INVITE PARTICIPANTS

GUIDELINE 8.8.1

Inform the participants that they have been chosen and that you will be interviewing them.

The notification of participation should come from the executive sponsor. In it, the sponsor should indicate support for the facilitation process and the interviews that occur in preparation for it.

GUIDELINE 8.8.2

Create the invitation as a letter from the executive sponsor to the participants, requesting full cooperation from the participants.

Such a letter asserts support for the approach and summarizes the expected deliverables. Send this out at the conclusion of the interviews. Ideally, send the invitation out a week in advance of the session. Therefore, aim to complete the session planning a week or two before the session is anticipated to take place. Include in the invitation the final agenda, schedule, location, purpose, scope, objectives, constraints, and list of participants.

STEP 8.9: IF NECESSARY, CONDUCT A PRESESSION MEETING

GUIDELINE 8.9.1

If the rule discovery roadmap is complex, the participants are new to facilitation or their roles in it, or the target system is complex, conduct a presession briefing.

Keep in mind, though, that a complex agenda may be an indicator that you need to refine the roadmap or assign homework prior to the session. The purpose of the session and its agenda should be to facilitate the pooling of knowledge and consensus decision-making, without being distracted by complexities of technique.

If you conduct a presession meeting to review the rule discovery roadmap, be sure the presession meeting happens within a few days of the facilitated session. Otherwise, the participants are likely to forget what you have taught them about rules and rule discovery.

CASE STUDY: STEP 8.9—CONDUCT A PRESESSION

Case Study Instructions:

- Suggest an appropriate presession agenda.

Case Study Solution:

You schedule a 1-hour presession the morning before the rule discovery session. At the presession, you will cover:

- What a business rules system is.
- What a business rule is, with samples from VCI.
- The relationship of business events, decisions, rules, and data.
- Classifications of rules, with samples from VCI.

Phase 2: Conduct the Facilitated Rule Discovery Session

You are now ready to carry out the facilitated session or several of them.

STEP 8.10: DELIVER THE INTRODUCTION

The objectives of the introduction are to review the approach, objectives, premises, and the expectations of each participant.

GUIDELINE 8.10.1

Introduce the participants and cover administrative points.

As the facilitator, introduce yourself and people assigned to document the session. Have each participant introduce themselves and their role on the project.

Review the session schedule, break times, meal arrangements, refreshments, facilities, and so on.

GUIDELINE 8.10.2

Review the management perspective on this session.

As the facilitator, use large sheets of paper on which these items are documented. Review the purpose, scope, and deliverables of the session.

GUIDELINE 8.10.3

Review the agenda.

The agenda should be approximately six simple bullet points. Explain the agenda in detail and step through an example. Doing so adds a strong business focus to the sessions from the start.

GUIDELINE 8.10.4

Review the ground rules.

As the facilitator, review the basic protocol and etiquette for the session. Be prepared to enforce these ground rules. Sample ground rules for facilitated sessions are:

- Be punctual.
- One conversation will happen at a time.
- There are no bad ideas.
- Accept the views of others.
- Disagreements will continue for only 10 minutes before the issue is placed on a parking lot.
- The group is responsible for the outcome.
- Consensus means that a participant can live with the decision.
- Absence or silence is agreement.
- Speak for self: "I" not "we."
- No wordsmithing. Every unclear term needs a definition.
- Issues that cannot be immediately resolved are placed on a parking lot.

Ask for additional ground rules from participants and add them.

While you can change the sequence of the introduction, do not review the ground rules as the first item on the agenda. Ground rules represent constraints on participant behavior and it is wise to begin with the approach and objectives, prior to introducing constraints.

GUIDELINE 8.10.5

Schedule the executive sponsor to provide a brief kickoff.

If you plan to have several sessions, the executive sponsor speaks only at the first session.

The kickoff presentation should be brief, about 5 minutes. It's an opportunity for the executive sponsor to express support for the process and ensure that participants are aware of their roles and expectations. It should include:

- What the project is about
- What management hopes to accomplish

- Why the participants present were chosen
- Support for the process and roles as defined.

GUIDELINE 8.10.6

Have the business and technical partners give their expectations of the session.

Again, this is only done at the first session. These are the technical and business partners responsible for executing the initiative in question, under the sponsorship of the executive. Either one can be responsible for taking just a few minutes to discuss, for example:

- Any earlier efforts on behalf of the project, as appropriate
- Probable steps after the workshop
- Any technology or other issues or initiatives that depend on or impact the project.

GUIDELINE 8.10.7

Review open items from previous sessions.

Discuss whether these items are still open. Close out those that have been addressed to the satisfaction of the group.

STEP 8.11: EXECUTE THE RULE DISCOVERY ROADMAP

Here is where the excitement begins. Walk the participants through the rule discovery roadmap. When you get to the steps where participants are to provide decisions and rules, allow participants to say first what comes to mind, and then clarify it, then all decide if the decision and rule belongs in the intended final list of decisions and rules. Place undefined terms on a large sheet of paper and do not move off of a rule until all such terms are defined to the satisfaction of the group (or assigned to someone).

At some point, you can divide the participants into smaller teams and have each team analyze the rules for a business event and present a final rule set. Or you can be creative and group rules by data subject (such as product, customer, credit check) and have the participants walk around the rule groupings posting questions or comments about each rule. You can then review these with the entire group.

GUIDELINE 8.11.1

As you complete each step of the process, as laid out in the agenda, check it off to show where you are in the process and demonstrate progress.

Use the rule discovery flowchart for this.

GUIDELINE 8.11.2

Consider capturing rule discovery metrics.

Sometimes it is useful to capture metrics about the session itself, as a guide for future planning or for improvement. Some sample metrics may include:

- Number of rules captured per time period
- Number of rules tested by a scenario
- Number of issues raised per rule.

CASE STUDY: STEP 8.11—EXECUTE THE RULE DISCOVERY ROADMAP

Case Study Instructions:

- Identify the decisions uncovered in the session.
- Identify the rules behind the decisions.
- Begin to identify underlying terms.
- Document follow-up action items.

Case Study Solution:

You highlight possible decisions from the session. Correlating these to business objectives, strategies and policies is left to the reader.

Decisions:

- Is credit check necessary for guardian?
- What credit rating is assigned to a guardian?
- Is guardian poor credit rating?
- Is guardian fair credit rating?
- Is guardian excellent credit rating?
- Is credit approved?

Below are potential rules behind the decisions:

- Is credit check necessary for guardian?
  - If guardian is employee, credit check not necessary.
  - If guardian selects prepay, credit check not necessary.
- What credit rating is assigned to a guardian?
  - If ??? Then guardian credit rating = poor
  - If ??? Then guardian credit rating = fair
  - If ??? Then guardian credit rating = excellent
- Is guardian poor credit rating?
  - If guardian credit rating = poor, then guardian credit not approved.
- Is guardian fair credit rating?
  - If guardian credit rating = fair, then guardian payment method must be prepay.
- Is guardian excellent credit rating?
  - If guardian credit rating = excellent then guardian selects payment method.
- Is credit approved?
  - If guardian credit approved then invoke assignment of member ID and member password.

■ If guardian credit not needed, then invoke assignment of member ID and member password.

You identify the following terms:

■ Guardian credit check needed flag

■ Employee

■ Guardian

■ Member

■ Guardian credit-rating code

■ Guardian credit approved flag

■ Guardian payment type

■ Member ID

■ Member password.

Note that the conditions by which actual guardian credit ratings are set are not yet defined. There was much discussion over how to assign these ratings and insufficient information since some of the input may come from an outside service bureau.

You decide on the following action items:

Action Item #1. Greg, from the Credit department, will investigate the kinds of credit rating schemes provided by the currently preferred credit bureaus and report back within 5 days. Greg will define the Guardian information items above.

Action Item #2. The participant from the Marketing department will obtain from the Human Resources department a definition for the term Employee to verify that the decision about employee guardians not needing a credit check makes business sense. These will be done within 5 days.

Action Item #3: The participant from Guardian Services will define Guardian and will contact the Member Services function for a definition of Member and its information items above, within 5 days.

STEP 8.12: REVIEW THE SESSION

In closing either a series of sessions, or an individual session within a series, it is important to review the session accomplishments, next steps, and how effective the session was.

GUIDELINE 8.12.1

Review deliverables.

Summarize the original methodology, highlighting the deliverables. This serves as a review of accomplishments.

GUIDELINE 8.12.2

Identify important lessons learned about the business itself, while attempting to discover its underlying rules.

This can be an extremely valuable consideration. Rules in a vacuum have little value. Even if you cannot agree on all rules, the process of searching for them and evaluating them can teach participants valuable insights about the business and how to improve it.

GUIDELINE 8.12.3

Explain immediate next steps.

As the session wraps up, it's critical that you clearly identify and assign responsibility for actions that must be researched. List all items to be undertaken and for each:

- Clarify the action item. Ensure that there's a good understanding among everyone as to what is intended by this item—a group activity
- Identify the participant who accepts responsibility
- Assign a date for completion
- Discuss possible next business subtask or business event for the next rule discovery session.

GUIDELINE 8.12.4

Explain the next steps in the rule capture process.

This is an excellent opportunity to reflect, as a group, on where the facilitated session led the participants and what is left to do, regarding rules. For the rules captured during the session, next steps may be the following:

- Review the business strategies supported by the policy.
- Review the business objective for the strategy.
- Refine the business metric for the business event based on knowledge gained.
- Discuss the effectiveness of the rule (and other rules in its set) in achieving that objective.
- Possibly discuss the expected timeframe and frequency of change for each discovered rule.

You can carry out those steps through another facilitated session or assign it as a follow-up activity to appropriate participants.

GUIDELINE 8.12.5

Recommend the next steps for the rule capture process.

Guide the participants in making a group decision about the next steps in this process. Do they agree with the next steps? Do they agree on who should be involved in accomplishing them and how they do so.

GUIDELINE 8.12.6

Review open items.

Open items are those questions that occurred through the course of the session, and are very important to achieving the objectives of the session, but which could not be addressed during the session itself. Review the open items and for each:

- Establish who is responsible for addressing this open item
- Determine when any action is to be completed
- Define how the resolution will be communicated to the group.

GUIDELINE 8.12.7

Review the effectiveness of the process.

Involve the whole group in measuring the effectiveness of the process and lessons learned. Invite them to evaluate the facilitator. Consider the use of evaluation forms. You can have the group evaluate the facilitator by filling out anonymous evaluation forms. Be sure to hold a group discussion to evaluate the process of the session. While forms can also cover the first items of lessons learned and overall process effectiveness, it is also a good idea to have the group discuss these openly as a final exercise.

GUIDELINE 8.12.8

Provide a final session wrap-up.

At the end of the session, or at the end of the last session in a series, encourage the business or technical partner to provide a final session wrap-up. This doesn't need to be elaborate. It is primarily a matter of:

- Defining how documentation will be distributed to the group
- Outlining their responsibilities for reviewing the documentation
- Thanking the participants

CASE STUDY: STEP 8.12—REVIEW THE SESSION

Case Study Instructions:

- Document lessons learned about the rule discovery experience.
- Document immediate next steps.
- Document the recommendations from the participants.

Case Study Solution:
The participants found it interesting to note:

- They were very unsure of which rules should be constraints and which should be guidelines, especially where credit checks are concerned. There was much discussion about communicating warning messages by the system, which can be overridden by a VCI park ranger with proper authorization under certain circumstances.
- There were unclear boundaries of jurisdictions between the Credit department and the Finance department (and the latter was not present).

- Some participants (Marketing) were interested in specifying the kind of guardian information to collect at the time of enrollment, specifically demographic/psychographic information and identification of sales channel that brought the guardian to VCI. Understanding the information that is input to the event can generate additional rules (such as constraint rules) to be sure the guardian enters the information correctly. If the information that is input to the event is not relevant to the facilitated session (in this case, Check Guardian Credit), this discussion is out of scope. If, however, the facilitated session is addressing the rules behind the part of the event that collects this information, the discussion is within scope and corresponding terms and rules should be captured.

The VCI participants make the following recommendations:

- Include more functions in the session (Member Services, Human Resources), whenever possible.
- Have a separate facilitated session to confirm and document policies, strategies, and objectives or have them readily available prior to the rule discovery session.

Phase 3: Complete Follow-up Activities

It is extremely important that you identify the follow-up activities that will clarify or add credence to the rules discovered.

STEP 8.13: OBTAIN RESOLUTIONS TO OPEN ITEMS

The facilitator should remind the business or technical partner to stay in communication with those participants responsible for open items. The participants need to obtain the resolutions and have the scribe add them to the session results.

STEP 8.14: DISTRIBUTE SESSION RESULTS

Every participant and the sponsor should have access to documented session results.

GUIDELINE 8.14.1

Assign final format of the session results to the scribe.

Establish a date by which you will publish the session results. Be sure that all participants, partners, and sponsors receive a copy.

GUIDELINE 8.14.2

Consider publishing the results of the session in the knowledge center.

If you have created a knowledge center for the project, include all results from facilitated rule discovery sessions in the knowledge center.

An Example of Planning a Facilitated Rule Discovery Session

For the sake of simplicity, Figure 8.2 illustrates the above steps as they apply to the planning of a 1–3 day facilitated rule discovery session. The schedule presumes that the rule discovery roadmap is fairly well known. The schedule allows time to tune the final agenda for the 1–3 day session. Ideally, you should complete the planning 1–2 weeks prior to the session to ensure that all the participants have received the invitation, that they have had a chance to review the approach and prepare, and that you have addressed all logistical issues.

However, it may be that the scale and complexity of the project, and number of participants requires planning a series of facilitated workshops (a cohesive group of 1 or more day sessions) over an extended period of time. In this case, the facilitator will need to collaborate with the partners and possibly a methodologist and one or more project managers to establish the timing, resources for, and length of sessions. The same concepts and tasks apply, however, and the schedule simply scales upward.

For example, it may take up to twenty days to conduct all interviews and complete thorough planning for a project that is to run many months. In such cases, the overall executive invitation may focus more on the purpose and scope of the project as a whole, and how facilitation will be applied to it in general terms. Kickoff and wrap-up may comprise complete separate sessions at the beginning and end of the process.

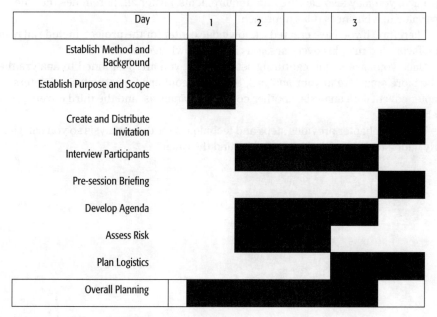

Figure 8.2   Sample schedule for planning rule discovery sessions.

For individual efforts, the main exercise is to ensure that the rule discovery session fits within the framework of the overall project.

While there are many techniques available to a trained facilitator, the most important aspects of a successful facilitation session are a well-structured and relevant rule discovery roadmap, well-defined deliverables, and thorough planning and preparation.

Summary

Typical facilitation sessions don't have a formal emphasis on the collection, management, and delivery of rules as a separate asset. Instead, emphasis is placed on items that surround (but don't quite address) the rules. These items include object design, process design, user interface design, database design, formal requirements gathering, and even business process redesign.

Facilitated rule discovery sessions, because they are a disciplined group working session, are useful because they limit the possibility of gathering conflicting rules among the participants, save time in reviewing and evaluating rules, and disciplined discussions yield better quality rules. Optionally, a data analyst is a useful addition to the sessions, especially if you want to gain a head start on the logical data model.

Thorough planning and preparation is key to the success of a facilitated session. To be efficient, you need a rule discovery roadmap that you can walk through with participants comfortably and to which they can easily relate. It must be compatible with the organization's culture. Most importantly, you want to capture the rules, evaluate them for quality as a group, and tie them to business context and metrics. (Depending on approach, you may also capture data requirements.) After all, herein lies the true business value in a business rules approach.

Therefore, if you have created a knowledge center for the project, include all results from facilitated rule discovery sessions in the knowledge center.

Once you have begun capturing sets of rules, you are positioned to analyze them. To be more complete in your analysis, this book contains three analysis chapters. One chapter covers data analysis, another covers rule analysis, and the third covers process analysis.

The next chapter provides steps and techniques for data analysis so you can gain an early understanding of the semantics behind the rules.

Analysis

Analyzing Data

You arrived at the data analysis phase because you have gathered sufficient discovery artifacts to begin building a detailed logical data model. If you are fortunate, you already have a conceptual data model. If you have followed the discovery approach in this book, you may have a list of terms and facts. Perhaps you developed a business object model to reflect those terms and facts. You may be participating in a rule discovery session during which you will uncover the terms and facts.

Worst case, you don't have a conceptual model, terms, or facts, or even rules, and you are simply trying to develop a logical data model to support the target business rules system. In that case, you may host facilitated data discovery sessions or conduct interviews with business experts. Or you may simply tag along while other analysts (such as process, business, or object analysts) conduct interviews or facilitated sessions with business experts. Your job is to listen for terms and facts and cast them into a high-quality logical data architecture.

Hopefully, you will not be creating a logical data model merely by inspecting existing physical data structures. If your only input to the data analysis activities is the existing physical data structures, follow the steps in this chapter with extra care. Reengineering data from existing physical structures is not likely, by itself, to lead you to data structures positioned for the future. It is just a starting point.

Figure 9.1 reminds you again of where in the full methodology the analysis phase fits. Specifically, you have completed the discovery tasks. You are now analyzing the data requirements in parallel with rule requirements. When analysis is complete in all tracks, you are ready for the design phase. Figure 9.2 illustrates how the three major analysis tracks (data, rules, process) relate to each other.

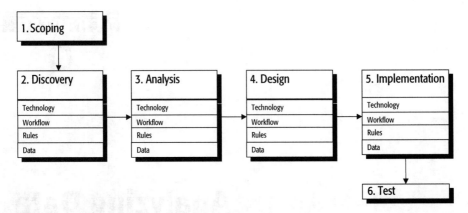

Figure 9.1   Business rule systems methodology phases.

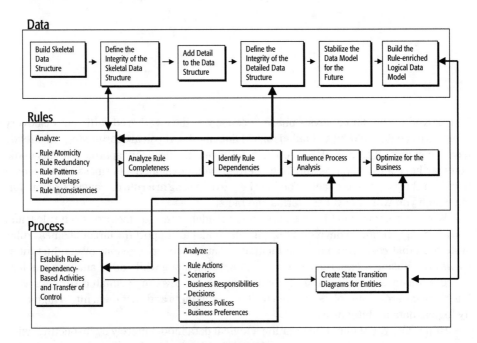

Figure 9.2   Integration of data, process, rule analysis.

The data track produces the data models and eventual database. When you follow the methodology steps in the data track, you uncover the vocabulary and grammar with which the rules are expressed and you create a stable data structure to represent that vocabulary. Specifically, as you uncover rules, you make sure each word or phrase is represented in the data model and database. Hopefully, you can understand that the transition from rule collection to data constructs is a very natural one.

The most important part of Figure 9.2 for this chapter is how the data and rule track connect. Notice that the boxes in the data track that address integrity have links to the rule track. That's because the integrity rules behind the data are truly rules and in the business rules approach, are addressed as rules. Also note in Figure 9.2 that the data and process track connect when the data track addresses the rule-enriched logical data model and the process track becomes concerned with uncovering process-related issues around changes in important entities.

What Is Data Analysis?

In this book, *data analysis* is the set of steps, techniques, guidelines, and tools for transforming data requirements into a rule-enriched logical data model. A rule-enriched logical data model represents a natural evolution of a basic logical data model. A *basic logical data model* is a representation of the data requirements (for a system or an enterprise) in a correct, consistent, stable, and shareable format (Fleming and von Halle 1989). Typically, a logical data model consists of a structural and an integrity representation. The structural representation is a logical data model diagram, with definitions behind it. The integrity representation is usually a set of very basic rules governing population of that data structure so that the data values are correct from a business perspective.

Keep in mind, however, that in a business rules approach, the integrity aspect of a traditional logical data model overlaps significantly with the logical rule model, discussed in Chapter 10. Therefore, there should be serious coordination between a rule analyst and a data analyst in capturing and managing the integrity rules.

In a theoretically perfect business rules approach, all integrity rules are part of the rule track and not the data track. These integrity rules include the basic ones that are commonly included in logical data models. It also includes advanced rules that you will find when you take a more serious approach to rules analysis. Most likely, you will find a middle ground where some basic integrity rules may be part of the logical data model, although some will become part of the logical rule model. Let's now discuss the role of a logical data model in more detail.

"At the heart of logical data modeling is an appreciation of data as a valuable resource for a business organization. Logical data modeling is a philosophy (as well as a technique) for recognizing and documenting the fact that business data have an existence, independent of how they are accessed, who accesses them, and whether or not such access is computerized" (Fleming and von Halle 1989). Therefore, the logical data model is logical, correct, consistent, stable, and sharable.

The logical data model is *logical* because it is unbiased by implementation target technology. That is, a database designer can adapt the logical data model to any target database technology solution.

The logical data model is *correct* because it represents the data from the business person's perspective, based on business definitions and business integrity constraints. It is *consistent* in that it does not knowingly contain contradictions in data names, definitions, and data structure or data integrity aspects. It is *stable* in that it will service changing business and application requirements with minimum disruption to the business and its systems. Finally, the logical data model is *sharable* in that it is unbiased by particular access patterns, hence can serve the needs of many applications and organizations.

A logical data model is a very disciplined representation of the information requirements for a target system or an entire enterprise. Some of that discipline (such as the application of normalization techniques and identification of foreign keys) yield a logical data model that is closely aligned with a first-cut database design using relational technology. If you will not be using relational database technology (perhaps you are using object or object-relational technology), you may not need to apply all of these disciplines. In these cases, refer to documentation from your product vendor for the most appropriate data modeling and design approach. (As indicated in Chapter 7, you can develop a fact-oriented model in place of a logical data model. This chapter presents the development of a logical data model for those readers who will be designing relational databases and for whom a logical data model is more familiar than a term/fact model).

A logical data model is not the same as a business object model or a class model. A business object model is usually a class model containing only those classes that have meaning to the business audience, such as customer, order, and product. As indicated elsewhere in this book, a business object model can be very useful for gaining an initial understanding of the problem domain, however it is often not maintained as a living document, but serves as a starting point for a design-oriented class model. This class model adds to a business object model those classes needed to make software work, such as interface and control classes. While the business object model and the class model are very useful for their purposes, they are not the most useful deliverable for representing terms and facts over the long term. This book advocates that a logical data model, because it structures data based on its semantic meanings and relationships (not based on a messaging or processing basis) is more appropriate.

If you disagree with the role of the logical data model and you prefer to use your business object model as the source for your terms and facts, you should still apply many of the data analysis ideas in this chapter to the naming and defining of those terms and facts.

Data Modeling Standards

Before you begin creating a logical data model, you will need to have data standards in place. Specifically, you will need to decide:

- What kinds of logical data models will you create?
- What kinds of naming conventions will you follow?
- What kinds of procedures will modelers follow to create integrated logical data models?
- What kinds of meta data will you capture about the models and where will you store it?

In the business rule methodology, we reference four different kinds of logical data models. The first is the *conceptual data model*, introduced in Chapter 4, which is a high-level representation of data needed for a specific scope. This book suggests you begin to create a conceptual data model during the scoping or discovery phase, as a starting point.

The second kind of logical data model is an application logical data model. An *application logical data model* is a detailed logical data model (contains all detailed data elements) needed for a target application or system, but not necessarily extended beyond that scope.

The third is an *integrated logical data model,* which is one logical data model combined with another logical data model to create one consistent representation of both. The source models can be representations of various perspectives of one system or across systems.

The fourth is an *enterprise logical data model.* By this, we mean a detailed model of the data across the entire business enterprise. An enterprise data model need not represent all data across the enterprise, but the data it represents is analyzed across the whole enterprise. Thus, it is possible to have an enterprise data model for customer data, but not for product data, for example.

As for naming conventions, this chapter contains recommendations for naming entities, relationships, and attributes. For now, consider that you might need at least five different kinds of names for entities and attributes:

Business name. Usually free form, no abbreviations

Logical data model name. Not free form, has disciplined parts and sequence of those parts (discussed below)

Database name. Usually an abbreviated form of the logical data model name due to DBMS length restrictions

User name or application name. Usually as appropriate for application development language or user interface tool.

If you need to develop abbreviated names (such as for the database or application), there are three general approaches to establishing standard abbreviations:

Option 1 is to use a data modeling tool that automatically generates abbreviations for you. This is the ideal solution because it will generate consistent abbreviations for every one. Option 2 is to apply an algorithm for deriving an abbreviation from a nonabbreviated word. A common algorithm is first to remove all vowels except a starting vowel, then remove duplicate consonants. If the resulting abbreviation is too long, you may need to apply additional logic to the abbreviation algorithm. Option 3 is to start a standard list of abbreviations for words.

When it comes to integrating various data models, you will need procedures for how data modelers should do this. Such procedures are beyond the scope of this book. Typically, however, the procedures are documented in a shared publication, available online to data modelers. Model integration may occur in concert among individual data modelers and designated model integrators.

The meta data about the logical data models is usually stored in a standard CASE or logical data modeling tool. You can often extend these tools to include additional meta data. Often, this meta data is transferred from the modeling tool into a central repository where the meta data is available to a wider audience for reference. It is good practice to establish meta data architecture. A meta data flow indicates where certain meta data is created (perhaps in a logical data modeling CASE tool) and how it finds its way to various destinations (such as the help facility for your upcoming business rules system).

Consider creating the logical data model in a standard logical data modeling tool, not in a commercial rules product, even though such products enable you to do so. The reason is that you should treat data as a shared asset. Mature model management and integration capabilities exist and will likely continue to mature in today's data modeling technology. Also, you will want to separate the logical data model from its physical implementation.

How to Measure the Quality of a Logical Data Model

Before explaining the approach to basic logical data modeling, let's first understand how to measure the quality of the model when it is finished. Simply put, consider the following criteria for its quality:

- Represents each business fact in one and only one place (no unnecessary redundancy of facts)
- Represents each business fact in the one correct place (based on normalization concepts)
- Represents each business concept in a consistent manner across the model (for example, if there is a concept of preferred customer, it is always represented either as a flag or as an entity, but never as both)
- Represents the data in a manner that is clear and discriminating to the model's audience
- Represents the data in a manner that is correct across organizational boundaries
- Endorses the integrity qualities of Codd's original relational model (such as in the depiction and integrity of primary keys, foreign keys, and so on).

More specific considerations include the following seven criteria by which you can judge the quality of a single attribute and three additional criteria by which to judge the quality of an entire logical data model.

For each attribute, you will aim for the following:

Relevant/Justified: Each attribute must be essential to the target scope of analysis. There is no sense wasting time on unnecessary attributes. You will ensure that each attribute is essential in two ways: by scoping the target data environment and by maintaining a close correlation between data and rules. You scope the target data environment during the scoping phase when you identify data subjects and start a list of conceptual data entities. You continue to scope your data environment during discovery as you evolve the conceptual data model.

You maintain a close correlation between data and rules by associating, during the discovery phase, decisions and rules with the information they reference and create. You may find it useful to create CRUD matrices from rules to data. Essentially, if there is no rule that references or creates a piece of information, you may want to question whether you should capture, analyze, design, and implement that piece of information. Who uses it and for what?

Atomic: Each attribute must represent one piece of information such that it cannot be decomposed without losing meaning. You want atomic attributes because each atomic attribute represents only one unit of change. A nonatomic attribute will make changes difficult. Consider a nonatomic attribute, called Address. It is nonatomic because it contains many different pieces of information within it, such as street number, street name, town name, state name, country name, zip code, and so forth. If you want to change someone's street number, you have to find it within a larger piece of information. Such a change would be much easier if there were one attribute called Street number.

You ensure that each attribute is atomic during data analysis by applying guidelines for adding attributes provided in this chapter.

Declarative: Each attribute must prescribe a piece of information and not how to navigate through the information. A *declarative attribute* is freestanding, shareable, technology-independent, and therefore serves as a piece of business information. It does not represent a symbol simply indicating how to access or navigate through data structures.

You ensure that each attribute is declarative during data analysis by naming attributes according to naming standards and defining attributes (and entities and relationships) following guidelines in this chapter.

Intelligible/Precise: The attribute's intended audience must understand it such that the audience can use it in a predictable manner. You do not want uncertainty, ambiguity, or confusion about attributes. You ensure this criterion during data analysis by naming each attribute according to standard naming conventions, defining each attribute with a business definition, and providing meta data (such as business examples) to supplement its definition.

Complete: Each attribute must possess all intellectual properties necessary for its usage. You do not want partially defined attributes. You ensure completeness of a single attribute during data analysis by making sure that every attribute is named according to naming standards that indicate its type (through class words) and by capturing relevant meta data for clarifying its meaning and intended usage.

Reliable: Each attribute must originate from a source authorized to decide that the attribute is as the business desires. This criterion differentiates a person's opinion as to what an attribute means from the business leadership deciding what an attribute means and how it is to be used properly. This criterion also encourages accountability for the data within the business organization. By knowing the authorized data steward, you save time when investigating proposed data definitions and changes. You do not want data definitions and names that are not sanctioned. You ensure the reliability of an attribute during data analysis by seeking its business steward who is empowered to approve it, change it, and watch it progress from draft form to tested form to production form.

Authentic: As each attribute is copied into various forms (from logical data model, to physical database design, to database specifications, to program names) each representation must remain faithful to the original intent and

expression of the attribute. You do not want attributes to deteriorate as you copy and distribute them electronically. You accomplish this from data analysis through database implementation by following proper data management procedures.

There are also three criteria against which to measure a collection of attributes into entities and entities into a logical data model:

Complete/Predictable: All data necessary to support a business event are present. Hence, the logical data model (and resulting database) supports a business event regardless of who accesses the data or how the data is navigated. You ensure this level of completeness during data analysis when you combine your logical data model with other relevant data models. You also ensure this criterion when you expand your logical data model to incorporate an enterprise-wide perspective. Finally, you seek adherence to this criterion when you test your logical data model against possible future changes.

Unique/Nonredundant/Minimal: There is no uncontrolled redundant data. You may decide to redundantly store a piece of data in the database environment, but you do not want to specify data redundantly during analysis. You ensure uniqueness of the data in the logical data model during data analysis through the application of normalization theory and the incorporation of supertype-subtype structures.

Consistent: A logical data model does not knowingly contain contradictions within itself. There is no piece of data or data structure that disagrees with other pieces of data or structures in the logical data model. You will ensure consistency of a logical data model through thorough understanding of data attribute definitions, integrity rules, and normalization principles.

Table 9.1 summarizes the criteria for logical data model quality, along with how you will accomplish each.

Table 9.1   Tips for Improving the Quality of a Logical Data Model

LOGICAL DATA MODEL QUALITY CRITERION	PHASE IN WHICH THIS CRITERIA IS ADDRESSED	HOW YOU WILL ACHIEVE IT
Relevant/justified	Scoping	Data subjects Conceptual data entities
	Discovery	Conceptual data model Rules correlated to information referenced and created
Atomic	Data analysis	Guidelines for adding attributes
Declarative	Data analysis	Naming conventions Business definitions
Intelligible/precise	Data analysis	Business definitions Naming conventions Meta data

Table 9.1 (*Continues*)

LOGICAL DATA MODEL QUALITY CRITERION	PHASE IN WHICH THIS CRITERIA IS ADDRESSED	HOW YOU WILL ACHIEVE IT
Complete	Data analysis	Naming conventions Meta data
Reliable	Data analysis	Data stewardship
Authentic	Data discovery, data analysis, database design, database implementation	Data management
Logical data model completeness	Data analysis	Combining relevant data models Expanding for enterprise perspective Analyzing for the future
Logical data model minimality/ nonredundancy/ uniqueness	Data analysis	Normalization principles Supertype-subtype structures
Logical data model consistency	Data analysis	Business definitions Normalization principles Integrity rules

The steps in this chapter provide guidelines for meeting the above criteria for high-quality logical data models.

Overview of Basic Logical Data Modeling

This chapter is an abbreviated version of a much more in-depth coverage of basic logical data modeling, presented in Fleming and von Halle 1989 (see References). As such, this chapter focuses primarily on the basics of logical data modeling, with enhancements related to rule considerations. Figure 9.3 details the steps in this chapter. If you are a seasoned data modeler, you may need to read only the summary of this chapter, followed by Steps 9.13–9.16, because you are probably not experienced in creating a rule-enriched logical data model. If there are items in the summary that are unclear, you can peruse through the details of the chapter.

For the novice data modeler, read all of the sections that follow. In the case study, don't become concerned if you feel that your modeling decisions at each step would have been different from ours. Keep in mind that data modeling is an iterative task and you may be ahead of or behind our step-by-step thinking. The most important point is that you learn to ask the right questions about the data and that you end up with a basic logical data model that is semantically equivalent to the one we propose at the end of this chapter.

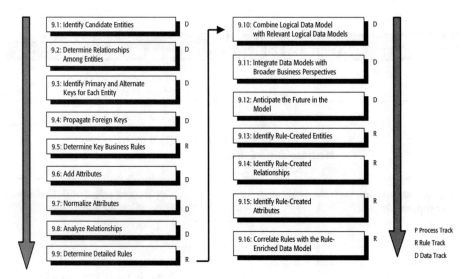

Figure 9.3   Steps for analyzing data.

Basic Logical Data Modeling Breakdown

Figure 9.3 depicts the steps covered in this chapter. The rest of the chapter divides the basic logical data modeling methodology into six sections. These sections alternate from a focus on data structure to a focus on data integrity and culminate in Section 6, a focus on knowledge.

The first section, "What Are the Steps for Defining the Skeletal Data Structure," addresses the initial identification and modeling of entities, subtypes and supertypes, and relationships. This provides an early visual understanding of the complexity of the target data structure.

The second section, "What Are the Steps for Defining the Integrity of the Skeletal Data Structure," specifically takes a look at the integrity rules governing the initial structure. Doing so enables the data analyst to make changes in the skeletal data structure to accommodate future rule considerations.

The third section, "What Are the Steps for Adding Detail to the Data Structure," contains steps and techniques for adding the detailed attributes to the existing data structure. This section serves to fill in the logical data model with most of the data details, but also validates the initial data structure.

The fourth section, "What Are the Steps for Defining the Integrity of the Detailed Data Structure," aims to add all the rules behind all of the attributes. Unlike other logical data modeling methodologies, this section is very intense as you aim to work with a rule analyst in documenting every data integrity rule, regardless of whether it is supported by the data structure, the DBMS, a rule technology layer, or an application-specific layer.

The fifth section, "What Are the Steps for Stabilizing the Data Model for the Future," is perhaps the most important section of all. Many logical data modeling approaches (and, indeed, systems development methodology approaches) consider the logical data model complete when it contains all data needed by a target system. The business rules approach is not content with that. Because the data foundation determines how easily the target system accommodates business change, this section presents steps and techniques for evolving the initial logical data model into one that has high probability of accommodating both anticipated and unanticipated business changes with minimal disruption.

The sixth section, "What Are the Steps for Building the Rule-Enriched Logical Data Model," is unique to a business rules approach. Traditional logical data modeling approaches do not include the creation of a logical data model, which is enriched with data created by rules. That's because such data is materialized through a rule and need not be persistently stored. A shortcoming to this thinking is that much of the knowledge and decision-making capacity of the organization is then lost, buried in program specification or code. A business rules approach aims to externalize logically the knowledge and decision-making so that the business knows the decisions and underlying knowledge, can analyze them, share them, and change them. In this section, you study rules and capture the pieces of information that those rules materialize. You treat the information materialized by rules as an asset to be captured, named, defined, and managed for the good of the business. It is no longer acceptable for information created by rules (knowledge) to remain buried and hidden.

How Is Data Analysis Different for a Business Rules Approach?

Logical data modeling is different for a business rule system in four ways, shown in Table 3.1, consistent with the principles of the business rules approach:

- Separating rules by recognizing their existence separate from (but related to) the logical data model

- Tracing rules by incorporating a reference to them in the rule-enriched logical data model

- Externalizing rules by capturing rules in natural language

- Positioning rules for change by representing rule-materialized knowledge, from a logical and semantic perspective, for sharing

The first difference supports the principle of separating rules because data analysis for a business rules system recognizes that rules have an existence separate from, but related to, the logical data model. Most logical data modeling methodologies include steps and techniques for capturing the basic integrity constraints (a subset of rules) about the data model. These are sometimes referred to as structural constraints. Most often these include primary key constraints, alternate key constraints, relationship referential constraints, relationship and attribute optionality constraints, and attribute domain constraints. Most logical data modeling methodologies leave responsibility for other kinds of constraints (multiattribute constraints, multientity constraints) to the application development methodology. So a difference in the business rules approach is that the logical data modeling methodology complements the rule analysis methodology in specifically capturing all data integrity constraints, some in the data structure but most in the corresponding rules.

Therefore, it becomes the responsibility of a rule analyst to collect and analyze rules. It is the responsibility of a data analyst to collect and analyze data requirements. When the data analyst discovers rules that have been traditionally part of the logical data model, the data analyst and rule analyst need to get together. Most rules should be separate from the logical data model, not tightly bound to it, to allow for flexibility in the future.

The second difference supports the principle of tracing rules because, while rules are captured separately from the logical data model, they are referenced in the rule enriched logical data model. A rule enriched logical data model contains data structures for information materialized through the execution of rules. Information materialized through the execution of rules is either computed by a computation rule or inferred by an inferred knowledge rule. More than that, a rule is assigned to an entity within the logical data model based on the knowledge it creates, thereby creating a predictable way of associating rules to entities. This does not imply that the information materialized by rules is made persistent in the physical database design. When you add to a rule-enriched logical data model a reference to the rules, you have a very useful deliverable that integrates the rules perspective organized according to the data perspective. Refer to Figure 9.4 to see where the rule-enriched logical data model fits with respect to other data models.

The third difference supports the principle of externalizing rules. That is, rules, when captured along with a logical data model, are expressed in natural language for business understanding.

The fourth difference supports the principle of positioning rules for change because a rule-enriched logical data model treats rule-materialized information as an asset. That is, these pieces of information are analyzed and expressed from a logical, semantic perspective so the business can understand them and change the rules that create and reference them. These rule-materialized pieces of information should have names, definitions, domains, and should be shareable across the enterprise, when appropriate.

Therefore, to summarize, a rule-enriched logical data model for a business rules system is a representation of all data referenced and created by a system (or an enterprise) regardless of whether the values for that data are nonderived or materialized through the execution of rules.

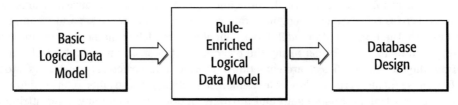

Figure 9.4   Data models in a business rules approach.

The steps in this chapter lead you to create, as a starting point, a basic logical data model representing the base, nonderivable information. The steps then use this model as the foundation for building a rule-enriched logical data model.

What Is the Purpose of Logical Data Modeling?

The purpose of logical data modeling is twofold. The first purpose is to capture business information requirements targeted for a business rule system. The second purpose is to cast the information requirements into terms with common business names and definitions and organized into high-quality data structures, supported with data integrity rules.

There exist many approaches for creating a logical data model. Sometimes such approaches reflect the capabilities of a specific logical data modeling tool. Most logical data modeling approaches, however, are similar in concepts and intent. They aim to understand the data from a business perspective, cast that data into a desirable data structure, and define the most important integrity rules that should protect that data structure from contamination.

As for the structural aspect of a logical data model, most methodologies endorse the concepts of entities, subtypes, supertypes, relationships, attributes, and normalization. The methodologies may differ in philosophy as to whether the model ought to include representations of computed or inferred data.

In a business rules approach, you will capture all computed and inferred data in your logical data model. Therefore, this book refers to a logical data model for a business rules system as a *rule-enriched logical data model*. The rule-enriched logical data model brings forth in a very tangible way a hidden aspect, called *organizational knowledge and decision-making*. This aspect, represented by the rule-enriched logical data model, is a fundamental new deliverable in the data analysis phase of the business rules approach.

What Are the Deliverables of Data Analysis?

The data track for the analysis phase has as its deliverables, the following:

- Data source quality reports, if migrating from or referencing existing data stores
- Rule-enriched logical data model
- Synonym list
- Logical data conversion specifications, if migrating from an existing data store
- Data integration and standardization issues, if integrating with existing data stores
- Documentation and recommendations on options in multitiered data architecture
- Data distribution requirements, if storing data in more than one location
- Requirements for storing historic data
- Requirements to meet auditing needs

- Estimated data volumes
- Data backup and recovery requirements
- Data security requirements.

This chapter focuses on development of the rule enriched logical data model. The other deliverables listed above are the same as you would create even if you were not following a business rules approach.

What Are the Steps in Building Skeletal Data Structure?

As indicated above, the skeletal data structure is the first-cut estimation of the *shape* of the data, how complex it seems to be. You may be developing a skeletal data structure for one business event or use case at a time, for example. A skeletal data structure contains the most important, visible aspects of the data requirements without concern for details. The emphasis is on gaining business understanding of the entities and relationships, but not for all detailed data items.

STEP 9.1: IDENTIFY CANDIDATE ENTITIES

An *entity* is a business object or thing of interest to the business, about which the business wishes to record information, but most importantly to readers of this book, about which the business wants to express and execute rules. Entities can be tangible objects (as in a person entity) or intangible objects (as in an organizational unit entity).

GUIDELINE 9.1.1

Start with a list of business nouns.

There are two basic ways you can start the search for entities. The first is to refer to the conceptual data model if you created one during the scoping phase. In the absence of a conceptual data model, the second way is simply to start an entity list by reviewing the discovery deliverables. These may range from the business events to the rule collection, looking for business nouns. The business nouns are terms.

GUIDELINE 9.1.2

Include an entity in the model for each term referenced in rule clauses, where the term is best represented by an entity.

As you study the list of rules gathered during the discovery phase to be sure that you have an entity (a container) that would house detailed information for each noun mentioned in each rule. Look for nouns, hence entities that represent people, places, or concepts.

Your list of entities will expand as you proceed through discovery, rule analysis, or data analysis.

It is important to understand that an entity is a business object with a definition, but which houses detailed information properties. Therefore, group your nouns into sets based on similarities in definition and properties. For example, group all purchase orders into one entity, called Purchase Order. Each individual purchase order is an instance of the entity called Purchase Order. The logical data model does not represent entity instances, merely entity types. However, inspecting possible entity instances is a good way to uncover the entities.

GUIDELINE 9.1.3

Name each entity according to naming conventions.

Follow standard entity-naming conventions when naming entities. Use single noun forms for entity names, without abbreviations. Start a list (if your modeling tool does not automatically do so) of entity names so that other modelers use the same names as entities when referring to a term with the same meaning.

GUIDELINE 9.1.4

Define each entity from a business perspective.

An entity definition should be meaningful to the business audience and should be defined unambiguously. The definition should also include examples (instances) that qualify for this entity as well as those that do not, where such examples are needed for clarity.

As a simple example, suppose you have an entity called Renter. The preliminary definition of this entity is "a person or organization who rents a property for payment." On the surface this definition may seem quite clear, but you will want to ask the following kinds of questions about it:

- What is meant by a person? Must it be someone 18 or older?

- What is meant by organization? Must it be a business organization or does a family constitute an organization?

- Is a person or organization that merely inquires about renting a property also considered a renter? Is a person who used to rent a property considered a renter? If so, what is the acceptable timeframe over which such a person or organization is still considered a renter?

- What is a property? Must it have a building on it? Is a building a property? Can multiple buildings be a property?

- What does it mean to "rent a property for payment"? Are there circumstances where a person or organization occupies a property for no payment and is still considered a renter?

GUIDELINE 9.1.5

Diagram each entity.

For our purposes, diagram each entity as a box with the entity name in it. See Figure 9.5.

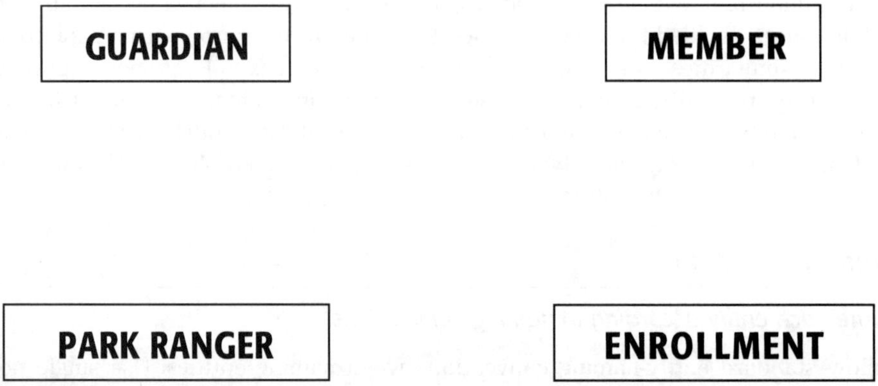

GUARDIAN		MEMBER

PARK RANGER		ENROLLMENT

Figure 9.5   Preliminary entities.

GUIDELINE 9.1.6

Place entities with the lower quantity of occurrences in the upper left-hand portion of the diagram.

You will want your logical data model diagram to be easy to read, hence you want to minimize the number of relationship lines that will cross over each other. If your modeling tool does not optimize diagram presentations, you can optimize the diagrams by following this guideline. That's because the entities with the most number of occurrences usually have many relationships to other entities and relationship lines will start out as fewer on the left side of the diagram and increase as you move down the page.

Figure 9.5 places the Enrollment entity on the bottom right-hand side, for this reason.

GUIDELINE 9.1.7

Capture meta data about each entity.

Often, your choice of modeling tool determines the kinds of meta data that you can capture most easily. Typical meta data to capture for an entity includes the following:

- Business name
- Business definition
- Whether the entity is a supertype or subtype (covered below)
- Estimated number of occurrences (minimum, maximum, average)
- Business steward (role that can change the meta data)
- Primary key (covered below)
- Alternate keys (covered below)
- Foreign keys (covered below).

GUIDELINE *9.1.8*

Verify that your entities are high quality.

The criteria for a high-quality entity are:

- Has one primary key always (discussed below)
- Has one unique business name
- Is well defined for business understanding
- Is supported with examples from the business.

GUIDELINE *9.1.9*

Group together entities representing persons, those representing organizations, those representing locations, and those representing things so you can look for the opportunity to denote subtype-supertype structures.

One of the most important structural and integrity aspects of a logical data model is its subtype-supertype structures.

A *subtype* is a subset of another entity (called the *supertype*) where occurrences of both designate the same object in the real world, but the subtype has additional more specific properties (Fleming and von Halle 1989). An intuitive example is that of the supertype, Employee, with subtypes Part-time Employee and Full-time Employee.

Depict subtypes with a supertype when the candidate supertype is likely to contain attributes and relationships that are common across all subtypes. For example, all employees (part time or full time) have first names and last names and are related to projects. Likewise, consider a supertype-subtype structure when there are attributes and relationships that differ from subtype to subtype. For example, while all employees have first names and last names, only part-time employees may have an hourly rate, whereas full-time employees may have a salary. At this early point in logical data modeling, you may not yet know whether there are common or distinct attributes and relationships among potential supertypes and subtypes. That's fine. For now, rely on intuition and limited knowledge. You will be able to confirm the existence of supertypes and subtypes as you proceed through the rest of the steps.

GUIDELINE *9.1.10*

When in doubt, err on the side of depicting more supertypes and subtypes than fewer.

Subtypes and supertypes are crucial because they allow for a subtype to inherit properties from its supertypes, hence you don't need to represent such properties more than once in the model. Therefore the use of subtypes and supertypes supports the desire to represent one fact in one place, one fact in the correct place, and to represent information requirements in a clear and discriminating manner.

You can diagram a supertype-subtype relationship in many ways, depending on your logical data modeling tool. For our purposes, we will simply show a line from a supertype to a subtype, label the line with "IS A KIND OF" (which means "*subtype* IS A KIND OF *supertype*").

CASE STUDY: STEP 9.1—IDENTIFY CANDIDATE ENTITIES

Case Study Instructions:

- Assume you have discovered twelve rules in the discovery phase. Identify candidate entities from these rules:
  - Rule 1: If a guardian exists in the Guardian set, the guardian is known.
  - Rule 2: If a guardian's credit rating code is "A", then the guardian has good credit.
  - Rule 3: If the guardian is known and the guardian does not have good credit, disallow member enrollment.
  - Rule 4: Member age is computed as current date minus member.birth-date
  - Rule 5: If member age < 16 and member age > 6 then member.age is appropriate.
  - Rule 6: If member age > 16 then recommend other theme parks for older members.
  - Rule 7: If member age is not appropriate then reject member enrollment.
  - Rule 8: If member is enrolled in the park then initiate Schedule-Park-Entrance event.
  - Rule 9: If a guardian's credit rating code is not = "A" and the guardian's special deal flag = "yes" then the guardian has good credit.
  - Rule 10: If the guardian's credit rating code = "B" then the guardian has good credit.
  - Rule 11: If the guardian exists in the Park Ranger set then the guardian has good credit rating.
- Review the candidate entities and rules. Identify possible supertypes and subtypes.

Case Study Solution:

By inspecting the rules, you can see many detailed data items, such as guardian credit rating code, but you are looking for the entities, which are the business objects described by those details.

Based on the above rules, a potential list of entities includes:

- Guardian
- Member
- Enrollment
- Park Ranger

At this time, you gain consensus on the business name and a business definition for each candidate entity.

In looking at the candidate entity list, you group together those entities representing people, those representing organizations, those representing locations, organization units, things, and so on. Then among each such group, you look to see if subsets seem evident.

In the case study example, Guardian, Member, and Park Ranger all represent types of people. Based on limited knowledge, you suggest that a Park Ranger is a subtype of Guardian. After verifying this with a business expert, you create the diagram in Figure 9.6.

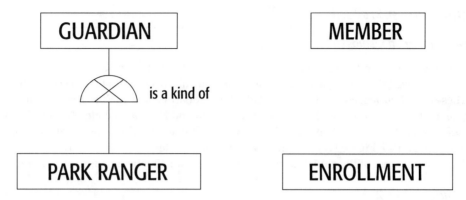

Figure 9.6   Preliminary subtypes and supertypes.

STEP 9.2: DETERMINE RELATIONSHIPS AMONG ENTITIES

A *relationship* is a fact about, or association among, entities. These may be difficult to discover because they are usually implied by rules or by descriptions of business events, but not typically explicitly stated.

It is common to name a relationship as "Entity [verb or proposition phrase] Entity", with the verb in present tense, such as "Customer places Order". On the logical data model diagram, for your purposes, draw a line among entities for each relationship, adding the relationship name on the line. It is usually good practice to name a relationship in both directions.

GUIDELINE 9.2.1

Include relationships among entities for facts that support rule clauses when those facts are best represented by a relationship.

Connections among nouns are best represented as relationships when the corresponding nouns are already depicted as entities in the logical data model. Later you will discover that you will represent connections among entity nouns and more detailed nouns as attributes within entities.

GUIDELINE 9.2.2

Name relationships according to naming conventions.

Use verbs or prepositional phrases to name relationships. Use the present tense rather than past tense or gerund. Avoid meaningless relationship names, such as "has," since this adds ambiguity. Common relationship names include:

- Business verb phrases ("teaches", "places order", "requests catalogue")
- "is composed of" to represent parts and subparts.

GUIDELINE 9.2.3

Diagram relationships.

For now, diagram relationships as lines between the relating entities.

Reviewing the case study description, you may discover at least two relationships. These are "Guardian enrolls Member" and "Member participates in Enrollment." You can represent the first one as a line between Guardian and Member, labeled "enrolls". You can represent the second one as a line between Member and Enrollment, labeled "participates in" (see Figure 9.7). You may want to label the lines in both directions.

Read the rest of the guidelines and sample diagramming techniques for this step.

GUIDELINE 9.2.4

Consider carefully whether cardinality properties of a relationship ought to be represented in the data model, as a rule, or both.

Relationship cardinality indicates the maximum number of instances of an entity involved in one instance of the relationship. Hence, cardinality restrictions are rules because they represent constraints over the relationship. The reason you consider relationship cardinality constraints while determining the skeletal data structure is that these restrictions influence how you will represent the data structure properly.

To uncover relationship cardinality for each relationship, ask a business expert to specify the maximum number of entities of one type that can exist in a relationship with the other type. Ask the question for both directions of the relationship.

If you were following other logical data modeling methodologies, you would diagrammatically indicate the cardinality on each end of a relationship line. This is sometimes shown as a crow's foot or an arrow or other marking. For a business rules system, however, you don't need to include cardinality restrictions (or lack thereof) on the logical data model diagram. For a business rules system, you may decide to simply record cardinality constraints as rules, not as part of the data structure diagram.

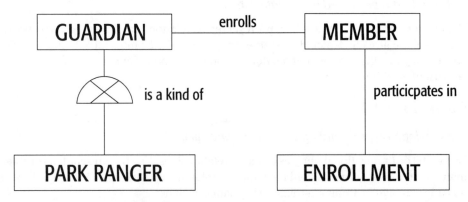

Figure 9.7 Sample relationships diagrammed.

Therefore, at this point, you identify the cardinality constraint rules so as to best draw the data structure diagram. However, record those constraints as rules, not as part of that diagram.

Note that the logical data model for a business rules system is strictly logical, that it is to represent the optimum logical data structure, and that it is to be devoid of rules as much as possible. If you will be enforcing cardinality constraints with your DBMS product, you will create a separate model (called a physical model) in which you will denote relationship cardinality restrictions and from which you will generate DDL.

GUIDELINE 9.2.5

Consider carefully whether relationship optionality properties ought to be represented in the data model, as a rule, or both.

Relationship optionality indicates the minimum number of instances of one entity that must exist in a relationship with another entity. It is referred to as optionality because if the minimum is one, the relationship is considered mandatory, but if the minimum is zero, the relationship is considered optional.

Again, if you were following a logical data modeling methodology for nonbusiness rules systems, you would denote optionality in the diagram at both ends of a relationship line, sometimes as dots and sometimes as hash marks, for example. In a business rules system, however, you may decide not to include optionality constraints as part of the logical data model diagram. You may record optionality constraints as rules.

As a reminder, your logical data model is technology-independent. It represents logical data structure. Rules are represented externally to the structure. Should you decide later to enforce optionality rules in your target DBMS, you may create a separate model (called a physical data model) in which you will depict your optionality rules and generate them in the corresponding DDL.

GUIDELINE 9.2.6

When in doubt, err on the side of higher cardinality for relationships over lower.

Consider carefully, 1:1 relationships and 1:M relationships for future growth. In particular, if you denote a relationship cardinality as 1:1 in your data structure, you make it very difficult for it to ever be more than one because you are imposing a limitation of one instance on each end. If you think one or both entity cardinalities may change to allow more than one such instance, denote the relationship in your logical data model diagram with the larger cardinality. Doing so will impact the key structure of your model (see steps below), but will accommodate growth.

For the same reasons, analyze the one-side of a one-to-many relationship. If you suspect that it could grow in the future to accommodate more than one instance, denote the relationship in your logical data model diagram with the larger cardinality. Again, doing so will impact the entity structure and key structure of your model, but will accommodate growth.

In addition, for every many-to-many relationship in your diagram, you may want to decompose it into two one-to-many relationships in a common intersection entity. Doing so will allow you later to place detailed attributes into the correct entity.

GUIDELINE 9.2.7

Capture meta data about relationships.

Again, your choice of modeling tool may determine the kind of meta data about relationships that is easiest to capture. Common meta data about relationships includes:

- Parent entity
- Child entity
- Relationship name
- Relationship cardinality
- Relationship optionality
- Estimated ratio of a parent occurrence to its child occurrences
- Insert rule (discussed later)
- Delete rule (discussed later).

CASE STUDY: STEP 9.2–DETERMINE RELATIONSHIPS AMONG ENTITIES

Case Study Instructions:

- Review the entities in the case study so far. Identify possible relationships among them.
- Consider the two relationships in Figure 9.7. Determine the questions to ask to determine the minimum cardinality of the relationships.
- Evaluate 1:1 and M:N relationships. Determine if the 1:1 should be expanded to 1:M. Determine if the 1:M should be expanded to M:N.

Case Study Solution:
In the case study, so far there are four possible entities. At first glance, reviewing the rules and asking questions of the business expert, the following relationships emerge, as already shown in Figure 9.7:

- Guardian enrolls Member.
- Member participates in Enrollment.
- For the relationship, Guardian enrolls Member, ask the business expert:
  - A guardian can enroll a minimum of how many members? (Suppose the business will allow a guardian to exist without a member, so the minimum is zero.)
  - A member can be enrolled by a minimum of how many guardians? (Suppose the business requires that at least one guardian must enroll a member, so we call it "one.")
- For the relationship, Member participates in Enrollment, ask:
  - A member can enroll in a minimum of how many enrollments? (Suppose the limit is zero, a member can exist without an enrollment.)
  - An enrollment can be for a minimum of how many members? (Suppose the limit is one. An enrollment must have a member associated with it.)

You now have two rules as follows:

- A member must be enrolled by at least one guardian.

- (A guardian can exist without enrolling a member, so this is not a constraint rule.)

- An enrollment must be for exactly one member.

- (A member can participate in no enrollments so this is not a constraint rule.)

For a business rules system, you do not need to show relationship optionality on the logical data model diagram since you capture optionality as a set of rules. If you wanted to show it on the diagram, one technique is to show a solid circle for the mandatory side of the relationship and a hollow circle for the optional side.

For the relationship Guardian enrolls Member, ask a business expert the following questions:

- A guardian can enroll a maximum of how many members? (Suppose the answer is no limit.)

- A member can be enrolled by how many guardians? (Suppose the business person indicates many. That is, each guardian can enroll the member in a different enrollment.)

For the relationship Member participates in Enrollment, ask the business expert:

- A member can enroll in a maximum of how many enrollments (Suppose there is no limit.)

- An enrollment can be for how many members (Suppose the limit is one.)

Refer again to Figure 9.7 and consider the relationship cardinality and optionality you uncovered so far. There are no 1:1 relationships to analyze. However, there is a 1:M relationship between Member and Enrollment. When you ask if this could ever be a M:N relationship, you discover something interesting.

The Enrollment entity in the diagram is nothing more than the intersection entity between Guardian and Member . The fact that a guardian enrolls a member results in an enrollment. The fact that multiple guardians can enroll a member results in possibly multiple enrollments. To more correctly represent these relationships, the M:N relationship between Guardian and Member is removed and replaced with two 1:M relationships to Enrollment. This is more correct semantically because an Enrollment is really defined as the enrollment parameters set by one Guardian for one Member. Figure 9.8 shows the revision in these relationships along with cardinality and optionality notation.

Analyze the relationships from Guardian to Enrollment and from Member to Enrollment in Figure 9.8. Can either of these ever grow to be M:N? The answer is no, since an enrollment by definition is by a guardian for a member, only one of each per enrollment.

Figure 9.9 indicates the revised relationships devoid of optionality or cardinality indicators in the diagram, since such depictions are redundant with stating them as constraint rules.

The rules now are:

- An enrollment must have exactly one member.

- An enrollment must have exactly one guardian.

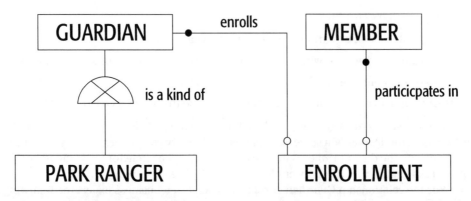

Figure 9.8 Revised relationships.

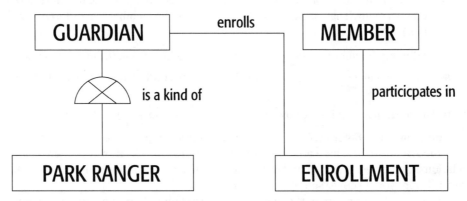

Figure 9.9 Revised relationships devoid of cardinality and optionality.

What Are the Steps for Defining the Integrity of the Skeletal Data Structure?

By the time you get here, you already have a very good idea of the evolving data structure to support your rules. In this section, you progress from understanding the data structure to uncovering its integrity. However, you have already considered some of its integrity when you analyzed relationship optionality and cardinality.

As you follow the steps below, keep in mind that you are aiming to confirm that the entities and relationships are complete. You do this studying the integrity rules behind them and incorporating any resulting modifications to the logical data model.

STEP 9.3: IDENTIFY PRIMARY AND ALTERNATE KEYS FOR EACH ENTITY

So far, you have identified entities and the relationships among them. You want to move onto adding details, or attributes. An *attribute* is an atomic unit of data about an entity. The first attribute you add to each entity will be its primary key.

A *primary key* is an attribute or minimum set of attributes that you select to be the standard way of identifying a specific instance of the entity. A *minimal set of attributes* implies that you cannot eliminate any attributes from the primary key without destroying the primary key's ability to identify a unique instance of the entity. A primary key can be one attribute or it can be a composite, more than one attribute.

A primary key is part of the integrity component of the logical data model because it confirms that the definition (and identification) of the entity is tangible and the primary key itself has rules about it by definition. Specifically, the attributes of a primary key must together be unique and each must be non-null.

GUIDELINE 9.3.1

Select a high-quality primary key for each entity.

Before you identify primary keys, let's analyze the properties of a good quality primary key. Most of these come from a landmark article published by Whitener (1989). The criteria for a good quality primary key are:

- Unique across organizational boundaries
- Never unknown in value
- Unchangeable in value
- Factless
- Legal
- Controllable
- Visible to the business people.

The first criterion requires that you select a primary key whose values are unique across the whole enterprise. Do not choose a product ID whose values differ by department, for example. If each department assigns its own product ID and those values can duplicate across departments, you may need to suggest the creation of a new attribute as primary key.

The second criterion is that the value of the primary key is always known, that is, every instance of the entity has a value for the primary key and each entity instance has an identifier from the creation of the entity instance. Not to know its primary key means not to know the entity instance. For example, if you do not know an employee's identifier, how do you know that you do not already have the employee in the database?

The third criterion is that the value of the primary key never changes. That is, the entity instance will forever be identified in this manner. For example, an employee's ID will never change, which means that the organization will never reuse employee IDs of employees who leave the company. The reason for this criterion is to be able to retain traceable history. A new employee should have a new employee ID and should never be confused with a previous employee.

The fourth criterion is very important in that a primary key should be factless, meaning that it contains no intelligence, it simply identifies an instance of the entity, but nothing more. Thus a combination of department number and employee number is not a good primary key because this primary key also indicates department number. It is probably likely that the department number may change over time, hence the employee's identification (the combination of department number and employee number) would also change. This then causes a violation of the third criterion. A historic example is the way telephone companies once identified telephone customers by the customer's billing telephone number. Thus if a customer moved and was assigned a new billing telephone number, the customer became a new customer (with a new identifier). Often this meant that the telephone company had difficulty understanding that this was the same customer as before (so credit history was no longer available for that customer) and it became frustrating to the customers, to say the least.

The fifth criterion cautions that primary keys ought to be data items that are legally available or useable as such. For example, there are personal data elements that a person does not need to share except under certain circumstances (such as USA social security number) and therefore, such attributes should not be used as primary keys.

The sixth criterion indicates that the primary key ought to be an attribute or attributes whose values are under the business's control. In other words, do not use as primary keys any attributes whose values can change at someone else' s whim. For example, while the business's partnering companies may assign their own product numbers to their products, you may want to consider creating your own universal product ID and using the partners' ID as an alternate. In this way, if the partners change the size of that attribute or the way the values are assigned, the impact on your business is minimal.

The seventh criterion is often subject to debate. It states that business people should see the primary key values. This comes under debate because often (as we see later in this chapter) the most stable primary key is a newly created meaningless value. Since this new value (for example, product ID of 4357) is meaningless to the business community (they are accustomed to seeing 45-size-red-chairs), it is better that they begin to see the new identifier on screens, Web pages, and reports. You can also show them the old identifier, but as a nonidentifying attribute.

It is of extreme importance that you choose good quality primary keys. Primary keys tie your whole database together. The combination of primary keys and foreign keys, in relational technology, allows you to navigate and relate data throughout the database. You want to select very stable glue for holding that database together to minimize impact on the business of future changes.

GUIDELINE 9.3.2

Consider surrogate primary keys wherever possible.

There is much industry debate over the value of surrogate primary keys. A *surrogate primary key* is an attribute without meaning, such that its value simply denotes a specific instance of an entity. For example, an arbitrary employee identifier of 30765 is a surrogate key if the digits have no meaning. Yet, the combination of first name, last name, date of birth, and a timestamp is not meaningless. Nor is an employee identifier of 30765 if 3 indicates the month of hire, the 07 indicates the department of hire, and the 65 denotes a room number. The identifier 30765 is only meaningless if no part of it carries any significance whatsoever.

Surrogate keys are not business intuitive. Yet, they provide very stable identifiers in database structures because the value of the key never changes over time no matter what other attribute values about that entity change. In the example above, an employee instance with a meaningless identifier of 30765 remains employee 30765 even if she changes her room number at some point.

GUIDELINE 9.3.3

Favor single attribute primary keys over multiple attribute primary keys.

This guideline often comes under debate. Single attribute keys are superior because they tend to be more stable. If you have multiattribute keys, usually each attribute means something other than identifier. Looking ahead to implementation, single attribute keys are easier for enforcing referential integrity, if doing so through the DBMS. From a physical perspective, because primary keys are propagated as foreign keys, single-attribute primary keys will take up less storage space.

The negatives are that, if you are using a DBMS that clusters rows (sequences rows) only in primary key sequence, the sequence of single attribute values may not be as useful as sequencing on multiple columns. Also, joins across tables are often more useful when done using business intuitive columns. However, these negatives apply to the physical design, not so much the logical considerations.

GUIDELINE 9.3.4

Be sure the primary key of subtypes is the same as the primary key of the supertype.

Recall that subtypes are simply entities that are a type of another entity. Therefore, an instance of a subtype should have the same identifier as its corresponding supertype.

GUIDELINE 9.3.5

Capture the primary key in the data structure.

Identify the primary key of each entity, with business input. Denote it in the data structure diagram if your modeling tool allows it. We will show it with a (PK) next to it in the diagram. The primary key is included as part of the data structure because it is usually propagated through relationships as foreign keys to other entities. Therefore, while it is part of the integrity of the data model, it is also part of its structure.

GUIDELINE 9.3.6

Capture the uniqueness and non-null properties of the primary key as rules.

We encourage you to capture the uniqueness and non-null properties of a primary key as a rule. Doing this allows you to determine where best to enforce them, in the DBMS, rule technology, both, or elsewhere.

GUIDELINE 9.3.7

Identify alternate keys, if any, for each entity.

An *alternate key* is an attribute or set of minimal attributes that can identify a unique instance of an entity, but that were not chosen as the standard primary key. Often, more business-oriented attributes can serve as alternate keys.

Alternate keys can sometimes contain nulls.

GUIDELINE 9.3.8

Capture the uniqueness and non-null property of each alternate key as rules.

Doing so allows you to utilize DBMS, rule technology, or other for enforcing these rules. Let's not denote these in the data model diagram, only as rules.

GUIDELINE 9.3.9

Identify subtype-supertype membership rules.

For each supertype-subtype group, determine if each instance of the supertype must be at least one instance of the subtype. This is called a *supertype exhaustion rule.*

For each supertype-subtype group, determine if each instance of a subtype must not also be an instance of another subtype. This is called a *subtype mutual exclusivity rule.*

CASE STUDY: STEP 9.3—IDENTIFY PRIMARY AND ALTERNATE KEYS FOR EACH ENTITY

Case Study Instructions:

- Review the entities in the logical data model. Determine a primary key for each one.

- Identify supertype structures in your logical data model. Determine the alternate keys present in these structures.

- Determine the membership rules within supertype and subtype structures in your logical data model.

Case Study Solution:
So far, there are four entities in the logical data model. Let's play it safe and assign to three of them a surrogate and assign a composite key to enrollment key as follows:

- Guardian: Guardian-ID

- Park Ranger: Guardian-ID (as a subtype of Guardian)

- Member: Member-ID

- Enrollment: Enrollment-ID, Member-ID, Guardian-ID

Each is unique and non-null.

In the case study, suppose your business expert reveals that Park Ranger (being an employee of VCI Park) has an alternate key of Employee-ID.

Rules for this alternate key are:

- Employee-ID is not null.
- Employee-ID is unique.

So far, there is a supertype of Guardian with a subtype of Park Ranger. Assume that there is another subtype of Non-Park Ranger. Some rules you uncover are:

- A Guardian must be either a Park Ranger or Non-Park Ranger.
- A Park Ranger cannot also be a Non-Park Ranger (obviously).

STEP 9.4: PROPAGATE FOREIGN KEYS

This chapter includes this step as part of building a logical data model, although it is one of those steps that is very much a part of the relational database concepts. For example, if you are not using relational technology, you may have other alternatives for representing relationships in your database design. Also, from a purely logical perspective, the appearance of foreign keys in a logical data model is often redundant with respect to the relationship line itself.

Regardless, this chapter includes this step for three reasons. First, most databases today are in relational technology. Second, it is useful to propagate foreign keys so you can determine if a foreign key is needed as part of the primary key of the child entity. Third, the propagation of foreign keys is a mechanical step, usually carried out automatically by most logical data modeling tools. We show them in the data model diagrams with (FK) next to them.

GUIDELINE 9.4.1

For 1:1 relationships, select one entity to serve as the parent entity and the other as the child entity. Then, propagate the foreign key of the parent entity into the child entity.

One-to-one relationships are very rare. In fact, it is difficult to come up with an example. But suppose you had an entity for University and another for Dean. Suppose that a university has only one dean and a dean can be dean of only one university. Also presume that the primary key of Dean is Person.ID and the primary key of University is University.ID. If you choose the dean as parent, the Dean.ID is propagated to the University entity as a foreign key. If you choose the university as parent, the University.ID is propagated to the Dean entity as a foreign key. Do not propagate the primary key of each as the foreign key in the other since doing so violates your goal of representing one fact in only one place.

STEP 9.5: DETERMINE KEY BUSINESS RULES

In this step, you are crossing into the rule track, but you are doing so by studying the data structure, not so much the rules gathered. Regardless, perform this step in conjunction with the person performing rule analysis.

Therefore, from a data integrity perspective, you now need to ask detailed questions about each relationship. You are looking for the typical rules about relationships shown in Table 9.2. The rule analyst is likely looking for the other kinds of rules about relationships. Specifically, you should ask about insert, delete, and update repercussions.

Table 9.2 Rules for Relationships

TYPICAL RULES FOR RELATIONSHIPS	OTHER RULES FOR RELATIONSHIPS
Insert rules	Count checks on cardinality (max)
Delete rules	Multientity/attribute constraints
Update rules	

GUIDELINE 9.5.1

Specify one delete rule for each relationship.

On delete of a parent entity instance, what should happen to the child instance? Options usually include:

- Delete the corresponding child occurrences (cascade delete)
- Disallow the delete if there are child occurrences (restrict delete)
- Set the child foreign keys to null (set null delete)
- Set the child foreign keys to default value
- Do nothing, leave the foreign key values as they are
- Customized logic.

GUIDELINE 9.5.2

Specify one update rule for each relationship.

On update of a parent entity's primary key, what should happen to the child instances? Common options are the same as those for delete.

GUIDELINE 9.5.3

Specify one insert rule for each relationship.

On insert of a child entity instance, what checks are needed? Options usually are:

- Reject insert if parent does not exist (dependent insert)
- Set foreign key to null if parent does not exist
- Set foreign key to default value if parent does not exist
- Leave the foreign key values as is
- Customized logic.

    Each insert, delete, update rule is called a *referential integrity rule*.

CASE STUDY: STEP 9.5–DETERMINE KEY BUSINESS RULES

Case Study Instructions:

- In the case study, determine referential integrity rules for each relationship.

Case Study Solution:
On delete of Guardian, what should happen to:

- Park Ranger: leave this child
- Enrollment: cascade to this child

  On update of Guardian primary key:

- Disallow the update always

  On delete of Member, what should happen to:

- Enrollment: cascade to this child
- On update of member primary key: disallow this update always

  On insert of Park Ranger:

- Automatically insert guardian instance

  On insert of Enrollment:

- Member: automatically created
- Guardian must exist

What Are the Steps for Adding Detail to the Data Structure?

When you get to this point, you have a very good logical data structure and you understand the rules that preserve it. However, you don't yet have the detailed content in that structure.

Sometimes it is frustrating for business people to review the model at this point. They may say, "You have spent all of this time and now you know that customers place orders for products and that products appear on line items, but you don't know any of the details?" The important point is that not only do you know those basics, but also you have documented them in common vocabulary so that everyone now knows them and knows them in the same way. Adding detail is the easy part, although it is also time-consuming.

It is time to uncover attributes, which are the detailed data elements that you will place properly into your logical structure. So far, the only attributes in the data structure are the primary, alternate, and foreign keys. You focus in this section, then, on uncovering the nonkey attributes and understanding the structure of the attributes.

STEP 9.6: ADD ATTRIBUTES

An *attribute* is a fact or nondecomposable unit of information about an entity (Fleming and von Halle 1989). You already understand the role of primary key attributes in identifying entity instances and the role of foreign key attributes in preserving relationship integrity. Nonkey attributes clarify the details the business wants to know about each entity, specifically the details that might be referenced by or created by a rule.

There are two basic ways you can start the search for attributes. The first is to refer to the conceptual data model if you created one during the scoping phase and if you included in it some important attributes. In the absence of a conceptual data model, the second way is simply to start an attribute list by reviewing the discovery deliverables.

Peruse the discovery deliverables again, from the list of business events to the rule collection, looking for detailed business nouns.

GUIDELINE 9.6.1

Include an attribute in the model for each base, nonderivable term referenced in rule clauses, where the term is best represented by an attribute, not an entity.

As you study the list of rules gathered during the discovery phase, be sure that you have an attribute that depicts detailed, base, nonderivable information referenced (not created) by each rule. Look for details such as names, descriptions, codes, amounts, dates, quantities, and numbers.

Your list of attributes will expand as you proceed through discovery, rule analysis, data analysis, and maybe process analysis.

GUIDELINE 9.6.2

Make sure each attribute is atomic.

This guideline highlights the properties of a good quality attribute. They are as follows:

- Nondecomposable (atomic)
- Values drawn from the same domain.

The first property indicates that a good quality attribute is one that cannot be further decomposed into smaller pieces without losing meaning. Take for example, an address field. As one attribute, it is not a good quality attribute. After all, it can be decomposed into smaller pieces, each with meaning. Some of the pieces might be:

- Street number
- Street name
- Town name
- State code
- Country code.

It is important to decompose candidate attributes into atomic attributes because each of the atomic attributes should have its own business name, its own business definition, its own possible value set, may normalize to a different entity, and each one changes independently of the others. For example, if a town name changes, the entire address does not change. In fact, a person authorized to change a town name may not be the same person authorized to change a street number.

To summarize, each atomic attribute represents the smallest unit of data that is changeable and represents the smallest unit of data about which integrity (rules) can and should be specified.

GUIDELINE 9.6.3

Make sure each attribute represents values drawn from the same domain.

The second property indicates that, after decomposing candidate attributes into atomic attributes, the values for each atomic attribute should be of like kind. For example, consider the candidate attribute called Product ID. Suppose you discover that the product ID for some products are 31 characters long, for others are 9 digits without characters at all, and for others, the primary key is 12 characters. These are not all from the same set of valid values. You should select one of these as the product ID attribute and make the others their own attributes (if useful). Or you should create a new attribute value set for Product ID that is drawn from one set of valid values.

If you use an attribute to store more than one kind of valid values, you overload the attribute, adding unnecessary complexity to the way someone accesses and manipulates data, not to mention you add difficulty in protecting its integrity.

GUIDELINE 9.6.4

Define each attribute from a business perspective.

Define each attribute with a clear business definition. Include examples, where examples add clarity.

GUIDELINE 9.6.5

Name each attribute according to naming conventions.

Use the attribute definition as a starting point for naming it. Consider naming attributes as follows:

Entity-Name.descriptive-words-class-word.

The *class word* indicates the type of attribute it represents. Common class words include:

- Date
- Quantity (a count of something)
- Text (a description of something)
- Amount (money)
- Percent
- Number
- Name
- Flag (yes, no)
- Code (series of possible discrete values).

GUIDELINE 9.6.6

Consider the advantages and disadvantages of "specific modeling" versus "generic modeling."

Usually, very experienced logical data modelers or enterprise data modelers prefer generic over specific modeling techniques. It is important to know the difference and to consider using generic modeling when possible.

Specific modeling is a technique whereby you represent pieces of information more or less how they sound to the business audience, very literally. For example, a business person may mention that there is a late fee for a guardian if the guardian does not pay the invoice on time. Using specific modeling techniques, you may represent this piece of information in a logical data model in an entity called Guardian and as an attribute called Guardian.Late-Fee-Amount.

An alternate approach is to use generic modeling techniques. *Generic modeling* is a technique whereby you represent pieces of information in a manner that is often less intuitive, but allows for easy changes.

For example, you can have one entity for Guardian with a 1:M relationship to another entity called Guardian Fee. The Guardian Fee entity would contain an attribute for Guardian.ID (as a foreign key) and two attributes to represent the guardian late fee. These would be a Guardian.Fee-Type and Guardian.Fee-Amount. An instance representing the guardian late fee would have a row with the Guardian.ID set to the proper Guardian identifier, the Guardian.Fee-Type set to "late fee", and Guardian.Fee-Amount set to the late fee amount. To understand the value in the Guardian.Fee-Amount, therefore, you would need to know the Guardian.Fee-Type also.

The advantage of the specific technique is that the data is very intuitive to a casual viewer. That is, the data in the attribute is exactly what the attribute name indicates that it is. A disadvantage is that adding various kinds of fees requires the addition of new attributes, which changes the visible data structure.

The disadvantage of the generic technique is that the data is less intuitive to a casual viewer. No attribute is called Guardian.Late-Fee-Amount. The viewer has to read two attributes and understand how to interpret them.

GUIDELINE 9.6.7

Document standard class words and their meaning.

Publish the list of acceptable class words so that everyone names attributes in the same way.

GUIDELINE 9.6.8

Do not abbreviate attribute names unless your logical data modeling tool requires it.

For business clarity, it is best not to abbreviate names. If you must abbreviate names due to size restrictions in your modeling tool, consider the next guideline.

GUIDELINE 9.6.9

Document a standard approach to abbreviating attribute names.

A standard approach to abbreviating attribute names can be a list of words and your standard abbreviations for them. It can be a formula for arriving at an abbreviation of a word. Or, it can be a procedure for obtaining a valid abbreviation, which might include approval by a data-naming stewardship group.

GUIDELINE 9.6.10

Place attributes common across subtypes in the supertype.

This rule is simply a reminder that common attributes are placed in the supertype and that only discriminating attributes (specific to a subtype) be placed in the appropriate subtype.

Even if the subtypes are mutually exclusive and exhaustive of the supertype (that is, every instance of the supertype is also an instance of the subtypes and only of one subtype), still place the common attributes in the supertype. You could argue that putting them in the subtypes is acceptable since they will not be duplicated. Yet, future access and joins, and so on, remain simpler if you stick to this rule.

GUIDELINE *9.6.11*

Place attributes specific to a subtype in the subtype, not the supertype.

Again, consider that you want one fact in one place and in the correct place. Placing an attribute in a supertype when there are instances of the supertype without values for that attribute causes unnecessary confusion and is not an accurate representation of what the attribute means in the business.

GUIDELINE *9.6.12*

Avoid codes, if possible.

Codes are simply abbreviations for real information. Consider the code "f" for full time and "p" for part time. Instead, create an attribute for the real information, such as "employment status text" where its values are part-time for part time and full-time for full time. (Imagine the simplicity!)

GUIDELINE *9.6.13*

When codes are intuitive to the business, be sure they are mutually exclusive.

More often than not, most codes, introduced in the past perhaps merely to save computer-based storage, are now very much a part of the business person's knowledge and familiarity. To remove the codes now may cause angst. If so, still examine those codes and correct them if they do not meet the criteria for a good quality attribute. For example, a code of "pf" for "part time" and "female" contains two pieces of information, not one. It contains hidden intelligence. To search for females, you need to search for "pf" and "ff" and maybe "%f" to accommodate females of all types of employment status.

It is better to make this two codes, one for employment status code with values representing part time and full time and one for gender code with values representing male and female.

GUIDE *9.6.14*

Collect meta data about each attribute.

Common meta data about attributes usually includes:

- Business name
- Business definition
- Domain
- Optionality (nullness)
- Data type and format
- Length

CASE STUDY: STEP 9.6—ADD ATTRIBUTES

Case Study Instructions:

- Refer to rules 1–11 in Step 9.1 looking for base, nonderivable attributes.

Case Study Solution:
The following candidate base, nonderivable attributes are relevant to rules 1–11:

- Guardian.credit-rating-code
- Member.birth-date
- Guardian.special-deal-flag

This chapter makes it easy for you in that these are already nicely named. Regardless, if you followed the recommendations in the discovery phase, your attributes should already be nicely named.

STEP 9.7: NORMALIZE THE ATTRIBUTES

This chapter does not go into the detail of normalization theory. However, you will follow third normal form principles and place your attributes into the correct places in the entities of our model.

GUIDELINE 9.7.1

Place all attributes into entities such that the logical data model is, at least, in third normal form.

This chapter contains the definitions of first, second, and third normal forms. *First normal* form specifies that each entity has a fixed number of single-valued attributes. This means that an entity does not have repeating groups of attributes in it. In our case study, consider a Guardian entity that contains information about its related members. For example, if the Guardian entity contained attributes for member1-first-name, member1-last-name, member2-last-name, member2-first-name, this would be in violation of first normal form. So, you would remove these and create a Member entity, which you already have done.

Second normal form specifies that the attributes in an entity are functionally dependent on the entire primary key. In our case study, suppose the Enrollment entity has a primary key of Guardian-ID and Member-ID. If you had put the member-first-name also in the Enrollment entity, the entity would violate second normal form because you do not need to know both the Guardian-ID and the Member-ID to know the member-first-name. You only need to know the Member-ID (part of the primary key) to know the member-first-name.

Third normal form specifies that each entity contains only attributes that do not depend on other nonkey attributes. In the case study, if you assign a park ranger to be responsible for a member, then you would add the Park Ranger.ID as a foreign key in the Member entity. If you also placed the Park-ranger-first-name in the Member entity, the Member entity would violate third normal form. That's because you can find out the park ranger name simply by knowing the Park Ranger.ID, which is not part of the primary key of Member.

If you are not familiar with the three normal forms, please refer to Fleming and von Halle (1989) for more detailed examples.

CASE STUDY: STEP 9.7—NORMALIZE THE ATTRIBUTES

Case Study Instructions:

- For the case study, determine which entities each attribute belongs to.

Case Study Solution:

The attributes are associated with entities as depicted in Figure 9.10.

Guardian:

- Guardian.credit-rating-code
- Guardian.special-deal-flag

Member:

- Member.birth-date

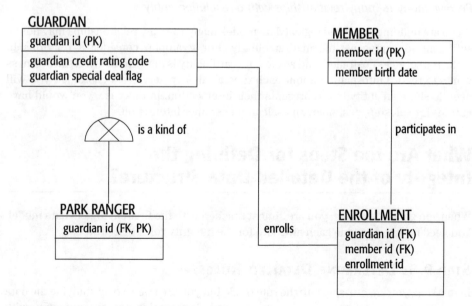

Figure 9.10 Attributed data model.

Enrollment:

- No nonkey attributes

Park Ranger:

- No nonkey attributes.

STEP 9.8: ANALYZE RELATIONSHIPS

It is now time to look closer at the relationships. So far, you have relationship structures and basic integrity rules. In some cases, relationships can become complex. We present two guidelines here for complex relationships. If these guidelines are unfamiliar to you, please refer to Fleming and von Halle (1989) for more details.

GUIDELINE 9.8.1

If a relationship is among three or more entities, create a resolution entity for their relationship.

Most relationships are binary, such as "customer places order" or "salesrep is assigned to customer account." However, you may find relationships among three or more entities, such as "salesrep sells car to customer." Even the "customer places order" relationship can be regarded as "customer places order for product." When you have this situation, simply represent each entity as an entity (customer, order, product) and create another entity for their intersection (line item). The second example would consist of entities for salesrep, car, customer, and sale.

GUIDELINE 9.8.2

Resolve many-to-many relationships with a resolution entity.

If you are building a detailed logical data model, many-to-many relationships may not be sufficient to represent information clearly. For example, consider a relationship "salesrep services customer" and assume its cardinality is many-to-many. If the business wants to record information about each time a salesrep services a customer, you will need to show an entity that represents their intersection. In this case, you would have entities for salesrep, customer, and salesrep-customer interaction.

What Are the Steps for Defining the Integrity of the Detailed Data Structure?

When you get to this point, you are almost finished with the first-cut logical data model. You need now to examine each attribute for the integrity rules that protect it.

STEP 9.9: DETERMINE DETAILED RULES

In this step, you are crossing into the rule track, but you are doing so by studying the data structure, not so much the rules already gathered. Perform this step in conjunction with the person performing rule analysis.

GUIDELINE 9.9.1

Capture detailed rules about attributes.

Table 9.3 illustrates the kinds of rules that exist for attributes. In this step, you are looking for the typical attribute rules. The rule analyst is likely looking for the other rules.

GUIDELINE 9.9.2

Document as a rule the value check (valid values) for each attribute.

If an attribute has a restriction on its values, document the restriction as a rule. Doing so allows you to enforce valid values through rule technology or otherwise.

GUIDELINE 9.9.3

Standardize on shared code values, using international standards, industry standards, or enterprise standards, over application-specific or organization-specific standards, where appropriate.

This guideline can be extremely important. Investigate the availability and usefulness of codes issued from industry standards organizations. If you can standardize on such code values, the business will find it easier to integrate and communicate with its suppliers and customers who may also adopt those standards. For example, you should investigate the purchase or subscription to address reference codes (such as state codes, country codes, county codes, and so on). As another example, you should also investigate use of standard chemical or substance codes.

GUIDELINE 9.9.4

For now, do not include domain entities in the logical data model.

When an attribute can take on one of a set of distinct predefined values (such as, day of the Western Work Week is Monday, Tuesday, Wednesday, Thursday, Friday), it is common practice to include entities in the logical data model to hold those values. Do not do this at this point. This decision can be made during the design phase because the designer will evaluate whether to enforce these through the database design or rules technology.

Table 9.3 Rules for Attributes

TYPICAL RULES FOR ATTRIBUTES	OTHER RULES FOR ATTRIBUTES
Uniqueness	Computations
Optionality (null)	Inferences
Value check	Multiattribute/entity constraints

Guideline 9.9.5

Document as a rule the optionality property for each nonderivable attribute.

The optionality property for each nonderivable attribute is similar to the optionality property for each relationship. For each nonderivable attribute, determine whether the entity must have a value for it or if the value can be set to null. You need to know this because these attribute values are not created by a rule, so a user enters them or the database is populated from another source. You need to know which of these attributes the system must demand an input value for.

Case Study: Step 9.9—Determine Detailed Rules

Case Study Instructions:

■ Study the attributes in Figure 9.10 and determine appropriate optionality rules and valid-value checks.

Case Study Solution:

■ Guardian.credit-rating-code (mandatory) value set (A,B,C,D)

■ Member.birth-date (mandatory)

■ Guardian.special-deal-flag (mandatory) value set (y,n)

What Are the Steps for Stabilizing the Data Model for the Future?

As hard as you have worked up to this point, you may only have built a logical data model for a portion of the target system. Your objectives in stabilizing the data model for the future are threefold. First, you want to extend your focus from present requirements to future possibilities. Second, you aim to understand the information changes that are costly in money and time. And, third, you want to deliver a logical data model that will accommodate potential information changes with minimal disruption to business operations.

Step 9.10: Combine the Basic Logical Data Model with Relevant Logical Data Models

Perhaps your logical data model represents the data needed for one or a subset of business events, or perhaps for one release of the system. If so, gather other data models for the system and combine them together. It is best to do this two models at a time and to use your logical data model tool, if possible.

Guideline 9.10.1

If you have been building a logical data model for each actor or use case or each business event or for any subset of your system, combine all of those models.

Look for similar entities. Compare and combine attributes and relationships. Look for subtypes and supertypes. Consider opportunities for creating such structures.

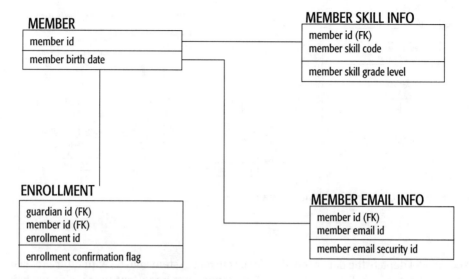

Figure 9.11   Member attributed data model.

CASE STUDY: STEP 9.10—COMBINE THE BASIC LOGICAL DATA MODEL WITH RELEVANT LOGICAL DATA MODELS

Case Study Instructions:

- Figure 9.11 shows a logical data model that represents another aspect of the target system. A data modeler who was taking a data subject approach to data modeling built this model. Specifically, the model represents all of the data needed about the subjects Member and Guardian. Combine this model with the one you have been developing.

Case Study Solution:

This is a fairly easy combination to accommodate. The model in Figure 9.11 contains more information about Member than does the model you have been working on. Fortunately, because all modelers are following the same naming conventions (and were very diligent about data definitions), the task of combining these models is made easier. The result is in Figure 9.12.

STEP 9.11: INTEGRATE DATA MODELS WITH BROADER BUSINESS PERSPECTIVES

Even after combining data models across various aspects of your target system, the most important integration is yet to come.

GUIDELINE 9.11.1

Where possible, integrate system logical data models with a broader scoped perspective, such as is available in an enterprise data model.

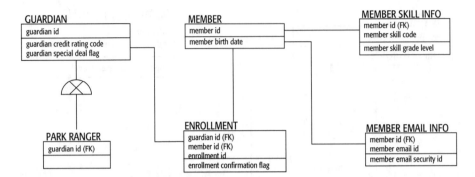

Figure 9.12 Combined attributed data model.

Your model depicts the data needed for your current system, maybe with future releases under consideration. Because the data foundation is so important to enabling business change, this is the best time to evolve your data model into one that resembles an enterprise data model, if possible.

As a reminder, an enterprise data model is a logical data model that represents data requirements across a business enterprise, transcending system and organizational boundaries. Because the data is analyzed from all business perspectives, the enterprise data model represents the data in a structure and with integrity rules that accommodate or can accommodate everyone . . . without imposing future and expensive database changes.

GUIDELINE 9.11.2

In the absence of an enterprise data model, refer to the CRUD from the conceptual model, and incorporate into the data model those data aspects from other business areas that fall within your entity scope.

Most likely, you are not fortunate enough to have an enterprise data model of any sort available to you. If so, see if you can take responsibility for expanding the scope of your data model. For each entity in it, refer to the CRUD matrix of your conceptual model, created during scoping, to see which other business areas have a use for that data entity. Make an appointment to meet with them and review your corresponding entity(s) with them. Discover additional attributes, relationships, and subtypes/supertypes that would impact the stability of your database.

CASE STUDY: STEP 9.11—INTEGRATE DATA MODELS WITH BROADER BUSINESS PERSPECTIVES

Case Study Instructions:

- Suppose there is an enterprise data model depicting data for business party data, as shown in Figure 9.13. Business Party is an entity that represents a person or organization that may be involved with VCI in any way. Business parties include

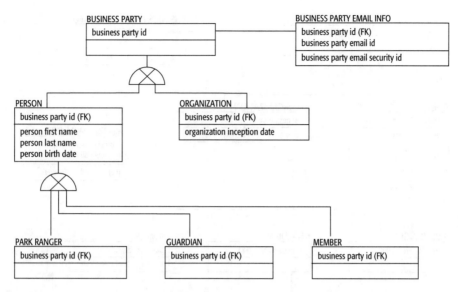

Figure 9.13   Enterprise business party model.

employees, customers, partners, and financial analysts perhaps. Update your basic logical data model to reflect valid aspects from this enterprise data model.

■ Fortunately, the business party enterprise model was a major assistance, improving the data model with much vision. You don't need to investigate further the Organization entity because your system is not, at this time, concerned with data about organizations. Or is it? Document areas to expand in your model.

Case Study Solution:
There are interesting revelations in the enterprise data model that you, investigating the business event for "Request to Enroll" did not discover. For starters, you thought that an email address appropriately belonged to a member. Perhaps you might have realized that a guardian, too, may have an email address. However, the enterprise data model informs us that an email address belongs to a business party, a person or an organization. The enterprise data model provides the capability to accommodate various email addresses for an organization, separate from email addresses for individuals.

You originally considered that birth-date was an attribute about Member because you needed to know member age. However, it appears that birth-date is an attribute common to Person and that Member is a subtype of Person. Integrating the business party enterprise data model with the evolving model, you may arrive at the solution in Figure 9.14.

The integrated data model posed a few interesting challenges. You had to evolve your data model to include the Business Party supertype, hence you needed to assign attributes from Guardian, Member, and Park Ranger to the appropriate places within a Business Party supertype/subtype hierarchy. Also, therefore, you needed to propagate the Business Party-ID everywhere it was needed.

There is yet another interesting challenge. Like before, there are two relationships into Enrollment. However, prior to the integration, these relationships were represented

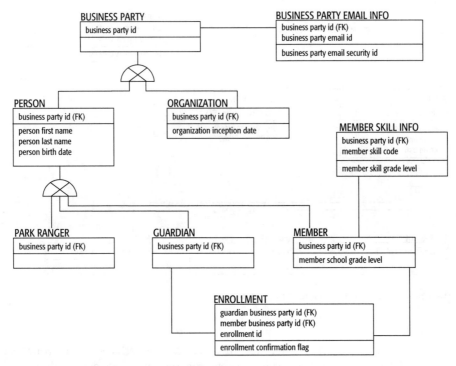

Figure 9.14 Integrated logical data model.

by different foreign keys (Member.ID and Guardian.ID). With the introduction of Business Party, you now have two relationships into Enrollment with the same foreign key, Business Party.ID. So you had to add a suffix to each to indicate from which entity it originated.

Imagine if you had not integrated your model with the enterprise data model and later needed to make these changes in your database and application. These are not simple changes. The cost to make these changes may be prohibitive. Therefore, without this integration and forethought, you might have inadvertently created yet another data and application deliverable that cannot be shared and leveraged.

You might want to expand the scope of Enrollment. Are there different types (subtypes?) of Enrollment? Do you want more information about the member's school? You also have not yet touched on billing information.

You should schedule meetings with the Marketing department (about school information perhaps) and the Customer Service department (about billing information).

STEP 9.12: ANTICIPATE THE FUTURE IN THE MODEL

There are two futures. There is the future you know about, reflected in the series of incremental system deliveries. Then there is the future you don't know about.

GUIDELINE 9.12.1

Begin anticipating the future by investigating data requirements for each incremental delivery piece.

It is always best to solidify the data requirements for the entire system scope, beyond the first incremental delivery piece. That's because, again, data changes can be very costly and time-consuming. It is worth spending the time, during the first delivery increment, to understand and model the data for all subsequent increments.

If this sounds unreasonable, consider the following idea. It would be ideal to have a fully subtyped, keyed, and attributed logical data model for the entire scope, which included all increments. However, if that is unrealistic, look to include all supertypes, only immediately relevant subtypes, and only immediately relevant entities. You can add nonkey attributes and new entities later, if need be.

So, if possible, look at the business events for each incremental delivery piece:

- Look at the data used by each business event.

- Look at the cross-organizational sharing of each of those data entities targeted for the first release and analyze those data entities across those organizations.

- Look, based on the data scope, at which other business events you might be able to enable quickly by delivering the data scope.

GUIDELINE 9.12.2

Consider future enhancements to the data model to accommodate changes or additional rules.

Even by looking at future releases, you may need to stretch your intuition and vision. Ask yourself how confident you are that the constraints represented in the data model will truly be relevant forever. You may want to deliver a more flexible data model (fewer structural constraints) and represent constraints as rules so as to accommodate a future as yet undreamed of, but which may seem reasonable from a business perspective.

GUIDELINE 9.12.3

Pay special attention to information changes that are most difficult to accommodate.

These usually include:

- Constraint changes
- Primary key changes
- Subtype-supertype changes and the movement of related attributes
- Relationship and attribute cardinality changes
- Optionality of attributes
- Change in default values.

GUIDELINE 9.12.4

Consider use of common data model patterns as relevant.

A *data model pattern*, according to Dave Hay (1995) is a common shape for common business information situations. There are data model patterns for sale addressing a wide variety of such situations, the most common being business party, product, address or location, manufacturing, and industry-specific models. Another useful reference is Silverston (2001).

GUIDELINE 9.12.5

Recast all rules in the language of the final, stable data model.

During the discovery phase, you may have captured rules only in natural language or reworded them to fit into templates. In concert with the data analysis activities, be sure the terms in the templates match logical entity or attribute names or properties in a business object model.

CASE STUDY: STEP 9.12—ANTICIPATE THE FUTURE IN THE MODEL

Case Study Instructions:

- For the case study, this is a difficult step. That's because VCI is a new business and is probably, as yet, much undefined. This is quite true with most new dot-com companies and many of these will be (or should be) developing business rule systems for e-business. It may be worthwhile to get the business leaders or investors together and embark on a strategy discussion, showing inherent constraints in the current data model. List the kinds of questions you would ask such an audience.

Case Study Solution:
For your model, these might be:

- Are you missing future persons who may play a role in memberships (billing role, enrolling role)?

- What about financial analysts? Should you worry about them, connect them to any of the entities, perhaps as special members?

- Which brings you to the question of whether there might be future types of members, each of which might be involved in different types of enrollments?

- Would you want to capture information about the members (hobbies?) so as to get insights into future offerings?

- Would you want to know about organizations? Might there be organizational memberships? Might schools sponsor special tutorials or electronic courses through VCI?

When Is a Logical Data Model Complete?

Building a logical data model is not a trivial task, especially if it is to stand the test of time and serve the business through change. It will take time. At times, you may feel like there is no end to the task. However, a logical data model is complete enough to turn over to the rule and database designers when it has the following:

- Stable diagram
- Entities with stable primary keys
- Entities with attributes for target rule implementation
- Entities and attributes with stable names
- Entities and attributes with complete definitions
- Attribute with data type, length, null, domains
- Stable structural constraints (from this chapter)
- Subtypes and supertypes designed with the future in mind
- Volume estimates reasonably known.

What Are the Steps for Building the Rule-Enriched Logical Data Model?

You now have a stable basic logical data model, which represents persistent data in a disciplined manner. At this point, you enrich that basic logical data model with pieces of information created by known rules. The information created by rules is called knowledge. In this way, these pieces of information can be leveraged and shared across the organization. After all, these pieces of information, or knowledge, rightfully should be named, defined, and normalized because they are referenced by other rules. You also want the data model to enable business change. Specifically, your data environment may need to change and your rules may need to change. By formalizing the dynamics between your data asset and your rule asset, you not only provide more insights to the database and rule designers, but you insure that the ultimate technical solution allows for dynamic business change in an optimum manner.

STEP 9.13: IDENTIFY RULE-CREATED ENTITIES

We use the phrase *rule-created entity* to mean an entity whose instances exist as the result of executing a rule. Rule-created entities are usually the result of an inferred knowledge rule.

GUIDELINE 9.13.1

Include an (inferred) entity in the logical data model for each term referenced in the THEN clause of an inferred knowledge rule when the value created by that rule is an existence of an entity.

An example makes this clear. Consider the following rule:

If a Guardian.credit-rating-code = "A" then the guardian has good credit.

In this example, when the *if* clause of this rule is true for a particular guardian, the *then* clause logically results in an instance of a Guardian-with-Good-Credit. That is, imagine that there is a set of Guardians-with-Good-Credit. The members in that set are those guardians who qualify based on this rule. Thus, guideline 9.13.1 instructs you to include in the rule-enriched logical data model an entity for the term referenced in the *then* clause of this inferred knowledge rule. In this case, then, you may consider creating an (inferred) entity called, Good-Credit-Guardian. This entity need not be persistently stored, however, because its members can be inferred using this rule. However, you want to logically externalize these entities so that the rule and database designers can consider various design options.

Entities that may be materialized by rules are ones that may be needed for regular existence checks (such as: is guardian a Guardian-with-Good-Credit?) as well as more complicated checks, including exclusivity tests (such as: a park ranger guardian cannot be in the set of preferred guardians).

GUIDELINE 9.13.2

Consider carefully whether to represent inferred terms as entities or flags.

Guideline 9.13.1 also instructs you to create an entity only when the value created by the rule seems to be an instance of an entity (rather than an instance of an attribute). So, remember the definition of an entity from earlier in this chapter. An entity is a business object with a definition, but which houses detailed information properties. Therefore, if the value created by the inference rule is likely to have other pieces of information about it, you should represent the term for it as an entity. In this case, if you think there may be other attributes about Guardian-with-Good-Credit (such as, effective-date when guardian attained this status), you would represent it as an entity. If you think there are no attributes about Good-Credit-Guardian, you can consider representing this term as a flag, Guardian-with-Good-Credit-Flag, that would be an attribute that normalizes to the Guardian entity.

GUIDELINE 9.13.3

If a rule analyst has not already done so, ensure the inferred knowledge rule is added to the rules repository.

Obviously, step 9.13 overlaps with the rule analysis activities. If you are a data analyst working with a rule analyst be sure both the data and the rules are documented.

GUIDELINE 9.13.4

Normalize the rule to the appropriate entity in the rule-enriched logical data model.

You (or the rule analyst) can correlate rules to a rule-enriched logical data model, in addition to having that model contain data constructs. In step 9.13, as you discover an inferred knowledge rule that creates an entity, you can correlate the inferred knowledge rule itself to the entity whose instances it infers. This is where the rule normalizes.

CASE STUDY: STEP 9.13—IDENTIFY RULE-CREATED ENTITIES

Case Study Instructions:

- Review, again, the following rules from earlier in this chapter. Which ones may suggest the need for an inferred entity?

  - Rule 1: If a guardian exists in the guardian set, the guardian is known.

  - Rule 2: If a guardian's credit rating code is "A", then the guardian has good credit.

  - Rule 3: If the guardian is known and the guardian does not have good credit, disallow enrollment.

  - Rule 4: Member age is computed as current date minus member.birth-date

  - Rule 5: If member age < 16 and member.age > 6 then member.age is appropriate.

  - Rule 6: If member.age > 16 then recommend other theme parks for older members.

  - Rule 7: If member.age not appropriate then reject enrollment.

  - Rule 8: If member is enrolled then initiate Schedule-Park_Entrance event.

  - Rule 9: If guardian's credit rating code is not = "A" and guardian's special deal flag = "yes" then guardian has good credit.

  - Rule 10: If guardian's credit rating code = "B" then guardian has good credit.

  - Rule 11: If guardian exists in the park ranger set then guardian has good credit.

Case Study Solution:
A possible answer is that Rule 1 may suggest the need for Known Guardian, Rule 2, Rule 9, Rule 10, and Rule 11 may suggest the need for Guardian-with-Good-Credit, and Rule 5 may suggest the need for Age-Appropriate Member.

STEP 9.14: IDENTIFY RULE-CREATED RELATIONSHIPS

We use the phrase *rule-created relationship* to mean those relations that involve a rule-related entity.

GUIDELINE 9.14.1

Revise or add relationships to derived entities.

Specifically, if you have added (inferred) entities into your rule-enriched logical data model, you now need to investigate whether those entities connect in a business sense to other derived entities or nonderived entities.

CASE STUDY: STEP 9.14—IDENTIFY RULE-CREATED RELATIONSHIPS

Case Study Instructions:

- If you included Age-Appropriate Member as an inferred entity, reevaluate relationships around it.

Case Study Solution:
If you had included Age-Appropriate Member as an inferred entity in your logical data model, the relationship represented by "Member participates in Enrollment" should rightfully be between Age-Appropriate Member and Enrollment.

STEP 9.15: IDENTIFY RULE-CREATED ATTRIBUTES

We use the phrase *rule-created attribute* to mean an attribute whose value is materialized by the execution of a rule. That is, the attribute value need not be stored, because you can derive it by applying the rule to existing (persistent or nonpersistent) data. Attributes whose values are created through rules include those whose values are computed and those whose values are inferred.

GUIDELINE 9.15.1

Include in the rule-enriched logical data model derived attributes for terms whose values are computed in a computation rule.

Some traditional logical data modeling methodologies already include these attributes in a logical data model. Some do not. In this book, we definitely include these attributes in the rule-enriched logical data model. Consider the following rule.

> Rule: Customer order total dollar amount is computed as the sum of the line item amounts plus tax plus handling.

This rule computes the value of an attribute called Customer-order-total-dollar-amount. So, you would identify the need for a computed attribute by this name.

GUIDELINE 9.15.2

Determine constraints on the values of the computed attribute.

The values for computed attributes are automatically constrained by the computation rule. However, you may want to specify additional constraints. In the above example, you may require that the customer order total dollar amount be greater than or equal to 0. The rule analyst will be searching for more complicated constraints, such as whether the customer order total dollar amount must be less than a credit limit amount.

GUIDELINE 9.15.3

Normalize the (computed) attribute to the appropriate entity in the rule-enriched logical data model.

In this case, you would add the attribute Customer-order-total-dollar-amount to the Customer-order entity.

GUIDELINE 9.15.4

If a rule analyst has not already done so, ensure the computation rule is added to the rules repository.

Obviously, step 9.15 overlaps with the rule analysis activities. If you are a data analyst, working with a rule analyst, be sure both the data and the computation rule are captured.

GUIDELINE 9.15.5

Normalize the rule to the appropriate entity in the rule-enriched logical data model.

Again, you (or the rule analyst) can correlate rules to a rule-enriched logical data model, in addition to having that model contain data constructs. In step 9.15, as you discover a computation rule that creates an attribute value, you can correlate the computation rule itself to the entity whose instances it infers. This is where the rule normalizes.

GUIDELINE 9.15.6

Include in the rule-enriched logical data model derived attributes for terms whose values are materialized in an inferred knowledge rule.

Most logical data modeling methodologies do not capture these kinds of attributes. In this book, in the rule-enriched logical data model, we want to capture all of these attributes, making them available for reuse across the organization.

As an example, consider the following rule:

> Rule: If customer is of preferred status, then customer discount is 20 percent.

In this example, when the *if* statement is true, there is a value assigned to the customer discount attribute. While this attribute need not be persistent (it can be inferred through the rule), this inferred value may be of use to others. Therefore, name and define it for your rule-enriched logical data model.

GUIDELINE 9.15.7

Normalize the (inferred) attribute to the appropriate entity in the rule-enriched logical data model.

In this case, you would add the attribute customer-discount-amount to the Customer entity.

GUIDELINE 9.15.8

For inferred attributes, identify constraints on values they can be set to.

Most often, an inferred attribute is a flag, usually set to a "yes" or a "no." However, as seen in the example with 20 percent discount, the inferred attribute need not be a flag.

GUIDELINE 9.15.9

Normalize the (inferred) attribute to the appropriate entity in the rule-enriched logical data model.

If a rule analyst has not already done so, be sure the inferred knowledge rule is added to the rules repository.

Again, step 9.15 overlaps with the rule analysis activities. If you are a data analyst, working with a rule analyst, be sure both the data and the computation rule are captured.

GUIDELINE 9.15.10

Normalize the rule to the appropriate entity in the rule-enriched logical data model.

Again, you (or the rule analyst) can correlate rules to a rule-enriched logical data model, in addition to having that model contain data constructs. In step 9.15, as you discover an inferred knowledge rule that creates an attribute value, you can correlate the computation rule itself to the entity containing the attribute whose value it infers. This is where the rule normalizes.

CASE STUDY: STEP 9.15—IDENTIFY RULE-CREATED ATTRIBUTES

Case Study Instructions:

- In the case study, consider the implications of an attribute for Member.age-count, Guardian.good-credit-rating-flag, and Member.age-appropriate-flag. Discuss constraints on these attributes.

Case Study Solution:

You will want to specify that the computed attribute for Member.age-count must be an integer greater than or equal to 0.

The inferred attribute for Guardian.good-credit-rating-flag must be "yes" or "no" and is mandatory.

Since you have an inferred entity for Age Appropriate Member, you do not also need an inferred attribute for Member.age-appropriate-flag as this would be redundant with the inferred entity. (Remember that you aim to represent one fact in only one place.) You also decide that you do not need an inferred attribute for Guardian.known-flag since this simply means that the Guardian row exists in the Guardian table, which is redundant.

STEP 9.16: CORRELATE RULES WITH THE RULE-ENRICHED LOGICAL DATA MODEL

This step overlaps with the rule analysis steps. It is included here because it may be most useful to correlate rules to the model you created with your modeling tool.

GUIDELINE 9.16.1

Consider correlating the rules or capturing the rules themselves in the rule-enriched logical data model.

Let's look at an example. Consider the basic logical data model in Figure 9.15. Now, suppose a rule analyst has gathered the rules in Table 9.4 that are to execute against the model.

Carefully study Figure 9.16, which depicts a corresponding rule-enriched logical data model. Notice that it contains additional attributes (and could contain additional entities and relationships) that represent values materialized by rules. The values of

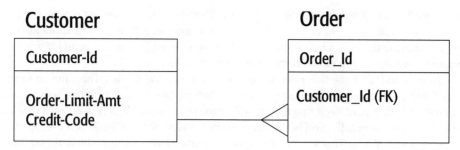

Figure 9.15 Basic logical data model.

Table 9.4: Sample Rules

RULE ID	RULE CLASSIFICATION	RULE IN NATURAL LANGUAGE
R1	Computation	The total dollar amount for a customer order is computed as the sum of the line item amounts plus tax plus shipping and handling
R2	Constraint	The total dollar amount for a customer order must be less than the customer order limit amount
R3	Constraint	A customer must not have more than 10 unpaid orders.
R4	Constraint	An order must be for a known customer.
R5	Inferred Knowledge	If the customer is a preferred customer, the order discount amount is 20 percent

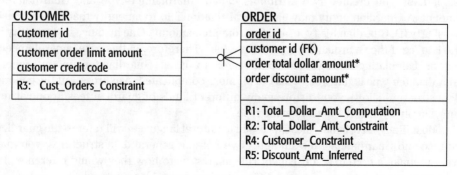

Figure 9.16 Sample rule-enriched data model.

these are known through execution of rules. Therefore, these are not pieces of basic information, but represent pieces of knowledge. Knowledge results from application of logic to information. So, a rule-enriched logical data model is a step beyond information management and a step closer to knowledge management.

Notice, too, that the five rules have been added to the model. The rules are numbered, but also named according to the entity they pertain to, a descriptive word, and a rule-related classword depicting the classification of the rule. Each rule is normalized to an entity where normalization is based on the data value or truth value (for constraints) the rule materializes. This kind of discipline results in very predictable rule-enriched (knowledge-enriched) models. A rule-enriched model provides a database designer and a rule designer with a common ground for designing the best implementation options for the rules and the data. The design should become a joint responsibility between a rule designer and a database designer, both working from one deliverable.

GUIDELINE 9.16.2

Conduct a walk-through of scenarios to ensure the rule-enriched logical data model is complete.

In practice, this guideline turn out to be extremely valuable. Review the concrete scenarios provided by the business people. For each one, point out in the rule-enriched logical data model exactly where and how every piece of information is represented. Not only does this assist in completing the model, but it also provides early insights into how rule logic will be expressed using the rule-enriched logical data model as the foundation for the database environment.

GUIDELINE 9.16.3

Make a note of special representations of pieces of information, for clarity.

Sometimes you will represent a piece of information in a very specific way. As indicated earlier in this chapter, perhaps you created an attribute called Guardian.late-fee-amount, which holds the total charges for a guardian when their payment is late. Any rule needing or calculating this value would refer to it as Guardian.late-fee-amount.

Now, suppose you represented this piece of information in a more general way. That is, perhaps you created two attributes called Guardian.fee-type and Guardian.fee-amount. A Guardian entity may have a 1:M relationship to an entity that houses BusinessParty.ID, Guardian.fee-type, and Guardian.fee-amount. One instance in this entity is the late fee if the Guardian.fee-type is "late fee". Therefore, in this case, any rule needing or calculating this value would refer to it as Guardian.fee-amount where Guardian.fee-type is "late fee". This is a bit more complicated to express, but the general data structure allows you to store many different kinds of guardian fees in one structure, simply by introducing a new fee type.

Most likely, an original rule, expressed in natural language, will refer to the guardian late fee and Guardian.late-fee-amount. If you create general data structures, you may want to make a note to a subsequent rule analyst as to how they would reference the original piece of data as expressed differently in a natural language rule.

Considerations for Iterative and Parallel Systems Development

After reading this chapter, you are in a better position to understand why it is so important to develop a solid data architecture for your business rules system. Hopefully, you can see, by the changes you made to the evolving data model, that some of those changes are significant. They are significant in effort and would be timely and costly if you had to make those changes, not only to the model, but to the corresponding database.

Because of the expense, effort, and time it takes to make major database changes, it is very difficult to develop a good data architecture in an iterative development situation. Obviously, this chapter led you through the development of a data model iteratively, by walking through the steps above. However, this is not the same as attempting to develop a data model iteratively by considering only a partial scope of the target system. Stable data architecture results from looking at the bigger scope and anticipating changes before you encounter them. Iterative systems development takes one piece at a time and iterates through analysis, design, and implementation. While this can work for the development of system code and screens, it may not be the optimum way to go about developing stable data architecture.

Therefore, should you need to develop your data model for an iterative development project, it is most important to start in scoping with a conceptual model, to understand as much as you can about all incremental delivery pieces, anticipate the future, and deploy common data model patterns.

Summary

The purpose of logical data modeling is to capture business information requirements (targeted for a business rules system) and cast them into common business names and definitions, as well as high-quality data structures, supported with data integrity rules. In a business rules approach, the logical data modeling methodology complements the rule analysis methodology in specifically capturing all data integrity constraints, some in the data structure but most in the corresponding rules.

By formalizing the dynamics between these two, you not only provide more insights to the database and rule designers, but you insure that the ultimate technical solution allows for dynamic business change in an optimum manner. We assume that the logical data model is strictly logical, that it is to represent the optimum logical data structure.

An enterprise data model is a logical data model that represents data requirements across a business enterprise, transcending system and organizational boundaries. Because the data is analyzed from all business perspectives, the enterprise data model represents the data in a structure and with integrity rules that accommodate or can accommodate everyone, without imposing future and expensive database changes.

Most likely, you are not fortunate enough to have an enterprise data model of any sort available to you. If so, consider expanding the scope of your data model. For each entity in it, refer to the CRUD matrix of your conceptual model, created during scoping, to see which other business areas have a use for that data entity. Make an appointment to meet with them and review your corresponding entity(s) with them. Discover additional attributes, relationships, and subtypes/supertypes that would impact the stability of your database.

Ask yourself how confident you are that the constraints represented in the data model will truly be relevant forever. You may want to deliver a more flexible data model (fewer structural constraints) and represent constraints in rules instead so as to accommodate reasonable changes in the future.

Most likely, you will be analyzing data and rules together since they are closely related to each other. While this chapter led you through steps for analyzing and optimizing your data requirements, the next chapter provides steps and techniques for analyzing and optimizing your rules.

CHAPTER 10

Analyzing Rules

You are ready to begin rule analysis when you have collected a set of rules that you now can study and improve. You may have collected these rules from people, program code, database constructs, procedures manuals, or any combination of these.

Regardless, you are ready to begin rule analysis because you have a set of rules that you now can study and improve. This is an important value of the business rules approach. A rule analyst, using rule-specific techniques, can assist the business in uncovering semantically disjointed (hence, potentially suboptimal) rule sets.

Specifically, the steps in this chapter apply familiar and new discipline to the rule collection, in much the same way that the steps in Chapter 9 applied discipline to a collection of data elements. The steps for analyzing rules lead you to find rule inconsistencies and redundancies. It includes steps for producing rule dependency chains, which unearth the essential "thinking flow" that emerges from knowing the rules.

Rule analysis includes tasks for analyzing rules into high-quality rule sets. You may validate rules through rule validation workshops. You make the decision whether to optimize the rule set for the business prior to initial rule implementation or to do so later.

If you have followed the steps in this book, you have as input, a table that correlates decisions to rules, a table that correlates rules to policy or high-level business motivations, and a table that correlates rules to the knowledge each creates and the information or knowledge each references. These position you for the most exciting part of the business rule methodology! This chapter focuses on rule analysis, which is where the business rules approach really becomes intriguing.

As intriguing as rule analysis is, however, this chapter may seem overwhelming on first reading. That's because it contains steps and techniques for analyzing rules in great detail. Keep in mind that you may not need to carry out all steps or even to apply all tech-

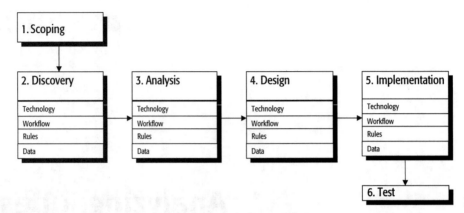

Figure 10.1   Business rule systems methodology phases.

niques, certainly not to all rules. Feel free to use techniques that work for you. Even if you decide to skip some of these steps, you will, at least, be aware of the possible consequences in rule quality. That may be acceptable since, if you followed the business rules approach correctly, you should be well positioned to make changes in rules later!

You may want to refer to Figure 10.1 to recall where in the full methodology the analysis phase fits. By the time you enter the analysis phase, you have completed the discovery phase. Specifically, in this chapter, you turn your attention to the deliverables from rule discovery, although you will be analyzing the rules in parallel with data requirements. After rule and data analysis, you move onto process analysis. All analysis in all tracks, in theory, precedes the design phase.

What Is Rule Analysis?

In this book, the core of *rule analysis* is the set of steps, techniques, guidelines, and tools for turning a set of discovered rules into a logical rule model. A *logical rule model* consists of three deliverables. The first is the set of rules expressed in standard terms and facts and analyzed for logical rule quality or semantic integrity. The second is a table or diagram depicting rule dependency relationships. The third is a table or diagram correlating rules to the data activities that depend on correct execution of the rules.

How Is Rule Analysis Different in a Business Rules Approach?

The primary premise throughout this book is the idea that a business rules approach encompasses a separate rule track. The focus of the new rule track is to separate the set of computations, constraints, inferences, guidelines, and action-enabling rules that utilize the information to guide actions. Therefore, the whole concept of analyzing rules with formalism and discipline represents a fundamental difference between a business rules approach and most other approaches for developing business information systems. Most other approaches rarely address rules directly with rule-specific discipline. There are seven important differences, in Table 3.1, to note:

- Separating rules by decomposing initial rules into atomic, stand-alone, reusable rules

- Tracing rules by uncovering dependencies among them

- Externalizing rules by assigning rules to rule patterns

- Externalizing rules to resolve inconsistencies

- Externalizing rules to resolve overlaps in rules and to ensure rule completeness

- Positioning rules for change by establishing well-defined rule jurisdictions and consensus

- Positioning rules for change by reconnecting rules to their business motivation and optimizing them to best meet business objectives.

Let's look at each of these differences.

The first difference supports the principle of separating rules by decomposing initial rules into atomic, stand-alone, reusable rules. The second difference supports the principle of tracing rules to their relationships to each other. Thus, the second difference is that a business rules approach not only applies discipline to a discovered set of rules, but also introduces the notion that an understanding of the logical rule set behind a business event should drive other aspects of the system. Therefore, rule analysis uncovers dependencies among rules and rule families, based on knowledge dependencies. Rule analysis refines the understanding of the system's process in terms of rule dependencies.

The next three differences relate to the principle of externalizing rules. Therefore, the third difference is the possible assignment of individual rules to rule patterns that create an interesting level of abstraction for business analysis. The fourth and fifth differences assist in externalizing rules because they aim to resolve inconsistencies and overlaps in rules and ensure completeness among them.

The sixth and seventh difference positions rules for change. The seventh and final difference is the deliberate attention to reconnecting rules to business motivation with the intention of optimizing rules to meet business objectives. Regardless, the system is designed with ongoing rule changes in mind. This is in stark contrast to other approaches where rules become buried, forgotten, lost, and difficult to change.

What Is the Purpose of Rule Analysis?

The purpose of rule analysis is to refine a set of discovered rules into a logical rule model. The concept of a logical rule model is a new one. To create a logical rule model, you clean up obvious shortcomings of a set of rules, thereby delivering a set of rules that are of higher semantic quality. By *semantic quality*, we mean that the set of rules exhibits integrity within itself. That is, the set of rules makes sense with respect to each rule's relationship to the other rules in the set. This does not mean, however, that these are necessarily the correct rules for meeting business objectives. It means that the set of rules chosen by the business to meet business objectives are a semantically complete, consistent, and minimal set.

We refer to a set of rules that you analyzed for semantic quality as *a logical rule set*, to differentiate it from a collection of rules that you have not yet analyzed. A *logical rule set*, then, is simply a collection of rules with two important characteristics. First, those rules meet this chapter's criteria for good semantic quality. Second, the rules are unbiased by implementation target technology. This means that a rule designer can adapt a logical rule set to any target technology solution.

In Chapter 9, you learned that data analysis focuses on understanding individual data attributes and how they semantically relate to each other, independent of how business processes access them. Likewise, in this chapter, you will learn that rule analysis focuses on understanding individual rules and how the rules semantically relate to each other, independent of how business processes execute them. Therefore, during rule analysis, you are not concerned with how or where you will implement the rules in the target system. Either you or a rule designer will make those decisions during the rule design phase.

Contrasting a Logical Rule Model and a Logical Data Model

Figure 10.2 illustrates again how the three major analysis tracks (process, data, and rules) relate to each other. Figure 10.2 contains the data analysis track as the top row of boxes. Notice that the data integrity boxes in the data analysis track are connected to the rule analysis track. That's because the data integrity rules are a common integration point between the rule and data tracks.

You will also see that the last two boxes in the rule analysis track connect to the first box in the process analysis track. Pay attention to this connection. It highlights the fact that rule family dependencies are a starting point for understanding essential process flow.

Finally, the last box in the process analysis track connects to the last box in the data analysis track where you analyze important entities in the rule-enriched logical data model through a state transition diagram to better understand process flow.

What Are the Deliverables of Rule Analysis?

The deliverables from rule analysis are as follows:

1. Rule management procedures (covered in Chapter 15)
2. Logical rule model
   a. Validated rules analyzed for semantic quality and expressed in templates
   b. Rule dependency chains
   c. Rule/data activity correlations

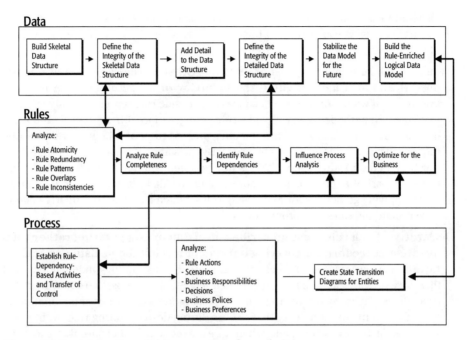

Figure 10.2   Integration of data, process, rule analysis.

During rule discovery, you should have delivered a rules repository and user guide so that rule analysts have a place in which to store rules. As part of rule analysis, you will need more sophisticated procedures and standards for managing and integrating rules from various sources, such as many different business persons or systems. The details of rule management are covered in Chapter 15.

How to Measure the Quality of a Logical Rule Set

Before you start the steps within rule analysis, you will need to understand how to measure the semantic quality of rules. Specifically, you can use criteria by which to assess the quality of each rule and of the entire collection of rules.

The first seven criteria are those by which you judge each rule. After all, every rule costs money. It costs money to think of it, document it, analyze it, optimize it, automate it, challenge it, trace it, and change it:

Relevant/Justified: Each rule must be essential to the target scope of analysis. There is no sense wasting time on unrelated rules. You ensure this criterion through proper scoping, defined in Chapter 4. That is, during the scoping phase, you select the business audience and source systems within the target scope. To further confirm a rule's relevance, during rule discovery, you correlate rules to business motivation. That is, in rule discovery, you associate rules with business policy or other aspects of business motivation. Doing so uncovers rules that no longer adequately serve the business's current objectives. It may be that the business has changed or is changing its objectives. Perhaps the business is fine-tuning itself. During scoping, you also uncover business metrics for measuring the effectiveness of a rule.

Atomic: **Each rule must represent one thought such that you cannot decompose it and still have it guide the behavior of an actor (human or electronic).** You want atomic rules because each atomic rule represents only one unit of change. Nonatomic rules will make rule changes more difficult. A rule is atomic if it cannot be broken down into smaller pieces, each of which represents one thought that can guide an actor's behavior. By the same token, a rule clause by itself (customer-credit-rating-code < "A") is not complete enough to guide an actor, but is merely part of a thought. You ensure that each rule is atomic during rule analysis by applying guidelines for expressing rules, which lead you to properly decompose nonatomic rules into atomic ones.

Declarative: **Each rule must prescribe a decision or computation rather than dictate a procedure for carrying out and enforcing the decision or computation**. A declarative rule is freestanding, shareable, technology-independent, and therefore provides a basis for rule independence. The truth is, there may be many procedures for carrying out the rule. Choosing among various implementation options for a rule is an activity that occurs during design. During rule design, you will investigate how, where, and when it best executes. You ensure that each rule is declarative during rule discovery and rule analysis by using only declarative templates for expressing rules, whenever possible.

Intelligible/Precise: **The rule's intended audience must understand it such that the rule is predictable and repeatable in its usage**. You do not want uncertainty, ambiguity, or confusion about rules to lead to undesirable behavior. You ensure this criterion during rule discovery and rule analysis by expressing each rule using a template prescribed for each business rule classification so that each reviewer understands the rule's intent. Further, you require that the nouns in the rules refer to data entities or business objects or attributes and that the data or business object model clearly depicts the underlying facts needed to evaluate rule clauses.

Complete: **Each rule must possess all intellectual properties necessary for its usage.** You do not want partially correct decisions or computations. You ensure completeness of a single rule during rule discovery and rule analysis by making sure that every rule clause necessary to make a decision is present. You also investigate the need for rule jurisdiction clauses.

Reliable: **Each rule must originate from a source authorized to decide that the rule is as the business desires.** This criterion differentiates someone's opinion from recognized business leadership. It also encourages accountability for the rules within the business organization. By knowing the authorized rule steward, you save time when investigating proposed rule changes. You do not want rules that are not sanctioned. You ensure the reliability of a rule during rule discovery and rule analysis by seeking its business steward who is empowered to approve it, change it, and watch it progress from draft form to tested form to production form.

Authentic: **As each rule is copied into various forms (from natural language, to templates, to declarative specifications, to executable code), each rep-**

resentation must remain faithful to the original intent and expression of the rule. You do not want rules to deteriorate as you copy and distribute them electronically. You accomplish this from rule discovery through rule implementation through proper rule management procedures.

There are also three criteria against which to measure a collection of rules:

Complete/Predictable: **All rules necessary to protect the integrity of a business event are present.** Hence, the rule set returns the same conclusion regardless of who invokes it or how it is invoked. You ensure this level of completeness during rule analysis through the use of rule patterns (checking for missing rule clauses or missing rules) and through the reference to the data model (in search of rules missed).

Unique/Nonredundant/Minimal: **There are no uncontrolled redundant rules.** You may decide to redundantly enforce a rule in the automated environment, but you do not want to specify rules redundantly during analysis any more than you want redundant data attributes in your data model. You ensure uniqueness of rules during rule analysis through the use of rule patterns.

Consistent: **A rule set does not knowingly contain contradictions within itself.** There is no rule that disagrees with other rules in the set. Again, you will ensure consistency of a rule set through analysis of rule patterns.

Table 10.1 summarizes the criteria for semantic quality rule, along with how you will accomplish each.

Table 10.1   Tips on Improving the Quality of Rules and Rule Sets

SEMANTIC RULE QUALITY CRITERIA	PHASE IN WHICH THIS CRITERIA IS ADDRESSED	HOW YOU WILL ACHIEVE IT
Relevant/justified	Scoping and rule discovery	Selection of stakeholders and source systems Correlation of rules to business motivation Business metrics for measuring a rule's effectiveness
Atomic	Rule analysis	Guidelines for expressing rules
Declarative	Rule discovery Rule analysis	Rule templates
Intelligible/precise	Rule discovery Rule analysis	Rule templates Correlation to data and knowledge
Complete	Rule discovery Rule analysis	Check rule clauses Jurisdiction rule clauses
Reliable	Rule discovery Rule analysis	Rule stewardship

(continues)

Table 10.1 Tips on Improving the Quality of Rules and Rule Sets (*Continued*)

SEMANTIC RULE QUALITY CRITERIA	PHASE IN WHICH THIS CRITERIA IS ADDRESSED	HOW YOU WILL ACHIEVE IT
Authentic	Rule discovery Rule analysis Rule design Rule implementation	Rule management
Rule set completeness	Rule analysis	Rule patterns Correlation to data and knowledge
Rule set uniqueness/ nonredundancy/ minimality	Rule analysis	Rule patterns
Rule set consistency	Rule analysis	Rule patterns

What Are the Steps in Rule Analysis?

In studying the above criteria for the semantic quality of rules and rule sets, you now embark on rule analysis. Therefore, to establish the above criteria, rule analysis consists of nine steps, depicted in Figure 10.3. The steps in rule analysis apply familiar and new discipline to the rule collection, in much the same way that the steps in data analysis add discipline to a collection of data elements. Note that step 10.8 in Figure 10.3 represents the connection to the process analysis track.

As rules technology matures, products are likely to introduce more automated assistance in carrying out some of these steps. For example, it seems likely that a rules repository or rules engine would be able to detect a redundant or inconsistent rule when you

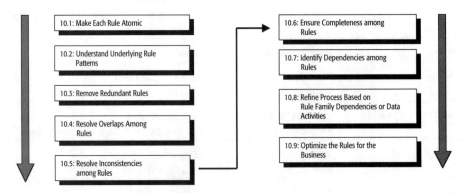

Figure 10.3 Steps for analyzing rules.

enter the rule into the product. For now, knowing that such functionality is often lacking, this chapter provides guidelines for carrying out these steps without automated assistance.

In practice, you can carry out most of the steps in rule analysis, at least steps 10.1 through 10.7, at the same time as you capture each individual rule during rule discovery. For example, as you discovery a rule, you can make sure it is atomic, that it is not redundant with other discovered rules, that you can identify its rule pattern, and that you can check for overlapping rules, inconsistent rules, and even for completeness of the rule itself. You can even add it to rule dependency diagrams or tables.

However, this chapter is separate from the discovery steps because you may have many rule analysts or rule miners capturing rules at the same time. If so, you will need to conduct rule analysis across many rule sets.

Let's now investigate the nine steps of rule analysis.

STEP 10.1: MAKE EACH RULE ATOMIC

Each rule should represent one complete thought, which means you should not be able to decompose it into pieces that represent complete rules.

GUIDELINE 10.1.1

Make sure each rule has only one result.

An atomic rule, by our definition, has one and only one result or conclusion. For an inferred knowledge or computation rule, the one result is the term whose value is created. For a constraint or guideline, the one result is the (simple or complex) condition that must or should be true. For an action enabler, the one result is the one action that is initiated. These become clearer through Guidelines 10.1.2 and 10.1.3.

GUIDELINE 10.1.2

When expressing an inferred knowledge rule or action enabler (as an If/Then statement), do not allow Ands on the right-hand side (the Then portion). Decompose these into separate rules.

An example clarifies this. Suppose you have a rule that states, "If a customer is preferred, then the customer's order qualifies for a 20 percent discount and for free next-day shipping." This represents two separate pieces of business logic and you can separate them without losing semantics. If you separate it, two atomic rules emerge:

1. If a customer is preferred, then the customer's order qualifies for a 20 percent discount.

2. If a customer is preferred, then the customer's order qualifies for free next-day shipping.

As stated above, these rules cannot be decomposed further without losing semantics. However, managed as separate rules, each becomes easier to change. Specifically, the business can change the order discount for preferred customers separately from changing the next-day shipping privilege. Likewise, the business can add restrictions more easily to the 20 percent discount privilege. The business may decide that only preferred customers living in New Jersey receive a 20 percent discount on orders, but that all preferred customers' orders qualify for next-day shipping. This requires only a change to the first rule.

GUIDELINE 10.1.3

When expressing constraints or guidelines, do not allow for Ands.

Again, let's rely on an example to make this clear. Suppose the business states that, "To place an order, the customer must be known (must be in the customer database) and the customer must have good credit rating." This is really two independent constraints, hence two atomic rules as follows:

1. Customer (placing order) must be known.
2. Customer (placing order) must have good credit rating.

Using the same justification as above, these two rules cannot be broken down further without losing meaning. Also, by making them separate, they can easily change independently. The business may decide later to deal with unknown customers by launching a quick credit rating assessment through an outside agent. Such a change requires only a change in the first rule.

Recall that you can also express the nonatomic constraint above using an If/Then expression. In this case, the rule could be stated as: "If the customer (placing the order) is not known (does not exist in the customer database) or the customer (placing the order) does not have good credit rating, then reject the business event." If you want to decompose it into two atomic rules, but express these using an If/Then expression, they become:

1. If the customer (placing order) is not known, then reject the business event.
2. If the customer (placing order) does not have good credit rating, then reject the business event.

The idea of decomposing rules into atomic pieces of semantics is very much like that of decomposing pieces of information (such as address) into its atomic pieces. The benefit is that, by isolating discrete pieces of knowledge (like isolating discrete pieces of information), you allow changes on those discrete pieces, without unnecessary redundancy in implementing those changes.

GUIDELINE 10.1.4

Make sure each rule contains only necessary conditions.

You want each rule to contain only the minimum conditions leading to its one conclusion. For an inferred knowledge and action-enabler rule, the conditions must all be relevant to the result. Computations, in our classification scheme, have no conditions. They are unconditional. (Recall that we classify a conditional computation as an inferred knowledge rule.)

GUIDELINE 10.1.5

When expressing an inferred knowledge rule or an action enabler (as an If/Then statement), do not allow Ors on the left-hand side (the If portion). Instead, decompose it into separate rules.

For example, consider the inferred knowledge rule: "If a customer is preferred or a customer is located in New Jersey, then the customer's order qualifies for a 20 percent discount." This is actually two atomic rules combined. You can separate them into two rules without losing semantics. They become the following two rules:

1. If a customer is preferred then the customer's order qualifies for a 20 percent discount.

2. If a customer is located in New Jersey then the customer's order qualifies for a 20 percent discount.

   Obviously you cannot decompose either of these further without losing semantics. By representing these as two rules, you provide the opportunity for the business to change each one separately. For example, suppose, the business wants to change the discount amount for preferred customers but not for customers located in New Jersey Since it is its own separate rule, the change is very straightforward.

CASE STUDY: STEP 10.1—MAKE EACH RULE ATOMIC

Case Study Instructions:

- Review the following three rules. Decompose those that are not atomic.

   A. For the member to enter the park, the Input Member Login ID must be in the set of Member Login IDs and the Input Member Password must match the Member Login Password.

   B. If the answer to the subject grade question < the guardian grade threshold then subtract the grade deduct time from the theme park allowed time and add the tutor bonus time to the tutorial park allowed time.

   C. If the guardian payment method is "credit" and the guardian credit rating is "good" then the guardian billing status is "sufficient for park entrance."

Case Study Solution:
Let's take these one at a time.

(A) For the member to enter the park, the Input Member Login ID must be in the set of Member Login IDs *AND* Input Member Password must match the Member Login Password.

   The above is an example of a constraint rule, as it will prevent the business event from succeeding. The presence of the emphasized *AND* is a hint that you can decompose it into two atomic rules as follows:

   The Input Member Login ID (of the member requesting to enter the park) must be in the set of Member Login IDs.

   The Input Member Password (of the member requesting to enter the park) must match the Member Login Password.

(B) If the answer to the subject grade question < the guardian grade threshold then subtract the grade deduct time from the theme park allowed time *AND* add the tutor bonus time to the tutorial park allowed time.

The above is an example of an inferred knowledge rule with two conclusions. The presence of the emphasized *AND* hints that there are two conclusions, hence two rules. You can decompose it into two atomic rules as follows:

If the answer to subject grade question < the guardian grade threshold then subtract the grade deduct time from the theme park allowed time.

If the answer to subject grade question < the guardian grade threshold then add the tutor bonus time to tutorial park allowed time.

(C) If the guardian payment method is "credit" *AND* the guardian credit rating is "good" then the guardian billing status is "sufficient for park entrance."

The above rule is an example of an inferred knowledge rule, but the *AND* on the left-hand side (the If clause) is needed for completeness and correctness. Therefore, it remains as one atomic rule.

STEP 10.2: UNDERSTAND THE UNDERLYING RULE PATTERNS

Before you move forward with steps 10.3–10.6, let's introduce the idea of a rule pattern. The rule pattern is a useful technique for analyzing certain criteria for rule quality. A *rule pattern* is a prescription for an atomic executable piece of logic, instances of which the business wishes to call into action. Stated another way, a rule pattern is a generalized form of a set of specific rules.

In this context, think of an entity in a logical data model as a prescription for organizing atomic data attributes, where the business is interested in storing and managing instances of the entity. So, then, think of a rule pattern as a prescription for organizing atomic rules, where the business is interested in storing and managing instances of the rule pattern. An example makes this clear.

Table 10.2 is a rule pattern table. A *rule pattern table* is a table that depicts in its left-most columns those rule clauses that represent the conditional in a rule (the If clauses) and depicts in its right-most column, the one result clause of the rule (the Then clause). Because you are dealing only with atomic rules, each rule pattern table will have a column for only one result.

The column headings of the rule pattern table define the rule pattern in much the same way that column headings of a relational table define the table's "pattern" or struc-

Table 10.2 A Sample Rule Pattern Table

RULE ID	IF GUARDIAN.CREDIT-RATING-CODE	AND GUARDIAN SPECIAL DEAL-FLAG	THEN GUARDIAN GOOD-CREDIT-FLAG
R1	Not = "A"	= "yes"	= "yes"
R2	= "B"	= "yes"	= "yes"

ture. The first column contains the Rule ID, for convenience. The second and third columns in Table 10.2 contain the conditions in the rule, and the fourth column depicts the rule's one result. The conditions and results are comprised of rule clauses.

Recall that a simple rule clause is a phrase of the form <term 1> <operator> <term 2>. A rule pattern table represents each rule clause by its "first" term (term 1), usually an entity or attribute name. The operator and the other terms appear as values in the rule pattern table rows, as shown.

Notice that Table 10.2 is populated with two atomic rules. Each rule has the same structure or pattern to its conditions. Each rule shares the same structure or pattern for its result. However, the instances of those patterns vary for each rule.

Rule patterns are interesting because a rule pattern provides a visual mechanism for achieving two analysis goals. The first goal is the *separation* of the *conditions* of the rule from the *result* of the rule. The second goal is the *abstraction* of those conditions and results into a general expression of the rule's structure. By abstracting individual rules into a general but precise rule structure, you are able more easily to examine the semantic integrity of those rules that conform to the same rule structure and across rule structures. For example, you can easily analyze each rule clause and each rule for a given rule structure against the whole set of rules in that structure to ensure that the set adheres to the semantic quality criteria.

The guidelines below provide insights into how to utilize rule pattern tables for rule analysis.

GUIDELINE 10.2.1

You may not have the time to create rule pattern tables for all rules. Be diligent in selecting the important or complex rules requiring rule pattern analysis.

Let's consider the different classifications of rules and what a rule pattern table for each would consist of. Refer to Table 10.3. It contains a collection of rules behind the business event "Guardian Enrolls Member." Let's uncover the rule patterns behind these rules, step by step.

Table 10.3   A Collection of Rules for Event Guardian Enrolls Member

RULE ID	RULE CLASSIFICATION	RULE
R1	Inference	If Business-party.ID in Guardian then Guardian.known-flag = "yes"
R2	Inference	If Guardian.credit-rating-code = "A" then Guardian.good-credit-flag = "yes"
R3	Constraint	Guardian must be known.
R4	Constraint	Guardian must have good credit.
R5	Computation	Member.age = current date—member.birth.date

(continues)

Table 10.3 A Collection of Rules for Event Guardian Enrolls Member (*Continued*)

RULE ID	RULE CLASSIFICATION	RULE
R6	Inference	If member.age < 16 and member.age > 6 then member.age-appropriate-flag = "yes"
R7	Action enabler	If member.age > 16 then recommend other theme parks for older members.
R8	Constraint	Member must be age-appropriate.
R9	Inference	If guardian.credit-rating-code not = "A" and guardian.special-deal-flag = "yes" then guardian.good-credit-flag = "yes"
R10	Inference	If guardian.credit-rating-code = "B" then guardian.good-credit-flag = "yes"
R11	Inference	If guardian.credit-rating-code = "A", then guardian.good-credit-flag= "no"
R12	Inference	If guardian.credit-rating-code = "A" and Business-party.ID in Park-ranger then Guardian.good-credit-flag = "yes"

GUIDELINE 10.2.2

For constraints, create a rule pattern table with a column containing the rule ID, a column for each primary term in a conditional rule clause, and a column for the event, indicating that the event must be rejected.

Let's look at R3, R4, and R8 because these are constraints. For constraints, you create a different rule pattern table for each distinct set of conditional clauses. Each of these rules, R3, R4, and R8 has a different set of conditions that rejects the event, so each rule is an instance in a different rule pattern table. Therefore, rule R3 belongs to the rule pattern table in Table 10.4, rule R4 belongs to the rule pattern table in Table 10.5, and rule R8 belongs to the rule pattern table in Table 10.6.

Table 10.4 Rule Pattern 1 (rejects event, constraint rule)

RULE ID	IF GUARDIAN.KNOWN-FLAG	THEN GUARDIAN ENROLLS MEMBER
R3	= "no"	MUST reject

Table 10.5 Rule Pattern 2 (rejects event, constraint rule)

RULE ID	IF GUARDIAN.GOOD-CREDIT-FLAG	THEN GUARDIAN ENROLLS MEMBER
R4	= "no"	MUST reject

Table 10.6 Rule Pattern 3 (rejects event, constraint rule)

RULE ID	IF MEMBER.AGE-APPROPRIATE-FLAG	THEN GUARDIAN ENROLLS MEMBER
R8	Not = "yes"	MUST reject

GUIDELINE 10.2.3

For guidelines, create a rule pattern table with a column containing the rule ID, a column for each primary term in a conditional rule clause, a column for the event, indicating that the event should be rejected.

Table 10.3 does not contain a guideline rule. However, let's suppose R8 were a guideline rule such that, "A member not of appropriate age should not be allowed to be enrolled, but there is room for negotiation." Table 10.7 shows a rule pattern table for this rule. While the rule pattern table looks similar to rule pattern 3, it is semantically different due to the Should versus Must as enforcement level.

GUIDELINE 10.2.4

For inferred knowledge rules, create a rule pattern table with a column containing the rule ID, a column for each primary term in a conditional rule clause, and a column for the one result.

Now you need to look at R1, R2, R6, R9, R10, R11, and R12 because these are inference rules. For starters, group together into one table those rules that infer the value of the same term. Doing this with these seven rules results in three preliminary collections of rules, one set that infers Guardian.known-flag shown in Table 10.8, one set that infers Guardian.good-credit-flag, and one set that infers member.age-appropriate-flag depicted in Table 10.9.

Table 10.7 Rule Pattern 4 (gives warning, guideline rule)

RULE ID	IF MEMBER.AGE-APPROPRIATE-FLAG	THEN GUARDIAN ENROLLS MEMBER
R8	= "no"	SHOULD reject

Table 10.8 Rule Pattern 5 (infers Guardian.known-flag, inferred knowledge rule)

RULE ID	IF BUSINESS-PARTY-ID	THEN GUARDIAN.KNOWN-FLAG
R1	In Guardian	= yes

Table 10.9 Rule Pattern 6 (infers Member.age-appropriate-flag, inferred knowledge rule)

RULE ID	IF MEMBER.AGE	AND MEMBER.AGE	THEN MEMBER.AGE-APPROPRIATE-FLAG
R6	< 16	> 6	= yes

Table 10.10   An Improper Rule Pattern Table (infers Guardian.good-credit-flag, inferred knowledge rule)

RULE ID	IF GUARDIAN.CREDIT-RATING-CODE	AND GUARDIAN.SPECIAL-DEAL-FLAG	AND BUSINESS-PARTY.ID	THEN GUARDIAN. GOOD CREDIT-FLAG
R2	= A			= yes
R9	Not = A	= yes		= yes
R10	= B			= yes
R11	= A			= no
R12	= A		In Park ranger	= yes

If you were to put the inferred knowledge rules for Guardian.good-credit-flag into a rule pattern table, it would look like Table 10.10. However, notice that some of its conditions for some of the rules are, in fact, null.

You can reduce the rule set in Table 10.10 to rule patterns by the use of a proper rule table. Recall that guideline 10.1.4 encouraged you to reduce your rules to those containing only the absolute necessary conditions. We use this guideline in creating a proper rule pattern table. A *proper rule pattern table*, then, contains a column for the same result and columns only for those conditions that are necessary for the result. That is, a proper rule pattern table does not contain columns for conditions that can be null. Nor does a proper rule pattern table contain a result column whose value can be null or set to some other value. Reducing your rule set to a collection of proper rule patterns can be very helpful in analyzing rules for semantic integrity.

You can reduce Table 10.10 to a set of proper rule pattern tables by gathering into one table all the instances with the same non-null conditions. This yields the rule pattern tables in Tables 10.11, 10.12, and 10.13.

Table 10.11   Rule Pattern 7

RULE ID	IF GUARDIAN.CREDIT-RATING-CODE	THEN GUARDIAN.GOOD-CREDIT-FLAG
R2	= A	= yes
R10	= B	= yes
R11	= A	= no

Table 10.12   Rule Pattern 8

RULE ID	IF GUARDIAN.CREDIT-RATING-CODE	AND GUARDIAN.SPECIAL-DEAL-FLAG	THEN GUARDIAN.GOOD-CREDIT-FLAG
R9	Not = A	= yes	= yes

Table 10.13   Rule Pattern 9

RULE ID	IF GUARDIAN.CREDIT-RATING-CODE	AND BUSINESS-PARTY.ID	THEN GUARDIAN.GOOD-CREDIT-FLAG
R12	= A	In Park ranger	= yes

It is interesting to note that, while an organization (or a subset of it) may operate with thousands of rules, the number of rule patterns should be significantly less. The same analogy holds in the data world. That is, while an organization operates with many entity occurrences, the number of entity types is significantly smaller.

Rule pattern tables are a useful technique for analyzing rules with the same structure and also analyzing rules of different structures but similar results. For example, using rule pattern tables, consider the following:

- Blatantly redundant rules within one rule pattern can become obvious.

- Overlapping rules (a subtle form of possible rule redundancy) can be detected through cross-rule pattern analysis if you group rule patterns together by similar result.

- Inconsistent rules within a rule pattern can become visible.

- Incomplete rule patterns can be detected by determining whether all necessary clauses are present in the rule pattern.

- Incomplete rule sets within a rule pattern are detectable by examining every combination of rule clause values.

GUIDELINE 10.2.5

For action-enabler rules, create a rule pattern table with a column containing the rule ID, a column for each primary term in a conditional rule clause, and a column for the action initiated.

Look at R7 because it is an action-enabler rule. Its corresponding rule pattern table is shown in Table 10.14.

GUIDELINE 10.2.6

For computations, create a rule pattern table with a column containing the rule ID and a column for the computation formula. You can optionally show a null If column to highlight that the computation is unconditional.

Table 10.14   Rule Pattern 10 (Recommends Other-theme-parks guideline, action-enabler rule)

RULE ID	IF MEMBER.AGE	THEN EVENT RECOMMEND OTHER THEME PARKS
R7	> 16	MUST initiate

Table 10.15 Rule Pattern 11 (unconditionally computes member age, computation rule)

RULE ID	IF	THEN
R4		Member.age = current date—member.birth-date

Look, this time, at R4 because it is a computation rule. Table 10.15 represents its rule pattern table.

Aside: There is at least one rule product that implements rules as rule pattern tables. Obviously, you can design your system around rule pattern tables, as an implementation option.

CASE STUDY: STEP 10.2—UNDERSTAND UNDERLYING RULE PATTERNS

Case Study Instructions:

- Table 10.16 contains a variation of rules R13 through R21 from the case study in Chapter 7. Rules R19–21 have been added for this exercise.
- Create rule pattern tables for these rules.

Table 10.16 Set of Rules Needing Rule Patterns

RULE ID	RULE CLASSIFICATION	RULE	EVENT
R13	Constraint	Guardian billing status must be sufficient for member entrance	MUST reject "Member requests entrance to the park"
R14	Inferred knowledge	If guardian payment method is "credit" and guardian good credit flag is "yes" then guardian billing status is sufficient for park entrance	
R15	Inferred knowledge	If guardian credit rating code is "A" then guardian good credit flag = "yes"	
R16	Inferred knowledge	If guardian is in park ranger then guardian good credit flag = "yes"	
R17	Inferred knowledge	If guardian payment method = prepay and guardian prepaid amount >= member theme park allowed time then guardian billing status is sufficient for park entrance	
R18	Computation	Guardian prepaid hours are computed as (to be determined)	

Table 10.16 (Cntinued)

RULE ID	RULE CLASSIFICATION	RULE	EVENT
R19	Inferred knowledge	If guardian good credit flag is "yes" and guardian payment method is "credit" then guardian billing status is sufficient for park entrance	
R20	Inferred knowledge	If guardian in park ranger and guardian hire date > 6 months from current date then guardian good credit flag = "yes"	
R21	Inferred knowledge	If guardian payment method = "prepay" and guardian prepaid hours > member theme park allowed time then guardian billing status is sufficient for park entrance	

Case Study Solution:

There are seven proper rule patterns. These are shown in Tables 10.17–10.23.

Step 10.3: Remove (Blatantly) Redundant Rules

In this step, you reduce the discovered set of rules to those that are truly distinct. You want the minimal set of rules that will achieve the desired results. Another way to say this is that you are aiming for rule economy.

Table 10.17 Rule Pattern 1 for this Case Study

RULE ID	IF GUARDIAN BILLING STATUS	THEN MEMBER ENTRANCE TO THE PARK
R13	Not = "sufficient for park entrance"	MUST reject

Table 10.18 Rule Pattern 2 for this Case Study

RULE ID	IF GUARDIAN PAYMENT METHOD	AND GUARDIAN GOOD CREDIT FLAG	THEN GUARDIAN BILLING STATUS
R14	= "credit"	= "yes"	= "sufficient for park entrance"
R19	= "credit"	= "yes"	= "sufficient for park entrance"

Table 10.19 Rule Pattern 3 for this Case Study

RULE ID	IF GUARDIAN CREDIT RATING CODE	THEN GUARDIAN GOOD CREDIT FLAG
R15	= "A"	= "yes"

Table 10.20 Rule Pattern 4 for this Case Study

RULE ID	IF GUARDIAN	THEN GUARDIAN GOOD CREDIT FLAG
R16	In Park ranger	= "yes"

Table 10.21 Rule Pattern 5 for this Case Study

RULE ID	IF GUARDIAN PAYMENT METHOD STATUS	AND GUARDIAN PREPAID HOURS	THEN GUARDIAN BILLING STATUS
R17	= "Prepay"	> = Member theme park allowed time	= "sufficient for park entrance"
R21	= "Prepay"	> Member theme park	= "sufficient for park entrance"

Table 10.22 Rule Pattern 6 for this Case Study

RULE ID	GUARDIAN PREPAID HOURS
R18	Is computed as . . .

Table 10.23 Rule Pattern 7 for this Case Study

RULE ID	IF GUARDIAN	AND GUARDIAN HIRE DATE	THEN GUARDIAN GOOD CREDIT FLAG
R20	In Park ranger	Prior to 6 months from current date	= "yes"

GUIDELINE 10.3.1

Compare logic among those rules that create a common data/knowledge value, common truth value, or initiate a common action. Remove redundancies.

Blatantly redundant rules are those that produce the same results and have semantically equivalent conditional rule clauses. This is why it is important to standardize on the nouns/terms in the rule expressions and why you standardize on rule templates. By standardizing on nouns/terms in rule expressions, you can easily group together rules that result in the same outcome and then compare their rule clauses for semantically equivalent meaning.

Rules that create a common data/knowledge value are either computation rules or inference rules. Rules that create a common truth-value are either constraints or guidelines. Rules that initiate common actions are action enablers.

Review each rule pattern table. Look for redundant instances of rules in each table.

In Tables 10.4, 10.5, 10.6, 10.8, 10.9, 10.11, 10.12, 10.13, only rule pattern 7 has more than one row. Inspection of those rows reveals that there are no blatantly redundant rules within this rule pattern.

Aside: Theoretical treatment of rule clause semantic equivalence can be found in other references. Those references usually discuss the reduction of clauses to horn clauses so as to reduce a rule expression into a common format for easy comparison of equivalences and inconsistencies. In this methodology, we simply rely on our templates to assist us.

CASE STUDY: STEP 10.3–REMOVE REDUNDANT RULES

Case Study Instructions:

- Review the rules in Tables 10.17 through 10.23. Identify redundant rules.

Case Study Solution:

This solution is easy. Inspection of Table 10.18 reveals that R19 is blatantly redundant with R14. However, it may not originally have appeared that easily because the rule clauses in the natural language versions in Table 10.16 were stated in a different sequence.

The revised rule pattern table is shown in Table 10.24.

STEP 10.4: RESOLVE OVERLAPS AMONG RULES

Overlapping rules are a form of potential redundancy. To keep it simple, *overlapping rules* are rules whose conditional clauses (the If clauses) are semantically equivalent except that one of the rules has an additional clause and the result clause (the Then clause) are semantically equivalent.

GUIDELINE 10.4.1

Compare rule clauses across rule patterns with the same result for potential overlaps in conditions.

An easy way to look for overlapping rules is to compare rule pattern tables that have the same result. (You are likely to have overlapping rules if your rule table is not proper in that it contains conditions that are null.) Let's continue with the examples.

Refer to Tables 10.11, 10.12, and 10.13. Notice that rule patterns 7, 8, and 9 all specify a result for Guardian.good-credit-flag. Look next to see if any of these rule patterns share a conditional term, but different sets of conditional instances. It turns out that all of these rule patterns share the conditional term, Guardian.credit-rating-code. However, only rule patterns 7 and 9 have a common instance. Both of these patterns contain a rule that compares Guardian.credit-rating-code to "A". Therefore, there is a potential for an overlap here.

Table 10.24 Revised Pattern 2 for this Case Study

RULE ID	IF GUARDIAN PAYMENT METHOD STATUS	AND GUARDIAN GOOD CREDIT FLAG	THEN GUARDIAN BILLING STATUS
R14	= "credit"	= "yes"	= "sufficient for park entrance"

Upon closer examination, you will see that this is so. Rule R2 in rule pattern 7 and R12 in rule pattern 9 both require the first condition (Guardian.credit-rating-code = "A"), but R12 has an additional condition not needed by R2 (Business-party.ID be in Park ranger).

The question arises: Is it sufficient for the Guardian.credit-rating-code to be "A" for a guardian to have a good credit rating? Or must the guardian also be a park ranger to have a good credit rating?

After checking with the business community, you discover that rule R12 is incorrect. All park rangers (they are employees) automatically qualify for having a good credit rating. Therefore Table 10.13 for rule pattern 9 is deleted.

CASE STUDY: STEP 10.4—RESOLVE OVERLAPS AMONG RULES

Case Study Instructions:

- Review the rule pattern tables in Tables 10.17 and 10.19–10.24. Find overlapping rules.

Case Study Solution:
Rule patterns 3, 4, and 7 set a value for the same term. However, only rule patterns 4 and 7 have a common conditional clause. Within that conditional clause, rule patterns 4 and 7 do, in fact, have an overlap. The question is whether any park ranger has good credit or if the park ranger must be employed for 6 months or more. The business states that all park rangers upon hiring are considered good credit. Rule pattern 7 is removed from the set of valid rule patterns. Rule patterns 2 and 5 set a value for the same term, but they do not have any overlapping conditional clauses.

STEP 10.5: RESOLVE INCONSISTENCIES AMONG RULES

There are two situations by which two rules can be *inconsistent*. The first is if the rules have semantically equivalent conditions but lead to contradictory conclusions. This situation is covered by guideline 10.5.1. The second is if the rules have semantically equivalent conclusions but result from contradictory conditions, which is covered by guideline 10.5.2.

GUIDELINE 10.5.1

Compare rule clauses among rules in the same rule pattern for semantically equivalent conditions but inconsistent result clauses.

Again, an easy way to look for equivalent conditions with inconsistent results is to study the rules within a rule pattern table. Search for the semantically equivalent conditions for which the result column has a different value.

Refer to rule pattern 7 in Table 10.11 and study rules R2 and R11. Looking at the left-hand columns, note that they have the same conditional clauses (Guardian.credit-rating-code = "A") but conflicting results (Guardian.good-credit-flag set to yes and no). One of these rules is either incorrect or incomplete.

Table 10.25 Revised Rule Pattern 7

RULE ID	IF GUARDIAN.CREDIT-RATING-CODE	THEN GUARDIAN.GOOD-CREDIT-FLAG
R2	= "A"	= "yes"
R10	= "B"	= "yes"

The business community informs you that R11 is incorrect. You remove it from the rule set. The revised rule pattern table is shown in Table 10.25.

As you can now appreciate, it is very important that you standardize on terms (and facts) in rule expressions. If you don't, it is much more difficult to analyze rules. Consider the following two rules as an example:

If Guardian.payment-method-type = "check" and Guardian.payment-status = "bounced" then initiate action Notify Guardian.

If Guardian.payment-method-type = "check" and Guardian.payment-status = "insufficient funds" then initiate action Notify Guardian.

Are these two rules equivalent? Does "bounced" and "insufficient funds" for guardian-payment-status have the same meaning? You cannot be sure without verifying the meaning of those terms. You should then standardize on one of them if they both mean the same concept.

GUIDELINE 10.5.2

Compare rule clauses among rules in the same rule pattern for inconsistent conditions that lead to semantically equivalent conclusions.

The explanation and examples for this guideline are left to the reader.

CASE STUDY: STEP 10.5—RESOLVE INCONSISTENCIES AMONG RULES

Case Study Instructions:

- Review the rule pattern tables in Tables 10.17, 10.19–22, and 10.24. Find inconsistencies.

- Rule pattern 5 in Table 10.21 seems to have an inconsistency. Rule R17 indicates that guardian prepaid hours can be greater than or equal to the member theme park allowed time, whereas R21 indicates that the guardian prepaid hours must be greater than this amount. The business people confirm that R17 is correct. R21 is removed as shown in Table 10.26.

Table 10.26 Revised Rule Pattern 5 for this Case Study

RULE ID	IF GUARDIAN PAYMENT METHOD STATUS	AND GUARDIAN PREPAID HOURS	THEN GUARDIAN BILLING STATUS
R17	= "prepay"	>= member theme park allowed time	= "sufficient for park entrance"

STEP 10.6: ENSURE COMPLETENESS AMONG RULES

In this step, you check for two different kinds of completeness. The first is rule pattern completeness, which is addressed by guideline 10.6.1. The second is logical data model completeness, which is addressed by guideline 10.6.3.

GUIDELINE 10.6.1

Check for rule pattern completeness by examining all possibilities for each rule pattern.

Let's now check for completeness of rule pattern 8 in Table 10.12 by asking if there are other values for Guardian.credit-rating-code in combination with Guardian.special-deal-flag that will turn the Guardian.good-credit-rating-flag to yes or no.

Table 10.27 represents rule pattern 8 with all possible permutations of rule clauses and results. A *complete rule pattern table*, then, is a proper rule pattern table that contains a row for each permutation of that term and relevant operators. You can populate your rule pattern tables until they are complete so that you know that you did not miss any instances of the rule pattern.

GUIDELINE 10.6.2

Check for the need for a jurisdiction clause in each rule pattern.

Another consideration in making sure a rule pattern is complete is to verify its jurisdiction clauses. A *jurisdiction clause* is a clause that indicates the territory (geographical,

Table 10.27 Rule Pattern 8 and Completeness Checking

RULE ID	IF GUARDIAN. CREDIT-RATING-CODE	AND GUARDIAN. SPECIAL-DEAL-FLAG	THEN GUARDIAN. GOOD-CREDIT-FLAG	COMMENTS
R9	Not = "A"	= "yes"	= "yes"	given
	= "A"	= "yes"	?	Overlaps with R2 in Table 11.11, investigate
	Not = "A"	= "no"		Don't know
	= "A"	= "no"		Overlaps with R2 in Table 11.11, investigate

political, etc.) over which the rule is to be enforced. For example, if a certain rule is pertinent in a certain U.S. state, be sure there is a clause in the rule indicating a test on state.

Suppose VCI issues special deal flags to guardians, but that this flag impacts the credit validation only of guardians in the state of New Jersey. Rule R9 in Table 10.27 may become:

R9: If guardian.credit-rating-code not = "A" and Guardian.special-deal-flag = "yes" and state-code = "NJ" then Guardian.good-credit-flag = "yes"

At this point, you should have a set of proper and complete rule pattern tables. That is, each rule pattern table has the same result clause and each has all combinations and permutations of that result clause and related condition clauses. We turn now to inspect the logical data model in search of any rules missed.

GUIDELINE 10.6.3

Check for completeness by examining the rule-enriched logical data model for missing rules.

Following this guideline, refer back to the evolving data model. Check that:

- Each attribute has a rule indicating whether it is mandatory or optional.
- Each attribute has a rule indicating its allowed values, if appropriate.
- Each attribute has a constraint rule if its values are dependent on testing other values.
- Each computed attribute has a computation rule.
- Each inferred attribute has an inference rule.
- Each primary key has a rule for its uniqueness and non-nullness.
- Each alternate key has a rule for its uniqueness and, as appropriate, for its non-nullness.
- Each inferred entity has an inference rule.
- Each relationship has cardinality and optionality rules.
- Each subtype/supertype structure has membership rules.

For this case study so far, you have captured constraints, inferences, computations, and a guideline. We have not mentioned the optionality rules. Below are the optionality rules for the relationships shown:

- A business party must be one of (park ranger, guardian, member).
- A park ranger must be a business party.
- A guardian must be a business party.
- A member must be a business party.
- A member must be sponsored by a guardian.
- A security officer must be a park ranger.
- A member privilege must belong to a member.

- A member privilege must be for a park service.
- A billing history must be for a membership.
- You can also add valid-value rules.
- Guardian.known-flag must be one of (yes, no).
- Guardian.good-credit-rating-flag must be one of (yes, no).
- Member.age-appropriate-flag must be one of (yes, no).
- Guardian.special-deal-flag must be one of (yes, no).

CASE STUDY: STEP 10.6—ENSURE COMPLETENESS OF RULES

Case Study Instructions:

- You review each rule pattern table (Tables 10.17, 10.19, 10.20, 10.22, 10.24, and 10.26) with the business people. The business expert informs you that VCI has just recently been experiencing credit difficulties with guardians with credit-rating-codes of "A" within Territory 1. Apparently, someone is assessing this credit-rating-code improperly. VCI wants to reject the enrollment of members for these guardians.

- Update the rule pattern tables with the required change. Evaluate the resulting rule pattern for completeness.

Case Study Solution:

There is a need for a new rule: "If Guardian.credit-rating-code = "A" and Territory = "1" then Guardian.good-credit-flag= "no." This rule requires a new rule pattern table as shown in Table 10.28. To study completeness, we filled in Table 10.28 with all possible rules for this rule pattern.

You now need to do more rule analysis. For starters, the new rule (R22) overlaps with R15 in Table 10.19 such that one of them is probably now incorrect.

STEP 10.7: IDENTIFY DEPENDENCIES AMONG RULES

In this step, now that you have reduced your rule set to proper rule patterns, you are positioned to study how these rules and rule patterns relate to each other.

Table 10.28   Revised Rule Pattern Table

RULE ID	IF GUARDIAN.CREDIT-RATING-CODE	AND TERRITORY	THEN GUARDIAN.GOOD-CREDIT-FLAG
R22	= "A"	= "1"	= "no"
R23	= "A"	Not = "1"	= "yes"
	Not = "A"	Not = "1"	??
	Not = "A"	= "1"	??

GUIDELINE 10.7.1

Create a dependency table or diagram for rules or rule families.

Let's discuss dependencies among rules first, then move onto defining rule families and their dependencies.

Fortunately, some rule products today can produce a rule dependency diagram or rule dependency report after you enter the rules into the product. It is also interesting to note that, with some products, you may not need to do in-depth analysis on dependencies among rules because the rule product will determine these and will execute the rules in the essential sequence. However, this section discusses how you can uncover the rule family dependencies so you have a better understanding of essential execution sequence.

You can create a rule dependency table that allows you to gain an understanding of the execution dependencies among rules. Table 10.29 is an example of a rule dependency table. A simple *rule dependency table* indicates, for each rule, those rules that must execute first before it can execute. For example, a rule that computes a value or infers a value must execute before another rule that tests that value.

In Table 10.29, the first column is the Rule ID, for convenience, and the second column is the rule's classification. The third column describes the rule and the fourth column indicates the rules that must execute prior to the rule referenced in the Rule ID column. For example, rule R5, which computes member age, must execute before rule R6, which determines the value of the member's age-appropriate flag based on the value of member age.

Alternately, you can create a rule dependency diagram. Figure 10.4 illustrates a sample rule dependency diagram using a UML Activity Diagram.

Let's now look at another technique that groups rule patterns into rule families. In this book, a *rule family* is a collection of rule patterns where each of those rule patterns results in a judgment about the same term (for computations and inferences and constraints). In the examples above, rule pattern 7 in Table 10.25, rule pattern 8 in Table 10.12, and rule pattern 9 in Table 10.13 all result in assigning a value to the term Guardian.good-credit-flag. All of these rule patterns happen to be patterns for inferred knowledge rules, but each pattern is different. Rule pattern 7 has only one conditional

Table 10.29   Sample Rule Dependency Table

RULE ID	RULE CLASSIFICATION	RULE DESCRIPTION	DEPENDS ON THESE RULES
R5	Computation	Computes member age	R6
R6	Inferred knowledge	Turns on the age-appropriate flag	R5
R8	Constraint	Rejects event based on age-appropriate flag	R6
R7	Action enabler	Recommends other parks based on member age	R5

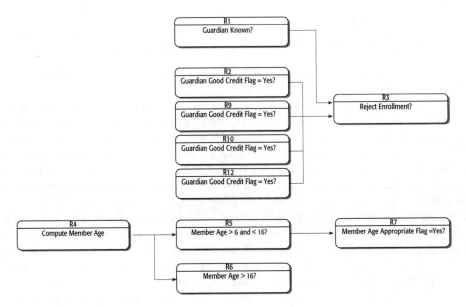

Figure 10.4 Rule dependency diagram using UML.

term, Guardian.credit-rating-code. Rule pattern 8 has two conditional terms, Guardian.credit-rating-code and Guardian.special-deal-flag. Finally, rule pattern 9 has one conditional term, Business-party.ID.

By gathering these rule patterns together into a rule family, you have all of the rules that set a value to the term, Guardian.good-credit-flag. Therefore, any rule or rule pattern that relies on this value has a dependency on the rule patterns in this family (and subsequently the rules within each rule pattern in this rule family) to execute. Let's show a detailed example.

Tables 10.30 through 10.39 repeat for your convenience a set of valid rule pattern tables.

If you study the results of each rule pattern table, you can group the rule patterns into only six rule families (if you group together into one rule family all constraint rules

Table 10.30 Rule Pattern 1 (rejects event, constraint rule)

RULE ID	IF GUARDIAN.KNOWN-FLAG	THEN GUARDIAN ENROLLS MEMBER
R3	= "no"	MUST reject

Table 10.31 Rule Pattern 2 (rejects event, constraint rule)

RULE ID	IF GUARDIAN.GOOD-CREDIT-FLAG	THEN GUARDIAN ENROLLS MEMBER
R4	= "no"	MUST reject

Table 10.32   Rule Pattern 3 (rejects event, constraint rule)

RULE ID	IF MEMBER.AGE-APPROPRIATE-FLAG	THEN GUARDIAN ENROLLS MEMBER
R8	Not = "yes"	MUST reject

Table 10.33   Rule Pattern 5 (infers Guardian.known-flag, inferred knowledge rule)

RULE ID	IF BUSINESS-PARTY-ID	THEN GUARDIAN.KNOWN-FLAG
R1	In Guardian	= "yes"

Table 10.34   Rule Pattern 6 (infers Member.age-appropriate-flag, inferred knowledge rule)

RULE ID	IF MEMBER.AGE	AND MEMBER.AGE	THEN MEMBER.AGE-APPROPRIATE-FLAG
R6	< 16	> 6	= "yes"

Table 10.35   Revised Rule Pattern 7 (infers Guardian.good-credit-flag, inferred knowledge rule)

RULE ID	IF GUARDIAN.CREDIT-RATING-CODE	THEN GUARDIAN.GOOD-CREDIT-FLAG
R2	= "A"	= "yes"
R10	= "B"	= "yes"

Table 10.36   Rule Pattern 8 (infers Guardian.good-credit-flag, inferred knowledge rule)

RULE ID	IF GUARDIAN.CREDIT-RATING-CODE	AND GUARDIAN.SPECIAL-DEAL-FLAG	THEN GUARDIAN.GOOD-CREDIT-FLAG
R9	Not = "A"	= "yes"	= "yes"

Table 10.37   Revised Rule Pattern 9 (infers Guardian.good-credit-flag, inferred knowledge rule)

RULE ID	IF BUSINESS-PARTY.ID	THEN GUARDIAN.GOOD-CREDIT-FLAG
R12	In Park ranger	= "yes"

Table 10.38   Rule Pattern 10 (Recommends other-theme-parks guideline, action-enabler rule)

RULE ID	IF MEMBER.AGE	THEN EVENT RECOMMEND OTHER THEME PARKS
R7	> 16	MUST Initiate

Table 10.39 Rule Pattern 11 (unconditionally computes member age, computation rule)

RULE ID	IF	THEN
R4		Member.age = current date—member.birth-date

that reject the business event). Let's look at each rule family. Refer to Figure 10.5. The box represents rule family A, which contains rule patterns 1, 2, and 3. The inputs to the rule family are Guardian.known-flag (for rule pattern 1), Guardian.good-credit-flag (for rule pattern 2), and Member.age-appropriate-flag (for rule pattern 3). There is only one output from the rule family, rejection of the business event.

Figure 10.6 depicts rule family B. It contains only one rule pattern, rule pattern 5, which creates a value for Guardian.known-flag. It has as input, Business-party.ID and its one output is Guardian.known-flag.

Figure 10.7 illustrates rule family C, which creates a value for Member.age-appropriate-flag. This rule family has only one rule pattern, rule pattern 6. It has one input, Member.age and its one output is Member.age-appropriate-flag.

Figure 10.8 highlights a more interesting rule family, rule family D, which contains three rule patterns, rule patterns 7–9, all of which materialize Guardian.good-credit-flag. Input to rule pattern 7 is Guardian.credit-rating-code. Input to rule pattern 8 is Guardian.credit-rating-code and guardian.special-deal-flag. Input to rule pattern 9 is Business-party.ID. The one output, of course, is Guardian.good-credit-flag.

Figure 10.9 houses rule family E. It contains one rule pattern, rule pattern 10, which initiates the event of recommending other theme parks. Its input is Member.age.

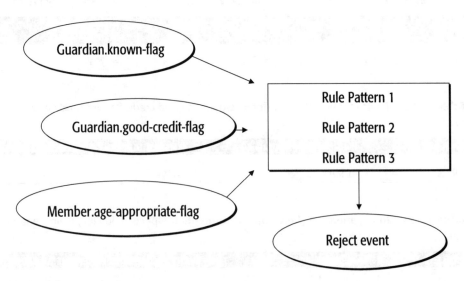

Figure 10.5 Rule family A.

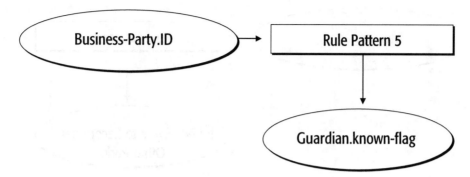

Figure 10.6   Rule family B.

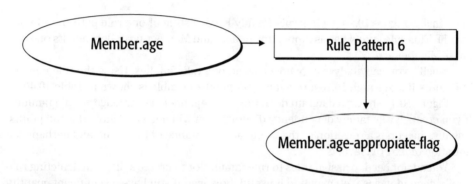

Figure 10.7   Rule family C.

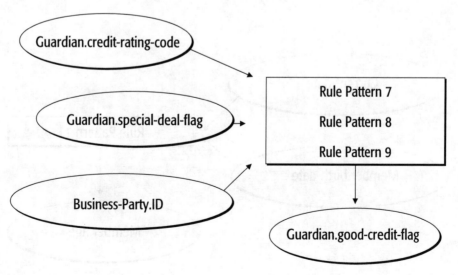

Figure 10.8   Rule family D.

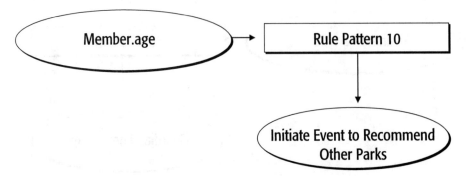

Figure 10.9 Rule family E.

Finally, Figure 10.10 depicts rule Family F, consisting of one rule pattern, rule pattern 11. This rule family has as input current date and Member.birth-date and its one output is Member.age.

Finally, you can analyze dependencies among rule families. Using the rule families in Figures 10.5 through 10.10 a rule family dependency table is shown in Table 10.40.

Figure 10.11 shows a diagram depicting the dependencies among the rule families. If you create a rule family dependency diagram, you will need to denote the end points. Usually, the end is a rejection of the event, an acceptance of the event, and perhaps the initiation of external events.

You do not need to assign rules to rule families or to create a diagram depicting rule family dependencies. You may find it useful, however, if you have a significant quantity of rules to analyze, and reducing them to rule families may simplify the analysis of dependencies. Keep in mind that rule families gather together rules that make a judgment about the same term, such as Guardian.good-credit-rating-flag, but does not distinguish

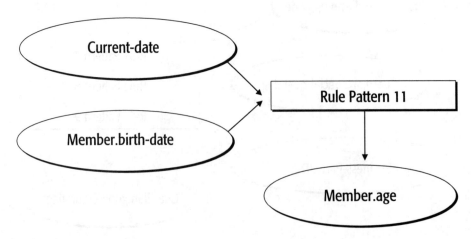

Figure 10.10 Rule family F.

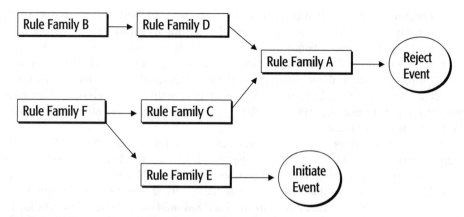

Figure 10.11   Sample rule family dependency diagram.

Table 10.40   Rule Family Dependency Table

RULE FAMILY	DEPENDS ON OTHER RULE FAMILY
Rule family A	Rule family D
Rule family A	Rule family C
Rule family B	
Rule family C	Rule family F
Rule family D	Rule family B
Rule family E	Rule family F
Rule family F	

between the different values that the term may be set to. The reason this may prove useful is that you will use rule family dependencies to better understand core process flow during process analysis. When understanding core process flow, you are only trying to understand the decisions made (hence, a rule family correlates to a decision about a term). When you get deeper into process analysis and analyze actual rule flow, then you will need to look at individual rules and the different values they may assign to the term.

GUIDELINE 10.7.2

Correlate each rule pattern to data activities.

You may want to understand in more detail the relationship between your rules and the data referenced. In this way, you understand the impact on rules should the definition or values of data change over time.

To correlate rules to data activities, you want to work with rule patterns. That's because each rule pattern represents one set of conditional terms that are referenced by all rules within that pattern. You want to create, for each rule pattern, a correlation from the rule pattern to the data activities that may cause a change in each of those conditional terms. After all, if the state of one of those conditional terms changes, the result or conclusion of your rule changes. Therefore, simply create a cross-reference from each rule pattern to the entity inserts, entity deletes, and attribute updates that should cause the rule pattern to execute.

Refer back to Tables 10.30 to 10.39 and study the kind of data activities that would change the one result value for each rule pattern. Rule pattern 11 should execute when an instance of a member is created (because rule pattern 11 computes the member's age). Table 10.41 indicates that this rule is associated with an insert of the Member entity.

Table 10.42 illustrates that rule patterns 6 and 8 should execute when specific attributes are changed. Take a close look at the three rows for rule pattern 6. Rule pattern 6 contains rule 6 as follows: "If member.age < 16 and member.age > 6 then member.age-appropriate-flag = "yes." This rule is should execute if the value of member.age is updated, if the rule's lower boundary (6) is updated, or if the rule's upper boundary (16) is updated. Perhaps you may want to assign terms to these upper and lower boundaries (such as member.maximum-age and member.minimum-age) rather than constants. Regardless, when those values change, the result of this rule may be different from the last time it was executed, and you may want it to reexecute.

CASE STUDY: STEP 10.7—IDENTIFY DEPENDENCIES AMONG RULES

Case Study Instructions:

- Review the rule patterns in Tables 10.17, 10.19, 10.20, 10.22, 10.24, and 10.26. Determine how many rule families there are. Create either a rule family dependency table and diagram.

Case Study Solution:
There are four rule families. These are depicted in Table 10.43.

Table 10.41 Rule Pattern Correlated to Entity Activity

RULE PATTERN	ENTITY	ENTITY ACTIVITY
Rule pattern 11	Member	Insert

Table 10.42 Correlation of Rules to Attributes

RULE PATTERN	ENTITY (OR RULES)	ATTRIBUTE (OR TERM) UPDATE ACTIVITY
Rule pattern 6	Member	Age
Rule pattern 6	Rule	Upper boundary
Rule pattern 6	Rule	Lower boundary

Table 10.43 Grouping of Rule Patterns into Rule Families

RULE FAMILY NAME	RULE PATTERNS	POSSIBLE INPUTS	ONE OUTPUT
Rule family A	Rule pattern 1	Guardian.billing.status	Reject event
Rule family B	Rule pattern 2	Guardian.payment-method-status	Guardian.billing-status
		Guardian.good-credit-flag	
	Rule pattern 5	Guardian-prepaid-hours	
		Guardian.payment-method-status	
Rule family C	Rule pattern 3	Guardian.credit-rating-code	Guardian.good-credit-flag
	Rule pattern 4	Guardian	
Rule family D	Rule pattern 6	To be determined	Guardian.prepaid.hours

A rule family dependency table is shown in Table 10.44. A corresponding rule family dependency diagram is shown in Figure 10.12.

STEP 10.8: REFINE THE PROCESS BASED ON RULE FAMILY DEPENDENCIES OR DATA ACTIVITIES

In this step, prepare the rule dependency tables or diagrams for review with the process analyst. The process analyst (with or without the rule analyst) can then compare the rule family dependencies with the process sequence.

GUIDELINE 10.8.1

Make sure the process sequence supports the required rule dependency sequence.

Refer to Figure 10.11. It shows us that the system can evaluate rule families B and F without evaluating any other rule families first. Therefore, these evaluations can actually

Table 10.44 Rule Family Dependency Table

RULE FAMILY	DEPENDS ON RULE FAMILY
Rule family B	Rule family C
Rule family B	Rule family D
Rule family C	
Rule family D	Rule family B
Rule family A	Rule family B

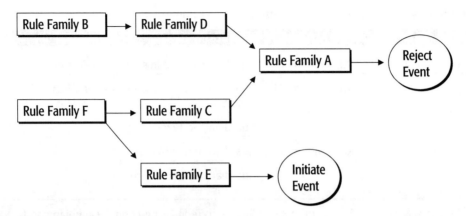

Figure 10.12 Rule family dependency diagram.

begin in parallel. Rule family C needs rule family F to execute first, as does rule family E. Rule family A, which represents all the constraints, cannot execute until rule families D and C execute.

GUIDELINE 10.8.2

Make sure the process analyst understands that other sequences can be altered.

Beyond the mandatory flow of knowledge, other workflow navigational sequences are by choice. The process or object analyst can then tailor them to accommodate performance or business requirements or preferences.

Look again at the rule family dependency diagram in Figure 10.11. Rule families B and D involve checking guardian existence and guardian credit while rule families E, C, and F involve determining the age-appropriateness of the member. The diagram shows that the system can, in fact, verify guardian existence and credit independently of verifying member age-appropriateness.

The process analyst can ascertain the merits of checking on the guardian's credit prior to, after, or in parallel with determining if the member is of the appropriate age. Part of the decision may be customer satisfaction issues. Would a guardian prefer to discuss their child's age before credit is checked, for example? Might it be better to do that since, if the member is ineligible, you can recommend another theme park prior to checking guardian credit? Or would you prefer to check the credit before troubling them with other recommendations?

STEP 10.9: OPTIMIZE THE RULES FOR THE BUSINESS

When you get to this step, you emerge with a set of rules that is semantically consistent within itself. This does not, however, guarantee that the rules make business sense. Specifically, the previous steps do not make sure that the resulting rules are consistent with business motivation. Moreover, these rules are likely to change either because the business motivations change (policies, objectives, tactics, and so on) or the rule set does not guide the enterprise effectively toward the business motivations.

GUIDELINE 10.9.1

Evaluate the need for change.

This is actually a business decision. There may be a need to change rules because the business wants consistent rules across organization boundaries. There may be a need to change rules because the objectives for the business event were not achieved using existing rules. There may be a need to change rules simply because the rules have not changed in many years, therefore, they should be analyzed for relevance.

GUIDELINE 10.9.2

Consider adding new rules.

More rules are not necessarily better than fewer rules. The question is how much human creativity should be permitted within the context of a decision within a business event? When does the business want to mandate or guide the actor and when does the business want to leave decisions up to the human actors? Lead the business people in evaluating business objectives, business strategy, and business policies. Look at business metrics. Assist them in deciding which business nouns require additional rules (constraints, guidelines, inferences, computations). Refer ahead to Figure 11.10 for insights into synchronizing new rules with corresponding analysis deliverables.

GUIDELINE 10.9.3

Consider changed rules.

Again, this is a business decision. Consider adding conditions to rules or removing conditions. Consider adding conditions for specific locations or a subset of scenarios and test the waters with those rules in place before changing the rule for all scenarios. Always, refer to Figure 11.10 to guarantee synchronization of changed rules with other analysis deliverables.

GUIDELINE 10.9.4

Consider retiring rules.

It may be most important to justify a rule's existence. Why is it there, does it assist in delivering benefits, meeting objectives, supporting policies, or to mitigating risks? If there is no current justification for a rule (it may simply be left over from outdated thinking or former business practices), eliminate it. Every rule costs money to enforce and audit and change. Again refer to Figure 11.10 to synchronize retired rules with other analysis deliverables. Hopefully, you will be changing rules often, be it adding, retiring, or updating rules.

GUIDELINE *10.9.5*

Assess the business impact of change.

Here is where your business-grouping scheme for rules from Chapter 7 pays off. Before changing a rule, identify the business events that share it, business processes that rely on it, and business organizations that will feel the change. Identify rules that depend on the outcome of the changed rule or those that provide input to it. If the rule is part of a group of rules behind a decision, study the business events and processes that make that decision, hence share the rule.

GUIDELINE *10.9.6*

Assess the impact of change on systems.

To accomplish this, your rules repository needs to point you to all relevant system changes. These might be programs, methods, database code, and so on. A rule might be implemented in various places using a multitude of technology; hence its change may require many information technology professionals.

GUIDELINE *10.9.7*

Create a plan for the change.

Your plan should include rule stewards to watch over the change, the time to plan the change, the professional needed to make the change, the time to make the change, mechanisms for testing the change (remember your concrete scenarios), and the time to put the change into production.

GUIDELINE *10.9.8*

Publish the plan.

This is very important and should be the responsibility of a rule management function. Be sure all effected parties (business people, customers, partners) are well aware of rule changes and when they will occur. You may wish to store in the rules repository rule-effective and expiration dates and broadcast planned rule changes as the time draws near.

GUIDELINE *10.9.9*

Implement the change.

This is simply carrying out the plan above.

Considerations for Iterative and Parallel Systems Development

As in rule discovery, there is very little that is rigid in rule analysis. Rule analysis, by defi-nition, is a deliberate opportunity to challenge and refine rules and decisions behind a use case or business event. If you are following an iterative development approach, you will evolve use-case descriptions, concrete scenarios, and process flow. Therefore, expect, within those changes, to find additional rules and decisions or to correct existing ones.

When rules or rule sets are simple, you do not need to iterate through all of the steps in this chapter for analyzing them. However, for complex decisions and challenging rules, the time is well spent. Of utmost importance is to tie rule changes to changes in other project deliverables, depicted ahead in Figure 11.10

The most rigid concepts, by definition, are the terms and facts behind the rules. You cannot change the meaning of a term without wreaking havoc upon all of the rules that reference it or create it. Therefore, while iterative development can discover new rule sources and new rules, analyze them, design them, deploy them, and start all over again, the whole foundation falls apart when the underlying data semantics and semantically stable structure changes. This is why, again, a stable information architecture is required not only for iterative development, but also for eventual changeable production systems.

But the rules must be free to change at any time. And iterative development is a way to test that freedom. How long does it take you to challenge a rule, assess the impact of changing it, change it, and test that change?

Summary

This chapter demonstrates the business value in analyzing rules. After all, the rules of the business represent its decision-making capacity. They govern how the business itself behaves with respect to its internal people and external partners and customers. They are a strong basis for business process reengineering as well as the transformation of systems from one technology to another. A rule analyst, by applying rule techniques, can assist the business in finding semantically disjointed rule sets that may be suboptimal or damaging to the business.

A final step in rule analysis is returning to the business motivation by optimizing rules. Specifically, many steps in rule analysis ensure that the rules you collected make semantic sense among themselves. However, you need also to make sure that the rules are consistent with business motivation, such as policies, objectives, and risk mitigation. Your rule analysis concludes by revisiting the connection between the resulting high-quality collection of rules and the business motivations the rules intend to support. You do this with an eye toward optimizing your rule sets for business purposes.

A business rules approach not only applies discipline to a discovered set of rules, but also introduces the notion that an understanding of the logical rule set behind a business event should drive other aspects of the system. With this in mind, rule analysis is a philosophy (as well as a set of techniques) for recognizing that rules have an existence independent of how the rules are executed, who executes them, and whether or not such execution is computerized.

However, this book assumes you will be computerizing these rules. With this in mind, now that you have analyzed your data and rules into high-quality deliverables, you are ready for the next chapter. You now begin to analyze the process that ties the rules together to service the business event or use case.

Analyzing Process

In this book, the term *process* means the dynamic characteristics of the system. The *dynamic characteristics* are the time-dependent behavior, specifically the sequencing of the system's logic, sometimes called the execution flow of the system. In this chapter, you start to analyze the "process" aspect of your system because you want to understand the execution flow behind each business event.

This chapter does not contain a complete methodology for analyzing the process behind a system. There are many excellent references on that topic, the most common approach today being an object-oriented approach. This chapter does not replace other process analysis techniques. Rather, it changes the emphasis to incorporate and leverage the separation of rule execution. Because of this change in emphasis, you may find that you do not need to create all of the common process analysis deliverables or that you need only to create them for a portion of your system's process. In fact, this chapter advocates that you delay the creation of your standard process analysis deliverables until you understand the influence on those deliverables of a separate rules capability. A *rules capability* is an automated functionality that manages and executes rules in a sharable manner. The rules capability can exist outside your system so that it is shared across systems. Or, most likely today, it exists within your system, but you will still implement it as a separate function or functions within your overall system logic. Once you understand the influence of a separate rules capability, you can then decide which additional deliverables you really need and what aspect of the system's process they need to address.

But, first, what does it mean, in the context of process analysis, to separate rule execution? For an answer, let's look at history. A long time ago, a system's internal logic included all logic needed to carry out its entire mission. That is, the system's internal logic not only addressed the business process logic for which the system was developed, but also details on how to access and navigate the data the system referenced. When commercial database management systems became available, this changed. At that time, the logic for accessing and navigating the data became the responsibility of the database management system, not the application system. That means that the logic for accessing and navigating the data was no longer internal to the system's logic, but separate and external to the system itself. The system's internal logic then focused only on the detailed business process logic (decisions and rules), the kinds of data it needed for those decisions and rules, and when it needed that data and decisions in the course of its execution.

With the separation of data from process came interesting analysis techniques. On one hand, there were techniques for analyzing the business process logic, which are usually either algorithmic analysis (such as functional decomposition) or object-oriented analysis. These process analysis techniques organize the business process logic into a structure of executing pieces, showing how those pieces relate to each other.

On the other hand, there were techniques for analyzing the data. Likewise, these aimed to organize the data into stable pieces, showing how those pieces relate to each other.

As you can see, there were two different kinds of techniques because there were two different target technologies: one for the business process logic and one for the data management. You leveraged these technologies by applying different analysis and design techniques.

Today, a business rules approach takes you one step further. With a business rules approach, the logic for accessing and navigating the rules now becomes the responsibility of a commercial or homegrown rules capability. This logic can be internal to the system itself or external as a shared capability. In either case, this book considers that the execution of rules is no longer part of the system's core process because the core process is the process that wraps around rule execution. With this perspective, rule execution becomes a separate aspect of the system. The system's core logic now focuses on the decisions it makes, the kinds of data it needs to make those decisions, and when in the system's execution flow it needs to make them.

Learning from history, it follows that you can be most efficient if you have three kinds of analysis techniques, because possibly you will implement on three different technologies: one for core process, one for the rules capability (even if homegrown), and one for data. Therefore, you need one technique that organizes data; one that organizes the revised process, devoid of rules execution and data navigation; and one that organizes rules execution.

Figure 11.1 reminds you where the analysis phase of a business rules approach fits with respect to other phases. The deliverables from the scoping phase that are most valuable during process analysis are the business context, such as strategies, objectives, policies, tactics, constraints, and risks. Also useful is the list of business events. The most valuable deliverables from the discovery phase are the event-response details (using your choice of notation, such as a use-case description), concrete scenarios, and the preliminary tasks or activities and decisions for each business event. The policies and rules you discovered during discovery may also be interesting. However, the focus of process analysis is likely to be on decisions (hence, flow of execution among decisions) and not on detailed rules.

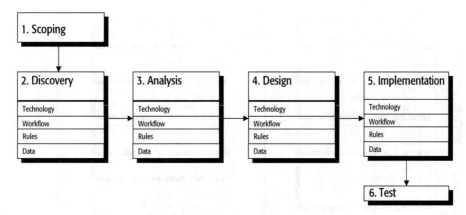

Figure 11.1 Business rule systems methodology phases.

You will also find that deliverables from your rule and data analysis become valuable now, such as the rule (family) dependencies and rule-enriched logical data model.

What Is Process Analysis?

In this book, *process analysis* is the set of steps, techniques, guidelines, and tools for transforming the process flow requirements from discovery into a somewhat technology-independent execution flow for the system. Because you are following a business rules approach, the deliverables from process analysis focus on the system's execution flow with attention to when the system calls upon the rules capability and when it calls upon the database software.

If you remove from traditional process analysis deliverables, the details of data access and rule execution, you have left over a revised process flow. Let's call this the core process flow. The *core process flow*, then, is the overall sequence of system execution with ties to both data and rule execution, but devoid of the details of how those data access and rule executions occur. In this sense, the core process flow integrates the data perspective and rules perspective into a holistic executable process that makes sense. The core process flow fills in the gaps that data analysis and rule analysis do not address, so as to create a cohesive execution experience for the interfacing humans and systems.

This chapter leads you in defining and modeling the core process flow and how it relates to rule execution. Figure 11.2 shows the steps covered in this chapter. Notice that most of the steps are most directly involved with the process track, although the assignment of decision and rules to the rules capability is shown to be part of the rules track. Notice that the last step, also shown as belonging to the rule track, creates a workflow diagram for the rule flow. You should only do this if you will be developing your own rules capability. If you will be deploying a commercial rules product, this step may be unnecessary.

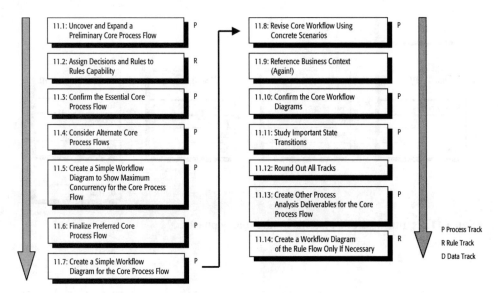

Figure 11.2   Steps in process analysis.

It may be beneficial to use prototyping as a way to uncover desired execution flow. You can build an initial prototype, especially if using commercial rules technology, and demonstrate it to the business audience. From here, the business audience can suggest changes and uncover desired flow and even rules.

To some of you, this chapter may seem like a deviation from object-centric analysis to algorithmic or process-centric analysis. This is not quite true, although the difference is subtle. In fact, this would be an injustice to the business rules approach. The subtlest differences can often bring the most significant value.

Therefore, a subtle difference in a business rules approach is that you decompose the problem domain into elements of thought, from decisions to rule families to rule patterns to individual rules. This is not quite the same as decomposing the problem domain into elements of process, from function to process to tasks.

This chapter leads you to look first at the intellectual aspect of decisions and wraps process around those decisions. If a beneficial way of carrying out process is to use objects, then the process wrapped around the decisions (and rules) will be comprised of objects. However, for now, you treat each decision as a raw element that serves a process needing that decision.

This difference is not so subtle when you use rules technology. That is because the actual execution of rules is not handled by the core process flow, but by other technology. This means you may need to do less analysis, less design, hence deliver your system faster.

To realize this benefit, you need to analyze process flow first in terms of decisions and second in terms of objects or classes, since not all decisions will require objects or classes.

How Is Process Analysis Different in a Business Rules Approach?

As in previous chapters, the differences in process analysis for a business rules approach relate to the STEP principles:

- Separating rules by understanding required rule flow before the rest of the system flow

- Separating rules by producing a workflow of the core process that may invoke shared decisions or rules

- Separating rules by exploring detailed rule flow as necessary

- Tracing rules by referring to business motivation to make sure the process flow, decisions and rules remain faithful to business objectives

- Externalizing rules by creating a state transition diagram and enhanced workflow diagram to illustrate results of decisions and rules on business objects and data entities

- Positioning rules for change by discovering alternate workflows that work

- Positioning rules for change by uncovering business preferences in workflow.

The first set of differences aims to separate the rules from other aspects of the system. You do this during process analysis by first understanding rule flow before analyzing the remainder of the system flow. You also integrate rules with the data and process aspects during process analysis. You produce a workflow representing the core process flow, which is devoid of rules but executes decisions. Finally, you will explore details behind rule flow if you will be writing code to achieve rule execution. You may not need to do much in this regard if you are using certain commercial rules products.

The second set of differences focuses on tracing rules. In this case, during process analysis, you revisit the business motivation for the system, thereby validating that your eventual process flow supports those objectives.

The third set of differences aims to externalize the rules so that people know what the rules are. During process analysis you do this by creating a state transition diagram for important business objects or data entities so the business audience can search for missing rules. You also enhance your workflow diagram to include correlations from decisions made to relevant business objects or data entities.

The final difference deals with positioning rules for change. Specifically, you discover alternate process flows that can correctly wrap around the essential rule flow. That is, you find various process flows that can work correctly in using the decisions to service the business event or use case. From here, you uncover the business preference among the alternate flows. Together, knowing the essential flow and the alternate flows, you have a better idea of which aspects of the systems logic may change over time. These changes may include changes in preferred flow at the gross level and changes in rules at the more detailed level.

To summarize these differences, process analysis in a business rules approach delivers a workflow, which assists in developing interfaces with humans and control flow. In principle, all business logic that you can express as decisions and rules is outside the core process. This can significantly simplify process analysis, design, and implementation.

An Interesting Difference between Discovery and Analysis

In scoping, if you followed the approach in this book, you gained an understanding of a business event by identifying its event-response process. Most of you will create use-case descriptions for this purpose. This is an intuitive starting point. However, you transitioned very quickly into analysis of the decision-making (and rules) needed by the process. Analysis of decisions and rules led you to analyze data or business objects. Finally, in this chapter, you turn back to analyzing the system's process so as to tie together the decisions, rules, and data or business objects into an executable script (a final process) that services the business event from start to finish.

Figure 11.3 illustrates this path. It shows that you started at scoping where you defined business events. You moved to discovery phase, where you defined event response processes or use cases, tasks or activities within the process or use case, business decisions within a task, and rules and data behind the decisions. Then you completed the data and rule requirements in analysis by adding to them and ensuring their quality.

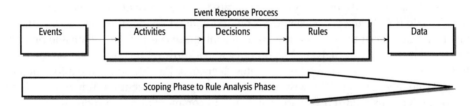

Figure 11.3 Order of process discovery.

In process analysis, however, you now reverse the order, as shown in Figure 11.4. That is, you have what you need to move backward through this chain to ensure that you have fully addressed the sequence of the system's process that is necessary to support all of the decisions and activities. To understand this necessary sequence, you start the

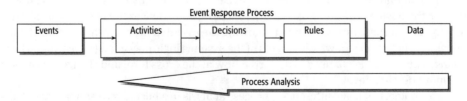

Figure 11.4 Order of process analysis.

process analysis by studying your rule (family) dependencies first, work (backward) toward defining the flow of business decisions and, eventually you tie it together by defining the cooperation among activities for processing it all together for each business event.

While you continue to separate the three perspectives (data, process, rules), you now integrate them into a solution that actually performs work. Note that all three perspectives carry out the work. The data perspective accesses data. The rule perspective executes rules. The process perspective carries out whatever is left over and ties all three together. It is important to note that the process track is really where it all comes together and either works correctly or does not. To ensure proper integration, you refer to rule dependencies to make sure you support the necessary sequence. You utilize the concrete scenarios to validate your process flow.

You produce a workflow of the core process where its tasks may invoke shared decisions or rules from outside the core system process. Therefore, you create a workflow diagram of the core process, independent of detailed rule process, but related. Therefore, you explore rule flow, but only to the point of logically grouping rules into system-executable decisions. Details on modeling rule flow are in this chapter, as a last step, because you may not need them. With some rules products, you may group rules for task execution preferences, but you may have no need to analyze rule execution flow by creating corresponding class models, sequence diagrams, activity diagrams, or others. If, however, you will be coding rules procedurally within your application or developing your own rules capability, you will need to produce more analysis and design deliverables for rules execution flow.

If you are developing your own rules capability, you can still leverage rules by separating them and you will, therefore, get possible rule reuse. However, you will spend time doing more process analysis, design, and implementation than if you had incorporated a commercial rules product. Naturally, more process analysis, design, and implementation means less productivity.

What Is the Purpose of Process Analysis?

The primary purpose of process analysis is to define the execution flow for the process behind a business event, integrating the processing with rule and data logic. Consider that a process, at the highest level, contains executable business tasks. For instructional purposes, think of four different kinds of tasks, as follows:

Interface-based. Tasks that communicate to and from the human actor or other system.

Action-based. Tasks that initiate an action external to the system, or reject the event.

Information-based. Tasks that make permanent changes to data storage.

Rule-based. Tasks that execute rules.

The goal in this chapter is to deliver a workflow model that includes all such tasks and how they interact with each other to complete the business event. The details of exactly how data will be accessed are part of the database design. The details of exactly how rule execution will occur are part of rule design. The details of how to accomplish what's left over are part of the core process design. But, first, process analysis must tie them all together logically.

What Are the Deliverables of Process Analysis?

The analysis phase has deliverables for each track. The analysis deliverables from the data track and the rule track are covered in Chapters 9 and 10 dedicated to those aspects of analysis. This book does not contain details on deliverables and techniques for the technology track. However, because the technology track is integral to process analysis, this is a good place to comment on the deliverables for the technology track.

During the scoping phase, a technology architect may have delivered a white paper or diagram for a high-level architectural vision, listing alternate technical solutions. During the discovery phase, the technology architect may have outlined detailed technical requirements for each target technology, created a detailed technology architecture diagram, and selected target technology products. These products may include a commercial rules product for executing rules.

Therefore, during the analysis phase, it follows that the technology architect may negotiate with corresponding vendors, conduct a proof-of-concept for technology that is new to the organization, validate that the technical solutions are the right ones, and begin to purchase, install, and customize hardware and software. Therefore, the deliverables during the analysis phase for the technology track are:

- Results from technology proofs-of-concept

- Validated and refined technical solution and selections

- The beginning of the technology architecture implementation.

Moving onto deliverables for the process track, which is the topic of this chapter, let's consider object-oriented analysis as the most commonly practiced approach. In most object-oriented projects, the major deliverables during the analysis phase are a class diagram and a sequence diagram. The class diagram depicts the business object classes representing real things in the business. The sequence diagram depicts an event-ordering sequence of interactions from the human actor and among object classes. Depending on the problem at hand, you may also produce collaboration diagrams, state diagrams, and activity diagrams.

In this chapter, we propose the possibility of fewer deliverables, depending on your target technology. Therefore, the essential deliverables of the process analysis phase are:

- A simple workflow model for each business event devoid of detailed rule and data processing, so you can communicate the flow to designers

- A state transition diagram for important data entities or business objects, so you can find missing rules

- A final set of concrete scenarios, so you can test all rules.

Additional deliverables, depending on your target technology and depending on whether you build or buy your rules capability are:

- A class model for the core process of each business event, so you can proceed with object-oriented design for them

- A sequence diagram for classes involved in the core process of each business event, so you can proceed with object-oriented design for them

- A class model for the rule flow, if you are building your own rules capability

- A sequence diagram for classes involved in rule flow, if you are building your own rules capability.

Notice the deliverables refer to a workflow model. A *workflow model*, in this book, is a diagrammatic way to show the dynamic aspects of the system, bringing together the sequencing of human interactions, decision processing, and data access. A workflow model defines a system's execution path. That is, it shows logical units and which ones must execute sequentially, which ones iterate, which ones form branches of execution, which ones can execute in parallel, and which ones must be synchronized. The system's execution path takes into account rule-mandated as well as business-preferred flows of control. An example of a workflow model is the activity diagram in UML.

State transition diagrams help in understanding the life cycle of the more complex entities in the rule-enriched logical data model or business object model. An *entity's or class's life cycle* consists of the sequence of allowable states an occurrence of an entity or object can assume during the processing of business events. You want to determine if you have missed any life cycle states because transitions among states usually imply additional rules and data.

At the end of process analysis, you will add to your growing set of concrete scenarios so that you have a solid basis for testing the system.

Process Analysis Standards

At the minimum, you will need standards for your workflow model, as follows:

- What workflow diagram notations should you use?

- What type of workflow model should you create?

- What workflow diagramming techniques are most useful?

- What model and symbol-type naming conventions should you use?

- What tools should you use when creating, storing, enhancing, and displaying your workflow models?

What Workflow Diagram Notations Should You Use?

As for the notations, there are a number from which you can choose. This book does not favor one over another. What is important is to choose a standard at the beginning of your project and use it consistently. However, there are a few symbol types that are essential. These include symbols to represent:

- Individual business tasks (activities) whether carried out by a person or by a system.

- Transfers of control from one task to the next, branching into parallel flows, consolidating flows and iterations of control.

- Business decisions, the outcomes of which affect transfer of control.

- External actors (people or systems) who interact with the system.

- Business functions or departments responsible for executing each activity.

- Business entities or objects and their statuses as they are created and changed during the processing of an event.

What Type of Workflow Model Should You Create?

As for types of workflow models, Table 11.1 is a list of the most commonly used workflow model types. Many of today's CASE tools and diagramming products support one or more of these models. If you have a CASE or diagramming tool available, then the models it implements may affect your choice.

Figure 11.5 depicts a sample UML activity diagram. The oval symbols represent business activities e.g., *Access Guardian Information*. The rectangular symbols depict objects and indicate their states, such as *Guardian [Active]*. The diamond-shaped symbols represent business decisions.

What Workflow Diagramming Tips Are Most Useful?

There are two workflow-diagramming tips to consider: naming conventions and content of a single diagram.

Table 11.1 Types of Workflow Models

WORKFLOW MODEL	WORK ACTIVITY SYMBOLS	DECISION SYMBOLS	FLOW OF CONTROL SYMBOLS (LINES)	PERSISTENT DATA SYMBOLS	RESPONSIBILITIES (SWIM LANE SYMBOLS)
Traditional flowchart	Preprocess Process	Decision	Flow	Online storage	Yes
ULM activity diagram	Activity (action state)	Decision	Transition	Object state	Yes
IDEF3 process flow	Unit of behavior	Junction	Precedence link Relational link Object flow link	Referent symbol used to represent objects	Yes

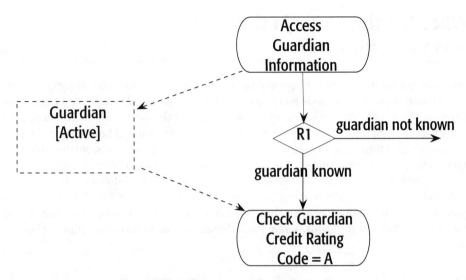

Figure 11.5 Enroll member UML activity diagram (fragment).

You should establish naming guidelines before you start modeling for each symbol type. For instance, use verb-noun or noun phrases for activity names. For example, *Calculate Invoice Total Amount*. Make each name unique and as meaningful as possible to a business audience. Do not introduce computer or technical language. In the case of decision symbols, use a statement of the question itself. For example, "Guardian Credit Rating OK?" It is a good idea to include the rule number or rule family number inside the decision symbol if known.

The second tip is to be consistent in levels on a diagram. That is, for the content of a single diagram, do not combine more than one level of activity on a diagram. For example, do not place a Process Order activity and a Validate Customer ID activity on the same diagram. Instead, attach a subdiagram to the Process Order activity symbol to show how processing an order includes validating customer IDs.

Where Should You Create and Store Your Workflow Models?

For creating and maintaining model diagrams, a CASE tool is usually a necessity, not an option.

Your team will be drawing and modifying many models during the life of your project. These models are investments that, if maintained and used, offer benefits well beyond the implementation of your business rules system. Enhancements made over the lifetime of a system should be based on these models. They are a key aspect of a system's specification.

What Are the Steps in the Analyzing Process?

Let's now begin the steps behind process analysis. Through them, you will apply a set of rule-enhanced process analysis techniques to the VCI case study. Each step employs a different technique. The sequence of steps represents the order in which you should apply them in your initial efforts for best results. However, you will find that, as you proceed, you will return to earlier steps from later ones. As with many system development approaches, the business rules approach is iterative, not a one-pass sequence of tasks.

The examples below are simple so as to focus mostly on philosophy and possible techniques. If all of your rule families are simple, you may not need all of these techniques. Or you may apply them to complex rule families only. Perhaps you will devise your own techniques or may be using tools that automate some of the thinking behind these steps.

STEP 11.1: UNCOVER AND EXPAND A PRELIMINARY CORE PROCESS FLOW

A goal of traditional object-oriented analysis is to determine the desired behavior of the system and the role of classes in carrying out that behavior. To determine behavior and class roles, typically you create, during analysis, a preliminary class model of business objects and a corresponding sequence diagram. You may, in fact, create the sequence diagram after the detailed use case descriptions and use the sequence diagram to drive the class model. Possibly, you would create collaboration diagrams, object diagrams, activity diagrams, and state diagrams, if you need more detail.

However, as you already know, the goal of business rules analysis has a different emphasis. Like object-oriented analysis, the goal is to determine the desired behavior of the system. But, unlike object-oriented analysis, the first emphasis is on the role of decisions and rules in carrying out that behavior, not on objects. Therefore, you want to understand execution sequence in the context of decision-making, not rush to understand it in the context of interacting classes. As you will see, it is premature to assume you need to model classes and their interactions because you may not need to do so for rule executions. Why so?

Until you separate the rules from the core system logic, you do not know what to model in your analysis deliverables. For example, if rule execution happens external to your core system logic, especially if you will use rules technology, you may not need to analyze and design models for executing those rules. In the interest of fairness, your target rules technology will influence the kinds of deliverables you should create during analysis. The more functionality your rules technology performs, the less functionality you need to analyze and design. You may, of course, need object-oriented static and dynamic models for whatever is left over. As indicated throughout this book, you will also need either a class model or a data model to depict the terms and facts that you reference in your rules. But it is possible (depending on your target technology) that you may not need much else.

Let's look now to the details of process analysis for a business rules approach. In this book, during the scoping phase, the deliverables that are relevant to execution sequence include the business event table, the event-response process table, and the scope diagram, which is most often a use case diagram.

During the discovery phase, you defined and modeled the event response process behind each business event. You uncovered possible or typical sequences by which the system may service a business event. Yet you did not rigorously specify complete interactions and cooperation among either detailed activities or how rule violations are handled. Depending on how you chose to document that preferred sequence, you may have any or all of the following:

- Use-case description for the interactions between the human actors and the system for a business event

- Decomposition of the use case into tasks and decisions

- Concrete scenarios that define specific instances of such interactions.

You now analyze the suggested execution sequence of the use case description to confirm that it is consistent with uncovered rule dependencies.

GUIDELINE 11.1.1

Review the correlation of task or activity to decisions.

Begin by selecting the business event or one of its use cases whose process you want to analyze. You now want to study, for a business event or use case, the human interactions with the system .

During discovery, you documented someone's perspective of the steps required to respond to business or human interactions involved. At that time, you were not overly concerned with sequence because you knew you would be analyzing sequence first based on rule dependencies. Now you need to revisit sequence.

Refer now to the simple use case for the business event Guardian Enrolls Member in Figure 6.4.

A useful technique at this point is to extend a decision, rule table to include the use case step and rule families that arrive at a result by which the decision can be made. Optionally, you can also include columns for the rule patterns within each rule family and the rules within each rule pattern. Refer to Table 11.2.

Table 11.2   Sample Use-Case Interaction, Decision, Rule Family Table

USE CASE INTERACTION	DECISIONS	RULE FAMILY	RULE PATTERNS	RULES
1. Guardian accesses VCI Web page.	None			
2. Guardian accesses the enrollment Web page.	None			
3. Guardian enters guardian information.	None			

continues

Table 11.2 Sample Use-Case Interaction, Decision, Rule Family Table (*Continued*)

USE CASE INTERACTION	DECISIONS	RULE FAMILY	RULE PATTERNS	RULES
4. System qualifies guardian.	Is guardian known?	Rule family B	Rule pattern 5	R1
	Is guardian of good credit rating?	Rule family D	Rule pattern 7	R2, R10
			Rule pattern 8	R9
			Rule pattern 9	R12
5. Guardian enters member information.	None			
6. System qualifies member.	Is member age-appropriate for this park?	Rule family F	Rule pattern 11	R4
		Rule family C	Rule pattern 6	R6
	Is member age-appropriate for other parks?	Rule family E	Rule pattern 10	R7
7. System displays complete enrollment screen.	None			
8. Guardian approves enrollment	None			

CASE STUDY: STEP 11.1—UNCOVER AND EXPAND A PRELIMINARY CORE PROCESS FLOW

Case Study Instructions:

If you followed an object-oriented approach during scoping and discovery, most likely you created use-case diagrams, identified scenarios, and perhaps started an ideal object class model. At this point, do the following:

- Create or review the use-case description for the business event Guardian Enrolls Member.

- Create a table correlating the use-case interactions to decisions, rule families, rule patterns, and rules.

Case Study Solution:

It is important to note that, at this time, the use-case description need not include references to which business objects perform which system actions or decisions. The use-case description simply describes the interactions and the decisions made by the system. Remember that objects may not make some of those decisions at all if the decisions are carried out by a rules capability.

Table 11.2 borrows the use-case description from Figure 6.4.

STEP 11.2: ASSIGN DECISIONS AND RULES TO THE RULES CAPABILITY

Before proceeding, you need to determine which decisions will execute through the rules capability. You need to determine this because whatever is then left over is the core system flow. You need to know now which analysis deliverables you need to represent in this core process flow.

GUIDELINE 11.2.1

Execute most decisions and rules through a rules capability.

Recall that you want to preserve the four basic principles of the business rules approach: separate, trace, externalize, and position rules for change. Therefore, this chapter assumes that all rules will be executed through a rules capability.

CASE STUDY: STEP 11.2—ASSIGN DECISIONS AND RULES TO THE RULES CAPABILITY

Case Study Instructions:

- For the business event Guardian Enrolls Member, determine which rules the rules capability will execute.

Case Study Solution:
The rules capability will execute all four decisions shown in Table 11.2. Table 11.3 contains a column to reflect this decision.

STEP 11.3: CONFIRM THE ESSENTIAL CORE PROCESS FLOW

So far in this chapter you have completed two steps. You correlated the preliminary process flow to decisions. You also assigned some or all of those decisions to the rules capability. In the third step, you take a look at rule family dependencies behind those decisions.

Recall that rule (family) dependencies highlight the absolute sequence of rules and rule families from the perspective of utilizing the knowledge created by rules. That is, one rule must create a piece of knowledge before another rule can reference that piece of knowledge.

You now use these dependencies to determine the essential process flow. The *essential process flow* is an execution sequence that must be followed based on knowledge dependencies for the decisions to make sense. You study rule dependencies to see whether they imply constraints or freedom on your core process flow. The business people will choose other execution sequence options based on reasons other than

Table 11.3 Sample Use Case Interaction, Decision, Rule Family Table with Rule Capability

USE CASE INTERACTION	DECISIONS	RULES CAPABILITY?	RULE FAMILY	RULE PATTERNS	RULES
1. Guardian accesses VCI Web page	None				
2. Guardian accesses the enrollment Web page	None				
3. Guardian enters guardian information	None				
4. System qualifies guardian	Is guardian known?	Yes	Rule family B	Rule pattern 5	R1
	Is guardian of good credit rating?	Yes	Rule family D	Rule pattern 7	R2, R10
			Rule pattern 8	R9	
			Rule pattern 9	R12	
5. Guardian enters member information	None				
6. System qualifies member	Is member age-appropriate?	Yes	Rule family F	Rule pattern 11	R4
			Rule family C	Rule pattern 6	R6
	Is member age-appropriate for other parks?	Yes	Rule family F	Rule pattern 11	R4
			Rule family E	Rule pattern 10	R7
7. System displays complete enrollment screen	None				
8. Guardian approves enrollment	None				

knowledge dependencies among rules. These reasons may be technology constraints or business preference.

GUIDELINE 11.3.1

Determine inconsistencies in the preliminary execution sequence based on rule family dependencies.

You can now use the rule (family) dependencies as a foundation behind your system's proper process flow. *Proper process flow* means a flow of activities that honor the sequence of rule execution based on dependencies among the rules (or patterns or families) themselves. Let's look at an example.

Note from Table 11.3 that the system decides whether the guardian is known before it decides whether the guardian has good credit. This implies the execution of rule family B before rule family D. Therefore, the proposed execution sequence of these decisions is consistent with the rule family dependencies. That is, it is true that rule family B must execute before rule family D as shown in Figure 10.11.

CASE STUDY: STEP 11.3—CONFIRM ESSENTIAL CORE PROCESS FLOW

Case Study Instructions:
Determine if the execution sequence in Table 11.3 for System qualifies member is consistent with rule family dependencies.

Case Study Solution:
The task of qualifying member, according to Table 11.3, is to execute rule families F, C, and E in that sequence. This sequence is consistent with the rule family dependencies in Figure 10.11 because rule family F must execute before rule family C and before rule family E.

STEP 11.4: CONSIDER ALTERNATE CORE PROCESS FLOWS

It comes as no surprise that there are many different ways to achieve the same result. This is especially true when determining process flow and taking into consideration the essential process flow and various opinions about the rest of the flow. This is why iterative development and prototyping is so valuable. Often, a business person does not know what their preference is until they see it. Often, a developer does not know how well an action will perform until it is done.

A business rules approach encourages you to find the absolute flow and then to experiment or discuss all alternatives, if useful.

GUIDELINE 11.4.1

Find rule (family) chains that are independent of each other.

Referring to Figure 10.11, notice that rule family C and rule family E are independent of each other. Rule family C determines whether a member is age-appropriate for this park and rule family E determines whether the member is age-appropriate for other parks.

While both of these rule families depend on rule family F to compute member age, neither of these rule families depends on each other. This means that these rule families can execute independently of each other, in parallel.

GUIDELINE 11.4.2

Find (whole) decisions that are independent of each other.

Refer again to Figure 10.11 and notice that because rule family C and rule family E are independent of each other, the decisions they represent are also independent of each other. That is, the decision about a member being age-appropriate for this park can happen in parallel with the decision about the member being age-appropriate for other parks. This is a simple example, because each decision is decided by one rule family. If there were a chain of rule families for each decision, the chains could execute in parallel.

GUIDELINE 11.4.3

Find (whole) tasks or interactions that are independent of each other.

Careful inspection of Figure 10.11 shows you that the rule family chains for the task Qualify Guardian and the task Qualify Member are independent of each other. That is, you can qualify guardian's credit rating without knowing anything about the member. You can qualify the member without knowing anything about the guardian.

GUIDELINE 11.4.4

Determine, for each rule pattern, where the information referenced comes from.

Now you identify where information comes from so you can determine if the effort and timeframe to obtain the information influences execution sequence. For example, within Qualify Guardian, where does credit information come from? Do you need to go outside the enterprise or to an internal database? You can extend Table 11.3 to include documentation on where information is sourced. Table 11.4 is an example. You can then refer to this table to be sure that your process flow makes sense. Can you access the information needed in an acceptable timeframe within the process flow?

For the purpose of this chapter, let's assume that none of the information sources, to our knowledge, constrain the core process flow.

STEP 11.5: CREATE A SIMPLE WORKFLOW DIAGRAM TO SHOW MAXIMUM CONCURRENCY FOR THE CORE PROCESS FLOW

A *simple workflow diagram* is one that does not contain activities for carrying out detailed data access or rule execution. After all, you don't show in a workflow diagram all the logic behind accessing a database, searching it, sorting it, and then committing changes. So, too, you won't show details in your workflow all the logic behind executing rules.

At this point, you create a workflow diagram that illustrates all possible concurrent executions of decisions and rule families. This workflow diagram assists in selecting a

Table 11.4 Sample Use Case Interaction, Decision, Rule Family Table with Information Sources

USE CASE INTERACTION	DECISIONS	RULES CAPABILITY?	RULE FAMILY	RULE PATTERNS	RULES	INFORMATION SOURCE
1. Guardian accesses VCI Web page	None					
2. Guardian accesses the enrollment Web page	None					
3. Guardian enters guardian information	None					
4. System qualifies guardian	Is guardian known?	Yes	Rule family B	Rule pattern 5	R1	Guardian information is from a local database
	Is guardian of good credit rating?	Yes	Rule family D	Rule patterns 7	R2, R10	Guardian credit rating information is from an outside source. How recent?
				Rule pattern 8	R9	Guardian credit rating and special deal information is from a local database
				Rule pattern 9	R12	Park ranger information is from a local database

continues

Table 11.4 Sample Use Case Interaction, Decision, Rule Family Table with Information Sources (*Continued*)

USE CASE INTERACTION	DECISIONS	RULES CAPABILITY?	RULE FAMILY	RULE PATTERNS	RULES	INFORMATION SOURCE
5. Guardian enters member information	None					
6. System qualifies member	Is member age-appropriate?	Yes	Rule family F	Rule pattern 11	R4	Member information comes from the screen
			Rule family C	Rule pattern 6	R6	Member information comes from the screen
	Is member age-appropriate for other parks?	Yes	Rule family F	Rule pattern 11	R4	Member information comes from the screen
			Rule family E	Rule pattern 10	R7	Member information comes from the screen, does the system initiate an action here?
7. System displays complete enrollment screen	None					
8. Guardian approves enrollment	None					

preferred workflow. It also allows you to refer to it later if you have the opportunity to increase concurrent processing through other technology.

This step illustrates the use of a UML activity diagram for delivering a workflow diagram. While an activity diagram is reminiscent of the more procedural flowchart, it models the process flow without relating it to classes or messaging sequence. An activity diagram is useful because you do not know yet what object classes you need to model. Rather, you are focusing on the decisions (intelligence) behind the tasks (actions) and not on the mechanism by which these occur or to what classes they might occur.

Essentially, you will build a workflow diagram that consists of activities for each interface-based, rule-based, action-based, and information-based task.

GUIDELINE 11.5.1

Create an activity for the task that interfaces with the actor in initiating the business event.

This is an interface-based task. Start with:

- Guardian starts enrollment service (interface-based).

GUIDELINE 11.5.2

Create an activity for each task that interfaces with the actor in passing information to/from screen.

These are also interface-based tasks. Add to the list such that you have:

- Guardian starts enrollment service (interface-based)
- Guardian enters guardian information (interface-based)
- Guardian enters member information (interface-based)
- Guardian approves enrollment (interface-based).

GUIDELINE 11.5.3

Create an activity for tasks that invoke the rules capability for a decision.

These represent rule-based tasks. You now have:

- Guardian starts enrollment service (interface-based)
- Guardian enters guardian information (interface-based)
- Check rule capability: is guardian known (rule-based)
- Check rule capability: is guardian of good credit (rule-based)
- Guardian enters member information (interface-based)
- Check rule capability: is member age-appropriate for this park (rule-based)
- Check rule capability: is member age-appropriate for other parks (rule-based)
- System displays enrollment (interface-based)
- Guardian approves enrollment (interface-based).

GUIDELINE 11.5.4

Create an activity for each task that passes information to/from a data source.

These are information-based tasks. Revise the tasks as follows:

- Guardian starts enrollment service (interface-based)
- Guardian enters guardian information (interface-based)
- Check rule capability: is guardian known (rule-based)
- Check rule capability: is guardian of good credit (rule-based)
- Guardian enters member information (interface-based)
- Check rule capability: is member age-appropriate for this park (rule-based)
- Check rule capability: is member age-appropriate for other parks (rule-based)
- System displays enrollment (interface-based)
- Guardian approves enrollment (interface-based)
- System updates enrollment database (information-based)

GUIDELINE 11.5.5

Pull the activities together in a workflow diagram that shows possible concurrencies.

An example of maximum concurrent core process flow for the case study is shown in Figure 11.6. Note the following about this diagram:

- Each box in the diagram represents an activity that occurs within the core process flow. Remember, the core process flow is devoid of rule and data details. There are ten boxes representing activities that happen in the core process flow. These are:
  - Guardian starts enrollment
  - Guardian enters guardian information
  - Guardian enters member information
  - System establishes prepay guardian
  - System displays enrollment
  - Guardian approves enrollment
  - System updates enrollment database
  - System recommends parks
  - Unknown action if guardian unknown
  - System rejects enrollment if member age not okay.
- Note that some of these are *interaction-based activities*, which represent communications with a human. (Interaction-based activities can also represent communications with electronic actors outside the core system flow.) There are five interface-based activities, as follows:
  - Guardian starts enrollment service
  - Guardian enters guardian information

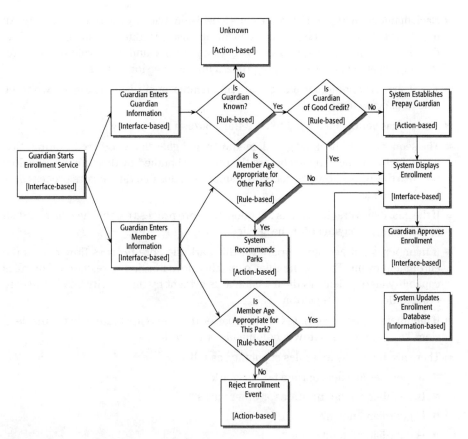

Figure 11.6 Simple workflow diagram.

- Guardian enters member information
- System displays enrollment
- Guardian approves enrollment.
- There are also *action-based activities*. These can reject the event, carry out action internal to the system, or initiate action external to the system. There are four of these, as follows:
  - System rejects enrolment event if member is not age-appropriate
  - System recommends other parks if member is age-appropriate for these
  - System takes an unknown action if the guardian is not known
  - System establishes a prepay guardian.
- There is an *information-based activity*, which causes an update to a database. There is one of these, as follows:
  - System updates enrollment database.

- Each diamond in Figure 11.6 represents a decision made by the rules capability. All details as to how those decisions are made are inside (hidden in) the diamond. The decision may involve many rules, many rule patterns, and many rule families. Yet the only aspect visible to the core process flow is decision results.

- The decisions about guardian credit and member qualifications are shown to be able to execute in parallel.

- No one has yet decided what to do if the guardian is not known.

- The sequence for checking guardian known and guardian good credit rating (that is, the fact that one happens before the other) is handled by the core process flow because these are shown as decision diamonds in this diagram of core process flow in this sequence.

- If the guardian's credit check is not good, the core process establishes the guardian as requiring prepayment for the service.

- If member is not age-appropriate for this park the core process flow rejects the enrollment event. That is, the rules capability does not do the rejection. The rules capability merely delivers the decision as is evident by the activity box in the core process flow for the rejection.

- If member is age-appropriate for other parks, the rules capability delivers the decision. The core process flow recommends other parks.

- There are four calls to a rules capability, as follows:
  - Is member age-appropriate for this park?
  - Is member age-appropriate for other parks?
  - Is guardian known?
  - Is guardian of good credit?

- These calls can be to four different rules capabilities, one for each decision. They can be to two rules capabilities, one for Guardian decisions and one for Member decisions. These calls can be to one rules capability that makes all decisions.

- The diagram implies that the rules capability accesses guardian information to see if guardian is known or has good credit rating because there is no activity box in the core process for accessing guardian information.

CASE STUDY: STEP 11.5—CONSIDER ALTERNATE CORE PROCESS FLOWS

Case Study Instructions:

- Study Figure 11.6. Identify alternative process flows.

Case Study Solution:
In studying Figure 11.6, one alternative is that you may want the core process to access guardian information and pass it to the rules capability, depending on rules technology, functionality, and performance. If so, you would add an activity box to access the guardian database prior to calling the rules capability for a decision. Another alternative is to combine the decisions about guardian (known and of good credit rating) into one call to the rules capability. Third, you may want to group member-age decisions into one call to the rules capability.

STEP 11.6: FINALIZE PREFERRED CORE PROCESS FLOW

You are now ready to document the preferred flow of interactions or tasks and decisions.

GUIDELINE 11.6.1

Create activities to capture metrics from scoping.

Review the needed business performance metrics. For example, during the scoping phase in Chapter 4, you uncovered a requirement to record the number of times a guardian begins to enroll a member but does not complete the process. This business metric will provide insights, perhaps, into how easy the enrollment process is.

You need to add an activity to count the number of unsuccessful enrollment attempts by a guardian. To handle this, you would add an activity box after Guardian Starts Enrollment Process, for an activity called action-based Start Enrollment Counter.

GUIDELINE 11.6.2

Consider business-preferred process flow.

You now know the essential process flow, source of information needed for decisions, and maximum concurrency process flow. To uncover the business persons' preferences, you are now in a position to ask two kinds of business process questions:

For the human interactions that can happen independently of each other, which sequence would the business prefer? As an example, within the business event Guardian Enrolls Member, does the business person want to carry out the interaction for qualifying member before qualifying guardian? Or vice versa? Does the business person want to qualify guardian and member at the same time?

For the decisions within an interaction that can happen independently of each other, which sequence would the business person prefer? As an example, within Qualify Member, does the business person prefer to check age-appropriateness for this park first or other parks first or at the same time?

CASE STUDY: STEP 11.6—FINALIZE THE PREFERRED CORE PROCESS FLOW

Case Study Instructions:

- Propose a realistic set of questions for the business people about their process preferences checking guardian credit.

Case Study Solution:
Sample questions may include the following.

- Do you want to update guardian credit information (through an online, real-time, outside service) each time a guardian logs on and inform the guardian, before any attempt is even made to enter a new member, that credit is bad?
- If you want to check the guardian's credit rating simultaneously with accepting member information, there are at least two options, both of which pertain to the flow of rule execution, not so much the core process flow. One option is accessing

an online credit service, while the other option is simply retrieving the latest credit information on file. Either can occur while allowing the guardian to begin the member enrollment process. You interrupt the enrollment process only if you find out credit is bad.

Regardless of the techniques you have applied to create your workflows, your business stakeholders must finally apply their experience and understanding of the current business environment to decide: "Does this processing make sense?"

STEP 11.7: CREATE A SIMPLE WORKFLOW DIAGRAM FOR THE CORE PROCESS FLOW

Create an activity box for each activity that the system or human actor carries out. Include also activity boxes for calls to the rules capability and to the database management system. Use the activities identified in step 11.5 as a starting point. Connect the boxes with arrows, indicating the final business-preferred process flow.

GUIDELINE 11.7.1

Do not show details of rules execution in the core process flow.

Remember that you have removed the details of rule flow from your core process flow. For the most part, these details are unimportant to the flow of your core process.

CASE STUDY: STEP 11.7—CREATE A SIMPLE WORKFLOW DIAGRAM FOR THE CORE PROCESS FLOW

Case Study Instructions:

- Review the activities in step 11.5. Create an initial simple workflow diagram for only the core process flow.

Case Study Solution:
Let's assume that the business wants to maximize concurrency, so the core process flow remains as shown in Figure 11.6. This means that each human actor may make some choices in process flow, that they may have a choice regarding the sequence they wish to walk through the business event. Let's also assume that the entire decision path for determining Guardian Known and Credit Status will occur within the rules capability, which will give back one, not two, results for simplicity's sake.

STEP 11.8: REVISE CORE WORKFLOW FROM CONCRETE SCENARIOS

The concrete scenarios produced in the discovery phase can be useful to enhance and validate your workflow diagrams. For instance, scenarios specify how rule violations should be handled. Your scenarios can serve as test cases through the workflows to be sure the workflows are complete and correct.

The rule analyst and workflow analyst should walk through each concrete scenario, step by step, comparing it to its workflow.

GUIDELINE 11.8.1

Map concrete scenarios actions to workflow activities.

Each concrete scenario should relate to the workflow in a straightforward manner. If you discover that the mapping of scenario steps to workflow decisions and activities is not complete, determine which you need to enhance: the workflow diagram or the concrete scenario.

You may also find problems with some scenarios. This can happen because the scenarios were written before you established and analyzed rule and data dependencies.

GUIDELINE 11.8.2

Study exceptional circumstances in the use case.

Those scenarios that document how to handle exceptional circumstances deserve special attention. For example, look through the concrete scenarios in search of those that will follow one of the alternate sequences in the use-case description.

For the example in this chapter, there are four alternate sequences for the business event Guardian Enrolls Member. Find a concrete scenario with an unknown Guardian. Walk through the scenario steps while pointing to the corresponding activity and decision in the workflow diagram. When you arrive at the decision where Guardian is not known, discuss what should happen.

Should the enrollment be rejected? Is this rejection done by the rules capability or the core system?

Should another business event for Enter New Guardian be initiated instead? Is this initiation done by the rules capability or the core system?

GUIDELINE 11.8.3

Assign responsibilities for interactions to external actors and internal actors (employees or agents).

Assigning responsibilities for interactions to actors is an essential part of workflow modeling. In complex processes, the system carries out most of the activities, but a business function or external agent may carry out other activities and interact with the system.

Document the assignment of interactions for each activity to actors. External actors, such as customers and suppliers, will carry out activities in support of interactions that are outside the system scope but which must be documented. This is because the procedures that external actors must follow, when they interact with the target system to achieve a result, must be congruent with your system's interface and procedures. Internal actors, such as employees and agents, may carry out activities in support of the business process and system scope.

You can use *swim lanes* to represent internal business functions and groups of external actors. That is, place activities carried out by an actor in its own horizontal lane on the diagram. In this way, the activities assigned to each function are drawn in its swim lane.

Add a swim lane to your workflow diagram for each external actor and internal business function or department involved in processing an event.

Move each activity and decision to its correct swim lane. Some transfer of control lines will cross between swim lanes indicating transfers of control between business functions during the processing of an event or between the system and its users.

When a transfer of control line crosses from one swim lane into another, it represents a transfer of responsibility from one business function to another or to/from the business and an external actor. Examine each situation to determine if the business rationale behind each transfer decision has been established. There may be new rules here.

GUIDELINE 11.8.4

If useful, add results of decisions to the workflow diagram.

For every decision symbol in the initial workflow diagram, determine the created or changed data entity or business object. Refer to the rule-enriched logical data model, if helpful. Identifying data entities or business objects that are changed will be helpful later in this chapter when you consider creating state transition diagrams.

Create another horizontal lane on your workflow diagram. Into this lane, add special symbols to represent the entity or business object changed or created. Connect each entity or business object to the decision that makes it so. An example is provided in the case study step below.

CASE STUDY: STEP 11.8—REVISE CORE WORKFLOW FROM CONCRETE SCENARIOS

Case Study Instructions:

- Review the use-case description for Guardian Enrolls Member. For the exceptional circumstance where a guardian does not have access to the Internet, discuss possible changes in workflow.

- Guardians are the external actors who usually initiate the Enroll Member process. Therefore, enhance your workflow diagram for the core process by adding a swim lane for the guardian. Move activities done by the guardian into the Guardian swim lane.

- Add to the diagram for this step, the decision results for Guardian.

Case Study Solutions:
Accommodating guardian's without Internet access can be a simple workflow change if it means that the park ranger simply carries out the role of guardian. You can then add an activity for Guardian Contacts VCI. You can change other activities to read Guardian Agent carries them out, not simply Guardian.

Figure 11.7 shows a simplified Guardian Credit Check portion of the workflow which contains a swim lane for the VCI Guardian Services (the system) and one for the Guardian. Notice that the diagram illustrates that the guardian is responsible for three activities:

- Starting the enrollment service
- Entering Guardian information

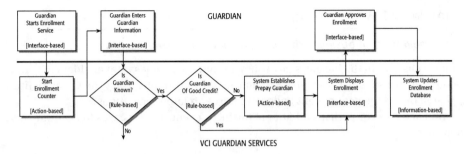

Figure 11.7   Simple workflow diagram with swim lanes.

■ Approving enrollment.

The other activities are handled by the VCI Guardian Services, which calls a rules capability twice, once for each diamond.

Figure 11.8 adds an additional swim lane in which to record decision results. Notice how the results of the rules capability point to statuses of Guardian. In this case, a Guardian will be known or unknown and of good credit or bad credit.

STEP 11.9: REFERENCE BUSINESS CONTEXT (AGAIN!)

At this point, you want to make sure the workflows remain consistent with business context information from Chapter 4. Business context information includes VCI's business strategies, its business objectives, tactics, and policies.

GUIDELINE 11.9.1

Revisit and apply business context documentation from the scoping phase.

Add activities to your workflow diagram, if needed, to supply additional activities required to meet business context requirements.

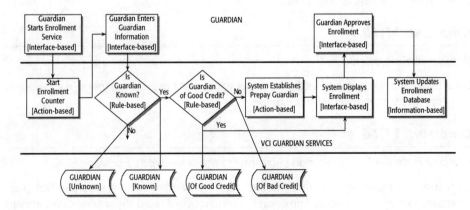

Figure 11.8   Simple workflow diagram with Guardian status.

GUIDELINE 11.9.2

Assess the impact of business changes on your workflow diagram.

Look for changes in the business environment that the business stakeholders may have become aware of since the project charter. For example: Have new competitors appeared or has the government imposed Internet-related regulations?

Add activities or perhaps additional business events or use cases to accommodate such changes.

CASE STUDY: STEP 11.9—REFERENCE BUSINESS CONTEXT (AGAIN!)

Case Study Instructions:

- Recall that a tactic from Chapter 4 is that the system should display for the guardian a thorough explanation of each game before the guardian is asked to select the games for the member. (A guardian may find some of the games inappropriate for their children.)

- Suppose the technology department informs the strategists that competitors are appearing on the marketplace. To keep VCI in the leadership spot, guardian services need to be provided from wireless devices such as cell phones and PDA devices. Discuss.

Case Study Solution:

You should add activities that can recognize a guardian inquiry, access service information, and display it. You will also need to add the Service entity as the source of services information.

The workflow may remain the same, but interface design may be impacted.

STEP 11.10: CONFIRM THE CORE WORKFLOW DIAGRAMS

To answer these final business questions and to complete your workflow models, you should meet with appropriate people.

GUIDELINE 11.10.1

Resolve final workflow.

Do a final review of your workflow models with your business partners (e.g., process owners), and with subject matter experts.

GUIDELINE 11.10.2

Communicate the final execution sequence to the screen/page designers.

It is extremely important that you communicate the workflow to the screen and Web page designers so they can get started on design. Alternately, in a rapid application development environment, you may have prototyped the screens and rules. Now you can communicate revisions in decision flow and task flow, which result in revisions in screen/page flow.

If using a data-change-oriented rules product, you may not have to do much process design. Once you define your data or objects and related rules, the screen and page sequence will determine the sequence of database updates, which will automatically execute rules that are needed.

STEP 11.11: STUDY IMPORTANT STATE TRANSITIONS

A *state transition diagram* is a graphic notation the purpose of which is to model the sequences of allowable states that can be held by a business object. The diagram also depicts how an object transitions from one state to another.

State transition diagrams help you determine if you missed states, decisions, or rules. Think of state transition diagrams as workflow diagrams turned inside out.

Each workflow diagram depicts major entities or business objects about which decisions are made. Each state transition diagram, in contrast, depicts a single entity or business object and all the states that an occurrence of it can assume during its processing by all event-response processes. State transition diagrams use state symbols to represent entity or business object states and transition lines the allowed sequences of state changes during its processing by all event-response processes.

GUIDELINE 11.11.1

Create a state transition diagram for the most complex entities or business objects.

You may not need to invest time in creating state transition diagrams for all entities or business objects within your project scope. Diagram only the most complex ones. Complex entities or business objects are those with many possible states and accessed by many activities in many workflow diagrams. These entities or business objects will be the most rule-rich, giving you the best return on your efforts. State transition diagrams can be especially helpful in discussions with subject matter experts for discovering new rules and data.

GUIDELINE 11.11.2

Create state transition diagrams only after you have completed workflow models for all business events.

Select an entity from the rule-enriched logical data model or a business object from a business object model for diagramming.

Locate all workflow diagrams containing occurrences of this entity or business object.

For each entity or business object state, create a state symbol on your state transition diagram.

Connect the state symbols with transition lines. From each state symbol, the transition lines point to the next allowable state(s) into which an entity in the target state can be transferred.

Finally, determine if your state transition diagram leads you to update other models. This determination is essential to maintaining the consistency in the system's description in all other model types and repositories.

CASE STUDY: STEP 11.11—STUDY IMPORTANT STATE TRANSITIONS

Case Study Instructions:

- In discussions with the customer service department, they are very interested in states of Guardians. Specifically, they identify four important states, from a customer service perspective: prospect, active, inactive, and closed or undesirable.

- Create a state transition diagram for these states.

- Discuss questions that would surface new rules as a result of studying these states.

Case Study Solution:

Figure 11.9 shows the completed state transition diagram for the Guardian entity for these states.

Some questions that arise that may lead to new rules are:

- Can a prospective guardian enroll a member? Or are prospective guardians considered Guardian unknown?

- Can inactive guardian enroll a member?

- How does a prospective guardian become an active guardian, by what rules or events?

- How does an active guardian become inactive, by what rules or events?

- What does it mean to be a closed guardian? Can a closed guardian enroll a member? (A closed guardian seems not to be the same as an unknown guardian.)

STEP 11.12: ROUND OUT ALL TRACKS

It is more important for analysis to be complete than it was for scoping and discovery. Therefore, you need to integrate your analysis deliverables across tracks to be sure all interrelated artifacts are present.

In a model-driven approach, you create several different models, for example logical data models or class models, state transition diagrams, and workflow models. Note

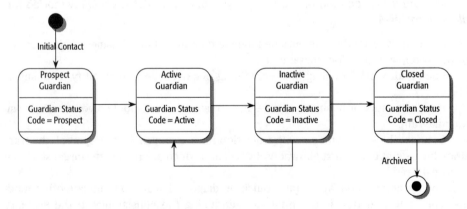

Figure 11.9 State transition diagram.

that each model type describes the same system. But each model type illustrates a different aspect of the system. Data models or class models depict the system's data requirements for persistent data storage, although they may include rule-materialized information. Workflow models show the system's processing requirements for responding to business events initiated in the external world.

Nevertheless, all models are highly interrelated. An addition or change in one usually dictates modifications to others. It is very important to keep the different system models and descriptions consistent with each other throughout a project.

GUIDELINE 11.12.1

Consider the implications on one deliverable when you make a change to another.

The list below includes all of the model types you may produce by phase. Each is correlated to a list of analysis tasks that you need to revisit when you add or change something in a model. In this way, you ensure the integrity of each model type and the consistency of system descriptions among models. Figure 11.10 shows the same integrity and consistency checks graphically.

Your rules repository can be useful at this point. You can query it to extract information about a model and all documentation related to it. For example, a query locating an existing rule should also obtain the data the rule references and creates, the scenario that validates it and the business policy that it supports. Queries of this type are called *impact analysis reports*. See Chapter 15 for more information.

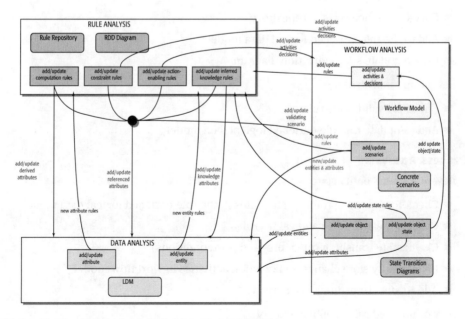

Figure 11.10   How rule, data, and analysis tasks relate.

Rule Analysis

If new or updated rule—all rule categories

- Check that the rule-referenced attributes are in the rule-enriched logical data model
- Check that there is a validating concrete scenario
- Add the rule to the rule repository with its links to other important artifacts
- Add the rule to a rule (family) dependency diagram and rule (family) dependency table

If new or updated constraint rule

- Check for integrity relationships in the rule-enriched logical data model
- Check for an implied exception handling activity in workflow model

If new or updated action-enabling rule

- Check business event and its process in workflow model

If new or updated inferred knowledge rule

- Check for the created knowledge attribute in the rule-enriched logical data model

If new or updated computation rule

- Check for referenced and derived attribute in the rule-enriched logical data model

Data Analysis

If new or updated entity

- Check existence rules in repository
- Add to the rule-enriched logical data model
- Create/update state transition diagram

If new or updated attribute

- Check for valid value rules
- Add to/update the rule-enriched logical data model

Process Analysis

If new or updated entity state

- Check for state-determining attributes in the rule-enriched logical data model
- Check state attribute valid values rules
- Check state transition rules (pre- and postconditions)
- Check entity state change and deletion activities in workflow model
- Add to state transition diagram

If new or updated rule-enabling activity

- Check for the rule in the rule repository with its links to other important artifacts
- Check for matching concrete scenario step
- Add to workflow model in correct swim lane

If new or updated rule-checking decision

- Check for the rule in the rule repository with its links to other important artifacts
- Check for matching concrete scenario step
- Add to workflow model in correct swim lane

If new or updated transfer of control line

- Check if change of functional responsibilities (swim lanes), that rule(s) in repository
- Add to the workflow model in correct swim lane(s)

If new or updated swim lane

- Check if business objects or entities of the same type in workflow model
- Check that all activities, decisions, and transfer of control lines added to swim lane
- Add to the workflow model

If new or updated scenario

- Check for business event
- Check for event-response process
- Add to scenarios

If new or updated scenario step

- Check for activities and decisions in workflow models
- Check for entities and attributes in the rule-enriched logical data model
- Check for rules in repository
- Add step to the scenario

CASE STUDY: STEP 11.12—ROUND OUT ALL TRACKS

Case Study Instructions:

- In reviewing the final workflow diagram, the business expert surfaces the question about how frequently the business should reevaluate a guardian's credit worthiness and update his/her good credit flag. What are the rules associated with a guardian who has existing members, but VCI now discovers the guardian's credit rating has gone bad? Not surprisingly, the business stakeholder answers to these questions will involve additional rules and data elements, for example, Guardian Last Credit Check Date.

- Devise additional rules and data elements. Discuss how these change deliverables in other tracks.

Case Study Solution:
This solution is left up to the reader.

STEP 11.13: CREATE OTHER PROCESS ANALYSIS DELIVERABLES FOR THE CORE PROCESS FLOW

In steps 11.1 through 11.12, you developed:

- Workflow diagram (such as a UML activity diagram)
- State transition diagram
- Additional concrete scenarios.

If you will be developing your own code for the core process flow, you need now to create the corresponding analysis deliverables. Since most of your projects are likely to be object-oriented, these deliverables may be:

- Refined class model with more details on business objects, perhaps adding infrastructure (boundary and control) classes.
- Sequence diagram, which traces the execution of a scenario or use case in the context of those object classes.

If you will be developing your own code for the rules capability, you need now to create analysis deliverables for the rules flow. These may include the same diagrams listed above, but focused on delivering rules capability, not a complete process flow. You would then use a workflow diagram as one of your deliverables for the analysis of rule flow, along with deliverables for the rule flow listed above (refined class model, and sequence diagram).

Finally, if you are using a commercial rules capability that is a complete application development environment, you may have very few, if any, addition analysis deliverables to create.

STEP 11.14: CREATE A WORKFLOW DIAGRAM OF THE RULE FLOW, ONLY IF NECESSARY

Chapter 10 presented a basic approach to analyzing the flow of rule execution. The useful deliverables were a rule or rule family dependency table and a rule or rule family dependency diagram. At this point, if you will be designing and developing your own rules capability, you may want to create more formal deliverables.

If so, create a workflow diagram of rule flow where that rule flow is internal to the rules capability, not part of your core system flow.

Start with the rule dependency table or rule dependency diagram that you created in the rule analysis phase for those rules to be executed within the rules capability. Refer to Figure 10.4, which shows the Enroll Member event rule dependency diagram.

For the purpose of this discussion, assume that all of these rules are to execute within the rules capability and that you will be implementing the rules capability using procedural code.

For each rule symbol representing an inference, constraint, or action-enabling rule, draw an activity symbol on a new workflow diagram. The activity should be named to describe the rule it represents. For example, for the rule dependency diagram rule R6 Member Age >16? the activity name could be Check Member Age >16. Place your activity symbols in the same sequence, left to right, as the parent rule symbols are arranged on the rule dependency diagram. Don't draw any transfer of control lines yet.

Figure 11.11 shows three activity symbols derived from rules R5, R6, and R7. For simplicity, the activity symbols show only the age-checking rules, not all rules in the diagram.

After each rule is checked, control must be transferred to the next correct activity based on the outcome of the rule firing. To represent the true or false result of the rule checking activity, draw a decision symbol after each rule activity symbol. Decision symbols can share the same name with their parent rule symbols, for example, Member Age >16? It is a good idea to place the rule number associated with each decision inside the symbol as well. Figure 11.12 shows decision symbols (diamond shapes) drawn to the right of their companion rule check activity.

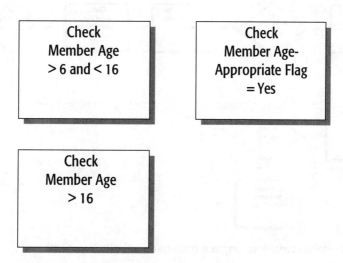

Figure 11.11 Activity symbols from rules R5, R6, and R7.

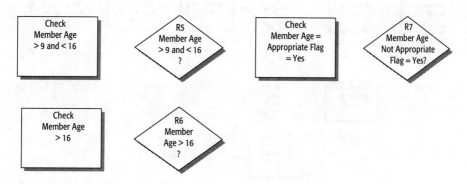

Figure 11.12 Decision symbols for testing rule check outcomes.

Connect activity and decision symbols with transfer of control lines in the same way as they are portrayed in the rule dependency diagram.

Name the transfer of control lines exiting decision symbols to indicate the outcomes of the rules check, for example, yes and no. You do not need to name lines indicating simple transfers of control, such as between the Compute Member Age and Check Member Age >6 and <16.

Figure 11.13 shows the completed initial workflow diagram derived from the member-qualifying rule symbols R5 through R7.

For each constraint, guideline, inferred knowledge, and action-enabling rule, draw an activity symbol that depicts the action that must be taken based on the results of the rule's firing. In Figure 11.13, the Recommend Older Member Theme Parks activity prescribed by action-enabling rule R6 has been added.

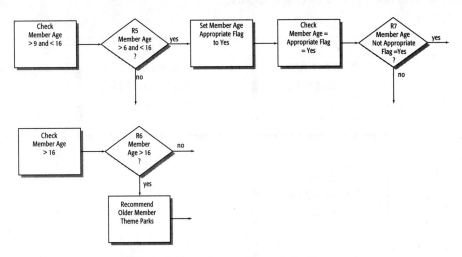

Figure 11.13 Initial workflow diagram from rule symbols (fragment).

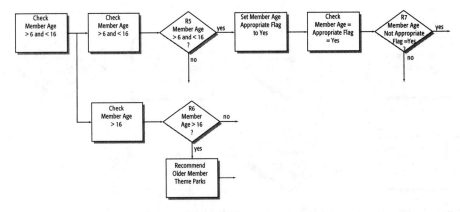

Figure 11.14 Computation rules added.

For each computation rule, draw an activity symbol to represent performing the prescribed computation. Place each symbol in the same location as its parent rule symbol on the rule dependency diagram. In Figure 11.14, activity symbols representing computation rules can share the same name with their parent rule symbols, for example, Compute Member Age. It is a good idea to note the rule number associated with each computation activity inside the symbol.

Considerations for Iterative and Parallel Systems Development

The most rigid aspects of process analysis are the data architecture and the rule dependencies. The other aspects you consider in process analysis are changeable and therefore lend themselves well to iterative development. These include business preferences for execution flow, corresponding screen flow, and eventually screen design. In fact, iterative development may be very valuable in prototyping variations here so as to understand the possibilities and to verify comfort level with the final complete process flow.

If you are following an iterative development approach, you will be evolving use-case descriptions, concrete scenarios, and these now lead you to alternate process flows.

As you test variations in process flow, expect to find additional rules and decisions or to correct existing ones. Naturally, when you add or change rules, you need to revisit the impact on rule flow and on the data architecture. As indicated in Chapter 10, you should be able to add, change, and delete rules from the decisions that group them, test out your new set of rules, and continue to refine them. This is especially possible when using commercial rules products.

Even when you finalize the process flow, the rules must be free to change at any time in the future. Again, iterative development is a way to test that freedom, although your data architecture needs to be flexible enough for you to add and change rules without disruptive database changes. How long does it take the business audience to challenge a rule, assess the impact of changing it, make the change in the system, test that change, and put it into production?

Summary

Many of the subtle differences in a business rules approach are not obvious without understanding the role of process analysis in tying together the three tracks. To make these differences clearer, Table 11.5 highlights some of them in comparing traditional object-oriented analysis to rule-enriched object-oriented analysis.

At first glance, the table seems to suggest that there are more tasks and deliverables for a business rules approach, so the approach would require more time. This is, in fact, quite untrue. The business rules approach aims to analyze and design business logic (rules) in a way that minimizes cost, where cost is measured in development time, testing time, maintenance and enhancement time, and system performance time. To see where that minimization occurs, let's study the rows in the table more closely.

Note that rows 1 through 3 in Table 11.5 are identical for both traditional object-oriented and rule-enriched object-oriented analysis. The deviation starts at row 4. This deviation occurs because the goal is to understand the intellectual content of the use case so that, from this understanding, you can determine which aspects of the problem domain are worth exploring in terms of objects and classes. Keep in mind that you may not need to analyze and design the dynamic aspect of objects or classes behind rule execution.

Therefore, row 4, by creating a logical rule model, views the problem domain first through a knowledge-based perspective. This perspective decomposes a use case into decisions, rule families, rule patterns, and rules and uncovers the essential dependencies among them. The essential rule dependencies serve as a critical foundation for the dynamic aspect of the system.

Row 5, by creating a rule-enriched term and fact model, views the problem domain through an information-based perspective by identifying and modeling terms and facts referenced or created by the decision and rules.

It is interesting that these two priorities (knowledge/decisions/rules and information) also represent two critical organizational assets that will become more and more important in the Information Age of commerce.

Row 6 continues the deviation from traditional object-oriented analysis by creating an activity model that is typically an optional deliverable for object-oriented analysis approaches. In this chapter, an activity model plays a more important role because, at

Table 11.5   Traditional Object-Oriented Analysis versus Rule-Enriched Object-Oriented Analysis

DELIVERABLES IN TRADITIONAL OBJECT-ORIENTED ANALYSIS	DELIVERABLES IN RULE-ENRICHED OBJECT-ORIENTED ANALYSIS
Use case diagram.	Use case diagram
Use case description.	Use case description
Scenarios	Scenarios
	Logical rule model (decisions, rule families, rule patterns, rules)
Ideal business object model	Rule-enriched logical data model or rule-enriched business object model
	Activity model for core process flow
Sequence diagram	For core process flow, sequence diagram
Class diagram	For core process flow, class diagram
	For homegrown rules capability, sequence diagram
	For homegrown rules capability, class diagram

this point in analysis, it is too premature to start viewing the "process" as objects or classes. Specifically, other than the terms and facts needed by rules execution, you do not yet know what other characteristics of such objects or classes you need to analyze (such as sequences, states, and collaborations).

Rows 7 and 8 are identical in both columns of Table 11.5, with a major difference. An analyst following traditional object-oriented analysis creates these deliverables for the entire scope of the system (or its current release). In a business rules approach, an analyst may only create these deliverables for the core process flow if rules execution will occur through commercial rules technology. This could be a much smaller portion of the system's behavior; hence the creation of these deliverables can represent significant and tangible time-savings. If rules execution will occur through a homegrown rules capability, rows 9 and 10 represent the creation of these same deliverables for the rules capability. In the latter case, there may not be a significant time-savings over traditional object-oriented development, but you will have delivered a separate rules capability that may be shared and reused, going forward.

Three more points are worth mentioning if you look closer at Table 11.5 because these points connect together the rule deliverables to object-oriented deliverables:

- The logical rule model (especially the rule family dependencies) serves as an excellent and natural input to the workflow model, as discussed at length in this chapter.

- The activity model serves as an excellent and natural input to the sequence diagram because the activity model represents execution sequence in the absence of objects or classes. The sequence diagram assigns control flow to objects and classes.

- The rule-enriched logical data model can serve as input to the class diagram because it contains the business terms referenced or created by rules (objects, classes, or attributes) along with relationships among them.

This chapter is not meant to replace traditional process analysis techniques (such as object-oriented techniques), but rather to change your emphasis to incorporate the separation of rule execution. Because of this change in emphasis, you may find that you do not need to create all of the deliverables you have used before or that you need to create them for a smaller portion of your analysis.

In the final analysis, it will be the business judgments of your business stakeholders that you must count on to complete your workflow models and validate that they represent processing that makes business sense.

At this point, armed with data and rule requirements and supporting them with core process flow, you are ready for the next part of this book. You now move into the design and delivery of the target business rules system or increment.

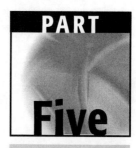
Design

Designing for a
Business Rules Approach

At this point, you are now ready to design your business rules system by integrating the three perspectives: rules, data, and process. This chapter is not meant to be a complete design methodology for designing systems. Instead, it highlights those aspects of system design that have a different emphasis and approach when delivering a business rules system. As such, this chapter focuses on the steps and guidelines for introducing a rules capability into your system design and how the rules capability influences the design of the rest of the system.

Recall that the term *rules capability* is the automated functionality that manages and executes rules, in a sharable manner across applications if possible. The rules capability may be a commercial product, homegrown software, or may be part of application code or the database management system. It may be a combination.

What Does It Mean to Design for a Business Rules System?

In many ways, designing a business rules system is very much like designing any system. A business rules approach is truly the integration of data-orientation, process or object-orientation, and rule-orientation. So, as for most other kinds of systems, you need to follow good design principles for the databases (most likely, relational) and processes (most likely, object-oriented design). This means designing at least three parts of the system (process or control flow, database, and rules). It means integrating these three distinct designs into a system that works.

How Is the Design Effort Different for a Business Rules System?

As indicated throughout this book, a business rules approach places deliberate emphasis, importance, and formalism on the delivery of rules within corresponding system logic. The differences in designing for a business rules system, shown in Table 3.1, are:

- Separating rules by aiming to implement them in a way that separates them from core process logic
- Separating rules by not burying them within application code
- Separating rules by housing them in or generating executable versions from a commercial rules product or a homegrown rules capability
- Tracing rules by tracking rule specifications to implementations
- Externalizing rules by making sure the natural language version of the rules serve as error messages when rules are violated
- Positioning rules for change by favoring changeable rule implementations (declarative specifications) over more rigid ones
- Positioning rules for change by favoring flexible data structures over more rigid ones

Let's discuss each difference.

The first differences in design supports the STEP principle of separating rules. That is, you aim to implement the rules in a way that separates them from traditional application logic. This means you want to house the rules in or generate them from commercial rules technology or build your own rules capability. In this way, the rules are shareable across application and components, if possible. Specifically, you don't want to bury rules within application, nonsharable code, where you cannot leverage them (and change them).

Another difference is that you trace rule specifications to their implementations. You do this through your own rules repository or through commercial rules technology.

Yet another difference is that you externalize the rules by making sure the rules themselves, in natural language form, serve as error messages when those rules are violated.

The final difference is that you position rules for change. That is, you favor changeable rule and database implementations over rigid ones. You can achieve changeable rule implementations by developing an environment that allows for rule specification in declarative language, where possible. You achieve changeable database implementations by delivering flexible data structures. That is, you want to deliver databases capable of accommodating easily new kinds of services, products, people, and other aspects important to business change.

Table 12.1 repeats the four basic principles of a business rules approach, but relates them now to how you can be faithful to them in your design.

Table 12.1   Four Principles of the Business Rules Approach and Their Relation to Design

PRINCIPLES BEHIND THE BUSINESS RULES APPROACH	REASON FOR EACH PRINCIPLE	HOW YOU WILL ACHIEVE IT IN YOUR DESIGN
Separate rules from traditional application logic.	Enable sharing of rule logic. Enable reuse of rule logic. Increase development productivity. Hasten change throughout the organization	Utilize rules technology. Build a simple automated rules service.
Trace rules to their implementations (human or electronic).	Facilitate impact analysis for rule changes.	Incorporate a rules repository. Utilize a systems development environment that manages rules.
Externalize rules to business and technical people.	Provide access for all audiences to business knowledge. Allow nontechnical people to suggest rule changes. Reduce the cost and time to implement changes.	Include rules as error messages. Launch the repository from within the application.
Position the rules for change.	Allow the organization to become whatever it wants to become whenever it wants to become it.	Favor changeable rule implementations over rigid ones, by: • Using declarative rule specifications and • Delivering flexible data structures.

What Is the Purpose of Design for a Business Rules System?

The purpose of design in this book is to translate the deliverables from data, rule, and process analysis into an integrated systems design that works well and is positioned for change. Looking at rule design, in particular, you want to translate the logical rule model into a physical rule design for the target technology. But you want to do so in a disciplined manner that preserves the integrity of the rules and the four principles behind the business rules approach.

Fortunately, rule design, like database design, is a process. Consider that *rule design* is a process for translating a logical rule model (discussed in Chapter 10) into a physical rule design (discussed in this chapter) so that you can implement, at least conceptually, a rules capability into your system.

Remember that a logical rule model consists of rules expressed in templates, phrased in standard terms and standard facts, and analyzed for quality. The logical rule model also consists of rule (family) dependencies and rules tied to information referenced and created.

Because the goal is to introduce the concept of a rules capability, the *physical rule design* addresses four considerations:

- Specifications on how the rules capability functions
- Assignment of rules enforcement to the appropriate system tier
- Detailed specifications on how each rule is implemented in its target tier, and
- Insights into how all layers communicate with the rules capability.

Like all methodology chapters in this book, this chapter presents a step-by-step approach. While it is easiest to learn about and teach these in a sequential stepwise fashion, in reality you will carry out these steps in an iterative fashion.

Figure 12.1 reminds you where the design phase fits into the full methodology. Because you have carried out portions of discovery and analysis first, you can use those deliverables in your design decisions. You will find, as useful input to the design process, the logical rule model (from Chapter 10), the rule-enriched logical data model (from Chapter 9), the process or workflow model (from Chapter 11), available technology options, and perhaps the database design..

Figure 12.2 provides an overview into how three of the tracks (data, rules, and process) relate to each other during the design phase. While you will see fifteen steps in this design chapter, Figure 12.2 summarizes these into five boxes in the rule design track. Essentially, the first box in this track represents your focus on planning for or acquiring a rules capability as part of your technology and application architecture. Naturally, all design specialists (database designers, rule designers, process designers, and network designers) should be involved in this aspect of design. While this book does not address network considerations, you will need network experts to assist in predicting and planning for the impact of network traffic on your system and considerations for times when you may distribute and replicate rule code.

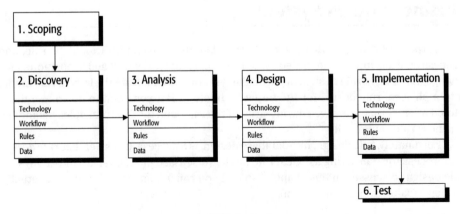

Figure 12.1   Business rule systems methodology phases.

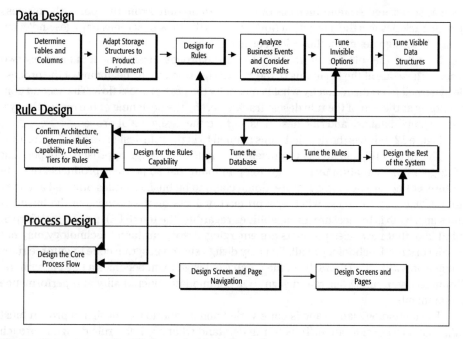

Figure 12.2   Integration of data, process, rule design.

The second box indicates that you will make some design decisions regarding the rules capability, whether you buy or simulate one. The third box illustrates that, should functionality or performance be an issue, you consider tuning the database design before tuning the rule design.

Finally, the last box indicates that you design the rest of the system. The rest of the system, if you have designed the database and rules, means designing for the process track.

Notice that the data design track and rule design track interrelate at two points. The first is a connection from the data design track where you design for rules in the DBMS layer. You should coordinate DBMS rule design considerations with the rule design track to make sure you design and implement rules into the right architectural components. Therefore, the design for rules box in the data design track relates to the very first box in the rule design track.

The data design track and rule design track also relate to each other when the rule design track recommends that you tune the database. Here, the arrow in Figure 12.2 points you back to the data design track where you would tune the invisible tuning options before doing so to the visible data structures.

Finally, Figure 12.2 presents a cursory process design track. This book does not intend to provide full details for this track since the steps you follow here are the same as you would when designing any system. Of importance, though, is that the first box in the process design track is that of designing the core process flow, not the detailed rule flow. You can design the core process flow using your standard process design approach, such as structured systems analysis or object-orientation. From this point, the process design track designs the navigation flow, which is the flow of screens or pages and eventually the design details of those screens and pages.

Note that the rule design track relates to the process design track in precisely two places. These are at the beginning of the rule design track to the beginning of the process design track to confirm exactly what is meant by the core process flow. The second connection is at the end of the rule design track whereby the designing of the rest of the system, beyond database and rule design, is, in fact, the designing of process.

Figure 12.3 shows the detailed steps alluded to in the rule design track of Figure 12.2.

The goal of this chapter is to present a generic rule design approach, independent of target implementation technology. Keep in mind that some rules products are quite mature. Others are new, less mature. Some claim to be business rules oriented and may not be. One way to assess whether a product delivers on the promise of the business rules approach is to measure its capabilities regarding the four STEP principles. Keep in mind, too, that new rules products are emerging. Also, your target technology may not be rule-oriented technology at all. You may design shared program code to enforce rules outside or within the DBMS. If so, the database design team becomes a key player here. Ultimately, you tune your rule design to accommodate functionality and performance requirements.

The technology landscape is quite varied and a generic rule design approach must take that into consideration. To better understand what a generic rule design approach ought to be, let's review a generic relational database design methodology as a useful

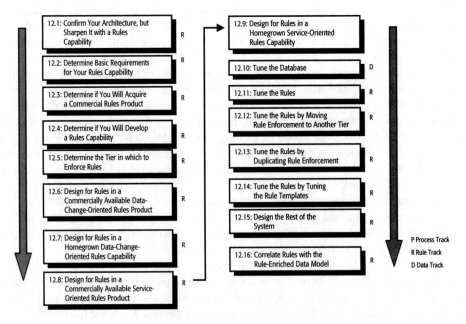

Figure 12.3   Steps for designing for rules.

framework. A generic relational database design methodology starts by translating a logical data model into a product-independent relational design. This is called a preliminary database design. By definition, it is faithful to the structure and integrity of the logical data model. But it builds on the simplicity, productivity, and flexibility advantages of relational database technology while remaining independent of your choice of RDBMS. You adopt the preliminary design to your product-specific environment. Finally, you tune it to accommodate functionality and performance requirements.

As a parallel, the generic rule design methodology translates a logical rule model into a product-independent rule design for delivering a rules capability into your system. This is called the preliminary rule design. By definition, it remains faithful to the structure (i.e., rule dependencies, rule patterns) and integrity of the logical rule model. But it builds on the simplicity, productivity, and flexibility advantages of current technology and a business rules approach.

You next adopt the preliminary rule design to your product-specific environment. Always keep in mind, however, that you are likely to measure the success of your design not by performance alone, and not by how correctly it reflects current business requirements. Rather, the business will measure your system's success by how easily it accommodates business changes and future needs. The ability to accommodate database changes was one advantage of relational database technology. The ability to accommodate changes in rules (business policy logic) is now an advantage with the business rules approach.

What Are the Deliverables of Business Rules System Design?

For most object-oriented projects, design deliverables can include class models enhanced with infrastructure classes, object diagrams, detailed operations, package diagrams, component diagrams, deployment diagrams, and screen or Web page navigation and designs. For a business rules design, you may need such deliverables for the core process flow (devoid of rule and data details). You would only need these for the rule flow if you are building your own rules capability. Otherwise, much of the design of rule flow is already designed and implemented into your commercial rules product and therefore, you need not design for it. This chapter considers where you may need or want to influence the sequence of rule execution.

With these ideas in mind, the deliverables from the design effort are:

- A rule technology diagram, showing the various layers (highlighting those in which rules execute)
- Physical rule design, consisting of
  - Assignment of rules to layers
  - Specifications for how the rules layer works
  - Implementation specifications for rules in the rules layer
  - Implementation specifications for rules in the database layer (triggers, etc.)
  - Insights into how the rules layer communicates with other layers.

■ Your standard design deliverables for the core process flow

■ Your standard design deliverables for screen and Web page navigation and layout.

Rule Design Standards

Before you embark on rule design, it is best to have certain rule design standards or guidelines in place. Many of these are covered in detail in Chapters 2 and 15. Standards you will need include:

■ What rule classification scheme do you need for rule design purposes?

■ What naming conventions do you need?

■ Where should rule designers document their recommendations?

■ What procedures should rule designers follow to be sure rule design is integrated and reviewed?

It is often useful to classify rules (or rule patterns) in a way that groups together rules that should have similar design requirements. Some organizations group rules according to what the rules aim to do. Sample classifications are data validation rules (that test data values prior to database updates), security/authorization rules (that allow or disallow operations by specific people or groups), workflow or sequencing rules (that indicate the order in which computations or logic is carried out), or rules that specify where data is to be retrieved (that indicate, based on conditions, specific sources for additional information).

Other organizations classify rules during the design process as to whether the rules represent core enterprise-wide rules, organizational-specific rules (such as for a division or a product), or geographically specific rules. This chapter does not utilize a special rule classification scheme for design purposes. Instead, it encourages you to understand the data access requirements for the rules. Data access requirements may significantly impact performance.

Rule-naming conventions will vary by rules product. Some products allow you to name a rule, a rule set, and perhaps a rule hierarchy.

As for where designers should document their recommendations, it is often useful to create a standard form or screen through which a rule designer documents recommended rule implementation. A typical form or screen for this purpose contains the rule, how a rule violation should be handled, classification of the rule for design purposes if useful, the recommended implementation for the rule, and a version of the rule expressed for its targeted platform.

Integrating a rule design means making sure that the target implementation for rules represents a whole solution. This becomes especially important if your developers will be writing their own rule-enforcement code (perhaps as methods in application objects) or are writing their own rules layer. In these cases, you will want to have well-documented methodology procedures that ensure that all relevant rule logic pertinent to an object class resides in that class. You will also want formal design reviews for rules just as you do for database design and other aspects of system design.

How to Measure the Quality of Your Total Rule Design across Tiers

Before embarking on rule design, become familiar with the ten criteria for measuring its quality. These are:

Rule Independence from Application: The rule code remains separate and independent from the application-specific logic. Many rules should be shared, hence used consistently within an application and across applications. Therefore, it is desirable to embed into application-specific logic only the rules that pertain to the specific application and to delegate the rest of the business's rules to a rules capability that is external to the system. (Keep in mind that sometimes the rules capability is an integral part of your system, meaning that the rules are not easily shared beyond your system boundaries.)

Full Support for Rule Classifications: The rule design supports all rule classifications. The methodology in this book is built to support a wide range of rule classifications: constraints and guidelines, computations, action enablers, and inferred knowledge rules. It is most desirable that your rule enforcement layers be able to enforce all of these rule classifications so that you can remove any of them from the application-specific logic, when appropriate.

Full Support for Rule Clauses: The rule design supports management and reuse of all rule clauses. Rule clauses can become very complex, especially for scientific or expert assistance applications. Some rule products provide limited syntax for scientific notation and some cannot provide complicated logic across multiple tables or record types or along long relationship paths. When this is so, you may need to alter your database design to accommodate a product's limitations or you may need to resort to writing procedural code to augment the rules layer enforcement.

Rule Independence from the DBMS. The rule design is independent of, hence can be shared across, various DBMS environments. This property is desirable because it allows you to access, from a rules layer, data housed in various sources. It also allows you to change your underlying database products while keeping your systems operational.

Ease of Implementation: Each classification of rule is easy to implement. A goal is for rule implementation to be as easy as possible. The more you need to rely on procedural programming languages for enforcing rules, the more you will need very detailed rule specifications, the more complicated the coding will be, and the more time-consuming the testing effort must be.

Difficult to Circumvent: Rules are difficult or impossible to circumvent. Because rules exist to ensure correctness of business events (and of underlying data), it is important that many of the rules are always followed. This is especially true of rules for regulatory compliance and for situations where the business wants consistent action. It is important that your rule design make it difficult for people or systems to circumvent rules for which the business cannot tolerate violations.

Ease of Change: The time within which you can change each classification of rule is reasonable from a business perspective. This criterion is closely related to the criterion for ease of implementation. Because the premise of this book is that the business will want to change its rules over and over again, it is important that your rule design and architecture allow this to happen in a timely manner.

Rule Traceability: The business version of the rule can be traced to its implementations. Traceability from the business's understanding of a rule to its technical implementation is necessary if you want to accommodate changes quickly.

Rule Externalization: People know where to find explanations of the rules. You will want to provide external access to the rules (from within and without your system) so that people know what the rules are and can request rule changes or put them into action.

Performance of Rule Execution: Performance of execution must be acceptable from a business perspective. This may be the most challenging criterion. In today's world of e-business and Internet networks, performance can be hampered by many factors. Similar to the database design process, rule design needs to start by assuming an ideal technological environment but make allowances for less than perfect technology. There are tuning techniques for rule design to improve performance. Table 12.2 summarizes these criteria.

Overview of Basic Business Rules System Design

This chapter divides the business rules system design process into five sections. The first section, Confirm the Architecture, takes into account the variety of possible tiered architectures for your system.

The second section, Translate the Rules, contains a step-by-step process for transforming rule classifications into a corresponding rule design idea. The section assumes you have already made important decisions reflected in your analysis deliverables, such as the ideal structure of the data, the essential rule dependencies, and the preferred workflow sequences. If you have not done so, you will need to do this during the design process. The result of the transformation is a preliminary rule design representing all logical perspectives: data, process, and rules.

The preliminary rule design is independent of your implementation environment, except for acknowledging at least three separate layers: one for core process flow, one for data management, and one for rule execution. The *preliminary rule design* represents, within your architectural tiers, the ideal data-driven, rule-driven, process-driven approach to design. If you do not carry out the tuning steps in the other sections of this chapter, you delegate total performance responsibilities to the technology you selected for each layer.

The third section, Design for Rules, provides insights and recommendations for designing rule implementations in the rules layer.

Even so, your initial translation into a preliminary rule design may be insufficient in performance and perhaps functionality. Therefore, you will tune for these in the fourth

Table 12.2 Summary of Rule Design Criteria

RULE DESIGN AND IMPLEMENTATION CRITERIA FOR QUALITY	PHASE IN WHICH THE CRITERIA IS ADDRESSED	HOW YOU CAN ACHIEVE IT
Ability of rules to remain separate and independent from the application's specific logic	Discovery, analysis, and design	• Separate rules service
Ability to support all rule classifications	Design and implementation	• Multitiered rule support (presentation layer, rule layer, DBMS layer)
Ability to support all rule clauses	Design	• Alter database design • Write procedural code • Commercial rules product
Ability for rules to remain independent of database management system	Discovery, analysis, design, and implementation	• Rule templates • Commercial rules product
Ease of rule implementation	Design and implementation	• Commercial rules product • Declarative DBMS rule implementation
Degree to which the rule is difficult or impossible to circumvent	Design and implementation	• Disallow direct database updates (force use of rule layer) • Enforce rules in DBMS

continues

Table 12.2 Summary of Rule Design Criteria (*Continued*)

RULE DESIGN AND IMPLEMENTATION CRITERIA FOR QUALITY	PHASE IN WHICH THE CRITERIA IS ADDRESSED	HOW YOU CAN ACHIEVE IT
Ease and time for changing a rule	Design and implementation	• Commercial rules product • Declarative DBMS rule implementation • Rules repository for traceability • Externalizing rules and proper rule management
Traceability of rules to implementations	Discovery, analysis, design, and implementation	• Rules repository • Rule management • Commercial rules product
Externalization of rules to business and IT people	Discovery, analysis, design, and implementation	• Rules repository • Rule management
Performance of rule execution	Design and implementation	• Run benchmarks with prototypes • Tune the rules themselves (e.g., duplicate rule) enforcement • Tune the underlying database

section, Tune the Design. The fifth section, Pull It All Together, addresses the rest of the system design and interfaces to the rules layer.

The next two sections of this chapter present two very basic design approaches that differ only slightly from each other. The first, called A Fast Path Solution, is a quick approach by which you put all rules into a commercial rules product and then test the result. The second, called A Most Common Solution, is also a quick approach by which you put traditional data integrity rules into the DBMS, the rest of the rules into a commercial rules product, and then test the result. These two approaches may be useful if you simply want to get something implemented as quickly as possible so as to test out the business rules approach and associated commercial products.

A Fast Path Business Rules Design Solution

If you are interested in conducting a quick prototype to test the business rules approach and corresponding technology, you can apply the steps below rather than spend a lot of time on detailed design decisions reflected in the fuller design methodology. These steps prescribe that you put all possible rules into the rules product.

1. **Select a rules technology product that is easy to use.** This means selecting a product based on only four criteria. First, the product supports either the data-change-oriented or service-oriented rules approach, depending on what your system seems most appropriate for. Second, it supports the rule classifications that are most important to your prototype. Third, it uses a rules language that is intuitive to you. And, fourth, it integrates easily with your technology environment.

2. **Select a relational DBMS product.** The reason to select a relational DBMS product is that most rules products work most seamlessly and effectively with these products. In a prototype, you don't want to spend time tuning the data structures or making up for deficiencies in integrating a heterogeneous data environment. You want to focus primarily on the rules aspect and how it can work for your organization. If you already are using a relational DBMS product, review its functionality for the prototype.

3. **Define the data or objects to the rules product.** Quickly sketch a logical data model (or object class model) and enter it into the rules product. Do not, at first, worry about how to share such models from your modeling tool with the rules product. Do not even focus on creating an extremely high quality model. The goal is not on how to create these definitions in the rules product. Instead, you want to focus on gaining an understanding of what the rules product needs to know to execute rules.

4. **Place all rules in the rules product.** Rather than agonize over selecting the optimum tier for rule execution, be brave and put all rules in your rules product that it can handle. You want to focus on learning how to manage rules separately from other components and on learning the advantages and disadvantages of your selected rules product.

5. **Determine, confirm screen/page flow and create screens.** You can accomplish this by creating the workflow analysis deliverables. Or you can simply sit down with business people and quickly sketch a preliminary flow. You need to do this because it establishes the first sense of rule execution sequence. Create the corresponding screens or Web pages. Do not focus too much on screen design. You want to learn how intuitive it is to make the connection from the screen to the application to the rules, as well as how to make rule violation messages intuitive to the business community.

6. **Change rules.** This is perhaps the most important step. Invite participants to suggest rule changes. Make the changes and illustrate the changed system. The focus is on how easy it is to change rules and how difficult it might be to change underlying data structures.

7. **Evaluate the experience.** Have participants document their comments. In particular, ask them to consider how such capability (to add and change rules easily) can change the way they perform their jobs and how this may positively impact the business as a whole.

A Most Common Business Rules Design Solution

If you are interested in using rules technology early, rather than spending time on the fuller design methodology, you can also consider the steps that follow. These steps prescribe that you put standard data integrity rules in the DBMS and other rules in a rules product.

1. **Select a rules technology product.** In this case, do a thorough product comparison and select the product you believe will be strategic for your organization.

2. **Select a relational DBMS product.** The reason for this step is the same as in the steps above. The first prototype or system aims to test the rules layer, not so much the idiosyncrasies of data integration and connections. Again, if you already are using a relational DBMS product, review its functionality for the prototype.

3. **Enforce all traditional data integrity rules in the DBMS.** This is often a common decision because people are most familiar with this enforcement of data integrity rules, performance is known and understood, and these rules cannot easily be circumvented. These include primary key constraints, foreign key constraints, column null constraints, and column value checks.

4. **Enforce computations and aggregations in the DBMS.** Often this is a good design decision because these are data-intensive operations and perform best or comfortably in the DBMS.

5. **Enforce other rules (inference, action enablers) in the rules product.** Many organizations view the rules layer as the place for inference rules and action-enabler rules. Inference rules control the flow of decisions within the system while action-enabler rules influence the flow of control to a component outside

the system. In this regard, the other rules (computations, traditional constraints) are seen as data-oriented rules and are delegated to the DBMS.

6. **Determine, confirm screen/page flow and create screens.** This is the same as the similar step above. In this case, you may need to design and develop application interfaces to the rules layer.

7. **Change rules.** This is the same as step 6 in the Fast Path list above.

8. **Evaluate the experience.** Again, document the advantages, disadvantages, opportunities, and lessons learned.

The remainder of the chapter contains a more complete rule design approach.

Confirm the Architecture

Assume that your application architecture consists of multiple layers.

STEP 12.1: CONFIRM YOUR ARCHITECTURE, BUT SHARPEN IT WITH A RULES CAPABILITY

Usually, there is a presentation *layer*, which manages the interactions between the human actor and the interface to the system (usually screens or Web pages). Some people refer to this as screen flow. Sometimes there may be a *workflow layer*, which manages interconnected tasks such as might be found in long transactions. Some people call this process flow. An example of a long workflow transaction is the processing of a stock trade from a person's request, to the brokerage service handling it, to the stock exchange at which the purchase takes place, to the depository where the exchange is recorded, and to the financial institutions where money changes hands. There is the *database layer*, which manages (shared) data on permanent storage devices and sometimes contains enforcement of rules.

Another layer is the *business logic layer*, which typically provides the application control flow for the targeted business events and application logic. In a business rules approach, however, think of the business logic layer as having two different types of functionality. The traditional functionality is that which controls the specific process flow for the target application, but not the rule execution. The new functionality is a rules capability that manages execution of rules on behalf of this application or many applications.

Once you understand the layers for your system, this chapter leads you in taking a closer look at the rules layer.

STEP 12.2: DETERMINE THE BASIC REQUIREMENTS FOR YOUR RULES CAPABILITY

This book assumes that you accept the need for a rules capability. You now decide functional and technical requirements for the rules capability that will best service your application. Do this regardless of whether you will buy a product or build a simple rules capability yourself. While this book often refers to a rules capability as if it is software that exists outside your particular system, it may, in some cases, simply be a conceptual aspect that is integral to your system.

Refer to your business requirements to determine what kind of rules service your system needs. Recall from Chapter 1 that, in general, it is useful to consider two different types of rules capabilities: data-change-oriented and service-oriented.

GUIDELINE 12.2.1

Determine which classifications of rules you want to leverage using a business rules approach.

Remember that leveraging a business rules approach means separating the rules, tracing them to implementation, externalizing them for knowledge and maintenance, and positioning them always for change. If you decide to apply these principles only to certain classifications of rules, this decision may influence the type of rules capability your system requires. For example, some commercial rules products are targeted mostly at enforcing constraints while others are stronger at executing inference rules. You may find it useful to create a correlation of the rule classification scheme you used during discovery and analysis to the rule classification scheme used by potential commercial rules products. This correlation will help you better understand which classifications of rules are handled by which target rules products.

The rest of the chapter assumes that you want to leverage the principles of the business rules approach for all classifications of rules. This makes the design more challenging, of course.

GUIDELINE 12.2.2

Determine if your business requirements lead you to a data-change-oriented rules capability.

Recall that a *data-change-oriented rules capability* executes rules in response to a running application touching data for which rules have been declared. With this approach, as an application attempts to update data, the rules capability watches for conditions that must be true about the data as well as conditions that should cause a reaction, such as the creation of new data. The data-change-oriented rules capability watches out for the complex conditions specified in rules.

With most data-change-oriented rules products, the order in which the system processes information (which is the sequence in which the knowledge worker enters information and requests interaction) determines the sequence in which rules will execute. That's because the person-system interactions correlate to database access (hence, data changes) and rules are associated with data changes. Therefore, the presentation layer and sequence of screens or pages forces the sequence of data changes which implies the sequence of rule execution. You can start with policies about the core process flow, such as, Don't ask for all Member details before checking Guardian credit. To make this policy concrete, you need to design your presentation layer and the flow of screens or pages appropriately.

What this means is that the rule product knows the rule executions that logically need to occur and in what sequence. When such sequence is not deterministic, such a product can make performance optimizations, if it is intelligent enough to do so. That's because the opportunity for parallel execution becomes apparent when you analyze rules, as this book has discussed. Over time, as rules change, the rule optimizer should be able to reoptimize rule execution.

A data-change-oriented rules capability has proven useful for many e-business applications. These include BtoB (business to business), BtoC (business to customer), BtoG (business to government), and BtoE (business to employee) applications. Commercial products with this capability are noted for enabling faster development of applications where those applications are easily changed.

In particular, a data-change-oriented rules capability is useful when your business events and requirements have the following characteristics:

- The business event has a relatively short life cycle, from actor input through several interactions, eventually to database updates, such as is the case for ordering products or placing reservations through the Internet.

- The business event is data intensive, as is typical for most online transactional processing.

- There are a few to medium quantity of rules per business event (< 100), which may correlate to 5 rules for 15–20 tables of data referenced or created.

- The rules are more complex than simple data integrity rules, usually involving multirow or multitable constraints, computations, multitable inferences, but not as complex as rules needed for advisory systems.

- The data integrity of the data in the database is of utmost importance, so you could deploy it as a service prior to actually updating the database.

- There is a need to integrate application workflow with shared business policies and rules.

- The data exists in data sources for which data integrity rules are not available (nonrelational sources), but where the data aware rules service can enforce such rules.

GUIDELINE 12.2.3

Determine if your business requirements lead you to a service-oriented rules capability.

As a reminder, a *service-oriented rules capability* executes rules upon request by a running application, not because the application directly attempted to touch data. In this case, the rules service waits until an application calls on it to apply rules to data. Usually the application passes the data to the rules service, the rules service may also retrieve and update data from a database, the rules service executes the rules, and the rules service sends the results of the rule execution back to the calling application. The application can then decide to abort the transaction, update the database, or carry out other actions. Also, the application handles all other logic such as session management, database calls, and user interface management.

Service-oriented rules capability has proven useful for many kinds of e-business applications also. Commercial products with this capability enable the reuse of existing rules by new systems as well as the delivery of shared complex advisory or judgment services to systems.

In particular, a service-oriented rules capability is most useful when your business events and requirements have the following characteristics:

- The business event involves many rules per transaction (> 100), such as is the case when assessing many conditions prior to making a judgment.

- The business event requires complex rules or very rule-intensive applications as are found in applications such as risk assessment of a transaction or for issuing an insurance policy, for example.

- The business events represent special classes of application processing, such as diagnosis, advisory, classification, scoring, predicting, monitoring, configuration verification, diagnostics, and computer-aided selling.

- There is a need for package customization, where you want to add business-specific rules to a generic software package.

- The rules capability is to plug into existing components, including non-packaged legacy solutions.

GUIDELINE 12.2.4

Determine if your business requirements lead you to more than one kind of rules capability.

It is entirely possible that your system may benefit from more than one kind of rules capability. For example, a data-change-oriented rules capability may be perfect for qualifying a customer who wants to buy stock. In this example, a data-change-oriented rules capability can check all relevant constraints, computations, and inferences regarding qualifying the customer's account and ability to pay for the stock. However, other aspects of placing a stock trade may be very complex. A judgment as to where to purchase the stock may require the execution of many rules. If a judgment as to whether this is the right stock to purchase requires many and complex rules, involving probabilities and complex ratings formulas, a service-oriented capability may be most appropriate.

GUIDELINE 12.2.5

Confirm your application layers.

Modify your technology architecture diagrams to illustrate your choice of rule layer or layers.

CASE STUDY: STEP 12.2—DETERMINE THE BASIC REQUIREMENTS FOR THE RULES CAPABILITY

Case Study Instructions:

- For the business event Guardian Enrolls Member, determine the requirements for the rules capability.

■ For the business event Member Requests Entrance to the Park, determine the requirements for the rules capability.

Case Study Solution:

The business event Guardian Enrolls Member actually involves very few and very simple rules. The rules qualify the guardian, mostly from a credit perspective, and qualify the member from an age perspective. Either type of rules capability can handle this event. For illustration purposes, we will propose a data-change-oriented rules capability.

The business event Member Requests Entrance to the Park has an interesting combination of rule requirements. Some of the rules are straightforward in that there are inferences regarding how the member answers guardian-specific questions. Recall, however, that the first release of the system is to allow only four rather fixed questions (about homework, chores, activities, and grades), but that future releases will allow the guardian more flexibility in customizing such rules. Either types of rules capability, too, can handle this business event. For illustration purposes, we will deploy a service-oriented rules capability, which provides the ability for guardians to customize rules on an as-needed basis.

If this is your first business rules system, you should prototype both business events in the target technology to verify your selection. In fact, ideally, you would have introduced the technology during the discovery phase so you immediately deployed rules to illustrate results to business audiences.

If in the previous step you decided that you would indeed deploy a rules layer, you now decide whether to buy one or build one.

STEP 12.3: DETERMINE IF YOU WILL ACQUIRE A COMMERCIAL RULES PRODUCT

Consider past history. How many of us followed good database design principles (based on the merits of the relational model), then implemented our design in nonrelational database products? It is not impossible to do, but it is not easy. You cannot easily gain all the benefits of relational technology.

The same is true when you take a business rules approach. You can follow good rule design principles (based on the merits of the business rules approach). To implement them without rules technology is not impossible, but it is not easy either. And full benefits may not be easily attainable.

GUIDELINE 12.3.1

Consider the benefits of rules technology.

Refer again to Table 12.1 for a summary of the principles of a business rules approach. Notice how many of the benefits are enabled by commercial rules technology. Let's discuss some of them.

First, utilizing rule technology can increase development productivity by reducing time and cost. This is because mostly a commercial product handles the rule management and execution aspect of your system. As C. J. Date (2000) states, "Application developers no longer write detailed code to paint screens or look for changes in forms on screens—they just invoke built-in *presentation services* to get those tasks done. Likewise, they don't write detailed code to manage data on the disk, they just invoke certain built-in *database services* to get *those* tasks done." In a business rules environment, developers no longer need to write detailed code to invoke rules and sequence their execution properly.

According to John E. Mann, a customer using Versata's Logic Server and Studio, "Yet2.com at first saw a 25 to 30 percent increase in productivity . . . but now, while making changes, the doubled or tripled speed the company is now experiencing is truly paying off" (Mann 2000).

Another boost to productivity for development comes from the fact that, with rules technology, you can test rule logic before you have full test data available and even before you have the rest of the application coded.

A second, perhaps more significant advantage to including rules technology in your architecture is that utilizing rules technology reduces subsequent maintenance costs. It does so because changing a rule or set of rules can often be accomplished without writing traditional code and can be tested independently of the rest of the application. This is especially true if the rules product supports a declarative specification of the rules.

Third, rules technology provides a single point of rule specification, usually in the form of a product-specific active rule repository. A single point of rule specification ensures that there is one point of traceability for those rules implemented in the rules technology.

Fourth, depending on the rules product, you can deliver executable rules that can be shared across applications, thereby providing independence from application-specific process flow and data access.

Acquiring a commercially available rules product is much like acquiring other types of software. You should create a list of requirements, contact relevant vendors, and conduct a paper evaluation. Sample requirements include the breadth of rule classifications the product supports; whether it represents a data-change-oriented approach or service-oriented approach or other approach; how easy the product is for technical people to use; how easily you can use the product to allow nontechnical people to access rules; how open the product is to interfacing with various DBMS products, application languages and messaging services; and performance. Some rule products provide very friendly front ends, even allowing you to view graphically the impact of rule changes on rule sets and rule flows. Once you select a product, you may want to perform a short (30-day) proof of concept study, where you provide the data or object model, sample workflow, and a set of rules. You and vendor representatives can implement these in a demonstration and also test how well the technology interfaces with your environment.

You will find that some rule products support only rules not easily supported in a relational DBMS, so these products are likely to support complex constraints and inferred knowledge rules. Some rule products provide heaviest support for inference rules and are light on computation rules. Still others provide capabilities for business people to customize rules. Since different products classify rules differently and support different classifications of rules, you may find it useful to correlate their rule types to the classification scheme in this book. That way you will be able to compare one rule product's capability to another.

We have discovered that each rule product we evaluated was capable of supporting all of the rule classifications in this book. The differences were in how you expressed them, how easy it was to express them in declarative form following the product syntax, how they were implemented within the software environment, and how easy it is to change the rules.

If you decide to acquire a commercial rules product, you need also to determine if the commercial product is to be used for your application only or if it is to be shared among multiple applications. This may determine not only selection of product, but also how it is used.

STEP 12.4: IF YOU WILL NOT ACQUIRE A COMMERCIAL RULES PRODUCT, DETERMINE IF YOU WILL DEVELOP YOUR OWN RULES CAPABILITY

There may be many reasons why you cannot acquire a rules product. You may not have the budget for it, although many such products are not overly expensive. You may not be authorized to bring in new technology. Perhaps you fear that the need for new skills, while better for the organization in the long term, may better be postponed.

If you cannot utilize rules technology, you can still design your system with rules in mind, but you have to be diligent about separating the rules or you will lose them again. You can do this by introducing into your application architecture a new kind of object, object class, component, or service targeted specifically to manage rule execution and nothing else. That is, you can design for and implement objects or classes that exist primarily to execute rules. The more you separate these rule-oriented objects from application-specific objects, the more shareable the executable versions of the rules will be.

GUIDELINE 12.4.1

Decide on your approach to designing a rules capability.

To keep it simple, you have two choices:

Option 1: Build a separate service or component that simulates a (simple) data-change-oriented rules capability.

Option 2: Build a separate service or component that simulates a (simple) service-oriented rules capability.

CASE STUDY: STEP 12.4—IF YOU WILL NOT ACQUIRE A COMMERCIAL RULES PRODUCT, DETERMINE IF YOU WILL DEVELOP YOUR OWN RULES CAPABILITY

Case Study Instructions:

- Determine whether to buy or build the two rule layers.

Case Study Solution:

For educational purposes, we illustrate several solutions. You will find these in Chapters 13 and 14.

This chapter also proposes insights for crafting a homegrown simple version of each kind of rules capability, keeping in mind that our ability to deliver a rules capability as sophisticated as a commercial one is minimal. However, you should consider doing so with the idea that it positions you easily for moving into commercially available products at some point.

Translate the Rules

Recall that the purpose of this section is simply to translate logical rules into a correct, consistent, and stable design. At this point, you have decided on the number of layers in your architecture and whether you will buy or build your rules layer.

STEP 12.5: DETERMINE SYSTEM TIER TO ENFORCE RULES

Just as it is a good idea to delegate relational data access to a relational database management system, it is a good idea, in theory, to delegate enforcement of rules to your rules layer. Assuming that you included a rules capability (commercial or homegrown), you now need to assign rules to appropriate system tiers for enforcement.

GUIDELINE 12.5.1

Assign most rules to the rules capability.

In your preliminary rule design, consider delegating to your rules layer the rules you want to manage as a separate, shareable, changeable asset to the rules layer. The phrase "delegate to your rules layer the rules you want to manage," includes rules that you define to a commercial rules product but that the product may actually implement in the DBMS. With some commercial rules products, in fact, you have a choice. That is, you can specify rules to the product and instruct it to execute a rule in rule code or in DBMS code. Regardless of where they execute, these rules have been delegated to the control of the rules capability.

If rules technology were perfect, the rules layer would contain all necessary logic for knowing exactly when and how to execute a rule with perfect performance and not allow rule circumventions where they cannot be tolerated. It would, in essence (as C. J. Date mentions), especially for a data-change-oriented rules capability, be the superpower above the DBMS, whereby it contained specialized logic for executing rules. Rule technology would provide for the ultimate independence among architectural components.

The truth is that rules technology, like other technology, is not perfect. It follows that you assign rule classifications to your tiers first without considering product-specific limitations. You will tune later.

With this in mind, this guideline places rules in the rules capability. When you tune your rule design, you will reconsider this decision for each rule classification.

Design for Rules

You are now ready to design the rule implementation. The steps you follow to design for rules in the rules capability vary depending on many factors, such as its basic characteristics (data-change-oriented or service-oriented), functionality limitations, rule classification limitations, and performance considerations, for example.

There are three steps that are common among most rules products and service-oriented rules products. These include a step for defining the terms used by the rules. In data-change-oriented products, you usually accomplish this by defining a data model (actually, a physical database model) to the product. In service-oriented rules products, you usually accomplish this by defining an object model (actually, an object model with attributes only, not methods).

Another common step is translating the rules you have (in natural language form or in template form) and translating them to the rule language or rule interface supported by the product.

A third common step is determining if there are rules that you cannot express in the product and for which you need to develop traditional, procedural, or nonrule code. And a fourth common step is the testing of the rules.

Differences between these two categories of products include variations in how you organize rules within the rules product and how and if you influence the sequence of rule execution. Another difference is, due to the close tie between the database and a data-change-oriented rules product, you may alter your initial database definition to meet product requirements.

It is beyond the scope of this book to show a complete design solution for all relevant products. Please visit the companion Web site for complete coverage of case study solutions by various vendors and products.

STEP 12.6: DESIGN FOR RULES IN A COMMERCIALLY AVAILABLE DATA-CHANGE-ORIENTED RULES PRODUCT

When working with a data-change-oriented rules capability, rule design and implementation tends to be data-centric. It involves first specifying the tables and columns to the rules product, usually in data or object model form. Then you express rules about the data that the rules capability is to watch out for. Concurrently, you create user interface screens or Web pages through which to test the rules and to design more detailed interfaces.

You usually express the rules in declarative form, although you may need to translate your rules in templates into the product's own language. For example, if you followed the approach in this book, you have captured most of your rules as If/Then statements. If your product does not support this syntax, you will need to rethink the expression of the rules for implementation.

Rule design for a data-change-oriented rules environment may also involve altering the table specifications to accommodate rule-processing restrictions. The design effort may also involve denormalizing data in the database for functionality and performance reasons.

Below is a generic set of design and implementation steps that are common among most commercially available data-change-oriented rules products. This chapter describes the steps, while Chapter 13 provides product-specific details.

STEP 12.6.1: ORGANIZE YOUR RULES FOR THE RULES PRODUCT

Most products provide a mechanism for organizing your rules. Usually, this means defining a subject or project area by which to group them for administrative purposes. Typically, this grouping does not imply sequence of rule execution. It is merely for your management purposes.

Step 12.6.2: Determine if You Need to *Add* Additional Data Constructs

If you followed the approach in this book, you have all required terms in your rule-enriched logical data model. Otherwise you may need to add some of them now.

For example, if you have rules that reference aggregate values (such as employee average salary), you may need to define to the rules product an entity or object class to contain this term or attribute so your rule within the product can reference it. Confer with your database designer as to whether this term needs to be persistently stored in the database for your product to function correctly.

Step 12.6.3: Determine if You Need to *Alter* Your Data Definitions

Some of these products have limitations on their ability to process multitable rules regarding how distant (across tables) a rule can reference terms. Therefore, if you have a rule with terms that are too distant in your database design, you may need to define that data from one table to another or to aggregate up to a higher level (such as for aggregate functions). You will need to determine whether such values need to be persistently stored or not. Again, confer with your database designer.

Most data-change-oriented rules products either require that values materialized by rules be persistently stored or recommend that this be so. You need to define to the rules product the data referenced by the rules. Often the data turns out to be your relational tables. You need to define, usually via a modeling technique, the terms that you will reference in the rules. Sometimes you can provide to the product your physical database design model from your data modeling environment.

Step 12.6.4: Define the (Revised) Data Design to the Rule Product

While most products allow you to define the data structure using the product's capabilities, it is best to feed your physical design structure directly from your modeling tool into the rules product. The modeling tools usually provide more sophisticated functions to assist with modeling, including model integration capabilities.

Step 12.6.5: Determine How to Express Rules Declaratively

Even if you used the rule templates in this book or devised your own, you may need to translate these into rule product syntax.

Step 12.6.6: Enter the Rules into the Product

Using the product's interface, enter rules. Sometimes you can write the rules directly and sometimes you can use drag-and-drop facilities for doing so. If you have a rules repository separate from the rules product, you will also want to be sure you enter the rules into the rules repository or create an interface between them.

Note USoft uses standard ANSI SQL as the specification language for explicit business rules, making it very easy to map to any relational database.

Note Versata captures and implements business policies and requirements using declarative rules that are written in structured English, not procedural code. The rules need to be identified during analysis and then applied to the relevant data objects, attributes and relationships.

STEP 12.6.7: DETERMINE IF SOME RULES NEED TO BE CODED PROCEDURALLY (SUCH AS IN JAVA)

Some products may lack a full set of operators for all possible calculations and logical phrases. You may need to implement very sophisticated algorithms in procedural code.

STEP 12.6.8: TEST THE RULES

This is the fun part. You can do this by entering data into the default user interfaces that the product automatically creates for you. Or you can spend more time designing the interface.

CASE STUDY: STEP 12.6—DESIGN FOR RULES FOR A COMMERCIALLY AVAILABLE DATA-CHANGE-ORIENTED RULES PRODUCT

Case Study Instructions:

- If you chose a data-change-oriented rules product, walk through the design steps. Use two rules as an example:
  - For enrolling a member: A member must be between 6 and 15.
  - For invoicing a guardian: A guardian's monthly invoice is equal to the sum of the monthly charges of the guardian's members.

Case Study Solution:
Solutions for Versata Inc.'s product and USoft Inc.'s product are shown in the next chapter.

STEP 12.7: DESIGN FOR RULES IN A HOMEGROWN DATA-CHANGE-ORIENTED RULES CAPABILITY

There are various ways you can build your own simple data-change-oriented rules capability. Let's review the logic behind a data-change-oriented rules capability.

If you recall, a business event is serviced by a business process, which consists of a flow of tasks and supported by screens or Web pages. The system behind the process processes input, as any other system, until it arrives at a point of updating persistent data. The data-change-oriented rules capability is invoked automatically when there is a request to update persistent data. The rules capability correlates the data structures targeted for update to rules that protect those structures from contamination.

So, for example, if the system were attempting to change a salary field, the rules capability would execute all rules associated with that update. These would include perhaps a constraint on the new versus old salary value, any constraints on the maximum or minimum value, and so forth. If the application were attempting to create an order, the rules capability would execute computation rules for determining violations of credit limits as well as those used to determine special pricing. It would compute taxes and shipping fees and it would verify that referential integrity rules are followed. If rules are violated, the database update is disallowed and the rules capability sends back an error message, which indicates the violated rule or rules.

Keep in mind that if you develop your own rules capability, the need for your own rules repository is even greater because you will not be using a rules product that provides a repository function.

GUIDELINE 12.7.1

Consider using DBMS facilities to simulate a simple data-change-oriented rules service.

Indeed, many readers have been delivering a data-change-oriented rules capability for years by coding rules using DBMS facilities. In the simplest form, then, you can implement each rule in the DBMS using table definitions, view definitions, triggers, and so on. In this way, when your application attempts to update the database, these rules execute automatically and disallow database updates that violate the rules.

GUIDELINE 12.7.2

Consider coding a rules capability that translates database updates into rule executions.

In many cases, the use of DBMS facilities may be unacceptable because it represents a two-tiered approach or is limited to only one DBMS. If so, you may consider building a simple rules capability that is called by an application when it wants to access data. Either the application itself or the rules capability needs to correlate the application request with its specific database accesses. Then, the rules capability associates those database accesses with the rules that protect those parts of the database, and execute those rules.

GUIDELINE 12.7.3

Consider including rules within methods of data-change-oriented object classes.

Another option is to create an object class for each target table or file where that object class contains a method for inserting, updating, and deleting rows or record instances. These methods would execute all rules that protect the target data. This option does not explicitly separate the rules execution from the rest of the application.

As you can see, as the number and complexity of underlying data structures and rules increases, your system would benefit greatly from an appropriate rules product. A commercial rules product may also automatically manage the generation and distribution of rule code.

STEP 12.8: DESIGN FOR RULES IN A COMMERCIALLY AVAILABLE SERVICE-ORIENTED RULES PRODUCT

If a data-change-oriented rules service is data-centric, it seems only natural that a service-oriented rules service is process-centric. Specifically, when using a service-oriented rules product, the rule design effort tends to be process oriented. It usually involves creating an object model with which to communicate or share data with the rules service. Usually, the objects for rule execution contain data only, no rules. After all, the rules are in the rules service. You express the rules sometimes in procedural code and sometimes not. If declarative, you may be able to use If/Then syntax.

You are not likely to need to change database specifications since a service-oriented rules capability is not so closely tied to the data. The rule design effort usually involves grouping rules into executable sets or hierarchies, sequencing the execution of rule sets, and possibly sequencing the execution of rules within rule sets. You do this so that, when your application calls the rules capability for rules execution, the rules capability has been set up to perform that service in a particular manner.

Below are generic steps that are common across most service-oriented rules capabilities. Again, this chapter discusses the steps while Chapter 14 provides product-specific details.

STEP 12.8.1: CREATE A COMPONENT MODEL OF APPLICATION SHOWING RULE SERVICE COMPONENT

A component model provides a graphical understanding of how the rules capability fits into your application architecture. The component model diagram illustrates the application component, the rules service component, and the database component. Remember, your system invokes the rules service, so it is useful to see how this fits together. You may even have various kinds of rule services.

STEP 12.8.2: DEVELOP AN OBJECT MODEL FOR THE RULES CAPABILITY

This object model refers to the objects about which you want the rules product to execute rules. As such, it is usually a subset of the full application business model and usually contains attributes only, no methods and no rules. This object model is a vehicle for communicating data to the rules service.

STEP 12.8.3: DECIDE ON RULE SETS, RULE HIERARCHIES, AND SEQUENCE OF EXECUTION WITHIN A RULE SET

This is usually accomplished by decomposing your use case or business event or event response process into tasks. If you followed the approach in this book, you already did this during process analysis. You may need to decompose tasks further and to meet with screen/Web designers. In this step, for a simple business event, you group rules together for one task or subtask. In this way, your application can call on the rules service to perform rule execution for that task or subtask.

For very complicated business events, with many sets of rules, you may have the option within your product of creating rule hierarchies. Rule hierarchies are another mechanism for determining the sequence of rule execution. Refer to your specific product documentation on how best to group rules for proper execution sequence.

Within a rule set, sometimes you can determine the execution sequence of rules. Often the default is the order in which you enter the rules. Usually, you can override this.

STEP 12.8.4: DEFINE THE OBJECT MODEL TO THE PRODUCT

Most often, you can import your object model from an object modeling tool into the rules tool.

STEP 12.8.5: DETERMINE HOW TO EXPRESS THE RULES

You need to become familiar with your product's rule language or alternate forms for entering rules. You may be able to investigate two alternatives. You will enter some rules using the native rule language of the product. To assist guardians in changing the rules pertaining to their members, you will create a rule interface through which the guardians can enter their own rules. The interface will limit the kinds of rules the guardians can enter to rules about homework, chores, and so on. It will provide a mechanism for entering rules that does not require technical expertise.

STEP 12.8.6: ENTER RULES INTO THE PRODUCT

The rules are entered into the rules product either directly using the rule language syntax or through graphical or a wizard capability. Again, if you have a rules repository separate from the rules product, you will want to ensure that the rules reside in the rules repository.

Note ILOG features a Business Rule Language (BRL). Business users can construct rules in a natural language like syntax, customizable—because no single BRL can fit all—to the terms and vocabulary of any business domain. If rules are to be defined as constraint, inference, action, and so on, then these classifications should be made in the BRL, where business users will benefit. Rules can be created in any editor or using the ILOG Rule Builder environment, and loaded into the engine as a file, stream, URL, in XML, or created on the fly from within application code using the ILOG Rule Factory API. An application may also remotely attach to the ILOG Rule Builder, allowing users to edit, debug, and execute rules, while the application maintains control of the rule engine. A point and click editor allows business users to create rules in a natural language syntax called the Business Rule Language. The editor is also available as a JavaBean or Web component, enabling it to be built directly into any application, allowing rule editing directly from within the application or Web browser.

Note For HNC Software's product, the business rules are written in the Advisor Structured Rule Language (SRL). While SRL is a programming language, the grammar is English-like, making it easy to read for nonprogrammers, and fairly simple to learn. The Brokat Advisor Builder IDE provides a range of graphical tools to assist you in developing your business rules.

STEP 12.8.7: DETERMINE IF SOME OF THE RULES NEED TO BE CODED IN PROCEDURAL NONRULE CODE

As above, this will depend on the full functionality of your rule language within your product.

STEP 12.8.8: TEST THE RULES

Again, this is the fun part.

CASE STUDY: STEP 12.8—DESIGN FOR RULES IN A COMMERCIALLY AVAILABLE SERVICE-ORIENTED RULES PRODUCT

Case Study Instructions:

- Design for the rules in the service-oriented rules product. Do so for rules about answers to the member questions and for invoicing rules.

Case Study Solution:
A solution for HNC Software's product is in the next chapter.

STEP 12.9: DESIGN FOR RULES IN A HOMEGROWN SERVICE-ORIENTED RULES CAPABILITY

There are various ways you can build a simple service-oriented rules capability. Keep in mind that a commercial rules product will likely be more sophisticated than one that you build. For example, as indicated earlier, a commercial rules product may also automatically manage the generation and distribution of rule code.

Let's review the logic behind a service-oriented rules capability.

Again, recall that a business event is serviced by a business process, which consists of a flow of tasks and is supported by screens or Web pages. The system behind the process processes input, as any other system, until it arrives at a point of needing a decision to be made by the rules capability. The application invokes the rules capability, passes required information, and requests execution of the decision. The rules capability recognizes the decision, accepts the input, and executes the latest set of rules required to make that decision. The rules capability passes the result of the decision, which is the result of executing the underlying rules, back to the calling system.

So, for example, if the system were processing an employee salary change, it would invoke the rules capability to determine if a change in salary is acceptable. The rules capability would execute all rules associated with that decision. These would include perhaps the same constraints as above on the new versus old salary value, constraints on the maximum or minimum value, and so forth. If the system were taking an order from a customer, the system would invoke the rules capability to make several decisions, such as whether the total amount of the order is within the customer's credit limit. Perhaps the system would ask the rules capability to estimate the day of delivery to that customer. Perhaps the system would ask the rules capability to find the least expensive way to deliver the products to the customer. Each of these would be a decision, requiring the execution of many rules. The rules capability executes those rules and sends back a message as to the result.

In concept, then, you create a rules capability that accepts decision requests from various applications and has a predefined process by which to execute the rules that arrive at that decision. You may decide to organize rules into rule sets where each set relates to a decision.

GUIDELINE 12.9.1

Create a rules capability that accepts invocation from your system and processes decisions requested.

To keep it simple, define an interface to your rules capability, by which an application requests a decision and passes arguments. You can create object classes for each business object for which the application passes data. Those object classes can contain the rules within corresponding methods, coordinated by the control object class that correlates those executions with the specific decision being requested. You may have a control object class that manages the rules capability by associating the decision request from the application with the execution of a specific rule set, hence execution of the appropriate methods.

As you can appreciate, complex decisions are probably best handled by the appropriate commercially available rules product.

Again, keep in mind that, if you develop your own rules capability, the need for your own rules repository is even greater because you will not be using a rules product that provides a repository function.

Tune the Design

Proper tuning can be the difference between a successful and unsuccessful implementation. Tuning, in a business rules approach, like all approaches, should be collaborative and iterative. Tuning should be done together by design specialists for data, process, and rules. In some cases, you will want to include representatives from your DBMS vendor and commercial rules product vendor so as to maximize performance of those pieces of software. Some rule vendors claim that their product performs well enough not to need much tuning.

This section focuses explicitly on ways to tune the data and rules layer so as to preserve them as shared resources as much as possible.

STEP 12.10: TUNE THE DATABASE

In this step, you address performance and functionality challenges by tuning the database. Every systems design effort requires database tuning. *Tuning the database* is, as always, specifying design options that improve performance or functionality of an initial database design. The rule designer and database designer should collaborate here.

GUIDELINE 12.10.1

Understand data access characteristics of rules.

Classify each rule pattern (or those that are functionality or performance challenges) according to its data access characteristics: single versus multiple tables, single row versus multiple rows, and those requiring aggregate functions and sorts.

Perhaps computation rules are the easiest to understand. Computation rules can involve data from a single row in a single table. An example is a column for employee.compensation.amount, which is the sum of the values in two columns in the same row: employee.salary.amount and the employee.commission.amount.

A computation rule can involve multiple rows from a single table. An example is the average of employee.salary.amount. Taking it one step further, a computation rule can involve multiple tables such as the sum of the commissions on each sale plus the employee's salary.

Let's also consider constraints. The simplest of constraints are those involving a single column. You probably recognize these as simple edit and validation rules. There are also constraints, which involve only one table, but more than one column in that table. Such a constraint may state that the sum of two columns must not exceed a certain value. Another single table constraint may involve aggregate processing of the table, where an average or sum of a column is needed by the rule. Even more complex constraints are constraints requiring multiple tables. A familiar example is referential integrity rules, which are constraints between two tables. Another example is the membership rules among subtypes and supertypes. The same situations may arise for guidelines.

Inferred knowledge rules may involve only one table, but usually involve more than one table. Action enablers can also require data from a single or multiple tables.

You can see that a rule can require data either from a single row in a single table, multiple rows in a single table, or multiple rows in multiple tables. Some data access requirements for a rule may require a sort, which can be the case for determining maximum, minimum, sum, and average.

At this point, review rules for those that may pose performance problems. From a data perspective, these are rules that access multiple tables and require sorts. Review access paths for these rules with the database designer. Please visit the companion Web site for a white paper on relational database design, called Designing Relational Databases. For this chapter, we present a few guidelines for the rule designer to understand.

GUIDELINE 12.10.2

Consider first those database tuning options that do not compromise the stable data structure.

To preserve the most stable data structure, tune first those tuning options that are transparent and do not compromise the stable data structure. *Transparent tuning options* are options that are not detectable to business users and to programmers. The goal is to tune these first because they are transparent to people and program code and rules that access the data. In most relational DBMS products, these include, as examples, specifying file allocations, primary and secondary space, free space, locking considerations, and indexes.

GUIDELINE 12.10.3

Consider last those database tuning options that compromise the stable data structure.

If transparent tuning options prove insufficient, consider tuning options that are not transparent, such as denormalizing the data in a way that makes the denormalization visible to programmers, applications, and people.

A *nontransparent database tuning option* is one that is apparent to the business community, programmer, or rule. That is, tuning a nontransparent option is the altering of the data structure so that it no longer maps to a database representing a rule-enriched logical data model. The most common ways to tune the nontransparent data structure include physically storing columns that are exact copies of other columns, columns whose values are computed according to a formula (a computation rule), or columns whose values are inferred from logic (from an inference rule).

You will want to work with the database designer to determine if some of these values should be stored redundantly. Reasons for this may be that performance of certain rules is unacceptable, such as certain complex and data intensive computations. Some rules products have restrictions on how many tables can be referenced in a rule, thus duplicate copies of column values may be needed to reduce the number of tables referenced.

STEP 12.11: TUNE THE RULES

You may need to tune the rule implementation itself. The phrase *tune the rules* means altering or adding to your preliminary rule design so as to meet functionality or performance requirements that the preliminary design does not meet.

You may be surprised to learn that tuning options for rules are similar to tuning options for databases, at least in concept. For example, you can move a rule implementation from the ideal tier to another tier to meet certain requirements. More drastically, you can duplicate rule enforcements across tiers.

GUIDELINE 12.11.1

Consider first those rule-tuning options that are transparent.

The best kind of tuning for rules, as for databases, are tuning options that are transparent to human actors, programmers, and application components requiring rules. These may include caching mechanisms, for example. Since each product is very different, refer to your product-specific manuals for insights on these kinds of tuning options.

In general, keep in mind that, if your functionality and performance are acceptable, do not engage in tuning rules. That's because the tuning options below, while done to provide missing functionality or improve performance, do so at a cost. The cost is a loss of some characteristic of your ideal rule design. Your ideal rule design was based on the quality criteria in this chapter. Overtuning rules, like overtuning a database, is not always a benefit.

GUIDELINE 12.11.2

Consider last those rule-tuning options that are not transparent.

If transparent rule-tuning options are insufficient for meeting rule functionality and performance, there are three nontransparent ways to tune the rule design itself. You can move rule enforcement to another tier, duplicate rule enforcement on another tier, or change the rule template for specific rules or rule patterns.

STEP 12.12: TUNE THE RULES BY MOVING RULE ENFORCEMENT TO ANOTHER TIER

This step suggests you consider moving your rules enforcement, which is not necessarily transparent. A very common approach to moving rule enforcement out of the rules layer is to put it into the DBMS layer. This is common practice for rules that are very easily supported by the DBMS, such as uniqueness enforcement through use of a unique index. With some commercial rules products, referential integrity rules can be enforced either through the rules product or through DBMS functionality.

To understand your options, consider the following possibilities for where you can enforce a rule outside the rules layer:

- Application-specific layer: This refers to application code for this application that is not shared with other applications. This code is usually procedural code (such as C++, Java, Visual Basic, and so on).
- DBMS layer:
  - Domain definition: This is database code intended to be shared among applications that share the database. It defines data types, lengths, and sometimes value restrictions on domains.
  - DBMS table definition: This too is database code intended to be shared among applications that share the database. It defines column types, lengths, sometimes value restrictions on columns (uniqueness, not null, values), and sometimes relationship restrictions (referential integrity rules).
  - DBMS view definition: This is database code defining a virtual table to be shared among applications if they specify use of the same view.
  - DBMS trigger: This is database code intended to be shared among applications that defines code to be executable automatically when a table or column is operated on. It is typically written in declarative code.

- Method in shared object class: This is code intended to be shared among other applications because it is in an object shared across applications. That is, you can use this as a mechanism for creating shared, standard maintenance logic for specific data structures.

Table 12.3 summarizes the advantages and disadvantages of enforcing rules in the various tiers.

Table 12.4 summarizes for each rule classification, the most interesting options for rule enforcement. The numbers indicate the desired sequence for preference. That is, a "1" is the most preferred option, in the absence of restrictions. Notice that the first choice in this book is the rules layer.

Let's make some comments about Table 12.4.

For computation rules, recall that a computation is a statement providing an algorithm on numeric data for arriving at the value of a term. The algorithm can include arithmetic functions (add, subtract, multiply, divide), aggregate functions (minimum, maximum, average, mean, and so on), scientific functions (sin, cosine, and so on), and a counting function.

If the computation involves large data volumes (many rows, wide rows, many tables), the DBMS is likely to outperform a rules engine in manipulating such data. The third choice for computations is to create a method in a shared object. This would be appropriate if you are building your own rules capability. In this case, you can create an object class for the target table and include a method for materializing the computed value. Make sure that any other methods that change input values to the computation will invoke this method to recompute the computed value. This computation logic, because it is likely in procedural code, is probably difficult to change.

Recall that a constraint is a complete statement that expresses an unconditional circumstance that must be true or not true for the business event to complete with integrity. For the design discussion, consider that there are two very basic types of constraints. There are basic data integrity constraints that have been traditionally included in logical data models and in RDBMS products. There are also complex data integrity constraints that usually involve more sophisticated logic and data from multiple tables.

There are various DBMS facilities for implementing constraints. DBMS domain definition can be used to specify domain constraints shared across related columns. DBMS table definition can be used for referential integrity, primary key, column constraints such as uniqueness and null constraints and value constraints. DBMS index definition can enforce uniqueness on an alternate key. DBMS trigger definitions can enforce complex constraints.

For constraints, a very common compromise (usually due to rules product limitations and performance considerations) is to enforce traditional data integrity constraints (primary key constraints, referential integrity constraints, uniqueness constraints, non-null constraints, and value checks) in the DBMS while enforcing complex constraints (multitable constraints) in a rules layer. Keep in mind, however, that this solution has disadvantages: A change in some rules require a database definition change; these rules cannot be shared across DBMS products without recoding its DBMS implementation. Another common practice is to enforce attribute validation in the presentation layer.

For constraints, a shared method in an object is appropriate if you are building your own rules capability. You can create a method in each object class relating to a table and

Table 12.3 Advantages and Disadvantages of Enforcing Rules in Different Places

TIER FOR ENFORCING RULES	ADVANTAGES	DISADVANTAGES
Application-specific tier	Value need not be physically stored.	Enforcement is not as easy to implement as with a rules product or DBMS option. Enforcement is not shared. The value does not automatically change when underlying values change without serious design effort. A change in rule requires a change to procedural code where it is not shared and probably difficult to change.
Shared object method	Enforcement can be shared across applications. The value need not be physically stored.	Enforcement is not as easy to implement as with a rules product or DBMS view. The value does not automatically change when related data values change without significant design effort. Enforcement can be circumvented by not using the shared object or method. A change in rule requires a change to procedural code.
Rules layer	Enforcement is easy to implement if using declarative rule technology. Enforcement can be shared across applications. The value may not need to be physically stored. The automatically changes when related data values change. A change in rule simply requires a change in one rule in one place.	Without a rules product, implementation may not be so easy. Enforcement can be circumvented if people or applications can gain direct access to the database.
DBMS domain, table, trigger specification	Enforcement is easy to implement. Enforcement is shared across applications.	Enforcement is not independent of DBMS.
DBMS view definition	Enforcement is easy to implement. Enforcement can be shared across applications needing that value by sharing the view. The value need not be physically stored. The value automatically changes when related data values change.	A change in rule requires a view change, which may be more involved than a rule change. Enforcement can be circumvented by not using the designated view.

Table 12.4 Summary of Implementation Options by Rule Classification

RULE CLASSIFICATION	RULES LAYER	DBMS DOMAIN DEFINITION	DBMS VIEW DEFINITION	DBMS TABLE DEFINITION	DBMS TRIGGER	SHARED METHOD	APPLIC- ATION- SPECIFIC
Constraints	1	2	2	2	2	3	4
Guidelines	1					2	3
Computations	1		2			3	4
Inferred knowledge rules	1					2	3
Action enablers	1					2	3

enforce all constraints for the table through methods in the related object class. However, the constraint's truth-value will not automatically change when related data values change unless the design effort ensures that related methods (that update related data) also invoke the proper method.

Recall that a guideline rule is a complete statement that expresses a warning about a circumstance that should be true or not true. A guideline does not force the circumstance to be true or not true, but merely warns about it, allowing the human to make the decision. Hence, a guideline rule is much like a constraint rule but does not automatically prevent the business event from completing successfully.

Some commercial rules products cannot support guideline rules. Guidelines are not easily enforced in the DBMS, except through triggers that issue warning messages and roll back a database update. Therefore, the second choice is to create a shared object class and include guideline rules in a method or methods within that object class.

Recall that an inferred knowledge rule is a complete statement that tests conditions and upon finding them true, establishes the truth of a new fact. These are, perhaps, the most interesting rules to the business rules approach.

It is difficult to implement inferred knowledge rules in the DBMS. Most likely you would need to code triggers and you would probably need to store the resulting value physically so that it could be reused.

Instead, then, consider creating a shared object class for the table in which the inferred value belongs and creating a method for inferring it. Again, you may need to code all other methods that change related values so that they call the appropriate method to reinfer the value should any of those related values change.

Recall that an action enabler is a complete statement that tests conditions and upon finding them true, initiates another business event, message, or other activity.

GUIDELINE 12.12.1

Think carefully about rules for which the business cannot afford violations.

If you have enforced rules in the rules layer for which the business cannot afford violations, you may want to determine if you can disable database access from everywhere other than the rules layer. If you cannot disable such access or if you need to allow applications to access and update the database without going through the rules layer, consider moving the enforcement to the DBMS or schedule consistency routines to detect violations.

GUIDELINE 12.12.2

Enforce rules in the DBMS layer if performance is unacceptable in the rules layer and the rules are data-intensive.

Study your rules, especially those that are complex: aggregate processing, multitable, or requiring significant sorts. For this processing, consider materializing values through the DBMS, using DBMS built-in functions (such as sum, max, min, average) and joins. You may also find it appropriate, for performance reasons, to move rule enforcement from the rules layer to the DBMS for referential integrity and primary key support.

STEP 12.13: TUNE THE RULES BY DUPLICATING RULE ENFORCEMENT IN MULTIPLE TIERS

This step encourages you to think about duplicating rule enforcement selectively.

GUIDELINE 12.13.1

Duplicate the enforcement of rules in the DBMS layer for protection purposes.

If your rule enforcement is not in the DBMS layer (it is in the rules layer or application-specific layer), but you cannot prevent people or applications from circumventing that rule enforcement, consider also enforcing the rules in the DBMS.

GUIDELINE 12.13.2

Duplicate the enforcement of rules in the presentation layer for performance reasons.

In the ideal scenario, you have enforced rules in your rules layer. However, it is quite common that there are some rules that are used very interactively with the actor. These tend to be very simple edit and validation rules for data entry, for example. It is common practice to enforce these rules in the presentation layer so as to provide immediate error detection and correction to the human actor. However, keep in mind that you may still want these rules reexecuted at the rules layer, since this should serve as the one point of rules specification and control.

STEP 12.14: TUNE THE RULES BY CHANGING THE RULE TEMPLATE

In this step, you reevaluate the way in which you expressed rules to the rules capability. It may be possible to increase performance, for example, by restating the rules in another way.

GUIDELINE 12.14.1

For If/Then rule implementation, consider making rules nonatomic.

Recall that all of your rules are in atomic form. That is, expressed as If/Then statements, there are no Ors in the If clause and no Ands in the Then clause. This creates smaller, but more numerous rules that are connected together based on their knowledge dependencies.

Consider also that rule products should be experts at processing rules just like database management products should be experts at processing relational data. Looking at the relational database world, good design principles lead you to create preliminary relational tables that are normalized. This results in smaller, more numerous tables than if you combined several of these tables into one table. Relational database management systems are designed especially to process (read, sort, scan, join) many smaller, normalized tables that are related to each other through foreign keys. In fact, often denormalizing and combining tables can actually degrade performance.

In the rules world, the corollary should also hold. Rule products should be designed especially to process (execute, chain, scan) many smaller, atomic rules that are related to each other through knowledge dependencies. It may be the case that making these rules nonatomic might actually degrade performance.

However, in the database world, sometimes denormalization is the right solution. So, too, in the rules world.

For example, you may want to combine two atomic rule patterns into one executable rule. Suppose you had two rules as follows:

- If a person lives in "New Jersey," then the person is a preferred customer.
- If person has an income > $300k, then the person is a preferred customer.

Some rules products process Ors in the If statement. You could combine these into one nonatomic rule as:

> If a person lives in "New Jersey" or a person has an income > $300k, then the person is a preferred customer.

From an execution perspective, it could be faster to execute this as one rule than as two rules, although it is hard to imagine a great performance savings. Notice, too, that changes to independent thoughts (changing the income level for a preferred customer) are a change to the rule that also contains location for a preferred customer. So changes are not atomic, as discussed under Analyzing Rules (Chapter 10).

GUIDELINE 12.14.2

For other kinds of rule implementation, consider alternative expressions.

For example, if you are using a data-change-oriented rules product and its language is similar to SQL, consider revising the statement to favor the optimizer choices in the DBMS.

Also, if you have a choice between expressing rules in a more natural form and expressing them in very rigid almost-data-access form, consider using the latter if it improves performance, especially for complex rules.

Pull It All Together

It is now time to tie up loose ends.

STEP 12.15: INTEGRATE YOUR DESIGN PIECES

In this step, you gather together your rule enforcements in the rules layer, the DBMS, and application.

GUIDELINE 12.15.1

Despite your classifications tied to tiers, verify placement for each and every rule.

At this point, you have decided where your rule classifications are to be enforced. Hopefully, many of your rules are enforced in a rules layer. For basic data integrity rules and data intensive rules, perhaps you have enforced them in the DBMS. Still other rules may have gone into methods in shared object classes, especially if you cannot acquire a commercial rules product.

Now consider each rule against your classification scheme, but evaluate where it best fits.

GUIDELINE 12.15.2

Protect the database(s).

For all rules you decided to enforce outside the DBMS and for which the business cannot afford violations, you may need to make two specifications:

Disallow all activities directly against the database that might possibly violate rules. Specifically, use the DBMS security mechanism to allow only the rules layer to update the database where rule violations cannot be tolerated.

Force all application access through the rules layer or shared method, wherever the rule enforcement lies.

GUIDELINE 12.15.3

Integrate the shared methods in shared object classes.

If your design includes the creation of shared methods within shared object classes, you may need to make the following four specifications:

- Integrate all rules for one object class into appropriate methods (insert, update, delete per object class) where each of those methods invokes all related rules.
- Identify changes in underlying data values that should also trigger these methods.
- Disallow all activities directly against the database that might possibly violate rules.
- Force all application access through the shared object classes.

STEP 12.16: DESIGN THE REST OF THE SYSTEM

After separating the rules and the data, the remainder of the systems design involves solidifying screen flow, screen design, and creating specifications for application flow.

SAMPLE RULE LANGUAGE SYNTAX

For ILOG, a business rule application is any application that benefits from abstracting business logic from the application and incorporating that logic in the form of business rules. ILOG does not impose upon the application or the technical architecture of the application. ILOG rules ultimately become Java or C++ objects, depending upon which rule engine is used. ILOG rule engines are at home in C++, Java, and EJB applications, or within the J2EE framework—whatever the architecture.

Multiple instances of the rule engine can be executed in parallel—because it is thread safe—making JRules scalable as well as suitable for high-speed parallel processing architectures, and embedding in EJBs. Using Java's synchronization capability, JRules is *thread-hot*, allowing multithreaded applications to share objects and rules, and multiple rule engines to operate on the same set of application objects. In cases where speed is critical, ILOG would recommend C++, as the ILOG rules product was developed for critical military and telecom problems that require optimization for speed. Applications that must integrate into a wide variety of architectures would benefit from the platform independence of JRules. The ILOG rule language (used by both the Java and C++ engines) also provides methods of optimizing individual rules. Again, most of the optimization is under developer control, allowing them to decide when it is best to apply a given optimization technique within a rule.

The USoft environment allows you to deploy your system on any supported physical environment without having to make many changes in your business model. In other words, the business rules you have defined will run just as well on Oracle or DB/2, and it is also possible to deploy your USoft application on the World Wide Web. In all cases, the rules engine is a small set of binary executable files generated from definitions stored in a relational repository.

GUIDELINE 12.16.1

Follow your organizational standards.

For Web development, most organizations follow a form of iterative object-oriented analysis and design. Utilize these techniques for the remainder of your process layer. Follow screen and Web design techniques for your presentation layer.

GUIDELINE 12.16.1

Determine interfaces to the rules layer.

Whether you purchase a commercial rules product or build your own rules capability, you need to design the interfaces from your application and data layers to your rules layer.

Files are handled differently depending on the deployment architecture. For example, in a conventional Windows client/server environment, the rules engine files are distributed to each client machine, and only the database itself is server-side. In a Web environment, USoft's Java Open Rules Server (JORS) handles client requests, starting and stopping rules engines on the server side (application tier) and allocating these to clients. In this case rules engine files are not, of course, distributed to client machines.

When USoft's distributed rules engine is applied, tasks similar to those of the JORS server are performed by a transaction monitor, and rules engines exist on both client and server machines. This allows for optimization through workload balancing: Some rules are evaluated on the client side, others on the server side.

USoft can also be part of an environment that is mostly component based, in which case it offers data manager services guaranteeing rule enforcement on the data it manages. Listener services are only an explicit concern where USoft is made to interact with third-party technology. In a standard USoft application, the only listener service is the rules engine itself (essentially an API to the database)—instead of directly accessing the database, users are connected with the interposed rules engine, which accesses the database on the user's behalf and enforces all rules in the process. USoft offers some configuration settings for manual tuning of transaction monitor services if these are used. In the case of the (proprietary) JORS server, it offers a server manager console.

Versata delivers an application server (Versata Logic Server) in which it runs Java. Versata rules are compiled as Enterprise JavaBeans or CORBA objects.

In this final step, you determine how your application components (screens, application flow) and database components will communicate with the rules layer. If you are using a data-change-oriented rules or service-oriented rules service, refer to product-specific literature for details on how to interface to the rules capability.

CASE STUDY: STEP 12.16—PULL IT ALL TOGETHER

Case Study Instructions:

- Describe your solution for the data-change-oriented and service-oriented product environment.

Case Study Solution:

For the data aware commercial rules engine, we used USoft WebRuler as USoft's Java applet oriented solution for the Web. The developer wrote no Java code, because the USoft WebRuler publication process generates all necessary Java code.

For the stand-alone rules service using HNC Software's product, an Entrance Servlet manages the http requests from Members accessing the VCI park service from Web browsers and invokes the Entrance Rule Service.

More details on both of these are provided in Chapters 13 and 14.

Critical Success Factors in Designing a Business Rules System

Needless to say, the design of your system is key to its success. A good quality design, however, is based on a solid foundation of good business analysis. This foundation is most solid when you have analyzed each perspective of the system (data, process, and rules) using techniques and criteria for quality that apply specifically to each of those perspectives.

To summarize, a successful design endeavor is likely to result from the following factors:

Work from high quality analysis deliverables. Conduct formal review sessions with data, process, and rule analysts. Review the rule-enriched logical data model, logical rule model, and logical workflow model. Include business experts to answer questions.

Give serious consideration to utilizing a commercial rules product. Use of a commercial product provides insights into how to manage executable rules as a separate automation artifact that can be leveraged by the business and reused to enhance developer productivity.

Consider both the structural deliverables and integrity deliverables. These include data structure and integrity, process structure and integrity, and rule structure and integrity. The structural deliverables are the rule-enriched logical data model and subsequent database structure design, the rule family dependency diagrams and subsequent executable rule code, and the workflow and object class models and subsequent specifications. The integrity deliverables are the rules themselves.

Understand roles and responsibilities. Show respect for all three perspectives and for the professionals who are responsible for them. In a first business rules project, the rule analyst and designer may have minimal experience in addressing only rules, since the rule analyst or designer may come from an application processing or database background. If possible, include experts in the target rules technology as a sounding board.

Separate generic design steps from product-specific design steps. This is important if you want the design process to be repeatable and applicable to various technology environments. Describe the approach and decisions made for generic design steps and add to these, product-specific details or deviations.

Use a repository. Almost every chapter in this book has advocated the use of a common repository in which to store deliverables. These include deliverables specific to rules (such as the rules themselves or rule family dependencies), rule-enhanced deliverables (such as the rule-enriched logical data model) as well as nonrule deliverables (such as workflow diagrams and use-case descriptions and concrete scenarios).

Conduct formal design reviews. Establish checkpoints in the design process for reviewing deliverables and clarifying issues.

Summary

Designing for a business rules system means introducing a rules capability into your systems design. A rules capability is an automated function that manages and executes rules in a shared way. In a business rules approach, we define the business logic layer to have two different types of functionality. The traditional functionality is that which controls the specific process flow for the target application, but not the (shared) rule execution. The new functionality is a rules capability that manages execution of shared rules on behalf of applications.

We have discovered that each rule product we evaluated was capable of supporting all of the rule classifications in this book. However, if you cannot utilize rules technology, you can still design your system with rules in mind, but you have to be diligent about separating the rules or you will lose them again.

You need to determine in which tier you will enforce rules. If rule technology were perfect, you would put all rule enforcement in the rules layer. You will need to tune the underlying database(s) for performance and perhaps functionality requirements. You can also tune the rules by relying on product-specific transparent tuning options. When performance or functionality limitations are not acceptable, you can tune rules by moving enforcement to another tier, duplicating the enforcement, or changing the expression of the rules.

In the end, the business is likely to measure the value of your system by how easily and quickly it accommodates business change.

You are now ready to walk through the design steps for your particular technology environment. Because commercial rules technology may be new to many readers, the next two chapters provide details on how these design steps are applied to parts of the VCI case study using representative products. Chapter 13 does so for two data-change-oriented products, while Chapter 14 presents a solution using one service-oriented product and provides explanations on how another product in that category would work.

Implementing Business Rule Systems Using Data-Change-Oriented Rules Products

Chapters 13 and 14 contain details for the interested reader in designing and implementing portions of the case study using two different kinds of commercial rules products: data-change-oriented rules products and service-oriented products, respectively. Both chapters follow the design rules presented in Chapter 12, but provide product-specific insights, instructions, and examples using the VCI case study. Recall that a data-change-oriented rules product executes rules in response to a transaction attempting to update a database. The data-change-oriented rules product automatically executes predefined rules to be sure that the transaction meets acceptable requirements specified by the rules. On the other hand, a service-oriented rules product executes predefined rules when requested to do so by a transaction.

Chapter 13 presents design and implementation of portions of the case study using both the USoft Developer from USoft Inc. and Versata Inc.'s business logic automation engine, the Versata Logic Server. These products have existed for many years and each has evolved from the generation of triggers and client-based rule support into business rule support that is more independent of the target DBMS. These products have provided a development foundation for e-business applications, especially because they provide facilities for developing the full application.

For additional details on these and other products, please visit the companion Web site.

Implementation in the USoft Environment

Recall from the last chapter that design and implementation with a data-change-oriented rules capability tends to be data-centric. While you can define the data environment to the product either by creating an object class model or a data model, the point is that you specify the tables and columns to the rules product. Then you express rules about the data that the rules product is to watch out for. Concurrently, you create user interface screens or Web pages through which to test the rules and to design more detailed interfaces.

Consider the following two rules from the case study.

> Rule 1: A member must be between 6 and 15 years old. A member is allowed to use the VCI Park from the day of his or her 6th birthday, until the end of the month of his or her 16th birthday.

> Rule 2: Each month, the total charges for a guardian are the sum of the charges for each of her members.

This chapter focuses only on implementation of these rules. You can find additional implementation details for other rules on the companion Web site.

This chapter assumes that you have completed design steps 12.1–12.5 from Chapter 12. In particular, you have decided to acquire or test USoft's or Versata's rules product and you will enforce all possible rules in it. We start now at step 13.6 (the same as step 12.6 but renumbered to reflect this chapter number). Recall that step 13.6 addresses the designing for rules in a commercial data-change-oriented rules product.

STEP 13.6.1: DETERMINE HOW TO ORGANIZE YOUR RULES WITHIN THE RULES PRODUCT

As indicated in the previous chapter, you organize your rules according to business or data objects. You will also create rule sets. But first, in the USoft environment, you define a business area, then you define business objects.

USoft Developer has a module called USoft TeamWork. The primary interface for USoft TeamWork is the TeamWork catalog tab page in USoft Definer, through which you can define and view those items managed by TeamWork. For the USoft environment, a *business area* is a logical part of the business that is reflected in the system as a subsystem. Major business processes of VCI, such as VCI Financials, VCI Park Usage, and VCI Party Administration, are examples of business areas. The companion Web site contains a listing of the TeamWork items for the case study, including the details behind the VCI Party Administration Business Area. The companion Web site also illustrates how you would define a business area to TeamWork.

In a USoft environment, a *business object* is a logical object that covers business events or (parts of) a business process (tasks). A business object, therefore, provides a means of clustering the functionality offered by the application. Transactions can be performed with or on business objects.

From a technical point of view, a business object consists of data elements (tables, relationships, domains), rule/process elements (business rules), and presentation features (windows, dialogs). The companion Web site illustrates how you define the business object, called Party, to TeamWork.

USoft maintains a log of changes to business objects, so that you can keep track of which project team member changed what and when. To facilitate effective logging, each project team member should have his/her own user name.

STEP 13.6.2: DETERMINE IF YOU NEED TO ADD ADDITIONAL DATA CONSTRUCTS

There is no need to add data constructs for this case study.

STEP 13.6.3: DETERMINE IF YOU NEED TO ALTER YOUR DATA DEFINITIONS

There is no need to alter data definitions for this case study.

STEP 13.6.4: DEFINE THE (REVISED) DATA DESIGN TO THE RULES PRODUCT

Figure 13.1 is a data model as it looks in the USoft TeamWork Business Object Diagrammer. This is a model of the database design, not the pure logical data model. Let's review this model.

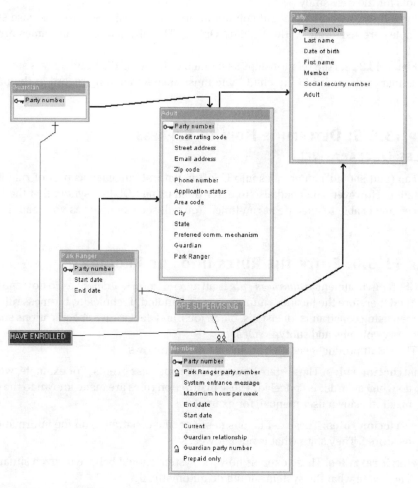

Figure 13.1   A partial data model for party in USoft.

The Party concept is implemented as a supertype table. Subtypes are Adult and Member. Adult is also a supertype table, with subtypes of Guardian and Park Ranger. There are two internal relationships involved here:

- Guardians have enrolled members.
- Park Rangers are supervising members.

Furthermore, the key icon denotes a primary key column and the lock symbol denotes a foreign key column. For completeness, the companion Web site contains corresponding data models in USoft for Account, Invoice, Park, and Park Usage.

Before you can define tables and columns, you need to define domains. A domain has a name, a data type, and a display type. The companion Web site contains a listing of domains in USoft for the case study.

In USoft, you can also specify a prompt and a set of allowed values for domains you want to restrict to those values. You can then present the prompt on the screen or Web page within a dropdown list box, or by means of radio buttons or check boxes. Again, the companion Web site illustrates a listing of USoft domains, allowed values, and prompts for the case study.

Figure 13.2 lists all table and column information from USoft for the case study. The tables are listed under the heading Object. The physical column names are not included.

Figure 13.3 lists the relationships as defined to USoft. If FK Mandatory is set to Y, it means that each record in the child table must have a matching record in the parent table.

STEP 13.6.5: DETERMINE HOW TO EXPRESS RULES DECLARATIVELY

You can (and should!) enter rules into USoft in natural language as part of rule documentation. However, you need also to enter them using SQL-like syntax that the USoft rules engine is able to execute at run-time. You will see examples as you read the rest of these steps.

STEP 13.6.6: ENTER THE RULES INTO THE PRODUCT

In a USoft environment, a *business rule* is an agreed upon statement as to how the business (and therefore the business information) is handled. Technically, business rules are enforced using constraints, decisions, batch jobs, and declarative specifications such as mandatory columns and subtype rules.

The USoft product classifies business rules as follows:

Instruction rules. These state how to handle business events. For example, what to do when an order is canceled. These instruction rules are made known to the organization using a user manual, for example.

Restriction rules. These define business specific constraints on the information to be stored. They state what is not allowed.

Behavioral rules. These express how the system should behave in given situations. They state what the system should do automatically.

OBJECT	K	M	D	Column prompt	DOMAIN	DATATYPE
Account	1	M	D	Account number	ACC_NUMBER	NUMBER(10)
	-	M	D	Guardian party number	PTY_NUMBER	NUMBER(6)
	-	M	D	Account balance	ACC_BALANCE	NUMBER(7)
	-	M	D	Account in good standing	TW_YESNO	VARCHAR2(1)
	-	M	D	Billing method	GRD_BILLING_METHOD	VARCHAR2(1)
	-	M	D	Automatic withdrawal info	TW_YESNO	VARCHAR2(1)
	-	M	D	Credit card info	TW_YESNO	VARCHAR2(1)
	-	M	D	Prepayment info	TW_YESNO	VARCHAR2(1)
Adult	1	M	D	Party number	PTY_NUMBER	NUMBER(6)
	-	-	D	Credit rating code	GRD_CREDIT_RATING_CODE	VARCHAR2(10)
	-	-	D	Preferred comm. mechanism	GRD_PREF_COMM_MECHANISM	VARCHAR2(1)
	-	-	D	Email address	GRD_EMAIL_ADDRESS	VARCHAR2(30)
	-	-	D	Street address	GRD_STREET_ADDRESS	VARCHAR2(30)
	-	-	D	City	GRD_CITY	VARCHAR2(30)
	-	-	D	State	GRD_STATE	VARCHAR2(20)
	-	-	D	Zip code	GRD_ZIP_CODE	NUMBER(5)
	-	-	D	Area code	GRD_AREA_CODE	NUMBER(5)
	-	-	D	Phone number	GRD_PHONE_NUMBER	VARCHAR2(20)
	-	-	D	Application status	GRD_APPLICATION_STATUS	VARCHAR2(1)
	-	M	D	Guardian	TW_YESNO	VARCHAR2(1)
	-	M	D	Park Ranger	TW_YESNO	VARCHAR2(1)
Automatic Withdrawal Info	1	M	D	Account number	ACC_NUMBER	NUMBER(10)
	-	M	D	Check bank name	AWI_BANK_NAME	VARCHAR2(20)
	-	M	D	Check	AWI_ACCOUNT_NUMBER	NUMBER(12)

continues

Figure 13.2 Table and column information in USoft.

Table	Key	M/D	Column description	Column name	Datatype
	-	D	Signature on file	TW_YESNO	VARCHAR2(1)
	-	D	Bank routing number	AWI_BANK_ROUTING_NUMBER	NUMBER(10)
	-	D	Current authorization	TW_YESNO	VARCHAR2(1)
Credit Card Info	1	D	Account number	ACC_NUMBER	NUMBER(10)
	1	M	Credit Card number	CCI_NUMBER	NUMBER(20)
	1	M	Expiration date	DATE_GENERAL	DATE()
	1	M	Name on card	CCI_NAME_ON_CARD	VARCHAR2(30)
	1	M	Credit card active	TW_YESNO	VARCHAR2(1)
Guardian	1	M	Party number	PTY_NUMBER	NUMBER(6)
Invoice	1	M	Invoice number	INV_NUMBER	NUMBER(6)
	1	M	Guardian party number	PTY_NUMBER	NUMBER(6)
	-	D	Issue date	DATE_GENERAL	DATE()
	-	D	Total amount	AMOUNT_MONEY	NUMBER(5)
	-	D	Payment status	INV_PAYMENT_STATUS_CODE	VARCHAR2(1)
Invoice Item	1	M	Member party number	PTY_NUMBER	NUMBER(6)
	1	M	Invoice number	INV_NUMBER	NUMBER(6)
	1	M	Park ID	PRK_ID	NUMBER(3)
	-	M	Invoice item paid	TW_YESNO	VARCHAR2(1)
	-	M	Actual time used	MINUTES	NUMBER(3)
	-	M	Base fee	AMOUNT_MONEY	NUMBER(5)
	-	D	Volume discounted fee	AMOUNT_MONEY	NUMBER(5)
	-	D	Additional child flag	TW_YESNO	VARCHAR2(1)
	-	D	Additional child discount	AMOUNT_MONEY	NUMBER(5)
	-	D	Default time	MINUTES	NUMBER(3)

Figure 13.2 Table and column information in USoft. (*continued*)

continues

Table				Description	Column	Datatype
	-	-	D	Bonus time	MINUTES	NUMBER(3)
	-	-	D	Deducted time	MINUTES	NUMBER(3)
	-	-	D	Final fee	AMOUNT_MONEY	NUMBER(5)
Invoice Member Section	1	M	D	Invoice number	INV_NUMBER	NUMBER(6)
	1	M	D	Member party number	PTY_NUMBER	NUMBER(6)
	-	M	D	Member total amount	AMOUNT_MONEY	NUMBER(5)
Member	1	M	D	Party number	PTY_NUMBER	NUMBER(6)
	-	-	-	Guardian party number	PTY_NUMBER	NUMBER(6)
	-	-	-	Park Ranger party number	PTY_NUMBER	NUMBER(6)
	-	-	D	Start date	DATE_GENERAL	DATE()
	-	-	D	End date	DATE_GENERAL	DATE()
	-	M	D	Guardian relationship	MBR_GUARDIAN_RELATIONSHIP	VARCHAR2(1)
	-	-	D	System entrance message	ENTRANCE_TEXT	VARCHAR2(100)
	-	M	D	Maximum hours per week	HOURS	NUMBER(3)
	-	M	D	Current	TW_YESNO	VARCHAR2(1)
	-	M	D	Prepaid only	TW_YESNO	VARCHAR2(1)
Member Entrance Criterion	1	M	-	Entrance Criteria ID	CRITERIA_ID	NUMBER(7)
	1	M	D	Member party number	PTY_NUMBER	NUMBER(6)
	-	-	D	Entrance criteria text	ENTRANCE_TEXT	VARCHAR2(100)
	-	-	D	Minimum good response	YESNO_NO_DEFAULT	VARCHAR2(1)
	-	-	D	Maximum bad response	YESNO_NO_DEFAULT	VARCHAR2(1)
	-	-	D	Impact minutes	MINUTES	NUMBER(3)
	-	-	D	Bonus park ID	PRK_ID	NUMBER(3)
	-	-	D	Remedial park ID	PRK_ID	NUMBER(3)
Member Entrance Response	1	M	D	Response datetime	DATE_TIME	DATE()
	1	M	D	Member entrance criteria ID	CRITERIA_ID	NUMBER(7)
	-	-	D	Response number of minutes	MINUTES	NUMBER(3)

continues

Figure 13.2   Table and column information in USoft. (*continued*)

Table				Description	Column	Datatype
Member Park Enrollment	–	–	D	Response text	ENTRANCE_TEXT	VARCHAR2(100)
	–	–	D	Response indicator	YESNO_NO_DEFAULT	VARCHAR2(1)
	1	M	D	Park ID	PRK_ID	NUMBER(3)
	1	M	D	Member party number	PTY_NUMBER	NUMBER(6)
	–	M	D	Enrollment start date	DATE_GENERAL	DATE()
	–	–	D	Enrollment end date	DATE_GENERAL	DATE()
	–	M	D	Enrollment current indicator	TW_YESNO	VARCHAR2(1)
	–	M	D	Maximum hours per month	HOURS	NUMBER(3)
	–	M	D	Default minutes per day	MINUTES	NUMBER(3)
Member Park Fee	1	M	D	Park ID	PRK_ID	NUMBER(3)
	1	M	D	Member party number	PTY_NUMBER	NUMBER(6)
	–	M	D	Actual time used	MINUTES	NUMBER(3)
	–	M	D	Base fee	AMOUNT_MONEY	NUMBER(5)
	–	–	D	Volume discounted fee	AMOUNT_MONEY	NUMBER(5)
	–	M	D	Employee discount	AMOUNT_MONEY	NUMBER(5)
	–	M	D	Final fee	AMOUNT_MONEY	NUMBER(5)
	–	–	D	Volume discount	AMOUNT_MONEY	NUMBER(5)
Member Park Usage	1	M	D	Park ID	PRK_ID	NUMBER(3)
	1	M	D	Usage date	DATE_GENERAL	DATE()
	1	M	D	Member party number	PTY_NUMBER	NUMBER(6)
	–	M	D	Allowed time	MINUTES	NUMBER(3)
	–	–	D	Actual time used	MINUTES	NUMBER(3)
Park	1	M	D	Park ID	PRK_ID	NUMBER(3)
	–	M	D	Park name	PRK_NAME	VARCHAR2(20)

Figure 13.2 Table and column information in USoft. (*continued*)

continues

				Description	Column	Type
Park View	-	M	D	Park function type code	PFT_CODE	VARCHAR2(3)
	-	M	D	Hourly rate	AMOUNT_MONEY	NUMBER(5)
	-	M	D	Volume discount threshold	HOURS	NUMBER(3)
(Logical View !)	1	M	-	Park function type code	PFT_CODE	VARCHAR2(3)
	1	M	-	Park ID	PRK_ID	NUMBER(3)
	-	M	D	Park function type description	PFT_DESCRIPTION	VARCHAR2(20)
	-	M	D	Park name	PRK_NAME	VARCHAR2(20)
	1	M	-	Park function type code	PFT_CODE	VARCHAR2(3)
	-	M	D	Hourly rate	AMOUNT_MONEY	NUMBER(5)
	-	M	D	Volume discount threshold	HOURS	NUMBER(3)
Park Function Type	1	M	D	Park function type code	PFT_CODE	VARCHAR2(3)
	-	M	D	Park function type description	PFT_DESCRIPTION	VARCHAR2(20)
Park Ranger	1	M	D	Party number	PTY_NUMBER	NUMBER(6)
	-	-	D	Start date	DATE_GENERAL	DATE()
	-	-	D	End date	DATE_GENERAL	DATE()
Party	1	M	D	Party number	PTY_NUMBER	NUMBER(6)
	-	M	D	First name	PTY_FIRST_NAME	VARCHAR2(20)
	-	M	D	Last name	PTY_LAST_NAME	VARCHAR2(30)
	-	-	D	Social security number	PTY_SOC_SEC_NUMBER	NUMBER(12)
	-	M	D	Date of birth	DATE_PAST	DATE()
	-	M	D	Member	TW_YESNO	VARCHAR2(1)
	-	M	D	Adult	TW_YESNO	VARCHAR2(1)
Prepayment Info	1	M	D	Account number	ACC_NUMBER	NUMBER(10)

continues

Figure 13.2 Table and column information in USoft. (*continued*)

Table	K	M	D	Column description	Column name	Datatype
System Parameter	-	-	D	Prepayment threshold	PPI_THRESHOLD	NUMBER (6)
	1	M	D	System parameter ID	SYSTEM_PARAMETER_ID	NUMBER (3)
	-	M	D	Minimum usage charge unit	MINUTES	NUMBER (3)
	-	M	D	Additional member discount	PERCENTAGE	NUMBER (3)
	-	M	D	Volume discount	PERCENTAGE	NUMBER (3)
	-	M	D	Employee discount	PERCENTAGE	NUMBER (3)
	-	M	D	Late fee	AMOUNT_MONEY	NUMBER (5)
	-	M	D	Bounced check fee	AMOUNT_MONEY	NUMBER (5)
	-	M	D	Late payment grace period	DAYS	NUMBER (2)

K: Key: 1 means: primary key column
M: Mandatory: a value has to be entered
D: Displayed

Figure 13.2 Table and column information in USoft. (*continued*)

```
Parent:                GUARDIAN
Child:                 ACCOUNT
Related Window Title: Accounts of this Guardian
Lookup Window Title:  Select a Guardian for this Account
Must Child Exist:     N
FK Mandatory:         Y


Parent:                GUARDIAN
Child:                 INVOICE
Related Window Title: Invoices for this Guardian
Lookup Window Title:  Select a Guardian to receive this Invoice
Must Child Exist:     N
FK Mandatory:         Y


Parent:                GUARDIAN
Child:                 MEMBER
Related Window Title: Members that have been enrolled by this Guardian
Lookup Window Title:  Select a Guardian to enroll this Member
Must Child Exist:     N
FK Mandatory:         Y


Parent:                INVOICE
Child:                 INVOICE_MEMBER_SECTION
Related Window Title: Invoice Member Sections on this Invoice
Lookup Window Title:  Select Invoice for Invoice Member Section
Must Child Exist:     N
FK Mandatory:         Y
Delete Rule: Cascading


Parent:                INVOICE_MEMBER_SECTION
Child:                 INVOICE_ITEM
Related Window Title: Invoice Items inside this Invoice Member Section
Lookup Window Title:  Select an Invoice Member Section for Invoice Item
Must Child Exist:     N
FK Mandatory:         Y


Parent:                MEMBER
Child:                 INVOICE_MEMBER_SECTION
Related Window Title: Invoice Member Sections linked with this Member
Lookup Window Title:  Select a Member for this Invoice Member Section
Must Child Exist:     N
FK Mandatory:         Y


Parent:                MEMBER
Child:                 MEMBER_ENTRANCE_CRITERIA
Related Window Title: Member Entrance Criteria for this Member
Lookup Window Title:  Select a Member to get this Member Entrance
                      criterion
```

Figure 13.3 Relationship information in USoft.   *continues*

```
Must Child Exist:        N
FK Mandatory:            Y


Parent:                  MEMBER
Child:                   MEMBER_PARK_ENROLLMENT
Related Window Title: Member Park Enrollments of this Member
Lookup Window Title:  Select a Member for this Member Park Enrollment
Must Child Exist:        N
FK Mandatory:            Y


Parent:                  MEMBER_ENTRANCE_CRITERIA
Child:                   MEMBER_ENTRANCE_RESPONSE
Related Window Title: Member Entrance Responses to this Member Entrance
                         Criterion
Lookup Window Title:  Select Member Entrance Criterion for this Member
                         Entrance Response
Must Child Exist:        N
FK Mandatory:            Y


Parent:                  MEMBER_PARK_ENROLLMENT
Child:                   MEMBER_PARK_FEE
Related Window Title: Member Park Fees of this Member park enrollment
Lookup Window Title:  Select a Member Park Enrollment for this Member
                         Park Fee
Must Child Exist:        N
FK Mandatory:            Y


Parent:                  MEMBER_PARK_ENROLLMENT
Child:                   MEMBER_PARK_USAGE
Related Window Title: Member park usages of a Member park enrollment
Lookup Window Title:  Member park enrollments have Member park usages
Must Child Exist:        N
FK Mandatory:            Y


Parent:                  MEMBER_PARK_FEE
Child:                   INVOICE_ITEM
Related Window Title: Invoice items concerning a Member park fee
Lookup Window Title:  Member park fees result in Invoice items
Must Child Exist:        N
FK Mandatory:            Y


Parent:                  PARK
Child:                   INVOICE_ITEM
Related Window Title: Invoice items concerning a Park
Lookup Window Title:  Parks appear in Invoice items
Must Child Exist:        N
FK Mandatory:            N


Parent:                  PARK
```

Figure 13.3 Relationship information in USoft. (*Continued*)

continues

```
Child:                  MEMBER_ENTRANCE_CRITERIA
Related Window Title: Member entrance criteria with bonus Park
Lookup Window Title:  Parks are bonus for Member entrance criteria
Must Child Exist:     N
FK Mandatory:         N


Parent:                 PARK
Child:                  MEMBER_ENTRANCE_CRITERIA
Related Window Title: Member entrance criteria with remedial Park
Lookup Window Title:  Parks are remedial for Member entrance criteria
Must Child Exist:     N
FK Mandatory:         N


Parent:                 PARK
Child:                  MEMBER_PARK_ENROLLMENT
Related Window Title: Member park enrollments of a Park
Lookup Window Title:  Parks are having Member park enrollments
Must Child Exist:     N
FK Mandatory:         Y


Parent:                 PARK_FUNCTION_TYPE
Child:                  PARK
Related Window Title: Parks are of a Park function type
Lookup Window Title:  Park function types concerning Parks
Must Child Exist:     N
FK Mandatory:         Y


Parent:                 PARK_RANGER
Child:                  MEMBER
Related Window Title: Members are supervised by Park Ranger
Lookup Window Title:  Park Rangers are supervising Members
Must Child Exist:     N
FK Mandatory:         Y
```

Figure 13.3   Relationship information in USoft. (*continued*)

Deduction rules. These state how information should be derived or calculated.

Presentation rules. These state how the system should present itself to the user, and how the work and tasks are to be organized.

USoft uses standard ANSI SQL as the specification language for explicit business rules, making it easy to map rules to any relational database. To USoft customers, SQL is a rich and powerful language in its ability to specify conditions about the data in a way that looks similar to natural language. You use the common SQL Select construct to specify restricting conditions, and you use Update, Insert, Delete to specify correcting conditions. Through the implementation of the rules in this SQL form, the rules engine protects the integrity of the database. Essentially, incorrect data cannot exist in the database. Data will not be allowed if it does not obey the business rules.

Another reason USoft selected SQL as a rule language is because it is a common skill in the industry, which means that USoft customers are likely to have employees with SQL skills and will, therefore, require little training to write rules. The USoft product eases the transformation from SQL to USoft rule development by providing the graphical SQL Definer. This feature allows the rule developer to drag and drop objects or relationships involved in the business rule. If the developer selects a relationship for a rule, then the USoft product displays both objects involved in the relationship, and incorporates the columns that join the objects.

Using USoft, you record all requirements as to what the system should be able to do, or how it should look as explicit business rules. The exceptions are the implicit rules already included in the data model. Even instructions for the end-user describing how to operate the system are ultimately business rules. Using USoft TeamWork for business rule documentation, you can capture instructions as business rules and refer to these in the user manual during the iterative process of development.

Let's take a look at one business rule: Member must be between 6 and 15 years old.

First, you should define it in a natural language sentence as shown in Figure 13.4.

Next, if you click on the Add rule button, you will see the Business Rule Wizard shown in Figure 13.5, through which you can begin to build the corresponding rule by first giving it a name. In Figure 13.6, you assign the rule to a table, while Figure 13.7 illustrates how you enter a condition for the rule. The companion Web site shows you how to enter additional conditions to a rule or modify or delete conditions. Figure 13.8 shows you how to add the error message associated with violations to the rule. Figure 13.9 shows you the completed rule for your approval. In USoft terminology, this rule is an example of a (restrictive) constraint. Notice that the USoft expression for the rule is similar to SQL and that you state the constraint in terms of seeking violations to it.

Recall that there are many invoicing rules for the case study. Most people think of the logic behind computing the Total Charge for a Guardian as a business process. How-

Figure 13.4 Defining a rule in natural language to USoft.

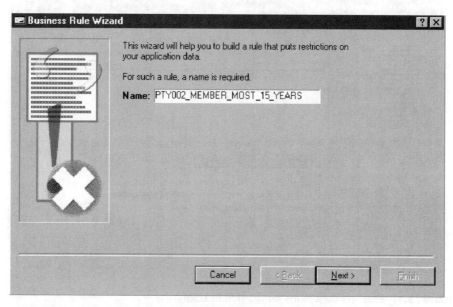

Figure 13.5 Using a wizard to name and build a rule in USoft.

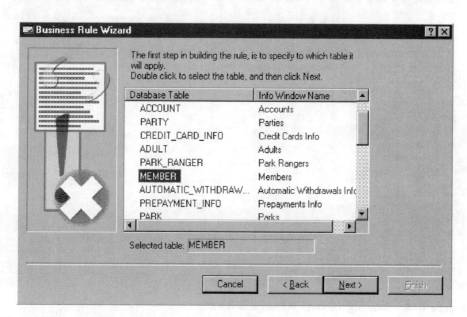

Figure 13.6 Assigning the rule to a table in USoft.

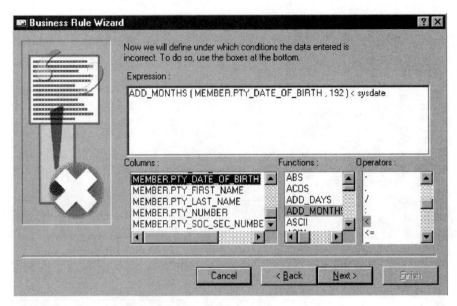

Figure 13.7 Entering conditions for the rule in USoft.

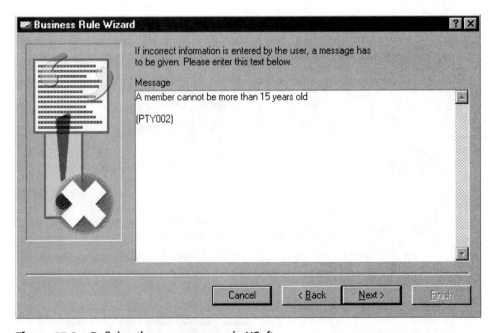

Figure 13.8 Defining the error message in USoft.

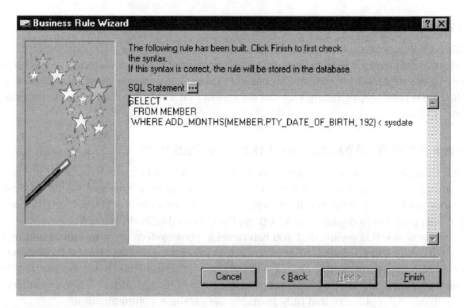

Figure 13.9   Viewing and approving the completed rule in USoft.

ever, in a USoft environment, you create a rule set to represent such a process. If you are interested in seeing how the invoicing rules for the case study are entered into USoft as a rule set, please refer to the companion Web site where six invoicing rules comprise the Invoicing Function rule set. The rules in this rule set are interesting because some of them involve arithmetic functions and some involve automatic updates to columns when the values of other columns change. Again, refer to the companion Web site for the detailed rules.

STEP 13.6.7: DETERMINE IF SOME RULES OR PARTS OF RULES NEED TO BE CODED PROCEDURALLY (SUCH AS IN JAVA)

This is not necessary. Once the business rules are captured and stored in the repository as SQL rules, no further programming is required to evaluate and process those rules. The USoft rules engine automatically takes care of this.

The rules engine enforces all business rules that govern the precise policies of the company. The rules engine prevents the user from violating the system, but also helps the user to perform their tasks. For example, it will display calculated values in the appropriate fields or update stock automatically when the user enters an order.

The rules engine balances its workload over the client and server part of the architecture, thus minimizing network traffic and maximizing the power and efficiency of the architecture. Load balancing of the application is dynamic. This completely bypasses the need for coding software and distributing software modules over your architecture.

STEP 13.6.8: TEST THE RULES

After implementing a business rule, you test its implementation. The companion Web site shows the error message displayed when one of the rules is violated. Finally, if your test of the rule has succeeded in all possible cases, you can record, within USoft, that the rule is tested. Specifically, you can document that a rule is defined, approved, built, and tested.

STEP 13.6.9: ADMIRE THE FINISHED PRODUCT

The USoft environment allows you to deploy your system on any supported physical environment, without having to make many changes in your business model. In other words, the business rules you have defined will run just as well on Oracle or DB/2, and it is also possible to deploy your USoft application on the World Wide Web.

In practice this means that you can develop your system on your laptop and then hand it over for deployment under a transaction processing monitor for use by hundreds of users. You will not need to change a thing. The rules engine has been tuned so that the rules are processed as efficiently as possible on any of the platforms. It also contains an intelligent SQL optimizer that fully manages the database communication.

Once the rules have been established, it is a trivial matter to replace the interface, whether it is a GUI screen, a Web browser, a batch job, a spreadsheet or a report. Likewise, once the rules are in place, it is a simple matter to change the data layer from one RDBMS vendor to another.

Let's look at sample screenshots of the runtime USoft business rules Web application.

An existing or potential new guardian logs in into the VCI system, either by providing the private entrance pass data or by logging in as an anonymous user. They see the screen in Figure 13.10.

Next, the potential new guardian decides to enroll as a new guardian, by selecting the First Enrollment tab in Figure 13.11.

From that tab, the system places the new guardian onto the first enrollment window in Figure 13.12.

A guardian can now enroll members and change existing entrance criteria or park enrollment. Figure 13.13 illustrates the window for doing so.

Figure 13.14 illustrates the window through which a guardian can choose park entrances for a member.

Figure 13.15 provides technical details for the applet that supports the enrollment of a guardian.

Implementation in the Versata Environment

Another commercially available data-change-oriented rules product is the Versata Logic Server from Versata, Inc. Oriented towards transaction-automation, the Versata Logic Server is one of two rules engines in the Versata suite. The second is the Versata Interaction Server, a process or workflow rules engine, used to model and control business transactions that span time and people. The Versata Logic Server and Versata Interaction

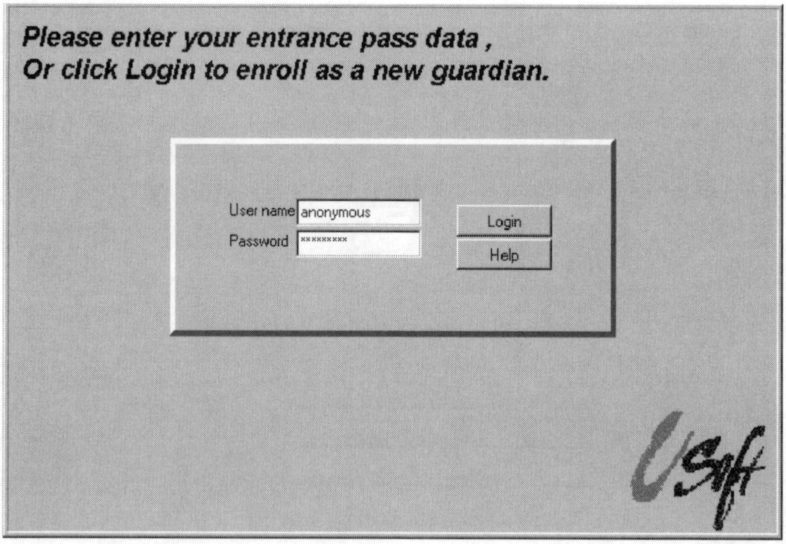

Figure 13.10 The initial VCI screen from USoft.

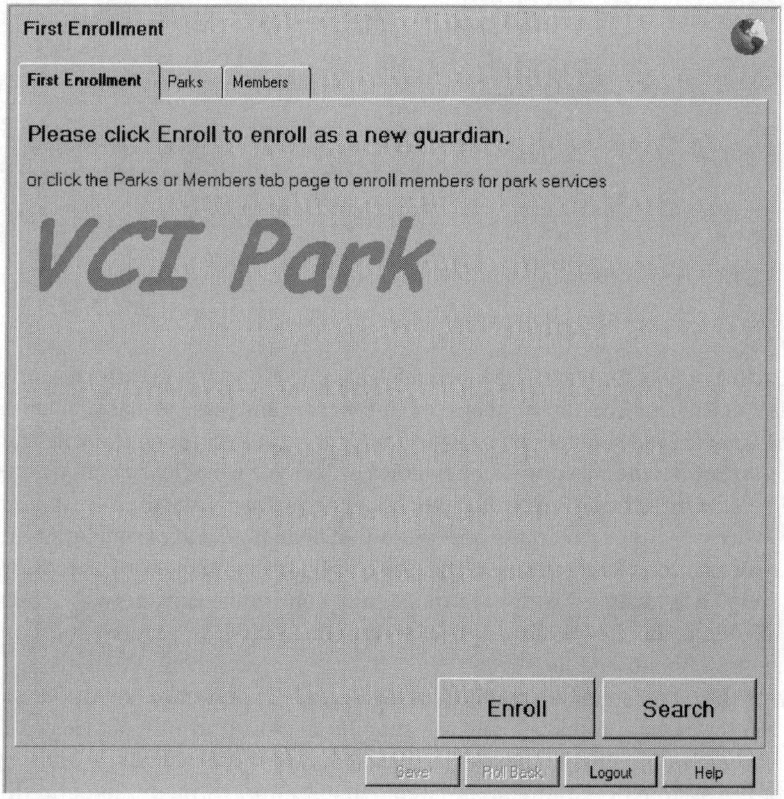

Figure 13.11 A guardian's view of starting the enrollment business event in USoft.

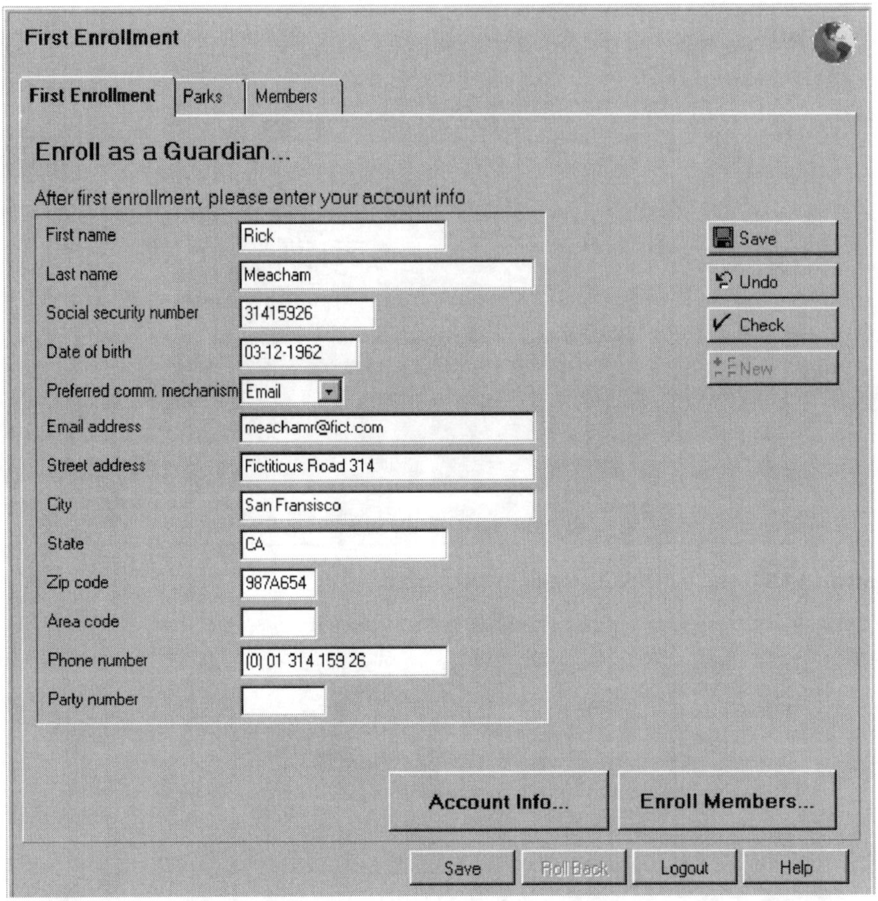

Figure 13.12   First enrollment window in USoft.

Server, with support for both CORBA and EJB application server platforms, provide the compilation and runtime environment for transaction and process-based business logic.

The Versata Logic Server can be used stand-alone or in conjunction with the Versata Interaction Server, the latter of which handles process or workflow rules. When employing the Versata Interaction Server, the developer or end user uses the Versata Interaction Server Process Designer to create processes that span time and participants. Within the Versata Interaction Server framework, processes are composed of activities and an object called a "transition" is used to model and control the flow between those activities—offering a number of process flow options, including parallelism, conditional branches, and time-based flows.

Given the complementary qualities of the Versata Logic Server and the Versata Interaction Server, both automation engines may be deployed to fully address a business event. Through this all-encompassing approach, Versata streamlines and automates much of the system development and deployment effort through the definition of the data model, business rules, and workflow or process rules.

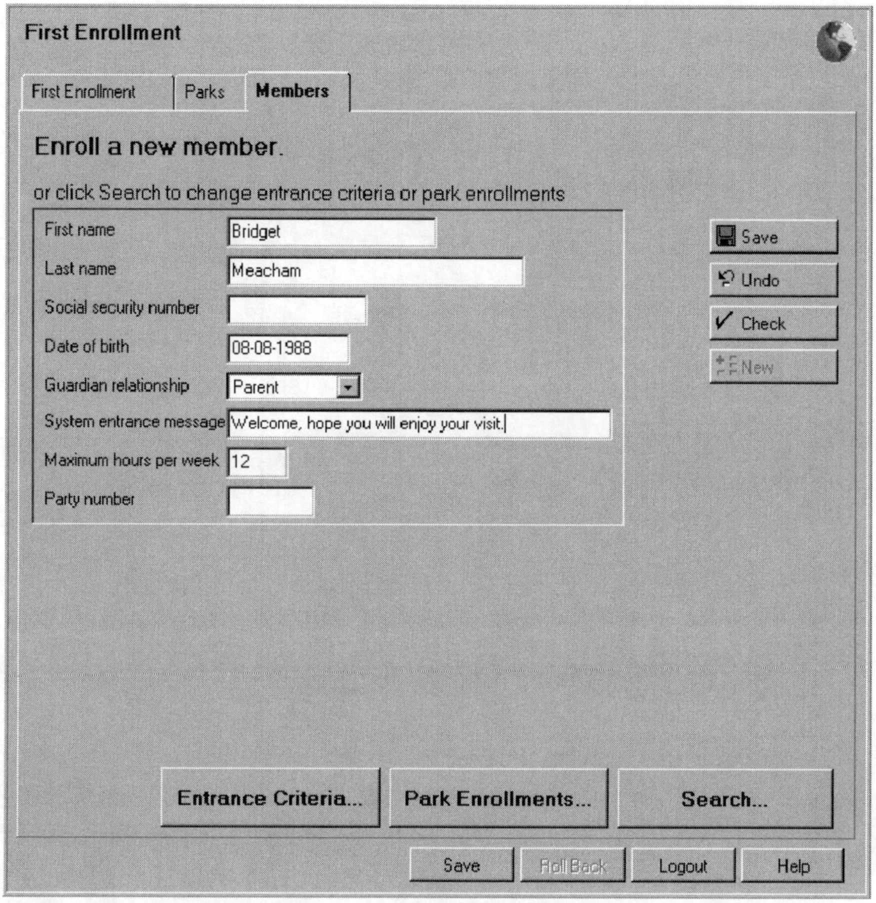

Figure 13.13   A guardian enters member information in USoft.

The Versata Studio is the development environment for the Versata Logic Server and includes the Versata Application Designer, Versata Business Rules Designer, and Versata Process Designer for manipulating rules stored in an XML repository. The Versata Presentation Services provide presentation interfaces to the Versata Logic Server. Versata Design Adapters provide integration between the Versata Studio and other development tools for data modeling, source code control, and content management services.

STEP 13.7.1: ORGANIZE YOUR RULES FOR THE RULES PRODUCT

The Versata Logic Server stores rule definitions in an XML rules repository. The Versata Studio provides capabilities for rule editing, compilation, and deployment for the Versata Logic Server. You define rules against data objects, such as Account and Guardian, and against relationship objects, such as Account_Guardian.

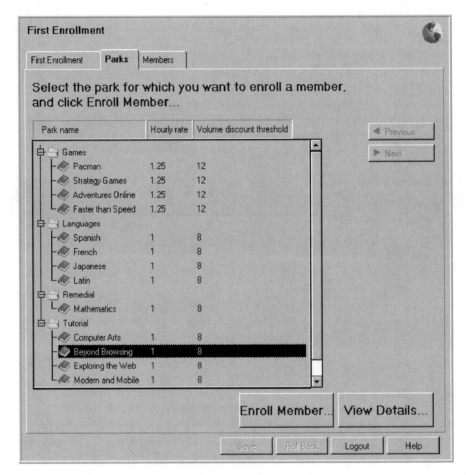

Figure 13.14 A guardian chooses park admissions in USoft.

Within the Versata Studio, the concept of data object includes the concept of terms as well as the constraint, computation, and inference rules related to those terms. Rules that react to data-change and existence-change (that is, inserting, updating, deleting) are correlated to a data object. Computations correlate to the attribute whose value is calculated according to the rule. You express inference rules against an attribute where the attribute holds the conclusion of the inference. You may enter constraints against an individual attribute (typically field validation-oriented) or a data object.

Relationships in Versata represent particular parent-child relationships between two data objects and you enter relationships into the Versata Logic Server as rules. You represent simple constraints on relationships, for example a "Member must have a Guardian" as relationship properties. You enter constraints involving terms as data object constraints. You may define simple referential integrity rules (such as defining what happens when a parent key is updated or when a parent is deleted) against the relationship.

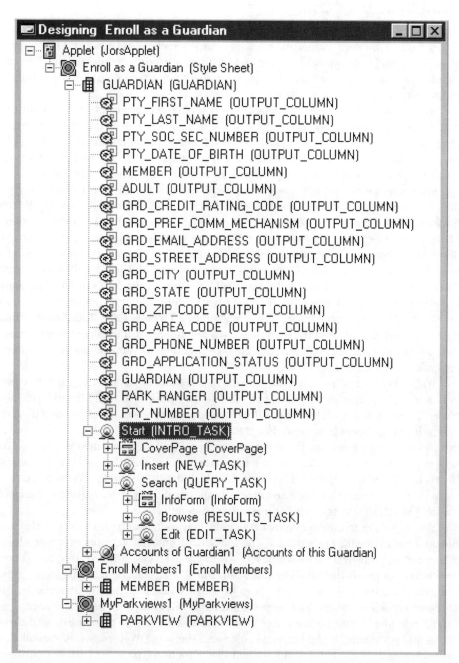

Figure 13.15 Design and implementation of the enrollment of a guardian in USoft.

STEP 13.7.2: DETERMINE IF YOU NEED TO ADD ADDITIONAL DATA CONSTRUCTS

To define business rules within the Versata Logic Server, you create or import a data or object model. You define rules on top of this model. Each rule is associated with either an entity (usually a relational table) or an individual attribute (column). Using Versata's simple rules language, you can declare permanent or virtual fields representing, for example, derivations or summations.

As rules are entered into the Versata Studio, it may be necessary to create additional data constructs. Most likely you begin with a logical data model as the initial basis for a physical database design and consider the need for additional data structures to support rules. The database designer can decide whether to make corresponding changes in the underlying data model by turning persistence on or off for a given data construct.

For computation and inference rules, the Versata Logic Server provides five types of derivation rules: (1) sum, (2) count, (3) parent replicate, (4) formula, and (5) default. Each of the sum, count, and parent replicate rules are associated with a named attribute of the data object. You may need to break more complex rules into smaller atomic derivations for entry. For example, to implement the VCI Park rule for computing account balance, two additional attributes come to mind, TotalBilled and TotalPayment. You can implement TotalBilled with a sum rule, the sum of the totals of billed invoices. Likewise, you can implement TotalPayment with a sum rule, the sum of the valid payments. Finally, the account balance is populated by a formula rule, "TotalBilled—TotalPayment". You do not need to make these two additional attributes persistent. That is, they do not necessitate a change to the database, but they will appear as attributes of the entity JavaBean used at runtime.

Within Versata, you may create new attributes that use declarative rules to create parent objects. For example, when you choose the option "On Child Insert/Update"— "Insert Parent If None" and a Child is then inserted, the rule will check to see if a Parent exists. If not, a Parent is created. For the case study, rules will execute and create an instance of InvoiceItem automatically whenever a ParkUsage instance is created. The new unique InvoiceItem (which represents a month full of ParkUsages for a given member) is initialized with MemberId, ParkId, and VisitMonth. To do this, Versata creates a relationship between ParkUsage and InvoiceItem (one did not previously exist) and adds the field VisitMonth to both ParkUsage and InvoiceItem.

Some changes to the case study data model may reduce complexity where the complexity is not needed. For example, the Party/Role objects were not referenced anywhere in the model or the case study. While they could be easily added later, one Versata solution is to simplify the model by combining Party, Guardian, Ranger, and Member into one table and using the surrogate keys of those objects instead of Party/Role. The entrance criteria questions and responses for the VCI Park were very similar to those for the individual theme park services. One Versata solution is to combine these into one set of tables, reusing many business rules and the same Web pages. A special Park instance was created with ParkId = 1 and ParkFunctionType = "VCI Park" in order to reference VCI park level questions and responses.

Some code tables are useful to support flags and types referenced in the data model or the case study notes, for example "Guardian Application Status" and "Guardian Known Flag".

A new data object InvoiceCycleStatus is useful for marking invoices as billed or mark balances as past due. Changing the record for the month from "Current Month" to "Billed" for example causes an automatic update to the status and balances of all that month's invoices and their accounts. InvoiceCycleStatus has a one-to-many relationship with Invoice.

When using Versata, it's important to keep rules declarative. As rules are entered into the Versata rules repository, you may need to tweak existing rules, create new rules, and delete others. It may even be necessary to go back to the business people to clarify certain questions. In the beginning, you may need to create new attributes and possibly change the data model as rules are expressed. As the development and maintenance cycle proceeds, however, the requirement to create new attributes is greatly minimized, although business rules can still be easily changed.

Implementation: Objects and Databases

Versata's data object represents both an object definition and a persistence definition. The data objects are deployed as java components running within the business-tier of an application server—typically the Enterprise JavaBean (EJB) container. The data object's attributes are visible as assessor methods prefixed by "get" and "set". Each attribute can be nominated as persistent or nonpersistent. The Versata Logic Server manages the persistence via a resource adapter to an enterprise information system (often JDBC to a relational database).

Some organizations may not be able to change the underlying database. For these situations, additional nonpersistent attributes aid in the declaration of rules and will automatically be recalculated each time the object is used. Typically, mathematical calculations using the object's own attributes have no negative performance impact. Keep in mind, though, that a count or a sum, because it spans objects, would require additional database access with related performance implications.

STEP 13.7.3: DETERMINE IF YOU NEED TO ALTER YOUR DATA DEFINITIONS

In the examples below, you will notice a few minor data definition changes in the VCI Park model. For example, the rule "AutoNumber" was used for surrogate keys (for example, ParkId), necessitating a datatype change from "integer" to "long integer."

STEP 13.7.4: DEFINE THE (REVISED) DATA DESIGN TO THE RULE PRODUCT

You may enter the data model into Versata by hand, reverse-engineer it from a relational database, or synchronize it with a Rational Rose class model.

STEP 13.7.5: DETERMINE HOW TO EXPRESS RULES DECLARATIVELY

The Versata Studio is an object-oriented integrated development environment (IDE) for designing, building, and deploying business components and Web-enabled applications.

The companion Web site provides a view of the first Versata Studio screen. Through the Versata Studio, developers can model database objects and their relationships to each other, reengineering from and deploying to databases. You input business logic to the Versata Studio as declarative business rules and then deploy as CORBA or EJB objects to an application server.

From Versata Studio, you can bring up the Business Rules Designer, as shown in Figure 13.16.

The Business Rules Designer models data objects and facilitates the entry of business rules. In Figure 13.16, the field ParkVolumeDiscPercent has been defined as an integer with a validation condition of being between 1 and 99.

You enter validation rules, derivation formulae, constraints and action-event conditions into the Business Rules Designer via an SQL-like business rules language. You can use the Rule Builder, shown in Figure 13.17 to express business rules.

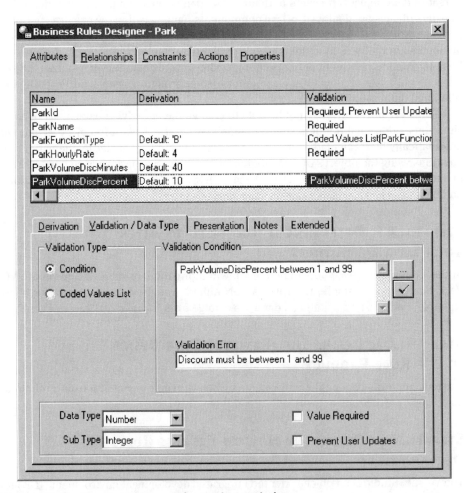

Figure 13.16   Versata Business Rules Designer window.

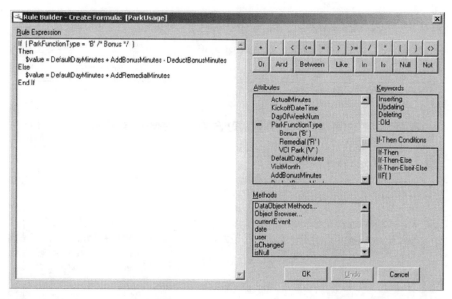

Figure 13.17   Versata Rule Builder.

You can create the rules by entering text, by selecting data object attributes, keywords, If/Then conditions, or by defining java methods and operators to limit typographical errors and help ensure rule syntax is correct.

Relationship Rules

Within the Versata Business Rules Designer, you edit relationships via the relationship tab as shown in Figure 13.18.

In the screen shot, the top pane details the relationships for a particular data object while the bottom pane indicates the properties associated with the selected relationship. On Parent Update and On Parent Delete refer to changes in the keys of that relationship by the Parent (typically the primary or alternate key). The On Child Insert/Update refers to the foreign key reference of the Child and defines actions to be undertaken should the Parent not exist. System messages may be overridden at the bottom of the panel.

Constraints

The Constraints tab of the Versata Business Rules Designer allows you to define data object-level constraints that enforce multiple attribute conditions. This tab provides a grid that lists information for all constraints defined for the selected data object.

The Condition field allows you to enter an expression describing the constraint's condition, optionally using the Rule Builder. The Error Message field allows you to specify a customized error message, to appear when the constraint is violated. The Error Attribute field allows you to specify the attribute in which the cursor is placed after a

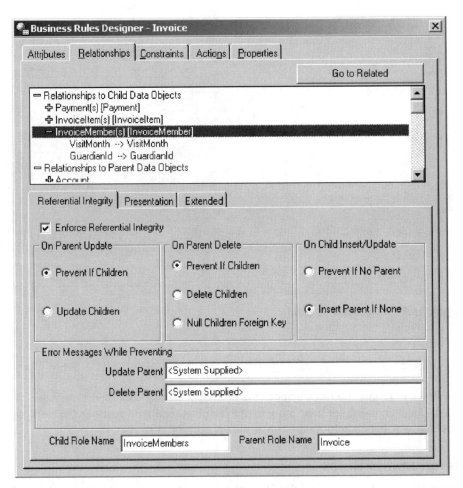

Figure 13.18 Defining relationships to Versata.

constraint is violated and the error message is dismissed. The screen shot in Figure 13.19 shows a constraint for the Invoice data object. In this case, Versata will not allow invoice totals to be changed once they have been sent out.

Action Rules

Versata action rules extend the declarative model by initiating actions outside the boundary of the business object. Actions include an "Action Enabler" statement, which Versata calls the "Event Condition," and an "Action" portion—which within Versata is a call to a Java method. The screen shot in Figure 13.20 shows the Actions tab within the Business Rules Designer.

The example demonstrates the business rule that a guardian may choose to receive by email the criteria responses of their members once they enter a park. Members enter

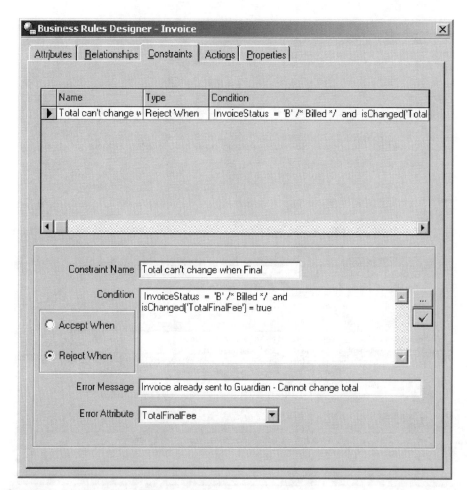

Figure 13.19   Constraint Rule in Versata.

a park once they have answered all the criteria for that park. The system can determine if the member has answered the criteria by checking the response flag. You establish this checking declaratively by creating a count rule in the ParkUsage object, called Num-UnansweredCriteria, that counts all criteria that the member has not answered. If that number drops to zero an email is sent if the guardian's preference is to receive email (PrefCommType = 'E').

Process Rules

Process rules establish the sequence of execution for business transactions that span time and people. You specify process rules to the process designer and they execute within the Versata Interaction Server rules engine. Figure 13.21 shows a screen shot of a process flow for Perform Credit Check.

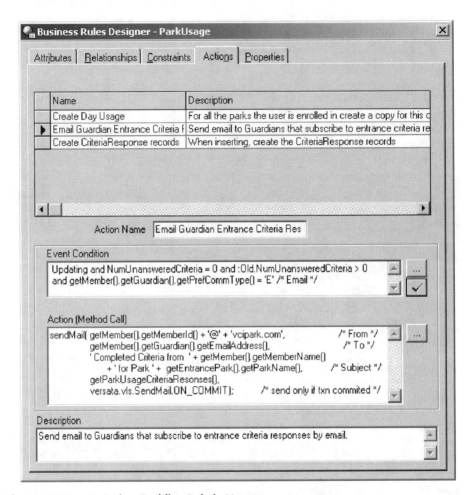

Figure 13.20   An Action-Enabling Rule in Versata.

STEP 13.7.6: ENTER THE RULES INTO THE PRODUCT

The discussion below illustrates the analysis behind entering rules in the Versata Logic Server.

Keep Rules Declarative: Create Parent Replicates To Control Side Effects

Consider the specification that "VCI identifies a volume discount threshold for each park." The initial data model lists a "Volume Discount Threshold" for Park. Further analysis identifies this as a threshold of minutes, at which point a percentage discount is applied to the BaseFee to yield the FinalFee (both existing attributes of InvoiceItem).

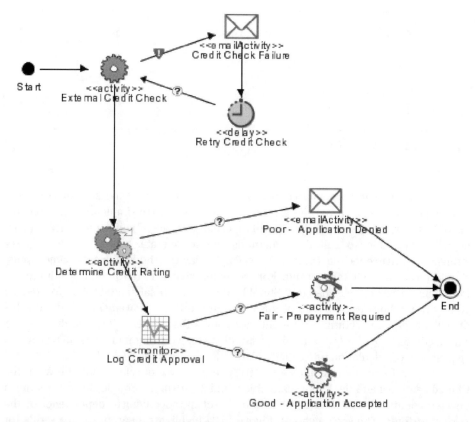

Figure 13.21   Process Flow in Versata

The Versata solution contains two attributes for Park: "ParkVolumeDiscMinutes" and "ParkVolumeDiscPercent". If you were to code such a rule within InvoiceItem in Java, it might look similar to Figure 13.22.

You can enter this calculation in the Versata Studio as a formula rule for FinalFee. However, the volume threshold and discount are associated with a Park. You can get to the Park object from InvoiceItem via a Child relationship called "Park", accessible via a Java assessor method called "getPark". The method getPark() returns the Parent Park object as referenced in Figure 13.23.

```
if ( getActualMinutes() >= getPark().getParkVolumeDiscMinutes() )
    setFinalFee( getBaseFee() * ( 100.0 -
getPark().ParkVolumeDiscPercent() ) / 100.0 );
else
    setFinalFee( getBaseFee() );
```

Figure 13.22   Final Fee rule in Java

```
if ( ActualMinutes >=  getPark().getParkVolumeDiscMinutes() )  then
    $value = BaseFee *  ( 100.0 -
getPark().getParkVolumeDiscPercent() ) / 100.0
else
    $value = BaseFee
end if
```

Figure 13.23   Final Fee Formula rule.

It is important at this point to remember two important characteristics of a business rules approach: (1) Business rules are unambiguous, and (2) the implementation and firing of business rules is under the control of a rules product, if you deploy a rules product. You are able to call Java methods within Versata, which makes it very straightforward to code rules in Java. However, the Java methods, given the same inputs, should return a predictable result. For example, what if ParkVolumeDiscMinutes or ParkVolumeDiscPercent changes? Should FinalFee be recalculated? Will you design your Java methods to take care of this? What if the Parent Park associated with this object changes, and returns a different ParkVolumeDiscPercent? Will you design your Java methods to do this? Because these situations are very common, Versata provides a special type of calculation rule called a Parent Replicate rule.

A Parent Replicate rule allows you to specify the exact relationship between the Child data object and the Parent data object and its attribute. You do this by creating a new term or attribute local to the Child data object and specifying its dependence on the Parent attribute. The screen shot in Figure 13.24 highlights a parent replicate rule for ParkVolumeDiscPercent.

Note that this field is chosen to be "nonmaintained" by not selecting the Maintained checkbox. In doing so, the Parent attribute will not reflect future changes of the parent attribute. That is, if next month you change the discount level for a Park, you don't want FinalFee to be recalculated. These nonmaintained Parent Replicates are also popular as defaults. For example, a future requirement that a Ranger can override a discount for a customer can be implemented by marking the ParkVolumeDiscMinutes field as updateable. Naturally "nonmaintained" Parent Replicates must be persistent in order to preserve their original value. However, "maintained" replicates don't need to be stored.

Now you can rewrite the rule using local declarative terms rather than Java methods as shown in Figure 13.25. Not only is this easier to read, it also alleviates possible undesirable side effects.

Calculation Rule Implementation

The Versata Logic Server run-time rules engine is a set of system services with data objects represented as Java entity beans. Figure 13.26 shows how Versata implements the calculation for FinalFee. Note that for FinalFee, Versata internally uses the BigDecimal Java data type—the only choice for accurate representation and arithmetic manipulation of currency data. The database representation is Decimal, which of course is also used by relational databases for currency datatypes. Note how the Business Rules Com-

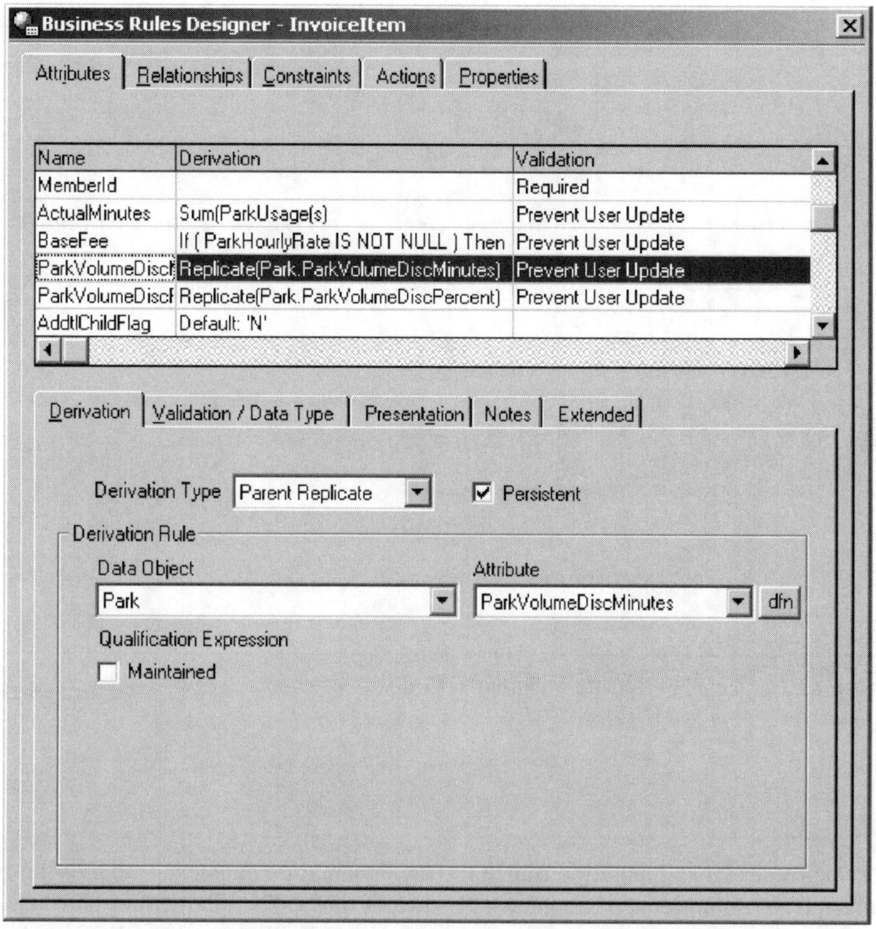

Figure 13.24 Parent Replicate rule in Versata.

```
if ( ActualMinutes >=  ParkVolumeDiscMinutes )  then
    $value = BaseFee *  ( 100.0 - ParkVolumeDiscPercent ) / 100.0
else
    $value = BaseFee
end if
```

Figure 13.25 Final Fee Derivation rule.

```
try {
  getParkVolumeDiscMinutes();
  getActualMinutes();
  getParkVolumeDiscPercent();
  getBaseFee();

  if ((  this.getActualMinutes() >= this.getParkVolumeDiscMinutes()
)) {
    setFinalFee(((this.getBaseFee()).multiply(( ((new

BigDecimal("100.0")))).subtract(getData("ParkVolumeDiscPercent").get
BigDecimal()) ))).
    divide((new BigDecimal("100.0")), getScaleConst(),
BigDecimal.ROUND_HALF_EVEN));
  } else {
    setFinalFee(this.getBaseFee());
  }
} catch (Exception ex) {
  handleAttributeFormulaException(ex, "FinalFee");
}
```

Figure 13.26 FinalFee Versata maintained Code.

piler expresses the computation rule in the implementation language—addressing type casting, type promotion, and rounding. The helper method handleAttributeFormulaException will catch common Java exceptions such as a NullPointerException and translate them into an exception that references the offending attribute. This is much easier for the rule developer to debug and much easier for the end user to understand.

Derivation Sum Rules

One of the most error-prone rules to code yourself is a sum calculation rule. Consider how you might maintain Account Balance by hand. You update the balance every time a change is made to an invoice's total amount, or a payment amount. You update the invoice total amount every time an invoice item's total is changed, or an item is added or removed. You write code such that the cancellation of an invoice subtracts the appropriate amount from the account balance. These detailed considerations are not usually explicit in specifications. They are, however, implicit in the definition of account balance. This means that the developer must address them all and the maintenance team must know how the developer made a change when the business rules change! What if an invoice is reassigned from one account to another? Did you remember to code to reduce the balance of one account and increase another? What if the status of an invoice changes from Cancelled back to Billed? Did you add the invoice amount back to the account balance?

Declarative rules let you define Account Balance as the sum of the billed invoice totals less the sum of the valid payment amounts. With Versata, sum rules are entered against specific attributes. For the case study, the Versata solution contains two new fields in the Account data object: TotalBilled and TotalPayment. In this instance, Account Balance then becomes the formula "TotalBilled—TotalPayment".

The screen shot in Figure 13.27 shows the sum rule for the TotalBilled attribute.

Note the qualification expression that TotalBilled only includes the total for billed invoices. Like any attribute, TotalBilled can be persistent or nonpersistent. Typically, recalculation is more expensive compared to the extra storage required, so in most cases it makes sense to persist these attributes unless the user is unable to change the underlying database schema.

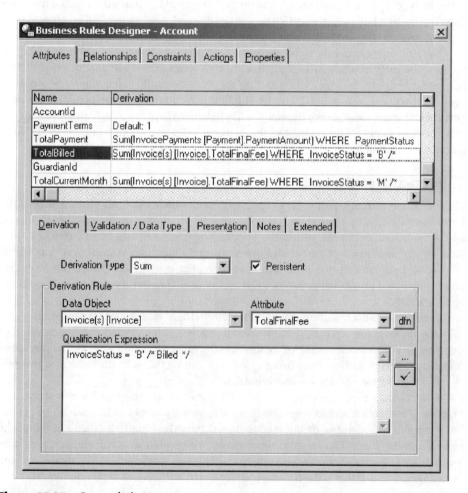

Figure 13.27 Sum rule in Versata.

Derivation Count Rules

The other aggregate derivation rule is the count rule. For the case study, the Versata solution uses a count rule to track the number of open balances. You started with the business rule that states that guardians must prepay when their accounts have an open balance for three months. An open balance is an account balance that remains positive when invoices fall due on the 25th of the month. There are several ways to approach this problem. One approach is to keep a count within the Account data object and update it when the balance is positive on the 25th of the month. The new count attribute is called "NumOpenBalances".

To implement the rule in Versata, you will want to consider how this rule might change in the future. Perhaps an open balance is one where the balance is greater than $5 rather than $0. Or perhaps the application should only consider balances existing over the previous two years. These changes will be easier to implement if you create a field in the Invoice data object to track the account balance at the point the invoice becomes due. The invoice billing cycle will include an additional state called "Billed (past due)".

Figure 13.28 shows the Versata Business Rules Designer for the count rule.

The rule only counts those balances that are positive. You could also create a qualification that only counted invoices in the last two years. When you use the current date in qualification expressions, it means that the system should recalculate the attribute every time the attribute is used. You would do this by marking NumOpenBalances nonpersistent. Figure 13.29 shows the rule for the BalanceWhenDue rule. Note the use of the ":Old." prefix to check the change of the InvoiceCycleStatus field from "B" to "D" indicating the due date has past.

Sequencing of Rules

The execution of rules of one data object may imply the execution of rules across the Parent and Child data objects, and the Parent and Child data objects of those objects, and so on. An object-cache within the Versata Logic Server rules engine reduces database access to at most one read and one write per object per transaction—providing very good performance for even the most complex operations. There are five data objects involved in invoicing: Invoice Cycle, Invoice, Member Summary, Invoice Item, and Park Usage.

The system must maintain rollup totals within these tables, but also must create all the records in the first place. Using declarative rules, you can map out the creation of these records and the summing of totals. Visit the companion Web site for a diagram of these data objects and how the firing of rules performs these operations from just one event—the creation of a ParkUsage record.

A ParkUsage record is created when a member enters the VCI Park. It tracks the number of minutes a member spends in a park on a given day. When the record is initially created, the number of minutes is 0, and thus the FinalFee is also 0. When the record is created, a create-parent-if-none-exists rule creates an InvoiceItem, which uses its own create-parent-if-none-exists rule to create a MemberSummary. Invoice is created the same way and, if this is the first invoice for the month, an InvoiceCycle record is created. Parent Replicate rules populate CycleStatus and InvoiceId into Invoice and MemberSummary respectively. Sum rules declare that the TotalFee for Invoice is the sum of

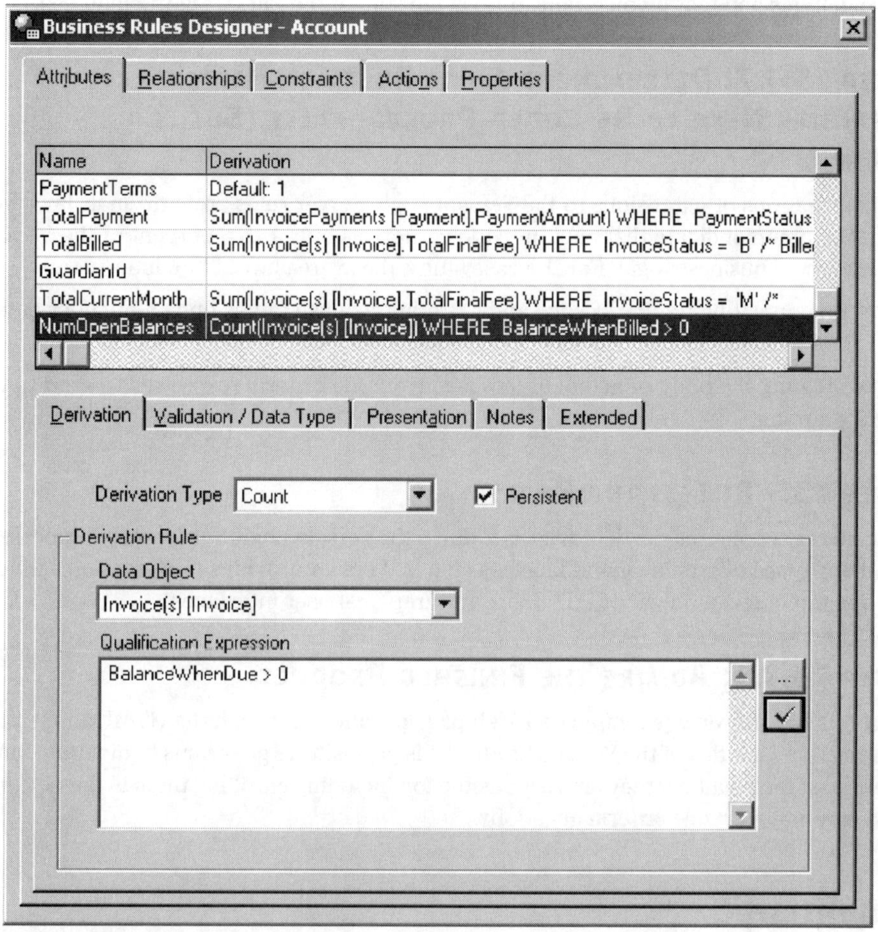

Figure 13.28 Count rule in Versata.

```
/* Invoice: BalanceWhenDue
 *
 * Remember the balance of the account when we bill for this
invoice
 */
if ( InvoiceCycleStatus is not null and
     :Old.InvoiceCycleStatus =  'B' /* Billed (open) */  and
            InvoiceCycleStatus =  'D' /* Billed (past due) */ ) Then
     $value = getAccount().getBalance()
End if
```

Figure 13.29 Calculation rule for BalanceWhenDue.

all the MemberSummary records; that the MemberSummary TotalFee is the sum of the InvoiceItems and that InvoiceItems total is the sum of the ParkUsage's FinalFees.

STEP 13.7.7: DETERMINE IF SOME RULES OR PARTS OF RULES NEED TO BE CODED PROCEDURALLY (SUCH AS IN JAVA)

Customizations or extensions to the Versata Logic Server rules are written in Java. Versata customers indicate that custom code comprises only 1 to 3 percent of the Versata Logic Server business logic. For the case study, these areas would include:

- Prepopulating the ParkUsage and CriteriaResponse tables once a member enters VCI Park for a particular day

- Creating the body of an email message from the criteria responses to send to the guardian

STEP 13.7.8: TEST THE RULES

The business components deployed as EJBs to the Versata Logic Server may be accessed by many types of graphical and faceless clients. Versata provides presentation services for the rapid development of HTML or Java graphical user interfaces.

STEP 13.7.9: ADMIRE THE FINISHED PRODUCT

Figure 13.30 shows an example of a Web page produced through the HTML application automation facilities of the Versata Studio. This page allows guardians to maintain information on the members they are responsible for, including enrolling them in theme parks and entering entrance criteria questions.

Summary

This chapter provided product-specific insights and details on how to design and implement portions of the case study in a data-change-oriented-rules product: USoft's Developer and Versata's Business Logic Server. The most important characteristics and benefits to using such products include:

- These products support a full transaction execution.

- As data-change-oriented products, the rules engine monitors database access and executes predefined rules in response to attempts at updating data.

- You define the rules in terms of underlying data objects, through specification of a data or object model.

- You define the rules in natural language first and then, declaratively, in the product's rule language.

- Usually, a rule wizard or rule builder provides assistance in expressing rules.

- The rule product determines when to fire the rules.

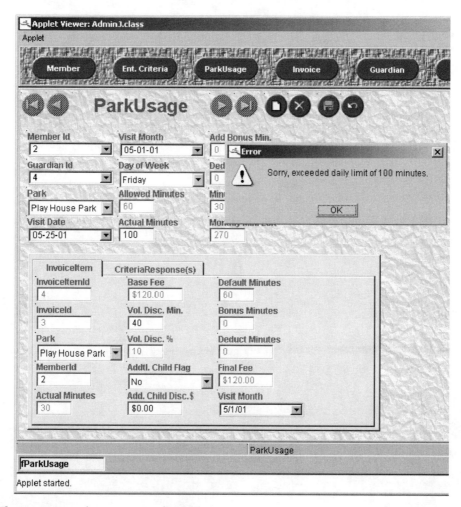

Figure 13.30   The Versata application.

- The rule product serves as a central point of rule definition and management.
- Often, there is very little need to write native programming code because most requirements are handled well by declarative rules.
- There is more detail on these solutions to the case study and on these kinds of products on the companion Web site.

As a comparison, the next chapter contains insights and details on portions of the case study using service-oriented rules products. These products execute rules when requested to do so by a transaction or component.

CHAPTER 14

Implementing Business Rule Systems Using Service-Oriented Products

This chapter continues the discussion of designing and implementing portions of the case study, this time using service-oriented rules products. Service-oriented rules products execute predefined rules when asked to do so by a transaction or component needing a decision. Typically, this means that a product in this category does not provide support for an entire transaction or system, in the way that data-change-oriented rules products do. Instead, a service-oriented rules product usually provides support for specific aspects of the transaction or system for which rules execution is the solution. Development of and implementation of other aspects of the system are addressed by other products or custom-developed application code.

This chapter specifically presents a look at the Blaze Advisor software suite from HNC Software, as well as products from ILOG Inc. A reason for selecting these products is that both of them represent mature product sets that have existed, in various forms, for many years, perhaps under different names. The vendors have great knowledge and experience based on historically providing support in expert systems environments, and now bring that expertise into supporting business rules as discussed in this book. You can consider using these products, because they function as components, in creative ways. For example, some customers have used these kinds of products to customize ERP packages so that such packages operate with organization-specific rules, rather than common ones. Other customers use these products to deliver personalization and intelligent dialogues between customers and an e-business application. Still other customers use these products to house all rules relating to certain business decisions. An example is the set of changing rules that match customer needs and qualifications with appropriate insurance carriers. Another example is the set of changing rules that select the optimum price and service available to a customer from various possible suppliers.

Implementation in the HNC Software Environment

Recall from Chapter 12 that using a service-oriented rules product tends to be process-oriented as opposed to data-oriented. Implementation in such a product, therefore, usually means that you create an object model with which to communicate or share data with the rules service. Usually, you need to define the objects needed for rule execution to the rule service, but you only define the data for the objects, no rules and no methods. The rules are in the rules service. In fact, your system may not even know what those rules are and those rules may change over time.

You express the rules sometimes in procedural code and sometimes not. If you express the rules in a declarative way, you may be able to use If/Then syntax. You are not likely to need to change your database specifications to better fit your rules product because a service-oriented rules capability is not so closely tied to the data. Your rule design effort usually means you need to think about how best to group rules into executable rule sets or rule hierarchies, what the sequence of the execution of rule sets is, and possibly what the sequence of rule execution is within rule sets. You do this so that when an application calls the rules capability for rules execution, the rules capability has been set up to perform that service in a particular manner.

Similar to the implementation with a data-change-oriented product, let's consider rule processing for an interactive business event (Member Requests Entrance to the Park) and a back-office functionality (Invoicing).

As in Chapter 13, we assume that you have completed designs steps 12.1–12.5, but you have decided to acquire or test HNC Software's or ILOG Inc.'s rules products. You want to leverage these products by enforcing as many rules as possible in them

We begin now at step 12.8 (renumbered to 14.8 to fit into this chapter) where you now design and implement the rules for your target service-oriented product.

STEP 14.8.1: CREATE COMPONENT MODEL OF APPLICATION SHOWING RULE SERVICE COMPONENT

Because service-oriented products function as plug-in components, you will need to understand the various ways that the product can fit into your technical architecture. Visit the companion Web site for more details on the Blaze Advisor product set.

To carry out Step 14.8.1, you need to describe the high-level components for the case study, confirm the target use cases in a use-case diagram for scoping, and create a sequence diagram to understand the use-case behavior for how the member enters the park.

Let's consider that the VCI case study, using Blaze Advisor, would need the following high-level components, depicted in Figure 14.1:

- The VCI database
- An Enterprise Java Bean container that manages the Entrance Rule Service
- The Entrance Rule Service that assigns entrance privileges and time allotments for various parks based on the input from a member

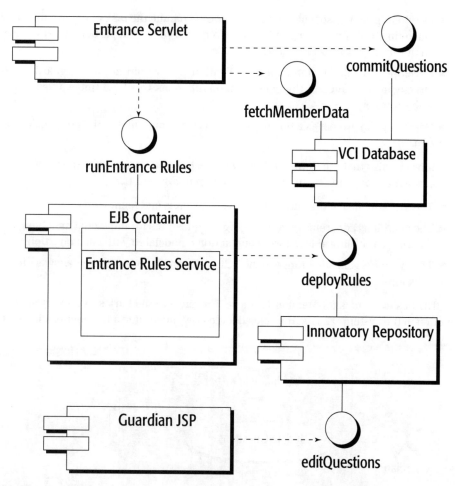

Figure 14.1   A high-level component model for the VCI case study with HNC Software product.

- A Blaze Advisor Innovator repository that stores the templates for the business rules and the rule values that the guardians can modify

- A Guardian servlet, also referred to as the Rules Maintenance Application and implemented as a set of Java Server Pages, that manages the http requests from guardians modifying the questions, answers, and actions.

An Entrance servlet manages the http requests from members accessing the VCI Park service from Web browsers and invokes the Entrance Rule Service.

A Blaze Advisor solution to the business problem posed by the VCI Park Entrance scenarios would include:

- Developing an Advisor rule project that would handle the task of determining how much time a VCI member is allowed or required to be in a particular park, based on the answers to a set of questions.

- Developing a rules maintenance application that would allow the guardians to directly access and edit the questions, possible answers, and time values from a Web browser.

- Deploying the project as a business rule service component of the greater VCI system.

Consider also that the Entrance Rules system has to accommodate the primary use cases, which are depicted in the use-case diagram in Figure 14.2:

- The VCI administrators add and remove guardians and members.

- The guardians add, remove, and modify the questions for individual members, and determine the allowable answers and actions associated with each question.

- The members gain admittance to the VCI Park system based on their answers to the questions.

The business rules for Member Requests Entrance to the Park serve a very specific function in the system. That is, the rules decide how much time a member is allowed in

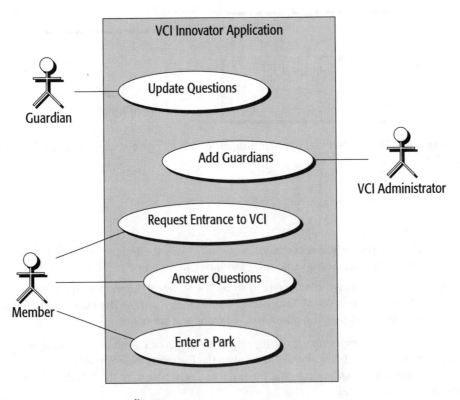

Figure 14.2   A use-case diagram.

each park based on the answers to a set of questions. This architecture separates the rules for deciding allowed park time for a member from other system activities such as managing session data, managing database transactions, and constructing the user interface. This accomplishes three important objectives:

- The rules are easier to update.

- The rule service can process the question and answer data, and set the appropriate time values.

- The system can be extended to include additional end-user touchpoints, such as PDAs, voice recognition systems, kiosks, and so on, without affecting the rule service.

- The rules can be invoked whenever a member logs on to the system from a Web browser.

The Blaze Advisor products provide all of the tools required to create the business rules, deploy them as an EJB[1], and update them on a regular basis without taking down the system. In fact, notice that guardians can update their rules (that is, the questions, answers, and allowed or required time in various parks based on a selected answer) over the Web through Java Server Pages generated by Brokat Rule Maintenance Application Generator.

To better understand the high-level components and how they serve the business event of Member Requests Entrance to the Park, Figure 14.3 presents a sequence diagram.

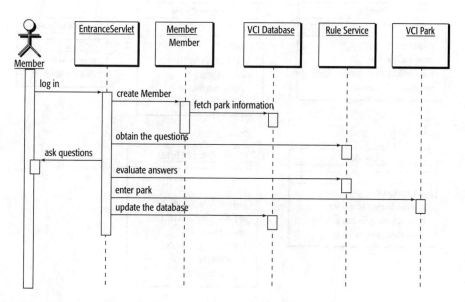

Figure 14.3   A sequence diagram.

STEP 14.8.2: DEVELOP AN OBJECT MODEL FOR THE RULES CAPABILITY

In this step, you identify the set of business objects that the rules will process. (You are not defining all of the business objects needed by your entire application. You may, of course, need to do so, but this step addresses defining only those objects that are the targets of rule execution.) The objects needed for rule execution must include properties for all of the data that the rules will evaluate, modify, or create.

You will implement the business objects for the VCI system as a set of Java classes that define the data requirements for the rules, as well as for the interactions between the Entrance servlet, the Entrance-Rules Service, and the VCI database. Figure 14.4 proposes a partial object model for the business event Member Requests Entrance to the Park.

Objects of the Member class serve as a container for the data about the questions that apply to a particular member, the parks the member is enrolled in, and the specific times allowed in each park, as determined by the rules. In the deployed application, the Entrance servlet is responsible for creating a Member object when a VCI member logs on to the system, and for managing the object's life cycle.

The Parks property of a Member object is a hash table that contains objects of the ParkEnrollment class. These objects include properties that correspond directly to columns in database tables. The Entrance servlet is responsible for connecting to the database through JDBC, and creating the ParkEnrollment objects from the result set.

Question objects represent the questions that VCI members must answer before entering the park. They include properties for the text of the question, the set of allow-

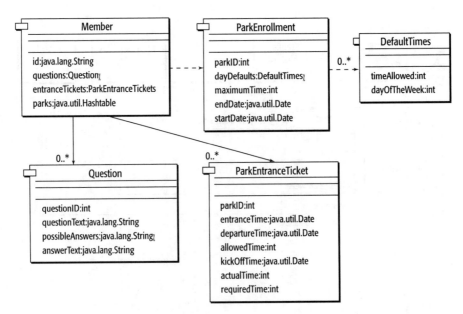

Figure 14.4   An object model for Member Requests Entrance to Park.

able answers, and the answer that the member selects. The responsibility for creating the Question objects is assigned to the Entrance Rule Service. This allows the guardians to manage the questions and determine the rules for the questions at the same time, through the Guardian JSP Rule Maintenance Application. The objects are created when the rule service is initialized, from the data supplied by the guardians.

ParkEntranceTicket objects are created as a result of rule actions, and appended to the entranceTicket array property of the Member object.

The Java classes are imported into the Advisor rule project so that rules can be written against the various object properties.

When a member logs in to the system, the member is authenticated by the Web server security system, and a Member object is created by the Entrance servlet and stored as a session variable. The member's ID is used to access the database to obtain the ParkEnrollment objects for the member.

The Member object is passed to the Entrance Rule Service. The first activity the rule service performs is to see if there are any Question objects in the questions array. If not, it adds the current set of questions defined for the member to the array, and returns the Member object to the servlet.

The servlet forms the http response to include the questions and the set of selectable answers as HTML form elements, and sends it to the member's Web browser. The member selects an answer to each question and submits the form. The Entrance servlet reads the answers from the http request and sets the answerText property in the Member object.

The Member object is again sent to the Entrance Rule Service. Since this time there are Question objects in the array, the rules evaluate the answers and set the entrance times accordingly. When the times are all calculated, the service generates a set of ParkEntranceTicket objects and adds them to the entranceTickets array.

The Entrance servlet passes the Member object to the Park Service, which uses the ParkEntranceTicket information to allow or deny access to the various parks.

The Entrance servlet writes the relevant question and answer data to the database.

Let's now consider the classes needed for the invoicing functions. Figure 14.5 illustrates an object model for this function.

STEP 14.8.3: DECIDE ON RULE SETS AND RULE HIERARCHIES

Related rules can be grouped into rule sets, providing fine-grain control over which rules will process for any given transaction. Rule sets provide a way to group related rules and local objects into functional units that can be invoked in much the same way that a function is invoked in a standard programming language. This both improves performance and simplifies the job of maintaining the rules. The rule flow for evaluating a member's questions is quite simple and is available on the companion Web site. In the VCI Park Entrance Scenario implementation, the rules that apply to each VCI member that logs on to the system are kept in separate rule sets. Even though all of the rules for the members are managed by the same rule service, only those rules that apply to the particular member are processed. In this case, each rule set is invoked by passing it the Member object as a parameter. Once the rule set is invoked, the rules execute until all processing is complete.

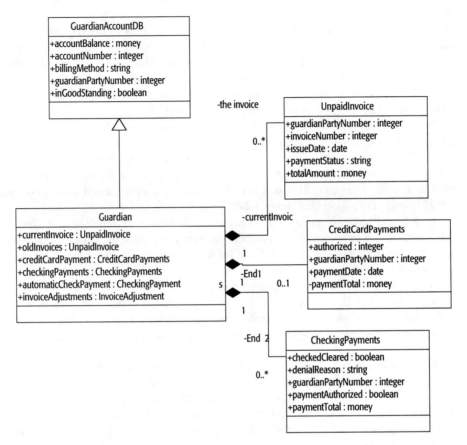

Figure 14.5   An object model for invoicing.

The rule set for a VCI member includes:

- A set of initialized Question objects, representing the questions for the member.

- A rule that tests to see if the question[] array of the Member object contains any Question objects, and appends all of the member's questions to it if it does not. This is the first rule to process, and it only fires when the rule service is invoked for the first time.

- The set of rules that correspond to the set of questions. There is a rule for each possible answer to each question.

- A rule that creates a ParkEntranceTicket object for each park that the member is allowed or required to enter. This rule is always the last rule to process, since it creates tickets based on the actions of the previous rules. To view the rule that creates the ticket, refer to the companion Web site.

Since an Advisor rule set can include local objects, all of the Question objects for the member are defined as part of the rule set. Even though Question objects are based on an imported Java class, you can declare them and initialize them in the Advisor project, using the Advisor Structured Rule Language. This allows you to maintain the questions and the rules written against the questions in the same place. (The section later in this chapter on rule maintenance describes how easy it is for the guardian to create the questions and rules without having any knowledge of the rule syntax or the actual implementation.)

The object representing the first question for Peter could be declared using this syntax:

```
    question0 is a Question initially {
questionText = "Have you completed your homework today?",
 possibleAnswers.append("Yes"),
possibleAnswers.append("No").
 }
```

Recall that this design dictates that the rule service will actually be invoked twice. When the Member object is passed into the rule set for the first time, the returnQuestions rule checks to see if the questions[] array has any elements. If it does not, it appends all of the currently defined questions to the array, and returns.

For the invoicing scenario of applying bank payments, there are more rules, hence more complexity. You can group the rules into three rule sets for CreditCard, AutomaticWithdrawal, and RegularChecking. You may want to create a rule flow diagram to illustrate the sequence of execution of three rule sets. The rule flow is depicted in Figure 14.6.

The rule flow starts as soon as a Guardian object is posted as an event. If multiple objects are posted as a batch, as in this design, they will be processed iteratively. The guardian is assigned to a rule flow variable. The variable can then be passed as an argument to any of the rule sets or functions.

The rule flow includes conditionalized branches that route the object to the appropriate rule set. The rules are grouped according to the billing method the guardian has adopted. Which branch the guardian object takes depends on the value of the billingMethod property of the GuardianAccountDB object.

STEP 14.8.4: DEFINE THE OBJECT MODEL TO THE PRODUCT

Advisor business objects are instances of classes that define sets of properties of specific data types. Advisor provides business object model adapters that let you define your Advisor classes by directly importing your enterprise Java classes, COM objects, XML schemas, or database schemas. This lets you assemble the data for your business objects from almost any system component.

Using Java and JDBC, you can define a set of classes for the business objects your rules require. You can then import these classes into your Advisor project. The objects are assembled in the application through JDBC, and then batches of the objects are mapped to the rule service. When the rules have finished processing, the application is responsible for writing the data back to the database.

Alternatively, you could use the Advisor JDBC wizard to define the classes for your business objects directly from the database schema, and then use the methods that are

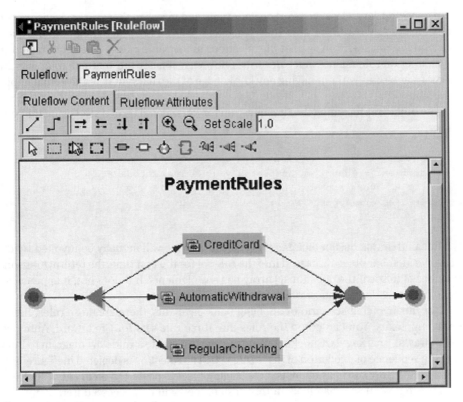

Figure 14.6 Payment rules flow.

included with the classes to fetch the data, and write back any changes when the rules have finished processing.

STEP 14.8.5: ENTER RULES INTO THE PRODUCT

You write your rules in the Advisor Structured Rule Language (SRL). While SRL is a programming language, the vendor states that the grammar is English-like, making it easy to read for nonprogrammers, and fairly simple to learn. Advisor rules are written as sets of *if . . . then . . .* or *whenever . . . then . . .* statements. The rules are written to evaluate the business object properties and trigger appropriate rule actions. The actions can modify the business object properties, create new business objects, invoke methods on business objects, or trigger additional rule processing. The Brokat Advisor Builder IDE provides a range of graphical tools to assist you in developing your business rules.

It may be interesting to consider two different ways of entering rules. The first way is the standard way, using Advisor Structured Rule Language. The second way is one you can develop by creating an interface by which a nontechnical user can enter rules.

You can write the rules for the first question that Peter must answer in the Advisor Structured Rule Language syntax as:

If (the answeredQuestion's questionText is "Have you completed your homework today?"
        and the answeredQuestion's answerText is "Yes")
then increment theMember.parks["Theme Park"].maximumTime by 30 minutes.
If (the answeredQuestion's questionText is "Have you completed your homework today?"
        and the answeredQuestion's answerText is "No")
then theMember.entranceTickets.clear(),
        return}

The rules are written in a natural, English-like syntax (which includes operations on time). In these rules answeredQuestion represents another pattern. It is defined to test all of the Question objects in the questions[] array of theMember.

Some examples of other rules would be:

if (the answeredQuestion's questionText is "You had a spelling test two days ago. If you received your test results today, what grade did you receive?"
        and the answeredQuestion's answerText is "C or worse")
then increment theMember.parks["Spelling Tutorial"].requiredTime by 15 minutes.
if (the answeredQuestion's questionText is "You had a spelling test two days ago. If you received your test results today, what grade did you receive?"
        and the answeredQuestion's answerText is "B or better")
then increment theMember.parks["Theme Park"].maximumTime by 15 minutes.

Let's now turn to how you can build a rule interface for nontechnical people. In the case study, guardians can add and remove questions and create and modify rules about those questions without knowing anything about object models, execution flow, or rule syntax. Brokat's Innovator is useful for creating the capability whereby a nontechnical person can enter or change rules, within limits. It lets you define pieces of your rule project as templates. A project can then include one or more instances of any or all of the templates. The templates include a unique system of Value Holders and PlaceHolders that effectively parameterize the template. Sets of values that represent the template instances are maintained separately from the templates. When you want to generate a complete rule project, the values are merged with the templates, at the places specified by the placeholders, to generate the runnable rule syntax.

The Blaze Advisor Innovator product provides a way to build a Web-based rule maintenance application that provides safe and simple access by nontechnical people to the rules. The VCI administrators can create sets of templates that separate the values that guardians can actually modify from the rest of the rule syntax. It generates a set of Java server pages that provide a clear and easy-to-use interface the guardians can use to edit the values. It explicitly controls how the values set by the guardians are incorporated into the rule set.

By creating templates for the rule set, the Question objects, the rules, and the rule actions, the amount of data a guardian actually has to modify can be cut down to a very manageable set of values. This set of values is made available to the guardian through JSP pages, with HTML form elements for editing the individual values. Innovator verifies that the string values entered through the HTML form will resolve into the correct data values at runtime.

In the rule project, each member has a rule set, and these rule sets are all alike except for the number and values of the Question objects, and the number and values of the rules. Furthermore, the rules are all basically the same except for the question and answer text, and which action to perform. There are only three types of actions, so choosing an action is just a matter of choosing one of the three, providing the time value, and selecting the park. These similarities make creating the templates fairly straightforward.

Look at the definition of the first question for Peter, and the rules for the two possible answers.

```
question0 is a Question initially {
questionText = "Have you completed your homework today?",
possibleAnswers.append("Yes"),
possibleAnswers.append("No").
}
    if (the answeredQuestion's questionText is "Have you completed your homework today?"
        and the answeredQuestion's answerText is "Yes")
    then increment theMember.parks["Theme Park"].maximumTime by 30 minutes.

    if (the answeredQuestion's questionText is "Have you completed your homework today?"
        and the answeredQuestion's answerText is "No")
    then theMember.entranceTickets.clear(),
        return}
```

Most of this is very straightforward. The guardian is only concerned with values that concern the text of the question, the text of the possible answers, and which action to take for each answer. For the action for the "Yes" answer, the guardian must also select the park, and provide the number of minutes.

The templates include value holders for these values. The guardians can supply the simple values, and select from the set of actions, to complete the template instance. When the rule project is regenerated, the current values that the guardian has set are merged with the boilerplate to generate the complete rule syntax.

Once the templates are constructed, Innovator provides a Rule Maintenance Application Generator that produces a complete set of Java server pages. These give the guardians access to their value instances, and HTML form fields for editing the values. A guardian can log in to the Rule Maintenance Application from a Web browser and be presented with HTML pages that offer clear and easy access to the questions, answers, and action values that they are allowed to modify. The guardian can enter or modify the text of the question, and add or remove answers.

Let's see how this would work. A guardian can operate within the screen shown in Figure 14.7. Consider that a guardian can add or change question text and possible answers. If the guardian clicks Add or clicks on one of the links in the Answer Text column of the table, the guardian is presented with the page in Figure 14.8. On this page, the guardian can edit the answer text, select which rule action(s) to take, and select park and time values. Additional pages are generated that manage the connections to the repository.

The repository contains the templates, and an instance of the rule set template for each member. Access controls can be applied to ensure that a guardian can only access and modify the rules for the members he or she is responsible for. The repository includes a complete API for generating the rule projects from the template instances when the rules in the deployed rule service need to be updated.

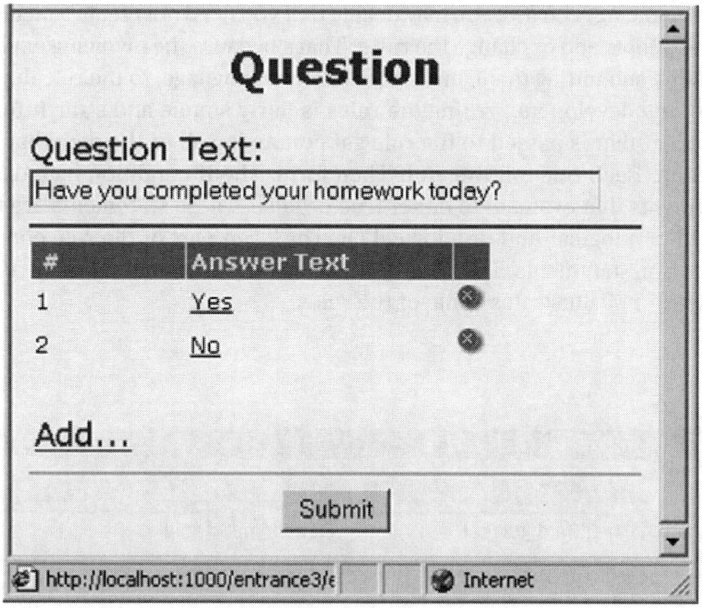

Figure 14.7   Guardian can edit question and answers.

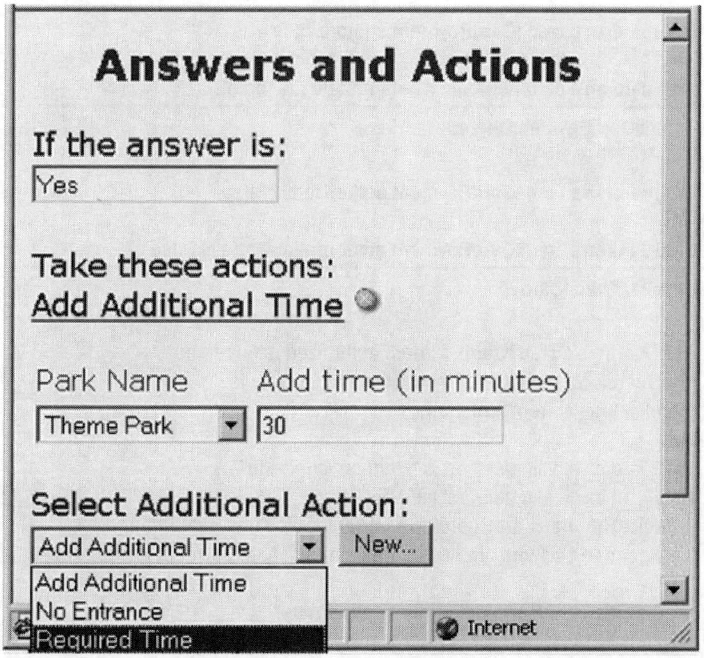

Figure 14.8   Guardian can specify actions to answers.

For the invoicing scenario, you may decide that you need not create a facility by which nontechnical people add or change the rules. That's because the invoicing experts request rule changes by submitting them, probably in natural language, to the rule developers.

For the rule developers, writing the rules is fairly simple and straightforward. The Guardian object that is passed to the rule set containing all of the data that the system is interested in. Each rule follows an If/Then form. The If condition includes any number of statements that evaluate to either true or false. These statements are themselves joined by either a logical And or a logical Or. The Then part of the rule consists of any number of action statements. The Then actions are only executed when the If conditions are true. Figure 14.9 illustrates some of the rules.

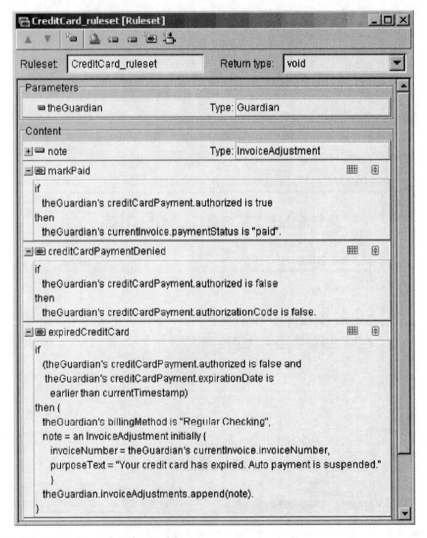

Figure 14.9   A rule set for Blaze Advisor.

The rule flow passes the guardian object to the rule set, which assigns it to a variable called theGuardian. The If conditions of the various rules test specific properties of theGuardian. The rule actions then perform whatever operations are required.

Notice that one of the actions of the expiredCreditCard rule is to create a new InvoiceAdjustment object, with the invoice number of the current invoice and the text of the message to be added when the invoice is sent to the customer. This object will be written to the database along with any other changes that are made by the rules.

The AutomaticWithdrawal_ruleset and RegularChecking_ruleset are very similar.

STEP 14.8.6: DETERMINE THE CONTROL OF RULE EVALUATION SEQUENCE WITHIN A RULE SET

This is covered above.

STEP 14.8.7: DETERMINE IF SOME OF THE RULES NEED TO BE CODED IN PROCEDURAL NONRULE CODE

This is not needed.

STEP 14.8.8: TEST THE RULES

As always, you should test the rules. In this case, you can simulate the data as input to the rules service and test the rules before the full system is finished.

STEP 14.8.9: ADMIRE THE FINISHED PRODUCT

The vendor states that the complexities of deploying the Advisor rule project as an Enterprise Java Bean (EJB) rule service are greatly simplified by the EJB implementation of the Advisor Rule Server and EJB Quick Deployer wizard are included with Advisor Builder. The Quick Deployer guides you through the process of defining the invocation methods for the service, and then generates the appropriate home, remote, and implementation classes, Deployment Descriptor, and script files that you can use to package and deploy the bean on your EJB server.

Implementation Using ILOG

ILOG Inc.'s JRules is another example of a service-oriented rules product, one that focuses on integration of its rules capability as a component of an overall application. When integrated into an application, the ILOG rules product monitors the state of various application objects in memory directly, without any proxy objects. Rules grouped into rule sets, and application objects are associated together into what is referred to as a context.

The ILOG JRules product is provided as a set of Java classes that you can extend with application specific data and methods. A Rule Kit is provided that includes a Rule Builder, a graphical Rule Editor, and is based on ILOG's extensible Rule Language. You can implement rules directly into Java classes and integrate into an application.

In ILOG, you can implement and integrate multiple rule engines. You can add, modify, and eliminate from any engine dynamically, without needing to recompile or redeploy.

The remainder of this section contains an excerpt from ILOG's JRules white paper, which gives a brief description of how rules are written for the ILOG engine.

- **Rule structure.** The basic structure of a rule is IF THEN. Typically, these are referred to as the Left Hand Side, LHS, and Right Hand Side, RHS, of a rule. The LHS contains conditions in the form of patterns and the RHS contains actions— things the rule should do if all the conditions on the LHS have been met.

- **Rule conditions.** The LHS of a rule is composed of a set of conditions or patterns that refer to Java objects. Each pattern is matched, if possible, with one or more objects in working memory. More precisely, a pattern comprises tests that are applied to each object in working memory and an object is said to match the pattern when it passes these tests successfully. Here is a typical pattern that might be useful in the shopping cart example:

  the item of type Fish is in stock

  - This pattern would match Item objects in working memory that are in stock and of type fish. Notice that this pattern references Item objects followed by specifications for attributes type fish and in stock. Another pattern could be

  the shopping cart value > 100.

- **Actions.** The RHS of a rule is said to execute or *fire* when all of the conditions on the LHS have been met. There are many actions that a rule might perform. Depending upon the requirements of the application, a rule may add an object to or remove an object from working memory, modify an object or execute a method on one of the objects. In the example below, an m percent discount is being applied to a customer's order.

  apply a 15% discount

  - Such an action might be executing a method on the shopping cart object modifying it by reducing the total purchase price by m.

Let us construct a set of four complete rules. The rules are written in a natural language-type syntax available in JRules and Rules and are readable enough to be self explanatory.

```
Rule GoldCategory:
IF
the purchase value is greater than the customer previous purchase amount
and the purchase value is greater than or equal to $100
THEN
Change the customer category to Gold and display the message "You're now a Gold customer!"
Rule GoldDiscount:
    IF
                the shopping cart contains between 2 and 4 items
                and the purchase value is greater than $100
                and the customer category is Gold
```

THEN

    apply a 15% discount

    and display the message "We're giving you a Gold discount!"

Rule SuggestFish

  IF

    the customer has previously bought fish

    and the shopping cart contains fish

THEN

    Suggest items related to fish

Rule JiffyFishFood

  IF

    The item is fish

THEN

    add free food sample to shopping cart

    and display the message "A free sample of Jiffy fish food!"

Application objects must be asserted into retracted from or updated in working memory before pattern matching in rules can begin. This can be done either by using keywords within rules or using the API from within Java code in application objects themselves.

Summarizing the tour at this point, an ILOG rule engine context working memory and rule set have been created.

```
//Create an ILOG rule engine
IlrContext myContext = new IlrContextO;


    // get the IlrRuleset associated with myContext
IlrRuleset myRuleset = my Context.getRulesetO;

// Add rules to myRuleset
myRuleset.parseFileName("fish-promo-rules");
```

and the rule set container loaded with fish promo rules. The application is ready to be run. Once a shopping session begins and objects are inserted into working memory, the rule engine will match objects in working memory against the LHS of rules placing rules that are successfully matched onto the agenda. When a rule or application object modifies working memory, additional rules may be put on or retracted from the agenda.

Summary

This chapter introduced you to the insights and details of implementing rules using a service-oriented rules product. The essential characteristics and benefits are:

- Rule development with these kinds of products is usually process-oriented rather than data-oriented, mostly having an object-oriented flavor.

- You can often express the rules declaratively.
- You define the data needed by the rules usually by defining a corresponding object model, devoid of rules and methods.
- You still need to design and implement the nonrule portions of your system.
- Rule design sometimes involves deciding on the sequence of rule execution, although this sequence is specified only once.
- The rules product serves as a single point of definition and management of the rules.
- There is more detail on these solutions and on these kinds of products on the companion Web site.

A business rules approach to systems development brings tremendous business value to any organization. This is especially true in the world of e-commerce and of the increasing need for business flexibility.

Hopefully, Chapters 13 and 14 introduced you to the world of commercial rules technology and how you can deploy it successfully. With the rapid pace of business change and customer demand, the use of a business rules approach coupled with business rules technology is the only way to keep up and to deliver quality and ongoing change.

You should now have a glimpse at the differences among such products, but also the similarities regarding the STEP principles. You should better understand now the directions that are set by these vendors and products and you can envision a future in which you position your organization for intelligent and timely change.

CHAPTER 15

Rule Management

Like any project, you need to manage the knowledge discovered during the project's life cycle and into system maintenance and enhancements. As you begin to interview the business community, you will need a repository in which to house the rules. You will use this repository throughout all phases of your project. You will also need to manage all your project deliverables and documents as a fundamental part of project management. This chapter focuses on rule management, so you'll need to integrate rule management with other project management aspects.

Rule management is necessary, not only during your project's duration, but also after implementation so you can manage the rules throughout their lifetime. Information and rules are two of an organization's intellectual assets. You will see that rule management, then, has many similarities to information resource management.

This chapter defines steps for identifying the scope of rule management, requirements for a rule repository, implementation options for that repository, and the beginnings of a rule management function.

What Is Rule Management?

Rule management is, obviously, the management of rules for the benefit of a rules community. The *rules* community, on the smaller side, can be the stakeholders for your system, but on the larger side, can be the entire enterprise and extraprise.

The very idea of rule management may sound scary or impossible to some readers but may sound powerful and enlightening to others. So, let's understand rule management in terms of its benefits, the risks of not managing rules, and the cost of managing versus not managing rules.

How Is Rule Management Different for a Business Rules System?

Rule management is different for a business rules system simply because rule management exists for such a system. Rule management, by existing, elevates the importance of business rules to the business and carries that importance into the organization's systems development function and approach.

As a comparison, in organizations that do not consider information important, systems are built without full understanding of the data and without recasting it into a shareable, flexible visionary architecture. However, organizations that consider information to be valuable build systems in partnership with an information management function, at best. Or, at worst, they build systems with careful attention to information resource management principles in designing or customizing databases.

Most organizations have undoubtedly thought that rules were important, but did not know how to make that importance really matter. Until recently, systems development efforts focused on designing system behavior usually through object-oriented approaches. Without a business rules mindset, even following object-oriented approaches, analysts, and programmers embedded rules in system specifications, program documentation, or did not formally capture them at all. These rules are held in bondage, resistant to change.

Before discussing the details of rule management, let's understand how other organizational assets are well managed.

Organizational Assets

To expand on Chapter 1, at the heart of a business rules approach is an appreciation for rules as a valuable, shareable, and leveragable asset of an organization. Your organization has other assets that are valuable, shareable, and leveragable, too, such as its employees, its money, its customers, and its legal obligations. Let's understand these more tangible assets so we can apply the concepts to rules as an asset.

Because these three resources (people, money, and customers) are so precious and critical to the organization's success, most medium-to-large organizations create specialized centralized functions dedicated to leveraging them. For example, you find a legal or contracts function that manages legal obligations of all kinds. A human resource function manages an organization's people. Let's look at the human resource function in more detail so you can see surprising similarities, benefits, risks, and costs for rule management.

The human resource function is often centralized so as to present a consistent interface to employees and agents (such as consultants). The human resource function handles contract negotiations, benefits administration, and other aspects of people management. A human resource function also ensures that internal organizations do not engage in unhealthy competition for an employee, for example. This function also handles the administration activities of people management so that other functions in the organization can focus more on their own mission, on what they do best. Therefore, establishment of a human resource function not only leverages the human resources across the entire organization, but also carries out human resource activities so that other functions don't need to redundantly do so.

It makes sense that an organization, wishing to leverage its people, establishes a human resource function to:

- Represent a consistent interface to its human resources

- Reduce redundancy in processes surrounding human resources

- Leverage benefits to human resources (for example, it is cost saving to obtain certain benefits for large quantities of employees than for each department to obtain those benefits for their subset of employees)

- Minimize internal unhealthy competition for human resources

- View enterprise-wide human resources as a pool from which to find talent as the organization grows and needs new skills

- Provide a single point of contact for human resource related issues and knowledge.

Another interesting asset is the organization's customers. While an organization would like to manage their customers, the truth is that customers in the Internet age are more empowered than ever to exercise freedom of choice in finding products and services. Therefore, many organizations establish a customer relationship function to manage, not the customer, but the relationship between the customer and the organization. This relationship is key to the organization's success and, interestingly enough, is deserving of careful rule management to guide that relationship effectively.

Information as an Intellectual Asset

Assets such as people, money, and customers are very tangible. Other assets, however, are less tangible. They seem more elusive. These include information, rules, and knowledge. Sometimes, intangible assets are extremely valuable.

Information resource management functions are found in organizations that are serious about managing information as a valuable, shareable, leveragable asset. Information is an interesting resource because it is nonconsumable. That is, a piece of information is not used up when someone uses it, like money is, for example. In fact, there is a great cost savings when many people use the same copy of the same information. The flip side is that there is an added cost to creating a separate copy of a piece of information rather than sharing it. Most often, this extra cost comes with no added benefit. Worse, the more copies an organization makes of the same piece of information, the more expensive that information becomes and the more it is prone to errors and inconsistencies.

For these reasons, information becomes a valuable asset when it is accessible to many and when its quality is good so that it leads to better faster business decisions and customer interfaces. Because information quality is of crucial importance today to organizational success, the chapter on data analysis (Chapter 9) contains detailed criteria by which to measure the quality of information.

On the other hand, information becomes a liability when it is inaccessible to those who need it, or when it is duplicated, inconsistent, or of such poor quality that it leads to confusion, frustration, untimely and incorrect judgments, and added costs.

For these reasons, an information resource management function aims to do the following, which resemble the goals of a human resource function:

- Reduce redundancy in processes surrounding information
- Leverage benefits to everyone regarding information (publishing available definitions, cleaning existing information sources, protecting information sources from contamination)
- Minimize internal unhealthy competition for information (minimizing unnecessary copies)
- View enterprise-wide information sources as a pool from which to find the right information as the organization grows and needs new information
- Provide a single point of contact for information-related issues and knowledge.

In summary, information management focuses on leveraging an organization's information asset; that is, leveraging what an organization can know through its information sources. Information management in general aims to establish the ability to conduct impact analysis based on a required change to a piece of data. For example, with proper information management, you should be able to identify the applications and databases that you will need to enhance to materialize the desired change. Therefore, this book advocates strong information resource management as well as rule management.

Rules as an Intellectual Asset

Rules, like information, also represent an intellectual asset. Like information, rules are also a nonconsumable resource. A rule is not used up when someone or a system executes it. Also, there is the added cost of storage to make copies of rules and the added business cost of rule copies being inconsistent with each other.

Rules become an asset when they are of good quality because rules are prescriptions by which the business makes decisions and interacts with others. Good quality rules lead to better, faster, more consistent business decisions. Good quality rules align with business motivation so that the rules lead the business to where it wants to go. To assist you in crafting high-quality rules, Chapter 10 on rule analysis contains details on exactly what it means for rules to be of high quality.

There are two significant differences between information as an asset and rules as an asset. The first is that, mostly, information is passive, in that it is a resource waiting for a business usage to reference it. (It is true that information has an active aspect, when it is created, for example.) Rules, on the other hand, are active in that, while a rule is a resource waiting for a business usage to execute it, rules actually guide the business.

The second difference is that a conceptual *information base* (collection of types of information for a business) does not change unless the very nature of the business itself changes. Rather, what changes are the rules about the business. The information resource's structure and definitions may remain somewhat constant over time, although its values change. But the *rule base* (collection of types of rules) needs very much to change. In a slow-changing world, rules do not change often. In a fast-paced e-driven world, rules need to change frequently and quickly. Therefore, rules are a very crucial asset for stewarding the business through change, and rule management becomes an instrument of organizational change.

That said, rules become a liability to the business when they are inaccessible, unknown, buried in program code or packaged software, duplicated, inconsistent, do not support business goals, and are difficult to change. When rules are in this state, they cost the organization a lot of money and possibly lost business opportunities. Consider, for a moment, how much of an organization's IT budget is spent supporting the execution of and maintenance of hidden rules.

In summary, rule management focuses on leveraging business policies (or customized policies), and the need to have these stated, understood, controlled, and dynamically changed by business stakeholders. Rule management aims not only to establish the ability to perform impact analysis based on a required change to a rule, but also possibly to establish an environment in which rules can change with minimal application coding changes.

What Is the Purpose of Rule Management?

The purpose of rule management is to provide access for all qualified stakeholders to the organization's rules while ensuring the security and integrity of related rule information. In addition, rule management provides business management with the ability not only to know its deployed rules but to request rapid deployment of rule changes. If you do not establish rule management, you may not meet this objective, even for the individual system(s) to which you applied a business rules approach. At best, the rules will serve only the target project in some way, while remaining contradictory to other organizational rules, or be redundantly implemented, difficult to change everywhere.

Ron Ross (1997) has defined business rule management as "activities and strategies that aim toward identifying and managing business rules; in order to:

- Understand business practices more completely

- Achieve greater consistency across functions, geographical areas, and systems

- Facilitate rapid change

- Achieve more adaptable business processes

- Move the company towards better Knowledge Management practices

- Improve communication between business users and IT professionals

- Enable easier migration of business functionality."

This book adds the following to the purpose of rule management:

- Reduce redundancy in processes (discovery, create, challenge, change, automate) surrounding rules
- Leverage benefits to everyone regarding rules (publishing available rules, mining rules from code, protecting rules from contamination)
- Minimize internal unhealthy competition for rules (minimizing unnecessary copies)
- View enterprise-wide rule sources as a pool from which to find the right rules and from which to change rules as the organization grows and needs new decisions
- Provide a single point of contact for rule-related issues and knowledge.

To realize the benefits of a business rules approach, rule analysts must be able to access and change rules during the project life cycle and business people must be able to access rules and, at least, be able to request changes. So, when you adopt a business rules approach, even for one project, you should also adapt continuous management of the rules, both during and beyond, the first system release. Managing rules means carrying out activities for:

- Collecting and recording rules
- Storing rules and rule deliverables
- Accessing and reporting of rules to the corporation
- Challenging rules
- Managing the change of the rules.

This chapter focuses on establishing rule management for your project. If your rule management proves its value and gains momentum (as we are sure it will), the organization may want to expand it to be a cross-project rule management function. Project-level rule management can serve as a prototype and foundation for larger scale rule management because management commitment and buy-in is essential prior to full roll out.

What Are the Deliverables of Rule Management?

Whether you consider rule management an integral part of your systems development project or a project of its own, you need to include rule management procedures, standards, techniques, and tools for all phases of your project. This chapter leads you through the steps and deliverables for establishing rule management practices.

It is useful to group the main deliverables of rule management under three main headings: rule stewardship, rule repository, and rule processes. Figure 15.1 lists the deliverables.

What Are the Steps of Rule Management?

Figure 15.2 summarizes the steps for achieving rule management.

This chapter divides the rule management steps into four sections. The first section contains the steps to Scope Rule Management. The second section, Establish Rule Stew-

Rule Stewardship:

    Rule Stewardship Roles
    Rule Stewardship Program

Rule Repository:

    Rule Metamodel
    Rule Repository Requirements
    An Implemented and Populated Repository
    Rule Classification Scheme
    Rule Templates and Standards
    Rule Security Profiles
    Rule Reports
    Repository Management Processes

Rule Processes:

    Rule Certification Process and Procedures
    Change Management Roles and Responsibilities
    Change Management Processes and Procedures

Figure 15.1   Deliverables of rule management.

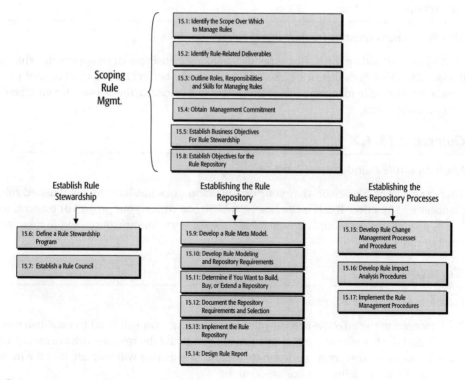

Figure 15.2   Steps for managing rules.

ardship, discusses an approach for recognizing and fostering business accountability for the rules. The third section, Establish the Rule Repository, is extremely important. It provides insights into requirements for your rule repository and how best to deliver one. The fourth section presents steps to Establish Rule Repository Processes by which rules entered, accessed, and changed.

Keep in mind that these steps are interdependent. Your approach to rule stewardship affects the rule management processes you put in place. These and your scope statement affect the rule-related information you store in the rule repository. The rule-related information you store in the repository affects your management processes and your stewardship responsibilities.

Scope Rule Management

You need first to define realistic boundaries within which you will manage rules.

STEP 15.1: IDENTIFY THE SCOPE OVER WHICH TO MANAGE RULES

Consider carefully what it means to identify the scope over which you want to manage rules. It is likely that the rules, while captured on behalf of one project, may have jurisdiction over many political, geographical, and project boundaries.

GUIDELINE 15.1.1

Identify business reasons for managing rules.

Start by understanding the business needs for taking a business rules approach. What is it about the target rules that rule management can make better? Stated another way, why is there an interest in managing rules? Document and prioritize the reasons for your project to manage rules.

GUIDELINE 15.1.2

Establish a rule management function.

There is a strong likelihood that your organization does not have an established rule management function. If this is the case, establish one within your project or external to it. For a small project, simply assign a full-time (or part-time) resource to the management of rules.

GUIDELINE 15.1.3

Establish success measures.

To demonstrate the effectiveness of rules management, you will need to establish metrics. Revisit the benefits of a business rules approach and the reasons you are managing rules. From these, determine appropriate measurements that will indicate that the management of rules is delivering business value.

Sample measurements to capture include:

- Time and money saved in analysis time due to reuse of existing rules
- Time and money saved in design and implementation due to reuse of existing rules, no redundant coding
- Time and money saved in testing due to separate testing of rules or existence of previously tested rules
- Time and money saved in maintenance due to speed of rule change and rule additions
- Time and money saved in proactively implementing changes in rules
- Time and money saved in training people on the new system because rules were available for reference and correction
- Time and money saved in future planning due to a common vocabulary and rule sets
- Level of satisfaction of business people due to more focused business/IT dialogue around rules
- Number of times a business rules system went through a change in technology (e.g., new release of DBMS, new release of operating systems, new release or emergence of browsers) and how much time it took to test and migrate rules
- Number of times the rule repository and rule management personnel are asked to participate in business process engineering efforts.

On a day-to-day level, track simple statistics, such as the number of changed rules and how often the most dynamic rules change. These statistics may provide insights into how rule management delivers value.

STEP 15.2: IDENTIFY RULE-RELATED DELIVERABLES

Rule-related deliverables are those deliverables that aid in documenting the rules and/or relate rules to other deliverables. Identify rule-related deliverables that are critical to the reasons you decided to manage rules.

GUIDELINE 15.2.1

Review the rule-related deliverables for each phase of the business rules approach.

Identify those rule-related deliverables for which there are benefits in managing formally. These represent a subset of the total deliverables formally managed as part of overall project management. Table 15.1 summarizes rule-related deliverables by phase, as presented in this book. These deliverables are described in detail in related chapters.

GUIDELINE 15.2.2

Evaluate the kinds of rule-related standards you will need.

Table 15.2 correlates rule-related deliverables to related standards. Identify and prioritize those rule-related standards that are needed for your project.

Table 15.1   Summary of Rule-Related Deliverables by Phase

METHODOLOGY PHASE	RULE-RELATED DELIVERABLES
Discovery	Decisions behind each business event
	Rule sources
	Rules
	Rules behind decisions
	Knowledge referenced and created by rules
	Concrete scenarios
Analysis	Rule-enriched logical data model
	Rule families
	Rule patterns
	Rule dependencies
	Data activities for rules
	Workflow diagrams
Design	Assignment of rules to architectural layers
	Specification of rule layer functionality

Table 15.2   Rule-Related Deliverables and Corresponding Standards

METHODOLOGY PHASE	RULE-RELATED DELIVERABLES	CORRESPONDING STANDARDS
Discovery	Decisions behind each business event	Naming conventions for decisions
		Mechanism for attaching decisions to business events
	Rule sources	
	Rules	Naming conventions for rules
		Classification scheme for rules
		Templates for expressing rules
	Rules behind decisions	Mechanism for attaching rules to decisions
	Knowledge referenced and created by rules	Mechanism for attaching knowledge to rules
	Concrete scenarios	Format for expressing
		Mechanism for attaching concrete scenarios to rules

Table 15.2   (*Continued*)

METHODOLOGY PHASE	RULE-RELATED DELIVERABLES	CORRESPONDING STANDARDS
Analysis	Rule-enriched logical	Mechanism for attaching entities or business objects to rules
		Mechanism for denoting inferred or derivable knowledge in the model
	Rule families	Naming conventions for rule families
		Mechanism for documenting rule families
		Mechanism for attaching rule patterns to rule families
	Rule patterns	Naming conventions for rule patterns
		Mechanism for documenting rule patterns
		Mechanism for attaching rules to rule patterns
	Rule dependencies	Mechanism for documenting rule (family) dependencies
	Data activities for rules	Mechanism for attaching data activities to rules
	Workflow diagrams	Mechanism for attaching workflow to rules
Design	Assignment of rules to architectural layers	Criteria by which to assign rules to architectural layers
	Specification of rule layer	Standard specification for various types of rule layers

GUIDELINE 15.2.3

Prioritize the list of deliverables and include the list within the business rule management scope statement.

Once you identify, prioritize, and review the list of formal rule-related deliverables, incorporate the list in the scope statement for rule management.

STEP 15.3: OUTLINE ROLES, RESPONSIBILITIES, AND SKILLS FOR MANAGING RULES

Adopting a business rules approach will require that you define new roles, not only in the IT department but also in the client community. Table 15.3 identifies some of the new roles and sample responsibilities that may meet your project needs.

Table 15.3 Roles and Responsibilities for Rule Management

ROLE NAME	SAMPLE RESPONSIBILITIES
Rule repository administrator	Ensures the quality of the business rule information stored in the repository by following the rule certification process. Ensures the data integrity and security of the business rule stored in the repository by administering the rule security profiles. Understands the basic principles and objectives of business rule management and the business rule templates and classification schemes. Understands the rule repository functionality and meta data model, and the requirements for meta data and meta data integration across all project phases. Participates in project scoping for the purpose of defining rule repository requirements and any needed enhancements. Defines required output reports from the repository. Understands rule management principles. Identifies inconsistencies in the repository and identifies processes for monitoring these. Interacts effectively with other team members to ensure all meta data reaches the repository and resolve inconsistencies. Designs and develop templates and standard reports needed.
Rule analyst	Promotes the benefits of rule deliverables. Leads the effort to integrate and coordinate reuse of existing rules amongt projects. Leads the establishment of the business rule naming standards and procedures. Documents the natural language-expression rule in the discovery phases. Completes the rule templates in the analysis phase. Supports the rule repository administrator in identifying and mapping rules clauses to the repository, and populating and refining these in the repository. Understands the basic principles and objectives of the business rule approach. Participates in the discovery, analysis, and design phases in terms of understanding system flow and how this relates to project scoping. Establishes the principles, definitions, and grammar (syntax) of business rules. Understands the rule repository functionality and meta data model, and the requirements for meta data and meta data integration across all phases. Identifies rule patterns. Identifies rule conflicts. Interacts effectively with business and system experts for the purpose of verifying rules, data models, and associated meta data.

Table 15.3 *(Continued)*

ROLE NAME	SAMPLE RESPONSIBILITIES
Rule steward	Is accountable for the quality of the rule produced. Validates rules. Controls use of rules. Resolves the issues across departments and groups relating to their business rules. Ensures that rules remain congruent with business policy. Proposes new versions of rules and documents the objectives of rule changes and cost justifications. Proposes retirement of rules and documents the reasons. Ensures that all required rule definition properties have been documented in the rule repository. Ensures that the business rules are uniformly applied across the company.

STEP 15.4: OBTAIN MANAGEMENT COMMITMENT FOR RULE MANAGEMENT

Obtaining management commitment on the rule management scope statement and corresponding roles and responsibilities is a critical success factor for your project.

GUIDELINE 15.4.1

Incorporate the rule management scope statement within the project scope statement.

As identified in Chapter 4, you will be developing a project scope statement. It is important that you synchronize the project scope statement and the rule management scope statement. The rule management scope statement should include why, what, how, who, where, and when:

- WHY bother to manage rules
  - Benefits
  - Goals of rule management
  - Risks of rule management
  - Risks of not managing rules
- WHAT to manage about rules
  - Description of rule-related deliverables
  - Specification of the rule-related information
- HOW to manage rules
  - Processes for adding, changing, archiving, accessing rules
  - Decision on the rule repository will be in place

- WHO will manage rules?
  - Organizational domain over which to manage rules
  - Roles needed
  - Where these resources will come from
- WHERE to manage rules?
  - Geographical boundaries over which rules are to be managed
- WHEN to manage rules:

Implementation strategy for a short-term timeframe in which to prove the benefit of rule management

Implementation strategy for a long-term timeframe in which to deliver full-blown management of rule

GUIDELINE 15.4.2

Conduct a formal meeting to present the rule management function and gain approval for it.

Both IT and business management should acknowledge and approve the scope and roles for rule management before moving on to the next steps.

Commitment means more than verbal directive. It means active support. To achieve active ongoing support for rule management, you will need procedures for resolving issues and for elevating the importance of rules to higher management should you feel rules are in danger of becoming lost again. This implies management commitment to oversee the political issues that might arise. Gaining top management support is generally not a simple task, but it is essential because rule management is new and change is difficult.

GUIDELINE 15.4.3

Offer formal and informal presentations on rule management, as needed.

To solidify ongoing management support, you will need to engage in consistent and constant communication to management about the rule management steps and what they accomplish as each project phase occurs. You can do so informally through one-on-one meetings. You can also offer formal presentations as introductory overviews of business rule management.

GUIDELINE 15.4.4

Consider creating a Web page as a portal for rule management activities.

An exciting communication technique is a rule management Web page. It can contain the rule management mission, standards, procedures, and the ability to launch the rule repository. It can also advertise status of rule-managed projects and successes. You can make it fun by exposing interesting discovered rules for the organization (only if this seems politically correct).

Another use of a rule management Web page is to design the Web pages by departments. Market how the different departments within your organization are benefiting by a rule-driven approach and rule management.

Establish Rule Stewardship

The term *steward* refers to one who has accountability for managing something that belongs to someone else (or another organization). For example, all employees are stewards of the corporation assets they utilize to perform their duties. Rule stewardship, like other forms of stewardship, is not ownership. It is accountability.

Information stewardship is defined by Peter Block (1993), as "the willingness to be accountable for a set of business information for the well-being of the larger organization by operating in service, rather than in control of those around us." The same principles that have been incorporated in information stewardship should be adopted for a rule stewardship program.

Therefore, *rule stewardship* is the willingness to be accountable for a set of rules for the good of the larger organization.

Rule stewards are people who have the responsibility to manage the business value of each rule. A rule has *business value* if the rule guides behavior in achieving a business benefit that justifies the costs of the rule's enforcement and maintenance. Some objectives for a rule stewardship program are primarily business oriented while others apply to both business and IT organizations.

STEP 15.5: ESTABLISH BUSINESS OBJECTIVES FOR RULE STEWARDSHIP

You need to establish business objectives for the rule stewardship program.

GUIDELINE 15.5.1

Establish accountability of rule stewardship.

To aim for rule accountability, be sure to document the properties of high-quality rules. You can use the criteria for high-quality rules from Chapter 10. For example, to be cost-effective, efforts at improving the quality of rules should focus on rules for which the business gain is highest. Rule stewards must assess the potential business gain of specific rules by correlating them to the business motivation (strategy, tactics, objectives, and so on) for which the rules exist or are proposed.

STEP 15.6: DEFINE A RULE STEWARDSHIP PROGRAM

Enlisting business rule stewards is an ongoing process, not a one-time event, for transforming rules into a manageable and valuable asset as well as ensuring the long-term protection of that asset.

GUIDELINE 15.6.1

Define the rule stewards' roles and responsibilities.

Table 15.3 contains a starting point for defining the roles and responsibilities for rule stewards. Identify candidate stewards, establish a method for evaluating which stewards are responsible for which rules, and build successful rule stewardship into the organization's reward system. Identify business people within your project team (or external to it) who have the business knowledge to steward rules and who would be empowered to suggest or judge discovered or proposed rules.

To determine which steward is responsible for which rules, refer to the rule-enriched logical data model or object model that you will develop during discovery or analysis. Start assigning stewards to entities, objects, or sets of entities or objects to specific stewards. In this way, these stewards are accountable for rules related to those entities or objects. For example, one steward might be responsible for all customer-related rules, another for all product-related rules, and so on.

At the same time, this approach integrates well with the information stewards who are likely to be assigned to entities, objects, or business processes. In fact, consider evolving such information stewards into rule stewards also.

Rule stewardship need not be a full-time role, depending on the quantity of rules and the activities around them. If there are active rule discovery activities in a particular area, the associated rule steward may be very busy. If rules are already established and rarely change for an area, the rule steward may not be very busy.

STEP 15.7: ESTABLISH A RULE COUNCIL

Rule conflicts will undoubtedly occur. These may be disagreements in rule definition or rule jurisdiction, for example. A *rule council* is a group of individuals representing multiple business functions who are empowered to discuss and resolve rule conflicts. This group should discuss and resolve real and apparent conflicts in rule definition and usage.

GUIDELINE 15.7.1

Establish the responsibilities of a rule council.

Essentially, the responsibilities of this council are to:

- Serve as the court of last resort for unsolved rule issues
- Maintain awareness of rule management within the scope of the project
- Provide business expertise in areas where rule issues arise
- Monitor the success of the rule stewardship program
- Set future direction, scope, and goals for rule stewardship.

GUIDELINE 15.7.2

Identify appropriate members for the rule council.

A rule council should be comprised of high-level business personnel who are empowered to resolve conflict, but who also have the organization's benefits at heart over personal domain issues. Most likely you will start with a rule stewardship program for your project only. Still, incorporate the concept of the stewardship council, especially if there are multiple business stakeholders involved.

For the case study, the heads of each of the relevant departments would make an excellent rule council. For starters, these departments would be Guardian Services,

Member Services, Marketing, Finance, Credit, and Theme Park Services. You can include representatives from other departments, such as Library, Tutorial, and University, as the system extends to include functionality and rules to support them.

GUIDELINE 15.7.3

Integrate the rule management approach with existing information resource processes, tools, and roles and responsibilities, if they exist.

If you have an existing information resource management function, study it for similarities and overlaps. For example, if there already is a working information stewardship program, extend it for rule management. If there is an information repository, consider extending it for documenting rules.

Establish the Rule Repository

Simply put, a *rule repository* is a database that contains an organization's rules and supporting information. The purpose of a rule repository is to provide all qualified stakeholders access to the organization's business rules while ensuring the security and integrity of rule information. It also facilitates the entire rule management process, through enforcement of standards, impact analysis, rule reporting, and automated access.

A rule repository, like other kinds of repositories, has many benefits. For starters, it provides the basis for common and consistent vocabulary among the rule community, which fosters quicker understanding and crisper requirements. It also provides a single point of contact for the rule community when searching for rules. Its browser capability enables people to seek rules or groups of rules. Very importantly, a rule repository allows an architect to get a wide perspective of the business logic (rules) across an application system or for a specific function or within a specific organizational unit.

Typically, a graphical interface allows entry to and maintenance of the rules. A reporting feature allows for the generation of rule reports. Remember that the rule repository should integrate with repositories for other deliverables for the project and, most importantly, your commercial rules product, if you use one.

STEP 15.8: ESTABLISH OBJECTIVES FOR THE RULE REPOSITORY

You need to identify your organization's specific needs for a rule repository.

GUIDELINE 15.8.1

Identify target audience, query and reporting, and rule reuse functionality.

Sample objectives for a rule repository are to provide:

- Access to all qualified business and technical stakeholders
- A facility designed to expedite business rule reuse across the company

- Query and reporting capability for rule analysis and traceability
- Storage of the rule documentation
- Security and integrity for rule-related information.

STEP 15.9: DEVELOP A RULE METAMODEL

A *rule metamodel* is a logical data model depicting the information you want to manage about rules. It is a good idea to develop a rule metamodel as a starting point for confirming your requirements. A rule metamodel is a yardstick against which to measure a commercial rule repository or against which to design your own. The rule metamodel should include all the metadata for rules that will be needed by both business and technical people.

GUIDELINE 15.9.1

Review rule-related deliverables for all phases.

In Step 15.2, you identified and documented the rule-related deliverables for your project. There are rule-related deliverables from each phase of the system development life cycle, and you need to determine which of these you will load into and manage through the rule repository.

GUIDELINE 15.9.2

Determine the kind of information you want to manage about each rule-related deliverable.

You will need to determine the kind of information you manage about each deliverable.

Spend time deciding what to record about rules themselves. The information you record about the rules will determine how useful the rule repository is. Some interesting pieces of information about a rule may be: its source (person, document, or system), date of last change, anticipated frequency of change, and business objectives it aims to support. You may also want to indicate the nature of the rule source, such as regulatory document, best practices document, casual or formal conversation/interviews, or tacit knowledge.

Repository support for the design phase should include specification and links from the natural language version of the rule, eventually to its technical specification. You will need to determine if you want to manage in the rule repository all possible expressions of the rule, such as the original free-form business conversation version, a templated natural language version, rule specification language version, and rule implementation language version. Or, you may only capture a subset of these. A common subset is a free-form natural language version that is understood by the business audience and the declarative specification version suitable for execution in a targeted rules product.

Refer to Figure 15.1, which summarizes the rule-related deliverables in this book. Create a logical data model of the information needed to create each deliverable.

The Business Rules Group produced an example of a publicly available rule meta-model, which focuses on the motivation row of the Zachman Framework (see Chapter 3). Publications from this group are available at www.businessrulesgroup.org.

STEP 15.10: DEVELOP RULE-RELATED MODELING AND REPOSITORY REQUIREMENTS

Once you complete the rule metamodel, review the technology and tools available for the project. It is best first to understand those technologies and tools already implemented and utilized at your company. You may, as part of your project, want to select or adopt tools for creating workflow models, object models, and data models as well as a means for capturing rules. When you select these tools, take into account integration of rule meta data with these tools, whether selected by you or provided as part of a corporate standard.

GUIDELINE 15.10.1

Determine where to capture terms and definitions.

For a small, simple project, you can capture terms (nouns with standard names), definitions in a simple word-processing document and, of course, the rules. Alternately, you can capture them in a rule repository, data-modeling tool, object modeling tool, or enterprise repository. Terms are the foundational pieces for data models and business object models. Regardless, this book, as you will see, encourages you always to define a term before using it in a rule expression.

STEP 15.11: DETERMINE IF YOU WILL BUILD, BUY, OR EXTEND A REPOSITORY

There are many options for a rule repository. Keep in mind that you want the rules to be accessible to the business audience as well as to systems development professionals.
    You can use as a rule repository, the following:

- Homegrown rule database
- Extended CASE tool
- Extended commercial repository tool
- Commercial rules product

GUIDELINE 15.11.1

Consider the advantages of a homegrown rule repository.

It is common for organizations to develop a homegrown database as a rule repository because it can be tailored to specific organizational requirements. Some organizations have done so using MS/Access while others have built sophisticated rule databases using robust DBMS products (such as Oracle) on various UNIX/NT platforms and even mainframe DBMS products (such as DB2). The disadvantages are that these rule databases are not integrated with commercial modeling tools. The advantage is that these rule databases are easy to query.

GUIDELINE 15.11.2

Consider the advantages of extending a CASE tool for rules.

Another common approach is to extend a familiar CASE tool to capture rules. In this way, you can associate rules with corresponding model components, such as process models, object models, use-case deliverables, and data models. Visit the companion Web site for examples of how to extend common CASE tools for capturing rules. A disadvantage is that the business audience does not typically utilize CASE tools. To compensate for this, create standard rule reports and make them available to the business audience. The rule management Web page is an excellent place to publish these reports or to allow business people to execute the reports themselves. Your CASE tool may have the capability to generate these Web pages.

GUIDELINE 15.11.3

Consider the advantages of extending an existing repository.

For organizations that already have widely shared repositories, the most acceptable solution may be to extend the existing repository to store rules. This way, those rules are available to a wider audience. The disadvantage is that most commercial repositories are not intuitive or accessible to the business audience. Again, in this case, create standard rule reports and make them available to the business community, perhaps through the rule management Web page.

GUIDELINE 15.11.4

Consider the advantages of utilizing the repository of a commercial rules product as your rule repository.

If you are implementing your target system using a commercial rules product, most likely it comes with its own rule storage and management capability. An advantage to storing rules here is that documented and executable rules are stored in one place. A disadvantage is that such repositories may not be extendable to include your other deliverables or to support other implementation environments (outside the target rules product). Also, business people may not have access to these repositories. The commercial rules product each approaches differently the idea of a rule repository depending upon their focus of their product. Therefore, the scope and emphasis of business rule meta data that they capture will vary. This is why it is important that you develop your own rule metamodel and compare it to the model behind these products' repositories.

In summary, there are several factors to consider in choosing between building, extending, or buying a repository for your rules, such as:

- Other modeling technology available currently within the corporation
- Project budget

- Capability of your current repository, if you have one
- Capability of your commercial rules product's repository, if you have one.

GUIDELINE 15.11.5

Determine rule editor requirements

As with any requirements phase, you must identify what are your requirements for editing, sorting, searching, and reporting rules captured for your project. When specifying requirements for a repository, there are different areas that must be addressed such as the repository interfaces, graphical user interfaces, and rule editor configuration. You may want to break down the rule editor requirements into the different rule expressions as identified in step 15.9 (business conversation rule expressions, natural-language rule expressions, rule specification language rule expressions, and rule implementation language rule expressions).

There are at least eleven requirements to consider regarding rule editor capability.

- The first is ease of entry. Will most people enter the rules manually? Perhaps the rules (or at least some of them) may result from business rule mining and may be entered through an automated interface. Is there a rule entry wizard that walks a person through the rule entry procedure with point and click capabilities?

- The second is ease of rule classification. After you categorize the rules, will the repository recognize all of your rule classifications?

- The third is ease of update. How easy is it to change rules once they have been entered?

- The fourth consideration is ease of selection. Can you find a rule easily by selection on any of its parts? Can you see all rules that have common themes or constructs?

- The fifth is ease of reporting. Will you need paper printouts? Will the output allow customized formatting of reports? How easy is it to select for report only those rules that a person wants to see?

- The sixth is ease of tailoring. Will it be necessary (and how easy is it to do) to tailor the output to show layers of rules to interested users? For example, an executive may not be interested in the lowest layer of rules (*if A then add B to C*), but would be interested in a higher layer (*if customer credit limit exceeded by potential order, do not fulfill order*).

- A seventh consideration is whether the repository offers graphic support to assist users in correlating rules, procedures, or scripts, and so on, to the data model.

- An eighth consideration is whether the repository can detect and explain potential conflicts, redundancies, and rule overlaps prior to run time.

- A ninth concern is whether you can list and inspect rules by any grouping relevant to the business problem, for example, by keyword, by data model construct (for example, data object, relationship type, attribute type), by processing component (for example, business process, script or procedure, transaction), by business motivation (for example, objective, critical success factor).

- A tenth feature is whether you can cross-relate rules to organizational roles (for example, stakeholders, stewards).
- An eleventh issue is whether the product supports rule versioning and is audit trail capability supported, along with effective and expiration dates so as to provide a historical as well as future perspective.

STEP 15.12: DOCUMENT THE RULE REPOSITORY REQUIREMENTS AND SELECTION IN A DOCUMENT

A suggested requirements outline is:

Rule repository objectives

Rule repository alternatives

Rule repository choice

Rule repository constraints

Rule repository project timeline

Rule repository enhancements

Assumptions

Budget—Technology and resource budget items.

STEP 15.13: IMPLEMENT THE RULE REPOSITORY

Implementing the rule repository means purchasing or creating or extending one, installing it, customizing it, defining the activities to establish it as a functioning product, and providing training.

In summary, this includes:

- Acquire or create the repository.
- Install it.
- Install it into the environment, including necessary interfaces and meta data exchanges and interface to a commercial rules product.
- Customize it.
- Determine security profiles of target user communities.
- Identify training needs.
- Acquire or create training materials.
- Schedule and conduct training.

Worth mentioning here is that if there are other tools, such as CASE tools involved in your system development process, you will need to plan for meta data exchange and management across these and the rule repository.

Also you may want to develop interfaces between the deliverable repository and your commercial rules product, if you select one. For example, it would be more efficient to download the rule specification rules to the rule engine instead of reentering them.

STEP 15.14: DESIGN RULE REPORTS

Most rule reports contain the rules, date of last maintained, whether the rule stewards have validated the rules, and so on. Rule stewards will be most interested in reports that highlight rule changes or suggested rule changes.

GUIDELINE 15.14.1

Consider basic rule reports.

In general, there are three commonly used rule reports. The first is a listing of rules grouped together in a logical group, usually based on what the rules aim to do. An example of such a report is shown in Table 15.4 produced by the USoft TeamWork Facility for this book's case study.

A second is a listing of rules associated with entities in a logical data model or objects. Table 15.5 shows such a report from TeamWork, as an example.

A third valuable report is a correlation of rules to their implementation, or at least to documentation about where the rules are implemented. Again, a TeamWork version of such a report is shown in Table 15.6.

You may want additional reports, too. Therefore, a third is an input report summary, which is a report of number of rules entered, number of rules validated, number of rules for each source type, and so on. A fourth is a report of rules reviewed and approved by rule stewardship council. The fifth and most important, however, is an impact analysis report. Such a report usually indicates, for a rule (targeted for change), the impacted rules, processes or events, use cases, data elements, business objectives, and, of course, existing automated code.

Table 15.4 Sample Rule Report from USoft's TeamWork of Logical Groupings of Rules

NAME	MOTIVATION	DESCRIPTION
Invoicing Function	REQUIREMENT VERSION 1	The park fee is computed for a member as follows: The base fee (1) is the actual time used (in hours) in a park rounded up to the next 15 minutes, multiplied by the hourly rate. The volume discount (2) is determined by multiplying the volume discount rate by the number of hours over the volume discount threshold spent in a park. The volume discounted amount (3) is the base fee (1) minus the volume discount (2). The employee discount (4) is determined by multiplying the employee discount rate by the volume discounted amount (3). The member park fee (5) is the volume discounted amount (3) minus the employee discount (4).

continues

Table 15.4   Sample Rule Report from USoft's TeamWork of Logical Groupings of Rules (*Continued*)

NAME	MOTIVATION	DESCRIPTION
Credit checks for guardian	CREDIT RATING POLICY	Checks for credit rating of Guardians: 1. When guardian enrollment data is entered, online or by a park ranger, the default value of the application status is (P)ending. 2. VCI Employees signing up as guardians automatically get the (A)ccepted application status. 3. Guardians with prepayment billing method also get the (A)ccepted application status. 4. At the end of each working day, all data of guardians with the (P)ending application status are mailed to our credit service bureau, for the external credit check. 5. When credit ratings are received (via email or snail mail) from our credit service bureau, these ratings will be entered in the system by our park rangers. 6. Credit ratings can be: (E)xcellent, (F)air, and (P)oor 7. Guardians with (P)oor credit rating get the (R)ejected application status. 8. Guardians with (F)air or (E)xcellent credit rating, get the (A)ccepted application status. 9. Accounts of guardians with (F)air credit rating get the (P)repay billing method code. 10. Once the application status of a prospective guardian is (A)ccepted, send a mail with the entrance pass (user/password) to a new VCI Member.

Facilitate a discussion with the business rule team to determine if additional customized reports are needed because of the project scope. Determine if a reporting schedule is necessary to run the repository reports.

At the end of this step, you may want to revisit your estimate for repository reporting tasks in the project plan. You may also want to consider publishing these reports on your rule management Web page.

Establish Rule Management Processes

The following steps assist you in determining the kinds of processes the rule management function defines and oversees.

STEP 15.15: DEVELOP RULE CHANGE MANAGEMENT PROCESSES AND PROCEDURES

You will need to document procedures by which business people can recommend rule changes, rule retirements, and additional rules. Include in these procedures a validation

Table 15.5 Sample Rule Report from USoft's TeamWork Showing Rules per Entity or Object

BUSINESS OBJECT	RULE ID	TYPE	SHORT DESCRIPTION	PRIORITY	MOTIVATION	DEFINITION
General	PRK013	Other Type	member communication	Should Have	BAN INAPPROPRIATE LANGUAGE	Communication can only be between a park ranger and a member. VCI monitors this communication for language content.
Invoice	INV001	Behavior	invoice date	Would Have	INVOICING POLICY	Invoice date is the first business day of the month.
Invoice	INV002	Restriction	one invoice a month	Would Have	INVOICING POLICY	One invoice is created per month per guardian, not per member.
Invoice	INV003	Restriction	account not in good standing	Would Have	INVOICING POLICY	An account is not in good standing if an invoice is more than 65 days overdue.
Invoice	INV004	Deduction	volume discounts	Would Have	DISCOUNT POLICY	Volume discounts are applied to current fees on a daily basis.
Invoice	INV005	Deduction	total charge for guardian	Must Have	INVOICING POLICY	The total charges for the month for a guardian are the sum of the charges for each member.
Invoice	INV006	Deduction	base fee	Must Have	FEE POLICY	The base fee for a park is the hourly fee times the number of hours spent in the park (rounded up to the nearest quarter hour).
Invoice	INV007	Deduction	base = final	Must Have	DISCOUNT POLICY	Without discounts base fee equals final fee.

continues

Table 15.5 Sample Rule Report from USoft's TeamWork Showing Rules per Entity or Object (*Continued*)

BUSINESS OBJECT	RULE ID	TYPE	SHORT DESCRIPTION	PRIORITY	MOTIVATION	DEFINITION
Invoice	INV008	Deduction	total charge per member	Must Have	INVOICING POLICY	The total charges for the month per member are the sum of the final fees for each invoice item in a member section.
Park usage	PRK005	Combination	entrance park questions	Must Have	WEB REQUIREMENT	A guardian must enter "Entrance to Park Questions." More specific: <Document: Entrance to Park Scenarios.doc> A member cannot enter a park unless the enrollment process is completed including the credit check and the guardian has entered their desired "Entrance to Park Questions." Many mentioned that VCI does provide some examples or templates of questions to assist the guardian. </Document: Entrance to Park Scenarios.doc>
Park usage	PRK006	Combination	enrollment	Must Have	WEB REQUIREMENT	Guardian sets default time per park.
Park usage	PRK007	Combination	enrollment	Must Have	WEB REQUIREMENT	Default time can be changed any time.
Park usage	PRK008	Behavior	enrollment	Must Have	WEB REQUIREMENT	When a prepaid guardian attempts to allocate more time in the theme park than allocated in the bank, display a warning message.

Park usage	PRK101	Restriction	possible responses	Must Have	REQUIREMENT VERSION 1	Currently, possible responses on entrance questions can be: (Y)es and (N)o
Party	PRK001	Presentation	enrollment	Must Have	WEB REQUIREMENT	Enrollment information may be entered by the guardian or by a park ranger on behalf of a guardian.
Party	PRK002	Restriction	guardian is a relative	Must Have	REQUIREMENT VERSION 1	A guardian may be a parent, grandparent, or other relative.
Party	PRK003.1	Behavior	default application status	Must Have	CREDIT RATING POLICY	When guardian enrollment data is entered, online or by a park ranger, the default value of the guardian's application status is (P)ending.
Party	PRK003.10	Behavior	mail entrance pass	Should Have	PROJECT REQUIREMENT	Once the application status of a prospective guardian is "Accepted", send a mail with the entrance pass (user/password) to a new VCI Member.
Party	PRK003.2	Behavior	employee accepted	Must Have	CREDIT RATING POLICY	VCI Employees signing up as guardians automatically get the (A)ccepted application status.
Party	PRK003.3	Behavior	prepayment accepted	Must Have	CREDIT RATING POLICY	Guardians with prepayment billing method get the "Accepted" application status.

continues

Table 15.5 Sample Rule Report from USoft's TeamWork Showing Rules per Entity or Object (*Continued*)

BUSINESS OBJECT	RULE ID	TYPE	SHORT DESCRIPTION	PRIORITY	MOTIVATION	DEFINITION
Party	PRK003.4	Other Type	mail credit service	Must Have	CREDIT RATING POLICY	At the end of each working day, all data of guardians with the "Pending" application status are mailed to our credit service bureau, for the external credit check. This includes corresponding account data.
Party	PRK003.5	Instruction	credit service ratings	Must Have	PROJECT REQUIREMENT	When credit ratings are received (via email or snail mail) from our credit service bureau, these ratings will be entered in the system by our park rangers.
Party	PRK003.6	Restriction	credit ratings	Must Have	CREDIT RATING POLICY	Credit ratings can be: (E)xcellent, (F)air, and (P)oor. These values are to be selected from a dropdown list box.
Party	PRK003.7	Behavior	poor credit rating rejected	Must Have	CREDIT RATING POLICY	Guardians with (P)oor credit rating get the (R)ejected application status.
Party	PRK003.8	Behavior	fair credit rating accepted	Must Have	CREDIT RATING POLICY	Guardians with (F)air or (E)xcellent credit rating, get the (A)ccepted application status.
Party	PRK003.9	Behavior	fair credit rating prepay	Should Have	CREDIT RATING POLICY	Accounts of guardians with (F)air credit rating get the (P)repay billing method code.

	ID	Type	Name	Priority	Category	Description
Party	PRK004	Presentation	member enrollment	Must Have	WEB REQUIREMENT	A guardian must supply the following information to enroll the member: guardian name, address, social security number, billing method, payment information, method of communication, member name, member ssn, member dob, relationship of guardian to member. Guardian info is shown on the Enroll as a Guardian task. The billing method and payment information are shown on the Account Info task.
Party	PTY001	Restriction	birth is in the past	Must Have	CONSISTENCY	A date of birth is be in the past.
Party	PTY002	Restriction	Member between 6 and 15 years old	Must Have	CUSTOMER POLICY	A member must be between 6 and 15 years old. A member is allowed to use the VCI Park from the day of his or her 6th birthday, until the end of the month of his or her 16th birthday.
Party	PTY003	Restriction	subtyping	Must Have	CUSTOMER POLICY	A Party is either a Member or an Adult.
Party	PTY004	Restriction	subtyping	Must Have	CUSTOMER POLICY	An Adult is a Guardian or a Park Ranger or both.

Table 15.6 Sample Rule Report Showing Notes on Rule Implementations

BUSINESS RULE	BUSINESS OBJECT	TYPE	CONSTRAINT	EXTERNAL ELEMENT	DESCRIPTION
INV005	Invoice	Non transitional constraint	INV005_TOTAL_ CHARGE		
INV006	Invoice	Transitional constraint	INV006_BASE_FEE		This constraint is transitional as a change in the hourly rate of a Park is not to affect the fees on an invoice.
INV007	Invoice	Non transitional constraint	INV007_FINAL_FEE		
INV008	Invoice	Non transitional constraint	INV008_TOTAL_ CHARGE_ MEMBER		
PRK001	Party	Info Task in WebRuler		Enroll as a Guardian info task	Enroll as a Guardian info task. Available online, built with USoft WebRuler, and implemented by a Java applet. The following attributes are not displayed online : Credit rating code, Application status, AND all checkboxes corresponding with subtype indicators.
PRK002	Party	Allowed Values			Allowed Values for the MBR_GUARDIAN_ RELATIONSHIP domain are: (P)arent, (G)rand-parent, (U)ncle or Aunt, and (F)riend.
PRK003.1	Party	Default Values			Default value of the ADULT.GRD_APPLICATION_ STATUS column set to (P)ending

ID	Type	Description	Name	Notes
PRK003.10	Party	Merely an instruction to our park rangers		Currently, this is a common and well-known procedure for our park rangers. In the near future, VCI plans to make use of the RDMI (Rules Driven Method Invocation) possibilities within USoft Developer to automate this business rule.
PRK003.2	Party	Non transitional constraint	PRK003_EMPLOYEE_ACCEPTED	
PRK003.3	Party	Transitional constraint	PRK003_PREPAY_ACCEPTED	
PRK003.4	Party	Batch Job		
PRK003.5	Party	Merely an instruction to our park rangers		This is already a common and well-known procedure for our park rangers.
PRK003.6	Party	Allowed Values		
PRK003.7	Party	Non transitional constraint	PRK003_REJECT_POOR_CREDIT	
PRK003.8	Party	Non transitional constraint	PRK003_ACCEPT_GOOD_CREDIT	
PRK003.9	Party	Non transitional constraint	PRK003_FAIR_CREDIT_PREPAY	

continues

Table 15.6 Sample Rule Report Showing Notes on Rule Implementations *(Continued)*

BUSINESS RULE	BUSINESS OBJECT	TYPE	CONSTRAINT	EXTERNAL ELEMENT	DESCRIPTION
PRK004	Party	Info Task in WebRuler		Enroll Members info task	New "Enroll Members" info task integrated as additional tab page on the existing "Enroll a Guardian" info task. This Member's tab page contains, among others: member name, member ssn, member dob, relationship of guardian to member.
PRK005	Park usage	Info Task in WebRuler		Member Entrance Criteria info task	Member Entrance Criteria info task.
PRK101	Park usage	Allowed Values			Allowed Values for the YESNO_NO_DEFAULT domain are: (Y)es and (N)o. This domain is displayed as a dropdown list.
PTY003	Party	Subtyping			The distinction between data of Parties that are Member and those who are grown-up and can not be member simultaneously is done via a Subtype Group PARTIES on PARTY.
PTY004	Party	Subtyping			The distinction between data of Adults that are Guardian and those who are Park Ranger or both is done via a Subtype Group ADULTS on ADULT.

process whereby the rule steward or rule repository administrator assesses the impact of new and changed. Rule stewards should confirm the final decision to institute the rule change.

GUIDELINE 15.15.1

Develop a rule certification process.

Before a rule can be added to the list of approved rules, the repository administrator must certify it. The certification process includes establishing that a rule:

- Is not a duplicate of an existing rule
- Does not overlap within existing rules
- Does not conflict with existing rules
- Has a name that complies with the rule-naming standard and
- Is adequately documented.

GUIDELINE 15.15.2

Develop a rule management process model.

Identify the processes needed to manage the rules within the rule management scope statement. Create a workflow for each of the rule management processes and deliverables.

Establish the information flow required on an ongoing basis between the project team and business clients, and how the rule repository or reports from it will be utilized to facilitate this. Also establish how the repository administrator will monitor rule, term, and source submissions/entries for consistency and completeness on an ongoing basis.

GUIDELINE 15.15.3

Develop rule change management procedures.

Once you define the processes for rule change management, you can define detailed procedures for carrying them out. The combination of detailed procedures and training makes the rule change management process trainable and consistent across the organization. You will need procedures adding, changing and versioning, and retiring rules using the rule repository. Figure 15.3 shows the flow of a rule change when using a project level business rule repository. Figure 15.4 shows the flow of a rule change when you also have an enterprise rule repository.

STEP 15.16: DEVELOP RULE IMPACT ANALYSIS PROCEDURES

Impact analysis is one of the most powerful capabilities of the rule repository and is made possible by linkages within the rule repository metamodel. The linkages help determine the impact of change a rule has on other rules—and data! It should be included as one of the first steps of your rule change management process.

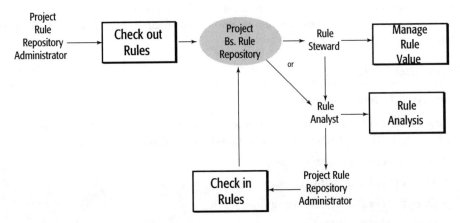

Figure 15.3   Sample rule change flow.

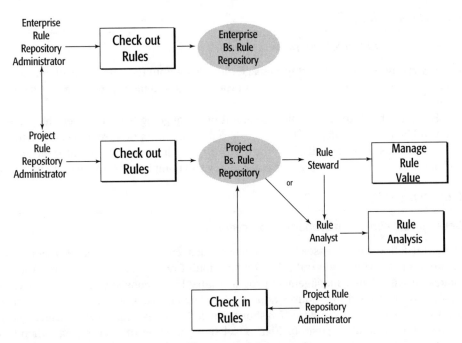

Figure 15.4   Sample rule change with an enterprise repository.

GUIDELINE 15.16.1

Develop Impact Analysis Reports.

Once you define the impact management process, review the rule repository metamodel to ensure that the process can occur easily.

Impact analysis implementation ensures that the change request is tracked through implementation and the sponsor of the change is notified of its status.

Step 15.17: Implement the Rule Management Processes and Procedures

Publish the rule management procedures to the technical and business team for your project. Also distribute the implementation plan to everyone who will be involved or affected. The plan will include any necessary training for these people.

Most likely, you will carry out two important parallel activities. First you will rapidly establish basic processes for the immediate project needs. Second, you may define the rest of them as you need them.

Guideline 15.17.1

Continue to market the business rules approach.

Whenever the opportunity arises, publicize the concept of business rules to the IT staff and business community in the form of written articles or Web page "marketing." Choose to share publications that are nontechnical and emphasize the benefits for specific job functions.

Another method of publicizing business rules is to provide a copy of relevant business rules to individuals when they request the authority to perform ad hoc reporting. Such sharing of business rules encourages consistent reporting and use of business information accessed through user queries.

Rule management, like most other processes, will have five levels of maturity: initial, repeatable, defined, managed, and finally optimizing.

If you are starting at the initial maturity level, your initial rule management efforts are likely to be a little chaotic as you learn how to be successful. Hopefully, this chapter provides you with enough guidance to understand the function well and to create a framework by which your rule management function emerges quickly into the repeatable maturity. Rule management becomes repeatable when you document, teach, and mentor its processes and procedures and your rule repository has a wide audience. Your rule management function becomes defined when rule management is understood and practiced with predictable progress. This is why success metrics are valuable to you. These not only measure the success, but also aid in predicting schedules, deliverables, and savings. When you are actively capturing and analyzing these metrics, your rule management function becomes managed whereby the metrics influence the process. Finally, as the metrics stabilize and your process becomes smarter, the rule management function becomes optimizing. It will deliver consistently high quality deliverables in predictable timeframes and at predictable costs.

Summary

Effective rule management is critical to the success of a business rules project. You can implement rule management for your project. Or the organization may decide to establish an organizational rule management function that spans projects or the whole enterprise. Most successes, however, will come from starting small (within a project) and proving value before attempting wider scale rule management.

The purpose of rule management is to provide access for all qualified stakeholders to the organization's rules while ensuring the security and integrity of related rule information. In addition, rule management provides business management with the ability not only to know its deployed rules but to request rapid deployment of rule changes. Without rule management, analysts and programmers embedded rules in system specifications, program documentation, or did not formally capture them at all. These rules are held in bondage, resistant to change.

Whether your project is large or small, the most important concepts to incorporate into your project about rule management are:

- Assets such as people, money, and customers are very tangible. Other assets, such as information, rules, and knowledge, are less tangible. Sometimes, intangible assets may be the most valuable.

- Rule management is most successful when there is active rule stewardship, where business stewards are accountable for the quality of the rules.

- You will need a rule repository. A rule repository is simply a database of the rules, with all related information. The best way to understand your needs for one is to create a rule metamodel of the information you want to manage about all rule-related deliverables. You can then build your own rule repository, extend an existing one or a CASE tool, or use one that comes with a commercial rules product.

- As always, you should take measurements so you can prove business value. Your goal is to quicken development time by encouraging reuse of rules, shorten maintenance time by delivering rules in changeable technology and tracing them to their implementations, and to allow the business to change as it sees fit.

Rule management may, indeed, be the only way to accomplish these objectives.

To Think About

Last but not least, a business rules approach gives you a philosophy and techniques that, along with business rules technology, represent a strategy and tools for tomorrow's business leadership. This book and its companion Web site gets you started on that road today.

If you follow a business rules approach to completion, your system will distinguish itself from all previous systems in four important ways, consistent with the STEP principles:

- Its rules will be **_separate_** from other aspects of the system so the business can know them, challenge them, and optimize them.

- Its rules will be **_traceable_** to the business objectives they aim to achieve and to all implementations where they are carried out so the business can know where the rules are actively guiding its operations and decisions.

- Its rules will be **_externalized_** so everyone can know what the rules are, thereby creating a knowledge-rich enterprise.

- Its rules will remain always **_positioned for change_** so that the business can proactively exploit those rules (its collective intelligence) to become whatever it wants to become whenever it wants to do so.

This brings you one giant step (S-T-E-P) towards building better business systems.

References

Block, Peter (1993). *Stewardship: Choosing Service over Self-Interest.* San Francisco: Berett-Koehler.

Brown, John Seely, and Paul Duguid (May–June 2000). "Balancing Act: How to Capture Knowledge without Killing It." *Harvard Business Review.*

Business Rule Studio (1999). "Managing Business Rules: A Repository Based Approach." Technology white paper. Available at www.RuleMachines.com

Business Rules Group (July 2000). *Defining Business Rules: What Are They Really?"* (3rd ed.). Formerly known as the GUIDE Business Rules Project Report (1995). Available at www.BusinessRulesGroup.org.

Date, C. J. (2000). *What Not How: The Business Rules Approach to Application Development.* Reading, Mass.: Addison-Wesley Longman Inc.

English, Larry (1999). *Information Stewardship: Accountability for Information Quality. Guidelines to Implementing Data Resource Management.* Data Management Association, DAMA International, P.O. Box 5786, Bellevue, WA 98006-5786.

Fleming, Candace, and Barbara von Halle. (1989). *Handbook of Relational Database Design.* Reading, Mass.: Addison-Wesley Longman, Inc.

Gottesdiener, Ellen (March 1997). "Business Rules Show Power, Promise." *Application Development Trends.*

Harmon, Paul, and Mark Watson (1997). *Understanding UML: The Developer's Guide.* San Francisco: Morgan Kaufmann Publishers Inc.

Hay, Dave (1995). *Data Model Patterns: Conventions of Thought.* New York: Dorset House.

Mallens, Paul (May–June 1997). "Business Rules-Based Application Development." *Database Newsletter.* Vol. 25.

Mann, John E. (April 2000). "Rules for E-Business." Patricia Seybold Group. Written for Versata Inc.

McMenamin, Stephen M., and John F. Palmer (1984). *Essential Systems Analysis*. New York: Yourdon Press.

Microsoft Corporation (1998). "Microsoft Repository." Available at msdn.Microsoft .com/repository.

Moriarty, Terry (April 1, 1993). "Business Rule Analysis." *Database Programming and Design*. Available at www.inastrol.com.

Moriarty, Terry (September 1998). "Business Rule Management Facility." *Database Programming and Design.*

Peck, M. Scott, Ph.D. (1993) *Further Along the Road Less Traveled.* New York: Simon and Schuster.

Phillips, Tony (2000). *Versata Method Handbook.* v 1.4. Oakland, Calif.: Versata Inc. Available from Versata Inc., 2101 Webster Street 8th Floor, Oakland, California, 94612.

Rosenberg, Doug, and Kendall Scott (1999). *Use Case Driven Object Modeling with UML.* Reading, Mass.: Addison-Wesley Longman Inc.

Ross, Ronald G. (1997). *The Business Rule Book* (2nd ed.). Houston: Business Rule Solutions, LLC.

Ross, Ronald G. (Sept./Oct. 2001), *The BRS Rule Classification Scheme. DataToKnowledge Newsletter* (29:5). Available at www.BRCommunity.com/a2001/b086.html.

Ross, Ronald, and Gladys S. W. Lam (1999). *Practitioner's Guide to Rule Management.* Houston: Business Rule Solutions, LLC.

Silverston, Len (2001). *The Data Model Resource Book, Volumes 1 and 2.* New York: John Wiley & Sons.

von Halle, Barbara, and David Kull, eds. (1994). *Handbook of Data Management.* Boston: Warren, Gorham, Lamont

Whitener, Theresa (January 1989). "Primary Identifiers: The Basics of Database Stability." *Database Programming and Design.*

Widom, Jennifer, and Stafano Ceri, eds. (1996). *Active Database Systems: Triggers and Rules for Advanced Database Processing.* San Francisco: Morgan Kaufman Publishers, Inc.

Wiegers, Karl. (1999). *Software Requirements.* Redmond, Wash.: Microsoft Press.

Index

529